China and the Shared Human Future: Exploring common values and goals

中国与人类命运共同体：探讨共同的价值观与目标

Globalization of Chinese Social Sciences book series ⑥
中国社会科学全球化系列丛书 ⑥

China and the Shared Human Future

Exploring Common Values and Goals

中国与人类命运共同体：探讨共同的价值观与目标

Martin Albrow · Edited by Xiangqun Chang

GCP Global Century Press
环球世纪出版社

Globalization of Chinese Social Sciences Series Vol. 6
Series editor: Xiangqun Chang

China and the Shared Human Future: Exploring Common Values and Goals
By Martin Albrow and Edited by Xiangqun Chang

This book first published in 2021 by
Global Century Press
23 Austin Friars, London EC2N 2QP, UK

British Library Cataloguing in Publication Data
A catalogue record for this book is available from the British Library

ISBN 978-1-913522-14-8 (hardback English); DOI https://doi.org/10.24103/GCSS6.en.2021
ISBN 978-1-913522-15-5 (paperback English); DOI https://doi.org/10.24103/GCSS6.en.2021
ISBN 978-1-913522-16-2 (hardback Chinese); DOI https://doi.org/10.24103/GCSS6.cn.2021
ISBN 978-1-913522-17-9 (paperback Chinese); DOI https://doi.org/10.24103/GCSS6.cn.2021

中国社会科学全球化系列丛书 第6卷
丛书主编：[英] 常向群

《中国与人类命运共同体：探讨共同的价值与目标》
马丁·阿尔布劳 著 常向群 编

此书由环球世纪出版社于2021年出版
23 Austin Friars, London EC2N 2QP, UK

该书编入大英图书馆的公开数据中的图书馆编目

ISBN 978-1-913522-14-8 (精装 英文); DOI https://doi.org/10.24103/GCSS6.en.2021
ISBN 978-1-913522-15-5 (平装 英文); DOI https://doi.org/10.24103/GCSS6.en.2021
ISBN 978-1-913522-16-2 (精装 中文); DOI https://doi.org/10.24103/GCSS6.cn.2021
ISBN 978-1-913522-17-9 (平装 中文); DOI https://doi.org/10.24103/GCSS6.cn.2021

Contents

Detailed Contents

Part Two: Practical themes

General Preface
The Globalization of Chinese Social Sciences Book Series

The phrase 'globalization of Chinese social sciences' came out of a discussion with Professor Stephan Feuchtwang at the London School of Economics in 2010 about the title of a book commemorating the 100th anniversary of Professor Fei Xiaotong (Fei Hsiao-tung)'s birth. The first volume (in both English and Chinese) was published in 2014 by Global China Press alone and in 2015 jointly with New World Press. The dissemination of 'Chinese social sciences' covers a very wide range, in which the promotion of Fei Xiaotong's work is only the first step. We therefore decided to use 'Globalization of Chinese Social Sciences' as the name of a book series in order to promote representative Chinese social scientific works. Here I shall briefly outline the key developments in 'Chinese social sciences' after 1949.[1]

Institutions and resources

In China, the National Philosophy and Social Science Planning Group of the CPC Central Committee is the highest body in the Chinese social sciences. The group operates through the National Planning Office of Philosophy and Social Science. Its National Social Science Foundation is commissioned by the Department of Social Sciences of the Ministry of Education, the Research Bureau of the Chinese Academy of Social Sciences (CASS) and the Research Division of the Central Party School, to be in charge of universities, the institutions of CASS and the central State organs, respectively, with responsibility for the application of research projects, management of funds and evaluation of results. The National Philosophy and Social Science Planning Group also owns the National Social Sciences Database, which was established by CASS and developed by its Library in 2013. It is a national-level, open-information platform for Chinese social sciences. In 2015, the Chinese Social Sciences Year Book series (15 volumes to date) was published, representing the high standard of work in the field. CASS consists of hundreds of research institutes, centres and related professional organizations, such as the Social Sciences in China Press (SSCP), Social Sciences Academic Press (SSAP), Chinese Social Sciences Net and its blogs and the journal *Social Sciences in China* and its site and blogs, the English version of which is now published by the Taylor and Francis Group. In 2015, the journal *Social Sciences in China*

---

[1] Yung-chen Chiang (2006), *Social Engineering and the Social Sciences in China, 1919-1949*, Cambridge: Cambridge University Press.

Review was founded. It aims 'to evaluate Fei Xiaotong Studies based on academic results based on national conditions, introduce a high standard of research results and create a system of academic discourse in contemporary China, comprehensively promoting Chinese philosophical and social scientific work in the world'. In recent years, the CASS Forum has also gained a strong reputation at home and abroad. In addition, there are a huge number of Academies of Social Sciences at province and municipality level.

They also have their own publications on social sciences based on their work at the local level. By September 2021, there were 3,012 colleges and universities of different types in China[2]. Some belong to the Bureau of Higher Education of the Ministry of Education, some to State ministries and commissions and others to provincial and municipal governments; more than a quarter are private universities.[3] In 2001, the Department of Social Sciences, Ministry of Education, built the humanities and social sciences services professional portal, the China Academic Humanities Information Network. It became the centre of information and online publications and for the dissemination, management and public enquiry services for humanities and the social sciences. All the universities have different faculties and departments and research centres for different topics. Almost all have their own publishers, producing academic journals and books. Social scientific work is published in philosophy and social sciences editions. It is worth mentioning a few examples of universities' contributions to providing services or promoting Chinese social sciences at the national level.

In 1998, Nanjing University and the Hong Kong Polytechnic University developed a Chinese Social Sciences Citation Index and the academic series of the Chinese Humanities and Social Sciences Citation index. It led to the foundation of the Chinese Social Science Research Assessment Centre in 2000.

Tsinghua University and Tsinghua Tongfang Holding Group established China's National Knowledge Infrastructure (CNKI) in 1999. It was supported by the Education Ministry, Science and Technology Ministry, Propaganda Ministry and General Administration of Press and Publications, with self-developed cutting-edge Chinese digital library technologies and grid resources as a sharing platform. It built the most comprehensive system of Chinese academic knowledge resources – the China Integrated Knowledge Resources Database – covering journals, dissertations, newspapers, proceedings, yearbooks, reference works, encyclopaedias, patents, standards, science and technology achievements and laws and regulations and some well-known foreign-language resources from Springer, Taylor & Francis and Wiley, forming a complete knowledge service network. The system is the core of the China knowledge resource base, totalling 101.9 million

---

2 List of universities in China. See: https://en.wikipedia.org/wiki/List_of_universities_in_China.

3 中国教育部:《2015年全国教育事业发展统计公报》，见：http://www.moe.gov.cn/srcsite/A03/s180/moe_633/201607/t20160706_270976.html [Ministry of Education of China (2016), *2015 National Education Statistics Bulletin*, 06/07/2016].

articles encompassing a large amount of social scientific work, some of which has been translated into English.

Fudan University is a top locus for the internationalization of Chinese social sciences. It founded China's first national institute for advanced studies of the social sciences (Fudan-IAS for Social Sciences). The founding Dean, Professor Deng Zhenglai, also founded the *Chinese Social Science Quarterly* in Hong Kong as early as 1992, which was re-established in 2008. In the same year, he founded China's first English-language journal on social sciences, the *Fudan Journal of the Humanities and Social Sciences* (FJHSS). He published an article discussing three issues of 'going global' (going-out 走出去) in Chinese social sciences in the era of globalization: the possibility of an open minded globalization; the necessity and possibility of 'going global'; and overcoming two major 'bottlenecks' which restrict Chinese social sciences from 'going global'.[4] Unfortunately, Deng passed away in 2013. His successor in Fudan-IAS, Sujian Guo, Professor of the Department of Political Science at San Francisco State University, USA, also became Editor of the FJHSS, which is now published by Springer.

Methodology

Some recent opinions should be mentioned here. In 2011, Professor QIAO Xiaochun of the Institute of Population Research at Peking University gave a lecture entitled 'Chinese social science: how far away from science?' at a number of universities, including his own and Shanghai University of International Studies, China Youth University for Political Science, Huazhong University of Science and Technology and Zhongnan University of Economics and Law. He believed that Chinese social science occupies no position or status in world academia, and therefore enjoys no right of discourse. This is because methodologically Chinese social sciences have a strong speculative character, in contrast to the empirical studies on which general social sciences are based. Details can be found in his book of the same name, published in 2017.[5]

However, in his 'Understanding the future' lecture in 2016, Professor Yu Xie of Princeton University and Peking University issued some more nuanced statements. Scientific studies, he observed, have three characteristics, namely objectivity, experience and repeatability. He also put forward three principles, variability, social grouping and social context, which provide a methodological basis for social scientific research. Xie suggested that in today's China it is more important

[4] 邓正来：全球化时代的中国社会科学发展，《社会科学战线》2009年第5期 [DENG Zhenglai (2009), The Development of Chinese Social Sciences in the Era of Globalization, *Social Science Front*, No.5].

[5] 乔晓春:《中国社会科学离科学还有多远？》，北京大学出版社，2017年版[QIAO Xiaochun (2017), *Chinese Social Science: How Far Away From Science?* Beijing: Peking University Press].

than ever to carry out social scientific research on China, since Chinese society has undergone comprehensive change and is still rapidly changing.[6]

In 2014, XIONG Yihan, Associate Professor at Fudan University School of International Relations and Public Affairs, published an article entitled 'The internationalization of social science and native language scholarly writing in China'.[7] He criticized the phenomenon of 'academic nationalism' that seeks to boycott internationalization, but also took issue with the 'colonial academic' who lacks local consciousness. He thought it very important that 'Chinese scholars should apply scientific research methods, actively participate in international academic dialogue and competition, invent dominant theoretical paradigms and set up research agendas with international colleagues. Even first-class Chinese writing with a global perspective is an integral part of the internationalization of social science in China.'

In 2015, Biao Xiang, Professor of Social Anthropology at Oxford University, who graduated from the Department of Sociology, Peking University, in the mid-1990s, published an article on 'The ending of the "intellectual youth" era of Chinese social sciences'.[8] Scholars born before the 1960s, who received an incomplete education but had experience in rural China, have nearly all left their leadership or teaching posts. In contrast, post-1970s scholars, who received continuous formal education but had little experience outside educational institutions, became the mainstream of academia. Xiang believes that the evolution of modern Chinese social science resembles the changes that have taken place between different generations of academic practice, knowledge acquisition and accumulation. Nevertheless, as Yefu Zheng, Emeritus Professor of Sociology at Peking University, pointed out, professors in the Department of Sociology at Peking University who were born before 1960 had still not retired; scholars' influence does not depend on their posts. Professor TIAN Song of Beijing Normal University also questioned whether the 'intellectual youth' era had ended. He maintained that the phenomenon of the post-1970s becoming mainstream is more of an academic management change.[9]

---

6 谢宇："今天在中国做社会科学太重要了，也太幸运了"，未来科学论坛演讲，《环球科学》，2017年7月，见：https://kknews.cc/zh-sg/education/r8eokx.html [Yu Xie (2016), 'Today it is so important and so opportune to be conducting social scientific research in China' (a speech at the Future Forum, Beijing), *Global Sciences*, Vol. 7].

7 熊易寒：中国社会科学的国际化与母语写作,《复旦学报（社会科学版)》，2014年第4期 [XIONG Yihan (2014), 'The Internationalization of Social Science and Native Language Scholarly Writing in China'. *Fudan Journal (Social Sciences)* 4].

8 项飙：中国社会科学"知青时代"的终结,《文化纵横》，2015年第12期，见：https://www.thepaper.cn/newsDetail_forward_1405189 [Biao Xiang (2015), 'The Ending of the 'Intellectual Youth' Era of Chinese Social Sciences, *Beijing Cultural Review*, 12].

9 田松：是代际替换，还是制度变更，《社会科学报》2016年3月10日第8版，见：https://www.sohu.com/a/150202304_472886 [TIAN Song (2016), 'Are We Experiencing Generational Change or Institutional Change? *Social Science Weekly*, Shanghai Academy of Social Sciences, 10 March].

The methodological character of Chinese social sciences is a large topic. Recently, a problem arose with translating the phrase '哲学社会科学' into English, which occurred in a speech at the Symposium of Philosophical Social Sciences by Xi Jinping, President of China, on 17 May 2016.[10] Xi obtained a PhD from the Department of Sociology, School of Humanities and Social Science at Tsinghua University, in 2002. Our professional translator translated 哲学社会科学 into English as 'philosophical social sciences', based on the context of the speech. Our editor accepted it, as did our academic adviser, Professor Martin Albrow, a founding editor of *International Sociology* and former President of the British Sociological Association. Moreover, inspired by it, when writing speech notes in preparation for attending a high-end international conference on China studies in October, 2016, he titled his speech 'Philosophical social science as a bridge from "Belt and Road" to global governance'. However, as the editor of this book series, I decided to change 'philosophical social sciences' to 'philosophy and social sciences' in the final English version of Xi's speech. This seemed to coincide with the letter of Xi's speech, although, from the methodological point of view, some important characteristics of Chinese social sciences were lost.

China's Chinese social sciences 'going global'

In recent years, great efforts have been made to encourage Chinese social scientific work to go global from China, ranging from social sciences forums and international conferences, academic exchanges, joint research projects or teaching programmes, to publications of journals and books abroad mainly sponsored by Chinese government funds[11] and encouraged by the government's policy.[12] They certainly promoted Chinese social scientific work globally.[13] The contributions of foreign publishers have also been acknowledged[14].

---

10 习近平：《在哲学社会科学工作座谈会上的讲话》，2016年5月18日，新华网，见：http://news.xinhuanet.com/politics/2016-05/18/c_1118891128.htm [Xi Jinping (2016), Speech at the Symposium of Philosophical Social Sciences, 18/05/2016 *Xinhua Net*,18/05/2016].

11 曲一琳：中国声音 世界回响——国家社科基金中华学术外译项目设立五年发展纪实，《光明日报》，2015年07月17日，见：http://www.nopss.gov.cn/n/2015/0717/c384417-27320824.html [QU Yilin (2015), Voice of China, Echoes of the World – Records of Five-year Development of the Chinese Academic Translation Project of the National Social Science Fund, *Guangming Daily*, July 17]

12 肖昊宸：打造一批卓越的中国特色学派，在世界学术体系中发出中国声音，《中国社会科学报》，2016-11-14，见：http://www.scio.gov.cn/zhzc/10/Document/1519460/1519460.htm [XIAO Haochen (2016), To create a group of outstanding schools with Chinese characteristics, to make a Chinese voice in the world academic system, *Chinese Journal of Social Sciences*, November 14].

13 段丹洁：让世界倾听中国学术思想的声音，《中国社会科学报》，2021-10-11，见：http://jspopss.jschina.com.cn/shekedongtai/202110/t20211011_7261955.shtml [DUAN Danjie (2021), Let the World Hear the Voice of Chinese Academic Thoughts, *Chinese Social Sciences Today*, October 11].

14 谢雨童、范家尧、吴碧宇：国外出版社对中国图书外译项目的贡献，《社会科学前沿》，

However, the process of Chinese social scientific work 'going global' is not as smooth as that of the nature sciences, finance, industrial products, culture, arts or language, etc. From 2006 to 2011, ZHANG Yaoming, the then editor-in-chief of *Xinhua Digest* published three articles addressing matters of urgency, situations and solutions for raising standards of Chinese social scientific journals.[15] ZHANG Nini selected 35 journal articles from 2012 to 2014, discussing Chinese philosophy and social sciences 'going global' in four areas: strategic significance, international publication and influence, the current situation of building academic platforms; and language problems.[16] In 2015, LIU Yang, a scholar with a background in management and communication, believed that whether Chinese social sciences can truly 'go global' depending on social science academic journals. Based on the comprehensive perspective of two kings of 'going global': disciplines and academic journals of Chinese philosophy and social sciences, he discusses effective ways of 'going global' for Chinese social science academic journals in the context of reforming its publication system.[17] He also explored quality assurance strategies for Chinese social science academic journals 'going global'.[18]

Since only two SSCI listed Chinese social science academic journals (in English) came from mainland China[19], Liu and his co-author found that the internationalization development of China's English academic journals of social sciences faces four contradictions in content organization, development scale, publishing mode, and management systems. They proposed a policy of building

---

2021, 10(05): 1204-1211 [XIE Yutong, FAN Jiayao, WU Biyu (2021), Contributions of Foreign Publishers to Chinese Book Translation, Advances in Social Sciences, Vol. 10, No. 05].

15 张耀铭：1) 中国学术期刊的发展现状与需要解决的问题，《清华大学学报 (哲学社会科学版).》, 2006(2); 2) 学术期刊的使命与魅力,《社会科学研究》, 2009(03); 3) 中国社科学术期刊的困境与出路,《现代出版》, 2011,(05) [ZANG Yaoming, 1) The development status and problems to be solved of Chinese academic journals, *Journal of Tsinghua University (Philosophy and Social Sciences Edition)*, 2006(2); 2) The Mission and Charm of Academic Journals, *Social Science Research* 2009(03); 3) The Dilemma and Way Out of Chinese Social Science Academic Journals, *Modern Publishing*. 2011(05)].

16 张妮妮：《中国哲学社会科学“走出去”研究》，北京：北京大学出版社，2016年 [ZHANG Nini (2016), *Studies on China's Philosophy and Social Sciences Going Global,* Beijing: Peking University Press].

17 刘杨:《中国社会科学学术期刊“走出去”研究》，社会科学文献出版社, 2015 [LIU Yang (2015), A Study on the Going-out of China's Social Sciences Academic Journals, Beijing: Social Sciences Academic Press (China)].

18 刘杨：中国社科学术期刊走出去的质量保障战略研究，《中州大学学报》，2015年第6期 [LIU Yang (2015), Research on quality assurance strategy of Chinese social science academic journals 'Going Global', *Journal of Zhongzhou University*, No.6]

19 姜志达：话语权视角下的社科学术期刊国际化研究，《出版发行研究》，2018（1），见：https://www.ciis.org.cn/yjcg/xslw/202007/t20200710_1104.html [JIANG Zhida (2018), Research on the Internationalization of Social Science Academic Journals from the Perspective of Discourse Power, *Publishing and Distribution Research*, No.1].

an academic discourse system with Chinese characteristics, Chinese style, and a Chinese manner to promote an international influence.[20]

It looks like there are some gaps between 'China's Chinese social sciences going global' and the 'Globalization of Chinese social sciences' that we promote.

Globalization of Chinese social sciences

The 'globalization of Chinese social sciences' is a live issue. The direction and outcomes of globalization of Chinese social scientific studies are neither Western nor Chinese, but add concepts, theories and methods derived from studying countries like China, which have a long history, huge population and complicated society, to the sum of human knowledge. This idea first appeared in 'A Chinese phase in social anthropology'[21], the Malinowski Memorial Lecture by Maurice Freedman given at the London School of Economics and Political Science in 1962. Two years later, Freedman made another speech on an occasion when area studies were being discussed, with the title 'What social science can do for Chinese studies[22], in which he distinguished sinology from Chinese studies and emphasized the need to study China social-scientifically. Both Martin Albrow and Stephan Feuchtwang were research students in, respectively, the Departments of Sociology and Anthropology at LSE, under the supervision of Maurice Freedman, and this influenced their academic careers throughout their lives.

Stephan Feuchtwang founded the China Research Unit at City University in 1973 when he worked there. It was the first organization dedicated to social scientific studies on China in the UK. Since 1998, when Feuchtwang was at the London School of Economics, he devoted himself to the creation of comparative studies of China. He appreciated Fei Xiaotong's comparative perspectives and theoretical conceptualization of the differential mode of association and the organizational mode of association (Gary G. Hamilton's translation of 差序格局 and 团体格局[23]) and elaborated them with his own translation.[24] In 2013, after the gestation,

[20] 刘杨、孙奕鸣：中国英文社科学术期刊国际化发展矛盾与破解，《中国科技期刊研究》，2020, 31(6): 644-650 [LIU Yang, SUN Yiming (2020), Internationalization development contradictions and countermeasures of China's English Academic Journals of Social Sciences, *Chinese Journal of Scientific and Technical Periodicals*, 31(6): 644-650].

[21] Maurice Freedman (1963), 'A Chinese Phase in Social Anthropology', *British Journal of Sociology*, 14(1).

[22] Maurice Freedman (1964), 'What Social Science Can Do for Chinese Studies', *Journal of Asian Studies*, 23(4).

[23] Fei Xiaotong (1992), *From the Soil: The Foundations of Chinese Society*, A translation of Fei Xiaotong's *Xiangtu Zhongguo*, by Gary Hamilton and WANG Zheng. University of California Press [Chinese edition: 费孝通：《乡土中国》，上海：观察社，1948年版].

[24] Stephan Feuchtwang (2015), 'Social Egoism and Individualism: surprises and questions from a Western anthropologist of China – Reading Fei Xiaotong's contrast between China and the West', *Journal of China in Global and Comparative Perspectives*, Vol.1 [Chinese version: 王斯福：社会自我主义与个体主义——一位西方的汉学人类学家阅读费孝通"中西对比"观念的惊讶与问题,《全球中国比较研究》，2017年第1期].

birth and early years of growth of the China in Comparative Perspective Network (CCPN) at LSE, he supported changing its name from CCPN to CCPN Global, as CCPN completed the process of becoming independent from the LSE.

In the USA also, some scholars are dedicated to Chinese social sciences. For example, Professor Daniel Little, Chancellor at the University of Michigan-Dearborn, presented a paper 'New developments in the Chinese social sciences' at a conference Mapping Difference: Structures and Categories of Knowledge Production, 19–20 May 2006, at Duke University. As early as 1989, he published *Understanding Peasant China: Case Studies in the Philosophy of Social Science*, which was translated into Chinese and published in 2009.[25] In 2010, Gary Hamilton, Professor of Sociology and International Studies at the University of Washington, presented a paper entitled 'What Western social scientists can learn from the writings of Fei Xiaotong'[26] at the international conference at LSE, Commemorating the 100th Anniversary of Professor Fei Xiaotong's Birth. Hamilton speaks highly of Chinese social sciences' methodological contribution to general social science methodology. A recent example was seen at the Young Scholars conference, Social Sciences and China Studies, 20–21 May 2016, organized by the Fudan-UC Centre on Contemporary China at the University of California, San Diego. These are joint efforts to promote Chinese social sciences from both Chinese and American scholars. All in all, a huge amount of work is being done all over the world in different disciplines studying China social-scientifically – too much to be mentioned here.

In the Preface of *Fei Xiaotong Studies*, the first volume of the *Globalization of Chinese Social Sciences* series, Feuchtwang states that Fei Xiaotong is probably the highest-ranking policy-influencing anthropologist of all time, who profoundly influenced social policies in China's development.[27] It is no accident that Xi Jinping mentioned in his 2016 speech LSE graduate Fei Xiaotong's name. In his Preface to *Peasant Life in China*, Malinowski noted that Dr Fei promised that, after he returned to China, he would work with Chinese colleagues to undertake a comprehensive reform of China's economic, social, cultural, political and belief systems.[28] Now Dr Xi Jinping, the highest-ranking policy-maker, in his speech on

[25] Daniel Little (1989), *Understanding Peasant China: Case Studies in the Philosophy of Social Science*, Yale University Press [Chinese edition: 李丹 (2009), 《理解农民中国——社会科学哲学的案 例研究》, 江苏人民出版社].

[26] Gary Hamilton (2015), 'What Western Social Scientists Can Learn from the Writings of Fei Xiaotong', *Journal of China in Global and Comparative Perspectives*, Vol.1, 2015 [Chinese version: 韩格理：费孝通著作对西方社会科学家的启示,《全球中国比较研究》, 2017年第1期].

[27] Editor's note: Stephan Feuchtwang. Preface, in Feuchtwang, Chang and Zhou (Eds) (2015), *Fei Xiaotong Studies*, Vol. 1 Globalization of Chinese social science series, and *Journal of China in Global and Comparative Perspective*, Vol. 1, 2015 [Chinese version: 王斯福：序言，《全球中国比较研究》, 2017年第1期].

[28] Bronislaw Malinowski. Preface, in Hsiao-Tung Fei [Fei Xiaotong](1939), *Peasant Life in China*, London: Routledge.

Chinese philosophy and social sciences, has promoted the comprehensive development of Chinese social sciences. We believe that this may not only affect the process of globalization of Chinese social science but could also have far-reaching historic impact on China's participation in global governance and society building and the sustainable development of a global society.

As early as the 1980s, when he was editor of the journal of *International Sociology*, Martin Albrow helped many Chinese scholars to publish their articles.[29] After 1990, he devoted himself to promoting the idea of globalization and became one of its international representatives. Nowadays, he helps promote Chinese social scientific work as part of the globalization of Chinese social sciences; at the same time, he attempts to insert the concept of transculturality into mainstream academia, as well as exploring the contributions of Chinese social sciences in the process of transculturalization. Details of this can be seen in my introductory paper launching the *Journal of China in Comparative Perspective*, entitled 'Transculturality and the globalization of Chinese social sciences: vocabulary, invention and exploration'.[30]

China and the Shared Human Future: Exploring Common Values and Goals (2021), by Martin Albrow, is volume 4 of the *Globalization of Chinese Social Sciences* book series. The title of Part Three is "Globalization of Chinese social sciences". It showcases how Albrow has been helping Chinese scholars and experts in China and the UK to fulfill their academic and social missions, and working towards social theory with Chinese characteristics over the past four decades. In the Editor's Preface of the book, in addition to Albrow's theoretical and methodological contributions, Chang emphasizes Albrow's involvement in the globalization of Chinese social sciences with five features. They are distinguishing a Chinese school of sociology from general social sciences; emphasizing the applicability of Chinese social sciences; encouraging theoretical work between the English- and Chinese-speaking worlds; promoting Chinese social scientific work in the international community; and disseminating the discourse of the globalization of Chinese social sciences.[31]

[29] Martin Albrow (2015), 'A Chinese Episode in the Globalization of Sociology', *Journal of China in Global and Comparative Perspectives*, Vol.1 [Chinese version: 马丁·阿尔布劳：社会学全球化过程中的中国篇章,《全球中国比较研究》, 2017年，第1期].

[30] Xiangqun Chang (2015), 'Transculturality and the Globalization of Chinese Social Sciences: Vocabulary, Invention and Exploration', *Journal of China in Global and Comparative Perspectives*, Vol.1 [Chinese version: 常向群：文化与中国社会全球化——词汇的发明与发掘《全球中国比较研究》，2017年第 1期].

[31] Xiangqun Chang, Editor's Preface, in Martin Albrow (2021), *China and the Shared Human Future: Exploring Common Values and Goals,* London: Global Century Press [Chinese version: 常向群：编者序，《中国与人类命运共同体——为了共同的价值与目标》，马丁·阿尔布劳著，伦敦：环球世纪出版，2021年].

I believe that with the joint efforts of Chinese social scientists and social scientists at home and abroad, the process of globalization of Chinese social sciences will be accelerated. The achievements can be integrated into the human knowledge and make contributions to benefit all mankind.

Xiangqun Chang FRSA
Founding Fellow and President of Global China Academy
Honorary Professor of University College London (2015–20)
Distinguished Professor of Nankai University
October 8, 2015
Revised on December 30, 2021
London, UK

Preface[1]

My original intention with this book was to draw a line under a personal period of intense concern for China and its place in the world. A line for an individual is, of course, utterly insignificant compared with the lines that can be drawn for the world.

Those lines in my lifetime include the period of the Second World War, 1939 to 1945. The events of the year it ended have left their mark on every year ever since. The obliteration of two Japanese cities with nuclear bombs, followed by countries of the world coming together to found the United Nations, left such a huge impression on the consciousness and language of the time that there was a general sense of a rupture with the past. For the great historian Arnold Toynbee it was the beginning of the atomic age.

The profound and widespread feeling of an endangered human existence on this planet meant that the language of the globe and the global came to accompany a general anxiety that was always in the background of the subsequent Cold War. In the Cuban missile crisis of 1963 this fear came very close to panic, only to pass, and for the global to acquire a new gloss of progress in the 1980s. The activities of the transnational corporations then brought the visions of the modern and the global together to shape the new idea of globalization. When to that was added the aspiration to address the growing environmental challenges, the global gained a critical cutting edge, especially for the younger generation.

The end of the Cold War in 1989 and the dissolution of the Soviet Union for some was more than the end of an epoch, it marked even the end of history. World events in March 2022 finally dispel that fairy tale. Human history cannot end, except in the eventual disappearance of our species, but the sense that the global age has a paradoxical conflicted unity (*xiangfan xianghe*) has prompted my own reflections, first in my book China's Role in a Shared Human Future: Towards Theory for Global Leadership, published in 2018, and now this sequel that is published today in London and Beijing.

Both books are inspired by the rise of China as a key actor in world events, and by my belief that no effort is too much to ensure that this is recognised worldwide, in both East and West. This has been the motive behind the efforts of Professor Xiangqun Chang and myself over the last decade in establishing an Institute, now the Global China Academy, and promoting the series of seven Global China Dialogues that concluded in December with the theme 'reforming global governance'. Together with Ingrid Cranfield and the Global Century Press we have worked together for a Global China.

---

[1] Editor's note: This is the author's speech note prepared for the launch of the book in Beijing and London during the London Book Fair, 5-7th April, 2022.

A former American Deputy Secretary of State and President of the illustrious Brookings Institution, Strobe Talbott, explained once how he wrote of the birth of the 'global nation' in 1992 to refer to a single world authority, and then found it being used for the role of the United States in an American century. By extension, however, any nation that saw itself committed to the safety and welfare of the whole of humankind could qualify as a global nation, and it was in that sense we set ourselves the objective of changing the discourse from one of East versus West, sometimes even of clashing civilizational states, into one where every nation can make its unique contribution to the global collective good.

China, by virtue of its continuous history over millennia, by its population size and its economic progress is now obliged to be a truly global nation. But that means it must, as any global nation must, engage directly with others who share the same perception. Exchange of knowledge and enhanced common understanding necessarily underpin the collective measures necessary for a future in which all can share.

For this reason I am sure all present at this event applaud the way President Xi Jinping has driven forward the phrase first used by former Party Secretary Hu Jintao, 'the community of common destiny for mankind' and how it now rests in the preamble to the Constitution of the People's Republic of China.

It has become the phrase that most fully expresses President Xi's philosophy for international relations. When he first used it in the Moscow State Institute of International Relations in March 2013 it was to expand on the meaning of living in the 'global village' a much loved Western idea. A year later at the UNESCO headquarters, it was to update the age old Chinese idea of harmony without uniformity, between cultures, including all people.

In the book we publish today I have aimed to emphasize the talent of the Chinese people in balancing commitment to values with setting goals that match the unique circumstances of any moment in time. It is an outlook, perhaps even a spirit, that I call 'pragmatic universalism'. In China you have no reluctance to think in terms of your own spirit and the spirit of our time.

Today, at this critical moment, when another line in world history is being drawn, I hope my book can add even the tiniest extra encouragement to China to realise its spirit as a truly global nation. It will then have achieved much more than the author could even have dreamed was possible in the years of its writing.

Martin Albrow FAcSS
Founding and Past Honorary President of Global China Academy
March 10, 2022
London, UK

Editor's Preface[1]

Professor Martin Albrow FAcSS (hereafter 'the author') was awarded the European Amalfi Prize for his book *The Global Age: State and Society beyond Modernity* (1996). His earlier books included *Bureaucracy* (1970), *Max Weber's Construction of Social Theory* (1990) and *Globalization, Knowledge and Society* (1990, ed. with E. King), the first book with the keyword 'globalization' in its title. Subsequently he has published *Do Organizations Have Feelings?* (1997), *Sociology: The Basics* (1999), *Global Civil Society* (co-editor; 2006/7, 2007/8 and 2011) and *Global Age Essays on Social and Cultural Change* (2014). These can all be regarded as contributions to mainstream Western social scientific work.

However, in recent years the author's writing has yielded two rather different books. They are *China's Role in a Shared Human Future: Towards Theory for Global Leadership* (2018, Foreword by Anthony Giddens, hereafter 'book 1') and *China and the Shared Human Future: Exploring Common Values and Goals* (2021, hereafter 'book 2'), published by Global Century Press (GCP). Book 2 is double the length of book 1 and together these companion volumes amount to approximately 300,000 words.

Based on his 60-year academic career, the author selected essential work on the theory and practice of globalization, which lays a solid theoretical foundation for book 2. As the editor of this book, I (hereafter 'the editor') collected the author's almost complete work, including academic papers and writings, newspaper articles, lectures, speech notes in academic and public conferences, academic and media dialogues or interviews, and remarks for China's special occasions during this period. They cover major themes like the Belt and Road Initiative (BRI), lifting the Chinese out of poverty and fighting COVID-19. This record would help readers to gain an understanding of how China participates in global governance and shaping global society. It can even be treated as an anthropological case study subject of a non-Chinese sociologist who has been participating in the field of 'global governance and China' through bidirectional engagements with Chinese academia, politics, publishers and media in the past 10 years.

To preserve the integrity of the author's academic and intellectual contributions relating to China in a global context, the editor considers them here as a single volume ('the work' thereafter) when writing this Preface. In addition to provide standard references as footnotes, the editor has also inserted a large num-

[1] Editor's note: The first part of this Preface is revised from the 'Postscript' of the Chinese edition of the book, published by Commercial Press in 2020 [Chinese editions: 马丁・阿尔布劳:《中国在人类命运共同体中的角色——走向全球领导力理论》, 北京: 商务印书馆, 2020年].

ber of notes throughout the book providing background and related information for readers. This Editor's Preface aims to emphasize the book's importance by highlighting 10 key features. They are divided into two parts: the author's theoretical and methodological contributions and his involvement in the globalization of Chinese Social Sciences.

1. The author's theoretical and methodological contributions

1.1 Producing equally high academic value work for mainstream Western publishers

Apart from family and friends, 45 names are listed in the Acknowledgements of the work, including 15 scholars each, coincidentally, in the West and in China, demonstrating the balance in the author's engagement with scholars both Western and Chinese. The work includes some writings selected from non-Chinese organised events and published books: chapters 11[2] and 14[3] in book 1; and sections 2.1[4], 2.2[5], 2.3[6], 2.4[7] and 2.5[8], 3.1[9], 6.1[10], 6.2[11] in book 2.

The author creates an academic collaborative model of interdisciplinary engagement with Chinese scholars. After tracing the changes in Max Weber's understanding of China over the last decade of his life, he has followed Weber's path over this last decade of his own life by engaging with Chinese scholars from multiple disciplines. The author's writing is mainly based on documentary studies, experiences of working with Chinese scholars (see Zhang, 2018: chapters 12 and

---

[2] Keynote address to the conference 'Transnationalization and Knowledge': The Ubiquity of Translation and the Crisis it Faces International Conference of the Research Network 'Trans/Wissen' (Trans/Knowledge) at the University of Trier, October 12–14, 2017.

[3] Keynote address to Hong Kong Baptist University's Faculty of Social Sciences 8th Global Social Science Conference on Trans-disciplinary Approaches to Global Social Science, December 11–12, 2014.

[4] Previously published in *Theory Culture & Society, Annual Review*, December. 2020, 37(7–8), pp. 315–327.

[5] Chapter 6.3 and sub-sections 3.1 to 3.6 are extracts from Martin Albrow (2014), *Global Age Essays on Social and Cultural Change*, Frankfurt: Verlag Vittorio Klostermann.

[6] A chapter in Ino Rossi (Ed.) (2020), *Challenges of Globalization and Prospects for an Inter-civilizational World Order*, Springer Nature Switzerland AG, pp. 143–156.

[7] Unpublished. Written originally in January 2018 at the prompting of Ino Rossi, to clarify ideas around the theme of a new paradigm for globalization research. The author's contribution to his project eventually resulted in the next section of the chapter.

[8] Opening Keynote lecture for the Conference 'Globality in the Space of Reflection of the Käte Hamburger Kolleg', Bonn, April 25, 2013. Published here for the first time.

[9] Speech at the 19th ISA World Congress of Sociology, Toronto, Canada, Research Committee 16 Sociological Theory, Panel 305, 'Populism and the New Political Order?', July 17, 2018.

[10] An invited conference paper entitled for Kalinga Seneviratne and Sundeep R. Muppidi (Eds.), (2021), *COVID-19, Racism and Politicization: Media in the Midst of a Pandemic*, Newcastle: Cambridge Scholars Publishing, Chapter 4, pp. 59–79.

[11] In Werner Gephart (Ed.) (2020), *In the Realm of Corona Normativities*, Frankfurt am Main: Vittorio Klosterman, pp. 497-502.

13; Jin, 2021: 9.2). The author's long period of engagement with Chinese scholars in China and the UK has enabled the discussion in Chapter 9: 'Towards Social Theory with Chinese Characteristics'. It is hoped to encourage the globalization of Chinese social sciences into human knowledge.

As a Weberian-based social theorist, the author believes academic 'exchanges with China bear fruits in every season, always fertilized by delving deeper into Weber'. He suggests that 'Weber today would be examining rationalization processes in the digital revolution and looking for ethical agents in a world of convergent global capitalism' (see 2.1). This thinking grows out of three related studies deriving from an international conference, 'Max Weber and China: Culture, Law and Capitalism', co-organized by CCPN Global, the predecessor of GCA, and published in book 1 (2018: chapters 12, 13 and 14). They may be seen as an example of 'transcultural academic products' (see next point below). These high-quality academic activities and publications complement the work of the Western mainstream academia.

This record would help readers to gain understanding of how China participates in global governance and shaping global society. It can even be treated as an anthropological case study subject of a non-Chinese sociologist who has been participating in the field of 'global governance and China' through bidirectional engagements with Chinese academia, politics, publishers and media in the past 10 years.

Coincidentally, the past decade covers China's President Xi Jinping's regime. From the time the author was making a very careful reading of *Xi Jinping: The Governance of China* (2016) he accepted the editor's view that Xi's work, including the volumes 2 (2018) and 3 (2020) are contributions from China's top elites, including scholars. Readers should treat them as representative of China's thinking for their policy making at the highest level during this historical period.

This book could be used for a historical comparative study from 1979-1989, then with Jiang Zemin (1993-2003), Hu Jintao (2003-2013), and Xi Jinping (2013-), and indeed for studies of China with global and comparative perspectives.

1.2 Reframing the 'community of common destiny' in terms of 'pragmatic universalism'

In the 1980s, Chinese sociologists employed Talcott Parsons's pair of concepts, universalism vs. particularism, to study Chinese society. There were three well-known ideas: China is a particularistic society, whereas Western countries are universalistic societies; particularism and universalism co-exist in Chinese society; and Chinese society would benefit from incorporating a more universalistic element which has emerged from comparative studies of China.[12] But what might that be? This question is still relevant.

---

[12] 郑也夫：特殊主义与普遍主义，《社会学研究》，1993年，第4期，第110-116页 [ZHENG Yefu (1993), Universalism vs. particularism, *Sociological Studies*, 4, pp. 110–116].

The author has offered a way of resolving this question by developing an approach to competing universalisms that he calls 'pragmatic universalism'.[13] The transcultural product that is generated by encounters between Chinese and other multicultural cultures is an example[14] In his speech to the 2nd Global China Dialogue, 'Transculturality and New Global Governance', in 2015, the author asserted that transcultural discourse makes possible a pragmatic approach to dealing with global issues (2018, Chapter 9).[15]

He also stresses that 'a community of common destiny' is embedded in Chinese culture, and is also Chinese leader Xi Jinping's formula for global governance (2018, Chapters 9–11). It is a community of common destiny applied to saving our planet. This is an example of the application of theory that the author calls 'pragmatic universalism', which does not deny the distinctive approaches of different cultures but shows how they can cooperate when there are common challenges.

In this book, the author distinguished his usage 'A shared human future' and China's usage 'community of shared future for mankind' (1.1), elaborating this distinction in answers to 10 questions that were proposed originally by a Chinese scholar but merged into the author's Q & A (1.2).

1.3 Breaking down the rigid division between purely academic work and popular work with theme-oriented work

Methodologically, this book can be viewed as theme-oriented work, thus breaking down the rigid division between purely academic work and popular work. It combines both academic work and popular work, i.e. there are some dialogues and interviews. They were previously listed as an appendix, but have been disassembled and added to the relevant theme, to enable readers to gain comprehensive views of the same theme.

As a practising social theorist or social theory practitioner, the author also created a model of 'engagement with independence' with Chinese officials and media. In his Acknowledgements, the author also expresses thanks to six Chinese officials and six media representatives. He has participated in many events held in China, where he also conducted several field visits arranged officially and involving Chinese media. Through the experience of interaction with them, on the one

---

[13] This goes in the same direction as the 'practical universalism' with transindividual perspective, in 'Pragmatic universalism – A basis of coexistence of multiple diversities' (2015), by Paola Maria De Cuzzani and Kari Hoftun Johnsen, *Nordicum-Mediterraneum*, 10(2).

[14] Shuo Yu (2015), Universal dream, national dreams, and symbiotic dream: Reflections on transcultural generativity in China–Europe encounters, *Journal of China in Global and Comparative Perspectives*, 1, pp. 36–73 [Chinese version: 于硕：普世价值梦、民族国家梦及环球共生梦：中欧相逢中的转文化生成性思考，《全球中国比较研究》，2017年第1期].

[15] Xiangqun Chang and Costanza Pernigotti (Eds.) (2016), *Global China Dialogue: Transculturality and New Global Governance*, London: Global Century Press, pp. 36–39 [Chinese edition: 常向群、裴可诗：《转文化与新型全球治理——全球中国对话》，第1–2合集，伦敦：环球世纪出版，2016年].

hand, the author gained knowledge of their views of China and the world[16]. On the other hand, the author's views were disseminated in the Chinese-language world. Book 2 includes 15 interviews (1.3, 3.13, 6.6, 6.7, 6.8, and 10 pieces under 7.4.2). With this kind of engagement, the author is both playing a public intellectual role and fulfilling a social mission (7.4).

The work consists of 123 pieces: 13 in book 1 and 110 in book 2. Of these, 70 per cent are theoretical studies (2018, Chapters 2 and 3; 2021, Chapters 1, 2, 3, 7, 8 and 9), whereas about 30 per cent are popular writing and interviews. Both Part One and Part Two of the book 2 are arranged in sequence starting with journal articles or book chapters, review essays or book reviews, forewords or prefaces, event speech notes, book or book series proposals, work in progress and media interviews. The aim is to help both Chinese scholars and the general public to be engaged in a mutual learning process. Part Three demonstrates the author's engagements with Chinese scholars to carry out academic and social missions in China and the UK.

1.4 Exploring the concept of 'transculturality' as an alternative conceptual tool for the study of globalization

The term 'transculturation' was first proposed by Cuban sociologist and anthropologist Fernando Ortiz Fernández in the 1940s, but it still occupies a marginal position in mainstream global social theory. American anthropologist Pamela J. Brink offered a clarification of the difference between 'transcultural' and 'cross-cultural'. According to her, 'transcultural' deals with the processes and results of multiple cultural transformations, whereas 'cross-cultural' is mainly used for a comparison between two cultures (1994).

In recent years, the author has been exploring the concept of transculturality, an analytical tool for understanding global society. In the English edition of book 1, the author uses the words 'transcultural' 78 times and 'transculturality' 31 times; book 2 uses the words 'transcultural' 73 times and 'transculturality' 20 times, a total of 202 times; whereas 'cross-cultural' is used only eight times in book 1 and six in book 2, a total of 14 times. The author believes that there is a fundamental difference between 'transcultural' and 'cross-cultural' and uses both terms precisely in this book. The author uses the concepts 'transcultural' and 'transculturality' in every chapter of book 1. In book 2 the author offers a section on transculturality (2.3.1). In the Chinese version, we translated 'transcultural' as 转文化 (*zhuan wenhua*), emphasizing the author's global perspective. It differs

[16] Many interviews published online, including those on *Xinhua Net* website, are no longer accessible now, although some of them can be seen via other websites. In the digital age things change very fast. If we had not made these interviews and dialogue materials available in this book, caught in the moment of their exchanges, we would not be able to find them again and gain a better understanding of how and when they evolved. This data is much more realisable and objective than data conducted from oral history, which mainly depends on people's memory.

from 'cross-cultural' (跨文化 *kua wenhua*), which represents a comparative perspective, commonly used in the Chinese-speaking world.

1.5 Transcultural communication between Chinese and non-Chinese readers

The British Academy report entitled *Language Matters* (2009) stated that 'the declining language skills are damaging the education system in a number of ways: […] it works against efforts to ensure that the UK is a world-class hub of research, which in turn is damaging to the UK's economy; it affects the UK's ability to address many of the most urgent global challenges […].' This report was published three decades after China's reform, which began in 1978. At the time, there was little literature in English on China's rapid growth and the impact of policies and research on China's development and social changes by Chinese scholars, compared with a huge number of studies on China in Chinese. This situation has not improved much since.

The author has throughout encouraged the editor to publish his work in both English and Chinese editions. This provides a way into transcultural communication between Chinese and non-Chinese readers. It is often said that a paper or book is written either for a Western or Chinese readership because they have different interests. That may be true. However, that view increases differences between people unnecessarily. Two-thirds of the above interviews were in Chinese. We have translated them into English, so that, on the one hand, readers can test how objective are the author's views that have been disseminated to Chinese readers. On the other hand, they show readers what questions Chinese media and readers are interested in. If we could learn from their interests, we might better understand them, communicate with them, find common values and goals from them and engage with them in working for the global public good.

2. The author's involvement in the globalization of Chinese social sciences

2.1. Distinguishing a Chinese school of sociology from general social sciences

In his Preface to *Peasant Life in China* (1939) by Fei Xiaotong, Bronislaw Malinowski wrote: 'The principles and the substance of Dr Fei's book reveal to us how sound are the methodological foundations of the modern Chinese School of Sociology.'[17] Fei's work represents the thinking and approach of the then Chinese school of sociology 82 years ago.

However, the development of Chinese sociology was interrupted for 30 years after the founding of the People's Republic of China. In 1999, Fei Xiaotong explicitly stated that 'we must develop a Chinese school of sociology'.[18] He also

---

[17] Bronislaw Malinowski (1939), 'Preface', in Fei Hsiao-Tung (Xiaotong), *Peasant Life in China*. London: Routledge, and New York: Dutton, pp. xxii–xxiii.

[18] 费孝通：重建社会学与人类学的回顾和体会（1996年），《费孝通全集》，呼和浩特：内蒙古人民出版社，2000年，第16卷，第439–469页[Fei Xiaotong (September 25, 1999), 'Review and Experience of Reconstructing Sociology and Anthropology', in *Complete Works of*

proposed that the 'Chinese school of sociology' should take the study of the social culture of civilized countries as the goal of social anthropology and in this way contribute to the construction of an international social anthropological discipline.[19] In recent years, Chinese sociologists and historians have also argued for a voice in world academia and the creation of a stream of outstanding schools with Chinese characteristics.[20]

The author regards 'philosophical social science' (哲学的社会科学 *zhéxué de shèhuì kēxué*) as the core of the Chinese school of social sciences. He distinguishes it from 'philosophy and social sciences' (哲学社会科学 *zhéxué shèhuì kēxué*) generally, as commonly used by Chinese scholars. He interprets and applies this idea in both books (2018, Chapters 2, 6 and 7 and Chapters 4, 5 and 6, respectively). Both book 1 and book 2 are Vol. 4 and Vol. 6 of the Globalization of Chinese Social Sciences book series. They are fine examples of constructing the discourse in this field. To a certain extent, they represent Chinese social scientists' voice in world academia because the author quotes many of their ideas which exemplifies how to develop social theory with Chinese characteristics.

2.2. Emphasizing the applicability of Chinese social sciences

The author believes that 'philosophical social science' in China is not purely speculative but carries the meaning of public philosophy and can guide the knowledge transformation of public policy. *Xi Jinping: The Governance of China* is a good example (2018, Author's Preface, Chapters 2 and 8), as it shows the way to bring China, the West and the rest of the world together in the concept of global governance (1.3). This breakthrough idea and its application may inspire Chinese scholars to carry out a stream of further empirical studies, such as identifying which social scientific and humanistic theories have been transferred into which policies in the 40 years since China's reform and opening up, and what roles they have played in its social and economic development. How have the policies been tested through practice and then refined into theory? Exploring these issues will bring Chinese contributions to the global social sciences to the fore.

Fei Xiaotong (2010), Hohhot: Inner Mongolia People's Publishing House, Vol. 16].

19 费孝通：重读《江村经济·序言》（1999年），同上，第15卷，第245-281页 [Fei Xiaotong, 'Rereading the Preface to *Peasant Life in China*' (March 25, 1996), Ibid., Vol. 15].

20 肖昊宸：打造一批卓越的中国特色学派　在世界学术体系中发出中国声音，《中国社会科学报》，2016年11月14日，见：http://www.ora.shisu.edu.cn/52/22/c3132a86562/page.htm [XIAO Haochen, 14/11/ 2016, 'Voices from China in the world academic system', *Chinese Social Sciences Today*].

2.3 Encouraging theoretical work between the English- and Chinese-speaking worlds

Based on the database of the Chinese National Knowledge Infrastructure (CNKI), Chinese sociologists have published 3,801 papers on Western sociology from classic to contemporary since 1980. Among them were papers on Weber (1,408, 37%), Bourdieu (542, 14.25%), Durkheim (467, 12.28%), Giddens (447, 11.76%), Simmel (123, 3.24%), Parsons (112, 2.95%), Comte (66, 1.74%), Harvey (65, 1.71%), Luhmann (52, 1.37%) and Collins (51, 1.34%). Studies of other Western sociologists by Chinese sociologists in the CNKI database amount to less than 1% of the total, largely because they do not know how to find other less well-known but equally important contemporary Western work. This means that Chinese sociologists' vision is very limited. At the same time, a huge number of interesting Chinese sociologists' work described in XIE Lizhong's paper[21] has been almost completely overlooked by sociologists in the English-speaking world. Thus, Western scholars, similarly, have little knowledge of what Chinese sociologists are doing and how their work is applied to policy and influences changes in Chinese society.

The above-mentioned two papers on Weber are produced jointly in collaboration with the author's former doctoral student, Professor Zhang Xiaoying of Beijing Foreign Studies University (BFSU), in an attempt to assimilate Chinese social culture studies into general sociological theories. In the book, they examine the premises of Weber's study of China, considering the 'world' from a Chinese as well as from a Western viewpoint, and then take the implications of that enquiry to arrive at judgments on other cultures that will enjoy cross-cultural (跨文化) acceptance. Relying on both objectivity and transcultural (转文化) communication, the co-authors try to reach a common view of the issues of cross-cultural understanding that Max Weber's study of Chinese culture raises (2018, Chapter 12). They also focus on the way in which Confucian ethics conventionalize a transcultural ethics of adaptation (2018, Chapter 13).

The work provides a template for Chinese social theorists to combine existing research with the research conducted by the masters of sociology. Similarly, the author engaged with Professor JIN Wei, visiting the UK from Wuhan University, to work on the concept of spirit and published two joint papers 'Spirit 精神 (*jingshen*) as a Key Contemporary Chinese Concept' (9.2) and 'Spirit in Chinese Culture and Western Culture Today' (9.3). These attempts to work with Chinese scholars are helpful for introducing Chinese social and cultural studies into the mainstream global social science community

[21] 谢立中:"当代中国大陆的社会学理论研究:学习、探索与争鸣",《学习与探索》,2017年,第6期,第39–52页 [English translation: XIE Lizhong (2017), Research on Sociological Theories in Contemporary Mainland China: Learning, Exploration and Contending, *Learning and Exploration*, 6, pp. 39–52].

2.4 Promoting Chinese social scientific work in the international community

The author was founding Editor of the journal *International Sociology*. He invited Dai Kejing of the Institute of Sociology, Chinese Academy of Social Science (CASS) to be an Associate Editor of the journal. For Chinese sociologists, the principles of *International Sociology* are very meaningful. The author wrote that, 'I stress "Chinese working in China", because the philosophy underlying the journal was that there should be no political, cultural or linguistic barriers to publication. This may well appear to be the policy for so many Western so-called "international" academic journals, but in practice those barriers exist, especially the linguistic one that requires authors to write in perfect English. Our policy was that no paper would be rejected on language grounds, which meant that we had to assess papers in the language of their origin first' (2018, Postscript; 2021, 7.1). In this way, as early as the 1980s, the author helped many Chinese sociologists publish academic papers in an international journal, partially realizing Fei Xiaotong's 'China Dream' of pushing the 'China school of sociology' into the international sociological community.

In 2017, the author was invited to take part in a panel discussion with South Korean sociologist Seung Kuk KIM, Chinese sociologist BING Zheng and an American–Chinese sociologist Yanjie Bian on different understandings of the meaning of globalization (7.3.2.2). The impact went beyond the boundaries of China.

There are some co-authored papers, dialogues or interviews with Chinese scholars in Chapters 12 and 13 of book 1 and in book 2 (4.1, 4.2, 6.1, 7.3.3.4, 7.3.6, 9.2). They are regular scholars in China who happened to be working with the author on different occasions (see the editor's notes for each of them in Chapter 7). If they can produce publishable work in the English-speaking world with help from the author, making contributions to the process of the globalization of Chinese social sciences, the international academic community should encourage more outstanding social scientific studies from China.

2.5 Disseminating the discourse of the globalization of Chinese social sciences in an enduring way

The work is pervaded throughout by dual global and comparative perspectives which broadens the horizons of China studies in time and space and expands comparative studies on China. China's image in global society can be illustrated in many ways. In the 40 years since the reform and opening up, China has achieved extraordinary results in going global with regard to material products, and its sciences, finance, culture and language have also gained increasing respect around the world.

As the then Honorary President of the Global China Academy, the author has helped in this process by disseminating the discourse on globalization in Chinese social sciences in an enduring way.

This root can be traced back 60 years to when the author was a Master's student under the supervision of Professors Thomas Bottomore and Maurice Freedman at the London School of Economics and Political Sciences (LSE) in 1961. They set up a comparative social institutions seminar programme. The author participated in it with course work on China's landed gentry. This laid an important foundation for the author's understanding of Chinese society with a comparative perspective. Thomas Bottomore is well-known by Chinese sociologists for his book *Marxist Sociology* (1975).[22] Maurice Freedman is well-known by Chinese anthropologists not only for his studies on Chinese family and lineage, but also for his phrase 'a Chinese phase in social anthropology' (see General Preface, p.7).

It is hardly known that the author published the first book review of *The Civilizing Process*,[23] by Norbert Elias, in the *Jewish Journal of Sociology* (vol. 11, 1969), edited by Freedman. This broadened the author's understandings of civilization and inspired him to focus particularly on China and global governance in the last 10 years of his academic life.

During the past 60 years (*huajia* 花甲) tthere have been many important works on China by Chinese and non-Chinese scholars, although few Chinese social scientific works have made their way into the body of mainstream English social scientific literature. The author has not only set an admirable example of how to engage with Chinese thinking, theory and academic work in a global setting, but also helped to found the Global China Academy and Global Century Press, whose mission is to add to the sum of human knowledge and participate in global society building and governance (see Chapter 8).

* * *

Before I end this Preface, I would like to express my gratitude to all the non-Chinese scholars and professionals for their help with the development of Global China Academy, Global Century Press and the Global China Dialogue series in every way without listing a very long list of names.

Here, my gratitude goes to the following Chinese scholars from China, China Hong Kong, France, the US and the UK for their support of the author's engagements to fulfil China-related academic and social missions, including whose who acted as speakers at the Global China Dialogues and associated events (see Part Three): BING Zheng, Hong Bo, Qing Cao, Yan Chen, CHEN Zhirui, Zhangfeng Cui, Kent Deng, FAN Lizhu, GU Yueguo, GUO Dan, GUO Fengzhi, GUO Xuefei, FANG Lili, Fei Hao, Dongning Feng, HAO Shiyuan, HONG Dayong, HU Bin, HUAN Pingqing, HUANG Ping, JIANG Haishan, JIN Wei, Walter Lee, Boyi

[22] Thomas Bottomore (1975), *Marxist Sociology*, London: Macmillan [Chinese edition: （英）托马斯·博特莫尔:《马克思主义社会学》，卢汉龙、费涓洪译，谈谷铮校，兰州：甘肃人民出版社，1985年].

[23] Norbert Elias (1969), *The Civilizing Process*, Oxford: Blackwell [Chinese edition: （德）诺贝特·埃利亚斯：《文明的进程：文明的社会发生和心理发生的研究》，王佩莉、袁志英译，上海：上海译文出版社，2018年].

Li, LI Chunling, LI Hong, LI Junfu, LI Peilin, LI Qiang, LI Wei, LIN Jian, LIU Shaojie, the late LU Xueyi, Baozhen Luo, LUO Jiaojiang, MENG Tianguang, MING Liang, PENG Kaiping, QI Jinyu, QIAN Hai, QIAN Hong, QIAN Yufang, RONG Ke, RUAN Ji, Xiaobai Shen, SHI Xiaojun, SHI Yijun, Lianyi Song, Lik Suen, TIAN Yuan, WANG Jufang, WANG Yigang, Jiaming Sun, Li Sun, WANG Aili, WANG Ping, WANG Ti, WANG Xi, WANG Wen, WANG Yanzhong, WANG Yiwei, WU Baojing, Yan Wu, XIAO Hong, XIE Lizhong, XU Baofeng, XU Jia, YIN Hong, YU Hongjun, Shen Yu, Linda Yueh, ZHANG Fengrong, Joy Zhang, ZHANG Letian, ZHANG Wei, ZHANG Yongfengg, ZHANG Xiaodong, ZHANG Xiaoying, ZHENG Lu, ZHAO Kejin, ZHAO Shu, ZHAO Yizhang, ZHOU Liqun, ZHOU Yongming and ZHU Guanglei.

Special thanks to Professor WANG Yiwei of Renmin University of China and his Master's student LIU Xuejun for their collections of a large numbers of media coverage and interviews of the author. My thanks also go to Mr DU Yichao, Director of Wuxi New Cultural Institute and PhD researcher of University College Landon, for his transcriptions of the author's two speeches and translating them into Chinese (1.3 and 1.4), for Professor XU Haiyan of Nanchang University (7.4.2.1), Mr YANG Bo, PhD researcher of University College Landon and Dr Ivan Hon of Global China Academy (7.4.2.8), and Professor SHEN Haimei of Yunan Minzu University and her doctoral and Master's students (5.5, 6.7, 6.8, 7.4.2.2, 7.4.2.3, 7.4.2.5), for their Chinese–English translation of all the journalists' interviews of the author, and transcription and translation of all the GCD VII video records for editing GCD VII proceedings (7.3.5.2), all at a very short notice and with high quality.

Finally, this book is published with support from the China National Publications Import & Export (Group) Co. Ltd of the China Publishing Group (CPG), to honour Professor Martin Albrow, the founding and past Honorary President of the Global China Academy (GCA), for his academic guidance in fostering and nurturing the Academy (see 8.1 of this book) and the Global Century Press (GCP, see 8.2) over the past decade; and for his intellectual input and activities in supporting and participating in the first seven Global China Dialogue (GCD) forums (see 8.3).

This book serves to demonstrate our collective efforts in exploring common values and goals for China and the shared human future.

Xiangqun Chang FRSA
Founding Fellow and President of Global China Academy
Honorary Professor of University College London (2015–20)
Distinguished Professor of Nankai University
November 8, 2021
Revised on March 16, 2022
London, UK

Acknowledgements

Whatever value this book may possess has depended on the generosity of so many people. They have shared their knowledge and experience with me, and have given their time to read the many drafts of the papers, both published and unpublished that eventually find their place in this volume.

Those whose names are listed below know just how much they contributed both to my thinking and in so many other ways, and it is impossible to document here what I owe to them individually. So to all of them I simply record my lasting gratitude. Thank you, both for the shared ideas generated in friendship, and for the friendship that arose out of working together:

Tom Albrow-Owen, Patrick Baert, the late Ulrich Beck, BING Zheng, Colin Bradford, Hugh Canham, Olaf Corry, Werner Gephart, Anthony Giddens, the late David Held, Stephen Kalberg, Mary Kaldor, Graham Leicester, LI Peilin, LI Qiang, LI Xuetao, Cecily Liu, LIU Kai, the late LU Xueyi, the late John Nurser, MA Hui, MA Lei, Susan Owen, Geoffrey Pleyers, Ino Rossi, Wolf Schafer, Hakan Seckinelgin, Sabine Selchow, Sam Whimster, SUN Youzhong, WANG Xin, XIANG Xiaowei, XIE Lizhong, XU Baofeng, YU Guo, YU Peng, ZHANG Dailei, Joy Zhang, Marian Zulean. It is a renewed pleasure to thank a previous editor of my work, Werner Gephart, of the Käte Hamburger Kolleg 'Recht als Kultur' in Bonn, for his contribution to this volume.

Three co-authors are represented in the pages that follow. It has been a pleasure and a wonderful learning experience to work with them. Therefore, my special thanks to ZHANG Xiaoying, of the Beijing Foreign Studies University and of the Confucius Institute in Tirana, Albania; JIN Wei of the School of Marxism, Wuhan University; and WANG Yiwei, of the School of International Studies, Renmin University.

Ingrid Cranfield has been indefatigable in her work for Global Century Press and shown unfailing kindness, tact and patience in sharing in the preparations for this book. Mark Lee, the Graphic Designer for Global Century Press, has turned every deadline into a showpiece of exemplary professional skills. For both, thank you very much for your professionalism.

Finally, for my editor, Xiangqun Chang, founder of the Global China Academy, I give immense gratitude for the opportunity over the last ten years to share in her unremitting intellectual entrepreneurship and enthusiasm for the causes of understanding and co-operation between China and the rest of the world. Without her encouragement and constant concern this book would never have appeared.

Martin Albrow FAcSS
Founding and Past Honorary President of Global China Academy
16 January, 2022
London, UK

PART I

Theoretical Exploration

DOI https://doi.org/10.24103/GCSS6.en.2021.1

Chapter 1
'A shared human future' and 'community of shared future for mankind'

This chapter starts with the author's speech on the occasion of the launch of his book *China's Role in a Shared Human Future: Towards Theory for Global Leadership.* It is followed by and forms an introduction to his answers to the ten questions he proposed for an extended dialogue initiated by Professor WANG Yiwei of Renmin University of China in April 2020. Together they point to the immense and diverse possibilities the idea of a shared future has for the responses to the global challenges that will determine the future of our species on this planet.

1.1 'Our shared human future' or 'All our futures' – the author's reflection on *China's Role in a Shared Human Future*[1]

One of the pleasures of being an author is being able to give a copy of one's own book to friends and family. Then one can write a personal message inside. Recently I inscribed inside a copy the phrase, 'for all our futures'. Quietly reflecting in my study a few hours later, it dawned on me that, yet again, I had failed to overcome some of the deepest Western assumptions about the human condition.

For President Xi Jinping's message, as it is conveyed in the title of my book *China's Role in a Shared Human Future*, is about a collective destiny, the common fate of humankind. By contrast, the sentiment expressed in my phrase 'all our futures' suggests not just diversity, but also divergent possibilities, even the babel of tongues the West imagined in the distant origin of our species.

Now, of course, both are valid scenarios, not even simply as alternatives, but equally possibly necessary complements to each other. For they grasp quite different aspects of the contemporary human condition, and the one much more pressing than the other. The shared future refers to the governance of the globe, to addressing the critical conditions that threaten human existence on this planet, above all nuclear insecurity and climate change.

Success in responding to these global challenges requires cooperation between the power holders at the apex of international relations, in particular between the USA and China. By contrast, 'All our futures' allows for, even emphasizes individual differences, the realization of uniqueness and the ever-present possibility of conflict. It is then a pure expression of Western individualism.

[1] Editor's note: This was a speech note delivered at the launch of Martin Albrow's book *China's Role in Shared Human Future: Towards Theory for Global Leadership*, at the London Book Fair, March 12th, 2019. It serves a comparative framework between the author's thoughts on 'a shared human future' and China's 'community of shared future for mankind'.

China now, with its Belt and Road Initiative (BRI), is for the first time in its history taking its unique national experience into a wider world far beyond its traditional boundaries. This venture is complementary to and draws upon some of the features of economic globalization and its institutional structures. But its main difference from the Western-inspired models of governance is that it looks to shared goals rather than the imposition of rules.

In other words, although the success of China's opening up depends on the adaptation and assimilation of both Marxism and Western economic and social science into its own cultural traditions, it does not approach other cultures from a standpoint of superior virtue or knowledge, but in the spirit of finding common goals and shared projects.

BRI is above all about the infrastructure of communications, of all kinds, air, land, sea transport and information technology. In this respect, engagement with other countries operates at a very basic level of recognized self-interest and a shared understanding of the indispensable requirements for a functioning economy. The shared goals can deliver precise outcomes and pave the way for future benefits that are yet to be discovered.

China operates the Piraeus port in Greece because that country has the world's largest shipping fleet and China is now the most important shipbuilding country. The advantages to both countries are manifest as trade expands between Europe and the East. This is not a commitment to shared values. It is a pragmatic arrangement to the advantage of both sides.

The Shared Human Future notion can be realized through this pragmatic approach to global issues. It does not minimize the importance of values, but crucially they are not to be derived by merging or aggregating national values or, worse still, imposing the values of one nation on another.

Rather, the values that guide global governance are ones that arise out of transcultural communication and the formation of global public opinion. Saving our species is not a national concern. It is a global imperative of which all human agencies must take account and the most powerful must cooperate to find the policies and practical steps that work. The values that inform global governance are to be those that are revealed in the course of our work together.

1.2 A dialogue of ten questions and answers for a dialogue on Xi Jinping's community of shared future for mankind[2]

Professor WANG Yiwei of Renmin University proposed to the author that they collaborate in framing questions on the nature and direction of Xi Jinping's community of shared future for mankind. The formula for that uncertain condition

[2] Editor's note: The author's contribution was invited by Professor WANG Yiwei. The text of other half of the dialogue is in Chinese and will not be included in this book [Chinese version: It is expected to be published as "王义桅：十问人类命运共同体——对话阿尔布劳院士（关于人类命运共同体的十个问题）"].

of the human future that I used in my *China's Role* book had been 'a shared human future', which translated in Chinese as 人类命运共同体 is the same as Xi Jinping's 'community of shared future for mankind'. In both cases, the emphasis is on 'shared', the indication that whatever arrangements develop in global governance or in the challenges of geopolitical relations mean there is no possible future for our species at all without cooperation and recognition of mutual obligations.

In our ensuing conversation we agreed that the value of the dialogue was precisely in the fact that we would each want to set different questions. In the following ten sections, my question is set out at the beginning and Professor Wang's question that treats of the same or related issues is printed immediately afterwards in parentheses. His full response to my questions will be included in his Chinese-language publication *Dialogue on Community of Shared Future for Mankind*, to be published by Renmin University of China Press in 2022.

This is the full list of Professor Wang's 10 questions:

What is the relation between a community of shared future for mankind and

1) China's Tianxia (all under heaven) doctrine?
2) anthropocentrism?
3) a harmonious world, also a foreign policy of China?
4) China's Great Rejuvenation?
5) the Belt and Road Initiative?
6) Communism?
7) globalization?
8) global governance?
9) the international order?
10) other communities in the world?

1.2.1 Which are the central global challenges that the community of a shared future will need to overcome in the coming period?

[cf. Wang Q 1 re: China's *Tianxia* (all under heaven) doctrine]

In the first place, the future challenges include all those from the past that we have not been able to overcome. They are the constant underlying threats to us all that have been with us since the beginning of the global age.

Nuclear security has been an ever-present concern since 1945, and indeed mounted as a risk to our future in the following years with the increase in the nuclear arsenal of the United States and the Soviet Union and then the addition of new countries to the list of those with nuclear weapons. Maybe there are five or six or seven, we can't be sure, and that in itself raises the level of anxiety. Or, perhaps, for the younger generations, say those born after 1970, nuclear proliferation is an accepted background fact of international relations and taken for granted, much as occasional crop failures might.

That level of acceptance however to my mind actually heightens the risk of a catastrophe, almost by accident. My generation saw, at a young and impressionable age, the first pictures of the mushroom cloud and devastation of Hiroshima and Nagasaki and the shock echoed through the public consciousness of the world's nations for many years. What is extraordinary to my mind is the extent to which the risks of catastrophe are discounted.

They were accepted even as the atomic bomb was being developed. The science behind it was not uncontested. There were distinguished scientists who pointed to a theoretical possibility of accidentally igniting the oceans with nuclear explosions. They were proved wrong in tests – fortunately![3] But what an extraordinary risk to put to test, for we should recognize that science always advances by debate, and those who are ridiculed sometimes are proved to be right.

The second challenge is the preservation of the natural environment, and this has to be seen in the first instance as distinct from combatting global warming. For, after the nuclear risk, the greatest alarm in the post-World War II years was raised by the unchecked use of chemicals on the soil and pesticides. The book by biologist Rachel Carson, *The Silent Spring* (1962), with its attack on chemical companies, caused a sensation, a change of public policy on pesticides and the creation of the US Environmental Protection Agency.

It was the beginning of a wave of public anxiety over a whole range of environmental issues, up to and including population growth, which were the focus of the Club of Rome report, *The Limits to Growth* (1972). This extended the scope of the environmental challenge to cover natural resources, food production, poisoning of the seas, air pollution and everything basically underpinning the way of life of the modern consumer, which could not continue unchecked without ending in disaster.

We should be clear that these environmental issues are still with us and that they represent a global challenge, since no country can develop industry or agriculture without consequences for its neighbours and countries beyond. This is obvious when it comes not only to managing the great rivers of the world and protecting the quality of the oceans, but also in agriculture, where over-cropping creates dustbowls, and in air pollution that knows no boundaries.

Over and above the ecological consequences of the way of life that has become standard for the developed countries of the world, we have the problem of global warming, the release of carbon dioxide into the atmosphere as a result of using fossil fuels. Combatting climate change should be seen as distinct from the other ecological issues, which remain as pressing as ever, even if fossil fuel use is eventually replaced by alternative energy sources. Nearly all countries of

[3] Professor Robert Robinson, described to me by the late editor of *Nature* as 'the outstanding chemist of the twentieth century', argued there was enough deuterium in the sea to start a conflagration if nuclear bombs were exploded in it. Other scientists treated him with scorn (Personal communication from John Maddox, 28.02.08).

the world are committed to the Paris agreements to become carbon neutral in time, and, most important, the new American administration has immediately announced its re-entry into them. The achievement of near consensus between governments on the need to replace fossil fuels is perhaps the most successful example to date of the recognition of our shared future.

Paradoxically, the most recent example of the common fate of humankind, the COVID-19 pandemic, has also shown the limits of a sense of shared future. The introduction of border checks and barriers to foreign visitors across the world in itself is not a rejection of our common humanity, but a sensible precaution to prevent the spread of the virus. But the willingness of countries to blame one another for its spread, the rush to secure vaccine supplies regardless of the needs of others and the challenges to the competence of the World Health Organization all detract from the recognition that human health is a global challenge.

Nuclear security, environment, climate change and health: all four are global challenges. The pandemic highlights also a fifth, namely digital security. The biggest transformation in recent times has been the advance of digital communication and the extraordinary rate with which digital technology has penetrated every aspect of daily life. This did not exist as an issue before the 1990s, since the application of computing technology to production lines and new appliances was only seen as an extension of automation and the advance of industry generally. The invention of the internet and the growth of social media have changed all that.

The range of issues raised by the new communication technology extend from the scope for control by the state and corporate surveillance of individuals at one extreme to the capacity of people to create subversive groups at the other. Big data and blockchains represent the extreme ends of the control spectrum, finding the characteristics of an individual among millions of others at one extreme and creating the new impenetrable identity on the other. At the moment, the technologies involved are largely in the hands of corporations like Facebook and Alibaba and state security services. The uncertain uses to which they can be put, however, are creating international tensions and recriminations.

Currently, attempts to regulate cyberspace are highly controversial and are resisted by the big corporate entities such as Apple and Amazon, which benefit from almost complete freedom from control both inside and outside the United States. In the new geopolitical condition where we have multi-polarity giving way to a duopoly of two superpowers, there is a grave risk of instability arising out of aggressive use of the new information capabilities. This is the global issue arising in the digital age, for which wise leadership and a willingness to cooperate are essential if the shared human future is to be secured. The sooner there are agreed standards for regulating digital communication the safer the world will be.

Looking further ahead, the prospects for the colonization of space open up potential both for conflict and cooperation, but we do have early examples in this area of profound political differences being overcome in the interests of a shared human endeavour. The cooperation of the Soviets and the United States in the early space stations was a wonderful instance of a shared quest for knowledge overcoming ideological differences.

Not all is doom and gloom. The challenges are persisting and great and, in the case of digital communication, new and pressing, but each of them is being met through a multitude of agencies, alliances and multilateral arrangements, as well as through the commitments of individuals who make global concerns into matters of personal conscience.

There are some who disregard these shared concerns as 'globalism'. But there is no more reason to dismiss an interest in the shared future of humankind as globalism than there is to regard an interest in the efficiency of a national government as nationalism. In each case, a common interest is best met through the commitment of individuals to the collective entities that have developed to meet the challenges that countries or the world as a whole face. In the case of the global challenges identified here, this is not globalism, it is global governance in practice.

1.2.2 How will a community of shared future allow for the diversity of identities and cultures?

[cf. Wang Q 2 re: anthropocentrism]

Let us recognize at the very beginning that diversity is not just a necessary feature of human society. It is the prerequisite for the survival of any living species. Every individual living representative of a species is in some respect different from every other and those differences provide the variety of responses that the species needs to meet the challenges to its daily existence.

In every society, even those that have high degrees of centralization, provision is made, either explicitly or in effect, for the differing characteristics of individuals to be attached to distinct tasks and roles. This is true even for the simplest societies, age and gender distinction being universal, but also provision for headship of the group. Personal achievements are relevant, even if only in physical strength. Those differences are directly related to the survival of the group as a whole.

The shape and character of a society's internal diversity will in part be determined by its natural environment. The steppes of Asia favoured the great riders of horses; the fjords of Norway were the home of the Viking warlords. But those selective conditions were tested in the context of relations with other societies. A society's hierarchy of prestige reflects the historical experience of conflict with outside forces. The longevity of that experience will support a cultural distinctiveness expressed in language, writing and literature with roots that can go back centuries or, in the case of China, millennia.

Diversity within and diversity between societies then arise out of distinct though related circumstances. Within, it is broadly a matter of the way qualities of individuals relate to the overall strength of the society. Differences between societies are determined by natural conditions and historical experience.

Those relatively simple distinctions become more complex in what is sometimes thought of as the conspicuously modern way in which diversity poses a problem, namely that which arises out of ethnic and cultural diversity within a society. Here China has a great advantage in having always contained other ethnicities within the dominant Han ethnic group. Their position is guaranteed in the Chinese Constitution. The great sociologist Fei Xiaotong wrote the original definitive account of minority nationalities in China and at this time 56 are officially recognized, of whom the Han people make up over 91% of the population, the next largest group being the Zhuang, with 1.27%.

For this diversity China has developed a variety of governance solutions, providing for autonomous ethnic areas and regions, prefectures, counties and townships. The magnitude of this complex achievement and its relevance to the integrity of China as a whole can be judged from the fact that 64% of the country's territory is under autonomous administration. Moreover, this arises out of a history where ethnic antagonisms often extend far into the past. The relevance of China's experience to a shared human future where diversity is a global challenge is therefore direct and immediate.

The other aspect of diversity in the global setting where China offers an instructive example relates to religious practice and belief. The Chinese Constitution guarantees freedom of religious belief and practice within the law. The Communist Party is itself an atheistic organization but exercises oversight through its United Work Department and religion in China retains an established place. Estimates of believers vary, anything between 40 and 80 million Christians, including about 12 million Catholics where the Papacy and the state have reached an accommodation, but there are estimates of nearly one-fifth of the population who profess some kind of Buddhist belief.

Other countries have experiences of multi-ethnic and multi-religious governance, so China is not alone in finding understanding elsewhere. However, these examples are all of sovereign nation–states with a unitary governance system, whatever the ideological differences between them. The difference with managing diversity worldwide is obvious. There is no world government and there is no prospect of one ever emerging.

If the world is to manage diversity in future under global conditions, then solutions have to be found that lie outside the experience of present-day national governance systems. We need to go back to first principles, first to individuals in society, then to relations between societies.

According to principles of comparative advantage, selection by merit applies within societies for the distribution of individuals between tasks and roles. But fundamentally those individuals share a common factor: they are all human. They share that too with all other human beings in the world. To that extent, the recognition by countries of common humanity is fundamental in approaching diversity.

That common humanity is the precondition for what cuts across national and ethnic divides in the world and is recognized in the practice of accepting in and out migration, mixed marriages, dual nationality, cross-border employment, international tourism and travel. This has long been the human infrastructure of what has been called globalization.

It is a fact of global society that national governments have long recognized in giving rights to their citizens living abroad and in maintaining special links with those who share ancestry or nationality with their country of origin. In their new country of residence, these foreigners very soon form communities of shared origin and create additional diversity. The process today is in full flow: think of Mexicans in the United States, Syrians in Germany or Ukrainians in Poland.

Every society balances what is common to human beings and what makes individuals unique. It relies on common features to provide comprehensive services and on unique qualities to fulfil special tasks. We are thinking here of extremes: care of children as universal, the scientific talent of an Einstein as rare. Those extremes are not in conflict with each other. Indeed, the wider the scope of educational provision the greater the chance is of finding special abilities. In the case of migration, both factors are in play, equal provision and expectations of a special contribution by the immigrant. Both envisage the new future.

China has for a long time extended its care and consideration to its citizens abroad, and for those Chinese communities who retain their special relationship with their country of origin, above all through language and tradition. They provide a bridge for their host country to China and in reverse too, and have been effective in the long run for creating the kind of cross-cultural understanding that the Confucius Institutes seek to provide on a more formal, governmental basis. On the basis of past experience, China can be a leader in promoting the understanding of the intimate and productive relationship between migration and diversity.

Migration is not irrelevant to relations between societies, but the issue of diversity for the global community is not restricted to flows of people. In a world where countries must cooperate to meet global challenges, there is a strong case for observing those universal rules of the division of labour that the eighteenth-century European enlightenment celebrated. Countries too have a predominance of special skills that they contribute to human well-being worldwide. Traditional Chinese medicine has fed into modern medical practice and China has provided an exemplary case of dealing with a pandemic in the current COVID-19 crisis. The United States' technological strengths have enabled it to provide worldwide digital services.

When it comes to meeting global challenges, then alliances between countries, especially on a regional basis, can achieve a level of capability beyond any one country. In the context of multilateral arrangements such as the European

Union, BRI and ASEAN, we see a differentiation beginning the reveals the comparative advantage of each in respect of communications, agriculture and shipping. This was the basis of a proposal I made with Colin Bradford for an explicit agreement between regional blocs to prioritize and specialize in specific policy areas as a contribution to overall global goals such as the MDGs. ('Regionalism in Global Governance: Realigning Goals and Leadership with Cultures', 2005).

Cooperation in the pursuit of global goals is a strategy where China can and does provide a lead, something most recently displayed in its commitment to green strategies to combat global warming. China has demonstrated its huge capability for goal achievement in the elimination of poverty. That has depended on cooperation between every national and local agency, diverse contributions to a single effort. It is a model, a demonstration of its comparative advantage in sharing with other countries for global goals.

1.2.3 How can we advance an idea of sharing that can be accepted by all cultures?

[cf. Wang Q 3 re: a harmonious world, also a foreign policy for China]

The act of joining concern for our future with the idea of sharing reshapes global public discourse. It shifts our focus of attention from the future, as a vista of open and endless possibilities, to an examination of what holds human beings together. It refers us then to basic existential issues.

This is President Xi's most fundamental contribution to creating a new world order. It follows Confucius' dictum for the ruler – attend first to the words. In keeping with ancient Chinese wisdom, when Xi introduced the idea of the 'global community of shared future' to a meeting of the CPC with world political parties (1.12.17), he quoted from the Book of Rites:

> All living things grow side by side without harming one another; the sun, the moon, the seasons rotate according to their own laws without hindering each other.

With this reference to the ancient appreciation of the fact that the laws of nature also govern human existence, Xi directs us to what applies to everyone on earth. It can't be ignored or, put another way, if ignored, the consequences are disastrous.

These sentiments relate to what is universal. They will be expressed differently in different languages and cultures. The ancient Greeks recognized it in the myth of the self-destruction of the chariot of Icarus as it came too close to the sun, pointing to inevitable limits on human ambition to master nature. The sun often figures in these intuitions of the universal conditions of existence. The ancient Indian Vedic texts equate knowledge with the sun's illumination.

Sharing space with nature means all human beings are subject ultimately to the same conditions. It is a sense of sharing that has been dramatically intensified with the recognition that the planet we inhabit is endangered by our own activities. But that very recognition equally also points to the limits of that idea.

For the sharing of our natural conditions can be a notion common to all peoples and individuals in a way that invites them each to follow their own inclinations. It allows for the isolated community, even for the Robinson Crusoe on a desert island as in Daniel Defoe's satirical novel. It can equally underpin the free market ideologies of the West.

It is only when the idea of sharing is extended to cover relations between living beings, and when we consider the consequences of each ignoring everyone else, that it reaches the top of the agenda of our contemporary crisis. Selfishness, greed, egotism, ruthless disregard of others, bring destructive consequences for society as well as for the environment. But then the organization of society becomes the frame for our understanding of sharing.

The diversity of societies, with their different histories, cultures and languages, inevitably brings different ideas of what sharing can mean in human relations. We may find a recognition of the universality of our shared world with nature, but sharing with other people is always accompanied by boundary definitions, them and us, citizens and foreigners, landlords and tenants, men and women, friends and strangers.

This is when space is subject to limits. It ceases to be the natural world without end, but a territory bounded by a separate piece of earth, guarded by other people. But we are of course sharing with them, that is, sharing a meaning, a definition of what is theirs and what is ours. International relations then are the sharing of the space on this planet, allowing each country to go its own way in its own territory. Nations are bonded in their shared understanding of their separateness.

Sharing then is also a dividing up. Interestingly, in European languages, English 'sharing', French '*partager*' and German '*teilen*' all link the ideas of dividing up and combining together in one and the same word. Since etymologically those words in the three languages have quite different ancient roots, it suggests that the meaning they bear, and their easy translatability, derives from a primordial common understanding that is independent of any particular language. Perhaps '*fēnxiǎng*' conveys the same duality, but I must leave that to my Chinese colleagues to confirm. In any case, Xi's speech in translation employs the English 'share' in his 'shared future', but in Google Translate that becomes '*gòngtong de wèilái*' and a 'global community of shared future' becomes '*yigè gòngxiǎng wèilái de quánqiú shèqū*'.

Undoubtedly, Xi's 'global community' emphasizes combining more than separating, in two ways. First 'community' as a concept has a deep meaning of 'held in common', of what joins people together, in ways beyond even their awareness, while 'global' has that comprehensive, planetary meaning that was given dramatic expression when World War II ended with the spectre of human extinction through nuclear weapons.

It is of course quite presumptuous of me to compare my own formula of 'a shared human future' with President Xi's, since the two occupy positions at the extreme ends of importance in global discourse, his being world-changing, mine being a minor contribution to scholarship. So it is only in this context of examining the meaning of sharing that I would point to the particular emphasis that adding the word 'human' gives, and dropping the word 'community'.

'Community' brings with it the sense of common culture and shared values that makes a great deal of sense at local levels, in villages or in distinct residential areas of large towns. For nations in the twentieth century, it must cover the functional differentiation of spheres like the economy, leisure, public administration, education and so on. Not for nothing is there often talk of the 'sporting community' or the 'farming community', meaning those who find common interest and understanding because of their similar occupations even if they do not know one another. But to put a whole nation under the heading of a community challenges those everyday senses.

Communitarianism, the American-inspired political ideology aims to reproduce those local- and interest-based senses of community at the national level. It has the noble aim of seeking to resolve differences and create a common consciousness, but to my mind risks easily descending into a narrow nationalism. The idea of a global community is even more speculative. How deep do we wish the sense of common identity to reach into every individual? Is there not a danger in global communitarianism?[4]

My formula of a 'shared human future' allows an openness about identity and an option about what common activities that implies. But the continuity implied in the survival of human beings places a premium on cooperating to face common dangers. We share the threat of climate change, we share the dangers of nuclear warfare. Combining with others to meet those challenges is the priority, and possibly the maximum to which identical striving is required. For the rest, we can each find our own destiny. Every person, every culture can agree that they have their share in the future of humankind.

1.2.4 How has the Xi Jinping idea of a community of a shared future developed since the Boao Forum for Asia in April 2013?

[cf. Wang Q4 re: China's Great Rejuvenation]

Theory can never stand still. If it does, it changes into dogma and can no longer inspire practice. It is on this understanding that President Xi has emphasized the need for Marxist thinking to develop. In his words: 'The lifeline of a the-

4 For an extension of the idea of community to a global scale see Amitai Etzioni's *From Empire to Community: a New Approach to International Relations*, Palgrave Macmillan, New York, 2004. There he sees the need for a new global authority arising out of common dangers. A 'global nation' would arise alongside a restructured United Nations. I am reluctant to see either 'nation' or 'community' attached to the new arrangements that are needed to meet challenges to humankind's existence on this earth. But that new arrangements are needed is beyond dispute.

ory lies in innovation and it is the sacred duty of Chinese Communists to develop Marxism.' (Xi, Vol. 3, p. 98).

The concept of the community of a shared future is of course in a direct line from one of the visionary passages in the *Communist Manifesto*, when the antagonism between classes and the corresponding exploitation of one nation by another will have come to an end.

When the Forum for Asia was founded in Boao, Hainan Province, on February 27th, 2001, it already included 26 countries and its Charter envisaged high-level dialogues 'to promote and strengthen economic exchanges, interaction and cooperation within the region, as well as between the region and other parts of the world'. This therefore was a very appropriate venue for President Xi in a keynote welcome speech to the delegates to recall its origins and point to a new start after a 12-year cycle of the Zodiac on April 8th, 2013.

His theme was 'A better future for Asia and the World' and he placed the Forum in the context of increasing interconnectedness and interdependence, where its aims both gained momentum and faced many challenges at the same time. He then made this pronouncement that introduced the concept of a community of shared destiny and shaped the rest of the speech:

'Ladies and gentlemen, dear friends, Mankind has only one earth and it is home to all countries. Common development, the very foundation of sustainable development, meets the long-term and fundamental interests of all the people of the world. As members of the same global village, we should foster a sense of community of shared destiny, follow the trend of the times, keep to the right direction, stick together in time of difficulty and ensure that development in Asia and the rest of the world reaches new heights.'

There followed the outline of four requirements for common development: breaking new ground to make it irresistible; working for peace through dialogue; cooperation in the interests of each and every country; being open to the world and its diversity.

Illustrating precisely its relevance to China in particular, Xi referred back to the 18th National Congress of the CPC and cited the Chinese Dream, the renewal of the nation and the creation of a modern, prosperous, strong, democratic, culturally advanced and harmonious socialist country. The following day, speaking to Chinese and foreign entrepreneurs, he referred again to the 18th Congress and the Chinese Dream of national rejuvenation, emphasizing particularly the quality of growth and the promotion of a green economy.

In the first week of October 2013, Xi reiterated essentially the same Boao message in two events in Indonesia. But in the following year, in a speech at the UNESCO headquarters in Geneva on March 27th, he offered the world an elaboration of the concept beyond its original focus on development. Now it was to be framed against the Western clash of civilizations thesis.

The West had been there in the sub-text of the Boao speech, in the reference to the global village, the concept that more than any other in the 1960s had expressed the West's sense of new global interconnectedness. But now Xi was highlighting Western divisiveness as opposed to a primary axiom in Chinese thought, 'harmony without uniformity'.

Harmony corresponded to the needs of 'a world with different cultures, ethnic groups, skin colors, religions and social systems and all people on the planet have become members of an intimate community with a shared destiny.' In an extra emphasis on mutual reliance in the world today, Xi thanked UNESCO for its contribution to preserving and disseminating Chinese civilization. From economic development the shared future has expanded its scope to culture.

In 2015 there were equally significant amplifications of the idea. In Volume 2 of *The Governance of China*, the final section bears the title 'A Community of Shared Future' and contains Xi's 2015 speech for the 70th session of the United Nations, where he called for inclusive development and an 'ecosystem that puts Mother Nature and green development first'. It was followed soon after at the second World Internet Conference by his call for a community of shared future in cyberspace.

In the UN Office at Geneva on January 18th, 2017, Xi's speech bore the title 'Towards a Community of Shared Future for Mankind' and this time it ranged over law, governance and democracy in international relations, common security, emphasizing actions as the key to building the community and committing China to the prevention of war, to common development, citing BRI as an example, to the formation of partnerships as a principle and commitment to multilateralism.

From economic development to culture, to green ecology, through cyberspace to international politics, the scope extends ever further, including perhaps the most decisive and far-reaching commitment to that shared future at the Paris Conference on Climate Change on November 30th, 2015. Efforts in that green direction held up a mirror to all aspects of working for a shared future. It was a shared mission for humanity, a new kind of win–win international relations.

We are able to point to the continuing development of the concept by attending to this sequence of Xi's speeches, and might, as a result, infer that it was simply a pragmatic application of the idea to different circumstances. Pragmatic responses to facts on the ground have long been well reflected in Chinese political culture and policies.

But there is also evidence that there has been a concerted theoretical impulse pushing the idea of a shared future forward. In a philosophy seminar in May 2016, 'to develop philosophy and social sciences with Chinese features', Xi emphasized the combination of Chinese identity and traditional culture with worldwide studies to boost innovation and creativity and he included the community of a shared future for mankind in a list of Chinese contributions that also included core socialist values and BRI.

This explicit and ongoing work on the idea is reflected in the recent volume 3 of *The Governance of China.* The relevant section is twice the length of its equivalent in volume 2, now bears the title 'A Global Community of Shared Future' and begins with a definition: 'As the term suggests, a global community of shared future means that the future of every nation and country is interlocked'. The aim is to build 'a single harmonious family, and turn people's longing for a better life into reality'.

Including the global with the community of a shared future actually indicates a shift in the frame of reference from earlier years. Whereas we have previously seen the idea expanding to include every sector of human affairs, from 2017 it is nuanced according to regions of cooperation. We now find encouragement for specific communities of a shared future, as with the BRICS countries, China and Africa, and Latin America. The global community then allows for more regional communities and there is an equivalent greater concern for binding them together in global governance.

He returned to the theme of the world economy at the G20 summit on June 28th, 2019, the same concern he addressed when he met the Asian nations at Boao in 2013. He now appealed to the responsibilities of the leaders of the top economies, and proposed four directions into the shared future: structural reform and innovation; improvement of global governance; breaking logjams with initiatives like Belt and Road (BRI); and promoting partnerships.

In the end, the shared future comes down to practical measures to realize, in his words, 'enduring peace and prosperity in the world and a better life to all our people'. The idea has to keep pace with the demands of the day.

1.2.5 What will be China's priorities for its contributions to this community in the next few years?

[cf. Wang Q 5 re: Belt and Road Initiative]

One of the four Confucian books, the *Liki,* offers advice that begins with the person and culminates in the world. Each step takes one to a higher level. First, get one's heart in the right place. Based on that is the right ordering of home life. The home is the foundation for rule in national life, and then, to quote, 'the restoration of peace in the world depends on ordering the national life'.[5]

The English have no equivalent doctrine, but the homespun wisdom of the saying 'charity begins at home' has some affinity with the spirit of these ancient Chinese ideas. But it was hardly charity that governed the quest for markets and the desire to convert the natives to Christianity that inspired the British Empire. Neither was it altruism that motivated the desire to spread the American way of life. For the Western powers, the world was to be built in their image.

[5] Lin Yutang (Ed. and trans.) 1938. *The Wisdom of Confucius.* The Modern Library, New York, pp. 144–48.[Chinese edition: 林语堂:《孔子的智慧》，黄嘉德译，太原：山西师范大学出版社，2006年].

It was ever so different for the Middle Kingdom. It has always regarded its own health as its first priority, and it remains beyond the rightful concern of any outside commentator to suggest anything different. It would, moreover, be completely presumptuous for me or anyone else to recommend how that might be achieved. All an outsider can say is that for more than 40 years China has made a remarkable job of ordering national life, and through its revitalization has now earned the right, and even responsibility, to attend to 'the restoration of peace in the world'.

I have tried throughout my answers to these questions on how the world can reach a community of a shared future to adopt a position outside any one country. After all, that future belongs to everyone, regardless of nationality. The citizen of the world who might once have challenged national identity has now become, at one and the same time, a national and global citizen, looking to all citizens and all nations to join in confronting and overcoming global challenges. The cooperation that this requires brings with it the prospect of a better future for all.

Every country looking first to its own welfare sounds rather reminiscent of an international order that in the West is often called 'Westphalian', after the peace of 1648 that ended a war in Europe lasting 30 years. The notion of independent sovereign states is sometimes dated from then. But the new global order is different. The degree of interdependence is such that the welfare of a country is intimately connected with others. China's opening up in 1978 recognized this, even as the rest of the world was only then beginning to grasp the idea of globalization.

Economic globalization has been central to China's policies ever since, with a key difference from most of the rest of the world, namely that there has been no blind faith in the market, and state intervention for specific purposes has always been a policy option. Balanced growth has always been the goal. In particular, the risk of globalization polarizing wealth as it has done in the West has been met by regulation. Thus, most recently, the integration of finance and technology with its intrinsically cross-border potential has led to the People's Bank of China sending out draft regulations for discussion.[6]

Managing globalization has a dual function, for the home country and for the system in which it participates. For the shared future, these two aspects are inseparable. Given China's size and weight in the global economy (at the end of 2019 two-thirds of national economies traded more with China than with the United States), it is a priority for the world as a whole that China continues on this path.

Equally, managing the global economy and global governance are intimately related. This is evident in China's membership of an ever-increasing number of multilateral trade relationships. What began in 1980 with partnership of the World Bank and then later in 2001 with membership of the World Trade Organization

6 Pan Gongsheng, 'How China tackles fintech risk and regulation', *Financial Times*, 28.1.21, p. 23. Pan is deputy governor of the People's Bank of China and heads the State Administration of Foreign Exchange.

has developed into an ever expanding, overlapping set of networks. Of the latest agreements, one signed in November 2020 is the Regional Comprehensive Economic Partnership for free trade with 14 other major Asia Pacific trading nations including Japan, the Philippines, Vietnam and Australia.

The other is the EU–China Comprehensive Agreement on Investment, agreed in principle on December 30th, 2020, whereby both sides effectively agreed to rebalance trade between Europe and China, meaning Europe gained most in terms of access to Chinese markets. The imbalance must be seen in geopolitical terms of making Europe more dependent on China. The agreement comes at a particularly delicate moment in geopolitics with the transition in the American Presidency. But, as the Trump presidency demonstrated, all multilateral arrangements have a geopolitical significance and their multiplication is on balance a contribution to a more secure future for the world.

With external investment China also contributes another side of its strength to the rest of the world, its success in goal attainment. China has just been able to announce the end of absolute poverty and the achievement of a moderately prosperous society in all respects, the first of its Centenary Goals. The road to that success has been a long one of repeated intermediate principles, rules, strategies, targets and goals, with its culmination at the end of 2020, the last year of the 13th Five Year Plan of the Central Committee of the Chinese Communist Party. The steady and long-term goal-directed nature of Chinese public policy is also accompanied by the capacity to move quickly and decisively to meet necessary short-term drives and emergencies. The latest example has, of course, been the dramatic curtailment of the COVID-19 outbreak in Wuhan.

This focus on goals means that China was a prominent supporter of the United Nations Millennium Development Goals and is now an enthusiastic partner in the 17 Sustainable Development Goals. Sustainable development has become an important component of its Belt and Road Initiative (BRI), with its six economic corridors taking trade and infrastructure investment to 140 countries. Renewable power now contributes more than half of the energy investment in the BRI.

Managing the natural environment has been part of Chinese cultural DNA since time immemorial, and the fate of the ruler was traditionally linked to the avoidance of famine, flood and natural disaster. The national success of the Communist regime in China and the global nature of the threat that climate change poses mean that China should take its rightful place as leader of the world's efforts to halt and reverse the trend to global warming.

There is another side to China's commitment to green development. Now that the United States has inaugurated President Biden, the world is finally near to unanimous commitment to combat climate change. The stocks of firms developing green technology are booming on Wall Street. But this is just the latest stage in a change in global public opinion that began in the 1960s with grassroots movements in the West. Engagement with Western public opinion must be the culminating and decisive contribution to the community of shared future.

The Chinese appreciation of this necessity is sometimes acknowledged in accepting Joseph Nye's formula of 'soft power'. It translates into policies to promote Chinese language and culture, most obviously in the Confucius Institutes. A more eye-catching initiative is the recent announcement of the planned establishment of a Chinese university in Hungary. Foreign, especially American and British universities have long had locations in China, taking advantage of the status of English as the main foreign language there. China now recognizes the need to promote Mandarin with equivalent institutions abroad.

There is more to soft power than language, and indeed more to culture than what has often been thought of as its main vehicles, films and entertainment. But in the end the contribution of China to our shared future must be to win recognition in the rest of the world for its profoundly different mind-set. This is what can do most to enable the West to come to terms with its own demons.

At its simplest, harmony, cooperation, family can be presented as replacements for control, competition and individualism. This is a start, but it appears more like the offer of an alternative menu, rather than an invitation to dine at a different place. The Chinese mind-set begins in a different experience of living and its concepts in reflecting that cannot be simply translated into English equivalents.

Xin, heart and mind together, a unity of response to others; *li*, the right way to do things, again thinking of others; *dao*, often simply translated as 'way', but carrying much more weight, as in the message of Jesus Christ 'I am the way, the truth and the life'; none can be understood without a wider appreciation of Chinese culture. And of course *yin* and *yang*, famous in the West as a symbol, is therefore useful as a kind of pre-verbal introduction to Chinese thinking.[7]

But this is just looking at pinyin script: Romanized letters are unable to convey the connotations of the written characters that occupy so much of the early education of the Chinese child. Their figurative representation of meaning allows for the same form of understanding as road signs do in English, except that they can bring with them allusions to primordial and centuries-old experience. Roman letters only represent sounds, Chinese characters depict meaning and, like mathematical symbols, can be translated directly into any mother tongue. We don't have to speak Mandarin to read the characters. In this respect, while English has become the world's spoken language, there is good reason to suggest that Chinese characters have the potential to become the world's reading language.

We are ending on a speculative note, but then the shared future is unknown and allows for imaginative possibilities. China has brought to the modern world millennia of alternative experience. In doing so, it is lending just that necessary counterweight to the tendencies of Western modernity that have accelerated knowledge and technology to the point of self-destruction.

---

[7] For a profound examination of the uniqueness of the Chinese outlook on life, see the French sinologist François Jullien's books, *In Praise of Blandness* (2004) Honolulu, University of Hawai Press; *A Treatise on Efficacy* (2008), Zone Books, New York.

A Western psychiatrist has allowed himself similar speculation at the conclusion of a masterly account of the historical importance of the differences between the two hemispheres of the brain. In his book *The Master and the Emissary: the Divided Brain and the Making of the Western World*, Iain McGilchrist has described how the history of the West has favoured the left side of the brain, a hemisphere that, following an equivalent division in animals, focuses on logic and precision, while the right side provides for empathy and a broader perspective.[8] His view is that East Asian cultures use strategies of both hemispheres of the brain more evenly and he cites in support an observation by the great scholar of Chinese science, Joseph Needham, that Western thought has a 'fondness for particles ... to which the Chinese were "perennially perverse".'[9]

If we add together the example of its own revitalization, the efficacy of its goal attainment, the cooperation of its multilateralism and the sustainability of its investment we already have the distinctive and essential Chinese contribution to making the global community of shared future. But perhaps the decisive factor in saving the world from itself will be if China can convey to others its sense that harmony is the fundamental principle for living at one with oneself, with others and with nature.

1.2.6 How will Marxism and socialist values help to shape the direction of change for the community of shared future?

[cf. Wang Q 6 re: Communism]

Contemporary China draws on an extraordinary store of wisdom from its own heritage. Additionally, it has absorbed the sometimes bitter experience of modern Western societies, without being drawn into an attempt to copy them. In this it is aided by its respect for Marxist thought.

Marx and Engels provided the prophylactic against Western liberalism. Their critique of the political economy of their day and the consequences of industrial capitalism has provided an abiding example of the need for constant theoretical vigilance. Social and economic development has advanced immensely since the middle of the nineteenth century but the example of their determination to resolve the contradictions between impersonal processes and human fulfilment is as relevant now as it was then.

The Marxist critique of Western capitalism arose out of both practical engagement and theoretical self-understanding of the conditions of nineteenth-century modernity. It distanced itself from its own time, reached out beyond its culture

---

8 Iain McGilchrist (2009) *The Master and the Emissary: The Divided Brain and the Making of the Western World.* New Haven: Yale University Press, p. 458.

9 Joseph Needham (1969) *The Grand Titration: Science and Society in East and West.* London: Allen & Unwin, p. 17.[Chinese edition: [英]李约瑟：《文明的滴定——东西方的科学与社会》，张卜天译，北京：商务印书馆，2016年].

and consequently still provides guidance for achieving an equivalent objectivity in the very different conditions of twenty-first-century global society.

Economic processes have social consequences. A state that remembers this simplest of all lessons to be drawn from Marxist thought will be protected against the self-serving arguments of the richest that economic principles must lead to an increase in their share of the collective efforts of its people. A state concerned to safeguard the future for all its people and itself will aim for growth that benefits everyone. China has demonstrated that this is possible by eliminating poverty and achieving a moderately prosperous society by 2020. There is nothing so practical as leading by example and China can continue to do so not just for itself but for the rest of world.

There has been no stronger statement emphasizing those elementary principles than President Xi's speech that he made to students and their teachers at Peking University in 2014 on the 95th anniversary of the May 4th movement. The events that followed that day and the New Culture Movement that followed can rightly be seen as the most important transition from the original Marxist theoretical advances to the present-day emphasis on socialist values. For Marxism does not provide a blueprint for a future society and the belief that it does has been the mistake of far too many revolutionary solutions in the past. It provides the theoretical basis for the structural reforms that allow the people to realize the values that build a better future for their country, society and themselves.

Xi's speech put it all very succinctly: 'The May 4th Movement gave birth to the May 4th spirit of patriotism, progress, democracy and science, kicking off the New Democratic Revolution in China, promoting the dissemination of Marxism in the country and laying the groundwork for the founding of the CPC' (Xi, 2014, *The Governance of China*, p. 185).

When we think of China's example for the rest of the world in the future, we should bear in mind the lessons of the past. Recall what happened in Europe in that period after World War I. The economic foundations of the international economy were so shaky that extreme distortions of values circulated widely. It was a period of acute value conflict that paralleled and often worked in tandem with Chinese events that led to World War II.

The subsequent settlement was very much one of an institutionalization of values in the United Nations but where China and the West went separate ways in important respects because of the profound differences in their cultural heritage. A distinguished German sociologist and former European Union commissioner for foreign affairs, Ralph Dahrendorf, for whom it was my privilege to work briefly as a young man when he was a professor in Tübingen, Germany, used to applaud the institutionalization of conflict in the West. Its political systems assume and encourage conflict on interests and values. China has always had harmony as its axial principle, even when it has experienced civil wars.

It is in that spirit that China has formulated its twelve socialist values, which it divides into three sets of four, for country, society and citizens. As Xi explained, these combine to 'represent the nature of socialism, to carry forward the fine traditional Chinese culture, draw on the best of world civilization and reflect the spirit of the times' (ibid., p. 188). Effectively he is pointing to the contemporary relevance of the Chinese grasp of socialism for the rest of the world, and who can say in the light of the last decades of China's opening up that it has not demonstrated that relevance in a spellbinding manner?

The threefold division of the values conceals a sophisticated distribution of their relevance for public and private life. They are proudly advertised in public places, but together they must prompt ample reflection on their balance and how they relate to one another. Since they are, in Xi's presentation, relevant to anyone in the world, I will be bold enough to offer my own very brief understanding of them.

The four that shape the country are prosperity, democracy, civility and harmony. The balance between them is notable, but also the depth of Chinese experience. Prosperity arises from observing economic principles, while its achievement has to be shared, that is, democratically distributed. Effectively the lessons of Marxism are summed up in the two words 'prosperity' and 'democracy'. Arriving at this balance requires civil relations between people, while harmony is an existential requirement for human beings in the natural world.

Freedom, equality, justice and the rule of law contain the governing principles for a rational and just society, for establishing the institutions that allow and encourage people to assume that others will accept their rights to pursue their chosen occupations and lead their lives in their own way while offering others the same assurance.

Patriotism, dedication, integrity and friendship direct and enhance energy. They strengthen the emotional bonds between people, not just with their immediate circle but also expanding out to the country as a whole so that the personal life is also a commitment to the welfare of their fellow human beings.

For the rest of the world, the impressive and instructive thing about Xi's and China's exploration of values is simultaneously its historical depth and its contemporary application. To quote: 'Values appear and develop in the process of human beings getting to know and shape nature and society' (ibid., p. 191). There could hardly be a more succinct statement of how values evolve and why we should expect their continuing evolution.

The Marxist moment was necessary to break the assumption that values are timeless and beyond human control. It undermined the idea of inherited social privilege and it clarified the dependency of contemporary society on economic principles. What was left was the recognition of values for reshaping society. In China's case, a rich heritage of thought could be revitalized under new conditions.

In the case of the West, there has been a failure to recognize the independence of values from economic principles. Industrial capitalism has morphed into the digital economy and money has become the measure of personal success. Paradoxically, the American Dream of rising in society has become the victim of the country's economic development. The China Dream, on the other hand, a formulation that nods to the success of the American economy in sheer wealth creation, is a much more encompassing vision of the Chinese citizen as a social being, growing with society as it develops.

The idea of community is far more applicable to Chinese society today than it is to the United States, where community has been associated traditionally with the original settlements, smaller towns and neighbourhoods. The value that has linked them has been the striving of the individual to realize the American Dream in their personal success. It is an open question whether the Chinese Dream or the American will contribute more to shaping the shared future for humankind.

The development missions of Western capitalist societies since World War II have led to the introduction of governance arrangements in other countries that replicate the institutionalized conflicts of the West. By contrast governance, in China is underpinned by the CPC, which ensures a power structure with a grassroots base coordinating the work of private and public agencies of all kinds, from education to transport, from farming to broadcasting, all aiming to implement national priorities.

In this way, the Communist Party is the motivating and governing force in a national community. As far as a global community is concerned, there is no equivalent to energize effort for global priorities. Since there are, as we have pointed out, global challenges that require an urgent and coherent global response, the CPC may well consider it important for China's global responsibility to reach out, not just to other political parties but also to groups and agencies in other countries, to encourage a collective response.

The resistance of Western countries to approaches from China to cooperate on global issues on ideological grounds may well be one of the most unfortunate distractions from mounting a truly global communal effort, a realization of global community. It will be a challenge for the CPC to develop a truly global strategy for influencing countries with traditions of Western representative democracy to cooperate with China on threats that confront us all. The CPC's success or failure in this will be a decisive factor determining the outcome of efforts to create a genuine global community of a shared future.

1.2.7 In what ways can we expect the nature and impact of globalization to change in the coming period?

[cf. Wang Q 7 re: globalization]

The world has come a long way since globalization became the slogan for the 1990s. By then, its story already stretched back over 20 years to the time when an American professor had used it as a chapter title in a politics textbook. In the 1980s, American corporations adopted it to describe their own vision for expanding into international markets. Then, at the beginning of the 1990s, academic debates about its meaning and impact took off in many different directions. Later, towards the end of the decade, the Clinton presidency in the United States adopted globalization as the narrative of a necessarily American-led future for the world.

So public rhetoric around globalization has been changing from the beginning and has continued to change, even as the underlying facts to which it refers have often moved independently of it. In particular, geopolitical events have interrupted any sense that there is a single direction to world history. '9/11', the destruction of the twin towers of the World Trade Center in New York in 2001, ended any euphoria that might have lingered from the celebration of the arrival of the third millennium of the Western calendar.

From my own earliest engagement with globalization as a theme at the World Congress of Sociology in Madrid in 1990, I have been concerned to distinguish the discourse of the global from geopolitics and trends in the world economy. The spiritual and the material are bound together in our experience of passing time and for humanity as a whole there are events that mark off periods of history from one another.

It was the explosion of nuclear bombs over Japanese soil in 1945 that initiated a new sense of the fragility of human existence, of an endangered globe. I argued in my book *The Global Age: State and Society beyond Modernity* (1996) that it was the threat of the nuclear holocaust that signalled the end of the modern age and its displacement by the global age.

It was this sense of our fate on this earth being in the balance that undermined the old belief in modernity as progress. The widespread sense of an endangered human existence on the planet was reinforced by the recognition that development could also mean a damaged natural environment. The label of modernization that the West tagged to its model of economic development for the rest of the world lost its appeal, to be replaced by the contested discourse of globalization.

Globalization was both a contested discourse and a master narrative. As an extension of the use of the language of the globe, it shared the sense of interdependence and worldwide communication that had been conveyed in Marshall McLuhan's inspired term 'the global village'. It picked up on the slogan 'think globally, act locally', to reflect the impact that Roland Robertson preferred to call 'glocalization'. Substituting for modernization, it looked to be the latest stage in a movement of world history that appealed so much to the American imagination.

But, regardless of the language, the economy rolled on with its own momentum, even as geopolitics conditioned its direction. With the Cold War as its background and with its war in Vietnam in the past, American capital was ready to engage with China as it emerged from the Cultural Revolution. China too was opening up and the Third Plenary Session of the 11th Party Central Committee in December 1978 declared China should 'be proactive in developing economic cooperation with all countries of the world' (Li Lanqing, 2009, *Breaking Through: The Birth of China's Opening up Policy*, p. 70).

Important symbolic events followed. In January 1979, Vice-Premier Deng Xiaoping was entertained by President Carter in the White House. It followed the normalization of diplomatic ties between the US and China at the beginning of the month. The next day, Coca-Cola signed an agreement with the authorities allowing it to open bottling facilities in China. This was more than just symbolic; Coca-Cola was the leader in developing the kind of global market strategy that became the ambition of every international corporation in the 1980s. This was the decisive moment for the framers of global marketing strategies in that decade.

But Coca-Cola represented both a drink and the American way of life, and for many it was only the most prominent example of the expansion of the global village, intimately associated with jeans, pop music and Hollywood. Globalization therefore also meant travel, crossing cultures and the development of global culture. It could also mean 'one world' and Coca-Cola exploited that sense by advertising its product in a song to teach 'perfect harmony'.

By the first decade of the twenty-first century, globalization could in one context mean the world becoming more interdependent, in another, greater diversification as national cultures spread globally, in yet another, more standardized tastes as value chains extended worldwide and the same products became available everywhere. On the one hand, the uniqueness of a place could receive global attention; on another, wherever one travelled the hotels could appear the same.

In academic accounts of globalization, homogenization, hybridization and individuation competed for space in the journal pages. In a way, those concepts illustrated the limits of the concept of globalization to identify any direction in contemporary history. The global might be the frame for human endeavour but it could not fix the content. Global governance might take globalization forward, global events might take it back. Global culture might seem to promote Americanization, yet Hollywood might make anti-American films (as the *Wall Street Journal* complained once about the global hit 'American Beauty'). In fact, Hollywood might not even be regarded as American at all, given its vast range of talent from all quarters of the globe.

China, by contrast, has resisted the extreme forms of what it sees as Western cultural imperialism and insisted on speaking of economic globalization. In his early reference to global governance and global development at the 5th BRICS meeting in March 2013, President Xi Jinping linked them to 'deepening economic globalization', and he has been consistent ever since in reserving globalization to the economic sphere (Xi, 2014, *The Governance of China*, Vol. 1, p. 356).

The story of economic globalization since 1978 has been intimately connected with the rise of the Chinese economy, and for China globalization has been effectively equated with the development of the global economy. But change in the economy has not been in one direction either and China has early on seen the importance of the digital revolution.

In sum, looking back, there is no single story of globalization. The twists and turns in discourse have reflected geopolitical events. There is no straight line in economic development. No one could have predicted the impact of continuing innovation in computing technology and the power of the internet. And the most recent shock has been COVID-19, which both upends the idea that countries' borders will become ever more open and also points to human dependence on scientific cooperation.

If we want to know the future of economic globalization, we need to look back and draw the lesson that there has been no single line of development, unless one simply regards the growth of the global economy as the one consistent feature over the last fifty years. That growth has been very uneven and its distribution over the continents and regions of the world has reflected political as much as economic forces.

The big story has been the growth of China and its success in bringing half a billion people out of poverty. The less prominent but in some ways more influential development for world stability has been the polarization of wealth within countries as a global class of billionaires has become more detached from national roots. This is the point where 'global' loses its claim to define the character of a historical period, when a new kind of politics emerges from the consequences of economic globalization.

The global age has ended much as the modern did, with the conjunction of a set of events and new circumstances that change outlooks throughout the world. Global challenges remain, global warming has not been defeated and the threat of nuclear disaster has never been eliminated. But the dominating discourse is now the digital and the digital age has become the frame both for policy makers and everyday life.

We are writing at a critical turning point in history, where the consequences of economic globalization are hollowing out the politics of liberal democracies, when the digital revolution has combined with social media to produce new kinds of opinion formation and when a global pandemic has activated a worldwide intensified control of personal behaviour.

Globalization no longer provides an answer to the direction the world takes at this juncture. Much as modernization lost its hold in the past, it serves only to indicate just one pair of alternatives among a multiple list of alternatives, such as: open up vs close down; preserve vs demolish; choose vs take orders; save vs spend; etc., etc. Global vs local is just another alternative. It can certainly offer no clue as to how the relations between two superpowers will develop. China and the United States will each draw on their own culture in shaping their stance to the other, and the world largely waits with both hopes and fears for the developing outcomes.

1.2.8 How must the existing institutions of global governance change to advance a true community of shared future?

[cf Wang Q 8 re. global governance]

Governance is the term that has been retrieved in the West from the pre-modern period of its history. It was in regular use before the sixteenth century to cover the various forms of social and political control, both of self and others, that preserved order, with or without a central government.

The recovery of the idea of governance in the 1990s was directly linked to the impact of globalization on institutions established after World War II. The United Nations and its affiliates like the IMF, the World Health Organization and UNESCO were all created with the idea that the world needed an order that would secure it against the catastrophe that overwhelmed it in 1939. In the 1980s globalization, especially in the form of the expansion of global corporations, effectively created new cross-boundary linkages that no longer fitted into that order.

This approaching obsolescence of the post-war order appeared to come closer with the apparent impending United States global hegemony after the demise of the USSR. The language of governance then gained a hold in international discourse reflecting resistance to what was increasingly seen as a potential world empire. It gained expression immediately after the end of the Cold War in the Stockholm Initiative on Global Security and Governance in April 1991, which under Willy Brandt's guidance proposed the Commission on Global Governance.

The report of the Commission, *Our Global Neighbourhood*, is one of the founding documents for global society in the twenty-first century. It effectively envisaged an order to social and political relations that was an unplanned but yet guided outcome of multiple interactions at different levels between state and non-state actors. In its words: 'What is new today is that the interdependence of nations is wider and deeper. What is also new is the role of people and the shift of focus from states to people.'[10]

That perception of the direction of change in the world led the authors to ask for a renewal of the international system, an expansion of the rule of law worldwide and the enabling of citizens to exercise democratic influence on global processes. All this was echoed in the academic discussion that paralleled the deliberations of the Commission. James Rosenau plied it with background papers and subsequently opened the contributions to a new journal, *Global Governance*, in 1995.[11]

[10] The Commission Our Global Neighborhood (Ed.) 1995, *Our Global Neighbourhood: the Report of the Commission on Global Governance*. Oxford University Press, p. xiv. The volume adopts a definition of governance that can apply to any level of human organization, from a local club to world society today: 'Governance is the sum of the many ways individuals and institutions, public and private, manage their common affairs' (p. 2).

[11] James N. Rosenau (1995), 'Governance in the Twenty First Century', *Global Governance*, 1(1), pp. 13–43.

Mainstream American academic work was then mobilized in the Visions of Governance project of the Harvard Kennedy School of Government in 1996, linking it specifically to questions of democracy. A subsequent volume that resulted from the project was edited by Joseph S. Nye Jr and John D. Donahue, who offered the following definitions:

By governance, we mean the processes and institutions, both formal and informal, that guide and restrain the collective activities of a group. Government is the subset that acts with authority and creates formal obligations.[12]

Parallel to the discussion of governance in the context of international relations there was a widening debate about the governance of Western corporations. This was a clear corollary of the recognition of the transformative effects of globalization, which meant that the transnational corporation, normally American-owned, was effectively escaping national governmental supervision, regulation and often responsibility to shareholders, employees or the citizens of countries in which it operated.

Mervyn King, South African judge and former chair of the steering committee reviewing governance within the UN, speaking at a conference in 2005, effectively acknowledged the degree of autonomy that corporations had achieved when he emphasized that 'good governance springs from integrity and intellectual honesty rather than compliance with external standards'.[13]

The debate about governance has arisen out of the tensions and dilemmas that globalization has produced for the older modern ideas of representative government in the West, and in particular those of the Anglophone countries that suffer from the hollowing out of their own societies even as they hold up their democratic experience as an example to the rest of the world.

Governance as a concept takes us beyond government and indeed into the preconditions for order between people in general. In this respect it is an open invitation for those outside the Western cultural complex to offer their own interpretations and accounts of what brings order and consider them in the context of a rapidly developing world society.

China was represented on the Commission on Global Governance by a person of immense experience, who had been permanent representative to the United Nations (1985-86) as well as secretary to leader Zhou Enlai, Ambassador Qian Jiadong. In the words of the report, 'we all agreed on the overall substance and direction …' and it appealed to humanity to agree 'a better way to manage its affairs'.[14]

---

[12] Joseph S. Nye Jr. and John D. Donahue (Eds.) (2000), *Governance in a Globalizing World*. Washington, DC: Brookings Institution Press, p. 12.

[13] Tomorrow's Global Company: the challenges and choices. Report of the conference held at Wilton Park, UK. September, 2005. London: Tomorrow's Company, p. 18.

[14] *Our Global Neighbourhood*, p. xvi.

The commitment of any one country to the report, including China (indeed of any individual, since, however distinguished, they were all there in a personal capacity), was left open for future exploration and argument. The terms of the report were such that it could only indicate general directions, but that in itself was sufficient to set the tone for a continuous development of debate about securing a stable global order ever since.

What is clear from examining the context of the subsequent debate about governance is that it mirrors the disintegrative experience of globalization in the West itself. The debate has been couched in terms of democracy, responsibility, representation and accountability that arise out of the unique historical development of Western nation–states and their subsequent worldwide expansion. But those effects of globalization include the rise of new agents who are products of processes quite distinct from those that created the nation–states in the first place. Environmental groups or anti-nuclear campaigners cross national boundaries and appeal to the common interest of humankind. In fact, they adopt the global vision to point to the essentially self-interested motivation of other transnational agents, the economic globalizers, to accuse them of their global imperialism rather than commitment to the global public good.

It is these contradictory directions in the emerging developments since 1990 that James Rosenau sought to express by inventing the term fragmegration, envisaging entities breaking up and new ones forming.[15] The rather dismissive response from Joseph Nye was that there was no need to alter the English language to realize that contradictory movements can happen at the same time.[16] The tone of that comment, let's leave language alone, was in line with Nye's argument that global governance required a large state to take the lead for it to use its power to benefit others.[17] In other words, global governance reproduced existing power relations and was an extension of American benevolence. Similarly, the language of the globe is the gift of the English-speaking world.

This is just one small example of the contradictions in Western approaches to governance. When it comes to national institutions, there is an assumption that representative institutions exist independently of the group that holds power. Parties alternate. But in global institutions there is an assumption of one party control – the United States. The fact is that rapid change in world society cannot follow a single blueprint. Indeed, neither of those solutions to shaping global governance is adequate and we must be prepared for novel solutions.

China, with its vastly longer experience of settled government, as well as of the impact of Western imperialism, is uniquely qualified to take a lead in the

[15] James N. Rosenau (1997), *Along the Domestic-Foreign Frontier: Exploring Governance in a Turbulent World*. Cambridge: Cambridge University Press, Chapter 6 Fragmegration, pp. 99–117.

[16] Joseph S. Nye Jr. (2002), *The Paradox of American Power: Why the World's Superpower Can't Go it Alone*. New York: Oxford University Press, p. 59.

[17] Ibid., p. 15.

evolution of global institutions. It begins with a quite distinct conceptual approach to political order, with relations between people and with nature having a pivotal place. It was the basis for President Hu Jintao's contribution of the unique Chinese concept of *Hexie Shijie*, world harmony, to the 60th anniversary of the United Nations in 2005.[18]

Over the centuries Chinese political culture has prioritized qualifications, experience and wisdom over voting and representation. In its twentieth century, the massive change in its own political system, while preserving that traditional respect for knowledge and experience, has seen socialism with Chinese characteristics replacing the imperial institutions but at the same time drawing its leadership at all levels from the people. The result has been a form of democracy that allows for consensual commitment to national goals with consultation at every level of decision making.

The success of achieving the goal of a moderately prosperous society in 2020 demonstrates the capacity of the governance system of China as a whole, with the Communist Party as the motivating agency, for the total national effort. If there is a case for one country to lead global governance, as Nye suggested, then China would now appear to be rather more qualified than the United States.

My own proposal, however, is that we treat global governance as a unique contemporary set of practices and institutions that are evolving all the time. In particular, the major development since the original foundations of 1945 has been the emergence of collective goal-oriented agreements, such as the UN Climate Change Conferences, implementing the Kyoto Protocol of 1997 that extended the Convention of 1992, which committed the parties to reducing greenhouse emissions, and subsequently the Millennium and the Sustainable Development Goals. These have penetrated through national layers of administration to motivate actors at grassroots levels.

In the West, the commitment of citizens to global goals has tended to be treated as civil society, or 'third sector', with domestic concerns swept up in the intersection of politics and business. The consequence has been the detachment of 'global citizens' from national politics, even as business itself has been drawn to the global market. The space is left open for the growth of populist movements attacking the remoteness of national elites from local concerns. The dynamic of these changes provides moments of high drama in the transition of power in the United States at the time of writing. They also impede any further commitment to the development of global institutions.

China, on the other hand, gives high priority to its national commitment to the United Nations, the WTO, the WHO and other multilateral agencies. For instance it commits the highest national share of the personnel of the UN peacekeeping forces. It establishes other multilateral bodies such as the Asian Infrastructure

[18] ZHANG Xiaoying (2012), *The Economist's Construction of Globalization (1985-2010): A Narrative Analysis with a Chinese Perspective*. Beijing: World Affairs Press, pp. 242–259).

Investment Bank (AIIB), and its BRI has since 2013 taken investment in transport and communications to more than 60 countries.

These are all contributions to developing global governance based in pragmatic responses to the needs of other nations, with a shared understanding of where cooperation will bring mutual benefit. The shared future is constructed out of each project's vision of improvement for the people it is to serve.

On the one hand, the outcome is to aggregate human benefit from cooperation across borders, on the other, global goals like ending global warming form consensual elements in those same projects and contribute to the global community as a whole. This is a mirror of any community that allows its members to find their own destiny within it, while at the same time contributing to programmes that affect the interests and well-being of them all.

It is the shared understanding of these respective aspects of a community that secures order and shapes its governance, rather than any plan that seeks to create a new order. It is a dynamic process of search and discover for the wellbeing of each and every member, collective and individual. No better sense of community is required, no blueprint will offer a better solution.

In the last year the world has experienced what global governance is like in the crisis precipitated by COVID-19. If a government policy adviser had been asked to design a hypothetical threat to test the resilience and effectiveness of global governance and had proposed imagining a virus with the global incidence of COVID-19, the response might well have been: 'Go away and produce something more realistic'. But a pandemic of lethal potential is what the world is experiencing.

Nuclear war imperils everyone on earth but, once it happens, governance has failed. In the case of a pandemic, the responses of and outcomes for individuals, organizations and countries reveal the scale and effectiveness of the governance they share. The event is ongoing, the overall health outcomes still uncertain, but we can be sure that governance at all levels will be subject to review and reform as never before. It could even result in improvements if we all look to our shared future.

1.2.9 What is the future of democracy in a community of a shared future?

[cf. Wang Q 9 re: international order]

We owe the word 'democracy', rule by the people, to the ancient Greeks, and in modern times the word has gone round that the Greek city states two and half millennia ago were democracies. That was only rarely true and in any case democracy was for them by no means something to be praised. It could easily turn into mob rule.

In fact, for the philosopher Aristotle, the best kind of government was a constitutional state, and democracy would distort it by serving the masses. His predecessor, Plato, had an image of the democratic man as someone who went about shouting for liberty and equality but in practice doing just what he pleased! The mass of the people on the one hand, individual freedom on the other, the two extremes combine in permanent tension in the idea of democracy. Under the best of circumstances they can exist in the idea of responsible citizens at ease with one another. In the worst cases historically anarchy or tyranny can result.

The contradictions implied in serving the masses, on the one hand, and allowing individual freedom, on the other, were obvious in the most famous account of American democracy in the middle of the nineteenth century. Alexis de Tocqueville viewed the advance of democracy as irresistible but 'according as we establish either democratic liberty or democratic tyranny, the fate of the world will be different'.[19] What he found 'most repulsive in America is not the extreme freedom reigning there but the shortage of guarantees against tyranny'.[20]

Fast forward to the present day. The United States' narrow escape from the chaos of a Trump coup makes de Tocqueville's words prophetic. The institutional framework of the American Constitution only just prevented tyranny – of the minority, however. But at the same time the deep divide between the Democratic and Republican parties seems destined to persist indefinitely. In the party system of Western democracies, conflict is institutionalized.

The names with which the West describes democracy, 'representative' or 'liberal', embody the contradictions already apparent to the Greeks. 'Liberal' meaning free, 'democracy' meaning rule by the people, can only be reconciled with institutions that seek to resolve conflicts that arise between people.

From the end of their domination by the Roman Catholic Church in the sixteenth century, the history of the Western countries has been one of endemic and persisting conflicts, over religion, about empire, between classes, over ethnicity and most recently about gender. In the governance of nation–states those conflicts have been both managed and amplified for the purposes of political parties.

In more recent times, the rapid globalization of the world economy has led to rising social tensions within nation–states. The wealth of the world grows but within countries polarization of rich and poor increases. The competing interests of capital seek to find advantage by ever-growing financial support for political parties, while the new communication technology allows for increasingly hostile exchanges and the mobilization of hate in the social media. Liberal democracy is in crisis.

Fifty years ago, the West thought of liberal democracy as the necessary accompaniment to modernization and economic development for the rest of the world. Governments and global governance agencies sought to tie economic aid to the reform of governmental institutions that mirrored Western models. Since the Millennium, confidence in this strategy has been shaken. The Iraq War and

[19] Alexis de Tocqueville (1994) [1848], *Democracy in America*. London: Fontana Press, p. xiii. The quotation is from the preface to the twelfth and next-to-last edition in the author's lifetime.

[20] Ibid., p. 252.

the failure of the so-called Arab Spring have dented both the prestige of Western democracy and hopes for exporting it.

Finally and most recently, the shock of the Trump presidency, with its departures from the Paris Accords on climate change and from the World Health Organization, has demonstrated that multilateralism and global governance institutions have no permanent guarantee to be supported by Western democracies. Instead, the rest of the world is bound to examine the Chinese example of consultative democracy with growing interest.

In this respect we need the same historical perspective on China as we have given to the West. Before the collapse of the Qing dynasty in 1911, any talk of democracy in China was associated with Western-style innovations like voting. But it should be recalled that the West at the time by no means had extended the suffrage to all citizens and debates among Chinese intellectuals had their own dynamic even if they paralleled Western ones.

For instance, before women got the same right to vote as men in the UK in 1928, the Chinese Communist Party from its foundation in 1921 supported women's equality. Socialism with Chinese characteristics has a prominent place in contemporary political rhetoric in China, and its debts to and affinities with traditional culture have received considerable emphasis. Less attention has been given to the roots of Chinese democracy, for some obvious reasons. Chinese imperial rule was distant from everyday life. The Chinese village might never see a government official and everyday affairs were the concern of the residents and their headmen.

Notwithstanding all the changes that have taken place since the nineteenth century, localism is still the basis of Chinese governance, that is, local people make local decisions. When a Western observer wrote about village life in the dying years of the Empire, he highlighted the talent for cooperation of village people as embodied in local self-government.[21] When Fei Xiaotong began his now classic studies of life in Kaixiangong village in 1936, he found the headmen still key for the performance of collective social functions.[22]

President Xi's own experience as a young man in Liangjiahe village and later as Party Secretary in Zhejiang province gave him a feeling for the grassroots that comes through in a speech he made on rural revitalization in September 2018: every village is different, give full play to local initiative, use creative experience of the grassroots to improve top-level design.[23]

---

[21] Arthur H. Smith (1909), *Village Life in China*. Edinburgh and London: Oliphant, Anderson and Ferrier, pp. 226–234 [Chinese edition: [美] 明恩溥：《中国乡村生活》, 译者: 陈午晴 / 唐军，北京：中华书局，2006年].

[22] Fei Hsiao Tung [Fei Xiaotong] (1983), *Chinese Village Close-up*. Beijing: New World Press, p. 22 [Chinese edition in: 费孝通：《江村经济》（含《江村经济》《重访江村》《三访江村》），厦门：鹭江出版社， 2018年].

[23] Xi Jinping (2020), *The Governance of China*, Vol. 3. Beijing: Foreign Languages Press, p. 307 [习近平：《习近平谈治国理政》，北京： 外文出版社，2016年].

When we read Xi's exhortation to the 19th Party National Congress to strengthen the people's position as masters of the country, we need to visualize a huge hierarchy that begins at local levels in towns and villages, with levels extending through provinces up to central government, where there is continuing discussion and decisions involving members of the public and Party officials. The Party leads but, stresses Xi, only through law-based governance.[24]

The Party is involved at every stage of the decision-making process, from the village and the factory, the town and the corporation. It acts in and with the decisions of the people up to and including the leadership of the government. It brings forward policies set by the top and conveys aspirations and information from below. It guides and it listens. It has its own internal democracy. The national co-ordination it achieves makes China the most powerful collective civil agency the world has ever seen. It offers the world to observe a model of consultative democracy, but it is unique to Chinese culture and ways of life.

Given the new power of China and its relative size in the world, the question arises how far it can influence the direction of global institutions. Its own model of democracy, socialism with Chinese characteristics, is by definition not transferable to other countries, which all have their own kinds of governance. At the same time, the special features of any one country are important for the global public good precisely because they can make a distinctive contribution.

In China's case, the deeply embedded emphasis on cooperation and the central place that harmony has within its outlook on the world are valuable assets for any alliance or multilateral arrangement between nations. Over and above this contribution of Chinese culture, socialism itself is an ideology promoting an outlook on human welfare beyond national borders. The success of Chinese socialism encourages people-to-people ties across the world, ones that will help to soften the acute competitiveness of Western capitalism.

Beyond any ideological contribution, however, what is most important for the future configuration of international relations is that China has broken the mould of the rift between first and third world countries, developed and developing. This opposition has shaped the debates in the United Nations and created predictable deadlocks on issues where it is in the common interest for all to agree. China is now the bridge nation, linking the poorer nations, through its past experience, to the richer nations by its presence among them.

Multilateral institutions are arrangements between equal partners. They are intrinsically democratic in the sense that each has an equal say. It is to the benefit of all if their culture is one of discussion with the shared aim of reaching agreement, consultative democracy, rather than one of agreement to differ, to carry on without a collective decision, in other words liberal democracy. China's democracy can help to shape the shared future for humankind, not by exerting its

[24] Ibid., p. 39 [Chinese edition].

newfound power but by example, by showing how the principles of its own governance work for the benefit of its citizens.

1.2.10 In the shared future, how will the differences between civilizations, nation–states and other bodies benefit a global community?

[cf. Wang Q 10 re: other communities]

A community is not a team, it is not a business and it is not even a family, although it may include them. The point is that a community has a distinct social composition, with sharing being an intrinsic element and the sharing of space being fundamental.

Best and universally understood is the sharing of territorial space that makes up communities as various as Kaixiangong, Banbury, Manhattan or Tepotzlan, to name just a few made famous by anthropological studies. Additionally, that shared space can accommodate all the diversity of activities that provide for the needs of everyday life.

Bonding within the shared space does not preclude sharing with those outside its boundaries. Indeed, the boundary between communities is itself a shared understanding, or it should be, if there is not to be conflict between them. Between neighbouring communities, the development over time is one that has been documented worldwide across the centuries and civilizations, namely they exchange goods, services and people.

Very frequently, neighbouring communities were once exogamous units, as was the case in China traditionally and is still mainly so in Kaixiangong when Fei Xiaotong was conducting field work there in 1936. Marriage was just one of the main ties that linked communities.

The bonds within and between small communities provided the ground for what became over time the science of economics. The etymology of economics, 'oikos', the ancient Greek household, gives the clue. There the division of labour between men and women, slaves and neighbours provided the basis for understanding, exchange and mutual support.

When Adam Smith formulated the fundamental principles of the modern discipline two millennia later, the world was still rural. He wrote of the hunter becoming skilled at making bows and arrows and finding that exchanging them for meat was a better way of providing food than by hunting himself.

The principles of the market, the idea of comparative advantage, apply as much to collective human bodies as they do to individuals, right up to countries and even civilizations. In the global community, the basis for specialization between civilizations was already there with the ancient Silk Road. These days as China has become the manufacturing workshop of the world, it has been left to the first industrial country, the United Kingdom, to specialize in financial services and higher education.

It is the notion of sharing that provides for the extension of the idea of community to occupations and interest groups. Those who belong to the academic or scientific community, or to the farming or business community, are ones with similar outlooks, experience and interests that mean they have a feeling of sharing, even as they live and work far from each other, even beyond their own country. This is important for a more specific notion of global community than simply sharing the earth's territory. It is relevant to the fate of our species and the response to global warming in particular.

In this respect we need to think of the community of the largest interest group of all, everyone on earth and of the need for us to cooperate. Here the division of labour is not based in exchange but in technical efficiency. It is the logic of organization that requires the appropriate skills to be attached to the tasks that provide the greatest benefit to the goal of the whole enterprise.

Again, the principles from which this can proceed have also long been evident. Adam Smith in fact actually began his *The Wealth of Nations* with an example from his own time, and he only turned later in his text to the origins of the division of labour and the wider implications for trade between nations. He drew his first example from the new industrial production of his time. He wrote of the manufacturer of pins who would divide up the work into special tasks between different groups of workers who, in consequence, could produce far more than they would have been able to do working singly.

When there is a shared goal, the elimination of global warming, we need to think in terms of the most efficient way in which all human agencies, individuals, businesses, countries and even whole regions and civilizations can contribute to its success. The conditions for that are all the more favourable because the international division of labour has progressed so far that specialized production already has areas of concentration, hotspots of activity that attract the persons of similar and complementary skills. Silicon Valley is only the most famous contemporary example, but for centuries the Netherlands has been renowned for the production of flowers, while the countries of South East Asia vie for the title of best rice producer.

We need to think in terms of the most efficient collective cooperative effort for the achievement of the most pressing global goal of all. This is different from the attainment of goals that every country can aim for in its way. The Sustainable Development Goals, SDGs, are within the scope of each country individually, even though cooperation is manifestly advantageous where it is possible. But in the case of global warming, the shared future means cooperation is essential.

It makes no sense for Brazil to compete with the United States in soya production by clearing the forests of the Amazon, and at the same time it would be to the world's advantage to assist Brazil to find alternative sources of revenue. Reducing greenhouse gas emissions is within the scope of every individual simply by switching off electric lights, and every country can encourage fuel efficiency. But some countries can develop solutions that others can emulate. Denmark has become a leader in green energy production and has been a pioneer in passing legislation committing to delivering climate finance to developing countries.

But it is the United States and China as the two biggest carbon emitters who can make the most effective contribution. The US under President Trump withdrew from the Paris Accords, President Biden will rejoin, but this turnaround only illustrates how climate change policy is just another aspect of a deeply divided country. But division also means there is some good news too. Many states such as Virginia and Illinois have passed legislation to implement clean electricity policies.

Yet it is China that has the best chance to show global leadership. Its historic axial value of harmony between humanity and nature, along with its own sense of being the 'Middle Kingdom', means that it can develop green policies that reflect the deeper impulses of its own culture. Along with the BRI, it ought to mean that this direction of travel operates not just in transport but also through the media and public opinion.

Currently official efforts are devoted mainly to repair the damage resulting from past economic growth, but now environmental risk has become a top priority for all investment, internal and overseas. Director General Xu Biju of the Chinese Ministry of Ecology and Environment announced at the beginning of 2020 the coming establishment of the National Green Development Fund (NGDF) to focus on green investment, even as this is emphasized in BRI investment. The NGDF was launched on July 15th, 2020 by the Ministry and the city government of Shanghai with capital of 88 billion yuan ($12.59 billion) to finance the green development of the Yangtze River region.

1.3 Interview and speech on *China and the shared human future*[25]

1.3.1 A pre-recorded interview with the China Global Television Network (CGTN): answers to questions prepared by LIU Xin

Albrow: Thank you for the invitation to speak, especially on a topic, regardless of vital importance, which I had spent many years thinking about.

1) You've done pioneering work on globalization. Professor Albrow, please tell us about your concept of globalization. What exactly does it mean to you?

Globalization is supported by lots of countries. How successful has it been internationally? Given the ongoing international political tensions, where do we stand *vis-à-vis* globalization? What's China's position there?

You ask me what my understanding of globalization is. Well, you know that there are two main directions, and they are often confused. In everyday life, one sense of globalization is that the world's becoming one place. Every part of the world is

[25] Editor's note: This interview was pre-recorded in July 2021 on behalf of Ms LIU Xin, CGTN senior host in the Global Thinkers programme, and subsequently edited to place each of Ms LIU's questions in the present text before each of Professor Albrow's answers.

connected with everywhere else, and we are able to access every part of the world. And that is the most obvious sense – when we're talking over the web to people the other side of the world, and when I talk to my school friends in Australia, for instance – the world is becoming one place.

So that's the broad sense of globalization, which people often say it is.

Now there's a more restricted sense, which is the globalization of some particular aspect of human activity going worldwide. Something that happens in one place, and then, everywhere in the world, people know about it. At this very moment, I may be at the Olympic Games: it's happening in one place, but the whole world knows about it, so it is being extended globally, and that can happen for a big event like that, but it can also happen, of course, for things that are much smaller.

We learn about the exploits of Chinese people, for instance, going into space. That is the globalization of the Chinese space programme. So, that's another sense of globalization, the globalization of one specific aspect of human behaviour. Some of those are the understandings I have of the idea.

You ask me about the success of globalization. After all, it is a process which nobody controls, so it's very difficult to talk of it in terms of success or not success, but I do understand, when you in China ask me about that, there is a rather specific sense and this is the sense of economic globalization. The world's becoming one market, and countries, in fact, are trading with every other country in the world. An open market and the sense of globalization you're using there is actually very similar to the age-old concept of free trade, which goes back centuries. How far is the world at the moment becoming more globalized in an economic sense?

Countries are putting up barriers at the moment between themselves, in all kinds of respects, as they try to, for instance, prevent the effects of COVID-19, so maybe economic globalization is possibly going backwards a little bit. But, on the other hand, if you think of the globalization of digital communication, that's advancing all the time, and very difficult to hold back.

2) Your book, *China's Role in a Shared Human Future: Towards Theory for Global Leadership*, was published in 2018. During the book launch, you said China was set to be a major player in shaping global ethics. What kind of 'global ethics' were you referring to? Do you still think the same way?

Yes, global ethics. Something that underpins international relations. International relations are often seen in power politics, too. But behind all international relations is the same sort of meeting others on their terms and seeking to understand their position. Indeed, you can't talk about power unless you're in a position to know the qualities of the people you're interacting with. Global ethics actually comes before, not after it. And by that I mean a sense of whom you're dealing with and the right way to deal with people.

From that point of view, I think China is in a very good position, because, of course, it's an age-old culture, it is ethically based. And clearly I'm thinking primarily about the Confucian system of ideas, the Confucian system of the five basic relations. And the fact that it is a very much earth-based concept, it's not a physical concept, it's not a religious concept, it's an earth-based ethic. And from that point of view, I think China has a very good position for promoting international relations, on an ethical basis, because, indeed, Chinese society fundamentally is also based on ethics of social relations and regard for other people.

From that point of view, it is very different, I think, from many of the positions that exist in the West, because the West has continually over the centuries been expanding, and subject to revolution: not in fact concerned primarily with sustainable society, but more with expanding the scope of its own power over the rest of the world. On the leadership role, maybe I've already suggested why I think China is in an appropriate position for undertaking global leadership,

3) The book is about China's readiness to assume a global leadership role. And you linked two studies under that subject, one by Max Weber, an important Western theorist during the global transition from the 19th to the 20th century, and the other one the study of Chinese President Xi Jinping's thoughts during the global transition from the 20th to the 21st century. Is there any connection between the two thoughts? What made you conclude that China will assume a global leadership role from these studies? Why not other countries?

You ask me about how that relates to my earlier work on Max Weber. Max Weber was the preeminent theorist of society and politics at the turn of the 19th and 20th centuries. One of the messages that he had, and especially subsequently, in the First World War, was that political leaders had to have a sense of responsibility for the consequences of what they do; responsibility for consequences was something that Max Weber emphasized all the time. As against that kind of leadership, which is simply fine words, is trying to excite populations rather than to lead them in a direction that would actually benefit them in their lives.

4) What do Western theories say about today's global cooperation? How can Xi's thinking help to promote global peace and collaboration instead of power rivalries? What are the benefits for the world in following both? What would be the consequences if one of the two was missing?

I would suggest that China today is in a very good position for getting global leadership. It has a strong sense of responsibility. And at one and the same time, of course, it is an immensely powerful and large country. There is no other country that can act with the same kind of coherence as China does today. So it's in a perfect position to take the position of global leadership, but by that I mean taking responsibility for the consequences of the actions you do. There are benefits for the world from reading and listening to President Xi, as I emphasized in my book. He is a thinking leader. He is a leader who bases his actions on an expansive set of concepts and ideas, which extend over the whole range of political and social action. This is unusual in the contemporary world in the sense that the pressures in the contemporary world are all the time on political leaders to display, to make statements that they don't have to answer for, to excite their populations. President Xi's method is to proceed steadily and consistently based on a set of concepts that has profound roots in social and political theory in both the West and the East. He brings Marxism together with Chinese culture. He brings Chinese culture together with Western thought on economic laws. He brings all these things together. And, at the same time, exercises a responsible leadership philosophy for his party and his country. So, from that point of view, we have an example of leadership for the rest of the world.

5) You said the concept of the community of shared future proposed by Xi is broader than globalization. Globalization is generally applied in areas of trade and economy whereas a community with a shared future is talking about the happiness of all humans and the efforts to realize it. How did you draw that conclusion? What's the significance and impact of upholding both the concept of globalization and faith in building a community with a shared future?

Well, you ask about globalization and the shared future. The two things are distinct. They are distinct ideas. As I explained earlier, the notion of globalization is making the world a single place integrating all countries. The shared future, on the other hand, is a question of addressing the problems and challenges the world as a whole. And from that point of view, the shared future is looking into the future and looking to solve the problems like climate change, and like the pandemic, setting up institutions. The shared future is a plan of action. Globalization is a set of processes, that sometimes derive from the plan of action, but nonetheless, that the plan of action has to respond to. So you've got two aspects. The objective processes of globalization, which are always potentially out of control, because the collective consequences of the actions of a billion people could never be completely controlled. The shared future idea is, however, to bring some sense into those collective actions and to arrive at solutions to the problems, the challenges. So the shared future is really a response, in many respects, to the problems globalization brings.

6) What role does China play in building such a community globally under Xi's leadership? How has the concept been regarded by the international community?

I think the notion of the shared future in the international community has not yet received the prominence that it deserves, partly because maybe a China has been a little bit reluctant to promote this idea. But, you see, the world needs Chinese ideas, mainly because they were rooted in a culture that is distinct and separate and with a history that is quite different from that Western-influenced world. The benefit that the world gets from China is, to put it very briefly, the result of five thousand years of Chinese thought and wisdom.

7) How does the Belt & Road Initiative fit into globalization in international trade and economic ties?

You said the Belt & Road Initiative can help to avoid great power rivalries. Exactly how? Some people say the initiative serves as a tool for China to spread its influence in other countries. What do you think of that? Has the initiative got an economic and political dimension as well?

Within globalization, the Belt and Road Initiative has got a very, very special particular place, primarily because globalization as such covers every aspect of human activity, economics and trade and politics and culture, everything could be included under that notion.

Belt and Road is very specifically concerned with infrastructure. It's concerned with making those connections of land, sea and air, facilitating the ability of countries to trade with each other to facilitate people to travel from one country to another and also to develop their own economies. That set of measures brings so many countries together. Belt and Road is a very special, coherent programme which can underpin globalization generally, but it has a very focused and directed set of policies connected with it. Of course, it has been suggested it extends China's power and influence. You should expect that any good policy coming from a country that is to the benefit of the people extends the influence of the country whose policy it is; so, if I were a Chinese person, I wouldn't regard that as criticism. Belt and Road extends China's power and influence? Of course. You wouldn't actually do it if it did anything else. And, from that point of view, the benefits that it gives to the people extends to those benefits reciprocated for China itself.

8) Why did you want to learn Chinese back in 2016? How do you see the international media describing China? For example, the Chinese Dream? Has the international community assessed Chinese values or stances on political affairs accurately?

Well, that's a very personal question, why I wanted to learn Chinese in 2016. Let's put it this way: I've always wanted to learn Chinese, or at least since I was a teenager. And never had the opportunity or possibly the determination to undertake it. And in 2016, I thought maybe I was old enough to attempt it. But I could say that my first interest in China goes back, very, very much earlier, to 1954. And indeed, I sent to Professor Li Xuetao in the Beijing Foreign Studies University the project documents that I wrote when I was at school for the study of Chinese history in 1954 when I was seventeen years old. So, if you like to see why I've always been interested in China, you can ask Professor LI Xuetao in Beiwai (BFSU).

Yes, the Chinese Dream. I do think the international community generally has difficulty in appreciating China. The notion of the Chinese Dream, I think, was a very smart way of China approaching Western thinking by adopting a terminology that of course arises from the United States. The notion of the American Dream, for the first time, was applied to relations between countries and the China Dream, I think, is the exact complement to that, although it does of course have a very different significance from the American Dream.

The American Dream is very much one directed towards individuals rising in society. The China Dream is one which is concerned with the prosperity of China as a whole. The China Dream is about raising everybody, the American Dream very specifically about the advantages to an individual, suggesting that any individual can rise to the top. That is not the kind of dream that appeals to China, and indeed it's very interesting in this respect, the recent initiatives that have been taken in China to dampen down that excessive zeal for education, which has resulted in overly ambitious parents paying so much money in order to get their children educated. That's not the China Dream. That's the American Dream. The China Dream is a collective dream for the prosperity of the country as a whole.

9) You said China is an exemplary model in combating the pandemic. And the most impressive part for you was how the Chinese people united and coordinated to overcome this challenge. Why do you think this kind of high solidarity could be achieved? What's the government role along the way? What's the relation between the government and the public on this matter? Could other countries gain anything useful from China's experience?

Finally, you ask about the pandemic. Of course, the first advantage that China has is its, shall we say, consensual attitude, the willingness of people to work together. Second, its respect for authority, consensus of respect for authority, of how things come together when there's a national crisis. The pandemic was a national crisis. These aspects of Chinese culture enabled people to work together and respond very rapidly. And that is something that has been present in China in my experience and to my knowledge for a very, very long time.

I mean, I always remember my first visit to China in 1987 when my wife and I visited a Chinese village, and the Chinese family planning workers there were talking in terms of messages that they perceived as coming direct from Beijing. In any Chinese village of the time, you could receive the messages that came from Beijing about the necessity for the one-child family policy. For me, this was a revelation, to recognize, as it were, the enormous coherence that is possible in a society which operates on the assumption that the leadership leads people forwards; that is the way you get collective tasks done. So I think the pandemic is yet another example, actually, of the way China can show the rest of the world what is necessary to achieve a goal, overcome a crisis and work for the benefit of the population.

Thank you very much for the time you've allowed me to talk. It's been a great privilege. Thank you very much.

1.3.2 Speech notes at the Beijing International Publishing Forum[26]

First, I would like to say I welcome very much this opportunity to speak at an event, which is bringing Chinese books to the world. And it's a great privilege for a Western British author to be able to speak when his book is being launched. I really need to say a little bit about what I hope the book will do.

First of all, and most important, it does express the view of a Westerner about the contributions that China can make to the wider world today And I know, as a Westerner, obviously, my view is a biased view. Namely, I come from the West, but I think it is important that people in the West try to understand China. Obviously, from the Chinese point of view, but it's always the case you have to reinterpret for a wider worldwide audience. I'm hoping this book will appeal to people from all cultures, who have an interest in what China can do for the world as a whole.

This is why the book begins with a discussion of the idea of the shared future, which President Xi Jinping has promoted for many years now. The shared future, the common future for humankind. This is the fundamental concept underpinning Chinese foreign policy. Unless you can contribute in your relations with other countries to an idea that there is something that they share, you will not have very great success. The elements of the shared future, of course, are the solutions to all the problems that the world has as a whole.

One of the characteristics of the globalized world is that we have challenges which apply to human beings as a whole. And for that reason, I begin the book with the idea, with Xi Jinping's idea of the shared future. This is not a vague concept; it is actually very precise. And it comes down to brass tacks: it comes down to building airports, it comes down to railways. It's very clear from the Belt and Road, which I mention later in the book. The Belt and Road Initiative is one which starts from infrastructure. But it has a wider vision. It connects to the notion that the world as a whole means the kinds of interconnections that make it possible to deal with global challenges.

COVID-19 is a prime example of what China can do towards a shared future. We have all seen examples of Chinese strengths. When it comes to dealing with the COVID-19 outbreak, the rapidity of the response, the coherence of the measures and the widespread nature of them covering the whole country made China perhaps the most successful country in dampening down and resisting COVID-19.

And this is demonstrating that the shared future involves coherent policies and practical measures to deal with global practical measures. I think one of the most important things that China does is not to offer a vague philosophy to the

[26] Editor's note: This was an invited conference speech about the present book, *China's Role in a Shared Human Future: Exploring Shared Values and Goals*, delivered at the Plenary Session, Beijing International Publishing Forum, September 12, 2021, in the Asia Conference Hall, Beijing Asia Hotel. It was organized by China National Publications Import and Export (Group) Co. Ltd., the sponsor of the Beijing International Book Fair.

world, nor to emphasize and prioritize institution building. We need institutions, and China contributes to them, of course, China contributes more peacekeeping troops to the world, UN peacekeeping troops, than any other country. So China contributes to global institutions, but it's more successful in actually dealing with concrete problems, of demonstrating to the world that this is the way forward.

Very much, we'll see China contribute to the Sustainable Development Goals. The United Nations has now for many years promoted the Millennium Development Goals. And then the Sustainable Development Goals are focused on goal measures, and that matches very much China's philosophy of its contribution to worldwide problems. Contributing worldwide in the global sense is one thing but you can also contribute to the world by giving an example from your own policies.

China has been exemplary in the last fifty years, specifically in dealing with its own domestic economy and raising people out of poverty. And it never ceases to introduce measures that will help people get out of poverty. Of course, its famous one-child policy originally was designed for that purpose, but now, finally, China has decided it has served its purpose. There are many measures it undertakes, which have the purpose of dealing with the problems as they are at the moment they occur. So, the Chinese policy on poverty reduction has always been highly pragmatic.

Even its household registration system, for instance, was designed to ensure that local people actually did sustain their relationships with their locality and the result in a way has been mass migration to the cities, but money has flowed back into the countryside. Similarly, very recently we've had an example in the last few days. They clamped down on the headlong rush to work, which gives advantages to your own child or children through extra lessons of private tuition and all the rest of it, a huge industry in China. And it's been recognized in China as a whole that this kind of individualism is not the best way to raise the standard of living of the people as a whole. Quite rightly in my mind, what is worse, China has put in place measures to restrict the scope of profit making out of people's ambition, for their child to get ahead of other children. This is not actually the fundamental Chinese way. The Chinese way is to bring everyone up together. So, the poverty reduction schemes over the years have been, I think, a fine example to the rest of the world of maintaining social solidarity and coherence, even as your country becomes more and more prosperous.

In so many countries in the West, the prosperity is based on growing inequality, but China is resisting those pressures to growing inequality. I mentioned the Belt and Road Initiative also as another example of the brass tacks approach, the pragmatic approach to the economy and to raising the profile of China in the rest of the world. People often criticize China, China's Belt and Road, saying, oh, it's all self-interest. It's done only to enhance China's power and influence. Well, a successful policy of building an airport or a railway in another country is a great benefit to that country, and bringing a great benefit to their country will also help the standing and status of China. The two things will go together. So the criticism that the BRI is actually helping China in its rise as a global power is beside the point altogether. It completely misses the point that China's rise is associated with the rise of other countries and China wishes, in fact, to bring other countries with it. So, these are lessons from China, the way they dealt with the pandemic, in the way it deals with poverty, in the way it's working on Belt and Road. These are all lessons that are actually contributing to the ideas of governance for the world as a whole.

The governance of the globe is something that emerges out of the concerted interactions of over two hundred countries. But, being about to become shortly the largest economy on the globe and one of the most powerful nations, the second most powerful militarily after the United States, China is going to have a huge influence on the world. The examples it's giving us at the moment mean that global governance will, with China's influence, be on the right path, going in the right direction. And its contribution to the future for us and for our children and generations to come will, I suggest, be huge.

Now, my book concludes with some more general considerations about the theoretical underpinning of the Chinese contribution, the theoretical contribution ultimately being a universal one that belongs to all countries. China again has shown itself entirely capable of absorbing the best of Western thought on, for instance, economics, on social structure, on Marxist thought, and assimilated it to the Chinese vision, which emphasizes social relations above all as the foundation of human society. The amalgam of Western and Chinese ideas in the current Chinese world view, is to my mind, one of the most optimistic elements there is in a world which today seems so often beset with insoluble problems.

In putting together this book, I'm extremely grateful to the editors of the book, of the amount of work that they put into it. I'm very grateful to Professor Xiangqun Chang and to Professor WANG Yiwei. They have contributed, and many other colleagues in China have contributed to my thinking. I am sorry if I don't mention everyone by name. But the book itself has given me a great deal of pleasure, reflecting many, many years of learning about China for the benefit of, first of all, of course, myself, but more importantly for the rest of the world.

Thank you very much for listening to me today.

DOI https://doi.org/10.24103/UCW5.en.2021.2

Chapter 2
The theory and practice of globalization

The coincidence of the international settlement of the Second World War with the threat to humankind that nuclear weapons produced made the language of the globe central to human endeavour. With capitalism's continuing worldwide expansion and technological advance, both structural changes and the practices of change-agents came to be called globalization, prompting an ever-intensifying debate around the concepts and propositions needed for understanding the current social transformations.

2.1 Max Weber: from modernity to globality – a personal memoir[1]

Extraordinary though it may sound in this, Max Weber's centenary year, 1920 does not, at my age, seem so long ago. After all, it seems like only yesterday that I spoke at a conference to commemorate the 50th anniversary of his tragically early death.

I came across him first in 1957. His was the last name to figure on a Cambridge course booklist on the history of historiography. The lecturer never got to the end of his list. I did, and it was a life saver. I had been enduring the derisory comments of a final year tutor who mocked my interest in theory and this was the antidote.[2] It turned out to be a life changer as well, but I couldn't know that then.

Here was an author who actually tried to make sense of history. I made up my mind to study him further, for which I had to learn German. So the next year was spent in war-ravaged Cologne, painstakingly working through Marianne Weber's (1926) biography with a dictionary, attending a language course at the *Volkshochschule*, while earning my fennigs as an assistant teacher in a suburban Gymnasium. ('Don't listen to him,' the English teacher told the class, 'he's got an accent'.)

Then to the LSE to register for a thesis on Max Weber and rationality. 'Why do you want that topic?' was the disdainful query from my supervisor, the venerable Morris Ginsberg, successor to Hobhouse in the first chair of sociology in the UK. 'Hobhouse is much more interesting.' I persisted, rationality fascinated me – and has done ever since, for its limits as well as its scope.

As it turned out, Ginsberg probably had his own reasons for trying to steer me in another direction. He was then a rather lonely figure left behind by younger

[1] Previously published in *Theory Culture & Society, Annual Review*, December 2020, (37)7–8, 315–327.

[2] That tutor was the young Maurice Cowling, later famous as the Tory guru in Thatcher's years. I had to argue against 'There's no such thing as society' from the very beginning of my career. Good training!

stars like Karl Popper, Ernest Gellner, Raymond Firth and Michael Oakeshott. Their lectures stimulated my growing conviction that serious work on Weber required a much deeper understanding of his time and antecedents than my thesis would allow.

So when I happened across a job advertisement in *The Times* for a post researching bureaucracy in Germany, I sent in a speculative inquiry. It turned out to have been placed by Tom Bottomore, who at the time was lecturing on both Marx and Weber at the LSE, and who was the British lead for the new European Centre of Sociology. There were only two applicants, he told me. The other was a retired clergyman. I had the job.

It involved a thoroughly Weberian topic, a sociological study of German civil servants, and meant living in Germany again, working with the young *Ordinarius*, Ralf Dahrendorf, in Tübingen. As well as him and Bottomore, another lead figure was Michel Crozier (1964), making waves in the study of French bureaucracy. The Centre was a veritable Weberian hothouse. It was headed up by none other than the great Raymond Aron (1957), whose book on German sociology was already an inspiration. What a golden opportunity to acquire that deeper understanding!

To cut a short story even shorter, the project lasted three months only for me. Aron invited me to his flat on the banks of the Seine to tell me I had made a good start, but the French authorities, charged with administering the Ford Foundation grant for the Centre, could not countenance funding a British citizen to do research in Germany. I was out on my ear, but, thanks to the informal LSE network, found myself a month later in October 1961, along with my friend and fellow graduate student, Tony Giddens, in an initial teaching job as an assistant to Norbert Elias in the University of Leicester.

Weber did not excite much interest in the recently established Leicester department. Bottomore, who had eased my arrival, was the informal network link between it and the LSE, but it was too busy flexing its muscles against the dominance of the much older department, and Elias was already casting his spell. There was, however, a chance to introduce Weber in the theory course. It was mainly via Edward Shils's edition of the methodology essays (Weber, 1949) and of course Parsons's translations of *The Protestant Ethic and the Spirit of Capitalism* (Weber, 1930) and the first volume of *Economy and Society* (Weber, 1947). But they were tough going for undergraduates and we were grateful for the help of a new book by a recent immigrant from South Africa, John Rex, whose reliance on Weber in his *Key Problems of Sociological Theory* (1961) was for years thence to be the best defence of a left Weber interpretation.

Two years later I was in Reading as the first tenured lecturer in sociology, coincidentally able to have a hand in the appointment of the first holder of a sociology chair there, Stanislav Andreski (1984), a Weberian in his own inimitable way. He encouraged me to develop organization theory and in an article in the *Penguin Social Sciences Survey* (Albrow, 1968), I was able to express my first tentative reservations on Weber's fact/value distinction.

The hectic expansion of British sociology in the 1960s then took me to Cardiff in 1967, still with unfinished ambitions and unrequited interest in bureaucracy and rationality. Unrequited, because the slim staffing in new sociology departments in those days meant you found yourself teaching comparative social institutions and research methods, as well as theory, and anything else that could contribute to a credible degree course.

I hope these reminiscences are not just self-indulgence. They intend to convey not only the magnetic influence of Weber's whole thought world on a young scholar, but also how the vast scope of his enquiries could encourage deep immersion in just one small aspect of them. There was something else too. Weber was an engaged intellectual, alert to and involved in all the political currents of his time. He delighted in controversy. These were qualities that persuaded me sociology was my calling.

Paradoxically, to my regret later, Weber's own unremitting polemics encouraged the same acerbic temper in my criticisms of other scholars. I was grateful when, 40 years later, Amitai Etzioni (1964) graciously accepted my apology for gratuitously savage comments ('simplistic', 'banal') on an early work. They appeared in my first novice publication, a review article of recent books on organization (Albrow, 1964). My tone was probably the displacement of my own deep but still incoherent dissatisfaction with the place rationality had in Weber's thought. Fortunately, I did also commend his earlier book as 'most remarkable' (Etzioni, 1961).

Given the centrality of rationality for him, both in concept formation and in his historical and comparative accounts of rationalization, adopting the true Weberian spirit entailed being critical of Weber's whole enterprise. Not that this was a lonely endeavour. Studies of bureaucracy and organization in the 1950s and 1960s were all proposing significant amendments to Weber's ideal type of bureaucracy. They contributed to a golden era for Weber-inspired empirical research, led by Robert Merton and taken forward by his students, Peter Blau and Alvin Gouldner. These were pioneers who would have a prominent place in my first book, the student primer *Bureaucracy* (1970a).

In the same year as the publication of that book, the British Association for the Advancement of Science gave me a wonderful opportunity for a more expansive public treatment of the same theme. In the conference I referred to earlier, the sociology section of the Association was commemorating Max Weber and I was invited to give its keynote Lister lecture, choosing the theme 'Public Administration and Sociological Theory'.

Considering Weber from widely different perspectives, of functionalists and systems theorists, of Marx, Alfred Schütz and political scientists, I concluded that Weber's ideal type could no longer be sustained as an appropriate model for contemporary civil services. Professionalism and personal responsibility were intrinsic to their operation. The lecture's final reflections may well be considered relevant even to this day:

> The professional official has achieved emancipation from the machine to follow the objectives of his professional conscience. It makes the content of that conscience of immediate concern to us all. (Albrow, 1971: 356)

Those sentiments rounded off ten restless years, searching for a position on Weber and bureaucracy between competing theoretical schools that would be both distinctively mine and provide a solid enough base to allow for the more comprehensive consideration of his corpus that was now my ambition. There followed a period that was to last, for many reasons, both personal and political, in national and academic settings, for another twenty years.

* * *

The 1970s and 1980s were turbulent times for academics in general and sociologists in particular. The rival theoretical schools became proxies for wider conflicts that had spread beyond the universities in 1968, and the atmosphere within universities often remained toxic. Running a sociology department challenged both personal and intellectual qualities.

Weber provided a lode star for me in this period, a stable reference point, all the more paradoxical since his work reflected the conflicts of his own time and was also the target of rival interpretations. But it was the very complexity and density of his work that encouraged so many rival standpoints and I was content to follow my own path between them. My intention had by then crystallized to provide my own distinctive synoptic account of Weber's theoretical position.

It was to be a long and protracted process. Buoyed up by the success of *Bureaucracy* and rewarded for past administrative duties with leave of absence, I accepted a Leverhulme Fellowship to join the legendary Johannes Winckelmann's Max Weber Institute in Munich in 1973/74. It was a heady time, bringing many new friends, including Weber scholars Horst Helle, Gert Schmidt and Stephen Kalberg, whose outstanding work on Weber, which includes applying his method to the contemporary United States (2014), has been a pleasure to follow to the present day.

But it was colleagues in Cardiff who prompted me to take another direction in Weber studies. On my return to Wales, the journal of the newly established Faculty of Law, *The British Journal of Law and Society*, invited me to contribute a paper on Weber and law, another vast segment of his concerns, though of course linked to his ideas on bureaucracy. I decided to concentrate on a formative early essay, his critique of the jurist Rudolf Stammler, and followed it up with a translation for the same journal (Weber, 1975-6).

Overall my sympathies were with Stammler, whose infringements of the is/ought dichotomy Weber castigated with the 'zeal of a reformer of sexual morality'. He was 'a little like a reviewer for a "quality" newspaper faced with the first issue of the Communist Manifesto deciding, because it falls neither in the category of "literature" [n]or "history", it has *therefore* nothing worthwhile to say' (Albrow 1975: 132).

Effectively in line with my commentary on that debate (Stammler had replied), I was shaping a position that was then commonly called social constructivism, arguing that, although one could concede that lawyers might focus more on the normative and sociologists on the empirical, nonetheless both engaged with real society where the two sides of the dichotomy intersected, and it was in that shared and disputed space that both professions became agents of social change.

It was a position that tallied with my other work as a sociologist, which had included acting as a consultant to a local community (Neath) in South Wales contesting proposals for a new road that would divide it in two. That practical experience had led me to arrive four years before at a position that much more closely approximated to a public view of the sociologist representing the 'human factor' than 'some self-deceiving concept of the value-free professional' (Albrow, 1970b: 18). That experience, of course, was also consistent with the reality of Weber's passionate, even at times reckless engagement in both public affairs and in academic politics. There he spoke from the heart, covering his commitments sometimes with reference to the irrationality of ultimate value standpoints.

On that point, I share a centuries-old Anglo-Saxon rationalism, reiterated in 1962 by Runciman at the beginning of the take-off period for British sociology, namely that, while Weber may be correct in saying disputes on rival philosophies may be in practice unresolvable, it is 'a mistake to argue that they can be shown necessarily incapable of ever being resolved' (Runciman, 1963: 168).

Value positions are always open to argument, even where their proponents refuse to argue, but the application of rational methods in the world around us has effects that go beyond argument. This is the nub of Weber's distinction between rationality and rationalization that became a focus for me in the 1980s.

Rationalization was a concept embedded in Weber's historical and sociological accounts that effectively bypassed his methodological reflections. It applied to the uses of either or both logical (formal) and ends/means (material) thinking, whether their application was in any ultimate sense correct or not. Rationalization could also be a cumulative process and its long-term consequences could be experienced in the capitalist system of his time.

His last statement on the matter, the famous introduction to the essays on the sociology of religion, with their poignant dedication to Marianne (1893 'bis ins Pianissimo des höchsten Alters'), dated June 7, 1920, just seven days before his death, pointed to the varieties of rationalization in different sectors and in different cultures, the specific nature of Western rationalization and its cumulative nature (Weber, 1920: 1–16). In the West it was associated with a general demystification of the world and an iron framework for people's lives that made them ready to accept the message of charismatic leaders.

When it came to his personal attitude towards rationalization, Weber occasionally lets his value-free guard down in an incidental comment like 'The path of human destiny cannot but appal him who surveys a section of it' (Weber, 1930: 29), but an idea that gained some traction with his critics, namely that he somehow prepared the way for Hitler, is preposterous.[3] I have to concede that my early and very jejune reaction to his rationalization account was similar to Alvin Gouldner's (1955) dismissal of 'metaphysical pathos'. It all seemed to smack of a non-Marxist historical determinism.

But in the course of the 1980s, more mature engagement with social realities in the UK in particular led me to give rationalization much more credence. It helped to leverage an angle on developments in Thatcher's Britain, a theme I explored in a paper for the World Congress of Sociology in Mexico in 1982. It increased contact too with the developing small community of young Weber scholars in the UK, beginning a discussion that continues pleasurably to this day with Sam Whimster, who has been pivotal in the growth of worldwide Weber scholarship by founding the journal *Max Weber Studies*.

Whimster invited me to contribute (Albrow, 1987a) to the book he edited with Scott Lash, *Max Weber, Rationality and Modernity*, in which I had the chance to explore in some detail how British legislative developments around data protection and artificial human reproduction illustrated an elaboration and intensification of the idea of rationality compared with its earlier treatments by Kant and Weber.

Another friend, Johannes Weiss (1987), who was already well ahead of me in writing on the foundations of Weber's thought, came to much the same view of rationalization in a paper in the same volume. The contemporary relevance of Weber made engagement with Marxism inevitable, and Weiss's prompting led to a contribution to a volume he edited (Böckler/Weiss, 1987) comparing Marx and Weber on their treatment of the idea of the social (Albrow, 1987b).

That theme was to have been presented in a Beijing conference in 1989, yet another Weber anniversary, 125 years since his birth. The events that year in Tiananmen Square meant it was called off. But, in any case, the tenor of the paper was already contained within the book that was the culmination of twenty years of struggle with Weber and myself.[4]

Wrestling with Weber and rationality had preoccupied me then for well-nigh thirty years. It had taken me in many different directions; challenging the split between rationality and emotions, grounding objectivity in social science, exploring bureaucratic culture, deconstructing linkages between rationality and rationalization, defending the idea of society against Weber, exploring his relations with

[3] For instance, his outlook was comprehensively rejected by the Nazi sympathiser Christoph Steding. What is true is that he was moving towards more sympathy with socialist positions towards the end of his life.

[4] Actually, it probably would never have been completed had Sue Owen not said she wouldn't marry me until I had finished it.

Marxist theory, culminating in a synoptic view of Weber's contribution to social theory in 1990. But it turned out to be mainly a personal satisfaction, one submerged in the tumult of the time, and too late to make any lasting impact.

Max Weber's Construction of Social Theory (1990) was written at a turning point, or rather many turning points, personal and political. My employer, University College Cardiff, to put it in recognizable terms, had 'gone into administration', and I had been pensioned off, even as I had begun editing a new journal in Cardiff for the International Sociological Association, *International Sociology.* All that paled into insignificance against the backcloth of subsequent geopolitical upheavals with the disintegration of the Soviet Union, the end of socialist regimes in Eastern Europe, the clampdown in China and announcements of 'one world' with a single superpower, the United States.

* * *

There was a new (relatively) term that went with the upheavals, globalization appearing in the print media as well as academic journals. The recently founded TCS was in the vanguard publishing Robertson and Lechners' rejection of Wallerstein's economism (1985) and headlining the idea of globalization. *The Economist* by 1990 was running a leader (May 4, 1990) declaring, 'For big companies further globalisation is a golden opportunity', followed by an article in the same issue on 'brand-stretching' that cited firms pursuing a strategy of 'globalisation of their brands'.

Editing the ISA's new journal, I was involved too in the planning of its 1990 World Congress to be held in Madrid. There was an intense if not torrid atmosphere among the planners debating how to capture the sense of historical turning point, to own a trope in public discourse as well as occupy the appropriate academic heights. Discussion converged on the theme 'sociology for one world', but pushback came from many directions, objecting to an implicit Western triumphalism, and the theme was amplified with 'unity and diversity'.

That in itself was not enough to satisfy sociologists eager to seize the moment. The new journal had, since its first issue in 1986, published papers reflecting just that balance, diverse viewpoints arising in different cultures, written originally in many languages, converging on common issues. Globalization was in the air and on its pages.[5] It represented the spirit of the ISA.

So it was decided every Congress delegate should receive a conference volume consisting of selections from the journal and entitled *Globalization, Knowledge and Society* (1990). Given as it was to over 4,000 delegates from every

---

[5] Piotr Sztompka had commented on trends variously described as the global village, the single network, de-differentiation, fluid borderlines: 'I put all these tendencies together under the label of globalisation' (1988: 52).

continent, it was a great marketing opportunity for the publisher, Sage, but also an effective promotion of globalization as the new central theme for sociology.

Weber did not loom large in the early globalization writing. He was cited in only six of the 23 contributions to another seminal globalization collection that also appeared in 1990, Mike Featherstone's special issue of TCS, *Global Culture: Nationalism, Globalization and Modernity*. But there were two incidental references in the two most influential books on globalization for sociologists that were highly significant.

Anthony Giddens, of course, had long before regularly lectured and written on Weber but in *The Consequences of Modernity* mention of him belonged only to the preliminaries. Based on lectures in Stanford in 1988, this book burst like a tornado on the rather stale modernity/postmodernity common room conversations, taking the consequences of global interdependence and the reshaping of social relations in everyday life in a direction that was to lead Giddens subsequently into public life. His mention of Weber was incidental, but allusion to rationalization as the key for his thinking on capitalism gave me pause for thought.

Robertson, on the other hand, acknowledged the formative influence on his own thinking of Weber's repeated return to two ideas of the world, the religious sense of the word and the arena of international struggle (1992: 2–3). At the same time, Robertson declared him '*relatively* [his emphasis] uninterested in what we now call globalization' (ibid: 143). My gloss on Robertson was that he considered Weber belonged to a period of modern history where globalization was advancing but had long since passed beyond him.

Weber provided Robertson and Giddens, then, with two different starting points and this was mirrored in their entirely divergent accounts of globalization. For Robertson, he was a voice from an earlier stage of modernity and that fitted with his version of globalization passing through historical stages. By contrast, Weber's account of rationalization in Giddens's eyes was an early intimation of the new technologies that underpinned globalization.

In both cases, Weber was enclosed within his own iron cage of modernity. At one level I could agree with them. He was the unrivalled commentator on his own time, effectively establishing its own self-image as modern. Yet neither Robertson nor Giddens gave him more than marginal importance for understanding their and my own time. Implicitly, then, our time was either postmodern, which occasionally they allowed, or a new period in human history altogether, which they never did.

The paradox for me was that my 1990 account of his work applauded Weber's capture of his time: 'his sociology, then, has succeeded in grasping the spirit of the twentieth century in an extraordinary manner'. His studies of religion, nationalism, power and the market linked to the 'universalisation of Western culture and the penetration of rationality into other cultures 'provide the basis for understanding the relationship between multiculturalism and globalisation' (Albrow,

1990: 284). But if leading commentators of our new world could say that it had moved on so much beyond Weber, surely we needed to grasp its radical novelty.

Could it be a coincidence that Robertson, Giddens and I converged on globalization at that time – just as, by happenstance, all three of us in 1960 used to relax together in the LSE graduate student common room? Our work had nothing that linked us then, only co-presence. Now being contemporaries was enough for us, and many others of course, to come quite independently to a similar sense that something fundamental had changed.

Where I differed from them was I felt that consigning Weber to an earlier period of an ever-advancing modernity simultaneously underestimated him and downplayed the rift with the past. Two things were then going on for me in the 1990s, one of which was the developing idea of a period that not merely came after the modern but represented a profound break with it. Given that I considered Weber not just to have intuited the deeper currents of his time but also provided intellectual tools to understand any time, I was then led to ask: What would Weber have made of the 1990s? And harking back to my days as a history student, I preferred to look at globalization against a background of shocks, crises and epochal change.

Of course, Weber could not foresee the catastrophic rupture with the past that came with the explosion of the hydrogen bombs over Japan in 1945, recognized by the leading intellectuals of the time such as Arnold Toynbee and Raymond Aron as ushering in a new age. This was the decisive turning point where the equation of modernity with progress could no longer be reasonably upheld. He was not a prophet, and he was famously scathing of his contemporaries who claimed to be, but the question remains whether his conceptual frame could allow for epochal change.

My view was that Weber's sense that rationalization brought values into conflict with one another and the allowances he made for the influence of charismatic individuals gave sufficient latitude within his conceptual frame to accommodate epochal shift. He had a profound sense of the novelty of modernity. A break with the past was after all the premise of his account of the Protestant Ethic and his method in no way precluded the possibility of similar future breaks.

I put these considerations to a meeting of the Max Weber Study Group of the British Sociological Association (Albrow, 1996a), arguing that it was his analytic methods that would have encouraged him to acknowledge an epochal break with the past. It is all the more plausible in view of the steady development of his thinking in theory and method throughout his career. I said we were 'all post-Weberians now'. That did not go down too well with a group of dedicated Weber scholars!

* * *

After 1990, then, my engagement with globalization, coupled with the sense of having established my own position on Weber's contribution, allowed him to be an inspiration but no longer a restraint. The sense of novelty of our own time I expressed in my *The Global Age: State and Society beyond Modernity* (1996b), which argued against seeing globalization as a one-way street into the future. Yet it was the global that was the signature of our time, displacing the modern as the dominant motif for public discourse.

Since then that predominance of the global has been challenged by the digital. In a way, that is the vindication of Weber's emphasis on advancing rationalization. For the digital operates in a direct line from the rational bureaucracy and Fordism of his time and it often supplants global issues in the public mind.

Globalization takes one in many directions, and in my case to China, which offers wonderful opportunities to pick up on Weber's own fascination with Eastern cultures. China's rise today is coupled with the desire to ride the tide of Western globalization for its own benefit while maintaining continuity with its own ancient culture. In this respect, a century after Weber, the questions he addressed to Chinese culture in relation to modernity have their close equivalent today.

The renewed relevance of Weber for understanding China prompted Whimster and me to join forces once again in mounting the conference on 'Max Weber and China: Culture, Law and Capitalism' in London in 2013. We were aided in this by Xiangqun Chang, who had recently established her Global China Institute to bring Chinese social science to the West. It prompted me to return to Weber's accounts of Confucianism and Taoism with the added advantage, that he didn't have, of collaboration with a Chinese scholar, Zhang Xiaoying from the Beijing Foreign Languages University, where for three years I lectured on globalization.

Those exchanges with China bear fruits in every season, always fertilized by delving deeper into Weber. In two papers (Albrow and Zhang, 2014; Zhang and Albrow, 2016), we have traced changing sequences in Weber's understanding of China over the last decade of his life. For example, he moved away from his earlier emphasis on adaptation as a key feature of Confucianism towards finding tension (*Spannung*) with the world and a striving to shape it. Nietzsche's ossified Chinaman gave way to the Mandarin chief executive of the railways.

His developing reflections on China give every reason to think that Weber's ideas would have continued to evolve with the changing times had he been spared the influenza in 1920. In a paper written specially for a volume on China's role in world society (Albrow, 2018b), I suggest that Weber today would be examining rationalization processes in the digital revolution and looking for ethical agents in a world of convergent global capitalism.

The commemoration of Weber in Beijing in 1989 had to be cancelled in the aftermath of a quintessential modern event, one entirely intelligible within his own political experience. There is a profound poignancy in the attempt to mount another one in Shanghai this year. There may well be another cancellation, this time in a global frame he never knew, but caused by something close in nature to the influenza that killed him. The COVID-19 virus demonstrates a universality beyond the modern and the global. Plagues kill people in all ages and cultures.

References

Albrow, M. (1964), 'The Sociology of Organizations', Review Article, *The British Journal of Sociology*, 15: 50–58.

Albrow, M. (1968), 'The Study of Organizations – Objectivity or Bias?, in J. Gould (Ed.), *Penguin Social Sciences Survey 1968,* pp.146-167. Harmondsworth: Penguin Books.

Albrow, M. (1970a), *Bureaucracy*. London: Pall Mall.

Albrow, M. (1970b), 'The Role of a Sociologist as a Professional: The Case of Planning', in P. Halmos (Ed.) *Sociological Review Monograph 16*, 'The Sociology of Sociology', pp. 1–19.

Albrow, M. (1971), 'Public Administration and Sociological Theory (Lister Lecture)', *The Advancement of Science*, 27: 347–356.

Albrow, M. (1975), 'Legal Positivism and Bourgeois Materialism: Max Weber's View of the Sociology of Law', *British Journal of Law and Society*, 2: 14–31.

Albrow, M. (1987a), 'The Application of the Weberian Concept of Rationalization to Contemporary Conditions', in S. Whimster and S. Lash (Eds.), *Max Weber, Rationality and Modernity*, pp. 164–182.

Albrow, M. (1987b), 'Der Begriff des Sozialen im Werk vom Marx und Weber', in S. Böckler/J. Weiss (Publisher), *Marx oder Weber: Zur Aktualisierung einer Kontroverse*. pp. 48-59.

Albrow, M. (1990), *Max Weber's Construction of Social Theory*. London: Macmillan.

Albrow, M. (1996a), 'Max Weber and Globalization', in M. Albrow (2014), *Global Age Essays on Social and Cultural Change,* Chapter 1.2, pp. 35–44.

Albrow, M. (1996b), *The Global Age: State and Society beyond Modernity*. Cambridge: Polity.

Albrow, M. (2014), *Global Age Essays on Social and Cultural Change*. Frankfurt am Main: Klostermann.

Albrow, M. (2018a), 'Max Weber, China and the Future of Global Society' in M. Albrow (2018b), *China's Role in a Shared Human Future*, pp. 149–65.

Albrow M. (2018b), *China's Role in a Shared Human Future*. London: Global Century Press.

Albrow, M and E. King (Eds.) (1990), *Globalization, Knowledge and Society*. London: Sage.

Albrow, M. and X. Zhang (2014), 'Weber and the Concept of Adaptation: the Case of Confucian Ethics', *Max Weber Studies* 14: 169–204. Reprinted in M. Albrow (2018b), *China's Role in a Shared Human Future*, pp. 124–48.

Andreski, S. (1984), *Max Weber's Insights and Errors*. London: Routledge and Kegan Paul.

Aron, R. (1957), *German Sociology*. London: Heinemann.

Böckler. S. J. Weiss (Publisher) (1987), *Marx oder Weber: Zur Aktualisierung einer Kontroverse*. Opladen: Westdeutscher Verlag.

Crozier, M. (1964), *The Bureaucratic Phenomenon*. London: Tavistock.

Etzioni, A. (1961), *A Comparative Analysis of Complex Organizations*. New York: The Free Press of Glencoe.

Etzioni, A. (1964), *Modern Organizations*. London: Prentice Hall.

Featherstone, M. (Ed.) (1990), *Global Culture: Nationalism, globalization and modernity. Theory, Culture and Society* Special Issue. London: Sage.

Giddens, A. (1990), *The Consequences of Modernity*. Cambridge: Polity.

Gouldner, A. (1955), 'Metaphysical Pathos and the Theory of Bureaucracy', *American Political Science Review,* 49: 496–507.

Kalberg, S. (2014), *Searching for the Spirit of American Democracy: Max Weber's Analysis of a Unique Political Culture, Past, Present, and Future*. Boulder and London: Paradigm.

Rex, J. (1961), *Key Problems of Sociological Theory*. London: Routledge and Kegan Paul.

Robertson, R. (1992), *Globalization: Social Theory and Global Culture*. London: Sage.

Robertson, R. and F. Lechner (1985), 'Modernization, Globalization and the Problem of Culture in World System Theory', *Theory, Culture and Society*, 3: 103–18.

Runciman, W. G. (1963), *Social Science and Political Theory*. Cambridge: Cambridge University Press.

Sztompka, P. (1988), 'Conceptual Frameworks in Comparative Inquiry: Divergent or Convergent', *International Sociology*, 3: 207–18.

Weber, Marianne (1926). *Max Weber. Ein Lebensbild.* Tübingen: J. C. B. Mohr (Paul Siebeck).

Weber, M. (1920), *Gesammelte Aufsätze zur Religionssoziologie.* Tübingen: J. C. B. Mohr (Paul Siebeck). In M. Weber (1930).

Weber, M. (1930) trans T. Parsons, *The Protestant Ethic and the Spirit of Capitalism.* London: George Allen & Unwin.

Weber, M. (1947) trans A. M. Henderson and T. Parsons, *The Theory of Social and Economic Organization.* Glencoe, IL: Free Press.

Weber, M. (1949) trans E. A. Shils and H. A. Finch, *The Methodology of the Social Sciences.* Glencoe, IL: Free Press.

Weber, M. (1975-6) trans M. Albrow, 'R. Stammlers "Surmounting" of the Materialist Conception of History', *British Journal of Law and Society*, 2: 129, 3: 17–43.

Weiss, J. (1987), 'On the Irreversibility of Western Rationalization and Max Weber's Alleged Fatalism', in S. Whimster and S. Lash (Eds.), *Max Weber, Rationality and Modernity*, pp. 154–63.

Whimster, S. and S. Lash (Eds.) (1987), *Max Weber, Rationality and Modernity.* London: Allen & Unwin.

Zhang X. and M. Albrow (2016), 'Max Weber, China and the world: in search of transcultural communication', *Journal of China in Global and Comparative Perspectives*, 2: 31–53. Reprinted in M. Albrow (2018b), *China's Role in a Shared Human Future*, pp. 100–24.

2.2 Global age issues on social and cultural change (chapters from the book *Global Age Issues on Social and Cultural Change*[6]

2.2.1 Basic information about the book *Global Age Issues on Social and Cultural Change* [7]

Abstract: In 14 previously unpublished essays, British sociologist Martin Albrow develops the global age thesis that he first proposed in the 1990s to capture the novelty of our own epoch. He absorbs insights from Max Weber, Emile Durkheim, Arnold Toynbee and Norbert Elias into a global discourse that shapes new approaches to abiding human dilemmas of faith, justice and responsibility. Even in resisting the idea that globalization and Americanization are inevitable, he argues that framing our time as global promotes a collective response to the challenges facing humankind. The hope for a human future depends on a normative ordering of global society, on global governance that allows local, national and global cultures to co-exist and thrive.

Contents

[6] Chapter 6.3 and sub-sections 3.1 to 3.6 are extracts from the book *Global Age Essays on Social and Cultural Change*, Martin Albrow, published by Verlag Vittorio Klostermann in 2014.

[7] Ibid., back cover.

2.2.2 Preface of the book by the editor Werner Gephart[8]

The global actor: observing a global moralist

Does globality change our categories of thinking about a world that – according to the sophisticated analysis of the anti-constructivist former fellow of the Center – does not 'exist' for logical reasons? Do we have to throw away the old-fashioned categories of the container theorists, as Ulrich Beck once called our much-cherished classical theorists Weber and Durkheim, because they never looked beyond the nation–state (Chapter 1)? Do we need a new theory of the social being we call global society (Chapter 2)? And if economics and society remain the main categories for analysing globality, then what is the role of culture beyond that of McDonaldization and *la civilisation du Coca-Cola*, i.e. Americanization or globalization as some say? And last but not least, what is the role of responsibility if the logic of functional differentiation – a term Ulrich Beck rightly borrowed from Luhmann – is one of the main reasons for accountability being shifted from one sphere to the next, because no overall system's competence is conceivable and therefore nobody is accountable in this system of structural irresponsibility?

[8] Preface of the book by the editor Werner Gephart. Ibid., pp. 5–7.

These topics, highly normatively loaded, have been critically discussed by our author for a long time throughout his travels around the world as a moralistic observer of globalization. Let me remind you of some of the major arguments in a work about the global age which has changed our world view, and let me add some personal opening remarks.

By now, it is hard to speak of globalization without assuming a mocking tone. Glocalization, globalization, McDonaldization, globalization of nothing – the list of neologisms continues unabated, without conveying any meaningful information. In a ritual manner, one has finally called the evil by its name and found an excuse for everything undesirable taking place in our world – excuse me: on our globe. The verve with which globalization is represented on the marketplace of novelties gives rise to the suspicion that we are merely dealing with a passing theoretical fashion. Historically, it can be hard to comprehend how globalization is tied to a second modernity.

After all, empires going all the way back to antiquity conceived of themselves as 'world empires'. And what about the 19th century? Marx offered the sweeping critical models and criticized the Saint-Simonians and their journal *Le Globe* for not factoring in their own living conditions when applying their ideas to Germany.

Huge international events took place, from the great exhibition in London with Paxton's Crystal Palace to the world fairs in Paris and St. Louis, where Weber discovered his America and Troeltsch was inspired to develop his sociology of religion. World literature, or 'Weltliteratur', to use Goethe's term, was created during this time, even if it originated in the little town of Weimar with just six thousand souls.

In other words, there is a long list of predecessors, even if they have nothing in common with international finance, internet portals, the human rights discussion and the interconnection of communications in the Luhmannian 'world society'.

With his pivotal work *The Global Age: State and Society beyond Modernity*, first published in 1996, Martin Albrow had a significant impact on the sociological discourse on globalization. In this study, Albrow broke with the dominant consensus regarding globalization, as represented especially by Anthony Giddens, and stated very early that 'globalization' did not provide an adequate account of what was happening globally. Globalization was not to be regarded in a purely mentally reflexive manner, or even as a process of global diffusion of modern norms and institutions. The new state of globality cannot be described by means of the narratives of modernity, or even deduced from them theoretically. Globality, Albrow states, is a new era 'with its own dominant features and shape'[9], which calls for a

---

[9] Martin Albrow (1996), *The Global Age: State and Society beyond Modernity*, Cambridge: Polity, p. 2 [Chinese edition: 马丁・阿尔布劳：《全球时代——超越现代性之外的国家与社会》，高湘、冯玲译，北京：商务印书馆，2001 年版].

new categorical framework that takes account of its 'social facticity', 'materiality' and 'spatial limitation'. The proposition of a 'global age' shifts sociological attention towards the fact that today modern culture and society have to deal with challenges which endanger the material and moral foundations of human life, or at least change them radically. Albrow approaches globalization by starting with its consequences and overall effects. It is not the functionalities of global systems, as stressed in system theory, that are most important to him, but the 'side effects' (Beck) of global dynamics and the rise of new global actors who can nowadays be found in the human rights, peace, environmental and women's movements and who contribute significantly to the emergence of new normative ideas and ideals that might overlap with or even challenge old organizational principles of communities and nation states. The call for new principles of global order is growing ever louder, and a new culture – or possibly cultures – of responsibility are on the horizon. For Albrow, the new globality does not require 'novelty, expansion, bureaucracy, male or white domination. But the vitality, richness and variety of the global age depend on the care with which its citizens preserve and tend the other more valuable achievements which were to the credit of the old modernity.'[10]

This raises the question of the normativity of the new transformations of global order, and of the normative consequences for the global age. It is therefore no coincidence that in his recent work Albrow increasingly concentrates on the challenges of global governance in the global age. How can global order be possible in this age and what is the role of law? These are some of the questions we were privileged to discuss with Martin Albrow during his extremely fruitful fellowship at the Käte Hamburger Center for Advanced Study in the Humanities 'Law as Culture', and we are delighted to now be able to share these intellectual pleasures with our readers. Nevertheless, we should not forget that reading Durkheim has left traces of some moralism, which in the global age is turned into a 'pragmatic universalism', as he calls it. That is why my pictorial homage to Martin Albrow depicts him as an observer whose habitus is inscribed by the globe's meridians, in sorrow for the world's destiny, but also incredibly optimistic in his youthful attitude towards the world.

Bonn, June 2014

2.2.3 Introduction: theorizing the global[11]

The year 1996, when *The Global Age: State and Society beyond Modernity* was published, seems an age away, a time of American triumphalism after the collapse of the Soviet Union; for some, the end of history, liberal constitutionalism driving alternatives out; for others, a new world order, following a single track to

[10] Ibid., p. 202 (emphasis added).

[11] Op. Cit. Albrow (2014), pp. 11–15.

greater prosperity with advancing globalization. It seemed as if good old-fashioned modern progress had immunized the world against genocide, a nuclear holocaust and environmental destruction. That sense of a resumed onward march of history was only marginally disturbed by projecting the American experience of culture clash to embrace the globe as a whole.

Every age writes its own history as it goes along, or rather we should say its histories, because *The Global Age* was written at that particular historical juncture as a dissident contribution, a considered critique of the globalization thesis that there was one direction the world had to follow, and that the unification of the world followed on from adopting a single set of modernizing precepts. I held the contrary position: that it was necessary to reject the then dominant globalization theorizing for what it was, a continuation of an older teleological narrative of advancing modernity, civilization and progress, blind to the real novelty that encompassed it, namely a pervasive discourse centred on the globe.

An orientation to the globe and an awareness of its endangered condition arising from the consequences of human activity had become an increasingly prominent feature of public discourse after the end of the Second World War. It was registered in the vocabulary of the globe, global, globality and globalism, as well as globalization. It was institutionalized in those governmental and intergovernmental agencies that handled global issues rather than globalization: problems of security, communications, international crime, climate change and world health.

Back in the 1980s, globalization as a concept, which had begun rather simply as a way of referring to the process of world unification, had been appropriated by the multinational corporation, then by Wall Street, and finally it became the centrepiece of the New Democrats' and President Clinton's recasting of American public and foreign policy. Equated to the spread of neo-liberal economic theory, it generated its own opposition in the anti-globalization movement, which has effectively succeeded in changing the discourse, allowing good things to be globalized, to include concern for human rights or environmental protection, and not just economic doctrine.

Globalization has thus been neutralized in ideological terms. As a reorientation to the globe of any human activity, of what was formerly simply local, national or regional, as a transcending of territorial boundaries and of exclusionary social boundaries, it has no necessary direction. It can promote global markets, and equally it can support global regulation; it may encourage a single authority, as for football, or multiple competing bodies, as for boxing. If, in the proto-history of the concept, the imagined future it portended was 'one world' or a 'new world order', we now recognize a 'variable geometry' world, a multipolar world, or simply multiple worlds.

Yet global discourse remains, even if globalization has been dethroned. The global as the frame for the contemporary human condition has outlasted the globalization of the 1990s and the 'global age' as an expression survives to capture key features of that frame. The reason is clear. The supervening problems of human survival on this planet have not been solved; they have become even more pressing. Summed up as global, they have a linchpin position in holding public concerns together with a worldwide scope as no other topic has done. The global has displaced the modern as the signature of our time, though there are growing challenges for that position, in particular the exponential growth of electronic communication, which is transformative of both social relations and technology. The digital age may displace the global so completely that it takes the fate of human beings out of their own hands. But we are not yet in a post-global age. It is only a matter of time. It will pass: all experience tells us that this is the case. Yet for the moment we are still global enough to respond to global challenges.

More than any other person, before or since, an early modern genius, Johann Wolfgang von Goethe, was sensitive to the changes of public mood, topographies of creativity, critical events, dominant opinion and social movement that make up what Voltaire before him had called the 'spirit of the age'. It is the configuration of people and their culture over a time and across a space that constitutes their world and which can be characterized in a word or a phrase, and thus distinguished from other epochs:

> The history of the sciences above all shows that for everything that counts as such there are specific epochs following faster or slower one on another. A significant view, new or renewed, is pronounced, recognition comes sooner or later, then collaborators; pupils take it forward, it is taught and propagated and unfortunately we note that it makes no difference whether it is true or false, for both take the same course, both are in the end a phrase, both impress themselves on the memory as a dead word.[12]

'It makes no difference whether it is true or false' carries a warning for all who write of their time, world, age or whatever word is used to refer to the diffuse context of life and experience which we sense as special or different from some other time, world, age, etc. Goethe is talking of what we have grown accustomed to call 'discourse', the power of making something through language and symbolic activity, a power which might well be exercised arbitrarily and have no basis in truth or reason – just like a proper name, in fact, accorded often quite whimsically by careless parents to be carried by the unfortunate infant for the rest of his or her life. Naming is arbitrary, description is not, and Goethe later sketched the outlines of epochs of what he called 'social formation' (*gesellige Bildung*) based on the degree of exchange between cultures. He identified four stages, which he named 'idyllic', 'social or civic', 'general' and 'universal'. It was all part of his reflections on world literature, an idea he conceived towards the end of his life. He too was willing then to risk his own strictures and impress a 'dead word', 'world literature', on our memories.

[12] Goethe: Aller Anfang ist heiter, p. 116 (this author's translation).

A name can just be a marker, even a number, as in bureaucratic society we all carry identification numbers. It can be more, and carry descriptive content, as old surnames did that indicated your place of origin. It may also be a self-assigned description: 'the special one', as the football manager José Mourinho famously named himself. The 'global age' is akin to a collective self-assigned name, an age that in its own language provides the obvious way of referring to itself. This is the condensation of a generation's experience that distinguishes it from other ages, like the 'babyboomer' generation, for those born after the Second World War, or Generation X of Douglas Coupland's novel, where a descriptive name could no longer capture the rootless existence his characters sought.

Can an age name itself? Yes, in the sense that with 'age', 'era' and 'epoch' we simply speak of people living, talking and writing in a particular period of time. Just as one would not talk of the modern age had not those who lived in it spoken of it in that way, then neither would we write of the global age if it were not prevalent in public discourse. We can then find an empirical base for the claim that we live in a global age in the public use of the term.

On page 83 (footnote 126) of my *The Global Age* you can turn to a rudimentary test carried out through a Google search on June 16, 2007 for the prevalence of 'global age' in digital sources. A similar search now, six years later, on June 7, 2013, gives the following results for hits on the same terms (earlier results in brackets): global age, 633,000,000 (446,000); atomic age, 15,500,000 (443,000); modern age, 414,000,000 (1,370,000); nuclear age, 87,100,000 (832,000); electronic age, 178,000,000 (793,000); computer age, 345,000,000 (932,000); digital age, 869,000,000 (1,180,000); industrial age, 145,000,000 (946,000); postmodern age, 5,544,000 (221,000); post-modern age, 254,000,000 (55,800).

Of course this is no more than suggestive, subject to the obvious limitations of search engine enquiries, and, since Google is a digital service, digital sources may reference 'digital age' more frequently, but already the intimations of what may come after the global age are there. What is plain too is that the global has overtaken the modern as the self-reference of the time, and, in its ratio of hits compared with the earlier search, it is catching up on the digital. (I leave comment on the reversal of popularity between 'postmodern' and 'post-modern' over the period to typographical experts.) There is another reservation Goethe expressed in a posthumous maxim about his own practice of describing the epoch in which he lived: 'Within an epoch there is no standpoint from which one can observe it.'[13] It is a view repeated by generations of historians who insist that their own time waits to disclose its secrets to their successors. Yet, since the future generation of scholars will insist that the primary sources for that earlier time are those which were written then, it would appear that the only people who *cannot* write validly about the present are historians. Effectively it leaves the present to journalists,

[13] Goethe, *Schriften zur Weltliteratur*, p. 303 (this author's translation).

political scientists and sociologists, who easily fall prey to some of the sins that historians have long dispelled from their accounts of the past: the tendency to see everything as preordained, to see everything in the past as leading to the present, to find a single direction to the future. This last fault has been particularly prevalent in accounts of globalization by social scientists and economists.

It is entirely possible to write about the present in the same way as the more distant past, provided the writer is aware of the processes of selective attention, of focalization and of narrative construction to which every historian is alert and which are involved in any account which seeks to be true to the facts while making sense of the course of events. Given that historians officially vacate the field of their own time, it is left to anyone to assume the task. But it extends beyond the boundaries of any discipline, for the good reason that the world of collective experience extends beyond the vision of any observer. My view of our global age inevitably bears the imprint of the sociologist escaping the disciplinary cage into narrating the present, but I make no apology for necessity. And in so far as my impression (hardly impartial, of course) is that the thesis of the book has stood the test of time, it may well be attributed to at least some of the merits of that discipline.

The original 1996 text was very much an introduction to thinking about the global age, offering a route to escape the clutches of a modernity without end.[14] For the second edition published in Germany there was an additional chapter covering the following decade.[15] Throughout the period I have been writing papers building in three main ways on the original thesis, either expanding on the theoretical and methodological implications, depicting features of the new social and cultural configurations or contributing to thinking on the normative and practical dilemmas that confront the global citizen. The following chapters are a selection from hitherto unpublished papers.

Since the chapters which follow were written over a span of twenty years, it would be beyond my powers and try the reader's patience to name everyone who has been personally helpful and influential over that time. In the 1990s I owed much to the discussion in the Thematic Group 6 on Local–Global Relations of the International Sociological Association, and I would like to thank Zdravko Mlinar and Henry Teune in particular.

The glorious years were in the mid-1990s when a group of us at the Roehampton Institute in London determined to resist all scepticism and make a research and teaching reality of global studies. John Eade, Neil Washbourne, Jörg Dürrschmidt, Darren O'Byrne, Patricia Alleyn-Dettmers, Laura Buffoni, Willemijn Dicke and Graham Fennell all helped to create one of those rare collective creative moments of which we all are beneficiaries, far beyond what we deserve

[14] Albrow, *The Global Age*.

[15] Albrow, *Das globale Zeitalter*.

from our individual contributions, and I am glad to be able to thank and pay my tribute to them here.

The United States is as exotic a culture as any in the world. In my time there I was fortunate to learn much more of it through the friendship of Colin Bradford of the Brookings Institution and Wolf Schaefer of SUNY Stonybrook, and it is my pleasure to acknowledge and thank them for a continuing intellectual stimulus that is global in every sense. The friendship of German sociologists has been greatly reassuring at times when Britain has seemed a foreign land and I owe a debt of gratitude for an ever-ready exchange of ideas to Johannes Weiss, Horst Helle, Richard Grathoff and Ulrich Beck.

Over the years of my association with the LSE's Centre for the Study of Global Governance, from 2004 to its untimely end in 2011, I was grateful for the pleasure and stimulus of collaborative authorship with Helmut Anheier, Marlies Glasius, Fiona Holland and Hakan Seckinelgin. Equally rewarding have been regular conversations with Geoffrey Pleyers, who has put the global age hypothesis to test in his extended empirical study of the activists who make it a reality.[16] Anthony Giddens cautioned me originally of the risk I was taking in writing *The Global Age* and was generous in his support both then and to this day.

Finally, I am especially grateful to Professor Werner Gephart, who invited me to join the Käte Hamburger Kolleg 'Law as Culture' at the University of Bonn and gave me the opportunity to publish this volume. He and Dr. Daniel Witte have given invaluable help in organising and editing this selection from a larger set of unpublished papers. Christian Neue has given valuable support and Simon Cowper's copyediting could not be surpassed. My warmest thanks go to them, the fellows of the Kolleg and their colleagues for providing a continuously stimulating intellectual environment.

2.2.4 Preface of Part I Classical perspectives and the global shift[17]

One commonly encountered criticism of the *Global Age* thesis is that a change of epoch ought to mean a different set of concepts for sociological analysis. This objection has partial validity. New configurations of social relations and cultural innovations will require revision of old concepts and the introduction of some new ones. In point of fact, colleagues and I have indeed revisited and reassessed old concepts and introduced new ones.[18] We have explored socioscapes, sociospheres, performative citizenship, extended milieux and tertiary relationships but equally drawn on much older notions of culture, structure and agency under the new global conditions.

---

[16] Pleyers, *Alter-Globalization.*

[17] Ibid., pp. 19–20.

[18] Cf. Albrow/Eade/Washbourne/Dürrschmidt, *The Impact of Globalization on Sociological Concepts*; Albrow, *The Global Shift and its Consequences for Sociology*; Albrow, *Situating Global Social Relations*; Albrow, Travelling beyond Local Culture; Dürrschmidt, *Everyday Lives in the Global City*; Eade (Ed.), *Living the Global City*; O'Byrne: *The Dimensions of Global Citizenship.*

The validity of the thesis does not depend on its author developing a wholly new vocabulary of his own invention. That would actually undermine the case the book makes, for it is a reflection on and of the age in which it is written, and the novelty of the age is out there in vast and fertile fields of research and scholarship on identity politics, lifestyle enclaves, hybridity, glocalization, disembedding, agentic states, structural coupling, network society, postcolonialism, etc. These have all been conceptualized in the period since 1945, and all make reference to contemporary transformations. It is hardly fanciful to suggest that they all relate, some more, some less directly, to a fundamental shift for human society, when it is no longer dominated by the modern project but labours under a comprehensive threat to its continued existence. Is this not the shift of historical tectonic plates?

But the demand for root and branch clearance of old ways of thinking owes more to a belief in postmodern deconstruction and to a refusal of the possibility of crafting any coherent narrative for our time than it does to a commitment to a new sociology. As I made clear in *The Global Age*, my aim was to move beyond the modern *and* the postmodern and write appropriately for the age in which we live. That emphatically does not mean consigning all contributions to our understanding from previous epochs to the dustbin of history. To adhere slavishly to the scholarly contributions of a previous period would be a mistake that their authors would never have countenanced. We neglect them at our peril.

The chapters that follow explore how we can draw – for the purposes of understanding epochal shift today – on classic figures in sociology, such as Max Weber, Emile Durkheim and Norbert Elias. They all worked with a profound sense of historical context and each engaged directly in making a sociological diagnosis of his own time. To them I add Arnold Toynbee as a great historian who ignored the strictures of his colleagues both in drawing extensively on the social sciences and in writing about contemporary history. In comparing Toynbee and Elias too there is the added interest that they straddle the modern and the global, and, in Toynbee, who wrote of both the atomic age and the postmodern, we have the example of an epochal imagination at work, which can reach out beyond its own time. He saw the atomic bombs as marking a turning point in human history and my fifth chapter has that as its inspiration.

2.2.5 Preface of Part II Towards theory for global society[19]

The four chapters that follow each involve a re-examination of what a global frame for social relations means for theorizing society. They all work outside the assumptions of what Ulrich Beck has called the thrall of methodological nationalism.[20] As a consequence of this change in basic cognitive assumptions, he asks for political engagement in the contemporary world, based on a cosmopolitan ethic. These essays ask for a more protracted examination of what a methodological

[19] Ibid., pp. 89–90.

[20] Cf. Beck: *Cosmopolitan Vision.*

globalism would look like before that kind of commitment. Moving out of the old comfort zone of nationally defined sociologies of social structure makes new demands on sociological analysis.

In particular, we have to resume a serious consideration, even rehabilitation, of the concept of society, once it is no longer equated with the boundaries of the nation–state. For too long, to my mind, sociologists bent before the prevailing political wind in the 1980s and 1990s and were happy to concur with a scepticism about society that comforted neo-liberal politicians and radical libertarians alike. Now, in British politics at least, society has come back into political fashion, this time in support of small government.[21] Either way, being denied or affirmed, society is combustible political material. That seems to make it even more imperative to develop analytical approaches that are detached from the politics of the moment.

The analyses that follow treat social relations as realities that constitute human collectivities of all kinds with variable components of human motivation, agency, norms, values, command over resources, attachments to territory and symbolic representations. Society in the widest sense is the sum total of those relations in the medium of which individuals inescapably pursue their lives and through the sum of which humankind explores its collective fate.

This is a humanistic view of society combined with a methodological globalism, in the sense that, given the potential for social relations to be conducted through any medium between any two or more people worldwide, research into society cannot in principle refuse to explore the consequences of those relations should they in fact be realized. There are political consequences to this position but they do not fit into old modern ideological divides. If one were to develop a political programme to safeguard a human future on the planet, it would contain elements from both left and right ideology, from communitarian and cosmopolitan ethics, depending on the current configuration of geopolitics and the means of mobilizing support.

This is a way of saying that the four chapters that follow seek to achieve the maximum analytical distance from commitment to politics or policies in order to provide maximum clarity for whoever has the global interest of humankind as their concern. They have that limited objectivity which Habermas's knowledge interest allows.

2.2.6 Preface of Part III Changing cultures: new norms[22]

No matter how far the social scientist pursues a cognitive interest, back to basic elements of the structuring of social relations as the last four essays did, its relevance to the normative component of human action can never be excluded. Rules of behaviour are so pervasive that even their breach is evidence of how

[21] Cf. Albrow: 'Big Society' as a Rhetorical Intervention.

[22] Ibid., pp. 141–142.

extensive and powerful they can be, and the scientist aiming to establish the degree to which they are observed necessarily judges their scope and meaning. An empirical sociology of norms and values, seeking to register their distribution, prevalence and persistence, is making judgments about the meaning of values and providing accounts of them, which, unavoidably, may either be at odds with or reinforce the beliefs of their adherents. Sociology in this respect is an intervention in the social and moral life of the time, even when the sociologist has no commitment one way or another to the norms and values under examination. It is an argument that depends on Weber's analysis of commitment to and freedom from value in social science but goes further than he did in detecting unavoidable value-laden elements in sociological research.

What for some is an irresolvable dilemma and therefore a fatal flaw in social science, the last five chapters acknowledge as an inevitability, which brings with it the obligation to demonstrate a positive contribution to the human future. The first chapter explores how in contemporary social theory the search for the grounds for social action ends up by identifying a substratum beyond the rational accounts of the actors, which, by the same token, harbours the faith commitments of new religious movements. (It is also, incidentally, the first time the author invoked the global age.) The postscript to that chapter documents how difficult it is to draw practical lessons from such an analysis by reporting the author's failed attempt to create an institutional commitment to multi-faith education.

The next two chapters explore the dilemmas that globalization has posed for American values and self-identity. The nation that both Alexis de Tocqueville and Karl Marx saw as quintessentially modern, and that has always seen itself as ahead of the rest of the world, has particular difficulty in recognizing that globalization has not been simply an extension of American values across the globe but exposes them to reinterpretation and retroactive application. To the United States the idea that the globe might colonize *them* is an oxymoron, but the new global culture only represents the apotheosis of all culture, which belongs potentially to all peoples, wherever it is generated. Now it travels from all parts of the globe, everywhere at once.

It is where global culture meets global governance that we find the issues that matter most for the future of humankind. The current institutional arrangements for handling the global economy and global issues have grown up piecemeal since 1945 and in many respects there is a mismatch between them, the goals they proclaim and the normative requirements of global society. Sociology needs to re-examine the whole basis of individual and collective responsibility in a world where nation–state authorities have declined in importance as monitors and arbiters of individual conscience.

Durkheim accorded the task of promoting universal human values to the *patrie*. Now individuals source their attachments to universality from a host of competing and conflicting collective entities within and beyond nations. There is no global court of appeal and the sociologist can contribute by examining the processes whereby accommodations are reached between those competing entities claiming to possess the true universals. One such process is where the different claimants to universal values engage with one another, respect one another's rights to live their lives in their own way and accept that, however long they debate those values, they may never agree on them. I call it pragmatic universalism. It is a position where the cognitive and normative come together and this unavoidably colours my own analysis. The last two chapters are reflections around that theme without in any way claiming to be more than preliminary to a much bigger task.

2.3 Goals, values and endemic conflicts in the new global culture[23]

In 1996, outlining the characteristics of a global age that was shaping the narrative of the time, I wrote in a section headed 'Culture and Multiple Worlds':

> Globality restores the boundlessness of culture and promotes the endless renewability and diversification of cultural expression rather than homogenization or hybridization (1996: 144).

It followed in the path of the seminal seventh volume of the journal, *Theory, Culture and Society* (TCS), also published as the book *Global Culture: Nationalism, Globalization and Modernity* (1990). Its editor, Mike Featherstone, captured the tone of its debates in writing of 'trans-societal cultural processes' giving rise to 'all sorts of "third cultures"' (1990: 1). Rightly, he rejected any suggestion that a single world culture was emerging, equivalent to and transcending national cultures.

Nearly three decades later, the early exchanges in TCS still resonate for the world of our time. Yet the profound changes since have left their marks on both public debate and new currents of ideas in the academic world. In particular, there has arisen a widely noticed political divide that has appeared in many countries between what are generally called globalists and populists.

Such a divide, where a clash of the global and the national has each side making transnational alliances, marks a development of political globalization that warrants speaking of a global politics beyond what is usually thought of as either national politics or international relations. It has of course its economic parallels in global corporate capitalism and its anti-capitalist campaigners and the clash is equally a cultural phenomenon transcending national boundaries.

The idea of global culture consequently has taken on quite another meaning from the single world culture Featherstone rejected in 1990. It is not the culture of a unified world society but of a global political system where dominant and oppositional segments contest the scope and penetration of the global into both national and daily life.

---

[23] A chapter in Ino Rossi (Ed.) (2020), *Challenges of Globalization and Prospects for an Inter-civilizational World Order*, Springer: Springer Nature Switzerland, pp. 143–156.

It is a public conflict conducted through media with unprecedented reach into everyday lives, inhabited by events and celebrities that have global recognition and conducted through conversations where distance is irrelevant.

The account that follows identifies elementary features that should aid the understanding of the novelty of this conflicted global culture. It will consider the ambiguous relation globalization has to the continual fragmentation and reconstitution of culture. It will deal with the inherent tensions in claims to control culture.

It can only in passing refer to the economic, political and environmental preconditions that are dealt with elsewhere in this volume. But three other defining features of the present world that have singular importance for culture need special mention.

The first is information and communication technology (ICT). In the broadest sense, technology is also a cultural product if we mean by that the outcome of human ingenuity harnessed to shared knowledge. Often enough too, it is human aspiration that leads technology. From the early speculations about satellite communication by the visionary scientist and novelist Arthur C. Clarke (1945) through path-breaking insights into the relation of media technology to the content of communication by Marshall McLuhan (1962: 31), who branded his time and ours with the 'global village', through to Tim Berners-Lee (1999), who tested out his dream of an interconnected world through the internet by inventing the World Wide Web, technology has been the main means to bring worlds together.

The second is the transformation of social relations, happening in parallel with technological development, both as a spur and being facilitated by it. Advances in the means of physical transportation have played a major part in travel within and between countries and have aided the migratory flows stemming from environmental pressures and diasporas induced by political conflict.

But equally important has been the possibility of real-time interpersonal communication over any distance in the world. As a result, we no longer associate community primarily with presence in a local area. It can now be generated equally out of networks that extend worldwide. The consequences of this disembedding are profound for nation–states confined within territorial boundaries, for ideas of citizenship and social control.

The third may be summed up as digitalization, but the pervasive use of 'digital' already renders too familiar processes that contribute to the transformation of every aspect of daily life, as well as to the infrastructure that makes industrial civilization possible, and to weapons systems that extend to outer space and threaten human existence. The computing power that increases exponentially takes us beyond global thinking into reconstructing the human being. Beyond human is no longer science fiction fantasy, but on the horizon of development in artificial intelligence (AI).

ICT, disembedding, AI, each sets boundaries to the analysis of contemporary culture. They are prime determinants of its future direction. They are incalculable too in their combined effects. But their impact is also under our scrutiny and can in part be controlled by our own efforts. These arise very much in the more narrowly defined sphere of culture. Current understanding of changes in this sphere is the theme of what follows.

2.3.1 The autonomy of culture

The boundary-crossing nature of globalization has been the catalyst for recognizing both the autonomy and creativity of culture. In the early 1990s, it was the threat of globalization to nation-state sovereignty that preoccupied public commentary. This was mirrored in academic debate by controversy around national claims to culture.

Featherstone's volume mentioned above, for instance, featured a sharp exchange between Immanuel Wallerstein (1990), for whom cultural analysis was only an extension of national power and ideology and in effect a 'non-subject', and Roy Boyne (1990), who argued that the concept of culture could not be confined to relations within and between groups.

Wallerstein's dismissal of cultural as distinct from social analysis has to be seen against the earlier widespread criticism of the dominant sociological paradigm of the 1960s. For Talcott Parsons (1951), culture and social relations were bonded in national societies integrated around central values. As a general theory of society, it came under relentless attack from Marxist emphases on class conflict throughout the 1970s and 1980s.

The inherent nature of culture to cross boundaries has long been recognized, as well as its potential for inspiring solidarity within and division between peoples. In early anthropology, acculturation was regarded as one of the effects of diffusion, where features of one culture were adopted by another. In the early twenty-first century, the same process may well be denounced as cultural appropriation.

Margaret Archer (1988: xxii) summed up the constant flux within and between cultures when she wrote of 'this shapeless, seething and shifting thing we call culture'. She went on to fix it for the purposes of sociological analysis with the concept of morphogenesis, the way in which interactions between people are constantly shaped by new cultural configurations.

There is now widespread recognition that social relations operate through cultural media with their own generative rules. The primordial case is a language, learnable by anyone, providing for personal expression but only within the limits of its syntax. At the same time, translation points to commonalities behind and between languages.

The success of the term Richard Dawkins (1976) invented, 'meme', to refer to a cultural element reproduced in multiple contexts, exemplifies the very message he wanted to convey. 'Meme' has become a meme. It also highlights the dissection of culture into basic factors, images, phrases, texts, all of which can be detached from their bearers, people or media, aggregated and analysed. Computing power today allows for the findings derived from assemblages of 'big data' in turn to be fed into product development, marketing and political persuasion.

2.3.2 Cultural differentiation

Culture is a site for conflict and competing claims to ownership. Yet attempts by human groups or organizations to monopolize what they claim to be their own culture, even to control symbolic expression in general, have never succeeded in the longer run. Globalization's controversial impact on national cultures reinforces what has always been evident, that culture is potentially open to all. It is prior to ownership, which can only be asserted after the event in an effort to control the creative expression that any culture generates.

The creativity of the counter-cultural movements of the 1960s was an obvious challenge to the dominant sociological theory that sought to accommodate them within its paradigm by means of the concept of deviant sub-cultures. But there was nothing 'sub-cultural' about the transnational spread of the student movement of 1968, nor the feminist, peace and environmental movements that drew on its energies into the future.

The discrediting of claims to exclusive ownership of a national culture by a state or a sectional group does not eliminate assertions of ownership of non-national cultures. Accusations of cultural appropriation can be aimed at anyone adopting the symbols of what were previously stigmatized cultures, e.g. at White persons displaying the dreadlocks associated originally with West Indian culture.

Those conflicts are all the more confusing because culture also produces the markers of belonging, from the special handshake of the secret society to the proud wearing of the shirt with a favourite team's logo. That shirt and its logo may itself cost more because of a sponsor's claim to ownership. Commercial interests thrive on creating new images and copyrighting them, inventing processes and then establishing patents. States underpin both corporate and individual claims to ownership with intellectual property law, extending it in the case of the United States to 99 years from the original creation. But the spread of culture always outstrips attempts to control it. Law can pursue smuggling or counterfeiting. No censorship can ultimately prevent every singing of a song, telling of a story or subversive joke.

2.3.3 Transculturality

The tension between a superordinate national culture and the culture of minorities, national or tribal, with the consequent fusions and variations, has generated state-sponsored attempts to preserve some stability in relations between cultures through the concept of multiculturalism, Related to it is the notion of hyphenated identity, where immigrant minorities are held to belong both to their original and to their host cultures. These ideas are hotly contested in both political and intellectual debates, as in Samuel Huntington's *Who Are We?* (2003).

Multiculturalism is a state-sponsored strategy for self-preservation. The institutional structure and values of the national culture are required to accommodate the religion and morality of minorities who in turn must adapt to state requirements. Frequently those minorities are not indigenous but share ancestry and culture with counterparts in other states. The result is hybrid transnational cultural relations. Hybridization has, however, inflammatory biological overtones at odds with the pressing state needs to defuse incipient racism in populations hosting influxes of immigrants. In an older religious discourse, syncretism was a favoured expression for an emergent mix of elements from different faiths. Under globalizing conditions, the concept of transculturality, emerging out of the anthropology of colonialism, conveys the quality of culture that arises out of contact between cultures, co-exists with them but frees itself from their control.[24]

The morphogenesis of transcultural values and institutions is especially obvious in the case of the discourse shared by multilateral institutions, transnational corporations and national diplomatic services. It is their business that constitutes much of what is called global governance. In the course of it, each governmental or non-governmental agency makes a contribution to a developing common discourse, reinterprets it for a domestic audience and returns to take the dialogue forward.

A prime example of this recursive process is provided by the idea of sustainable development that was brought to the world's attention by the Brundtland Report 'Our Common Future' (1987). Sustainability has become a transcultural theme, part of a wider global discourse on the future of the planet. In different countries, sustainability is related to specific social and environmental conditions and re-interpreted to engage with their own cultural definitions. Thus in China, for instance, what is ecologically sustainable is then tied to national political and social sustainability (Zhang and Barr, 2013: 9). National leadership then returns the message to the global discourse, in this case in President Xi Jinping's (2018) speeches that pick up the Brundtland meme and point 'Towards a Common Future for Mankind'.[25]

Transcultural communication in a common discourse can never preclude disagreement, indeed provides precisely the opportunities for opposing views to confront one another. President Donald Trump's announcement of his intention to withdraw the United States from the Paris Climate Change Agreement of 2015 highlights the ever-present potential for conflict between national and supranational culture, but it is also extremely contentious within the United States.

2.3.4 Pragmatic universalism

It has been a feature of Western culture since its ancient roots to aspire to universal truths. From Thomas Jefferson's self-evident truths in his American Dec-

[24] Fernando Ortiz (1951) coined the term to capture the quality of the music that developed in the West Indies from the intermingling of African and indigenous traditions.

[25] For an account of the challenges that concept might pose for China see Albrow (2018).

laration of Independence, through the French revolutionary dedication to rights, liberty and justice, to the British missionary zeal to spread civilization to the rest of the world, each state has proclaimed its unique status in promoting universal values. That states could come into mortal conflict with one another, not just in spite of but even because of these claims, was subsequently tragically demonstrated in the two World Wars.

The founding of the United Nations and the Universal Declaration of Human Rights represented a collective effort to realize universal values for the whole world. They have been subject to continual debate and development ever since. At the same time, there has been growing recognition that the simple declaration of human rights does not guarantee a shared understanding of their meaning. The extension of the idea of human rights from juristic notions of freedom, justice and equality before the law to economic and social rights has been a continual source of deep differences between states. In the ongoing exchanges, pragmatic compromises have been made on individual freedom, parents' and children's rights, collective bargaining, religious expression, etc., that cross value systems, East and West, South and North.

In comparing different claims to universality, what becomes apparent is that it is only the *striving for the universal* that captures human imagination everywhere. When one culture's universality claims meet another's, then accommodations between them, respect for difference and compromise become necessary means to avoid conflict.

This is an outlook variously praised or denounced as pragmatism. Frequently, it involves the substitution of goals for abstract values, an orientation to material outcomes, reductions in carbon emissions, halting desertification, eliminating infectious disease, preserving endangered species. This is the global materialism of the present age that may outlive the abstract notions of global markets and national sovereignty. It recognizes that it is easier to meet common challenges than to change minds. It is the ethos of a pragmatic universalism, where the emphasis is on striving rather than perfection, agreement to differ rather than imposition of absolute truths.

In terms of civilizational encounters in a globalized world, the main testing ground for the success of pragmatic universalism has to be in exchanges between the West and Asia. The worldwide adoption of similar technology and associated lifestyles is one aspect of bridging cultural divides. But at the fundamental level of contrasting value systems the emphasis in Asian cultures on harmony between opposites while maintaining the difference, coupled with increasing economic power, may mitigate the effects of the unqualified claims to possessing universal truths that have fuelled Western expansion in the past.

2.3.5 Negotiated identities

The conditional nature of nation–states' relations with one another, their sense of common threats, their shared technologies and participation in a global market, all of which are regularly bracketed under the general heading of globalization, have as a counterpart individual, group and corporate mobility and the formation of ties across boundaries.

Diasporas and the maintenance of personal ties across long distances and through long absences have increased recognition of community as a continuing set of close relations without a fixed or necessary land location or boundary. Detachment from the soil and the intermittent nature of contact between its members make community the imagined social framework for everyday life, rather than the sum of real-time interactions with known persons. Benedict Anderson's (1983) account of contemporary nationalism shows that even the largest social entities depend on this presumed fellow feeling with unknown others.

The omnipresence of strangers, dispersion of families, emotional attachment to causes and iconic figures, chains of economic dependency, instant communication over any distance, social media, local presence of global enterprises all contribute to complex networks of social relations.

The coalescence and dissolution of social entities, or the growth of entities of a hybrid kind (natural, cultural and social, as Bruno Latour [1993] has highlighted), becomes a major narrative theme of our time. Individuals now experience their personal social environment as a socioscape with no primary organizing image like community, class or even household. Their social networks are extended in space and time lodged in sociospheres with their own characteristics and rules (Albrow 1997). The theoretical basis for understanding the interdependence of multiple group membership with personal social identity was established at the beginning of the twentieth century by Georg Simmel's (1971) emphasis on overlapping group membership as constitutive of personal social identity. In the flux of globalizing conditions, both groups and individuals are engaged in constant redefinition of self-identity in negotiation with others. This extends through gender, race, ethnicity, nationality (as a personal attribute), nationhood (as a collective quality) and partnership, both sexual and economic. 'Trans' has become a prefix as prevalent in gender identity discussion as in debates about culture.

In the case of collective agencies, globalization, in forcing the most powerful, namely states, to engage with the conditions of their own existence, has brought the multiply contingent nature of all social entities into sharper focus. However large an entity is, it depends for its existence on *beliefs* in its existence (e.g. sovereignty recognition), just as in the simplest case an agreement between two persons depends on each believing the other believes it has been agreed, double contingency.

Widespread recognition of this indeterminacy, the purely conventional facticity of all social arrangements, from friendships to global agreements on climate change, is coupled with the continuous creation of new entities with novel structural features. This applies to innovative partner relationships, through business relations up to multilateral arrangements between nations. Binary classifications of entities into open or closed, authoritarian or democratic, networks or hierarchies, only capture single dimensions of multi-dimensional arrangements. Developing internet technologies permit vastly diverse circles of contacts to establish unique collective identities with greater or lesser investment of personal time and energy. Facebook, with billions of users, is only the largest of the hosts to these friendship groups, online communities or businesses.

This indeterminacy clashes with an old image of the nation–state as the guarantor of social order. In a globalized world, a myriad social relationships and entities criss-cross national boundaries and the demand for trust at every level of society increases. Arguably the nation–state can no longer meet the demand, and the touchstone of the advance of globalization has often been seen as the diminution of the power of the nation–state.

2.3.6 Integrity

The imagery of flows has become a conventional way of describing society rather than structure or system. Identity maintenance in an environment of flows and contested values makes integrity, both of individuals and of collective entities, a focal point for aspirations and accusations. The dual-linked meanings of integrity, wholeness and high morality provide clues to its contemporary prevalence. Fluid boundaries and negotiable identities under globalized conditions create existential anxiety for individuals, as well as producing in others uncertainty about their trustworthiness.

The demand for integrity applies equally to relationships and social entities of all sizes. Their putative existence, capacity to be recognized as responsible agents, depends on it. The claim to integrity in human affairs, then, is a declaration of a certain kind of existence, durable enough to be counted on to behave in a way that also confirms the claims to recognition of and respect for the existence of others. Over time we may see the usage 'an integrity' or 'integrities' come to register this underlying social transformation.

For individuals, the fluid, often ephemeral existence of social relations has ambiguous consequences. At one extreme, identity itself may become a fungible asset, put to use as the occasion demands, as John Eade (1997) described in his study of young Bangladeshis in London who alternated between being British and Bangladeshi depending on who happened to be with them. But equally, experience of self in multiple social relations may impart an urgency to the quest for integrity, to find core, durable elements. An equivalent search may occur too after sharing in diverse kinds of social relations in multiple contexts. Anthony Giddens's (1991) examination of self-identity sees it resulting in a quest for the pure relationship, beyond the conventional definitions of the wider society.

In collective and corporate settings, the integrity of members and employees is demanded as intrinsic to the integrity of the organization as a whole. Thus the British civil service makes it a core value for the service as a whole. It crosses ideological divides. It also appears as one of the Chinese Communist Party's twelve socialist values. It is proclaimed by business, but also in politics, art and literature. It extends too to the artistic or literary product. When it is challenged, it becomes a media story. It is a key marker for existence in the culture of the global age.

The search for integrity as an existential quest appears in acute form in a phenomenon that is not intelligible in an old modernist frame of reference that treated religion as a survival of pre-modern times. The vast profusion of religious movements, as documented in the work of Eileen Barker (1989), and so-called cults offers adherents a world view, deep personal experience and firm boundaries to relationships. Existential religiosity is as much a feature of the new global culture as the radical politics of the Occupy movement.

2.3.7 Global culture

In the 1990s, global culture was still a term in search of a concept. It could refer to worldwide cultural connections and expressions that were shared by national cultures. It might intimate Western ideas and practices that had achieved worldwide penetration, as with the cultures of transnational corporations. It could reflect the aspirations of intellectuals to shape a cosmopolitan outlook.

Cosmopolitanism has roots deep in history, since it is the reflex of encounters with strange cultures and seeks to accommodate that strangeness in a common ethic that emerges from each side to the encounter. Harking back to my earlier account of universalisms, it may be seen as the attempt to universalize the experience of otherness. It has, as Joy Zhang's (Chapter 5) contribution to this volume makes clear, deep affinities with the practices of science.

But a brief résumé of the sources of contemporary global culture shows how far it extends beyond science and technology, though that they are vital constituents. Global culture has arisen out of diverse sources coming together: satellite communication; the commercial media, information and entertainment industries aiming for world audiences; the commitments of multilateral institutions and their staff; the global consciousness of civil society organizations; the lifestyles of the employees of global corporations; the networking of global elites; the growth of social media. These forces have long crossed national boundaries and in the digital age inhabit a cyberspace that governments struggle to control. Global culture is both transnational and transcultural. In promoting dialogue between cultures, it generates new culture, and the receptiveness of national and local cultures to the reformulation of values that each has regarded as its own is one of the key dynamics in globalization.

But neither the transnational nor the transcultural is yet global. The global reference returns culture to the fate of the globe as a whole. Until the rise of the 'digital', 'global' was the most successful meme of recent history, capturing, in succession: the sense of common fate in the aftermath of the Second World War; the threat of nuclear warfare in the Cold War; environmental threats to human life on this planet: the interconnectedness produced by worldwide media transmissions; and real-time communication (social media) made possible by advancing communication technology.[26]

Phrases like Marshall McLuhan's (1962) 'global village' and René Dubos's (1965) 'think globally, act locally' were widely quoted before global corporations latched on to the global for marketing purposes and globalization was adopted as a master narrative by economists, policy makers and politicians. The pervasiveness of global references by both the advocates of globalization and its opponents reflected the sense of a shared and single world, even when the contests over its future were bitter and prolonged.

The global, then, is not a summation of national, transnational or even transcultural experience. It concerns the fate of the human species on an endangered planet.[27] Those who made that their concern were the first globalists, and their globalism predated and was appropriated by the later apostles of economic globalization. When the opponents of economic globalization coalesced and became the alter-globalization movement at the turn of the millennium, political conflict became embedded in global culture.

If today both the advocates of economic globalization and its opponents are spoken of in one breath as globalists, it is because the development of the global economy is itself one of the dangers to life on this planet. They are locked in a fateful and shared engagement with the human future, even when their motives and proposed courses of action may be deeply at odds with each other.

2.3.8 Globalism versus populism

The shared community of interest between the cultures of global corporations, national and multilateral agencies, international non-governmental organizations and civil society activists is a central component of global culture, but not the only one. They have a presence in the global media that also are tied to the global entertainment industry and the manufacture of celebrity. Together they provide for worldwide public viewing the lives and lifestyles of an elite that is truly global in the scope of its wealth and separation from 99% of the world's population.

Global culture now has matured to achieve something like the hegemony that Antonio Gramsci (1957) attributed to the cultural practices of the old industrial ruling class of the early twentieth century. But now it is global in nature rather than Western imperial. The sign of this late maturity is the emerging struggle between globalists and populists.

---

[26] Sabine Selchow (2017) has documented how 'global' has become inextricably intertwined with 'globalization' and argued that together they belong to a 'new world' discourse.

[27] Cf. Martin Albrow: 'global age' refers to a period of time when there is a prevailing sense of the interconnectedness of all human beings, of a common fate for the human species and a threat to its life on this Earth', in George Ritzer (Ed.) (2012), *Encyclopaedia of Globalization*, Vol II, p. 823.

The intensification of transnational relations since 1945, the growth of multilateral institutions and the worldwide scope of the activities of global corporations have between them created a global elite vastly separated in wealth and lifestyle from the general citizenship of nation–states.

Globalization has been the practice of this elite, globalism provides the set of ideas that legitimizes the practice, the belief that it is the globe as a whole that is the field and object of concern for human activities. As such, globalism is an outlook shared as much by the opponents of globalization as its practitioners. Indeed, as the extensive research of Geoffrey Pleyers (2010) has shown, the activists who demonstrated against globalization, like those who caused the suspension of the WTO talks in Seattle in 1999, were as much, if not more concerned about the future of human well-being across the globe than were the politicians and trade negotiators.

The anti-globalization movement morphed into alter-global, but the worldwide spread of globalist ideas opposing the global elite corresponds with Gramsci's analysis, where emerging classes generate their own organic intellectuals outside the traditional intellectual training programmes of the new elite. Taking the similarities with the international situation of industrial workers in the nineteenth century still further, the ambitions of a global opposition to the global elite are in fundamental contradiction to national resentments to anything global. Global activists, with their intellectually based moral commitments to saving the world and their international connections, are no longer seen as belonging to 'our people'. For nationalists, the activists are seen as part of the problem.

The boundary-crossing forces of global culture had their antecedents in earlier periods. The national problem for global activists is as much an acute issue today as it was for the international working men's movement of Marx's time. They were identified as cosmopolitans, which became a term of abuse for nationalist and anti-socialist movements. Today, where cosmopolitanism has an added ingredient of global consciousness, of attending to global issues and the fate of the planet, then it qualifies as globalism. Globalism is the apotheosis of cosmopolitanism. It also incurs the added odium of hostility to cosmopolitanism by those who feel threatened by changes that can be portrayed as benefitting the globalists at the expense of the masses.

2.3.9 Agency and responsibility

The two most prominent dynamic elements of globalism are the agents and forces operating in the global market on the one hand and the agencies and activists committed to global causes on the other. Taken together, they constitute a transformative force in world society that supersedes and should be distinguished from the world domination impetus of the older nationalist/imperialist configuration. We are talking here about the contrast between two ages, the modern and the global. In each there is a collision of opposites.

The rampant industrialization of the modern age was accompanied by romantic nostalgia for the past, and ruthless imperial exploitation of peasant producers could combine with Christian missions. Yet the extremes could sink their differences in the idea of progress, the advance of civilization, and the results, often enough, were public sanitation, education and even democracy.

In the global age similar accommodations are made, as corporations compete to take charge of the sustainability agenda, to claim 'green' credentials, while civil society's campaigns on climate change use modern selling techniques and all the promotional opportunities that the new media technologies provide. In both cases, they participate in the culture of consumer capitalism.

The contrast between the cultures of the modern and the global extends into the way purpose is woven into human activity. Max Weber famously made goal-oriented, rational activity a distinctive feature of modern society as compared with traditional societies. We can develop that idea in many ways and one of them is to point to both the nuances of purposive action and its distribution in global society. Modern culture made goal-directedness central to culture. Progress meant continuing achievement. Goals extended into a limitless future. As Jürgen Habermas (1997) put it, modernity was an unfinished project. At the same time, those goals were established through authority, delivered by bureaucracy, coordinated through the division of labour in the market and in organizations. Agency operated through well understood institutions and structures.

That whole cultural complex of modernity crumbled under the impact of two world wars, the Holocaust and nuclear destruction. Globality came as a shock, or a series of shocks, the biggest in 1945. Like Hegel's owl of Minerva taking to flight when dusk is falling, social theory was rather slow to register the change, except in capturing a sense of postmodern disorientation. It was the late lamented Ulrich Beck (1992 [1986]) who first pointed to social consequences of the repositioning of purpose in human agency. He argued that perception of risk brought about a new conditionality of action. It came also with differential exposure to risk for different groups, and its shared nature had become a structural feature of society quite as important as class formation. Later, he was to extend his understanding of the break from the past with a series of publications around the theme of a second modernity ensuing from the rupture with the older modern culture.

One has to dig deep to identify the theoretical shifts underlying the cultural history of the second half of the twentieth century. They were obscured in any case by the ideological conflict of the Cold War. But beneath those bitter exchanges between collectivistic and individualistic views of human society there was a deep, shared insecurity about human purpose and how it related to social structure.

Outside that ideological conflict, this insecurity surfaced in counter-cultural movements, until achieving some kind of resolution in the resurrection of the idea of civil society in the 1990s. With it came the recognition and acceptance of new ways of infusing individuals and society with purpose. Linked with the understanding of culture as autonomous boundary setting rather than being bounded, values came to supersede authority. The sharing of values came to define goals.

Value orientation provides for debate and updating of goals. Linked with the networking capabilities of new communication technology, it results in the de-centring of organization. Two quite distinct moments then provide for goals to be shared across boundaries. One is value orientation in decentred organization and the other is the sense that global challenges should govern the choice of goals. The present time is characterized as never before by goal definitions shared by nearly all governments and served by innumerable governmental and non-governmental organizations. The Millennium Development Goals, followed by the Sustainable Development Goals, represent the most ambitious project ever for human society to work as one in pursuit of values held by all.

If success followed plan as night follows day then the future would be bright indeed. The reality is that the new value-driven global goal-seeking society has difficulty in attributing responsibility and holding both individuals and organizations to account. Philosopher Hans Jonas (1984) argued that new technology meant new ethical ideas of responsibility had to be developed to meet the challenges to our species' existence. By the end of the first decade of the new millennium there was hardly a leader of a nation state who did not call for responsibility. That was the essence of America's promise its new President Barack Obama declared (Albrow 2014: 189).

This political call to reattach responsibility to human action is paralleled by a theoretical re-examination of purpose led by philosophers. John Searle has argued at length for the rehabilitation of shared purpose with the concept of collective intentionality. As in the performance of a symphony, players contribute to the collective intention without knowing each other's part in it (Searle, 2010: 45). It is an argument that can be extended: 'the entire structure of existing society depends on collective intentionality' (ibid.: 166). We can go further and ask 'Why not global society'?

Another concept, 'distributed agency', approaches the same issues of action towards common goals from an angle closer to the experience of decentred organization and human/machine co-operation. It is more closely related to the study of socio-technical systems and ideas of hybrid entities (the 'car-driver', human and mechanical, still purposive).

This last conceptual development, however, brings to the fore the issues of responsibility and accountability in a global culture. When intention, goals, design pervade the lives of all on the planet, what contribution can any one agent, individual or collective, make to meet the global challenges, so many of which are the aggregate effect of human activities? Should the driver of the diesel car who bought it in good faith, when told that it would help to reduce carbon emissions, now need to scrap it when told it increases pollution? What price progress or advancing civilization in the global age?

2.3.10 Global citizenship

In the recognition of threats to the species and the resulting mobilization for global goals, the goal-directedness of all forms of human activity has become ever more prominent, even as the goals themselves have an increasingly indeterminate relation to human agents. The depersonalization of goals is a characteristic of the global age.

At the same time as the individual lives and breathes in a telic culture, institutionalized purpose drives states and multilateral agencies, expressed for their collective direction in such formulations as the Sustainable Development Goals. Global governance may be conceived more in terms of 'governance objects' (Corry. 2013), fields for which partnering agents, both state and non-state, set shared goals, rather than in terms of governmental institutions.

Commitments to global causes, often in the face of local and populist opposition, require an awareness of the nature and limits of citizenship in the modern state. The ancient universalist subordination of duties to the city state in the idea of world citizenship is translated into global citizenship in response to globalization. It transcends the earlier oppositional focus of the anti-globalization movement and operates to use globalization for global ends, sustainable food production, green energy, eliminating communicable disease, cleaning up the oceans and combatting injustice and poverty.

Implicit in the performative nature of global citizenship is the virtual global state. Existing only in the actions of the global citizen, it has no constituted form other than in the aggregate, repeated and connected instances of those actions. The order that is the outcome of those actions is the global social order, and global governance is the continuous attention to perpetuating that order.

Global citizenship breaks with the modern nation–state idea by having no acknowledged central authority or institutionalized leadership. The new global culture does not entail world government. But that meets with incomprehension. The historic and deep-rooted hostility to the autarchy of the world citizen has had its recent, much cited public expression in the words of the British Prime Minister Teresa May, 'The citizen of the world is a citizen of nowhere'. Implicitly, that remark is a rejection of the abstract universalism of the Western Enlightenment, but it fails to challenge the global activist whose commitments are strongly material, to ecologically sound ways of living, elimination of disease and the provision of clean water. The globalism of the global citizen both detaches materialism from Marxism and rejects the abstract individualism of neo-liberal ideology.

2.3.11 Conclusion: The digital challenge

The last decade has seen dramatic change geopolitically, with upheaval in the Middle East and the rise of China; economically, with the stagnation of the global economy after the 2008 financial crisis; in Western national politics, with the rise of populism; in technology, with the advance of computing power; and culturally, with the growth and influence of the social media; the two last factors being generally combined under the broad heading of the digital age.

These all have ambiguous, often contradictory relations with globalization when it is deemed to be an overall trend towards the greater integration of world society. Geopolitics has become multi- rather than uni- or bipolar; populism is directly hostile to globalization even though populism itself thrives on transnational alliances. The 2008 global financial crisis forced unprecedented multilateral cooperation in the shape of the G20 meetings. Computing technology and social media together have brought the globe into their frame of reference and vision, yet also advance artificial intelligence and the pluralization of views and outlooks that ignore the globe.

It is the agnosticism of advancing technology towards global issues that encourages the adoption of the language of the digital age to displace that of the global age. There is a new nightmare scenario for our species in addition to a nuclear holocaust and the destruction of our natural environment, both ever-present possibilities. Artificial intelligence raises up the new spectre of the re-engineered human being, even human beings supplanted altogether by machines.

The digital and the global now occupy the same narrative space, threatening human existence on this earth, but they tend to compete for attention rather than find common cause. But what the digital does to the narrative of the global is to force recognition that it could too be consigned to a past era.

Not every factor in human life contributes to the advance of globalization. It can spawn its own countervailing forces, such as the localization of transcultural elements or the fusion and hybridization of cultures. The proliferation of local centres of globally oriented communities, special interests and organizations may easily lead to a redirection of their focus towards each other, to competition and conflict with disregard for a shared human future.

Currently the greatest force that is neutral in respect of world society, pushing technology forward, is digitalization, the direct-line successor to the rationalization that Max Weber saw as the pervasive factor in advancing modernity. Digital technologies can be developed to serve human welfare, health and prosperity or to control free speech and weaponize cyberspace. They could serve a world society with effective answers for global issues and social order based in good governance. Or they could underpin global inequality and the authoritarian rule of a few oligarchs.

Either way, the digital age operates transversally to the global age, can deflect human projects away from global concerns towards technologies for their own sake and shift the balance of value commitments away from human well-being and fulfilment towards innovation and power. The risk is global catastrophe through attention deficit, the disaster the world allowed to happen in a memory lapse.

References

Albrow, Martin (1996), *The Global Age: State and Society beyond Modernity.* Cambridge: Polity.

Albrow, Martin (1997), Travelling beyond Local Cultures: Socioscapes in a Global City, in Eade (Ed.), *Living the Global City,* pp. 37–55.

Albrow, Martin (2012), Global Age, in Ritzer, *Encyclopaedia of* Globalization, pp. 823–826.

Albrow, Martin (2014), Responsibility in the Global Age, in *Global Age Essays on Social and Cultural Change.* Frankfurt am Main: Klostermann, pp. 189–202.

Albrow, Martin (2018), *China's Role in a Shared Human Future: Towards Theory for Global Leadership.* London: Global China Press.

Albrow, Martin and Elizabeth King (Eds.) (1990), *Globalization, Knowledge and Society.* London: Sage.

Anderson, Benedict (1983), *Imagined Communities: Reflections on the origin and spread of nationalism.* London: Verso.

Archer, Margaret (1988), *Culture and Agency.* Cambridge, UK: Cambridge University Press.

Barker, Eileen (1989), *New Religious Movements.* London: HMSO.

Beck, Ulrich (1992 [1986]), *Risk Society: Towards a New Modernity.* London: Sage.

Berners-Lee, Tim and Mark Fischetti (1999), *Weaving the Web: The original design and ultimate destiny of the World Wide Web by its inventor*. London: Orion Business.

Boyne, Roy (1990), Culture and the World System, in Featherstone (Ed.), *Global Culture*, pp. 57–62.

Brundtland, Gro Harlem (1987) (World Commission on Environment and Development), *Our Common Future.* Oxford: Oxford University Press.

Clarke, Arthur C. (1945), Extra-terrestrial relays: Can rocket stations give world-wide radio coverage?, *Wireless World*, LI No.10, pp. 305–308.

Corry, Olaf (2013), *Constructing a Global Polity: Theory, discourse and governance.* London: Palgrave.

Dawkins, Richard (1976), *The Selfish Gene.* Oxford: Oxford University Press.

Dubos, René (1965), *Man Adapting*. New Haven, CT: Yale University Press.

Eade, John (Ed.) (1997), *Living the Global City: Globalization as local process.* London and New York: Routledge.

Featherstone, Mike (Ed.) (1990), *Global Culture: Nationalism, globalization and modernity.* London: Sage.

Giddens, Anthony (1991), *Modernity and Self-Identity: Self and society in the late modern age.* Cambridge: Polity.

Gramsci, Antonio (1957), *The Modern Prince and Other Writings.* New York: International Publishers.

Habermas, Jürgen (1997), Modernity, an Unfinished Project, in Maurizio Passerin d'Entrèves and Seyla Benhabib (Eds.), *Habermas and the Unfinished Project of Modernity.* Cambridge, MA: Harvard University Press, pp. 38–55.

Huntington, Samuel P. (2004), *Who Are We? America's great debate.* New York: Simon and Schuster.

Jonas, Hans (1984), *The Imperative of Responsibility: In search of ethics for the technological age.* Chicago: Chicago University Press.

Latour, Bruno (1993), *We Have Never Been Modern.* Cambridge, MA: Harvard University Press.

McLuhan, Marshall (1962), *The Gutenberg Galaxy.* Toronto: Toronto University Press.

Ortiz, Fernando (1951), *Los bailes y el teatro de los negros en el folklore de Cuba.* Havana: Cardenas y cia.

Parsons, Talcott (1951), *The Social System.* London: Routledge & Kegan Paul.

Pleyers, Geoffrey (2010), *Alter-Globalization: Becoming actors in the Global Age.* Cambridge, UK: Polity.

Ritzer, George (2012), *Encyclopaedia of Globalization.* Vol II. Malden, MA and Chichester: Wiley-Blackwell.

Selchow, Sabine (2017), *Negotiations of the "New World": The omnipresence of "global" as a political phenomenon.* Bielefeld: Transcript.
Simmel, Georg (1971) (Ed. Donald Levine), *On Individuality and Social Forms.* Chicago: Chicago University Press.
Wallerstein, Immanuel (1990). Culture as the ideological battleground of the modern world system, and Culture is the world system, in Featherstone (Ed.), *Global Culture*, pp. 31–56 and pp. 63–66.
Xi Jinping (2018), *The Governance of China.* Vol. II. Beijing: Foreign Languages Press.
Zhang, Joy Y. and Michael Barr (2013), Green Politics in China: Environmental Governance and State-Society Relations: London: Pluto Press.

2.4 Theory and narrative in a globalizing world[28]

Globalization has been one of those terms that occasionally emerge as markers of a period, capturing the experience of a generation. In it, theory and narrative are interwoven, assaulted by events, absorbing the shocks and finding lessons from them.

Research prises theory and narrative apart. The critical enquiry and empirical findings inspired by public debate around controversial issues covered by such a portmanteau term as globalization could tend to render it obsolete, but its continued currency has been sustained not just by powerful interests in the changing geopolitical context but also by the mutually reinforcing nature of its elements. The growth of multilateral institutions, the global reach of mass media, the ubiquity of social media, global movements to save the environment and for human rights, the global financial market, worldwide supply and value chains, foreign direct investment, the growth of air transport, migration and the growth of a cosmopolitan class, all these factors reinforce one another in creating an ever more integrated global society.

Whether it will retain its commanding position in the future depends not on the theory associated with it but with emerging issues in global politics. Cybersecurity and the digital economy may already be diverting attention away from global issues. Great power rivalries can yet arrest the movement as they did in 1914. Irrespective of these uncertainties, globalization debates have served to advance our understanding of society and culture.

From its earliest reception in public discourse, globalization has been intimately bound up with visions of the future, attempts to take charge of events and efforts to generate support for world views, ideological campaigns and political party mobilization. We should expect, then, over a half a century of geopolitical turbulence that it has adapted to a wide variety of circumstances.

Recently I distinguished three overlapping stages in the development of globalization discourse, as story, as strategy and as ideology. We can date the story from its incorporation into international relations literature by George Modelski

[28] Unpublished. Written in January 2018 at the prompting of Ino Rossi to clarify ideas around the theme of a new paradigm for globalization research. My contribution to his project eventually resulted in the next section of this chapter.

in 1972 referring to the increasing interconnectedness of the world and the growth of a global consciousness. It was a story that reached a culmination around the end of the Cold War, paralleled by a clutch of academic accounts around 1990, Albrow and King, Robertson and Giddens. In the 1980s, globalization was assimilated into a different expert language, that of business administration. A celebrated article in the *Harvard Business Review* by Theodore Levitt was the prompt for American-owned multinational corporations to name their strategies 'global', and this has since been mimicked by all kinds of entities from campaigns and charities to countries 'going global'.

In the mid-1990s story and strategy merged in neo-liberal ideology and in the championing of globalization by the United States as the necessary direction for the world economy and as the underpinning of liberal democracy. Two shocks have dented that imperial vision, quite apart from the opposition of the anti-globalization movements: 9/11 and the aftermath of the second Iraq War highlight the limits of democracy. But above all, the financial crisis of 2008 has turned out to be the biggest shock to the global economy since the Wall Street crash of 1928.

Douglas Kellner drew compelling lessons from the first of these shocks in an account in *Frontiers of Globalization Research* that challenged any easy equivalence between globalization and the unity of the world. In his words, 'it showed the objective ambiguity and contradictions of globalization and need for a more dialectical and contextualising optic'. Kellner's inferences from the 'war on terror' were reinforced and became even more persuasive with the subsequent impact of the crash of 2008.

What I conclude from both those shocks follows on from his account. I shall emphasize the collapse of the unity of theory and history that underpinned the ideology of globalization. But my main purpose will be to survey the advances in the theory of society and culture that the controversy around globalization discourse has promoted.

The features that accrued to a term originating in relative academic obscurity to make it the signature of a dominant ideology were those common to all ideologies: a declaration that history has direction; a theoretical explanation of why that direction was inevitable; benefits for and advocacy by the holders and servants of political power; the claim on everyone's moral obligation to it; retribution to those who might venture into opposition.

And opposition there was, from the very beginning, in every respect. The democratic direction envisaged by Fukuyama was soon confronted by Huntington's clash of civilizations. Successive crises, the East Asian of the early 1990s, the dot com bubble at the turn of the millennium and above all the financial crisis of 2008 shook confidence in the equation of market freedom with national prosperity.

American power itself as the main bearer of the message suffered numerous setbacks. It was embroiled in conflicts in Afghanistan and Iraq and never secured wholehearted support either abroad or at home. The main beneficiary of globalization appeared to be China, with a political system at complete odds with Western representative democracy. A vocal internal opposition of civil society activists advocated a different kind of globalization based in a green economy.

The overall coherence of a vision of a globalized world following the American pattern, as promoted in Thomas Friedman's *Lexus and the Olive Tree* and *The World is Flat*, no longer fits the facts on the ground. The drivers of history appear no longer in a political project to unify the world but in a rush of digital innovation into an unknown diversification of culture.

Globalization is therefore already appearing as a stage in an historical sequence. We can see its antecedents in the rationalization of the 1920s and the modernization of the 1960s. It has had its heyday in the period 1989 to 2008 and increasingly is being ousted by digitalization.

* * *

This is a history of four phases of public discourse in a century, rational, modern, global and digital, each adjective a cultural gloss on an ever-advancing synthesis of economic interests with the technologies of calculation. Each is an overlay on what has gone before, absorbing the past rather than erasing it, dethroning the older and assuming its place as the master narrative. In each of the four phases, opposition focuses on the contradictions that arise out of any belief that the future is based in theory. Theory can never contain the future, even though that is often seen as the implicit premise of the –ization suffix, the suggestion of a lawlike process, progressing relentlessly.

The challenges to master narratives invariably disentangle the theory from the story and take it forward to accommodate the new realities that the unfolding present always discloses. The stories that are sustained by political power lose their persuasiveness as opposition to it mounts and new theory advances as the politics fails to meet ideological expectations.

Beyond rationalization, emerging realities found counterpart concepts of charisma and informal social relations. Modernization discovered limits to its scope in cultural diversity. Globalization has provoked the politics of identity, from gender to nation and anything between and beyond. In the response to digitalization, it will be the very nature of the human being that becomes the contested territory for theory and practice. These are dialectical processes with open outcomes. In retrospect, we can document the interplay of power conflicts and theory. We can also point to the resulting advances in theory, and this, I would contend, applies to the social sciences especially.

Globalization and opposition to it, to both real processes and the master narrative, have been accompanied by, but also helped to inspire a deeper, more sophisticated understanding of the nature of human society and its relation to culture. My own version of that understanding follows.

2.4.1 Disembedded community

In the classic distinction of *Gemeinschaft* and *Gesellschaft*, the association of intimate, face-to-face relations with rootedness in a local territorial space was very much the default position for thinking about community in early twentieth-century sociology.

Diaspora and the maintenance of ties across long distances and through long absences has increased recognition of community as a continuing set of close relations without a fixed or necessary land location or boundary. Yet that detachment from the soil and the intermittent nature of contact between its members gives the community a place more in the imagination than in daily interaction.

2.4.2 Negotiable identity

Building on Simmel's emphasis on overlapping group membership as constitutive of personal social identity, developing Parsons's distinction between ascribed and achieved status, under globalizing conditions there has been increasing emphasis on the fluid nature of identity. Both individuals and groups are engaged in constant redefinitions of self-identity in negotiation with others. This extends through gender, race, ethnicity, nationality (as a personal attribute), nationhood (as a collective quality) and partnership, both sexual and economic.

The imagery of flows has become a conventional way of describing society rather than structure or system. Identity maintenance in an environment of flows and contested values makes integrity, both of individuals and collective entities, a focal point for aspirations and accusations.

2.4.3 Pluriform social relations

In classic early twentieth-century sociology, social relations were dichotomized between the primary, face-to-face with emotional involvement, and the secondary, impersonal and at a distance. It was a classification roughly corresponding to the distinction between community and wider ('the big') society.

The omnipresence of strangers, dispersion of families, emotional attachment to causes and iconic figures, chains of economic dependency, instant communication over any distance, social media and the local presence of global enterprises all contribute to a complex matrix of relational types rather than a polarized dichotomy between primary and secondary.

The coalescence and dissolution of social entities, or of entities of a hybrid kind, (natural, cultural and social, as Latour has highlighted) becomes a major narrative theme of our time. Individuals now inhabit their immediate personal spatial environment as a socioscape with no primary organizing image like community, class or even household. Their social networks are extended in space and time lodged in sociospheres with their own characteristics and rules

2.4.4 The autonomy of culture

Increasingly, there is recognition that social relations operate through cultural media that have their own generative rules. The primordial case is a language, learnable by anyone, providing for personal expression but only within the limits of its syntax. Attempts by human groups or organizations to monopolize culture, even what they claim as their own invention, or indeed to control symbolic expression in general, have never succeeded in the longer run. Globalization's controversial impact on national cultures makes very clear that culture is essentially owned by no one and potentially open to all.

2.4.5 Global culture

Conversely, the generative nature of culture is only activated by human beings, singly or in groups, and in their creative activity they craft, design and invent new things and forms of expression. National cultures only develop through the efforts of powerful political agents with the support of workers, artists, writers, administrators and soldiers. All kinds of human association can develop culture specific to them, created and claimed by their members but always diffusible beyond their control.

Global culture has arisen out of diverse sources coming together: the universalism of science and technology; satellite communication; the commercial media, information and entertainment industries aiming for world audiences; the commitments of multilateral institutions and their staff; the global consciousness of civil society organizations; the lifestyles of the employees of global corporations; the networking of global elites; the growth of social media. These forces always crossed national boundaries and in the digital age inhabit a cyberspace that governments struggle to control. Global culture is both transnational and transcultural. In promoting dialogue between cultures it generates new culture and the receptiveness of national and local cultures to the reformulation of values that each has regarded as its own is one of the key dynamics in globalization.

2.4.6 Globalism versus populism

The boundary-crossing forces of global culture have always had their antecedents in earlier periods. Formerly they were identified as cosmopolitanism, contrasting with local attachments. Where cosmopolitanism has an added ingredient of global consciousness, of attending to global issues and the fate of the planet, then it qualifies as globalism.

Globalism is the apotheosis of cosmopolitanism. It also attracts, and carries forward with added odium, the hostility to cosmopolitanism from local and national populations who feel threatened by the changes that can be portrayed as benefitting the globalists at their expense.

The two most prominent dynamic elements of globalism are the agents and forces operating in the global market on the one hand and the agencies and activists committed to global causes on the other. Both should be distinguished from the world domination impetus of the older nationalist/imperialist configuration and from the emergent digital revolution that has no terrestrial limits.

2.4.7 Global citizenship

Commitments to global causes, often in the face of local and populist opposition, require an awareness of the nature and limits of citizenship in the modern state. The ancient universalist relativizing of duties to the city state in the idea of world citizenship is translated into global citizenship in response to globalization. It transcends the earlier oppositional focus of the anti-globalization movement and operates to use globalization for global ends, sustainable food production, green energy, eliminating communicable disease, cleaning up the oceans and combatting injustice and poverty.

Implicit in the performative nature of global citizenship is the counterfactual global state. Existing only in the actions of the global citizen, it has no constituted form other than in the aggregate, repeated and connected instances of those actions. The order that is the outcome of those actions is the global social order, and global governance is the continuous attention to perpetuating that order.

Global citizenship breaks with the modern nation–state idea by having no acknowledged central authority or institutionalized leadership. The historic and deep-rooted hostility to the autarchy of the world citizen has had its most recent and public expression in the words of the British Prime Minister, 'The citizen of the world is a citizen of nowhere'.

Implicitly, that comment is a rejection of the abstract universalism of the Western Enlightenment but it fails to challenge the global activist whose commitments are strongly material, to ecologically sound ways of life, elimination of disease and provision of water. The globalism of the global citizen is a retrieval of materialism from political ideology.

2.4.8 The interrogation of agency

The original sociological problem setting of the relation of individual and society under nation–state conditions became a question of agency and structure, how individuals were shaped by, limited by and resisted a structure supported by the state. In Marxist terms, the structure of bourgeois society, class society under capitalism, was the state. But under globalized conditions, agency and culture are the defining co-ordinates for individuals and collective entities of unlimited variety, while power belongs to a global class controlling the means of cultural production.

The question of who is responsible for what extends from the ingredients of a meal to the retreat of the polar ice caps, from school discipline to the content of the child's mobile phone, from dress codes to Jihad. Structure, a settled and durable set of enabling and constraining positions in a network of social relations, appears far less to define the nature of agency than beliefs, values and chosen associates.

In relationships among individual human beings, collective intentionality is widely invoked and distributed agency accepted as normal.

Whereas the old modernist assumptions of what Archer (1988) called the conflation of structure and culture and what Garfinkel (1967) called its accompanying cultural dopes have now become obsolete; the widely accepted fungible nature of culture renders individual agency always open to interrogation, and agency itself can be imputed to cultural products that make human beings redundant. The advance of artificial intelligence is the culmination of an anxiety about the future of human beings that modernity harboured from the beginning in its search for laws of nature.

* * *

The rubric of cultural and social globalization tends to encompass all the eight features of our contemporary world that are listed above, disembedded communities, negotiable identities right through to the ambiguities of agency. Taken together as a field of research, they define the paradigm for the study of culture and society under globalizing conditions. Yet in each case what we see highlighted are features of human social relations and culture that can be studied retroactively, in previous periods and cultures.

Which raises again questions that have dogged globalization accounts from the earliest attempts to define its scope, as for instance: Is globalization a new phenomenon or is it a name for processes that have long been features of human society? This is to state the question in its extreme form by suggesting polar alternatives.

Debate is more finely tuned when globalization is viewed as a historical trend, with roots in time immemorial reaching a recent crescendo. That position is challenged by pointing to periods of history where features seen as central were more prominent than was the case later. Hence there could be no case for saying the trend was either inevitable or indeed could not be arrested. This point has been supported especially by evidence of world market integration before the First World War with the subsequent retreat into economic nationalism afterwards.

If attention is focused on economic processes, then the case for ebbs and flows, advances and retreats of globalization becomes stronger, but, looked at overall, as a comprehensive development across all sectors of human activity, then the case for recognizing an overall and intensifying process of growing interdependence and complexity of human interactions across the face of the earth becomes overwhelming.

Dense connectivity of one place with others anywhere else exists alongside the possible mobilization of a billion adherents to a single cause worldwide. The recognition of the shared fate of its human inhabitants and other species that have the globe as their home has as counterpart places of global unique significance, the Great Wall of China, Silicon Valley, the Taj Mahal, Vatican City, Hollywood, Hiroshima.

Achieving global recognition, 'going global' has become an aspiration not just for corporations and countries but also for political movements, cities, civil society associations and fame and fortune seekers of all kinds. Taken together, these factors reinforce one another and are the culmination of a historical development going back far in time. And going forward …?

This is where the huge momentum of the overall trend gives rise not just to misgivings and outright opposition but also to misapprehensions. 'Going global' as a strategy has no guarantees of success. Globalization as a historical trend has all kinds of contradictory possibilities and no necessary direction for any particular aspect.

The power and connectivity of computing roughly double every two years but in both its organization and social impact it varies between extremes of high centralization and extended distribution. The old mainframe computer was replaced by the personal computer, then the cloud gathered data from those computers, only for applications now to be putting immense computing power at the users' fingertips.

If the advance of technology has no necessary consequence for the direction of social organization, the same is even more true for globalization. Developments in the last few years clarify the difference between globalization as an overarching historical trend towards the unification of world society and globalization as a process extending the scope and range of any particular invention, product, fashion, idea or ideology across the globe.

Nothing makes this clearer than the advance of free market or neo-liberal ideology to dominate economic thinking in the 1990s, to be regarded by many as synonymous with globalization as such and the subsequent backlash in the anti-globalization movement and demands for control of markets, environmental protection and the defence of human rights. This later became what Pleyers has documented as the alter-global movement because its scope was equally global to that of neo-liberalism and yet its thrust was exactly opposite. In others words, globalization as such has no inherent direction when it comes to a particular feature of social and cultural life.

This is even true of what has often been regarded as the touchstone of the advance of globalization, a diminution of the power of the nation–state. Again, it was the advance of neo-liberal ideas and the power of the international financial institutions, which made this a prominent theme in the 1990s. But this was very much a cover for American triumphalism in that period with its talk of a new world order.

In fact, the position of nation–states has changed over the last thirty years so that they are now the main agents for a globalized world order, rivalled of course in their efforts to control events by the global corporations and especially the giants of the internet. Certainly populist reactions against the global system may project states back into a search for the lost sovereignty of a previous era, as is the case of the United Kingdom with its impending departure from the European Union, but detachment from the new multilateral institutions means a loss of power and influence even as sovereignty is recovered.

Globalization has transformed the world, not as a programme or an ideology but as the aggregate result of a set of interacting forces. Those have been factors set out above underlying the rise of global culture more than anything else: the universalism of science and technology; satellite communication, the commercial media, information and entertainment industries aiming for world audiences; the commitments of multilateral institutions and their staff; the global consciousness of civil society organizations; the lifestyles of the employees of global corporations; the networking of global elites; the growth of social media.

We can add to those cultural forces obviously with ones that are more economic, the integration of financial markets, the growth of global production and value chains, led by global corporations and the growth of consumer demand, the standardization of tastes.

Political moments are less obviously unambiguously globalizing. The imperial ambitions of great powers can just as easily delegitimize global institutions as support them. More potent are global and environmental pressures on internal national politics that lead countries to agree on the Paris Climate Change Accords. Similar pressures operate in the context of the G20 meetings, where agreement on global issues is the lowest common denominator of their shared interests.

2.5 Responsibility as a fundamental category in the global age, or recognizing the new collectivism[29]

It is more than a matter of courtesy to express my gratitude to the Käte Hamburger Kolleg in Bonn and its Director, Professor Werner Gephart, for inviting me to give the opening lecture in this conference on globality. As a Fellow of the Bonn Kolleg, I have been impressed by the appropriateness of the theme of globality for the general mission of the Kollegs. For, as never before, Germany is beginning to assume the responsible role in world politics that fulfils the aspirations Max Weber expressed at the beginning of the last century and which were to be so cruelly destroyed in the carnage of two world wars.

Weber formulated his *Verantwortungsethik*, which we translate in English as the ethic of responsibility, with political leaders specifically in mind. It is a theme which Chancellor Merkel has readily embraced within the Christian tradition. 'I commit myself explicitly to the co-responsibility of politics for a community consciousness based on norms, ideas and attitudes. Ethical striving is a question of

[29] Opening Keynote Lecture for the Conference 'Globality in the Space of Reflection of the Käte Hamburger Kolleg', Bonn April 25, 2013. Published here for the first time.

survival for the modern state. It is not for nothing that the preamble of our basic law begins 'In the consciousness of its responsibility before God and humanity.[30]

She is not alone in invoking responsibility. Few political leaders will not appeal to it at one time or another, whether in times like the financial crisis or in leading a fight against crime. It is a repeated refrain in Barack Obama's speeches. Only nine days ago, immediately after the Boston Marathon massacre, he announced that 'any responsible individual, any responsible group will feel the full weight of justice.'[31] In this case, as opposed to the positive sense of responsibility he normally prefers to invoke, he is pointing the finger of blame. Responsibility is for good and evil.[32]

In the words of the liberal thinker Friedrich Hayek, who more than any other wanted to draw a line under the collectivism of the interwar era, 'responsibility, not to a superior, but to one's own conscience [is] ... the very essence of any morals that deserve the name.'[33] Unlike other human qualities, such as intelligence, consciousness or happiness, responsibility involves choice and therefore is a proper subject for ethical consideration. But then, what is the responsibility of the group to which Obama refers? As a trained lawyer he is fully aware that the complexity of imputing responsibility to persons or groups is a central issue in legal considerations. These aspects of responsibility, the ethical and the social, and the way they are bonded in the legal, are together the first of two interwoven themes that make up the substance of my remarks today.

The other theme is globality and the way it requires us to rethink the conclusions that Hayek drew about collectivism and to consider again its place in human affairs. To an extent, irrespective of the topical allusions I have just made, a concern for responsibility might appear to be exclusively universalistic and abstract, more appropriate for a philosopher than for the humble sociologist that I am. But Hayek's concerns were indeed for proper social arrangements in which responsibility could be lodged and he expressed his belief that it was in social organization of a small scale where that could best happen.

Like him, I want to scale responsibility, in this case bring it to earth or at least to the globe, which we should never forget is the rough shape of the earth, and

---

[30] Rede von Bundeskanzlerin Dr. Angela Merkel 'Deutschland dienen – ethische Grundsätze politischen Handelns' anlässlich des 60-jährigen Bestehens des Rheinischen Merkur am 13. Juni 2006 in Königswinter. Meine Damen und Herren, ich bekenne mich ausdrücklich zur Mitverantwortung der Politik für ein Gemeinschaftsbewusstsein aus Normen, Ideen und Einstellungen. Die ethische Anstrengung ist eine Überlebensfrage des modernen Staates. Die Präambel unseres Grundgesetzes beginnt nicht ohne Grund mit dem Satz: *'Im Bewusstsein seiner Verantwortung vor Gott und den Menschen'.*

[31] CNN newscast, April 16, 2013.

[32] *Die Welt Kompakt* provided an example of the dual nature of responsibility in a single article reporting on those responsible ('Die Verantwortlichen') for the Boston massacre and those responsible for the forthcoming London marathon. ('Der vergebliche Kampf um absolute Sicherheit', April 17, 2013, p. 5).

[33] *The Road to Serfdom* (1944), London: Routledge, p. 157.

which I suppose is a scaling up rather than scaling down. So let me begin with remarks about globality, an equally abstract concept, to be sure, but one that should never allow us to escape from the material conditions of life on this planet. Hayek wrote in 1944. Those conditions have been transformed since then and it must be appropriate to revisit the fundamental issues he raised. We have not followed the road to serfdom that he warned us not to take, but we are in another place of some confusion.

For those who have finally got used to the word 'globalization', 'globality' might seem a neologism too far, in which case even this conference's theme might seem dangerously fashionable. They might, however, recall that in the 1950s and 1960s the word 'global' took some time to become commonplace. Carl Schmitt observed how the circumnavigation of the globe first brought the division of its surface into the imagination of merchants, rulers and lawyers but it was only in 1950 that he expressed that as 'global linear thinking'.[34]

It was in the immediate post-Second World War period that 'global' became a common term rendering a meaning distinct from universal, international or oecumenical. As opposed to those ideas, it had a spatial reference, one that enabled Marshall McLuhan to coin the 'global village' metaphor as our lived paradox of community beyond local connection and René Dubos to point to the global and local defining each other in the slogan 'think globally, act locally'.

The elaboration of cognate terms in subsequent discourse with globalization, globalism and globality was easily achieved in European languages and made it possible to speak with only a little hesitation of global culture, global society or global politics. Indeed, the sociologist Roland Robertson who wrote the first book-length treatment of globalization also explored in it global culture, globality and the less widely recognized glocalization.

When I went on a little later to publish *The Global Age*, it was in full recognition of this wider shift of discourse. The book didn't invent the term, there were occasional previous uses, and however often it has been used since this is not because of my invention but because it expresses the time in which we live. We collectively reference our time as the global age, a frame that numerous authors and publishers have found useful in book titles. And since then, recognition of the global has extended to global governance, global civil society, global elites and so on.

Why not the age of globalization, as some would prefer to call our time? Well, there is a case to make for that, but I deliberately rejected it on the following grounds, namely that globalization became too intimately linked with modernization and with a sense of a necessary direction of history. It became the persuasive catchword of neo-liberal ideology. It did not reflect the shock to human existence brought about by the nemesis of the modern project in the atomic bombs of 1945.

[34] *Der Nomos der Erde im Völkerrecht des Ius Publicum Europaeum* (1950). Köln (Cologne): Greven, p. 54.

This is what sparked off the recognition of human life on this planet as a contingent and not a necessary development, a matter for collective human choice.

The threat of a nuclear holocaust convinced Arnold Toynbee and others that the atomic age ushered in postmodernity, and subsequent writers on that contested term that expresses so much of our contemporary confusion have failed to find any coherent direction in globalization. They are in this respect right. An orientation to the globe means we can go round in circles and also bump into each other coming from opposite directions. We can globalize markets, but we can also globalize regulation. Neo-liberals have persuaded those of the left as well as of the right that globalization means unfettered markets but that is an ideological success of hegemonic intellectuals, rather than an analytical necessity.

At its triumphant peak, the thinkers of the modern age saw it as a story of human progress in the scientific control of nature and society. In the global age, we live in the shadow of the threats to human existence that very progress produced. We have been forced to recognize globality, a condition where the viability of the planet as a living space for the human species becomes a matter of collective concern and where the totality of human environmental interrelations affects us all down to the details of our everyday lives. This is what our conference reflects in its opening statement: 'Globality seems to permeate all cultures and social spheres today'. And in the lectures that follow we find displayed the vast scope that the examination of globality can assume, from the media, to democracy through human rights, religion, theatre, up to and including global ethics.

All of this without reference to the national, and since Hayek associated collectivism with nationalism it could appear that his ideas have triumphed, in a way that he did not imagine. For, along with a widely acknowledged advance of individualism of which he would have approved, we have, as it were, at the opposite end of the social spectrum, a globality beyond national boundaries, which, when viewed through its lens we detect global problems extending far beyond our personal capacity to solve.

How can an individual person address resource depletion, overpopulation, environmental degradation, species loss, climate change, nuclear security, energy security, global poverty and epidemics, terrorism, international migration, crimes against humanity, human rights and the crises of global capitalism? Do we not have to call upon what appropriately are termed agencies, collective ones, even the most powerful ever yet developed, the state? Have we not to address the place of collective agency in the global age as much as its individualism?

Indeed, when we consider responsibility in the frame of globality it may be that our leaders invoke it so often precisely because the number and scale of the issues which face them are so great that what is within their power, even when the will to do something is there, is heartbreakingly inadequate. These calls to responsibility sound almost the equivalent to the calls to courage and patriotism that led millions to sacrifice lives in vain as they ran forward from their trenches towards their deaths at each other's hands in the First World War.

To call for responsibility in Hayek's sense of following conscience is paradoxical in this context. It can provoke pacifism as much as patriotism. The calls for responsibility then may represent an appeal to commitment, to follow the leader, as much as to follow conscience. But is not this the collectivism that Hayek abhorred? The conclusion we have to draw is surely that, with the idea of responsibility, we cannot avoid addressing both the individual and the collective.

Picking up the thread of responsibility may provide one route out of that place of confusion to which the globality of our time has brought us, but it will force recognition of the bonds of society. Which is why the Bishop of London in his funeral address for Hayek's greatest admirer, Margaret Thatcher, was at pains to say that her famous statement, 'There is no such thing as society', had been taken out of context and misunderstood. She only wanted to dismiss the notion of 'an impersonal entity to which we are tempted to surrender our independence'.[35]

And yet, of course, it is the fulfilment of duties for the state, Hayek's responsibility to a superior without reference to personal feelings or opinion, that is often hailed as responsibility. We are bound then to examine responsibility as not just personal conscience but a social bond and it is in the shaping of the relation between the two aspects where we may expect to find the new influence of globality on our lives.

It is a deep irony of contemporary global and not just British society that the funeral of the iconic figure of neo-liberal ideology, Margaret Thatcher, should have taken place in St. Paul's cathedral in London, where in the space in front of it, a year before, the Occupy movement, the street protest against that ideology and the greed of its beneficiaries, attracted worldwide attention. Before the authorities dispersed the Occupy tents, the protest had split the cathedral hierarchy and prompted deep heart-searching and discomfort in the wider religious community. Did the ceremonial farewell mark her victory? Possibly, but the wider movement against unrestrained global capitalism, of which the Occupy movement is just the latest manifestation, lives on. Indeed, and yet on the other hand in some ways, it also vindicates a Thatcherite theme, responsibility itself in following conscience.

The anti-globalization movement or, as its more recent supporters have named it, the alter-globalization movement represents the assumption of responsibility for realizing global goals at a personal level. It is the answer of millions of its supporters to the question of what role individuals can play in responding to that array of global issues which, when they were listed above, appeared so imposing no person could possibly address even one of them. It is the successor to waves of social movements in the second half of the twentieth century, the peace, green, feminist movements which have mobilized worldwide and in each

[35] Richard Chartres, Bishop of London, 'The end is where we start from', Lady Thatcher's funeral, Supplement *The Guardian*, April 18, 2013, p. 8.

case operated through like-minded individuals joining in common causes across national boundaries.

In the case of the alter-globalization movement, we are fortunate to have an outstanding empirical study of its adherents by a sociologist who has shown the equal amount of dedication to his research as his respondents to their cause, over eight years, attending 250 activist meetings, present at seven World Social Forums, as well as the anti-G8 and anti-WTO gatherings between 2001 and 2009. Geoffrey Pleyers's book *Alter-Globalization: Becoming actors in the Global Age* has as its main theme the interplay of self-definition and reasoned engagement with global issues in opposition to the dominant players on the global stage. But in that process there is a continual formation and reformation of collectivity and exploration of organizational form. Protest camps may appear to the passing journalist as an ongoing party to the sounds of the samba, but intensive organizing over the internet and into the nights, internationally, will have taken place to set them up. In Pleyers's words, 'The individual lived experience intersects with collective history' and, as opposed to revolutionaries in previous eras, 'these activists consider social transformation to be an ongoing collective process'.[36] As Hayek would have wanted, in general they are suspicious of large organization, preferring to replicate small groups, rather than produce large organizations with representative structures. They are the bottom-up response to the dominant collectivities of our time, nation–states and global corporations.

These activists may in the main disdain the official channels and discourse of the multilateral and national institutions through which policies on global issues are engineered. Yet the language of state and citizenship is also employed by others who are committed to goals beyond the nation–state. In citizenship there has always been recognition of responsibility beyond any specific duties in employment by the state. It is held to be a moral requirement of those belonging to a political community to participate responsibly in its institutions in return for enjoying the protection and entitlements they provide. Extended to the global, for many the corollary of human rights is a duty to act as a global citizen.[37] That in turn may involve lobbying national government to act in the global interest, to ensure that they think globally and not just nationally. The prime example in our time is of course the popular pressure to commit to the reduction of carbon emissions in the atmosphere, a global issue which until the global financial crisis dominated all others.

Yet the agencies of the contemporary nation–state do not simply have to be prodded by popular pressure to adopt policies on global issues. They are locked

---

[36] Pleyers, Geoffrey (2010), *Alter-Globalization: Becoming actors in the Global Age*. Cambridge, UK: Polity, pp. 86, 91.

[37] See Darren O'Byrne (2003), *The Dimensions of Global Citizenship: Political identity beyond the nation state*, London: Frank Cass. He finds both the poor farmer on the periphery of the West and himself equally responsible in their actions to the world as a whole (p. 225).

into an immense and intricate web of obligations to which they are committed, either as members of the United Nations or adhering to agreements with multilateral institutions. In the names of their citizens, they sign up to the Millennium Development Goals, to establish an International Criminal Court or to affirm that they have a responsibility to protect human beings. Responsibility extends to the apex of the international system.

Responsibility for good deeds or bad, responsibility to people or in office, responsibility for people or to conscience, shared responsibility, collective responsibility are all variations around a theme where the nuances are as varied in everyday life as they are in public affairs. In some ways the English language is not well suited to making these distinctions – just the one word for all of them. At least the German language can distinguish *Verantwortung* in the task or deed from the *Verantwortlichkeit* of attitude or ethos.

Now, these illustrations of the sheer breadth of applicability of the idea of responsibility, its unlimited relevance to any context of human behaviour, warrant us in considering it a fundamental category in the analysis of human society altogether, not just in the global age. One of the followers of the classic Durkheimian school of sociology, Paul Fauconnet, came to that conclusion over 80 years ago. His monograph on responsibility remains a vital source for deeper reflection and it begins in the true Durkheimian fashion recognizable to every beginning student of sociology by declaring that responsibility is a social fact. This is not an intuitive statement; it depends on a theoretical analysis of what is involved in declaring someone is responsible for something. A rule, which is inherently open to general application, is employed to single out a person who shall be punished. 'A theory of responsibility presupposes a theory of sanctions.'[38] The rule is applied as a judgment to determine that X is responsible and should be subjected to an appropriate punishment. In the penal law of contemporary societies, only adult, healthy people are suitable subjects for punishment, children, the insane, corpses, animals and inanimate objects are excluded, but that hasn't been the case in all societies at all times and Fauconnet examines at some length the penal codes of other times and cultures.

His was a focus which in a later period was the subject of an excellent set of papers edited by the South African anthropologist Max Gluckman, which confirmed Fauconnet's original judgment that no society has existed without attributing responsibility. The title of that volume was the somewhat awkward *The Allocation of Responsibility*. It could have been 'attribution' or 'imputation'. But English doesn't do it well. Neither, as Fauconnet pointed out, does French, and in an informative footnote he comments that only German adequately renders his concerns exactly with the term *Zurechnungsfähigkeit* and he offers the definition of the concept in von Lizst's *Lehrbuch*: 'In purely formal terms

[38] Paul Fauconnet (1928), *La Responsabilité: Étude de sociologie*, Paris: Alcan, p. 26.

Zurechnungsfähigkeit can be defined as the capacity of action to be punished at law, that is actions which have the capacity to incur relevant legal sanctions that follow on from their punishable illegality.' If that seems verbose, then I refer my German-speaking audience to the original!

Now, there is a slight oddity about Fauconnet's approval of *Zurechnungsfähigkeit*, namely that it does not fit what he calls is the rule for all responsibility, namely 'X is responsible' where X is a person. For, according to Lizst's definition, it is the action and not the person which is *Zurechnungsfähig*. Does this matter? Well, according to a substantial comparative study of legal causation by two eminent British jurists, it does. The starting point for H. L. A. Hart and A. M. Honoré is that commonsense principles everywhere make it easy in practice to identify the causes of events and the part people play in those causes. The caution us against accepting what textbook writers say about the difficulties of establishing causation on the grounds that 'we do after all succeed in communicating with each other over a great area of discourse where we use this notion' but they also concede that finding the principles behind everyday judgments is fraught with difficulty.[39]

From this point of view, legal responsibility, the attribution of blame for an act which requires punishment, is a restricted notion of responsibility which in its fullest extent includes all voluntary acts of the free individual.[40] Between this definition of what it is to be a human agent, which they trace back to Aristotle, and the legal judgment that someone deserves to be punished is a whole realm of voluntary acts that attract varying amounts of praise and blame depending on the moral codes of the wider society, the broad area of which these days we are becoming accustomed to calling normativity.

It follows from this account that, since law is encapsulated within the wider discourse of a society in identifying causes and attributing agency to individuals, then principles of legal responsibility will also vary from one culture to another. And this is the case they say with *Zurechnung*, which they call 'a curious strand in German philosophical thought' going back to Kant's sharp distinction between *Zurechnung* and causation and the identification of causes with physical processes. The agent's acts can then be regarded as facts and treated as subject to laws.

Hart and Honoré's objection to the reasoning that they find enshrined in German legal thought is that often it is relevant to consider voluntary conduct as causal, quite apart from questions of blame, as for instance in the case of poisoning where the causal account is different if is self-administered knowingly or unwittingly swallowed. They comment too on the huge European continental output of legal treatises on causation compared with an almost complete absence in the common law countries, and they clearly regard the search for principles in this area inferior to a tradition close to commonsense reasoning. Which reminds me of

[39] H. L. A. Hart and Tony Honoré (1959), *Causation in the Law*, Oxford: Oxford University Press, p. 24.

[40] Ibid., p. 39.

the joke among lawyers told me by my very old friend, distinguished lawyer himself, Dr Hugh Canham, about the English judge musing before his judgment that 'common law is common sense' – hearing which, one lawyer in the courtroom says to another, 'Get ready for an absurd verdict.'

We can of course jump too readily to culturalist conclusions about law. The contrast between the rationalistic, principled basis of Continental law and the case-based common law has often been made, but when it came to German criminal law the authors point out that it was reinforced by adopting John Stuart Mill's theory of causation in the late nineteenth century. By contrast, in civil law the predominant theory of causation was one of probability and adequate causation advanced by von Kries, which was later to be influential on Max Weber's theory of action. However, in both cases, theory-led argument prevailed in legal decision making and Hart and Honoré conclude on this dry note, that nonetheless 'it is impossible entirely to suppress the promptings of common sense'.

Is a theory about the deed as fact being prior to the motive more or less rationalistic than one which insists on the unity of deed and motive? One is reminded of Goethe's Faust declaring that in the beginning is not the Word, not Thought, not even Power, but the Deed, or again elsewhere Goethe's 'All theory is grey, dear friend, green is life's golden tree'.[41] But even though Hegel may declare that the Owl of Minerva takes to flight when first the dusk is falling, nonetheless a theory that puts life and deeds first and itself last is still a theory. You will not shift the English self-image of commonsense realism so long as its counterpart is the image of the other, the Continental theorist.

What we can conclude, however, from considering the idea of responsibility across cultures is that it is not only legal rules that vary. This leads us no further than reciting long lists of cultural differences in punishments, the age of responsibility, the definition of mental incapacity and so on. The comparison of common law and Continental law brings into consideration the methods of reasoning about responsibility, the concept of the human agent and relations between individuals and society. From this point of view we can contemplate the possibility that a theory which dehumanizes society, as Niklas Luhmann's famously does, is more plausible when it can start from considering the act not as motivated but as a material fact.

The idea of responsibility is then lodged in a set of universal existential and ontological concepts known through the human experience: self and other, knowledge, action, causation, chance, the surrounding environment, the individual, identity and the group, which will vary in the way they are construed from one culture to another. Responsibility both in its broadest sense of results than can be attributed to human action and in the narrower sense of acts which provoke

[41] Grau, teurer Freund, ist alle Theorie und grün des Lebens goldner Baum.

retribution or reward from others and in the still narrower sense of performing a prescribed duty belongs to that set of fundamentals.

When the configuration of that set shifts over time we easily talk of the end of one age and the beginning of another. This is epochal shift. We recognize it readily in the transformation of fundamental concepts of the world that took place during the Western renaissance and then the Enlightenment. There is very little dispute that the shift from seeing knowledge as arising in the contemplation of divine truth to regarding it as the result of experiment and instrument of human progress was such a shift that helped define the modern age.

The shift to the global age is equally profound. Like the advent of modernity, globality has not arrived in human experience all at once. But over the last seventy years it has transformed the parameters of human experience. Knowledge no longer delivers control of nature, it prepares for the incidence of eventualities it cannot predict. Individuals may define themselves and others in relation to the fate of the human species. The collectivity to which we all belong contains the seeds of its own destruction. The public sphere is sustained through global media of communication. There are endless possibilities of collective self-organization.

These are features of our time. Notice, please, they do not mention the end of the nation–state, the loss of community, the rise of anomie or any of the usual laments about dislocated modernity. For good reason too, because the nation–state is transforming into an agency for global governance, because community has become a translocal affair and because anomie may or may not be more prevalent than in Durkheim's time. The transformation is more fundamental: it concerns the relations of individuals to collectivities, of norms to people and interaction on a global scale.

Let me illustrate the scope and scale of the new collective responsibility with three very high-profile examples.

The first is clause 231 of the 1919 Treaty of Versailles.[42] This is perhaps the most famous historical instance of the imputation of collective responsibility to a nation. Two American legal counsel drafted it, one of whom arguably provides the most influential example of the power of Hayek's individual conscience in the twentieth century, the deeply religious John Foster Dulles. For if his part in drafting that clause was not enough, he was also the intellectual driving force behind the foundation of the United Nations and the Universal Declaration of Human Rights and as American Secretary of State the resolute designer of the Cold War with the Soviet Union. The world has wrestled ever since with the consequences of clause 231, but, despite the widespread condemnation of nationalism, it is of

[42] Clause 231 of the Treaty of Versailles: The Allied and Associated Governments affirm and Germany accepts the responsibility of Germany and her allies for causing all the loss and damage to which the Allied and Associated Governments and their nationals have been subjected as a consequence of the war imposed upon them by the aggression of Germany and her allies.

course an endorsement of the principle of collective responsibility which operates between nation–states to this day, and in that sense legitimizes nationalism.

The second is various affirmations since 2005 in the United Nations of the Responsibility to Protect.[43] Arguably this normative commitment of the international community to intervene in the affairs of member states is the most important extension of the United Nations collective agency since its foundation. It underpinned recent British and French intervention in Libya, French and German in Mali and the African states in the Central Africa Republic. It has not yet been invoked in Syria, because the great powers cannot agree.

The third is quite likely to incense some of those who fervently support the second, namely Corporate Social Responsibility; often regarded as the figleaf that conceals the rape of the poor people of the world, it is the rubric widely used by the global corporations to express their concern for wider responsibilities than their legal duties to their shareholders. It is then a normative commitment and a direct response to the agitation of civil society organizations and campaign groups pointing to exploitation of workers in poor countries, or to environmental damage. The pressure they exert works. Even if CSR is hypocrisy, as those groups so often go on allege, that is the homage vice pays to virtue, to borrow from Rochefoucauld. Global corporations do monitor their supply chains to identify reputational risks and take steps to reduce them.

Collective responsibility is then a widely acknowledged feature of our world today. How does it work if we accept the Weberian principle of reducing all collective agency to the actions of individuals? In brief, it is enforced by global public opinion, if one likes, by the Durkheimian conscience collective, and works through the individual conscience. The problem is it operates unevenly and imperfectly and it is hampered by an intellectual reluctance either to acknowledge the power of the new collective responsibility or to examine how it operates in the individual conscience. We might almost say that the backwardness of our academic assimilation of global responsibility and normativity is the result of the ongoing failure to bridge the cultural divide between French collectivism and German individualism. In principle, given theoretical acceptance, it can easily be explored empirically in surveys of the relative weight of commitments that individuals declare to family, community, nation and the globe, as in the kind of work pioneered by Alex Inkeles's on modernization and Ronald Inglehart's World Values surveys.

Theoretically conceivable, empirically surveyable, but is the balance of collective and individual responsibility practically possible? Here I want to affront all of the West's cherished self-images with my fourth high-profile example of

[43] A state has a responsibility to protect its population from mass atrocities; the international community has a responsibility to assist the state to fulfil its primary responsibility; if the state fails to protect its citizens from mass atrocities and peaceful measures have failed, the international community has the responsibility to intervene through coercive measures such as economic sanctions. Military intervention is considered the last resort.

collective responsibility, namely by citing the Chinese rural responsibility system. The backstory of Chinese economic resurgence since 1979 is becoming increasingly known in the West, but still too often regarded through ideological spectacles and without taking the substance of the reforms seriously. The rural responsibility system established the households and individuals as basic units for Chinese production, in a chain of responsibilities for national production targets, up to and including the state. Elaborate systems of contract specify respective contributions and rewards. It is a management of individual/collective relations of vast scope inspired in large part by the fieldwork of China's most famous sociologist, Fei Xiaotong.

The Chinese economic miracle began in the countryside. It provided the basis for the subsequent development of industrial capitalism on lines closer to Western models but we should recognize that corporate organization varies greatly between countries in terms of defined mutual responsibilities of different stakeholders, owners, shareholders, directors, managers, workers and the wider community.[44] At one extreme we have co-operative organizations owned by workers, at another the limited liability company where shareholders have no responsibilities and directors only are responsible for making profits. The narrowness of these definitions in Anglo–American capitalism produces the abuses of corporate power which lead to debacles like the Enron or Lehman Brothers collapses. The German model of *Mitbestimmung* lodges *Mitverantwortung* more effectively in a social market economy.

But these are national models of shared responsibility. There is also a political difficulty in the management of global issues of course, namely that there is no global government to accept the collective responsibility on behalf of the global community. For some, this is a completely disabling fact that means appeals to global action are entirely specious, indeed a way of avoiding responsibility, since labelling an issue as global simply means passing it up to a level where there is no collective authority.[45]

But that argument is negated by the existence of multilateral institutions, global governance and global cooperation between nations, as the Duisburg-Essen Käte Hamburger Kolleg will surely testify. Shared responsibility is no less responsibility and Chancellor Merkel's affirmation of *Mitvertantwortung* illustrates how that is effectively rendered in the German tongue.

---

[44] 'We must adhere to the principle of democratic management. As in the selection of the form of the responsibility system, any improvement or revision of the responsibility system should follow the mass line. The masses should be aroused to hold discussions and their wishes should be respected. The leadership should assist the masses in evaluating their experiences and seeking ways to improve the responsibility system.' In Wang, Guichen and Zhou Qiren et al. (1985), *Smashing the Communal Pot: Formulation and development of China's responsibility system*, Beijing: New World Press, p. 74.

[45] As Emery Roe argues in *Narrative Policy Analysis* (1994), Durham: Duke University Press, chapter 6, Global warming as analytic tip, pp. 108–125.

In relation to the Bonn Käte Hamburger Kolleg's responsibility, *Mitverantwortung* alludes to norms underpinning a national commitment on which a constitution is based. It affirms the embeddedness of law in the normative order widely accepted as the basis of contemporary German politics. It is expressed in terms specific to German culture. But we have to address the new global culture too. Globality is the invitation to recognize its existence. In centring individual and collective action on responsibility to the globe and humankind, in reinforcing the discourse of human rights, it re-establishes norms as the premise for any possible legal system. It makes the normative the new dynamic contribution to a re-examination of law in relation to society which Werner Gephart demanded in his comprehensive study of the relations of law to social theory.[46]

Globality also asks of us what contribution we can make to solving the challenges facing the globe. We can all individually and in the multitude of collective entities to which we belong, including the nation–state, assume global responsibility. What might be the specific contribution of Germany?

Without daring to venture an answer to that vast question for German citizens, let me conclude by drawing on the life experience of another British Germanophile, Lord Noel Annan, whose memoirs *My Age* encourage me in the recognition that biography and the sense of passing epochs are closely interwoven. An academic before the Second World War, in it he served in Churchill's cabinet office in the underground bunker, and afterwards he became a member of the British Control Division in Germany. Later he was Provost of Kings College Cambridge. He accorded to eighteenth- and nineteenth-century German thought the title of 'the German Renaissance', 'as remarkable as the outburst of creativity we call the Renaissance in Italy'[47] For him, it was the recognition both of national culture and impersonal forces that was its great gift to the world, and that meant being eloquent champions of nationalism, which the English practised but saw only in terms of individuals.

Like the English before the world wars, the world has been practising collectivism without recognizing it. Indeed, recognition has been repressed, Hayek's strictures on the back of the terrible experience of those wars has made collectivism a dirty word. The time has come for those inhibitions to be thrown over and I can think of no other intellectual tradition on which it is more suited to build a profound understanding of globality and the relations between individual and collective responsibility in the contemporary world than the German one, which includes Kant, Hegel, Marx, Weber, Luhmann and Habermas.

---

[46] *Gesellschaftstheorie und Recht: Das Recht im soziologischen Diskurs der Moderne* (1993), Frankfurt am Main: Surhrkamp.

[47] Noel Gilroy Annan (1990), *Our Age: Portrait of a generation*, London: Weidenfeld and Nicolson, pp. 247–251.

DOI https://doi.org/10.24103/UCW5.en.2021.3

Chapter 3
Global governance and China[1]

The example China provides in its own governance system has lessons for the rest of the world, not in the sense that other countries should try copy cultural features that are unique to China, but because it is underpinned by theoretical ideas of a high order, that, however, also allow for pragmatic responses to pressing needs. This balance of theory and practice in national contexts is equally relevant for considering governance for the globe as a whole.

3.1 National solidarity under conditions of globalization: the theoretical basis of Xi Jinping's Governance of China[2]

Our World Congress session proposes we examine 'Populism and the New Political Order?' – with a question-mark. I propose to remove the question-mark. Let us go a step further and replace 'New' with 'Current'. Now further still, and talk of the 'global political condition' instead of the world political order.

Those small changes allow me to cut out the usual preliminary discussion. I'm then picking up on globalization in the title of my presentation because I think the common interpretation of populism as a response to globalization is broadly correct. But then there have to be many qualifications to that sweeping assessment. Here are two:

Qualification number one: Globalization is not the first way or time when outside forces have penetrated what we call countries or societies and scared sections of their inhabitants.

Qualification number two: Populism has arisen in the past under many different conditions, including urban revolts, under colonial oppression or in economic collapse. We just have to add globalization to that list. In all these circumstances, the leaders of a populist movement exploit their followers' sense of threat to a preordained and cherished social order. Is the threat real? Well, we have a famous sociological tenet that tells us that at least their perception is real in its consequences.

We can add to that perception a real feature of the situation where populism thrives: the concerns of the one side will be denied as real by the other. One side

---

[1] Editor's note: Sections 3.1 and 3.2 are journal articles, and 3.3 is a special lecture at Wuhan University. The remaining pieces are invited articles or remarks by Chinese officials or journalists

[2] Originally prepared for the 19th ISA World Congress of Sociology, Toronto, Canada, Research Committee 16 Sociological Theory, Panel 305, 'Populism and the New Political Order?', July 17, 2018. The Chinese version is translated by Xu Jia and Ma Lei. 2019, Northeast Asia Forum, 28(03), 3–9+127 [Chinese version: 作者马丁・阿尔布劳，译者许佳、马蕾：全球化条件下的国家团结——习近平治国理政的理论基础，《东北亚论坛》，2019年第3期，第3–9页，见：https://d.wanfangdata.com.cn/periodical/dbylt201903001].

will be accusing the other of losing a sense of reality, of promoting fake news, for instance. And the other returns the compliment. There arises then a special condition, a disorder, one where cognitive, evaluative and expressive orientations to social relations are so disconnected and at variance with one another that the very existence of the social entity comes into question.

* * *

At this point I am not sure whether I will have lost the attention of a younger generation of sociologists, or even indeed their sympathy. I rely on you to tell me, for it will not have escaped you that my introduction harks back to discussions that dominated sociology in the mid-twentieth century (when I was around) and indeed in its founding period over a hundred years ago (before my time!), namely what holds a society together.

The feverish intellectual excitement of the 1960s and 1970s largely dismissed the centrality of that theme for our discipline. We may recall the objections to it: they pointed to conflict as a permanent feature of society; saw societies as always enmeshed in wider systems; in the end saw only one world system. Still later, arriving at the postmodern turn, societies didn't even exist.

I don't suppose for one minute anyone here adopts those positions in the crude way my summary expresses them. But as a respectful nod to the postmoderns I will speak of social entities rather than societies. Families, communities, organizations, clubs, armies, sects – they are all social entities. We can discuss their formation and dissolution and what requirements they have to meet to continue in existence. What are called variously nation–states or countries are also social entities. We have been reminded recently that they are imagined. Longer ago Arnold Toynbee called them myths. But all human social entities are imagined in much the same sense.

There are cycles in our discipline when what holds these imagined entities together becomes the focal point of its ongoing debates. It was so for Emile Durkheim, for Talcott Parsons and I would suggest it is once again central. In each case it was politics that made it so.

In Durkheim's time, it was the politics of solidarity in France that framed his work. For Parsons, the background condition was the fate of his national collectivity, the United States, in the contest between Western capitalism and Soviet communism. In our time, it is the struggle over control of the human future.

In each case, the theoretical focus turns to the motivational factors that link individuals with the wider social entity, precisely because it is these that are brought into question under conditions of social transformation. Technological innovation in the broadest sense has driven all these transformations, whether in industrial production (assembly lines), weaponry (nuclear) or communication (digital computing).

The Durkheimians and Parsonsians were integrationists, looking to find the formulae that would guarantee the survival of the encompassing collectivity, from the nation to the civilization. The continuation of that perspective is to be found in Samuel Huntington's work. But to my mind, only Amitai Etzioni has projected it forward in sufficient depth to explore the foundations of a possible global community.

* * *

The politics of populism today confronts sociologists with a theoretical problem as large as, and equivalent to the problems that Durkheim and Parsons faced. How does the nation–state fit within a global community when globalization appears to undermine its solidarity and its future stability?

The kind of answer early professional sociology provided can be illustrated by what Parsons held to be 'the central empirical insight from which Durkheim's theoretical development starts', namely the 'vast complex of action in the pursuit of individual interests takes place within the framework of a body of rules, independent of the immediate individual motives of the contracting parties.'[3] Parsons traced the development of Durkheim's thought through his early formulations of organic solidarity arising out of the division of labour to the fully-fledged theory of normative rules, where social life rests upon 'a system of ultimate common value attitudes'.[4]

Solidarity, interests, rules, motives, norms, values, these are the components of a general theory of what holds a society together. I will not labour their intellectual history here, since after all they still, I believe, form, or should form, part of Sociology 101.

Instead, I want to provide a contemporary example of social theory concealed in political advocacy. I quote:

> We should … intensify education in public morality, professional ethics, family virtues and individual integrity, promote basic moral standards such as patriotism, dedication to work, integrity and friendliness, and cultivate social trends of recognizing honor and disgrace, practicing integrity, encouraging dedication and promoting harmony.[5]

It is a statement not so very far, I suggest, from a position that Durkheim would have recognized and commended. But I have tried to delay recognition of the source by omitting a key phrase coming immediately after 'We should …'. But I will reveal it now, to avoid being accused of covert propaganda. (I can leave it to you to judge whether I'm an open propagandist).

---

[3] Talcott Parsons (1949), *The Structure of Social Action*, Glencoe, IL: The Free Press, p. 314.

[4] Ibid., p. 464.

[5] Xi Jinping (2014), 'Strong ethical support for the realization of the Chinese Dream'. In: *The Governance of China*, Beijing: Foreign Languages Press, pp. 176–177.

The phrase is 'pay close attention to advocating socialist morals'. The source is a Xi Jinping speech in 2013 at a ceremony for national ethical model awards. There is a problem in the Western world about taking any such statement prefaced by a commitment to socialism as anything but ideological window-dressing. That is even more the case if it comes from the leader of a country with a Communist Party regime. So I must ask for patience while waiting for my full argument.

Socialism in China comes with Chinese characteristics. It attaches to Chinese culture. I quote again, this time from a speech in 2014 to a seminar for provincial officials:

> We should ... accelerate the building of a value system that fully reflects the characteristics of China, the Chinese nation and the times. To safeguard our value system and core values we must let culture play its due role. A nation's culture is a unique feature that distinguishes that nation from others.[6]

What are the core values? In a speech to the staff and students of Peking University, Xi says this is a 'theoretical and practical question'. His theoretical answer is, They are socialist and twelve in number, as follows: 'prosperity, democracy, civility, harmony, freedom, equality, justice, the rule of law, patriotism, dedication, integrity and friendship'. These are divided up into sets of four: the first four are for the country, the second for the society, the third for citizens.[7]

These remarks are not merely incidental to a speech that contains an extensive consideration of values in relation to past, present and future and in relation to China's place in the world. Those three types of value, related to the different facets of the social entity, in turn relate to three aspects of social reality. They 'represent the nature of socialism, draw on the best of world civilization, and reflect the spirit of the times'.[8]

After this implicit ontological taxonomy for any national society, Xi then turns to address China's role in the world, to restore worldwide respect while retaining a hold on traditional values handed down from the classics. He illustrates this with a selection of aphorisms including: 'When the Great Way prevailed, a public spirit ruled all under Heaven' (*The Book of Rites*); 'the people are a foundation of the state' (*The Book of History*); 'harmony without uniformity' (*The Analects of Confucius*).[9]

From the most general principles, Xi turns to specifics of Chinese culture via referencing the way the uniqueness of any culture arises out of different natural conditions and course of development. You have to know who you are: 'There are no two leaves exactly alike on earth.'[10]

* * *

---

6 Xi, 'Improve the governance capability through the socialist system with Chinese characteristics', ibid., pp. 116–119.

7 Xi, 'Young people should practise the core socialist values', ibid., p. 188.

8 Ibid.

9 Ibid., p. 190.

10 Ibid., p. 191.

I hope I have at least made out a plausible case for considering Xi's treatment of values on a level with Durkheim's and Parsons's. In which case, we are bound to ask if his account of the centrality of values is likely to succumb to the same criticisms and arguably failure as did the accounts of our illustrious professional predecessors.

As a sociologist aspiring to create a science, Durkheim left the question of the social bases of values – which people held which ones – to be established by research. He had concluded early on that their origin had to be in society (an intoxicating term for him according to my first teacher, Morris Ginsberg). The question, 'Of which society?' remained open for empirical investigation.

In his early lectures in Bordeaux, Durkheim argued for democracy, 'as the political form by which society arrives at the purest consciousness of itself. A people is more democratic in so far as deliberation, reflection and the critical spirit play a more considerable role in the conduct of public affairs.'[11]

But this moral superiority of democracy was exposed to the anarchic forces of capitalism and sectional interests. The collective consciousness of pre-industrial societies that held them together was, in his view, reduced to abstract norms of equality and individualism. He had no faith in the solidarist movement for social reform, but rather called for social integration based in a renewal of moral values through education.

From our own vantage point of hindsight and in the current state of Western confusion over values, we may regard with foreboding the lameness and inadequacy of Durkheim's attempt to reposition French society around values. This was especially so given that his own educational principles emphasized a secular internationalism that was consistent with scientific sociology. Where could France be in this 'nowhere world'?

Parsons's revision of Durkheim's value theory was no more successful in finding plausible national agents for central values, though to his credit he recognized it was necessary to identify their social base. They had to be grounded, he said, in existential beliefs about the world, in motivational needs as a personality and in relations with others in society – a tripartite division that bears some resemblance to Xi's later one.[12]

But Parsons introduced a factor that took him further than Durkheim along the road to grounding values, namely power. Values determine what is worth doing. But power, in his famous definition, is 'the generalized capacity to mobilize resources in the interest of attainment of a system goal',[13] and goals are selected to accord with values.

---

[11] Quoted by Steven Lukes in *Emile Durkheim, a Historical and Critical Study, His Life and Work*, Harmondsworth: Penguin, 1975, p. 273.

[12] Talcott Parsons (1960), *Structure and Process in Modern Societies*, Glencoe, IL: Free Press, p. 174.

[13] Ibid., p. 41.

One might expect that the introduction of power into the analysis of social stability would provide the guarantee for the maintenance of the common value system. But there is a paradox here, namely that the institutionalization of the separation of powers in the American constitution reflects, in Parsons's terms, 'our suspicion of commitment to overly specific national system-goals'.[14] Emphasis on occupational achievement meant there was no top elite or ruling class.[15]

So while Parsons pointed to common values as necessary for the stability of the system, for him the society of the United States fell short of that requirement. He contrasted his position with that of the immensely popular thesis of C. Wright Mills in *The Power Elite* (1956) that control of American society had passed into the hands of an organizational elite. The strains produced by industrial development were compounded by new demands in the international situation. He likened McCarthyism of the 1950s, the hounding of alleged Communists, to the populism of the 1930s that attacked Wall Street and helped to destroy the League of Nations.

As one rereads Parsons's essay from 1955, 'Social strains in America', the parallels he draws between the 50s and 30s have striking echoes in the situation today.[16] He writes how it '*cuts clean across the traditional lines of distinction between "conservatives" and "progressives"*' (his italics),[17] how Republicans advocating high tariffs and withdrawing from international responsibilities are utopian about the consequences, how 'Communism symbolizes "the intruder"'.[18] He even points to what he calls the fantasy, 'clean up the Chinese situation quickly and then our troubles would be over'.[19]

* * *

One must stress that Parsons's social system was *counterfactual*. It was an analytical template for a perfectly stable society that did not exist. It brought power into the equation with values as a necessary condition but in the case of the United States power was too diffused to be effective in securing that stability. In which case, it is instructive to see how Xi's speeches address precisely that issue in China.

A problem for a Westerner reading Xi,s speeches is that the concepts that figure in the theories of liberal democracy are buried in a completely different context, namely the Chinese political system. They are there, but not being the main focus they fail to be indexed. Check out 'governance' and it is indexed once as 'governance capability' but I have counted over 30 references that are not indexed. 'Integrity' is listed with eight entries for political integrity, but I found over

[14] Talcott Parsons, 1954, *Essays in Sociological Theory*, Glencoe, IL: Free Press, p. 418.
[15] Ibid., p. 431.
[16] Talcott Parsons (1960), op. cit., pp. 227–247.
[17] Ibid., p. 244.
[18] Ibid., p. 243.
[19] Ibid., p. 246.

30 more mentions. Similarly, 'responsibility' has over 40 mentions, 'rights' more than 10, spirit at least 20 and values no fewer than 30.

Xi's main focus is indicated by the really big index entries: the Chinese people (over 60 mentions), the Communist Party of China and its Central Committee, (over 150), leadership of the Party or by leading officials (over 50), socialism with Chinese characteristics (over 50), opening up (over 50) and reform well over 100. 'Reform and opening up' is a separate additional entry with about 50 page references. The entries that mention the Party and entries for reform and opening up provide by far the most numerous page references and are a good reflection of their thematic weight in Xi's speeches and their intended audience at the time they were delivered.

The Party and its relations with the people are at the core of the institutions that bring values and power together in China. In a review article from 1957, Parsons criticized Mills on power because he overemphasized power over people as opposed to the power to get things done, the most important distinction in all discussions of power in society.[20] The fear of power over people is at the heart of the division of powers that institutionalizes the domestic weakness of American central government.

In China's case the political system is designed to channel power through to its apex. 'Power over people' and 'power to get things done' are brought together in a tripartite relationship between people, Party and government. In that system, explicit attention has to be paid to the potential for power to be abused by its holders.

Xi's campaign against corruption in his first term of office received much attention in the West, mainly because it gratified those who are keen to observe defects in the Chinese system. What received little attention was how it was embedded in a wider account of the way power and values need to be coordinated in a united society.

In a speech on January 22, 2013, 'Power must be caged by the system', before he was elected to be President of the People's Republic, at the Second Plenary Session of the 18th Communist Party Congress, Xi spoke of the Chinese Dream and declared, 'We must enhance checks and supervision over the exercise of power, make sure that power is 'caged' by the system. This was a plea directed not just to the Party: 'We must extensively solicit public opinions [sic] and suggestions, steadily accept public assessment and supervision by the whole of society.' 'We must let the whole Party and the people oversee power.'[21]

This is contained in a speech that also emphasizes trust, integrity, leadership, reform, discipline, theory, principles, goals, rules and responsibility. None of that list would be out of place in a Western treatise on public policy, but it is impossible

[20] Talcott Parsons (1960), 'The distribution of power in American society', in: *Structure and Process in Modern Societies*, Glencoe, IL: The Free Press, pp. 220–225.

[21] Xi, ibid., p. 429.

to imagine any current political leader who could deliver a speech to a party conference on those lines. But the Western reception of the Chinese leader's speech is completely dominated by its theme of corruption.

Corruption is about abuse of power, both by Party and government officials. 'All officials must use state power to serve the people' is Xi's command.[22] Collectively, the Party and the people can work to realize the Chinese Dream, and that extends to Chinese people at home or abroad. Speaking to a conference of Friendship of Overseas Chinese Associations, Xi spoke of the way overseas Chinese could draw on their common cultural heritage and, united with those at home, 'marshal great power for realizing this dream'.[23]

While China today emphasizes its unique culture, it is also working to bring concepts entirely familiar to the West into a completely different institutional frame, with a unitary conception of power that contrasts with Western pluralism. It also combines with a distinctive concept of consultative democracy in contrast with the Western representative type.

* * *

The solidarity of the Chinese kind is not without explicit use of Western theory. That is obvious in the prominent place that Marxism retains in political education and more generally. But equally there is a readiness to learn from more recent Western thought and experience where it can be put to good use.

Deng Xiaoping's early announcements of the opening-up policy in 1978 had been in preparation for two years, after sending a state delegation to learn about post-war reconstruction in Europe. In 1979 he arranged for an expert on the social market economy of Germany, Armin Gotowski, to explain the theory behind that country's solution to China's party leaders, government officials and social scientists. This was truth from facts, put into practice.

The same spirit has been present in the China's response to globalization. With a firm understanding of accounts of the expansion of the world market by Marx and Engels, the Chinese were never likely to let the self-interested nature of American accounts of economic globalization go unrecognized and they explicitly encouraged their own companies to go global.

In a speech entitled 'A Deeper Understanding of the New Development Concepts', delivered to the 5th Plenary Session of the 18th CPC Central Committee (18.1.16), Xi has called this policy 'multidimensional opening-up', making China, in his words, 'the biggest driver of global trade liberalization'.[24] The results,

---

[22] Ibid.

[23] Ibid., p. 70.

[24] Xi Jinping, Speech to the 5th Plenary Session of the 18th CPC Central Committee 18.1.16, 2017, *Governance of China II*, p.233 [《习近平谈治国理政》，第二卷，北京：外文出版社，2018年].

he said, were positive changes in power structures and a change of political landscape.[25]

This changed context and increasing Chinese role in the world economy and global governance combined with emphasis on the people leads on naturally to a 'people-centred development philosophy, fulfilling their expectations for a better life.[26] But this has its antecedents in Chinese history. Xi tells how 'moderate prosperity' and 'great harmony' are also described, in the Book of Rites.[27] This is where explicit engagement with issues of wealth distribution, fair shares, gathering the wisdom of the people, practising democracy and inclusive development are China's answer to the fragmentation associated with globalization in the West and the resulting populism.[28]

Populism is best controlled with policies that promote inclusion and the sense of a common cause, in other words solidarity. The irony of China's rise is that Western theory has been put to good use through political institutions far removed from Western liberal democracies. The result is a solidarity and a collective agency more powerful than any other the world has ever produced. Our shared human future now depends in large part on how the West and China together can develop global institutions that accommodate their differences.

3.2 China's contribution to the future of governance[29]

The term governance once had a relatively safe but obscure place in the scholarly thought of the West. It became more contested in the late twentieth century with the idea of global governance. But it is China that has made the greatest contribution recently by bringing it out of the shadows of academic discussion and into the limelight of public discourse.

We owe it in the first place to the two volumes of Xi Jinping's *The Governance of China* for demonstrating the richness and vast scope of an idea that encompasses justice, law, principles, rights, responsibility and much more. It includes the whole range of concepts that underpin a healthy society, one that enables people to pursue their values and share their aspirations in peace and security.

The last decade has been one where China has breathed new life into an old concept with original ideas and practical innovations. Governance has become a dynamic concept with China's unique approach, based in culture, ideology and practice. This applies both to global and national governance and I will consider each in turn.

---

[25] Ibid., p. 234.

[26] Ibid., p. 235.

[27] Ibid., p. 236.

[28] Ibid., p. 238.

[29] 马丁·阿尔布劳：中国对未来治理的贡献，《世界汉学通讯》，2020年第一期，见：http://get.blcu.edu.cn/info/1090/1289.htm [Martin Albrow, China's contribution to the future of governance, *World Sinology Information* (01), 2020/04/28].

The definitive account of global governance was contained in the report of the Commission on Global Governance, *Our Global Neighbourhood* (1995). Distinguished public servants with great international experience from 26 different countries joined to make recommendations covering the security of people and the planet, managing economic interdependence, reforming the United Nations to give civil society a greater say and extending the rule of law on the global stage.

China's voice on the Commission was heard in the person of Qian Jiadong, former ambassador to the United Nations in Geneva, who had worked as Zhou Enlai's secretary for foreign affairs from 1964 to 1976, but who had earlier been part of the delegation to the Geneva conference on Korea and Indochina in 1954. He represented China's growing engagement in international affairs, which included the time when it was rightfully reinstated in the United Nations in 1971.

The People's Republic of China has followed a path of steadily increasing its participation in international institutions. Deng Xiaoping famously promoted Mao Zedong's theory of the Three Worlds at the General Assembly of the United Nations in 1974, and, with reform and opening up, China fully supported the United Nations in its peacekeeping activities to the extent that it now has more peacekeepers on the ground than any other country.

Multilateralism has been a core principle in China's engagement with global governance and it has always sought to have a voice that matches its contribution. This applies as much to its membership of the International Monetary Fund as it does to its leadership of the Shanghai Cooperation Organization that grew from an initial a group of five nations in 1996 to eight in 2017 when India and Pakistan joined.

Sometimes the Belt and Road Initiative that began with President Xi's speech in Kazakhstan on September 13, 2013 and now has the cooperation of more than 70 countries, is bracketed with those multilateral institutions. In my view, that is a mistake that leads to a failure to appreciate the fundamental difference between an inclusive development strategy and a rule-based service organization.

Multilateral institutions are membership-based and provide frameworks both for specific kinds of collective action and also rules and regulations that govern the behaviour of the members in pursuing their own interests. Such a definition covers bodies as diverse as the IMF, ASEAN, OPEC and the EU. They may or may not have development as part of their aims, but they all depend on officials who are dedicated to the institution rather than to their own country.

In this sense, the United Nations is of course the greatest multilateral institution of them all, with a workforce exceeding 40,000, recognized career paths and lifetime service possibilities. It is not a world government but, in the eyes of many, especially in the United States, has the features of a central government that traditionally in that country has attracted hostility. Often the favourable conditions of employment of the officials of the public institutions compared with private sector employees who have less security bring denunciations of bureaucracy.

Multilateral institutions in the eyes of Western populist politicians attract even greater criticism than those of their own countries, but the rhetoric is very much the same. Officials are accused of being detached from their homelands and nations are urged to regain their sovereignty. Critics can focus on abuses where some staff members may indeed promote the organization more for their own benefit than for the wider community it is meant to serve, what is sometimes called 'institutional capture'.

The populist reaction against multilateralism is compounded by globalization. Indeed, the multilateral institutions are intimately connected with the rule-based global economic order that permits corporations to trade freely across national boundaries. National reactions against economic globalization then reinforce the hostility to the institutions that underpin it.

But what I want to emphasize here is the profound difference between the Belt and Road Initiative and previous development programmes. It is neither globalization nor a new multilateral institution. Of course many nations participate, but they do so on a bilateral basis, or sometimes in multiple bilateral relations. Each participant reaches an independent understanding with the authorized Chinese agency to borrow or to lease or to invest for a specific joint purpose, say to develop a port or to build a railway. These will form part of a coherent strategy to develop connectivity between countries with China as the leading partner.

Professor Wang Yiwei, whose book *The Belt and Road Initiative: What Will China Offer the World?* was the first authoritative account in English, put it very well when he wrote that BRI 'is not an entity or institution, rather it is a concept and initiative for cooperation and development'. In conjunction with that idea, I would like to stress the goal-centred nature of BRI.

The cooperation BRI requires is to accomplish specific projects, to achieve definite goals that contribute to the public good, in communications, trade, financial integration and prosperity. These all have measurable outcomes that bridge cultural divides.

The spirit of BRI is in its goal-centred nature. It matches the needs of contemporary times, allowing partners to put differences to one side in joining for agreed mutual benefit. It overrides utopian visions of a world where all have to understand one another in order to work together. It represents instead an outlook I prefer to call pragmatic universalism, where all preserve their distinctive cherished values while contributing to the common good.

Global governance from the perspective of pragmatic universalism ceases to be a framework of institutions but more a network of multiple projects dedicated to securing the future of human beings on this earth. Or, in Xi's famous formula, a 'community of shared future'.

I have argued that China is developing an approach to global governance that diverges from the orthodox Western views and opens up new possibilities for international cooperation. The West has so far mainly responded in ways that discount ideological preconceptions. Indeed, arguably Western countries that are as diverse politically as Greece, Italy and Poland, who have already signed memoranda of understanding with China, are inspired by the same pragmatic outlook that drives BRI.

In respect of national governance, however, the response to China is far more ideologically driven. This is understandable because, in Western eyes, the social and political order of China is determined by the position of the Communist Party and that leaves no option but to oppose its ideas for national governance.

The fact that China adopts not only ancient Western ideas such as governance, democracy and justice but also the modern language of values, responsibility and integrity is a huge challenge to all those in the West who have, ever since the Russian Revolution of 1917, regarded Communism as a conspiracy to destroy their basic freedoms.

China has long made Communism in its own image, and socialism with Chinese characteristics has roots in Chinese culture that long predate Karl Marx. Indeed Marx's insistence on production based in social relations has profound affinities with the ancient Chinese emphasis on social relations as the foundation of a prosperous society. In this respect, Marx was more Eastern than Western, which is only one of the many reasons why he was rejected in his homeland.

As I have pointed out in my book *China's Role in a Shared Human Future: Towards Theory for Global Governance*, it is the sophistication of the theoretical ideas, drawing on the Chinese classics as well as on Marxism and Western political economy, that underpin the governance of China as Xi has expounded it. They challenge the West to respond in a similarly sophisticated way. Instead, it resorts to slogans, about autocracy, dictatorship and authoritarianism, only some of the milder insults that are the daily language of the Western media.

Social governance in the new Chinese sense takes us beyond the old vocabulary of liberal democracy and into a transformation of the relations between people and government. In some respects, the crisis that is current as I write, the spread of the COVID-19 virus from its original source in Wuhan through China and out into the wider world, illustrates much of what is special in Chinese governance.

I have elsewhere added to the regular description of China as a civilization as well as a country by calling it a corporation too. That is something of an exaggeration to make a point. But it certainly is a corporate entity, on a scale that the world has never seen before.

The people are bonded into a programme of change and reconstruction that requires each and every one of them to contribute to the Centenary Goals and a vast number of subsidiary targets. The Party requires an ideological discipline of its members as well as commitment from the people to the 12 socialist values. Every community, enterprise, governmental organ and social body must have its accompanying Party group.

The result has been the remarkable growth in the power and prosperity of the Chinese people. Corporate bodies with a hierarchic structure can pass instructions downwards with speed and reliability. What they find difficult is to facilitate feedback from the lower levels to the top.

This is not peculiar to China. In the West, governments and corporations time and again try to silence whistleblowers, who aim to draw the attention of the leadership to misdeeds by employees lower down or sometimes bring to public attention criminal behaviour by the leaders. Equally, those at the top find it difficult to learn from the good ideas those at the bottom might have. This is an endemic structural problem for all large organizations.

By contrast, the upside of China's governance was demonstrated very soon after the outbreak of the virus was recognized. The world gasped in amazement as a hospital in Wuhan was built in less than 10 days. The measures that have been taken to contain the virus have demonstrated the extraordinary discipline and courage of Chinese people when called upon to support a national cause.

The dramatic achievements of China, both in this example and also ever since reform and opening up, are in part a product of its governance system, but in this case very much attributable to its specifically Chinese features rather than ones it shares with all large organized bodies. China's social governance has features that remove it from any facile comparisons with Western ideas of representative democracy. Indeed, as I argued recently in a newspaper article in *Reference News* (*Cankao Xiaoxi*, January 3, 2020, p. 11) it really deserves to be recognized as a new type of rule for the global age in which we live.

The big challenge for any nation at this time is to maintain control over and guide the technologies that drive our economies and social relations. At the height of the triumphalism of modernity in the early part of the last century, the term 'technocracy' arose to describe the way technical experts and impersonal systems were dominating government.

At this time in the West, populism is very much a reaction against the class that benefits from that expertise. China's leadership of the people through the Party provides oversight and checks over the machine at all levels in the great hierarchic system that constitutes any modern nation–state. It aspires to human control over the system that has led me to suggest that we need to describe it with a new term, 'humanocracy', rule by human beings.

In the coming period, where technology creates robots, vehicles carry us without human drivers and artificial intelligence designs vaccines, it is precisely the place of human beings in the system that surrounds them that becomes an existential problem, matching the very survival of our species on this planet.[30]

[30] Editor's note: This is the author's original note when the article was published: 'The author is currently a Fellow of the Academy of Social Sciences in the UK. In the past he has been President of the British Sociological Association, Editor of its journal, *Sociology*, and founding editor of *International Sociology*, the journal of the International Sociological Association.'

3.3 What the world can gain from China's global leadership[31]

Dean SHE Shuanghao, Vice Director Professor Wei Jin, colleagues of the School of Marxism of Wuhan University, may I first of all express my very great appreciation for your invitation to give a university lecture in the Sakura Top. It is a particular honour for a scholar from the West, especially from the United Kingdom, as I hope to make clear later.

My theme today is the desperate need for global leadership when our very existence on this planet is so severely challenged. When, as a Western scholar, European and British, I consider China as the nation best equipped to fulfil that role today, it is in part because it engages creatively with the legacy of Karl Marx.

In this speech I shall point to four main ways in which I consider China is shaping the direction the world should take in the coming years. First, President Xi's own formulation of the shared future for humankind. Second, one that has its roots in China's ancient culture, namely the emphasis on harmony. Third, the human unity with nature that your environmental policies today take forward, and finally, not least, your emphasis on the human spirit.

Marx is, of course, also admired by many in the West too, especially by those who are critical of the direction capitalism is taking. In any case we need to recognize that Marx belongs to both East and West. After all he was brought up in a German–Jewish family, and Jews are as much from the East as the West.

He took a standpoint as a citizen of the world. It is that position I try to occupy today. I am asking what it is the people of the world need and may expect from China, a country that has shown its ability to bring its vast population out of poverty. They can ask this because China has proved itself now ready to assume the responsibilities of global leadership.

World citizenship has a pedigree that goes back to the ancient Greeks, the philosopher Socrates in particular. It is a concept often derided in the West. 'Citizen of nowhere' was the scornful comment of a former British prime minister. A recent book by a German philosopher actually declared the idea of the world to be meaningless.

That would have been derisory in the middle of the eighteenth century when the imagination of the Irish writer Oliver Goldsmith depicted, in his volume *The Citizen of the World*, a Chinese narrator who embodied such a citizen, who was able to laugh at the absurd habits and stories of the Europeans, inventing gods as the Chinese have never done.[32]

[31] Editor's note: This is the 316th Luojia Lecture, which was delivered at Wuhan University, China, November 14, 2019, when the author participated in an international conference there (7.3.3) [万蕊嘉：英国社会科学院院士马丁·阿尔布劳做客珞珈讲坛，"珞珈讲坛"，武汉大学人文社会会科学院，2019-11-21，见：http://ssroff.whu.edu.cn/info/1171/2539.htm].

[32] The full title of the collection was *The Citizen of the World or Letters from a Chinese Philosopher Residing in London to his Friends in the East* and was published in London in 1762. They originated as twice weekly articles in a new daily newspaper, *The Public Ledger*, from 1760.

Karl Marx was never reluctant to use a term so widely employed in everyday language. Of course every student of Marx encounters his use of it in his epigrammatic announcement in the *Theses on Feuerbach* 'the philosophers have only interpreted the world in different ways; the point is to change it'. Of his later uses of the word, probably 'world market' is the most famous, and there he is deliberately contrasting it with limited national markets, leaving it without any predefined boundaries. How far did this 'world' extend? Its limits were not territorial, they were conceptual, in the same way as capital had no territorial limits and its scope was unconfined. Similarly, when in Chinese culture you speak of 'tianxia', everything under the sky, the sky has no limits.

What has no limits impels us to make limits for it. We divide up the world into 'my world' or 'your world', the 'human world' or the 'animal world'. (Though there, in a funny trick of the English language, we often speak of the 'animal kingdom', suggesting a further step, bringing the world under the control of a sovereign.)

That limitless quality is what challenges us most as we confront our world extending into the future. In that respect President Xi has provided the direction to shape our response to the world, and to change it. The newest and most publicized contribution to the world that China makes today is therefore to promote the shared future for humankind. It is that shared future where we join together both as world and national citizens, the national identity contributing to the task of finding our common future. Sociologist Joy Zhang tells me that you draw on the thought of Lu Xun to express the idea we share: national (identity) is the basis for the global (citizenship) (民族的就是世界的, *minzu de jiushi shiji de*).

As a British citizen I also have to ask what my country can contribute and whether it has any special qualities to bring to the common effort. Then I have to be honest about how my country has shaped me and my contemporaries. For what we have been able to do has been based on the past history of our country and that also includes a burden. I should explain myself.

When I went to school my teachers would point proudly to the world atlas and tell us to look at the parts that were coloured pink, to South Africa, Australia, Canada, India, and countries whose names are part of history, like Tanganyika, now Tanzania, or Ceylon, now Sri Lanka, Nyasaland, now Malawi. And Pakistan and Bangladesh did not exist. In 1945 they were all part of the British Empire.

Later I learned that the British Empire was built on trade and the exploitation of native populations. Fortunes were made from slavery and from forcing opium on the unwilling Chinese people. I recognize today that the wonderful Georgian and Victorian architecture of London and other cities like Bristol and Liverpool depended on the capital amassed from these awful practices. Those buildings make me realize that I benefit even now from the wealth created then. It is for this reason I think it right, when I have the privilege of speaking in a distinguished seat of learning in China, to apologize for my ancestors' part in the humiliations the

Chinese people suffered in former centuries. And I can only express my gratitude for the generosity you never fail to show to me, and to so many other citizens from my country, when we visit you.

It is a special feature of Chinese culture that you forgive, and not just foreigners. You forgive one another too, as I have discovered in talking with different generations, within families where past conflicts that have divided them have been overcome. They have learned how to share a future in families, in villages, townships, cities and provinces. What you have learned at home is what you are now offering the world. If the prospect of creating a shared future is your first contribution to the world today it is based on what I want to single out as the second contribution. This is that distinctive and core aspect of Chinese civilization that marks it out from Western countries in particular, namely the idea of harmony, the value that holds all other values together.

Your history is far more varied than is often realized in the West. Early Western accounts of China emphasized not just its durability but also stability. But you have overcome many periods of disorder and conflict, with the ideal of harmony always prevailing in the end. The contrast with the West is profound and I will try to say why. The West is built on conflict and in a very specific way. It seeks to manage it and use it, but not to remove it.

Marx and Engels of course recognized the importance of conflict in asserting that all history was the history of class struggle. Conflict in the West extends further than class struggle. It pits individuals against one another. The crucial period was when the mediaeval order of the Roman Catholic Church was challenged by the Protestant Reformation of the sixteenth century with its assertion of the direct relationship between the individual and God, with each finding their own way. Oliver Goldsmith's fictional Chinese observer commented that 'priests are eternally disputing against each other'.

Western individualism created a constant succession of new beliefs, lifestyles, communities, and escapes to new worlds. Conflict within and between them and between new and old worlds became and continues to be endemic.

I learned on only my second visit to China in 1988 how well you understand Western individualism. Visiting a village household while on a tour as the guest of the State Family Planning Commission, I asked to interview an individual about the one-child policy. The extended family opposite me burst into laughter. My interpreter explained they were laughing at Western individualism. On reflection, I recognized that a group interview would be more valid as a predictor of behaviour than one with a single person.

Individualism fed into the creation of representative democracy, the institutions of the nation–state and the wars that have gone with it. How, then, you might well ask, can one account for that degree of order that undoubtedly does exist in the West, even if conflict is unending? There have been many attempts to answer a profound problem, and I shall single out three.

As you can understand, I'm drawing you into the kind of discussion beloved by both academic sociologists and political scientists, namely the relative importance and interplay of conflict and consensus in the formation and persistence of societies. But its relevance today extends far beyond the classrooms.

Perhaps the most famous early answer, which to this day has its advocates, was that of Thomas Hobbes. In the wake of the Protestant Reformation, he argued that people living in a state of nature, where famously life was 'nasty, brutish and short' had to relinquish their natural rights and hand them to a sovereign power which would guarantee their security. And if they didn't? Here a modern answer was provided over a century ago at the beginning of the establishment of sociology as an academic discipline. The German philosopher and sociologist Georg Simmel argued that the alliances and cross-cutting ties that conflict produced in a complex advanced society were actually the source of its cohesion. That was before two world wars.

In the aftermath of those wars, with the collective effort to establish a new international order, sociological thinking inclined to a different answer to the problem of conflict. It was not to be suppressed, since that was inherent in modern society, but managed to the collective benefit through institutions. Subsequently that idea was developed as the theory of the institutionalization of conflict. It has been very much associated with someone I was privileged to learn from, namely the late Ralf Dahrendorf, who after a distinguished career as a professor in Germany was at one time the Commissioner for External Affairs for the European Union and later the Director of the London School of Economics. His idea was that, if conflict is acknowledged as inevitable, then the task is to manage it to the best advantage of society. Competition between firms is regulated, strikes are permitted and arbitration is available. 'Conflict is liberty,' he wrote. 'Liberal democracy is government by conflict.'

Dahrendorf was a great admirer of the United Kingdom as opposed to his homeland and was rather scornful of German attempts to create solidarity and social markets. The UK had a much healthier and productive acceptance of conflict, he thought. It was a view that became harder and harder to support in the years when the German post-war economic wonder amazed the world and the UK suffered years of damaging industrial disputes. Today I think he would be compelled to revise his thesis if he were alive to experience the toxic atmosphere of Brexit. Certainly his view must be increasingly open to question with the rise of populism in the West. In fact, what appeared once as solidarity through multiple cross-cutting ties now looks like social fragmentation.

The national institutions designed to accommodate conflict, like the division between judiciary, executive and legislature that the United States constitution enshrines, are failing to prevent increasingly bitter divides on party lines. The British constitution is being tested to its limits. The rise of the welfare state in Western societies in the last century has often been judged to have dampened or even rendered class conflict insignificant. But the expansion of the global market, backed by international financial institutions, with global financial capital and the global strategies of multinational corporations, all summed as economic globalization has, just as Marx foretold, produced class conflict on a global scale. The support that populist leaders give to one another across borders is a symptom of the resulting global nature of politics today. As I write, the uproar in the United States about the conversation between President Trump and the Ukrainian President Zelensky is a symptom of that global nature of politics.

So too were the worldwide marches by children that preceded the meeting of world leaders to debate global warming in New York on 23 September this year. There, a 16-year-old Swedish girl, Greta Thunberg, electrified a world audience by accusing those leaders of stealing a generation's dreams by failing to meet what China called 'a challenge common to all countries', namely that of climate change.

The Chinese people may look across to the West with a degree of self-satisfaction today. Socialism with Chinese characteristics is working. But the issues confronting the world require leadership of a very high order and currently it is to China the world must look. In that respect harmony is a message for the whole of the West. Harmony in China works primarily not through institutions but in the willingness on the part of every citizen to work in a common cause. It begins with the two Centenary Goals but they cascade down through every factory target and community agenda. The whole nation mobilizes towards ends that are diverse, coordinated and pragmatic. They are underpinned by values, but it is the goal-seeking nature of Chinese harmony and the cooperation it generates that provide the motive force in individual behaviour.

It is this goal-seeking quality that provides such a good match between China and the Sustainable Development Goals of the United Nations. These hope to inspire the nations of the world to provide a future for their children. That spirit is not equally shared among the nations. On my account, they are most congruent with Chinese culture.

Harmony in Chinese thought relates not just to human relations and to peace within and between nations. It comprises the three harmonies of Heaven, Earth and Man. In that trinity, human activity is dedicated to representing and reproducing nature. The commitment to 'modelling after nature' corresponds perfectly with the target that, among all the targets that drive the global community, is more pressing and important than any other, namely the creation of a sustainable environment. This, then, is the third great contribution China is making for the future of our species.

It was exemplified in President Xi's work promoting sound ecological policies in Fujian to make it the province with the best water and air quality. Early in his role as a leader in Zhejiang Province he called on the people to join in environmental protection and he called for balance between economic and environmental protection. From its beginning in 2013 the Belt and Road Initiative has been committed to 'clear waters and green mountains'. In the first Belt and Road forum for international cooperation in May 2017, President Xi emphasized the new vision of green development and the need to realize the goals of the 2030 Agenda for Sustainable Development.

Not just aspiration but achievement has followed. In a recent issue devoted to the climate, the influential Western magazine *The Economist* declared China had upheld its pledges on greenhouse gas emissions. China produces one third of the world's energy from wind-power, and has a quarter of the world's solar panels in use. In 12 years up to 2017 China reduced the rate of carbon emission per unit of GDP by 46%. At the same time, the magazine says China's choices are critical for the future of the world's temperature. The Belt and Road countries produce 28% of global carbon emissions.

Though the West likes to portray China as a top-down country, with every activity initiated from the top, the profound sense of harmony shapes everyday engagement with nature. It is a normal and traditional aspect of a farmer's work to take account of the long-term management of the soil as well as the immediate prospects for this season's crops.

Since 2011, University of Kent sociologist Joy Yueyue Zhang has been researching how, in line with government policies, non-governmental organizations are doing remarkable work at the grassroots level in educating both urban and rural publics in sustainable practices. One problem is that government has often to run to catch up with market forces. (She has told me, incidentally, that Wuhan scientists are in the forefront of developing genetically modified crops to defeat soil pollution and also to help ethnic minorities to expand sustainable traditional farming practices). 'Environment sustainability' or, more poetically and profound, 'harmony with nature' is a spirit that pervades China. And it is understood as spirit in China. And it is 'spirit' I want to identify as my fourth and last major contribution that China's leadership can offer to our world today.

When President Xi worked in Zhejiang he mentioned the Zhejiang spirit on nine occasions in his newspaper articles. He invoked 'spirit' no fewer than 69 times. The Party spirit gained 14 mentions as in 'Leadership transition Tests the Party Spirit of Leading Officials' and a whole article was devoted to the Typhoon Spirit. I can safely say no Western leader would make such copious use of a term that has had a special history in the West. In mediaeval Christianity, spirit came to be associated with God and with his son Jesus Christ to form the Trinity.

In the eighteenth century, when Goldsmith was writing, when China was a shining light for so many in the West and an important reference point for the Enlightenment, 'spirit' was adopted by the philosophers as a term without a religious dogmatic meaning. In tune with the dialectical spirit of the Enlightenment (or perhaps reflecting the need of Westerners to disagree with one another), it also prompted some like the Frenchman Helvetius to advance a new theory of materialism.

But the non-religious idea of spirit was to gain in strength and reach all-embracing scope in the philosophy of Hegel. As you know very well in a Marxist university, Hegel interpreted the whole of human history as the spirit coming to consciousness and reaching perfection in the European state. This was a philosophy to inspire a whole generation of young intellectuals, only for characteristic Western dissidence to bring it down to earth in the historical materialism of Marx. His rejection of Hegel and his dismissal of organized religion, combined with the advance of natural science, especially Charles Darwin's work on evolution, effectively removed spirit from public discourse.

Except in a mundane sense of enthusiasm, spirit in the West now as a reference belongs largely to the churches and new religious movements. Not so in China! I owe it to Professor Jin Wei here in Wuhan for drawing my attention to the multiple occasions your leadership asks the people to follow some spirit. It might be of an individual, Lei Feng for instance, or of a significant event, the cruise of the Red Boat, or of a place, the Shanghai City Spirit. I am sure there is bound to be a Wuhan spirit. In all these instances, spirit is referring to the ways in which multiple factors are bonded together through human activity to produce something new. Spirit is that bonding that creates an entity both material and spiritual, that takes on an existence of its own in human affairs.

The great Western social scientist Max Weber once sought to grasp the differences brought about by economic changes in the modern Western world by describing the 'spirit of capitalism'. But then he felt he had to reduce it to single factors in his famous analysis that followed as *The Protestant Ethic and the Spirit of Capitalism*. And he took a sideways swipe at Marxists for producing what he called a one-sided view of history.

But Marx himself was actually not one-sided. From his earliest writing, he declared the opposition between the spiritual and material was a false one, for they form a unity in human activity. Their separation in philosophy is only an abstraction from real life, where human beings are continually creating new things. Our collective practices lead to the creation of new kinds of existence, and that includes the renewal of society.

I conclude then with what for Western listeners will be a paradox that shakes them to the foundations of their beliefs. I have singled out four contributions that China can, indeed must make to the whole world today if it is to survive: a sense of shared future; the value of harmony; unity with nature; and the creative force of spirit in human life. And the greatest of these is spirit.

The economic success of China has been deeply disturbing for the West. Socialism is not meant to work. Currently all kinds of explanations gain popularity, cheating, spying, exploiting developing countries, manipulating currency … and the list grows. What the West cannot grasp is that socialism with Chinese characteristics works because of Chinese culture and civilization, and the spirit that has always been central to it. Westerners are trapped by their history into thinking spirit belongs to a separate compartment in life, indeed outside everyday life altogether. China does not compartmentalize spirit and as a result the West concludes it hasn't got it. The contrary is the case. It is everywhere in China, and survives in the West mainly in alienated forms, in cults, in sport and in mass concerts.

Thank you.[33]

3.4 Diversity and cooperation in the shared future[34]

There were many lessons for the whole world, and not just for China, conveyed in the first two volumes of President Xi Jinping's speeches. This was the main point of the speeches I made when it was my privilege to speak at the launch of the English versions in London in 2014 and 2018.

It was the choice of governance for the title that signalled the desire to reach out beyond China's borders. At the same time it carried an invitation to the diversity of the world's peoples. For governance is not government. It is the order that is generated out of the popular desire to lead a full life in harmony with one's neighbours.

Necessarily, then, the governance of China must embrace peace and cooperation with the rest of the world, and in this month of September, 2020 we welcome the added strength that Volume 3 of *The Governance of China* gives to that message. Xi's personal formulation of that idea, a community of shared future for mankind, with which he concluded Volume 2, now has the added emphasis of a larger section of extracts from nine speeches in this volume.

In them, the scope of the idea is further expanded by speaking of that community as 'global'. Yet its diversity is emphasized at the same time by pointing to the variety of shared futures: of the Shanghai Cooperation Organization; of the BRICS countries; China and Africa; Asian countries; and in specific sectors like the economy and maritime relations. The globe then is not a straitjacket but a field for a multitude of different endeavours.

Xi endorses rule-based global governance and emphasizes that it must be based in consultation and cooperation between all the people. He therefore asks for more democratic rule, taking in the multilateralism of the United Nations. At the same time the future of the world is not safeguarded by rules alone. What is fundamental for the human future is the creative cooperation of the world's peoples in battling poverty and disease, safeguarding the environment and providing the prosperity that is the basis for both personal and collective development. It is particularly significant, then, that the section on the shared future is followed by one on the Belt and Road Initiative. Deeds speak louder than words.

---

33 I am very grateful to Joy Zhang and Cecily Liu for their helpful suggestions at different points in the preparation of this lecture. They are of course not responsible for any errors it may contain.

34 Editor's note: This is a book review for *Xi Jinping's Governance of China,* Volume 3 [马丁·阿尔布劳：书评，《习近平谈治国理政》，第三卷，北京：外文出版社，2020年].

Yet, when all is said and done, *The Governance of China* is directed towards the Chinese people, and in particular to the Communist Party of China. That is emphasized this year by the devotion of the final section to the self-reform of the CPC. Yet, for an outside observer like myself and for all foreigners, this is immensely informative and deserves close attention since China's leadership in this century requires the rest of the world to become familiar with its unique features.

For me, the very first of Xi's volumes highlighted a special feature of Chinese governance. It represented the distillation of ideas from deep in Chinese history and culture linked to those of modern Marxist socialism. 'It demonstrates how much we should value systematic thought in political leadership,' I wrote. The same thought occurs to me repeatedly in reading Xi's addresses to the Party.

He begins with its founding and history as the inspiration for the present and then turns to the requirements for self-reform, rooting out the four malfeasances, formalism, bureaucratism, hedonism and extravagance. These all hinder a focus on the practical tasks of delivering socialism. But this emphasis on practice must be underpinned by familiarity with the ideas of Marxism with Chinese characteristics. Self-reform is then an ongoing process of practice and reflection.

Xi moves back and forth between pairs of ideas that are complementary and dynamic, between ideals and today's realities, between discipline and rejuvenation, integrity and innovative thinking, leadership and serving the people. The sound is not of the relentless drumming of a machine, but of the expanding repertoire of an accomplished orchestra. It's a performance that aims to benefit the people of China, to uplift their spirit and provide for their long-term rejuvenation.

The combination of continuing engagement with ideas and involvement in the practical demands of a shared future makes the Chinese regime the most coherent and far-seeing in the world today. It has proved itself in sharing its progress with its own people. The task for the future is to lead when its people are not its own. Volume 3 of *The Governance of China* provides the early indications of the direction of that leadership.

3.5 Provincial development, global vision: Xi Jinping in Zhejiang[35]

Readers of the earlier two volumes of speeches by the President Xi Jinping, published in the rest of the world under the title *The Governance of China* (Foreign Languages Press, 2014, 2017), will be surprised by this book – and probably will welcome it all the more.

For it represents the experience of an early part of his career, full of the energy and zest of a senior, though still youthful, official in the province of Zhejiang between the years of 2003 and 2007 and was first published in China in 2007.

---

[35] Editor's note: This is a speech at the first release in German and English of *Zhejiang, China: A New Vision for Development*, by XI Jinping, Beijing: Foreign Languages Press and Zhejiang People's Publishing House, at 71st Frankfurt International Book Fair, October 15, 2019.[Chinese edition: 习近平：《之江新语》，杭州：浙江人民出版社， 2017年].

It was my honour to be invited to speak at the launch in London of those earlier two volumes. I commented on their intellectual ambition beyond anything contemporary Western leaders care to or even generally are able to offer.

They combined Marxism, traditional Chinese culture and relevant Western theory to illuminate the prospects for China and to open the way to a shared future for humankind. So, very substantial, even daunting for the reader!

This volume has a lighter quality, though its basis in the same profoundly felt world-view is already clearly apparent. The difference is it is closer to the soil, rooted in Xi's work in Zhejiang. Rather than speeches, it contains no fewer than 232 short essays written originally for the *Zhejiang Daily.*

Addressed to officials and party members, they make compelling reading because of their directness and plain talking. Workers and farmers are the political foundation of the party (176) and it is farmers who should be empowered to solve rural issues.

The higher-ranking officials should share difficulties with officials at the grassroots level (190). The grassroots are the pillars on which the Party must base its work (192), and that echoes the earliest experience of Mao Zedong in the Autumn Harvest uprising of 1927.

Ancient wisdom comes into play when Xi wants to emphasize the importance of self-awareness. He quotes Confucius saying, 'I should reflect on myself thrice a day' (196) and that was part of the sense of responsibility of officials that had origins going back to the Han dynasty.

Historical depth goes hand in hand with global vision. But wrestling with Zhejiang's local problems, Xi has no need to use the rhetoric of multilateral bodies. He turns to a ninth-century Tang dynasty poet Bai Juyi (772-846), who lamented the boundlessness of human desire and the limits of the earth's resources.

China, writes Xi, must avoid the trap of Western modernization and achieve sustainable development. That was particularly true for Zhejiang, lacking natural resources, needing to create a conservation-based society (207).

Two days after that article, which was entitled 'Create a conservation-based society', Xi followed it with another: 'Stability and harmony are integral to the scientific outlook on development'. These were written as long ago as February 2005.

In them we find conclusive evidence of how long-standing and deeply rooted are Xi's beliefs about the direction China should take. He reflects on the experience of other countries in raising living standards and the resulting disharmonies. He points to the research and policy changes the Party in Zhejiang has introduced to bring peace and stability. Xi's words here are worth more than any summary of mine:

> Chinese culture is closely tied to the pursuit of a peaceful and harmonious society that enjoys sound government and allows people to live and work in contentment. We need only look to our Chinese ancestors for proof. They cherished such values as peace, harmony without uniformity and inclusiveness. The past

> has shown the overwhelming importance of stability. Without a stable environment, we never would have accomplished anything. Reform and development would just be empty talk, and any successes would have been lost. (208)

If I were still teaching in universities, as I did for 40 years, and I was giving a course on the basis of Chinese public policy since reform and opening up, and I wanted just one text for prescribed reading, this article would be my choice. And if the student reflected long and hard on it there would be enough in it to pass the examination. All in just 250 words!

This is the statement of the governing philosophy of the Scientific Outlook on Development. The next month it is all brought down to earth. In a series of articles Xi proceeds to outline the need to develop Zhejiang's service industry, to attract Fortune Global 500 companies to invest, to balance heavy and light industry and to look beyond Zhejiang for further development.

Thus, at the end of 2003, 4 million Zhejiang citizens were based in other provinces, they had invested 532 billion yuan, their revenues were more than 1 trillion yuan, 70% of their production was made in Zhejiang and that accounted for 30% of the output in the relevant industries.

I am only selecting some of the data from his article of March 21, 2005. The message for his readers was clear. He told them to think broad, strategic and pragmatic. But they needed to know the facts.

That was his message for the people of Zhejiang. I would suggest we can also draw a lesson from this article for us in the West. China has risen on a platform of policies that have the maximum intellectual range and depth but also command relevant data that reach into the intricate interactions of people going about their daily work and lives. Just think of the sophistication and complexity of the administrative operations needed for collecting the data in that article. That is replicated all over China.

President Xi's book provides a unique window on the processes that underpin China's renewal. But it deserves to be read not just by China specialists. It requires the attention of all those concerned to understand what is necessary for a country to survive and prosper in a world of unprecedented change.

3.6 Help for the world[36]

The Western media have reported extensively on President Xi's speech to the 19th Congress of the Communist Party of China. But, as you might expect, they have seen it largely through the prism of geopolitics or the global economy.

Even the highly respected magazine *The Economist* raised expectations of the Congress and the President by featuring him on its cover as 'The world's most

---

[36] 马丁·阿尔布劳：《探究十九大报告的深层思想》，《人民日报》2017年12月22日03版，见：http://dangjian.people.com.cn/n1/2017/1222/c117092-29722689.html [Martin Albrow (2017), Exploring the Deep Thoughts of the 19th National Congress of the Communist Party of China, *People's Daily*. December 22].

powerful man' (October 14, 2017). This may or may not be right, but it personalizes the issues in a way that does not contribute to greater understanding of China in the West.

Xi's speech deserves to be treated for what it is, a profound assessment of China's direction, not just for the coming five years, but over centuries past and decades to come. We have a saying, 'Still waters run deep.' His speech was calm and measured. The Western press only looked for surface excitement. We in the West should dive down to examine the currents below.

We need to begin by recognizing the significance of the Chairman's speech to the Party and of the Party to China in relation to Chinese history. In 1949 China began an experiment as significant for democracy as was the American War of Independence that began in 1775.

Each event threw off the relics of imperialism and each engaged with a new modernity, though at different stages of development. In each case there were visionary leaders who could both anticipate pwossible future directions of history and steer them to their own people's advantage.

Quite aside from any personal frailties and mistakes by the leaders of these revolutions, their countries recognize their unique and lasting contribution to founding a new order. Sometimes they have successors whose achievement is to take that order forward into a New Era.

US President Bill Clinton was such a leader in the West, though still not appreciated as such in his own country. He brought the world as a whole to consciousness of globalization, made it the dominant theme of his presidency and made the Millennium Development Goals the signature project of the global age.

There is no doubt that the rhetoric of globalization was designed to serve American interests and, more widely, the interests of the global capitalist class. I pointed this out in an article for *China Daily*, 'Globalization is not necessarily in the national interest'. It has to be managed by every country to serve national goals.

China understood this from the very beginning and has been careful to establish clear criteria for foreign participation in its economy and to take advantage from the benefits that free markets can provide. Xi's speech makes it very clear that China's participation in the global economy is first and foremost to be judged by what it delivers for national rejuvenation.

What is impressive in this commitment to openness to trade and investment across boundaries is also the recognition that with economic development the principal contradiction facing Chinese society also evolves. Development is unbalanced and has many defects that clash with the people's demands for a better life.

We in the West also recognize the contradictions of the modern economy, though it is expressed in different terms. Both growing inequality and environmental degradation can be attributed to a global capitalism that so often is successful in escaping national controls.

It does not have to be that way. Some countries are more successful than others in adapting to a global market and satisfying their people's demands for education, health and dignified old age. Germany is one of the best examples in Europe, Canada in the Americas.

But China is pursuing a path quite distinct from the West, developing a model of governance based on socialism with Chinese characteristics, capable of overcoming the current contradictions and looking towards a time when it is a global leader in innovation, with a harmonious society that makes its soft power all the more appealing.

This model depends on a profound partnership between people. Party and government. Xi's speech places huge emphasis on relations of Party and people, based in the Constitution and law. It contrasts profoundly with Western accounts of modern societies that revolve around the state, capital and electorate.

The model is dynamic, not static. It is a project for society, taking it forward from its present state with an emphasis on values, goals and policies that are based on theory and fact. To carry it forward requires leadership and that is the task of the Party, its mission to 'realize the Chinese Dream of national rejuvenation'.

Rejuvenation completes the process of recovery from the century of national humiliation, in which my own country, the United Kingdom, played a disgraceful part. Xi demonstrates Chinese magnanimity by avoiding any mention of these past injustices and offers a positive message for the world as a whole.

The optimism of Xi's message relies on his confident belief that traditional Chinese culture continues to provide the basis for any future modernization. It will continue to let 'a hundred flowers bloom' and encourage transformation and development.

This is an affirmation of culture that extends far beyond art and literature. It owes more to the findings of the scientific study of human culture worldwide. It extends to all aspects of human life and connects the habits and moral outlook of everyday life with the highest expression of human creativity.

If that sounds very theoretical, that is because it is. And because in Xi Jinping China has a leader with a profound grasp of theory and its relevance to people and to governance. In the West there is a saying 'Nothing is so practical as a good theory', but it is a saying forgotten by Western leaders today, who often give the impression that their thought is only as deep as their tweets are short.

The theory required for holding together and taking forward a country of more than 1.3 billion people covering nearly 10 million square kilometres must continually reflect on practice, digest a vast amount of current information on its condition and organize it around policies that reach every part of its life.

It is theory that relates goals to cooperation, values to markets, diversity to innovation, morality to work, leadership to equality and explores the drivers of social and economic transformation. In all of these sectors, West and East can exchange and benefit from each other's huge stores of ideas.

The biggest obstacle to that exchange is the West's dogmatic insistence that it alone understands democracy. This is at a time when the flaws in its democratic systems are obvious in countries where personal and corporate wealth underpins political parties and the chances of gaining office.

President Xi advocates consultative democracy, not the representative kind. Each has its distinct historical origins. In China today democracy depends on the intimate relation between Party and people. 'Our Party comes from the people, has its roots among the people, and is dedicated to serving the people.' With the people, it shares in and exercises oversight over government.

The intimacy of that relation depends to my mind on the historic willingness in Chinese culture to respect higher status, authority and knowledge. At the same time, it is the closeness of those bonds that make law so important in preventing the abuse of power and explain the drive against corruption in Chinese life that Xi has spearheaded.

The underlying strength of China in its social relations is yet to gain due recognition in the West. But it allows China now to extend its reach beyond its own borders. It is open to exchange with other cultures, confident in the value of what it offers. It puts its economic power to the advantage of other countries through One Belt One Road. Extending transport and communication infrastructure through Eurasia and Africa is a win–win for other countries and for China.

Xi speaks as leader of the Communist Party of China. It has the leadership of the most powerful peacetime collective agency the world has ever seen. He offers China's help in shaping what he calls a 'community with a shared future for mankind'. It is for the rest of the world to accept that the offer is made in good faith.

The underlying strength of China in its social relations is yet to gain due recognition in the West. But it allows China now to extend its reach beyond its own borders. It is open to exchange with other cultures, confident in the value of what it offers. It puts its economic power to the advantage of other countries through One Belt One Road. Extending transport and communication infrastructure through Eurasia and Africa is a win–win for other countries and for China.

Xi speaks as leader of the Communist Party of China. It has the leadership of the most powerful peacetime collective agency the world has ever seen. He offers China's help in shaping what he calls a 'community with a shared future for mankind'. It is for the rest of the world to accept that the offer is made in good faith.

3.7. Reflections for the 70th anniversary of the founding of the People's Republic of China[37]

Three score years and ten in the West traditionally were thought of as the normal lifetime of a human being. In that light, the 70-year period since the found-

[37] 马丁·阿尔布劳：《交流互鉴中书写辉煌故事》，《人民日报》2019年12月19日03版，见：http://www.scio.gov.cn/31773/35507/35515/35523/document/1670191/1670191.htm [Martin Albrow, Writing brilliant stories in exchanges and mutual learning, *People's Daily*, December 19, 2019].

ing of the People's Republic of China should prompt us to reflect on all those who have given their life's energies to securing its future.

A lifetime is just a passing moment in five thousand years of Chinese civilization. But it is from this extraordinary history that the Chinese people have drawn the inspiration to devote their lives to their country's defence, growth and rejuvenation.

It begins at infancy. All Chinese children learn to reproduce that civilization as they strive to master their written language. In so doing they come into touch with its roots in the past, with nature and the conditions for our existence on this earth. The uniqueness of the Chinese written characters is the most vivid symbolic expression of a civilization like no other.

All civilizations are different. They rise from very specific material conditions and they embody the traces of the unique experiences that make up their history. Many of these arise out of contact with other civilizations. China has assimilated these for millennia, from India, the Middle East and the Asian steppes as well as from the West.

In the 70 years of its existence, the People's Republic has presented the most dramatic example of the processes of cultural exchange by adapting ideas from the West to help build Chinese prosperity and the recovery of China's proper place among the world's powers. Economic globalization has been welcomed and in return China now offers the Belt and Road Initiative to all who want to share in the benefits of its own hard-earned wealth.

Cultural exchange often works best through example rather than slavish copying. China's Communist Party has since its earliest days found that Marxism best provides the analysis that both fits China's social conditions and offers the guidelines for its future development. But Marxism will have different results in different countries, which is why China's 'socialism with Chinese characteristics' inspires others to find their own distinctive paths.

Those very early language learning efforts of Chinese children mirror China's continuous response to the changing world around. Early on, Chairman Mao encouraged the modernization of Chinese characters to ease their acquisition. The simultaneous development of pinyin has not only assisted foreigners to learn Chinese but has become the initial entry point into reading for the young child in China today.

The massive effort educators have put into foreign language learning and especially into English has had enormous impact both on capacity to learn from experience of other cultures but also to guide foreigners who may visit China. This is cultural soft power, even more extensive and pervasive than its official representation in Confucius Institutes or English-language media like CGTN or *China Daily*.

From the early days of the founding of the People's Republic through the great opening up and reform to the Centenary Goals, the story of China has been one of continuous contact with other cultures. The adaptation and absorption of those elements of others' experience contribute to the fulfilment of the China Dream.

It is what happens between civilizations that shapes the wider human future. In trade, travel and the exchange of ideas, a common stock of knowledge is built. We share a worldwide technology and have done so ever since the taming of fire, the making of pots, harnessing of steam, taming the energy of the atom and now in digital communication.

None of these epoch-making advances in the use of natural forces has ever been confined for long to their place of origin, often unknown, or at least forgotten. I did not realize until this year, when I joined with others to celebrate its renovation, that the very first iron frame building in the world, a flax mill, was built in my own country, in the town of Shrewsbury in 1797. This was the very beginning of the technology that underpins those vast displays of skyscrapers that have in very recent times come to dominate the skylines of your cities.

For these reasons of technological diffusion and reception, the attempts in the West to exclude Huawei from the development of 5G communication technology are ultimately doomed to failure, even if they damage both sides of the dispute in the short run. The past experience of revolutionary new forms of communication, from printing to telecommunications, to air travel and in our time to the internet, suggests there is a general interest in developing common standards across the globe.

The International Telecommunications Union (ITU) provides a good example. Founded in 1865, and now a United Nations agency, it creates standards for communication technology that are shared by its 193 member countries. It must be a matter of pride for China that its current Secretary General, Mr. Zhao Houlin, had a long and distinguished research career in the Ministry of Posts and Telecommunications before being its delegate to the ITU.

Shared technologies and technology standards are the necessary basis for all those cooperative projects across boundaries that are required to meet the global challenges of today. The wisdom of Belt and Road involves the recognition that countries of widely diverse cultures can equally well appreciate the value of airports, roads, ports and railways.

This is where the shared human future, President Xi Jinping's guiding principle for China's contribution to worldwide development, has its beginning. Shared practical projects provide the basis for cooperation between diverse cultures. It was somewhat embarrassing recently at the Belt and Road Studies Network in Beijing to find myself being quoted on the placards in the entrance corridor to the meeting: In a 'shared human future you talk about the things we do together, not a future where we are all the same.'

On this basis depends the hope of the world that the catastrophe of unchecked global warming may be averted through the cooperation of every country and above all of China and the United States. The deep divergences between them in history and ideology can be overcome in the recognition of the practical measures that the solution of this existential crisis requires.

The next 70 years will be a global challenge for every civilization, above all for China, as it commits both its cultural heritage and its uniquely powerful collective agency to work for the welfare of all human beings. To this end, the more it invites others to share in its own civilization the more likely it is to win the willing cooperation the world so desperately requires.

The task is not hopeless. The West can be won over. In 1920, very soon after the end of the First World War, the greatest Western philosopher of the twentieth century, Bertrand Russell, stayed in China for several months. The very first banquet he attended on arrival in Shanghai made a vivid impression on him with its witty after-dinner speeches. He wrote later of his surprise. 'I had not realized until then that a civilized Chinese is the most civilized person in the world.'

3.8 Can the world follow China's democratic path?[38]

The impact of the global pandemic and recent political events in the United States have made the future of democracy a live issue. But the West persists in shutting its eyes to the relevance of China's developing system of social governance. Its consultative democracy can both rescue the modern state and take a lead in overcoming the challenges to our continuing presence on this earth.

Following the election of Joe Biden to the American presidency, Western thoughts have turned to democracy. Of course, after the storming of the Washington Capitol building, some think it has had a narrow escape and can carry on as before. But others prefer to look ahead and think about a future league of democracies. One thing you can be sure of: China will not be invited to join.

Yet, on nearly all indices, China is far more democratic than any of the countries that are touted as possible members of such a league. Universal adult suffrage, high voter participation, guarantees of equality before the law and redistrib-

[38] Editor's note: This article was written at the request of *People's Daily* in March 2021. The abridged version is entitled 'China's Democracy is Full of Vitality'. It was agreed that the article would not be published because the last two paragraphs were not written by the author. They are: 'At the global level, China has been committed to promoting democracy in international relations. China proposes extensive consultation, joint contribution and shared benefits in global governance and promotes equal rights, equal opportunities and equal rules for all countries. China advocates harmony without uniformity and coexistence and harmony, and encourages countries to work together to build a community with a shared future for mankind. This will provide a strong driving force for building a more democratic global governance system. It will be a democratic delivery of the global goals, the answer to today's global challenges of climate change and nuclear proliferation, of pandemics and digital communication standards. The achievements of the Belt and Road Initiative demonstrate that countries can work together to address common challenges and benefit the whole world.' Also: 'China's democracy, realized by Chinese people under CPC's leadership, is a continuous process with ceaseless exploration. The future of global democracy is a hotly debated topic. A further understanding of China's democracy can both tackle the problems of modern states and overcome the challenges to our continuing presence on this earth.'

utive government policies all work towards very great popular satisfaction with its political system.

When one also considers the efficiency and effectiveness of China's public policies, conquest of poverty and unrivalled economic growth over four decades, it is understandable that some in the West, including myself, have likened China to a corporation rather than a civilization. For the West knows such success only in the business world. But then add to business democratic features and ask: How would the most successful Western corporation, say Apple, react if told to vote for its leaders at every level?

China has its own democracy, consultative at every level, from village and factory up to the People's Congress. But it is an upright pillar with two supports: the Party that guarantees national values and policy making at all levels and the state that delivers the policies, centrally, in provinces, counties and locally. In the West, the popular vote selects representatives of political parties to actually run governments, whether they have the skills and experience or not.

The dominant countries in what is now a very fragmented West equate their representative systems with every democratic virtue, overlooking evidence that is repeated generation after generation. Parties rule in the interests of their supporters, and, competing for votes, they are dominated by moneyed interests and simplistic slogans that appeal to the largest number. In societies ever more polarized under the impact of globalization, populists fan the flames of racism and hatred of immigrants and minorities.

In its short history, Western democracy has seen the American Civil War, Hitler coming to power through democratic election, the rise of military dictatorships in Africa and Latin America and wars to impose democracy in the Middle East. The fact is that Western democracy has arisen out of conflict and depends for any success on the management of conflict.

Western political institutions presuppose conflict, even foster it and then to seek to contain it. Far too often, they fail because the institutionalization of party conflict can only provide a very unstable equilibrium. Often this is called 'liberal democracy' but 'conflictual' is a far better description. Indeed, we should cast our thoughts back over the long and chequered history of democracy.

* * *

The ancient Greeks had a much longer experience of democracy than the modern West and were rightly sceptical of its capacity to ensure stable government and secure the interests of citizens. For them, democracy was at its best when it was combined with other components of government rather than becoming its sole principle. Unchecked, they saw that it could far too easily degenerate into mob rule.

China has an unrivalled history of centuries of sophisticated administration and now, in the last hundred years, has been able to develop a new form of democracy that fits both its unique culture and contemporary globalized economic conditions. At this moment, the rest of the world still does not have the language that expresses the novelty of the system of governance China is developing.

Through the geopolitical prism of the present, as the world prepares for a bipolar power structure, the West's preferred binary code to describe its relations with China is 'liberal' versus 'authoritarian'. 'Liberal', seen as positive, is intended to convey freedom from government control, 'authoritarian', with negative connotations, control by a central power. But this opposition reflects a failure to understand the trust and confidence Chinese people have in their leadership.

We might consider a more adequate binary description of West/China relations to be 'conflictual' versus 'consensual'. A sense of democracy as generating consensus corresponds with the most elementary idea of democracy that goes back to preliterate conditions when we lived in small communities. The men (almost always men!) would gather in a circle to debate and resolve issues that concerned the group as a whole. A collective will always hovered over the discussions, and often enough determined the outcome.

A view, a judgment or a decision arising from the discussion of a group of equals is the elementary understanding at the basis of democracy. Sometimes, but not always, that equality is carried through to the point of voting on an issue. Representation of the decision comes later and its type becomes critical once the size of the group expands beyond the local community.

In the modern nation–state, this primordial democracy so often is submerged because the important issues have become technical and require expert knowledge. The complexity of issues that arise for a state with a population in millions, even over a billion, demands far more than democracy. Often this is expressed as the rise of technocracy.

To be sure, the governance of a country under present conditions does require expertise which democracy cannot supply. But it also needs common understanding of priorities, shared values and a sense of belonging to the same national community. Having added technocracy to democracy, we also need a third element, which previously, only half in jest, I have called 'humanocracy'. The guardians of those necessary components of national solidarity are the third pillar of modern governance. In China's case this is the Communist Party.

* * *

The Party's role in China today is the antithesis of technocracy. It has the task of ensuring that the executive actions and technical procedures of the state correspond with the principles, values and policies that the Central Committee has announced and the People's congresses have endorsed over the years.

Thus it is the Party that provides the leadership for the people in the governance of China, even as it supervises the state's delivery of policies. It is continuously listening to popular opinion and monitoring the well-being of the people while providing the moral encouragement to work for common goals and values. The people are the life-blood of the nation, the state is the brain, but it is in the Party that the heart beats.

China now has a fully developed kind of democracy that is an alternative to all previous models. Its success in providing for the people has been proven in eliminating absolute poverty, delivering moderate prosperity and in exceeding the growth rates of all major countries over the last 40 years.

China has shown the rest of the world what socialism can achieve when aligned with the culture and specific conditions under which a nation works and lives. It demonstrates the vitality of consultative democracy, or consensus as opposed to conflict. In dealing with the contradictions and disputes that arise in any society, it promotes the expansion of law-based governance at every level.

But where does China go from here? It resolutely refuses to propose a model for other countries to follow, precisely because it knows how its system is embedded in its own historical and cultural experience. But I suggest that its contribution to the global system will be decisive in promoting a law-based democracy everywhere. The reason is to be found in the universal recognition of that elementary and primitive democracy that I mentioned above and which prevails in the meetings of the multilateral institutions where consultation among equals is the taken-for-granted basis for decisions.

China's commitment to the international system, to its regional groupings, multilateral and bilateral agreements, always under the auspices of an acceptance of law, is the strongest component yet of a drive towards global governance that will promote the idea of consultative democracy throughout the world. This will be a top-down democratic delivery of the global goals, the answer to today's global challenges of climate change and nuclear proliferation, of pandemics and digital communication standards.

This is where China finds common cause with the bottom-up demands of the world's social groups and the Western civil society activists who have long campaigned in vain for an adequate response from their own failing political systems. With China's lead, the world has the chance to bring democracy into the digital age and to tackle head-on the issues that have brought human existence on this planet into question.

3.9 The significance of China's social governance to the world[39]

Very warm greetings to all my fellow delegates from around the world. May I first thank the Initiators Council of the Belt and Road Studies Network for your invitation to come to Zhili and to be able to observe at close quarters, even if only

[39] Editor's note: These are the author's remarks at International Forum: The Significance of China's Social Governance to the World, at Zhili, Huzhou City, November 18, 2019. See: China shares wisdom of social governance with world, *Xinhua*, November 20, 2019, http://en.people.cn/n3/2019/1120/c90000-9633927.html.

briefly, the experience of one of the many extraordinary communities that have developed since China's opening up.

In such a context it is a great privilege and truly humbling to be invited to speak on social governance on this special occasion. For as experience is the true source of knowledge it is from you that we should be learning.

In your invitation you have asked me to speak in particular about two topics, first, how social governance may contribute to the development of a society and its people's welfare, and second, how President Xi's thoughts on social governance might help towards solving Europe's social tensions. I am grateful for your suggestions.

On social governance, let me make some preliminary remarks. First, all governance is social in the sense that it is about sustaining social order, creating a stable social environment in which people can go about their daily lives, work and plan their futures. But of course you have a special reason for emphasizing the social in governance.

Effectively you are distinguishing governance that government delivers nationally from what it provides for the people, and to which they contribute, in their own communities. In Britain we make the rather simplistic distinction between central and local government, but that serves unfortunately to push people's initiatives into a third sector or civil society, seen as distinct from government.

As I said in my speech at the launch of President Xi's first volume of speeches, the choice of *Governance of China* for the English title was inspired, because it conveys that more intimate connection between government and society that is the hallmark of Chinese culture from the earliest times.

This is very evident in the examples of community involvement in Zhili local government that you were kind enough to supply before our meeting. The Ping An Welfare Alliance is made up of volunteers but they are sustaining public services. The Veterans Station is directly involved in public safety. Incidentally they both seem to attend to fire safety. Perhaps they both go to the Wu Meili to resolve the dispute about who puts the fire out. No, I'm joking of course, but the example of the Ping An Big Sisters shows how dispute resolution has long been regarded in China as an area where people can and should sort things out for themselves.

Social governance in China is rooted in a centuries-old culture where government is integral to people's relationships with one another. The Confucian five fundamental relations, after all, included the Emperor.

Now let me turn to President Xi's thoughts on good governance and their possible relevance to Europe. For this purpose I refer to his speech to provincial level officials on February 17, 2004 on the resolutions passed at the Third Plenary Session of the 18th CPC Central Committee on continuing reform. He declared then that the Party must improve its 'capability for scientific, democratic and law-based governance' (English edition, *The Governance of China*, p. 116).

Let me expand very slightly on each of the key terms: 'scientific', truth from facts, evidence-based; 'democratic', in accord with the people's aspirations; 'law-based', relying on legitimate, enforceable rules. Those are my elaborations, very condensed, but not too brief, I hope, to convey a train of thought.

Governance today needs all those qualities, in particular because the modern world is one of ceaseless change and development. This arises out of the capabilities of people today as they seek to master extraordinary digital technologies. The consequences for society demand continual efforts to bring science, democracy and law together.

In China the Communist Party has built on a combination of Marxism and your ancient governance traditions to ensure that those three qualities are always in play, interacting with each other. Now let me conclude by trying to answer the second question you put, namely how Xi's thought can help European countries in their troubles today.

The direct answer is that the content of his messages cannot be lifted from China's culture and transferred to the West. There are many specific reasons for this apart from the general comment that cultures are unique. One reason is that, since the eighteenth century, European countries, and we might add the United States and English-speaking countries generally, have operated on strict separations between law making, government policy and democratic practices. Such separations arose out of battles, often violent between central authority and new classes, and they represent a historic settlement that now comes under great strain, to my mind, largely because of unrestrained financial capitalism.

In many countries those constitutional arrangements are now in pressing need of reform. Such reforms will not reproduce the Chinese system. They will be specific to each country, although the affinities between the representative systems suggest they may arrive at similar solutions to each other. But how do they find those solutions? Where President Xi's ideas are relevant to the West is in their demonstration of the practical uses of theory. No Western leader today exhibits the comprehensive intellectual scope of his thinking on governance. *The contemporary world requires leadership that commands ideas more than it commands people*. This is the kind of exemplary leadership that European countries today so sadly lack.

When we leave Zhili, I am sure we will take with us astonishment and admiration for the achievements of its people, both of older residents and newcomers from all over China. We will return, I believe, with our imaginations fired up. We will search for the ideas that might lead to similar results in our own countries. But they will probably differ from each other as much as do the languages we speak. For intellectual inspiration, however, I recommend reading *The Governance of China* in any language.

Thank you for listening. May I conclude by expressing my personal thanks to our hosts, and, I am sure, on behalf of all of us, immense gratitude to the people of Zhili.

3.10 Remarks on the CCP's 100th anniversary celebration[40]

We should look at the Chinese Communist Party, in relation not just to its success for China but also to its success in offering a novel form of governance for the world as a whole. It is an extraordinary experiment, I would suggest, in developing a form of government where the moral quality of the nation is employed to direct and restrain the economic and social forces which are continually being transformed in the present world. This is where it is so important.

The Chinese Communist Party has proved itself an adaptive, pragmatic and learning party because it has narrowed down on the task really of offering the world an alternative model of how you run a society as large as China, in the conditions of extraordinary technical transformation, which we now tend to summarize as a digital age.

The Chinese Communist Party seems to me to be the only example in the world of a party which keeps pace with this digital revolution and is continually monitoring it for the benefit of the people of China as a whole. This is an example it has given, and, while it is absolutely the case China has never wanted to impose its will on the world,

I think it's a model which we will find increasingly the rest of the world will seek to emulate. So may I congratulate the party on its performance in the past hundred years, and look forward towards what it is going to achieve over the next hundred, which will be there, I trust, for our children and grandchildren.

Thank you very much.

3.11 Remarks on the PRC's 72nd anniversary celebration[41]

A National Day is always special for a country's citizens, and it is a particular honour for this foreigner to be invited to join your celebrations. Thank you very much, Ambassador Zheng Zeguang, for your invitation to speak on this occasion. Just like your Moon Festival, this day reminds us that Chinese celebrations increasingly attract a worldwide following. The message of Home, Harmony, Health and Hope for good fortune in the future has a universal appeal. It also conveys to the world, as President Xi suggested on May 31, the thoughts and spirit behind the China story.

May I then take this opportunity to congratulate your Embassy's Cultural and Tourism team for the good use of the mid-autumn message, to make its meaning available to the general public in the UK and more widely, across so many fields of Chinese culture in the coming three months with its 'All Under One Moon' programme.

---

[40] Editor's note: This is an invited remarks made at the Chinese Embassy in the UK held a Symposium on the Centenary of the Founding of the Communist Party of China, London, June 22, 2021.

[41] Editor's note: These are remarks for the Online Reception given by the Chinese Embassy in London celebrating the 72nd Anniversary of the Founding of the People's Republic of China, September 28, 2021.

The programme was launched as a multi-media series of events making full use of up-to-the-minute digital resources and ranging from presenting cooking classes to exploring nature reserves, from commemorating the 1911 Revolution to poverty alleviation. It includes over 40 projects and we in Britain can be proud that so many involve this country's collaboration.

It is the announcement of the forthcoming documentary series on poverty alleviation, entitled 'A Long-Cherished Dream' that has a special interest for me. It is my privilege to be associated with a Chinese charity 'Visionary Education', which, under the inspiring leadership of Cecily Liu, brings highly qualified educators and children from the most impoverished parts of China together in intensive programmes of learning.

This in itself has been but one small stream flowing into the river of China's poverty alleviation policy, which has come into full flood this year with the announcement of the elimination of absolute poverty. This was the aim set by the Chinese Communist Party to be fulfilled as part of the first centenary, the one of building a moderately prosperous society a hundred years after the founding of the Party.

This National Day has come in a centenary year and carries therefore a message of optimism, not just for the 72nd year of the PRC, but for the coming century. Let me then express the hope that the celebrations of this year signal the beginning of a second century of the same kinds of achievement that the Party has inspired in China in the past.

Moreover, just as the message of Hope, Home, Harmony and Health extends far beyond the borders of China, may we express the wish that everyone should benefit from the efforts of the people of China to make a better world of a shared future for us all.

3.12 Comments on Tell China's Stories – a Collection of Speeches by Ambassador Liu Xiaoming [42]

During Ambassador Liu Xiaoming's 11-year tour of duty in the UK, which began in 2010, he delivered over 700 speeches. For his mission he coined the acronym IDEA to summarize its purposes: expanding common Interests; promoting Dialogue; Exploring cooperation; Accommodation in bilateral relations.

Tell China's Story contains just 41 gems from that extraordinary IDEA treasure trove. They were offered to the military, to young leaders, to business people and many more, and delivered in all the corners of the UK. They reflect the most positive aspects of China/UK relations in what he called its Golden Era.

Two aspects of his thinking contribute much more widely to our shared future than just to the UK and make his speeches worthy of attention by a worldwide readership. One is a continuing emphasis on the core ideas that China brings to

[42] These are comments invited for the book by Ambassador Liu Xiaoming in November 2021.

international order, cooperation, openness, harmony, rule-based governance. The other exposes fully the special features of China's culture that provide its unique selling points: Marxism with Chinese characteristics, the wisdom of Confucius and Sun Tzu, the century-old Communist Party.

Throughout, incidental remarks make the reader sit up and think. China has more neighbouring countries on its borders than any other state. China provides more UN peacekeepers than any other nation. Let us reflect on how those two facts might be connected. Then go back and read more of this remarkable collection of insights.

3.13 Dialogue with global thinkers: What's the Chinese contribution that the world needs today? by LIU Xin[43]

Prof. Albrow says China's 'great contribution' is to convert their value commitments into practically possible projects. 'The world needs Chinese pragmatism.' The views expressed in the video are his and do not necessarily represent those of CGTN.

Liu Xin: In terms of global ethics and providing inspiration to global ethics, what do you think the West cannot do? Or do you think that the West can also offer something in addition to what the Chinese ethics can offer?

Martin Albrow: I don't think there's any one agency that can do everything. All agencies in the world which have any influence can and must contribute. China is setting an example to the world currently in how to manage all those other agencies within their own country. Certainly, I think it's quite fascinating for the rest of the world at the moment how the Party is managing to bring the big financial forces under control and is implementing policies that will reduce the gross inequalities which can develop under strange capitalism. So, this is an example to the world. The Chinese system is one that tries to balance all those factors in order to produce a harmonious country. And it's those principles that can be extended to the world as a whole. But of course, China can't do this on its own. One of the important things for the world is not just that China sets an example, but that China must also try to exercise an influence. I would distinguish between example and influence. You can set an example and not do anything for the rest of the world. But you've both got to set an example and to exercise influence. And there are several ways I think China can do that.

[43] Editor's note: This dialogue was with Ms LIU Xin, CGTN senior host in the Global Thinkers programme. The video is entitled 'Global Thinkers – What's the Chinese contribution that the world needs today?' See: https://www.youtube.com/watch?v=zW-HisiSFWM&ab_channel=CGTN. The version with English and Chinese dual language texts has a different title 'The world needs the spirit of China's pragmatism' [Chinese version: 对话思想者：全球中国学术院创始荣誉院长——世界需要中国的务实精神, CGTN 2022-01-04 13:01. See: https://mp.weixin.qq.com/s/Vec84pKdo7Y6_vSaKrPTHg].

Liu Xin: One of your arguments is that maintaining a common shared value can also lead to higher tensions, for instance, China and the United States, two countries that both say they value democracy, human rights, equality and justice are actually in a standoff over the different perceptions of what they value in common. How do we deal with that? Is that the case?

Martin Albrow: Values ultimately are guidelines. They are visions, they look to the future. Now, how does one prevent values themselves from becoming so dominant in one's imagination that you don't lead, shall we say, a balanced life? I would suggest the Chinese have found the way very well because the Chinese are very pragmatic people. When it comes down to values they look always to what is practically possible. And one of the great, I think, contributions that the Chinese make always is when they get down to it, they convert their commitments to values into particular projects and goals, things that they can achieve. And from that point of view, what we need in the world is Chinese pragmatism, China is often thought of in the West as an ideologically-driven country. In actual fact, the West is far more ideologically-driven, in the sense of promoting values as such, than China is. China has a complex system of ideas. It's a system that combines traditional Chinese thought with modern Marxist thought and with modern science and putting them all together produces then a complex of ideas that are ultimately practical. You have to do practical things with the Chinese ideas. They're not just floating in the atmosphere.

3.14 Online greetings at the Online Chinese New Year Reception[44]

May I wish the people of China a wonderful and happy New Year.

Let the Year of the Tiger endow them with its strength and vitality.

Let it empower them to bring the rest of the world together and to inspire us all to overcome the global challenges of our time.

3.15 Xi Jinping in my eyes: his view on global governance is full of wisdom[45]

Narrator: Martin Albrow is a Fellow of the Academy of Social Sciences. Since the 1980s, he has visited China many times. He was one of the first scholars in the West to propose the concept of globalization. More than 20 years after the

[44] This is an online greeting invited by the Chinese Embassy at the Online Chinese New Year Reception in celebration of the Chinese New Year of the Tiger, on January 24, 2022.

[45] Editor's note: On March 13th, 1972, China and the UK signed the Joint Communiqué on an Exchange of Ambassadors to establish ambassadorial diplomatic relations. To mark the 50th anniversary of this significant event Xinhua New Agent published a piece entited 'Xi Jinping in my eyes' with a video on March 12, 2022 [Chinese version: 新华社国际部、中国新华新闻电视网，新华国际传播融合平台：我眼中的习近平：他的全球治理观充满智慧，2022年3月12日，新华社，见：https://xhpfmapi.xinhuaxmt.com/vh512/share/10654430?channel=weixin]. Thanks to YANG Xiaoqiang（杨晓强）who transcribed speeches by the author and translated the narration in English enabling this piece to be included in the book.

concept of globalization was proposed, the world pattern has undergone major changes. In 2013, Chinese President Xi Jinping proposed the Belt and Road Initiative. In April 2015, a promotional meeting of Xi Jinping's book *The Governance of China* was held in London, England, and Albrow was invited to give a speech at the event. The book allowed Albrow to find new perspectives with which to study China.

Albrow: I think it was probably a year or so before. I really focused on it. Obviously reading the speeches, you realized – wow, this is important.

Narrator: Afterwards Albrow studied the book very carefully. He believed that the book embodied Xi Jinping's leadership art, which was of great benefit to his research. He started a new research project on globalization and the Belt and Road Initiative in 2016, at the age 79. On April 10, 2018, his book *China's Role in a Shared Human Future: Towards Theory for Global Leadership* was launched at the London Book Fair. This book interprets the concept of community with a shared future for mankind advocated by President Xi Jinping. In Albrow's view, the Communist Party of China has great determination and perseverance. It is able to battle with unyielding determination and stay true to its original aspirations. The Party united and led the Chinese people with one heart and one mind, and strives for its goals.

Albrow: I would say one of the reasons for its success is its great determination; its unwillingness to accept defeat.

Narrator: At present, the epidemic of the century and the changes of the century are intertwined. Unilateralism, protectionism and bullying still jeopardize the sovereignty, security and development interests of all countries. Albrow visited China many times for inspections and academic exchanges, and highly agrees with China's views on globalization. He believes that China has a profound understanding and foresight regarding globalization and the common destiny of mankind. Chinese leaders have a very clear concept of globalization development, which benefits the world. He sees the Belt and Road Initiative as an example in line with the trend of economic globalization.

Albrow: We all live on the same earth, and the fate of the earth is common to us all. And in, this respect, China has a wonderful opportunity to take on leadership in respect of creating the shared future. This isn't leadership in a military sense. This is leadership in a moral and value sense, but also in a pragmatic sense. And here, the Chinese capacity to achieve goals is so important to demonstrate to the rest of the world how you can achieve things.

I do think that one of the most important ways of approaching contemporary global problems is to treat them in terms of projects and goals, and this is what One Belt One Road does. When you talk about a shared human future, you talk about the things that we can do together in the future, not a future where we're all the same.

PART II

Practical Themes

DOI https://doi.org/10.24103/GCSS6.en.2021.4

Chapter 4
The Belt and Road Initiative

Since the launch of the Belt and Road Initiative by President Xi Jinping in 2013 not a year has passed without debate about what it means. From one viewpoint it is simply an investment programme in communications that link countries to China. Seen differently, it demonstrates how the collective efforts of the Chinese people to bring prosperity for themselves can change the global balance of power. Beyond those positions we can explore multiple consequences the BRI has for the diverse sectors of life it touches.

4.1 Dialogue on the BRI with WANG Yiwei[1]

The Belt and Road Initiative (BRI) refers to the Silk Road Economic Belt and the 21st-Century Maritime Silk Road.

The BRI includes three key ideas, the first of which is ‘The 21st century’. The BRI is first and foremost an integrated and interconnected transport network of railways, highways, air and sea routes, oil pipelines, power transmission lines and communication networks. The core word is ‘connectivity’, in which all things and all humans are connected – vividly representing the unique features of the 21st century.

The second key idea is the word ‘belt’, referring to the economic corridors and economic development belts– reflecting the experience and model of China’s reform and opening-up endeavours. The building of the Silk Road Economic Belt was designed to promote the development of all areas involved by gradually expanding growth and carrying out greater regional cooperation.

The word ‘road’ has a broader meaning. It plays the role of ‘the Way’ in the Chinese classic *Tao Te Ching*, which believes that the Way creates everything we know in the world. The Way in today’s world requires us to build a community with a shared future for humankind. The BRI is open and inclusive so that everyone can make contributions and share the benefits.

The China-proposed Belt and Road Initiative refers to the Silk Road Economic Belt that links China with Europe through central and western Asia, and the 21st-Century Maritime Silk Road connecting China with Southeast Asia, Africa, and Europe. Since the initiative was proposed six years ago, it has been the

[1] Editor’s notes: 1) The original title of this section was ‘Dialogue on the Belt and Road Initiative in celebration of the 70th birthday of the People’s Republic of China: 10 Questions about BRI with Martin Albrow and Wang Yiwei’, in the *Dialogue on China*, published by Renmin University of China, 2019, pp. 75–102. [Chinese version: 编写组：王义桅与马丁·阿尔布劳: 中华人民共和国成立70周年之际关于“一带一路”倡议的对话，《对话中国》，北京：中国人民大学出版社, 2019年]. 2) The Belt and Road Portal is at: https://eng.yidaiyilu.gov.cn.

popular means for the transfer of public goods and for building a community with a shared future for humankind – a platform for international cooperation to push forward inclusive globalization. It received a very positive response from all over the world.

However, questions still remain following its implementation. The following 10 are representative of some of the more important queries.

4.1.1 Does the BRI degrade the environment?

Albrow: Bringing the preservation of the natural environment into the debate provides critics with unlimited freedom to raise objections to BRI. For all economic development takes the gifts that nature provides and converts them into products for human use. This has been the case ever since the first apple was plucked from the tree of wisdom.

Human relations with nature are symbiotic. Still more, they are integral to it. The apples we pick today are from orchards and varieties of tree, hybridization is generally understood: that would never have existed without human intervention. We human beings are agents in the evolution of the environment on which we depend – and with which we struggle. No one should imagine it is automatically benign – cyclones, earthquakes and mortal disease are also natural.

The issue then is one of balance. A sainted figure of the environmental movement, American Henry Thoreau, famously retreated to the forest to find himself, but simultaneously applauded the railway that brought products from every corner of the globe and gave him the sense of being a citizen of the world. He admired the opportunities for work that new railways brought to neighbourhoods and the increased pace of life that they encouraged. He was an early prophet of connectivity and the stimulus it provides for personal exploration. It is an intuition shared by every tourist agency that advertises the beauty and isolation of the tropical island while advertising cheap air fares.

Finding the balance between economic development and environmental protection depends on the scale on which they are assessed. China is criticized for helping countries to build new coal-burning power stations, but it can rightly point to its own global leadership in solar energy applications. In doing so, it is adding together the impacts of its domestic energy policies and its foreign economic activity to assess their overall carbon emissions neutrality in a global balance sheet. It is the very globality of human-induced climate change that requires the largest carbon emitters to assess the total impact of their energy policies on a global scale. In this respect, China is taking the lead and the world has to hope it can bring others along with it.

Wang: As Confucius said, 'If one wishes to stand on one's own feet, one must help others to stand on their own feet; if one wishes to succeed, one must help others to succeed.' Every country has its own development needs and China's Belt and Road Initiative aims to help other countries achieve the goals set down by the

United Nation's 2030 Agenda for Sustainable Development. For instance, 70% of world poverty alleviation has been attributed by China. In today's world, 1,100 million people are without electric power (350 million in India). The Chinese trinity comparative advantage of 'Smart Grid + UHV + Clean Energy' helps to bring energy to them while cutting carbon emission. This is what president Xi put forward at the UN General Assembly in 2015: 'The Global Energy Interconnection Plan' (http://www.geidco.org/):

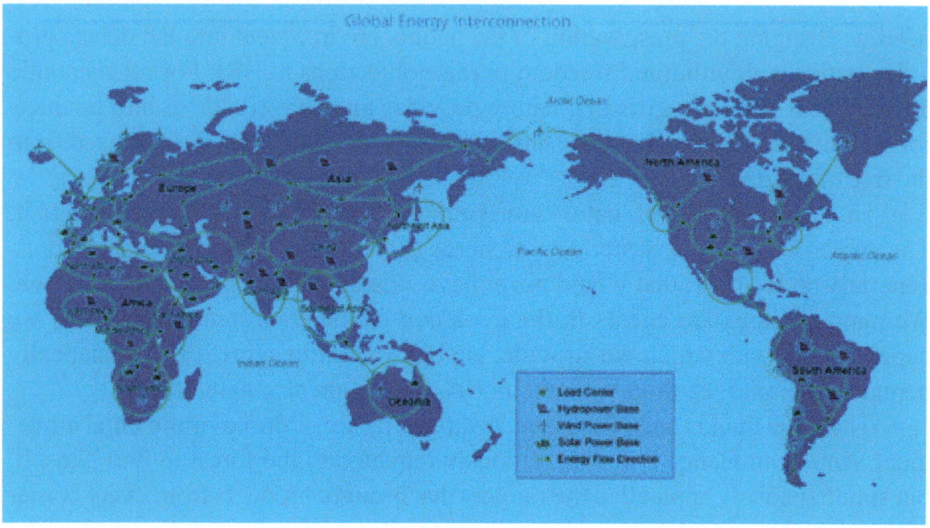

Map courtesy of http://www.geidco.org

In fact, green development is a very important objective for China. On May 2, 2019, China officially launched the International Coalition for Green Development on the Belt and Road Initiative, which could serve as an international platform for Chinese and leading foreign agencies to work closely together to conduct research and make policy recommendations on key issues as well as facilitate an international dialogue.

A NASA report shows that a quarter of the Earth's vegetated lands have shown significant greening over the last 35 years, thanks to China's contribution. China shares its experience with other BRI countries and has also made clear its commitment to incorporate green strategies into the BRI by releasing the Guidelines on Promoting Green Belt and Road and the Belt and Road Ecological Cooperation Plan. These documents outline a vision for sustainability.

4.1.2 Is the BRI a new form of debt imperialism?

Albrow: William Shakespeare has the wise old royal official in the play Hamlet say, 'Neither a borrower nor a lender be; for loan oft loses both itself and friend.' Indeed, the West has never been wholeheartedly capitalist, if one regards credit and debt to be inherent in capitalism. In the Christian story, Jesus threw the moneylenders out of the temple.

Thomas Piketty, whose vast tome Capital in the Twenty-First Century is held by some to bear comparison with its forerunner by Karl Marx, goes as far as to say that in all civilizations there has been a hostile reaction to the idea that owners of capital can earn a return on it without working themselves. Yet he points further to the failure of Soviet-style experiments in eliminating private ownership of capital as demonstrating the usefulness of markets in 'coordinating the actions of millions of individuals'[2].

The whole experience of Chinese reform and opening up has been one of learning how to control capital markets for the greatest social benefit. There is a profound recognition that capital represents a store of value that can be put to use for future benefits and it is the way those benefits are distributed that determines social stability. Piketty points to the advantage China has compared with European countries in being able to determine how to control capital.[3]

Recognition of the fundamental nature of capital and its control is essential to avoid the kind of crude moralism involved in the rejection of debt. For debtors and creditors are in a social relation where each has a commitment to the other and both have confidence in the future benefits of investment to both the borrower and the lender.

There is then no moral superiority on one side over the other. We have seen the trouble caused in the European Union by the assumption by one side, in this case German citizens, that the people of Greece are in some way morally corrupt because of their difficulty in managing their national debt. Those who lend to others earn interest, and if their investment proves unsound they have themselves as much to blame as the other side.

All this is relevant to the accusation that China, by investing in the infrastructure of other countries, lending them money to build railways or taking part-ownership of ports, is in some way building an empire. The answer to that is that the BRI depends on country-to-country deals on the assumption of equal responsibility and knowledge of their own interests. This is the basis of win–win calculations.

None of these considerations excludes the possibility of exploitative relations of the kind that Marx analysed, where one side owns the capital and the other nothing but labour power. But in the current world system of international relations, recognition of state sovereignty is the guarantee that country-to-country relations can be conducted on the basis of equality.

The risks of economic imperialism are enhanced when multilateral institutions operate outside national control and impose conditions on debtor countries that limit their independence and legitimacy for their own citizens. This has been illustrated dramatically in the treatment of Southeast Asia by the International Monetary Fund in the 1990s.

---

[2] Thomas Piketty (2014), *Capital in the Twenty-First Century*, Cambridge, MA: Belknap, pp. 531–532 [Chinese edition: (法) 托马斯·皮凯蒂：《21世纪资本论》，北京：中信出版社 2014年].

[3] Ibid., p. 536.

The reforms of the global financial system since the crisis of 2008 have done little to reduce the risks of future crises arising in part from the failure to recognize the moral equivalence of lending and borrowing. So long as it is not accepted that bad debts are inevitable features of working for future returns that can never be guaranteed, not something that deserves punishment, then risk will be inadequately factored into public policy and irrational scapegoating of the victims of misfortune will result.

The BRI in this respect is like any investment, as dependent on the debtor countries to deliver and as vulnerable to their failure. Indeed, more than that, the very connectivity that is such a benefit for all the countries involved in the BRI is itself dependent on all. The failure of any link in the chain can bring traffic to a halt. In the past, British imperialism often led to complaints of 'the white man's burden', a way of refusing to acknowledge the benefits of empire. China welcomes win–win, but it must also factor in a burden, the risk of lose–lose. As Piketty says, China has many advantages when it comes to managing capital. The rest of the world will rely on China for the success of the BRI.

Wang: 'Give a man a fish and he eats for one day. Teach a man how to fish and he can eat forever.' It's a common saying and underpins much of the Western foreign aid budget. 'Give a man a chicken and he has a choice. He can make chicken soup, or he can save the chicken, collect the eggs, raise more chickens, have more eggs and also have chicken soup.' It's a very different way of thinking because it emphasizes the way a skill or product or asset is used. It comes from a Chinese proverb and in many ways is a good description of the philosophy underpinning the BRI.

The BRI is not only about infrastructure per se but also about the impact of infrastructure and the way it enables economic growth and independence. In other words, the BRI is paving the way to paying back the debts that came into being in the past, not creating a debt trap.

'If you want to get rich, build the road; if you want to get rich quickly, build the motor road; if you want to get rich immediately, build the Internet road; if you want to get rich jointly, build the road that connects with China.' Such a slogan has encouraged many developing countries to join the BRI.

China has officially acknowledged the rising criticism about the so-called 'debt trap' for some participating countries, and has designed related institutions to avoid financial risk. On April 25, 2019, the Ministry of Finance of the People's Republic of China published the Debt Sustainability Framework for Participating Countries of the Belt and Road Initiative, which encourages China and related countries to use this framework as an important reference for lending decisions to conduct debt sustainability analysis and manage debt risks according to the risk rating results. It is a remarkable fact that this framework, a non-mandatory policy tool, can also serve as a supporting policy tool for the Multilateral Cooperation Center for Development Finance for usage on a voluntary basis.

The procedures of the Debt Sustainability Analysis (DSA) include the following steps: (i) debt coverage, (ii) macroeconomic projections, (iii) realism tools, (iv) country classification and debt carrying capacity, (v) stress tests, (vi) risk signals, (vii) the use of judgment, (viii) the final risk ratings, and (ix) the DSA write-up.

The DSA write-up contains the following: (i) public debt coverage, (ii) background on debt, (iii) background on macro forecasts, (iv) country classification, (v) determination of scenario stress tests, (vi) external DSA, (vii) overall risk of public debt distress, (viii) application of judgment, (ix) final risk ratings, (x) authorities' views, and (xi) tables and charts.

The DSA write-up for applicable countries may be compiled annually. With comprehensive assessment of the country's future development potential, debt-carrying capacity, debt sustainability, the 2030 Agenda for Sustainable Development and other common development agendas, the DSA results can serve as an important reference for the financial institutions of China and other BRI countries to conduct categorized management of debt risks and make rational lending decisions.

4.1.3 Can the BRI be transparent?

Albrow: Ever since the crises in the global economy of the 1990s, the introduction of greater transparency in economic policy has been hailed as a key contribution to avoiding their repetition. Crises recur nonetheless, notably in 2008, and the demand for more transparency rises every time.

In the face of this apparent paradox, the suspicion might arise that transparency provides fuel for crises rather than dampening them. It is not as simple as that but it is instructive to examine the dynamic processes involved. It is axiomatic that economic decision making by agents of all kinds, individuals, companies or governments, is improved when they have greater knowledge of market conditions, of their customers and of their competitors. They also need to know and rely on the enforcement of the regulations that govern economic activity.

The International Monetary Fund, in which China became a founding member in 1945 and in which it has been strengthening its position in the 40 years since opening up, has been the main guardian of the international economic order. Through enforcement of its principles for loans to struggling economies, it has been a key player in economic globalization. In its own words: 'The IMF has policies in place to ensure meaningful and accurate information – both about its own role in the global economy and the economies of its member countries – is provided in real time to its global audiences.[4]'

The problem in market economies is that it is always an advantage to have more knowledge about the policies and plans of others than they have of you. It is one thing to have the level playing field where everyone knows the common rules

[4] IMF *Factsheet.* March 20, 2019.

that govern it, but quite another to share with the other players your plan to win the advantage in the game. Moreover, this is respected in all kinds of rules and conventions about commercial confidentiality, official secrets, intellectual property, patents and individual rights to privacy.

Relationships between individuals, businesses and governments involve the management of an intricate set of balances between transparency and secrecy that is changing all the time. New forms of ownership and investment are continually created to avoid rules governing existing forms of credit within national economies. Another key area where economic agents seek to elude the constraints of transparency is by operating outside the boundaries of their nation–state. This in turn has been a main factor in economic globalization, the quest for profit beyond borders and the escape from national taxation. In the globalized economy, governments are equally rational agents using sovereign wealth funds to advantage overseas.

In two main respects, the BRI will be challenged on transparency. The first is China's acknowledged policy of keeping close connections between the state and business. Socialism with Chinese characteristics therefore supports distinct forms of corporate governance. The second is that the size of China's vast sovereign wealth with the autonomy it gains from state ownership gives it an advantage in competition with foreign investors.

The BRI will have to develop adequate responses to these challenges if it is to become an integral part of the global economy. There are precedents. The BRI is a hybrid of the bilateral, country–country agreements, and the multilateral, countries bonded by shared infrastructure and facilities. Major multilateral institutions such as the OECD and the IMF have developed multilateral surveillance for their members.

But perhaps the closest example of agreement to share information between countries is that of the European Union in its Treaty of Lisbon in 2000, when member states undertook to share goals with guidelines and timetables for achieving them, to adopt indicators of best practice, adopt policies from one another and monitor results. The BRI will need to develop similar kinds of surveillance if it is to retain the confidence of its partners and the esteem of the wider international community.

Wang: From bilateral to multilateral cooperation, the BRI takes transparency as the natural goal of high-quality demand, making sure it is more transparent to the international community.

Speaking at the forum on April 26, 2019, Chinese president Xi Jinping promised to ensure transparency and the 'fiscal sustainability' of all projects. 'Everything should be done in a transparent way and we should have zero tolerance for corruption,' he said.

There is no single dominant party, but instead equal participants; no operations under the table, but openness and transparency; no 'winner takes all' scenario, but mutual benefits and a win–win situation. China wanted to set up a mechanism under which countries involved in projects were bound by international accords and standards. Some countries, for example, think that because China is so rich they should squeeze every penny they can out of it. To combat this way of thinking, Beijing needs to work with developed countries in third-party markets, as it is doing with Switzerland, on assessment, supervision and arbitration in project construction and design.

4.1.4 Is the BRI just a geopolitical strategy?

Albrow: It is very easy for critics in the West to point to the BRI and dismiss it as simply a strategy for consolidating China's position as a global power. Since, in the United States at least, that is one of the main reasons to be anxious about the BRI, especially since its own status as the sole and unchallengeable super power has been declining for some years, it is worth taking the criticism seriously.

The fact is that China's geopolitical power has increased and will keep on increasing but that is not the main purpose of the BRI as I understand it from all its stated intentions and the projects it has already completed. The interests of the Chinese people are of course paramount. It would not make sense to anyone inside or outside China otherwise.

will bring with the immediate neighbourhood and further with the wider world. Additionally there will be the benefit of creating peaceful exchanges with other cultures and the enhancement of mutual understanding. There is no interest as far as an observer can discern in creating a power bloc or an international political movement, since the linkages binding countries cover every kind of ideological difference and often are with ones where there have been tense relations in the past.

Paradoxically, the projection of Chinese harmony into foreign policy itself creates suspicion in the West, where so-called realist theories of international politics retain an intellectual hold on strategic analysis. Moreover, from a realist point of view, if harmony increases Chinese power, if those countries in the BRI are brought into constructive cooperation with China, then harmony itself must be treated as a weapon in the hands of a potentially hostile power!

Fortunately, realist views are not the only ones that count in the foreign policies of Western powers. 'Divide and rule' may be one such strategy but that very often only achieves half its objective, namely it succeeds in dividing but fails to rule. China needs to recognize that the pluralism of Western political systems always allows for alternative views about China, as well as for internal strife and indecision about the direction of national policies. Brexit is a prime example in the United Kingdom, and a heated debate about China and the role of Huawei accompanies it, partly as a result.

China then needs to reach out to those views in the West that can recognize a common human interest in peace and cooperation and do not view harmony as a threat. They do exist. Those working with peace and reconciliation strategies have had notable successes in contexts as different as South Africa, Northern Ireland and the Balkans, while of course the European Union itself is an ongoing project to bring harmony between nations.

In none of these cases can one say the work of bringing peace is complete. But then no end is in sight either for the greater project of creating a shared human future. This is an ongoing task that we hope to pass to later generations for an indefinite time to come. The BRI is a step along a road that has no end.

Wang: With the goal to build a community with a shared future, the BRI's theme of mutual connectivity aims to embrace peace, security and prosperity globally, while at the same time being confronted with some serious challenges. The misinterpretation of the BRI stems from a wide range of reasons – especially that the BRI reflects Chinese He-he（和合）culture going beyond the Western divide. The BRI is a geo-economy and a geo-civilization rather than a geo-political strategy.

Many observers have mistaken the BRI as a counter to the US Indo-Pacific Strategy because they follow a Cold War mentality. The BRI does not limit joint construction only to the countries along the Silk Road route; it also includes other relevant countries. Projects might be located in countries along the route, but the standards, rules, funds, technology and talent are global. US companies, American citizens and the US dollar have already participated in the BRI construction in large numbers, while the Asian Infrastructure Investment Bank (AIIB) uses US dollars. The United States is thus a BRI-related country and a de facto participant. Owing to its international status and commitments, the United States functions as a neighbour of all countries in the world. China's wisdom means it will not and cannot exclude the United States. The BRI is China's overall strategy based on openness – promoting the transformation of the prevailing economic development model to encourage aspiring new global markets to achieve globalization, from partial globalization to inclusive globalization.

4.1.5 Does the BRI neglect the social responsibility that belongs to development projects?

Albrow: The BRI produces another paradox for the West, about the Chinese idea of social responsibility. 'Socialism with Chinese characteristics' is understood largely through two long-established stereotypes. There is the widespread view that Communism is a system where all individual behaviour is controlled to realize the goals of the wider society. Although the Chinese Communist Party aims only to develop a socialist society, this reinforces an even longer-held view of China as a culture where the maintenance of social ties takes precedence over individual aspirations.

The paradox then arises when Chinese people move to other countries. For there their sense of obligation to their compatriots can tend to exclude building ties with their hosts. Chinese enclaves then develop, often with resulting tensions with surrounding communities. In the past with earlier development projects, Chinese workers have come and gone leaving nothing but the results of their labour.

All of that, one might say, is understandable and no different from relations between foreign workers and host peoples anywhere. But then the accusation arises that Chinese development projects are irresponsible in failing to respond to the wider needs of the communities where their work has been based.

From the Chinese side this has been difficult to understand. In China today it is taken for granted that communities, especially those belonging to the 56 recognized minority ethnic groups, will exercise a great deal of autonomous responsibility for each other. Equally, the responsibility of enterprises for their workers has been assumed, in the past, as an almost total commitment to their welfare. Social responsibility then is not a controversial issue. It is taken for granted.

It is different in the West. The history of capitalism there has made the corporate entity entirely responsible to the shareholders and not to the wider society. Social responsibility then is controversial, high profile in political debate about corporate power, extending too to the activities of transnational corporations. Tragic and scandalous consequences of events like the Union Carbide explosion in Bhopal in India in 1984, generally considered the world's worst industrial disaster, have brought the responsibility of corporations operating abroad into lasting focus.

Put these two factors together, the Western sense of particularly strong Chinese social solidarity together with the controversial status of social responsibility in the West's dominant capitalist ethos, and you will find that the BRI will face intense scrutiny in respect of its impact on the communities where it is based. To some degree you can expect the West's own unease about social responsibility to be displaced and projected onto China – it eases the conscience!

As with all such phenomena that are basically aspects of collective psychology, all that China can do is to demonstrate particular concern for the localities involved in the BRI by offering, for instance, assistance in building community facilities, like hospitals, stadiums and homes for the elderly. In this respect, China indeed has the advantage of a long tradition of caring for the old. Deeds will count for more than words.

Wang: Do not hire local workers? The local working salary is only one-third less than China. Why not hire local workers? It takes time to train them. Chinese companies are learning to cater to social responsibilities – for instance, build hospitals, schools and provide public goods around the ports they are building. There are more and more social functions and services appearing in the industrial parks.

According to an industry report co-published by the State-owned Assets Supervision and Administration Commission of the State Council and the Chinese Academy of Social Sciences, over 90% of central SOEs prioritize training in local legal systems for their staff. About 74% of central SOEs impart training in local environmental protection, and 68% of central SOEs have initiated other measures to strengthen their staff's awareness of energy-saving measures, emission reduction and protection of ecological habitats.

For example, Power Construction Corp of China, or Power China, is one of the central SOEs that has made great efforts in strengthening relationships with local communities. The group has helped renovate local churches, schools, roads and many other infrastructural facilities in Karuma of Uganda, where it has set up a hydropower plant.

4.1.6 Does the BRI simply reinforce corrupt regimes?

Albrow: It is not always easy to decide that corruption is worse when it is in the news or when it is out of it. Media amplification of a political decision to mount a drive against corruption will always raise public awareness and thus a feeling that corruption is on the increase. It can even result in what Western sociologists have called a moral panic, when concern for a problem is quite disproportionate to any increase in its incidence.

In this respect, China's drive against corruption makes it a key talking point in Western commentary on the BRI. This is especially pronounced when, as is often the case, the agreement to proceed with a BRI project is with a regime that is highly personalized and under the control of a leader with a close circle of advisers.

There are several points to make about corruption concerns with the BRI. The first is that autocratic regimes are not necessarily corrupt, if by that is meant bribery of the ruler and his supporters. Indeed the fewer people at the top, the fewer who are available to bribe.

Second, systems of dispersed power are not faultless in this respect. For instance, the British parliament was rocked by a scandal in 2009 when newspapers revealed widespread false claims by its members for expenses. Western democracies can create so many checks and balances that bribery is the only way to get something done.

A third point is that the very connectedness of the BRI means that each agreement with another country must adopt similar principles, since disparity between countries in close relations with each other would create lasting dissatisfaction and attempts to reopen agreements.

Fourth, the BRI is hybrid in nature, bilateral in that there are country-to-country agreements, multilateral in the sense that the connectedness between countries requires overall administration. The result is a very strong incentive to maintain maximum transparency to avoid disputes and challenges about unequal treatment.

Fifth, the financing of the BRI will involve multiple parties, of course China, the AIIB and national and international funding bodies in the partnering countries. There are too many eyes focussed on the same project for there to be anything less than the maximum transparency.

None of this is to say there will be no problems with attempts to leverage advantage from the key position that any country holds as a link in the chain.

The very dependency of each on all, the fact that any point along the road can potentially threaten to disrupt the whole line of communication, makes the BRI dependent on all-round goodwill and fair treatment. There is a premium on good behaviour on all sides. Far from the BRI promoting corruption, it may be the best method yet devised for spreading good practice in development projects.

Wang: According to the Beijing Initiative for the Clean Silk Road released at the Thematic Forum on Clean Silk Road of the Second Belt and Road Forum for International Cooperation, on April 27, 2019, 'We propose countries involved in the BRI strengthen oversight over various cooperation programmes according to laws and regulations and strictly follow laws and regulations in bidding, construction, operation, and management of the projects, to leave no room for corruption and create a regulated and law-governed business environment.'

According to The Belt and Road Initiative Progress, Contributions, and Prospects released on April 22, 2019, all countries should encourage their enterprises to strengthen self-discipline, establish rule-based managerial systems, foster an enterprise culture that values integrity, monitor corruption risks and oppose commercial bribery.

4.1.7 Isn't the BRI just another exercise in neo-colonialism?

Albrow: Neo-colonialism has been a favourite accusation from left-wing critics, among them Jean-Paul Sartre and Noam Chomsky within Western countries, for practices that include using trade, aid, political education, technical support, health and cultural campaigns to boost a developing country's dependency on the donor state.

Old colonialism relied on stationing troops and officials within a territory to oversee local political structures, sometimes establishing communities of expatriates and in effect creating a dependent state, even to the extent of annexing it to the colonizing country. Neo-colonialism means control at a distance, the ability to draw revenues and to enforce compliance with political demands from a territory without occupying it or making any claims to rule it.

Leaders of countries that have freed themselves from the control by colonial powers since 1945 have frequently invoked neo-colonialism and charged their previous occupiers with maintaining covert control or subverting the new regimes. This has been especially the case in Africa, where, compared with Asia or Latin America, regimes have had little experience of statehood except as colonies. The PRC has then been particularly successful in displacing the old colonial masters in the public policies of the new states and has become the largest trading partner with Africa since 2009.

This success in Africa for China's overseas relations has not exempted it from the accusation of neo-colonialism, but, as is the case with transparency, the extremely divisive and hotly contested nature of the West's involvement in its former colonies diverts attention away from China. Western left-wing critics still focus on former colonial countries and right-wing critics have little credibility in what appears as an attempt to draw attention away from their domestic debate in their own country.

China, of course, through its century of humiliation, has bitter experience of what old-style colonialism meant and has, through its own efforts, avoided newer forms of colonialism. At the same time, its own historical experience gives it the depth of perspective needed to get behind the rhetoric and identify exploitation when it occurs. The size, scope and multilateral nature of BRI, the sheer number of equal partnering countries should provide additional protection against neo-colonialism.

The methods of the Bretton Woods international financial institutions that operate on a country-by-country basis allow for very different forms of foreign involvement in each, and in this respect make them vulnerable to practices that exploit local conditions or are open to corruption. If China was open to accusations of neo-colonialism in Africa, certainly the way the BRI is developing would appear to exempt it from any serious criticism on that score.

Wang: The World Bank Report Belt and Road Economics: Opportunities and Risks of Transport Corridors released in April 2019 says that BRI transport projects could contribute to lifting 7.6 million people from extreme poverty (less than PPP$1.90 a day) and 32 million people from moderate poverty (less than PPP$3.20 a day), mostly in corridor economies.

This is a clear denial of the accusation that the BRI is a new form of colonization. To help African countries become regional hubs for trade, finance and transport, the BRI makes industrialization the key to decolonization. For instance, compared with the metre-size narrow railway built by the British empire, with a speed of only 40–50 km/h, sending materials to Europe, the Mombasa–Nairobi railway is the first African standard-size high-speed rail (120 km/h), carrying both passengers and cargo, which contributes 2.5% economic growth for Kenya. All eastern African countries can benefit from access to the sea.

China has helped Africa in its industrialization and what has been achieved in a dozen years has outnumbered the results of Western colonization of hundreds of years. In addition to sharing the experience of realizing modernization through industrialization and building networks of high-speed railways, expressway, and regional airlines, China has also engaged in projects for improving African people's well-being.

The West believes that China has adopted the BRI to export the Chinese model – this is a big misunderstanding. The Chinese model can also be called the Chinese development model. It consists of a combination of problem-oriented and goal-oriented focuses, and its core ideology is to have an effective government plus an efficient market, thus using both the invisible hand and the visible hand to create and cultivate the market. In the end, the market plays the decisive role. This provides a new choice for countries that have not fully developed their market economy and creates new options to solve issues that the West's preferred free market model cannot or will not solve, such as market failures, dislocations and distortions. For example, you must first build roads before you get rich. However, developing countries have no funds to build roads and are unable to get financing from the international market, which means they cannot achieve industrialization. It is a vicious circle. To achieve a win–win outcome, China provides financing for development through asset-based mortgages and the construction of development zones, and it helps with road-building; at the same time, Chinese enterprises set up long-term operations in these countries. This is the common practice of the BRI. If market rules are so effective, why do 1.1 billion people in the world lack electricity? Since reform and the opening up, China has lifted 700 million people out of poverty, representing over 70% of the contribution to the United Nations Millennium Development Goals for global poverty alleviation, undeniably proving that the Chinese programme is effective. Getting rid of poverty, becoming better off and eliminating the gap between rich and poor in coastal and inland areas alike, as well as achieving the 2030 UN Sustainable Development Goals – these are the BRI's highest priorities.

4.1.8 Is the BRI just the Chinese version of the Marshall Plan?

Albrow: There appears to be a mainly Asian-, if not Chinese-inspired criticism of BRI based on a number of shaky premises. There is a widespread misunderstanding of what the Marshall Plan was. It was a hastily prepared American expedient to deal with the fast-developing stand-off between the Soviet Union and the Western allies in Europe.

It was set in motion by President Truman in April 1948, was directed to European powers (as well as Turkey) that had fought against Germany in the Second World War and who remained outside Soviet control. But one of the main recipients of around $13 billion over the following four years of aid was West Germany, the part that was occupied by American, British and French forces.

The idea behind what was officially called The European Recovery Programme was to safeguard the commitment of the countries that remained outside Soviet control to the system of Western representative democracy and to guarantee their social stability by assisting in the rebuilding of their economies after a devastating war. But the political aim was paramount and the plan is only intelligible in the context of the emerging confrontation between Soviet communism and Western powers who developed rapidly coalescing security interests around the North Atlantic Treaty Organisation (NATO), established a year later as a military alliance that survives to this day. Effectively, this is the core of what is known as the West today.

The general verdict on the Marshall Plan today is that it was successful in its aims and set Western Europe off in a direction which has culminated in the European Union (EU). NATO has remained as a distinct military alliance under

American leadership while the EU has not succeeded in developing a distinct defence function, even though this has been the aspiration of those leaders who have wanted to reduce dependency on the United States.

Parallels drawn between the BRI and the Marshall Plan are very misleading. For a start, the countries concerned in the latter were in a small corner of the Eurasian continent and were effectively the front line of an epic confrontation between capitalism and Soviet communism. Their economic recovery was promoted to secure them and the United States from the advance of the Soviets. It was an adversarial contest between two great powers, each with its subject states.

The BRI is not part of a contest between two rival blocs. It is as open to Italy as it is to Russia, to Myanmar as it is to Bangladesh. There are no inherent limits to its guiding principle of connectivity and world peace and prosperity, overarching aims that place no restrictions on its territorial extent or length of time it survives.

The true comparators with the BRI are the development programmes of the Western powers in the second half of the 20th century that went under names like 'modernization'. These have largely been conducted under the auspices of institutions set up in 1944 as the World Bank Group and spearheaded by the International Bank for Reconstruction and Development (the 'World Bank') and the International Development Association.

These institutions, today counting 189 member states, including China, have been the effective thought leaders and co-ordinators for development programmes worldwide. Along with the United Nations Development Programme and national programmes, there is an immense interlocking network of development projects with a cosmopolitan body of professional workers that is in effect a single global programme.

The main distinctive output with which the BRI needs to be compared is the Sustainable Development Goals (SDGs) of the 2030 Agenda for Sustainable Development. This is the true comparator for the scale and scope of the BRI, rather than the Marshall Plan conceived in what in effect were the local interests of one of the powers in a great power contest.

The comparison with the SDGs is far more instructive. They, like the great majority of development programmes, rely on nation–states as the operational base and the reporting units. The BRI has member states signed up to it and its success will be measured in infrastructural connectivity, trade and cultural exchange. As such, it challenges the world to think in terms of relationships and not in terms of the rank ordering of nation–states.

Wang: No. It is investment, not foreign aid. It is for mutual connectivity, not divide and rule. It is economic cooperation, not an ideological game. People in the West do not understand the BRI and lack proper historical perspective, as they simply compare it to Western examples such as the Marshal Plan.

There are three major differences:

- The Marshall Plan was a foreign aid strategy, while the BRI is an investment plan.
- The Marshall Plan was to export US overcapacity and standards to Europe, while the BRI seeks international capacity cooperation.
- The Marshall Plan was a geo-political strategy to divide Europe, while the BRI is a geo-economy meant to connect the world.

China is working to address the issue of excessive production capacity through peaceful cooperation, not through war – as Japan and Germany did during the Second World War. China has learned with great success from the models of Japan's official development aid (ODA) and Singapore's industrial parks.

Seek cooperation, while addressing obstacles. These struggles are for solidarity, not for engaging in the war of words or venting anger. It has to be emphasized that the BRI will accelerate the navigation of global capital to infrastructure and real economy so that available money can be harnessed and put into effective use, and so that blind investment will be turned into result-oriented investment.

By aiding the recovery of Europe's economy, the Marshall Plan turned Europe into an important tool in America's confrontation with the Soviet Union. The plan also enabled the United States to control and occupy European markets. The Marshall Plan came with stringent political conditions, and all pro-Soviet countries in Europe were excluded. The United States even set criteria and rules for its allies' participation in the plan, leaving aid-receiving countries with no choice but to fully comply. We can say that the Marshall Plan shouldered the strategic mission of stabilizing Europe with a view to confronting the Soviet Union.

The Belt and Road Initiative, on the other hand, is essentially a platform for cooperation among the participating countries. Considered as a public good that China is providing to the international community, the BRI emphasizes the principles of mutual consultation, joint development and shared benefits; advocates a new set of rules for international relations; and proposes a 21st-century model for regional cooperation. Founded on the basis of mutually beneficial cooperation, the Belt and Road Initiative calls on the countries involved to engage in equal and friendly economic and cultural exchanges in order to realize common development.

In a special period of history following the Second World War, the Marshall Plan played a role in stabilizing the situation in Europe and restoring the European economy, but its motive of paving the way for US hegemony was clear. The Cold War is now long behind us. China's BRI has abandoned the Cold War mentality and the zero-sum mindset of the past. Responding to the new trends of peace, development, cooperation and mutual benefit, it transcends the Marshall Plan in terms of both its content and significance. Thus, there is no historical or factual basis to support the claim that the BRI is China's Marshall Plan.

4.1.9 Rules or goals in the development process?

Albrow: There is a deep historically based assumption in the West that goals are the product of individuals and rules are set by governments. It is closely associated with what is widely understood to be Western individualism.

In practice, however, the situation from early in the 20th century has been different in a complex way. With the development of corporate capitalism, increasingly goals have been set by large organizations, up to and including the state, and rules have developed out of associations of individuals, professions and processes that cross the boundaries of organizations and states.

The most prominent example of the contemporary way of generating new regulations is the International Organization for Standardization (ISO), whose work was made obligatory in the Uruguay Round trade negotiations that ended in 1994 for all members of the World Trade Organization (WTO). WTO members are countries, but the ISO excludes states and is basically a centrally coordinated network of technical committees of experts.[5] Similar composition is found in bodies like the International Accounting Standards Board (IASB) or the Internet Corporation for Assigned Names and Numbers (ICANN).

These rule-generating and -administering bodies arise in the global economy out of the needs of goal-seeking agents to have predictable and widely accepted standards in dealing with other parties. Those others might be individuals, corporations or countries, or anything between. For the sake of pursuing their interests, countries then are often conceding limitations on their sovereignty to experts.

The legitimacy of the rule-making then derives not from the legislative authority of a single state but from multiple stakeholders' acceptance of the knowledge and expertise available to an independent rule-making body. The rules follow the goal-seeking and not the other way round.

It is in relation to these fundamental considerations of rule-making processes and goal-directed activity that we should aim to understand the special place the BRI holds in economic development. In the operation of the international financial institutions, held to be at the heart of what is generally called global governance, the requirement to follow rules is prior to the setting of objectives. The so-called Washington Consensus advocated by those institutions in the 1990s required states applying for loans to follow a precise set of prescriptions before they were considered eligible for support.

Even where goals become part of the shared understandings of the international community, as in the Sustainable Development Goals (SDGS), it is initial rules that define the goal that govern the activity to achieve it. In the BRI, rules are generally accepted technical standards independent of the goals and the sharing of goals sets up new rules among partners to a joint project.

---

[5] For an in-depth discussion of the processes of global private rule-making see Tim Büthe and Walter Mattli (2011), *The New Global Rulers: the Privatization of Regulation in the World Economy*, Princeton: Princeton University Press.

Just like the original Silk Road, the BRI is a journey of discovery, where the cooperation of partners in a new project produces new understandings, novel rules, procedures and products. No template is being imposed from above and the only requirement is a willingness to work together for common objectives that can only be achieved through cooperation. By comparison, the SDGs envisage the autonomous efforts of individual states to meet pre-defined targets. This is the contest, on the one hand, competitive behaviour characteristic of Western neo-liberalism, and, on the other hand, the BRI's alternative cooperative goal seeking, old wisdom put to new ends, ready to challenge the assumptions that underpin Western capitalist models of development.

Wang: Of course it is rule-based. But whose rules? We need to coordinate different rules to match the local conditions of the host countries. Development is the key to solving all other problems. But for sustainable development, we need to build of all, build by all and build for all.

The BRI emphasizes enterprises as the mainstay, along with market operations, government services and adherence to international standards. So, why do Westerners feel that the BRI consists solely of Chinese government projects? This is due to the national conditions of the countries along the initial route of the BRI and the specificity of the infrastructure construction itself. Among the 65 countries along the BRI's six major economic corridors, eight of them are least-developed countries, 16 are not WTO members and the Human Development Index of 24 of them is well below the world average. How can high-standard market principles like those advocated by the European Union be applied to all? That would be like a race between a child and a professional runner – in this light, such demands seem disconnected from reality.

China maintains that development is the key to solving all problems. Rules are of course important, but they should go through a process of gradual formation and continuous maturation. The state-guided economic development model explored by China's market reforms provides a complement to the development shortages of countries along the BRI. The initial boon is to bring infrastructure construction to these nations. By 'taking the eggs and not killing the chickens,' their ability to develop independently will be enhanced. At the same time, the BRI will help cultivate new markets. China's reform and opening up was piloted first in coastal areas and then later in inland areas so that cities could serve as economic hubs to drive the reform and opening up of China as a whole. Now, to get rid of poverty altogether, the BRI wants to grow the African market through building interconnected infrastructure (ports, cities, railways, roads, trade routes, etc.), so that Africa can gain its own development momentum, form economic development zones and realize industrialization and agricultural modernization. Relying solely on the market is like throwing a child into the sea – we can all imagine the result. Through development zones, China prefers letting children learn to swim in a pool before jumping into the sea. This is the BRI way.

4.1.10 Is the Chinese way of doing things different?

The differences between BRI and Western models of development are examples of what at the extremes are fundamental contrasts in the general outlook on life and the place of human beings in the world. They are differences that have long prompted reflections by scholars who recognise that such contrasts between cultures point to deeper insights than can be achieved by remaining within any one single culture.

A classic account of Chinese culture from a Western point of view by one of the great intellectual figures at the beginning of the twentieth century, Max Weber insisted that traditional faith in ritual and magic stood in the way of capitalism originating in the East, but allowed for its enthusiastic welcome when once established in the West.

With a century of further experience of East/West relations behind us and with the expertise of Western sinologists we can reach more sophisticated understanding. The French scholar François Jullien has pointed to the exploratory rationality of the Chinese way, the *dao*, where action seeks the best outcomes in an ongoing endeavour rather than the constraints of a pre-given goal.[6] This is rationality but not of a pre-set ends-means kind.

Goal-seeking in the Chinese way is precisely that, the seeking of desirable outcomes with the determination to realise values and human potential, and always under specific conditions. The Chinese way responds to situations not as impediments and interferences with a set course of action but as guides to future courses of action, suggesting change and opportunities. In economic terms it is the importance of revealed preferences. In philosophy it is the kind of pragmatism which John Dewey, its famed American champion, was delighted to find so prominent in Chinese thought.

These contrasts with the West are exhibited in a range of basic Chinese concepts. *Li* for instance covers what for the West is both law and appropriate behaviour, *xin* brings what in the West are almost opposite, 'heart' and 'mind', emotion and rationality, together in the motives for action.

It would be mistaken to assert that these differences of outlook represent unbridgeable divides between cultures. There is as much to bring cultures together as there is to separate them, as the history of cultural exchange demonstrates. But it is one distinctive cultural characteristic that BRI brings into play, with its emphasis on connectivity and the potential for growth, that makes it a whole new venture in development and marks a sharp contrast with the flat world image that distorts Western ideas of globalization. The rest of the world should welcome the distinctiveness of this new development paradigm and be grateful for the cultural diversity that makes it possible.

---

[6] François Jullien (2004), *A Treatise on Efficacy, Between Western and Chinese Thinking*. Honolulu: University of Hawaii Press, Honolulu [Chinese edition: (法）弗朗索瓦·朱利安：《功效——在中国与西方思维之间》，林志明译，北京：北京大学出版社，2013年].

4.2 The prospects of the Belt and Road Initiative in the post-pandemic era: A dialogue in the Guangming International Forum[7]

China's achievements in fighting COVID-19 should be attributed to the characteristics of China's national governance.

Xu: After the COVID-19 pandemic broke out all across the world, China actively participated in the international community's anti-pandemic cooperation. While actively cooperating with the World Health Organization, China has provided medical supplies and assistance to many countries, sent medical teams, held bilateral and multilateral video meetings for sharing treatment experience and proposed to strengthen cooperation for international public health and safety. China calls on improving global governance and continuously promotes global governance improvement by practical actions, which is compatible with the common interest of the international community.

Albrow: With reform and opening up, the People's Republic of China has followed a path of steadily increasing its participation in international institutions. For example, China fully supported the United Nations in its peacekeeping activities to the extent that it now has more peacekeepers on the ground than any other country. Over the years, China has attached great importance to global governance during the process of actively involving it in the globalization. Multilateralism has been a core principle of global governance

Xu: In the 1990s, you completed *The Global Age: State and Society beyond Modernity*, which established your pioneering position in research on globalization.

Albrow: The world is transiting from the modern era to the global era. Modernity is being replaced by globality, resulting in a decentralized phenomenon in various fields such as countries, governments, cultures and communities. Therefore, it is necessary to rebuild the relevant systems and theories. Neither modernists nor postmodernists have realized that a new era has come in discussing globalization. It would be more appropriate to replace globalization with 'global era' to name the current historical changes. A new theoretical framework is needed to understand the epoch-making historical changes, and this book is an attempt to understand issues from the perspective of a new theoretical framework.

Xu: China has been a facilitator in the process of globalization, which is based on the cornerstone of multilateralism rather than a single country. Both China and the international community have been deepening their understanding on globalization, and benefiting the world with the outcomes of globalization. However, a mo-

7 马丁·阿尔布劳、徐宝峰：后疫情时代，"一带一路"倡议的前景会更好' ——光明国际论坛对话，《光明日报》，2020年05月27日15版，见：https://news.gmw.cn/2020-05/27/content_33862928.htm [In the post-pandemic era, the Belt and Road Initiative will see a brighter prospect, A dialogue with Xu Baofeng. *Guangming Daily*, 27 May 2020].

mentum of deglobalization emerged in recent years. In particular, the COVID-19 pandemic has intensified the questioning on globalization. How do you explain the problems arising from the prospect of globalization?

Albrow: Multilateralism has been a core principle of global governance. The pandemic spread across the world has highlighted the inadequacy of global governance. Multilateralism and globalization are still the primary trend in the post-pandemic era, and only international cooperation could solve the global problems and create a shared future for mankind, because no country can tackle global challenges individually. Of course, globalization also faces new situations and needs to be upgraded.

Xu: China's Belt and Road Initiative is consistent with its position to uphold globalization and multilateralism. How do you evaluate the prospect of the BRI in the post-pandemic era?

Albrow: The BRI began with President Xi's speech in Kazakhstan in September 2013, and now China has signed related cooperation documents with 138 countries and 30 international organizations. Sometime people think that the BRI is bracketed with those multilateral institutions. In my view, that is a mistake that leads to a failure to appreciate the fundamental difference between an inclusive development strategy and a rule-based service organization.

Multilateral institutions are membership-based and provide frameworks both for specific kinds of collective action and also rules and regulations that govern the behaviour of the members in pursuing their own interests. Such a definition covers bodies as diverse as the IMF, ASEAN, OPEC and the European Union. They may or may not have development as part of their aims, but they all depend on officials who are dedicated to the institution rather than to their own country. The United Nations is of course the greatest multilateral institution of them all.

Multilateral institutions in the eyes of Western populist politicians attract even greater criticism than those of their own countries, which is due to the close relationship between multilateral institutions and global economic order, the latter enabling cross-border free trade by companies. It could be said that multilateral institutions support economic globalization, therefore intensifying populism's hostility towards multilateralism.

The BRI is an inclusive development strategy, whose vitality has been shown. It matches the needs of contemporary times, allowing partners to put differences to one side in joining for agreed mutual benefit. It overrides utopian visions of a world where all have to understand each other in order to work together. It represents instead an outlook I prefer to call pragmatic universalism, where all preserve their distinctive cherished values while contributing to the common good.

Global governance from the perspective of pragmatic universalism ceases to be a framework of institutions but more a network of multiple projects dedicated to securing the future of human beings on this earth. In the post-pandemic era, the BRI will see a better future.

Xu: China has always adhered to the idea of common development of all countries in the world, and the Chinese government neither exports certain doctrines nor changes others' domestic ideology. China's development path is deeply rooted in its own culture, and China's reform dividend and development achievements can be shared globally.

Albrow: China is developing and fulfilling an approach to global governance that diverges from the orthodox Western views and opens up new possibilities for international cooperation. Up to now, China makes no ideological requirements in its cooperation with countries all over the world. Indeed, arguably Western countries that are as diverse politically as Greece, Italy and Poland, who have already signed memoranda of understanding with China, are inspired by the same pragmatic outlook that drives the BRI.

In respect of national governance, however, the response to China is far more ideologically driven. This is understandable because in Western eyes the social and political order of China is determined by the position of the Communist Party and that leaves no option but to oppose its ideas for national governance.

The fact that China adopts not only ancient Western ideas like governance, democracy and justice but also the modern language of values, responsibility and integrity is a huge challenge to the West. China has long made communism in its own image, and socialism with Chinese characteristics has its roots in Chinese culture. As I have pointed out in my book China's Role in a Shared Human Future: Towards Theory for Global Governance, it is the sophistication of the theoretical ideas, drawing on the Chinese classics as well as on Marxism and Western political economy, which underpins the governance of China as Xi has expounded it.

They challenge the West to respond in a similarly sophisticated way. Instead, it resorts to slogans, about autocracy, dictatorship and authoritarianism, only some of the milder insults that are the daily language of the Western media. Social governance in the new Chinese sense takes us beyond the old vocabulary of liberal democracy, and should not be simply compared with the Western representative democracy. In the current global era we live in, the governance of China should be viewed as a completely new governance approach.

4.3 The meaning of Belt and Road for global governance[8]

On the 23rd March this year, President Xi came to Rome to witness the signing of agreements between Italy and China covering multiple sectors of the economy, including energy, agriculture and finance, as well as the ports of Trieste

[8] Editor's notes: 1) this was a speech at the 2nd Belt and Road Forum for International Cooperation. Beijing. April 24/25, 2019. 2) It has been translated into Chinese as the Preface of the Special edition 'BRI and international communication' of *Chang'an Communication Studies*, vol. 2, Xi'an: Shanxi Normal University Press, 2022 [Chinese version: 马丁·阿尔布劳：一带一路对全球治理的意义，"一带一路与国际传播"专栏，代序言，《长安传媒研究》，第二辑，西安：陕西师范大学出版社，2022年].

and Genoa. Of greater symbolic significance was the signing of a memorandum of intent that made Italy a member of the BRI.

Italy was the prime destination for the ancient Silk Road trade and from there Chinese products and culture circulated through the West, with their origin often unrecognized. The prophet of the new age of science, Lord Francis Bacon, wrote in 1620 that printing, gunpowder and magnetism had 'changed the whole face and state of things throughout the world', nothing had 'exerted greater power and influence in human affairs'. Yet, their 'origin, though recent is obscure and inglorious'.

A hundred years later and all that had changed, with praise being heaped on China, though not for inventions, but for the scale and grandeur of its imperial rule. Reactions to China in the West continue to oscillate wildly, but now almost simultaneously, rather than with a lapse of a century from one extreme to the other.

The BBC reported concern about the Italian agreement among European allies and the United States, with critics pointing to 'a bold bid for geopolitical and strategic influence', even as a US National Security Council spokesman had called the BRI a vanity project. It is kinder perhaps to speak of Western ambivalence towards the BRI rather than of incoherence, but the lack of understanding is palpable.

Among the many reasons for this Western failure to appreciate the positive nature of the BRI, I would single out one. It is seen as threatening and misplaced because it departs from many of the assumptions that underpin dominant views of global governance.

In scale and scope it has a global profile, rivalling any development programme of national or intergovernmental funding agencies. Around a third of the world's countries are involved. Huge, yes, but making no claims to universality. It is non-prescriptive and offers only the shared benefits of win–win deals. It is based on government-to-government agreements and not on free market principles. In other words, this is a unique formation, emphasized by the branding 'Belt and Road', expressing the special history of China's relations with the rest of the world. There is nothing else like it! It can tell us a lot, but only if we know about China.

Imagine if the Washington Consensus had been named 'The Gold Rush', evoking America's Wild West, and we would have been bound to consider its unique and very real nature, rather than seeing it as the outcome of the iron laws of the economy. The banality of naming agreements by a place name is probably why Beijing Consensus has never caught on.

Though it has ongoing global impact, the BRI is not global governance as commonly understood, namely as a set of rules and institutions with the aim of establishing order between nations and thus realizing universal human values. It does not deny global governance, but its relation to it is much more nuanced and indirect than simply being a subsidiary agent for it.

I think this is worth emphasizing in the context of the shared human future for which President Xi is such an eloquent advocate. When we share something in common, we rely on each recognizing the other's interest in it and expect that each will contribute to its maintenance. A shared human future stipulates the dependency by each on all, and all working for each.

The BRI is a step in that direction, or rather a multiplicity of steps as each partner makes agreements with others to build the links in the chains of connections it projects into the future and trades and communicates along the routes that have already been built. The resulting interconnectedness facilitates the experience of diversity and the enjoyment of products across the boundaries of countries and regions.

All depends on mutual interest in and understanding of the technologies needed to build the infrastructure. Shared goals underpin the BRI and these are neutral in respect of the values of the partner countries. A road is a road, whether it is used for a pilgrimage, a march or the way to work. Of course, those varied uses may well require regulations that prevent them from interfering with one another, but the rules come after the use.

The progress of the BRI will be measured by the increases in traffic of all kinds along its routes and the value that is added to the economies of the countries involved. Those are outcomes everyone expects. But I want to point to the consequences beyond those results in the exemplary character of its fundamental assumptions about international cooperation for the shared human future.

There are today global challenges in the shape of global warming, nuclear insecurity and the control of the internet and artificial intelligence that require the same kind of understanding and cooperation that the BRI depends on and promotes. To meet those challenges we need deals beyond boundaries, the pooling of knowledge, sharing of technologies and a common understanding of the requirements for action.

These imply practical projects to which those of vastly different values and world outlooks can subscribe and indeed need to support if they wish to pursue their own very different values in harmony with one another. The shared future will depend on such projects and the Belt and Road Initiative is only one step, but a very important one along the way to realizing it.

DOI https://doi.org/10.24103/UCW5.en.2021.5

Chapter 5
Lifting Chinese people out of poverty

The story of lifting people out of poverty forms an integral part of the rejuvenation of Chinese society. It is not then a special set of measures imposed as a development programme by outside experts. It is the consequence of the socialist expansion of the productive forces, drawing on the distinctive heritage of China and its unique human and natural resources. Xi Jinping's early leadership in rural areas exemplifies that spirit when those who go forward do so by bringing up those from the back.

5.1 Beyond poverty: a review of *Up and Out of Poverty*[1]

The title of this book could equally have been *Beyond Poverty*, since it puts poverty in its place, not as the issue that overrides all others, but as the one that will be best addressed by attending to the overall improvement of people's lives in a developing economy. It is an entry point into a programme that extends all the way from forestry practices to handling people's petitions, to the place of ethnic minorities and to the historical mission of the Communist Party.

The book contains speeches and articles covering the short period of just over 18 months when Xi was responsible for the prefecture in Fujian province, from November 1989 to July 1991. The messages he conveyed were entirely consistent with and anticipated the later policies and programmes he has promoted and described as China's top leader in the three volumes of his *Governance of China.*

These are the speeches of Xi as a young official, his youth made more vivid by the series of photographs at the beginning of the book, showing Xi at Party meetings, visiting factories and meeting ethnic minority villagers. He looked then considerably younger than his 37 years, but the speeches that follow showed it was an old head on young shoulders.

In fact he was a young man following a path clearly set out by Deng and Mao, on a journey continued too by wise heads around him. The Foreword to the book was written by Xiang Nan, who died in his 80th year in 1997 after a lifetime of service to Fujian Province. He wrote how, in 1988, Xi's 'four grassroots initiatives' were an inspiration for the departments in Ningde Prefecture. They called on officials to listen to the grassroots, both ideas and complaints, to work locally, to engage with them in research and in promoting the Party's ideas. When Xiang

[1] This is book review of Xi Jinping's, *Up and Out of Poverty* (2016), Beijing: Foreign Languages Press [Chinese edition: 习近平：《摆脱贫困》，福州：福建人民出版社，1992年].

visited his old haunts in his later years as chief consultant of the China Foundation for Poverty Alleviation, he could testify to the continuing influence of Xi's work.

This emphasis on the people was reflected in November 1989 when Xi applauded the work of people's congresses in Ningde Prefecture. We can find a direct line from that emphasis to the speech he made nearly 40 years later in his Report to the 19th National Congress of the CP when he emphasized the leading role of the congresses in lawmaking (The Governance of China, 2020, Vol. 3: 39–40). This book, then, is an entry point and at the same time points the way ahead.

The relief of poverty has now become an output of the four-pronged comprehensive strategy Xi outlined in 2015, and not just of the first prong, the creation of a moderately prosperous society in all respects, but also of the other prongs, reform, rule of law and Party discipline. It would not succeed without these other features of the strategy. For instance, 'Correctly handling the relationship between "breaking down" and "building up" in promoting intellectual and cultural progress' is integral to the whole strategy and Xi was emphasizing this as early as 1989 (p. 158), demonstrating that it went hand in hand with material progress, backing this up with illustrations from the second century BC Sima Qian, Biographies of Guan and Yan.

Already in these early speeches we find the trademark Xi use of literary sources, reflecting both the popular wisdom of age-old sayings and the insight of contemporary writers. He quotes 'fish leaping' and 'birds soaring' from a Tang dynasty Buddhist monk to inspire the farmer as easily as he refers to 'the extended hand will be caught' from the Marxist poet Chen Yi as a warning to greedy officials.

The underlying reason why the speeches also pointed the way ahead is that they were carried forward by the momentum given to Chinese society by Mao and Deng in mobilizing the historic economic, social and cultural capital of its people. Their comprehensive vision meant that those who were given the responsibility for leading its implementation had also to be closely in touch with local conditions, and this is what Xi's work and thought at the time illustrated.

Socialism with Chinese characteristics consequently becomes 'socialism with Ningde characteristics', given 'the unique geographical locations and specific economic development conditions of impoverished areas mean that development and change in those places can only be a gradual process' (p. 14, 'The Basic Proficiency of Officials — Maintaining Close Ties with the People', January 1989). The specific conditions in Ningde meant forests above all. They covered 65.2% of the whole prefecture and Xi directed his attention to them in a speech, 'Forests Are the Key to Ningde's Revitalization' (p. 116). This meant more attention to planting than logging, resolving the dilemmas of ancestral rights versus ownership of buildings, linking clearance to food production and generally creating the virtuous circles of development that favourable ecological conditions made possible. And fiscal revenues would increase.

While it is beyond the scope of this review to provide a precise estimation of Xi's personal contribution to the development of Ningde, it is now 35th out of 130 cities in the 2017 ranking of China's Integrated City Index and has an overall population of 3,393,698, of whom 25% are She minority people. In Xi's time, he spoke of a population of 2.7 million with over 100,000 She people, so their numbers now may well reflect the success of his championing of She commodity trading.

There are lessons for the West in a set of speeches dedicated to the people and Party officials of one small area of China 30 years ago. In the capitalist economies of Western nations there are many ways in which poverty is often regarded as a regrettable but inevitable accompaniment of economic success. It is argued that innovation and the need for new skills will necessarily leave some people behind.

Fiscal responsibility supposedly limits the scope for public support for those on low incomes. More radical thinkers are more Marxist than Marx in accepting a 'reserve army' of unemployed who keep wages down. Others point to rising average living standards and treat poverty as a relative concept rather than one that points to real material deprivation.

The Chinese example shows that these arguments are specific to the ideological capture of the levers of a capitalist economy by corporate controllers and owners of the vast proportion of its wealth. There is another way. It begins with the grassroots and integrates their needs with the organizational imperatives of a state that cares for all its people. Elsewhere I have called it 'humanocracy'. Whatever the name, China is showing that it can be done.

5.2 Preface to *Overseas Experts on China's Poverty Alleviation*[2]

The world is only just absorbing its astonishment at the speed and thoroughness of China's response to COVID-19. That has all happened within a calendar year. Soon it will have to cope with another lesson from China, its success in a much more protracted and deep-seated challenge, the conquest of poverty.

---

[2] Editor's notes: (1) In: *Overseas Experts on China's Poverty Alleviation* (in Chinese–English) (2021), by Stephan Petermann, et al. (Eds.), Egelsbach: Flieder-Verlag GmbH, in collaboration with CNPIEC (China National Publications Import & Export Co.), pp. 4–10. (2) A video speech was delivered at the 2021 Beijing International Publishing Forum, at the Beijing International Book Fair, August 23, 2021: 'Well, first I would like to say I welcome very much this opportunity to speak at an event, which is bringing Chinese books to the world. China has been exemplary in the last 50 years [...] in dealing with its own domestic economy and raising people out of poverty, and it never ceases to introduce measures which will help people get out of poverty. Of course, its famous one child policy originally was designed for that purpose, and now, finally, China has decided it served its purpose. There are many measures it has undertaken, which have the purpose of dealing with the problems as they are at the moment of time they occur. So the Chinese policy on poverty reduction has always been highly pragmatic. Even its household registration system, for instance, was designed to ensure that local people actually did sustain their relationships with their locality and the result is a great success. Thank you very much for listening to me today.'

By the end of 2020, according to the measurement standards set by the World Bank, China will have eliminated poverty in its population. In 1978, when the country began its reform and opening up, there were 700 million people in poverty. In less than half a century, an ever-intensifying succession of measures culminates in this moment of triumph, in the achievement of a 'moderately prosperous society in all respects'.

Back in 2016 I wrote that contemporary China is 'the most powerful collective human agency the world has ever seen'. Many assumptions lie behind the statement, about consensus, mobilization, aspiration and as well as about capability. Beyond those factors we might look at it relative to past achievements. If we do, then China's conquest of poverty must rate with the most celebrated, with the Great Wall or with the Pyramids of ancient Egypt, as a new wonder of the world.

This book is an appropriate tribute from the rest of the world, from foreign experts who can appreciate the context and scope of China's achievement and can see it from the perspective of their own cultures. They come from different continents, Asia, Africa, Latin America and Europe, bringing together their own diverse personal expertise and engagement with China to provide what the rest of world so greatly needs, an understanding of its poverty alleviation programmes with any lessons that may be applicable elsewhere.

The reports and reflections of the experts in this book are the outcome of close attention to the specific features of Chinese history and culture that go a long way to explain the appropriateness of its socialist system for today's conditions. Mohammed Khalil from Morocco has been a participant in China's period of reform from its beginning in 1978 when he began his medical studies in Beijing, and he has observed what foreign observers so often miss, the pragmatic approach, 'truth from facts' and attention to local conditions. All of these factors were key aspects of President Xi's early experience in Fujian Province and underpinned the targeted poverty alleviation programme he announced in 2013.

These emphases are a long way from the assumptions that so often underlie Western approaches to China. When Jeffrey Sachs published his acclaimed The *End of Poverty: How We Can Make it Happen in Our Lifetime* in 2005 (Penguin Books), he predicted that China would be first among the big poor countries of the twentieth century to end poverty in the twenty-first. So far, so good. But then he linked its future to Western-style institutional reforms. They didn't happen. So, in his book published this year, *The Ages of Globalization*, he mentions China's achievement of essentially zero extreme poverty as 'an economic miracle by any standard'. No mention of socialism with Chinese characteristics!

But direct observation of poverty alleviation at the village level will impress the open-minded investigator with the extraordinary commitment of local people to collectivist goals that have been set for the whole of China and adapted to local conditions. This is what Norbert Medina found in his visit to Donghan village in Xi'an Hu District with the development of the New Socialist Countryside, with agriculture, small manufacturing and tourism combining to raise incomes. He also found the same success in a Muslim quarter of Xi'an.

The book contains an important statement of the theoretical implications of the Chinese achievement for the rest of the world in Yuri Tavrovsky's chapter. Interestingly, when he lectures to Russian audiences on the success of China's poverty reductions, he tells us that their reaction is the same as in Sachs's comment quoted above – it must be a miracle. So much have they been persuaded of Western economic wisdom! But then he goes on to disclose the secret of the 'miracle'.

Tavrovsky, Director of the Centre 'Russian Dream and Chinese Dream', points to the Communist Party as the agency that resolves the contradictions between market and government. Poverty alleviation in the Deng Xiaoping reform and opening-up era changed Confucius' xiaokang, 'society of small prosperity', to 'a society of average prosperity', In turn, that was replaced by Xi's comprehensive well-off society and the China Dream. Tavrovsky writes: 'For the first time in the CCP strategy neither ideology nor economy but human society was given priority.'

The centrality of the Party for a strategy that brings the whole society into focus is also endorsed by Kim Seung Il of South Korea, who sees it gives China a unique national organizational system and institutional advantage that cannot be copied elsewhere. In particular, an 'elite' legion of leading officials is dedicated to implementing the poverty alleviation strategy.

But at the same time Kim points to distinctions that take us beyond the success of China's policies to date by suggesting that their very success introduces the problems of 'relative poverty', the growing gap between the top and bottom of income distribution that calls for attention to the values of society. He proposes that in this respect attention can usefully be directed to the Korean Saemaeul Undong, or the New Village Movement, which South Korea launched in the 1970s and which emphasizes the spiritual elements in life.

Saemaeul Undong was a government-led programme for village development emphasizing cooperation and values, raising both civic awareness and patriotism. Kim acknowledges that ethical values, such as those Mencius advanced long ago, have been incorporated into China's socialist values but implies that sufficient emphasis is lacking. What is intriguing his how far his proposal actually can address directly the problem of growing inequality that moderate prosperity has brought.

What Kim proposes does lead us directly into a sophisticated discussion by the authors of the next paper, Antonia Finnane and An Dongli, of the range of concepts that have been proposed to cover the cultural and social correlates of poverty that are experienced at a personal level.

Inequality, exclusion, social disqualification, disaffiliation, vulnerability are all concepts that are advanced to capture experience in the context of specific configurations of social relations. All of these have very different causes and consequences in Asia cultures where kin obligations are so extensive and strongly upheld compared with Western possessive individualism.

Kazakh researchers Aliya Anipina and Ardak Kaliolla provide an overview of the sheer diversity of policy initiatives that China's pragmatic approach has generated, which has also extended to the benefit of other countries. As they write: 'Over 70 years, China has transferred 400 billion yuan to 170 countries and international organizations to eradicate poverty, sent more than 600,000 people as humanitarian personnel and built about 5,000 humanitarian facilities. Thanks to China's efforts, 12 million specialists have been trained in developing countries. These figures speak volumes about China's mission for its own people and as a responsible world power.'

Global figures speak volumes, and yet, in the end, each one of us experiences the world in a unique way. Therefore it is entirely appropriate that the culmination of the volume is of the special insight gained through exploring how the countryside is changing beyond recognition.

Since 2017, Dutch design consultant Stephan Petermann has been a key collaborator with the world-famous architect Rem Koolhaas (appropriately, since he designed the CCTV headquarters building in Beijing) and with colleagues at the Beijing Central Academy of Fine Arts Visual Arts Innovation Center in a research project about the future of the Chinese countryside that figures in the 'Countryside, the future', an exhibition at the Solomon R. Guggenheim Museum in New York, which opened on February 20, 2020.

Through this experience, Petermann has been led to speculate on the role of the countryside in this global stage of development. Anticipating the national declaration of the end of poverty by the end of 2020, he travelled to three very different Chinese villages to explore the possibilities they had for making their own future.

Dazhai village in Shanxi was famous in Mao's time for a farmer–leader Chen Yonggui and a group of villagers who created new agricultural lands from a bleak terrain. But the land turned out to be too difficult to maintain and the legend of Chen is now only maintained by a larger-than-life statue in a village reoriented to tourism. Liuzhuang in Henan, on the other hand, remains as a model village, an example of agricultural and infrastructure development that Chinese leaders make a point of visiting. Yubulu in Guizhou is a tiny village, the target for rejuvenation that preserves old crafts but also, and perhaps consequently, caters for urbanites' growing desires for relaxing experiences in the 'real' countryside. It 'comes close to this mythic idea,' says Petermann.

There are no conclusions, the future course is not determined and that really is a diverting and entirely appropriate note on which this book concludes. After arriving at the moderately prosperous society, the Chinese future remains open for its people to shape.

5.3. Preface to *Levelling the Mountain-high Gap: Lessons from China's Leading Rural Educators*[3]

Levelling the Mountain-high Gap: Lessons from China's Leading Rural Educators has been included in the 'Understanding China and the World' book series and is to be published by Global Century Press (GCP). This is a book about Chinese socialist education in practice. The English edition should be required reading for Westerners with open minds and a global perspective who are keen to understand China in this field.

The whole world is the source of educational knowledge. In this book you will find references to the deaf–blind Helen Keller, to Jean-Jacques Rousseau, inspirer of the French Revolution and proponent of child-centred education, to the Ukrainian humanistic educator Vasily Sukhomlinsky, and to three Americans: philosopher John Dewey; Alex Osborn, theorist of creativity; and Lyman Bryson, educational broadcaster.

2020 was the year when China declared its victory over absolute poverty. The accounts in this book were written by the agents of a programme lasting 13 years that was conceived as a key contribution to that eventual success. We should congratulate every one of those dedicated educators who took part and equally the far-sighted leaders of voluntary action whose vision they turned into reality.

In this book, the 59 stories of principals of Chinese schools in rural areas contain every aspect of how socialism with Chinese characteristics works. They tell of education, with special concern for the poor rural areas, but the same message can be heard in every sector of society: sharing in a collective vision, trust in leadership, pursuit of excellence, respect for difference, help for the needy, generosity from the fortunate, eagerness to innovate, readiness to learn and joy in accomplishment.

Such an abstract list, read in isolation, can easily squeeze the life out of the unique experience of the individual teachers who took part in the programme. Each of their accounts is a fascinating story of how the pursuit of those values involves a unique individual struggle in circumstances that will never be exactly repeated, but which joined together contributes to a collective wisdom from which all can learn. Every one of them tells us something different.

The boarding school for primary pupils in Qinghai Province brings parents to the children in order to educate the parents. This is 'home–school co-education'. Teachers, parents, children sit down together to eat. Their green food and the administration of the restaurant testify to the care of the Party and government.

---

[3] Editor's note: This Preface was invited for the English edition of a Chinese book *Levelling the Mountain-high Gap: Lessons from China's Leading Rural Educators,* edited by Visionary Education at the China Association for NGO Cooperation (CANGO), published by China Economic Publishing House in 2020. The English edition is translated by DU Yichao, published by Global Century Press, London, 2022 (see 8.2.5) [Chinese editions: 中国国际民间组织合作促进会教育扶贫志愿项目编：《嘉言善行：山区校长谈教育》，北京：中国经济出版社，2020年出版；同名海外中文版，伦敦：环球世纪出版，2022年].

The ancient earth primary school in Gansu Province celebrates festivals to bring the enjoyment of ceremonies into every child's experience. Every year, around April, there is a spring tour. In the annual Tree Planting Day, children join in the planting of trees and flowers and in cooking a meal for the teachers. The etiquette they learn contributes to long-term social stability.

A poor rural woman in 27 years of service has risen to become the principal of ethnic schools in Heilongjiang Province. She runs a school 'that truly belongs to the students'. She takes forward General Secretary Xi Jinping's message to the Central Leading Group on Deep Reform to make teachers key agents in rural development. She lectures to them on advanced educational concepts and teaching methods.

In Yunnan Province, the principal of one primary school puts happiness at the heart of education. Teachers and students growing together can share an inner experience of happiness, which will include not only teaching and learning but also respect for each other, punctuality, good manners, appropriate dress and a regard for safety.

In a rural school in Sichuan Province, the left-behind little girl Qi, so joyful at school, breaks into tears at home telling how she hasn't seen her parents for a year and is looked after by grandparents. The principal cultivates a love climate through 'support pairs' for poor children and helps them through a 'warm sunshine' fund that he, his relatives and friends have set up.

In Hebei Province, there is a centre specifically founded to promote innovation in education, not just for the powers that be but also to inspire the students to innovate, where they can develop self-reliance, be unafraid of making mistakes and enjoy the spirit of innovation. 'Hands can be the soul' is the saying that brings knowledge together with practice.

Mathematics has long been integral to Chinese culture. In a primary school in Chongqing District, the emphasis on symmetrical beauty in Chinese traditional art and design is linked with the teaching of axis symmetrical graphics, while study of the origins and uses of the abacus brings the student close to traditional culture.

In the Inner Mongolia Autonomous Region, a primary school has emphasized campus football as a means to ease learning pressures on students. It promotes participation for all, boys and girls, and linked to teaching materials encourages learning. The result has been, over a five-year period of campus football, a continuing improvement in academic performance as well as good results in provincial competitions.

As a final example of the rich diversity of the levelling-up experience of education in China, we may take the role of the Party in a county of Xinjiang Province where it runs the only complete primary school. Its 2,180 students are drawn from Mongolian and Kazakh minorities and 13 other ethnic groups. It aims to implement fully the Party's 'Sunshine Project' for building a modern primary school. It integrates national customs with 'Red culture' to create a new campus culture.

I have cherry-picked nine cases from an abundant crop of educational innovations and avoided page references. This obliges you to look for them in the other 50, where you are bound to be diverted by others equally or even more sumptuous. My choice has been dictated only by the wish to reflect diversity and not by any implicit ranking of quality.

But highlighting the range and diversity of these contributions by educational leaders only emphasizes China's sense of education as the entry into a total national experience, drawing on both ancient wisdom and contemporary theories. To be expected are insights from Confucius, the Book of Morals and from the educator of the Republican period, *Tao Xingzhi* ('life is education').

The levelling-up theme of the book is a tacit contribution to China's second great Centenary Goal of 'building a modern socialist country that is prosperous, strong, democratic, culturally advanced and harmonious'. Its counterpart is the recent measures announced by General Secretary Xi Jinping to restrict incomes of the wealthiest, to limit private education and to rein in the tech companies. Here we have the two sides of the one socialist coin, so often underestimated in the West as the driving force behind China's advance.

In this book we are exploring the education Petri dish for an ever-renewing national culture, for a global world where a country grows by mixing the universal with the indigenous. No textbook about China today will tell you more first hand material about its vitality and strengths in rural education.

5.4 Seeking truth from facts[4]

Abstract: The decisive moment for China's poverty reduction came 50 years ago when the responsibility system in agriculture was initiated. This was the culmination of experience, of scientific work and of political leadership. The experience was of the limits of collective control, the science was of social experimentation and the leadership was of Deng Xiaoping. This was reform that freed country people to work and see the results of their own efforts, and it began the wider reform of the economy that spread to the cities and China's opening up. In these respects, China's lessons for the rest of the world are not in the setting of targets, but in a comprehensive, holistic approach. Even the measurement of poverty is less relevant than the motivation to change and to grow. The greatest poverty is the poverty of spirit, the sense that there is no future for oneself, one's children or one's country. The problems China has now are the results of success. Children left behind with their grandparents are a problem that results from the efforts of their parents to improve their lives. Then we find there are willing volunteers who bring help from afar to those children. The Chinese diaspora also contributes to

[4] Speech at the Parallel session 2 Poverty reduction in China: path and experiences, International Forum on Sharing Poverty Reduction Experience, China Academy of Social Sciences, etc, 14/15, December 2020.

China's rise out of poverty, but more importantly shows the Chinese spirit working wherever it is found in the world.

May I first express my gratitude to CASS for this privilege of speaking at a great event, an intellectual celebration of achieving the First Centenary Goal, the elimination of basic poverty in the People's Republic of China. The last time I had the pleasure of speaking here in Beijing, at that time in person, was in 2013, when Professor Li Peilin kindly invited me to speak on the topic of global inequality.

That is a theme for which the lessons of China's path and experience in eliminating poverty are highly relevant too, as the worsening condition of poorer countries under the impact of COVID-19 becomes ever more critical for our shared future. I will return to that in my conclusion.

There are many lessons the rest of the world can draw from China's elimination of poverty. I can only point to some of these in this short speech. But the first is the simplest and the most universal, namely, we can all learn from each other. So may I ask for your understanding for using the old English saying, 'The darkest hour comes before the dawn.'

Your darkest hour lasted a decade, but we have another saying, 'Cometh the hour, cometh the man', to point to the leadership of Deng Xiaoping, the inspiration for the transformation that followed. He exhibited the very qualities – cooperative spirit, worldly wisdom, open-mindedness to new ideas, respect for science, the courage needed to rise above misfortune – that were all combined in the Chinese people's rise from extreme poverty.

China's experience of escape from poverty began with recognition of the peasantry's experience, accepting the need for personal responsibility in agricultural production. Recalling those beginnings must also give particular pleasure to CASS because it was the re-establishment of sociology at that time in China and the research of its sociologists that supplied much of the scientific understanding for this liberation of the energies of the poorest people of the nation.

It also provided a lesson for other poor countries. Simultaneously China's opening-up policies provided the access, the encouragement and the chance to learn from the outside world. With the agricultural reform, confidence grew to develop foreign trade, to initiate the special economic zones and to begin joint ventures, especially with the Hong Kong business community. The journey out of poverty was a vital component in a comprehensive programme of modernization that continues to this day.

It is this holistic approach, where the relief of poverty is a key component of a comprehensive development programme, that provides an example to the rest of the world. As early as 1981, China resumed its membership of the World Bank so it could apply for development loans. It easily qualified for them since per capita income at $312 per annum was far below the qualifying maximum of $400.

In this context it is particularly appropriate to pay tribute to a World Bank President of the greatest distinction, who sadly died just a few days ago. James Wolfensohn, who was a great friend of China, was clearly inspired by its achievements, when he proposed that each country should have its own Comprehensive Development Framework.

What the West so often fails to recognize, or indeed even more often wilfully ignores, is the continuing ideological basis for this comprehensive approach and the role of the Communist Party in its governance. 'Opening up' and 'socialist democracy' were aligned with Deng's 'four cardinal principles' set out as early as March 1979: keeping to the socialist road, upholding the people's dictatorship, the leadership of the Party and Marxist–Leninism and Mao's thought. They were emphasized again in October 2017 in the Central Committee's Report to the 19th National Congress.

Those connections between the people and the Party were epitomized in the early career of President Xi Jinping. His book *Up and Out of Poverty* is a record of how he brought the people's congresses of Ningde Prefecture in Fujian Province and the Party officials together for the common task of the 1990s. In Zhejiang Province after the Millennium he was calling on leadership at all levels to assist those in difficulty. He pointed out that the moderately prosperous society still required the observance of the 'Five Guarantees', provisions for social security in the rural areas, that were made as long ago as the 1950s.

In the socialist outlook, targets, such as the one that has just been achieved, are only one aspect of the overall development of society. This contrasts with their place in Western political economy, where increase of GDP is often regarded as the decisive measure of national success, a paradox, of course, because it makes China the most successful of all economies in Western terms!

Increasing overall wealth of a society brings its own problems and in the West any accompanying unemployment and poverty for some may well be justified as an inevitable result of a dynamic economy. China's economic success challenges those assumptions fundamentally.

Its successful achievement of the First Centenary Goal leads naturally to the second, where the commitment to a modern socialist country that is not just prosperous but also harmonious can address the issues arising from the elimination of poverty. These are issues that arise from success. There are always those who are the casualties of the last step forward. What other countries can learn from China is that China learns from experience.

To give just one example, the children left behind in the country by their parents migrating to be urban wealth creators have emotional needs. These are now being met by the vision of the new generation of enlightened educators. The charity Visionary Education supports their work. Led by its managing director Cecily Liu, former *China Daily* journalist, this year it brought practitioners together to write the book *Levelling Mountain-High Gaps: Lessons from China's Leading Rural Educators* to bring those needs and remedies for them to the wider public.

The problems of success in one country are replicated when we consider them on a global scale. In my earlier CASS speech in 2013, I pointed to the in-country rise in inequality as a result of globalization. Relative deprivation, the sense of lacking respect and being disregarded replaces absolute poverty as a social problem. Now worldwide, although countries' borders are closing due to COVID-19, the impact of the virus is more severe on those poorer and socially excluded sections of their populations.

China's historic commitment to making the needs of the poor the top priority provided a model for the rest of the world. But even more important than the original goal is the example it gives of learning from experience, of seeking truth from facts and responding to them in a pragmatic and responsible manner.

5.5 China will strive fight resolutely to fight poverty and set an example for the world[5]

International Online Report (Reporter Liang Tao, Xijia): Recently, British sociologists and China experts stated that China's 'two sessions' (NPC and CPCC) in 2020 will send a clear message to the world.

Professor Rana Mitter, director of the China Centre of Oxford University in the United Kingdom, said in an exclusive interview with reporters that the Chinese government has sent a clear message to the world during the 'two sessions' (NPC and CPCC) in 2020. While overcoming the difficulties that COVID-19 has brought to economic development, China must also resolutely win the battle against poverty. Professor Mitter spoke highly of China's achievements in poverty alleviation, and he also said that China's achievements have attracted the attention of the world. 'In the past four decades, China has led hundreds of millions of people out of poverty in a record-breaking manner. This has become an important part of its development strategy and an important achievement for China. What has happened in China has impressed the world.'

Martin Albrow, an 82-year-old academician of the British Academy of Social Sciences and a well-known sociologist, said in an interview with reporters that China's ensuring that it completes the decisive goal of poverty alleviation is a huge achievement and has set a model for the world. 'For China, this is a great sense of accomplishment. This is an amazing thing. It also proves to the world how China can accomplish great things. It also sets an example for the world.'

As the initiator of the concept of 'globalization', Professor Albrow has devoted himself to the study of China's governance system in recent years, and has authored the book *China's Role in a Shared Human Future: Towards Theory for Global Leadership*. He said that, after China eliminates absolute poverty, the focus of the fight against poverty will shift to solving relative poverty, and solving relative poverty is an important core content of future poverty alleviation work.

---

5 梁弢、西佳：英国专家表示中国决战决胜脱贫攻坚为世界树立榜样，中央广电总台 2020-06-03，杨晓强 译，见：http://news.cri.cn/20200603/167bc846-d428-d552-3bc7-1aa940378dc2.html [LIANG Tao, XI Jia, British experts said that China will strive decisively to fight poverty and set an example for the world, China Central Radio and Television International Online, March 3, 2020. Translated by YANG Xiaoqiang].

DOI https://doi.org/10.24103/UCW5.en.2021.6

Chapter 6
Fighting COVID-19

COVID-19 is a singular moment in human history. For the first time there has occurred an emergency that has both impinged on the personal lives of every human being and at the same time preoccupied every government in the world. I call it the first total-global moment. It brings into focus the capacity of governments to deliver for their citizens as well as the potential for and limits of cooperation between them.

6.1 The moral foundation of the cooperative spirit in China's English media in combatting the COVID-19 crisis[1]

Zhang Xiaoying, Martin Albrow[2]

Abstract: China's mainstream English media, such as *China Daily*, *Global Times*, CGTN, Xinhuanet.com/English and China.org.cn/English, have emphasized global cooperation in combating COVID-19 crisis, instead of contributing to the blame game and politicizing the issue. What lies behind this cooperative spirit? This paper traces it back to three main Chinese philosophical traditions – Confucianism, Daoism and Mohism – to identify the sources of its theoretical framework. It argues that the cooperative spirit as represented in China's English media is essentially grounded in the ancient Chinese political–cultural values of these three traditions, which have all contributed in different degrees to the idea of *tianxia* (天下) as one family, taking '*ren*'(仁), '*shangshanruoshui*' (上善若水) and '*jianai*' (兼爱) as its core values, and maintaining a human-centred orientation.

Keywords: cooperative spirit, China's English media, COVID-19, moral foundation, human-centred orientation

The first aspect that Westerners should learn from Easterners is modesty and broad-mindedness… The second aspect that Westerners should learn from Easterners is the wisdom of accommodation… The third aspect that Westerners should learn from Easterners is mildness or compassion… The fourth aspect that West-

[1] This section was first published as ZHANG Xiaoying and Martin Albrow (2021), China: The moral foundation of the co-operative spirit. In: Seneviratne Kalinga and Sundeep R. Muppidi Eds., *COVID-19, Racism and Politicization: Media in the Midst of a Pandemic*, Newcastle: Cambridge Scholars Publishing, Chapter 4, pp. 59–79.

[2] Dr. ZHANG Xiaoying: Professor of the School of International Journalism and Communication, Beijing Foreign Studies University.

erners should learn from Easterners is the wisdom of enjoying a time-honored culture… The fifth aspect that Westerners should learn from Easterners is the spirit of *tianxia* (天下) as one family.[3]

Mou Chung-san, Hsu Foo-kwan, Carson Chang and Tang Chun-i

6.1.1 Introduction

China's mainstream English media, such as *China Daily*, *Global Times*, CGTN, Xinhuanet.com/English and China.org.cn/English, have been calling for global cooperation in combatting the COVID-19 crisis, instead of engaging in the blame game and politicizing the issue. What is meant by cooperation? This paper adopts a broader sense of cooperation that eschews a Western winners-and-losers concept and underscores the principle of inseparability of one and many, the worldview in traditional Chinese culture. The concept of cooperation, in a broader sense, can be seen as the philosophical ideal underpinning world citizenship. This paper traces the concept back to three main Chinese philosophical traditions of Confucianism, Daoism and Mohism to identify the sources of the theoretical framework for cooperative spirit. It argues that the cooperative spirit exhibited in China's English media is essentially grounded in the faith of the ancient Chinese political–cultural values of these three traditions, which have all contributed, to a greater or lesser degree, to the idea of *tianxia* (天下) as one family. The three different schools of thought all maintain a human-centred orientation, emphasizing the values of 'ren' (仁), 'shangshanruoshui' (上善若水) and 'jianai' (兼爱). We will start with a comparative study of the concept of cooperation between Chinese and Western philosophical culture. Then the ancient Chinese political–cultural values of Confucianism, Daoism and Mohism will be explored. Finally, we will identify the representation of the three main Chinese philosophical traditions in China's English media, China Daily, Global Times, CGTN, Xinhuanet.com/English and China.org.cn/English, in combatting COVID-19 through both a quantitative and qualitative analysis of the media texts between January and June 2020.

6.1.2 Western and non-Western interpretations of cooperation

In the Chinese context, cooperation consists of two words, '*hezuo*' (合作). According to Chinese hieroglyph characters, the first word '*he*' (合) in the oracle bone script, the earliest known form of Chinese writing, looks like a food container with a cap above and a vessel below. Its original meaning is 'closing', implying that the cap and the vessel match each other well and stay in harmony with each other. The second word '*zuo*' (作) looks like the shape of a standing collar in the

[3] 牟宗三、徐复观、张君劢、唐君毅：为中国文化敬告世界人士宣言——我们对中国学术研究及中国文化与世界文化前途之共同认识，附录，见张君劢：《新儒家思想史》，北京：中国人民大学出版社，2006年，第 585–591页 [Mou Chung-san, Hsu Foo-kwan, Carson Chang and Tang Chun-I (2006), A Manifesto on the Reappraisal of Chinese Culture: Our Joint Understanding of the Sinological Study Relating to World Cultural Outlook, in Carson Chang, *History of New Confucian Thoughts*, Beijing: Renmin University Press, pp. 585–591].

oracle bone script and bronze script, which is writing on Chinese ritual bronzes such as bells and tripodal cauldrons from the Shang dynasty (1600–1046 BC) to the Zhou dynasty (1046–256 BC). Moreover, in the lesser seal character, an ancient style of calligraphy adopted in the Qin dynasty (221–207 BC), the left side of '*zuo*' (作) looks like a person and the right side means 'sudden'. The original meaning of the word '*zuo*' (作) thus suggests that a person stands up suddenly, with the implication of rising or flourishing. In short, '*hezuo*' (合作) together refers to social interactions characterized by harmonious relationships that serve the purpose of making all flourish.

However, cooperation is described differently in the West. In his co-published book Cooperation in Primates and Humans: Mechanisms and Evolution, German professor of zoology and anthropology Peter Kappeler defines cooperation as 'social interactions characterized by costs to an actor and benefits to other conspecifics'[4]. This definition embodies current mainstream Western thinking, highlighting cooperation of individuals of the same species and dualism between benefactor and beneficiaries. It is in line with game theory, as pioneered by Professor John Von Neumann from Princeton University, where the interests of the players contradict each other totally, and one person's gain is always the loss of the other.

The contrast between China and the West in respect of their approaches to cooperation is profound. Whereas cooperation is a clear and natural corollary of the core value of harmony in Chinese culture, in the modern West, the pervasive influence of individualism means the starting point for any common venture or shared activity is to ask, 'What is in it for me?'.

The usual historical reference point for the origin of Western individualism is the religious Reformation of the sixteenth century in Europe. This removed the controlling social and political power of the Roman Catholic Church from large parts of Europe that it had held in its grasp for the previous millennium. The Church had claimed to mediate between the believer and God, but the Protestant Reformation declared that the believer had a direct and personal relation to the Creator.

One consequence of this religious revolution was a personal anxiety to prove oneself in the eyes of God. Max Weber famously pointed to this as a key factor in the origins of Western capitalism. Economic success was reassuring and correspondingly became a sign of personal salvation.

Another result was political chaos, to which there were two main responses. The contemporary observer of the religious wars of the seventeenth century, Thomas Hobbes, asserted that, since individuals were basically self-interested, only a strong sovereign state could provide for the order needed to prevent continuing conflict. But many sought to escape these conflicts by fleeing to the new

---

4 Peter M. Kappeler and Carel P. van Schaik (2006) (Eds.), *Cooperation in Primates and Humans: Mechanisms and Evolution*, New York: Springer, Preface.

lands recently discovered across the oceans. The United States grew out of the series of colonies founded by religious believers hoping to create a new life for themselves. They had to band together for basic economic and security reasons, surrounded as they were by uncomprehending and frequently hostile native peoples. But this cooperation for common purposes was strictly secondary to their deeper religious motivations and personal convictions.

The classic, still regarded as definitive, account of the early drivers of American ideology is that of the nineteenth-century French nobleman Alexis de Tocqueville. In his *Democracy in America* he described the outlooks of the early settlers in New England in this way:

Each individual is assumed to be as educated, virtuous and powerful as any of his fellows. Why then should he obey society, and what are the natural limits of such obedience? He obeys society not because he is inferior to those who direct it, nor because he is incapable of ruling himself, but because union with his fellows seems useful to him.[5]

Clearly, cooperation was strictly the consequence of a more basic self-interest or what the great authority in the new political economy, Adam Smith, called self-love. This eighteenth-century intellectual development was focused on finding a point of agreement between the ever-increasing demands and power of a centralizing state and the individualism that was driving trade and capitalism. One could have thought, as indeed the French physiocrats did, that the union of state and economic interests would be a possible way forward, but Smith's answer is epitomized in the well-known passage of his *The Wealth of Nations*.

It is not from the benevolence of the butcher, the brewer or the baker, that we expect our dinner, but from their regard to their own interest. We address ourselves, not to their humanity, but to their self-love, and never talk to them of our own necessities, but of their advantages.[6]

Out of their trading interest, out of self-love, arose a division of labour dictated by the market, and this has been a fundamental principle for Western economic thinking ever since. But it would be a mistake to assume that the individualism of the modern period meant that cooperation had been ruled out from the earliest days in the West. The ancient origins of Western thought in Greece and through until the Reformation relied on Aristotle's declaration that human beings were essentially social and made to live in communities. In other words, close to the time that Confucius was stressing human social relations in ancient China, in the West too there was an equivalent emphasis on the social nature of human beings.

It was those ancient roots that were evoked again in the nineteenth century by Karl Marx and socialists in many Western countries. It was a theme that per-

---

5 Alexis de Tocqueville (1994) (Ed. J. P. Mayer), *Democracy in America*, London: Fontana, p. 66. [Chinese edition: (法) 托克维尔：《托克维尔文集：论美国的民主》（第一、二卷），董果良译，北京：商务印书馆，2013年].

6 Adam Smith (2003), *The Wealth of Nations*, New York: Bantam Classic, pp. 23–24. [（英）亚当·斯密：《国富论》（上下册），郭大力、王亚南译，北京：译林出版社，2011年].

sisted into the mid-twentieth century when one of the family used to go with his or her mother to shop at the local cooperative society grocery store. It was part of the cooperative movement that had grown in popularity in the country ever since its founding in 1844, though today it is a shadow of its past.

But what Western socialism illustrates in its advocacy of cooperation is precisely opposition to the dominant forces in a capitalist economy based on self-interest. Indeed, socialist campaigning for cooperation to combat those forces both recognizes and contributes to the conflicts that have been pervasive in the West throughout the modern period, culminating in the two world wars of the last century. To this day, self-interest and conflict continue to predominate over appeals to cooperation as the ideas that shape Western public discourse and outlook on world affairs.

Clearly, cooperation was strictly the consequence of a more basic self-interest or what the great authority in the new political economy, Adam Smith, called self-love. This eighteenth-century intellectual development was focused on finding a point of agreement between the ever-increasing demands and power of a centralizing state and the individualism that was driving trade and capitalism. One could have thought, as indeed the French physiocrats did, that the union of state and economic interests would be a possible way forward, but Smith's answer is epitomized in the well-known passage of his *The Wealth of Nations*.

It is not from the benevolence of the butcher, the brewer, or the baker, that we expect our dinner, but from their regard to their own interest. We address ourselves, not to their humanity, but to their self-love, and never talk to them of our own necessities, but of their advantages.[7]

Out of their trading interest, out of self-love, arose a division of labour dictated by the market, and this has been a fundamental principle for Western economic thinking ever since. But it would be a mistake to assume that the individualism of the modern period meant that cooperation had been ruled out from the earliest days in the West. The ancient origins of Western thought in Greece and through until the Reformation relied on Aristotle's declaration that human beings were essentially social and made to live in communities. In other words, close to the time that Confucius was stressing human social relations in ancient China, in the West too there was an equivalent emphasis on the social nature of human beings.

It was those ancient roots that were evoked again in the nineteenth century by Karl Marx and socialists in many Western countries. It was a theme that per-
sisted into the mid-twentieth century when one of the family used to go with his or her mother to shop at the local cooperative society grocery store. It was part of the cooperative movement that had grown in popularity in the country ever since its founding in 1844, though today it is a shadow of its past.

But what Western socialism illustrates in its advocacy of cooperation is precisely opposition to the dominant forces in a capitalist economy based on self-in-

[7] Ibid., pp. 23–24.

terest. Indeed, socialist campaigning for cooperation to combat those forces both recognizes and contributes to the conflicts that have been pervasive in the West throughout the modern period, culminating in the two world wars of the last century. To this day, self-interest and conflict continue to predominate over appeals to cooperation as the ideas that shape Western public discourse and outlook on world affairs.

6.1.3 The moral foundation of cooperative spirit in Chinese philosophical tradition

6.1.3.1 Confucianism

The key concept in Confucianism is *ren* (仁). It is the highest moral principle, moral standard and moral state of humans. Centring on the concept of *ren* (仁), Confucius (551–479 BC), born in the Age of Spring and Autumn, established a system of ethical thought, with a set of connected concepts such as family reverence, loyalty, forgiveness, appropriateness, conscience, courage, courtesy, magnanimity, sincerity, diligence and kindness. *Ren* (人) is such a central term that it is mentioned 109 times in the *Analects of Confucius* and actually all the twenty chapters of the book dwell on *ren* (仁).

The Age of Spring and Autumn (770–476 BC) witnessed the moral degradation of the society. Rites and rituals collapsed and elegant music disappeared. Confucius suggested that the rulers should govern their country by restoring rites of the Zhou dynasty(1100–221 BC). As Duke Jing of Qi asked about how to govern a country, Confucius said: 'Rulers, subjects, fathers and sons should observe their respective rites.'[8] To restore these rites one must develop *ren* (仁) first, because it would be hypocritical to observe rites without *ren* (仁). In the words of Confucius: 'If a man has no *ren* (仁), what can his propriety be like?'[9] Confucius' ethical system with *ren* (仁) as its core spirit thus aims to restore rites and rituals and maintain a cohesive social order.

What is *ren* (仁)? The Chinese character for '仁' is composed of two parts. The left part means 'person' and the right part means 'two'. From this character we see *ren* (仁) means mutual love between two persons. In chapter 12 of the *Analects of Confucius*, there is a dialogue about *ren* (仁) between Confucius and his student Fan Chi: 'Fan Chi asked about *ren*' (仁). The Master said, 'It is to love all men.'[10] In chapter 17, Zi Lu, one of Confucius' students, asked Confucius about *ren* (仁). The master said, 'He who could practise five things wherever in the world would accomplish *ren* (仁).' 'What are they,' Zi Lu asked. The Master said: 'courtesy, magnanimity, sincerity, diligence and kindness. He who is courteous will not be humiliated, he who is magnanimous wins the multitude, he who

---

8 程昌明注:《论语》, 北京: 远方出版社, 2017年, 第12页 [CHENG Changming (2007, annotated), *The Analects of Confucius*, Beijing: Yuanfang Press, Chapter 12, p. 120].

9 Ibid., Chapter 3, p. 19.

10 Ibid., Chapter 12, p. 124.

is sincere is trusted by others, he who is diligent succeeds in all he undertakes, he who is kind can get good service from others.'[11]

According to the Chinese Confucian philosopher Mencius, *ren* (仁) originates from a spontaneous feeling of compassion and commiseration within the human heart-and-mind (*xin*, 心). For example, when a woman sees a child on the verge of falling into a well, she would rush over to save the child as if it was her own child. By doing so, the woman has developed compassion and commiseration into *ren* (仁).

How to approach *ren* (仁)? According to Confucius, the practice of *ren* (仁) starts from oneself, family and workplace and then extends towards the wider society. In chapter 1 of the *Analects of Confucius*, the Master said, 'family reverence is the root of *ren*' (仁).[12] And family reverence starts from oneself. In chapter 6, Zigong asked the Master, "What do you think of someone who gives extensively to the common people and provides aid to the multitude? Would you say he has possessed *ren* (仁)?' The Master answered, 'He is far more than having *ren* (仁). He must be a sage. Even Yao and Shun could not have done as much. A person of *ren* (仁) is one who helps others establish what he himself wishes to establish and to achieve what he himself wishes to achieve. To be able to correlate one's own feelings with those of others may be the way to approach *ren* (仁).'[13]

What is a man of *ren* (仁) like? In chapter 13, Fan Chi asked about ren *ren* (仁). Confucius said, 'Be respectful to parents, be conscientious in official affairs. Be loyal and honest to friends.'[14] A man of *ren* (仁), in the first place, must practise these three basic moral principles. In another chapter, Confucius explained that 'fine words and insinuating appearance are seldom associated with *ren* (仁)'.[15] From this we can see that a person of *ren* (仁) must place high value on inner cultivation. Inner cultivation is more important than words and appearance.

Ren (仁) has something in common with the notion of love in Christianity, but there is a difference between them. On the one hand, they share similarities in the promotion of the doctrine of universal love in the first place, encouraging people to connect to the source of all human love. On the other, they are different in terms of the nature of love. Confucian *ren* (仁) stresses hierarchical order, with love starting from oneself, family and workplace and then to the wider society, and with rulers, subjects, fathers and sons observing their respective rites to develop mutual respect and trust so as to establish a harmonious social order. However, Christian love is first of all the love of God as God loves all and then the love of your neighbours who have helped you in the name of God.

---

[11] Ibid., Chapter 17, p. 175.

[12] Ibid., Chapter 1, p. 1.

[13] Ibid., Chapter 6, p. 59.

[14] Ibid., Chapter 13, p. 133.

[15] Ibid., Chapter 1, p. 2.

6.1.3.2 Daoism

According to Laozi's Daoist cosmogony, Dao is the very origin of the universe. Dao is both Nonbeing and Being. In its original state, Dao is formless, thus Nonbeing. When it takes on form but still remains undifferentiated, it becomes Being or the chaotic One. One bifurcates into Tian and Di, which in turn form the interaction of Yin and Yang, the two opposite principles in nature. When Yin (female) and Yang (male) exchange their vital energy (Qi) and copulate, the Two generates Three, a number symbolizing plurality. This process multiplies generation after generation, generating all things. Thus all things in the world consist of Yin and Yang elements. Harmony emerges when the vital energy or Qi of Yin and Yang interacts and converges. As chapter 42 of *Daodejing* wrote:

> Dao gives birth to One;
> One gives birth to Two;
> Two gives birth to Three;
> Three gives birth to Ten Thousand things.
> All things have Yin on their back and Yang in their embrace;
> The Qi of the two converge and become harmony.[16]

As we are living in a world of opposite energies, Laozi teaches us how to establish ourselves and manage to get along in the world. It is his fundamental principle not to be rude, arrogant and overbearing but to be good, humble and soft instead. This becomes the ultimate standard of value.

Laozi further explains what is the highest good. He sees water as the embodiment of the highest good. Water, from Laozi's point of view, is one of the symbols of humility and competence. Being morally good without accomplishing anything amounts to 'good for nothing'. Being competent without a good heart is fundamentally flawed. All in all, water symbolizes the highest good because it is capable of accomplishing things but keeps itself in a low profile, taking no credit for its accomplishment. Chapter 8 of *Daodejing* gave a detailed description of water and those people who are like water:

> The highest good is like water;
> Water brings good to all things and does not contend;
> It goes to places which most people detest
> And is therefore akin to Dao.
>
> Stay low key;
> Keep a broad mind;
> Treat people kindly;
> Speak in good faith;
> Rule with good policy;
> Serve with good competence;
> Act with good timing.[17]

---

[16] 吴千之：《老子如是说–<道德经>新注新译，北京：外语教学与研究出版社，2013年，第120页 [Charles Q, Wu (2013), *Thus Spoke Laozi*, Beijing: Foreign Language Teaching and Research Press, p. 102].

[17] Ibid., p. 20.

'The great virtue is like water' (上善若水) thus becomes Laozi's philosophy of life. He described it to be 'akin to Dao', a symbol of humility, the origin of the universe, and the source of power. In chapter 78 of *Daodejing*, he mentioned water again: 'Nothing in the world is softer than water, yet nothing can better attack the strong than water.'[18] Laozi believed in the power of humility and humbleness.

6.1.3.3 Mohism

Mohism was founded by Mozi in the early Warring States. As one of the most important figures in Chinese history, Mozi was often linked with Confucius from the Warring States period (403–221BC) to the beginning of the Han dynasty (202BC–AD220).

The cornerstone of Mohism is *jianai* (兼爱), commonly known as universal love in the West. However, this translation is misleading if we truly understand the original meaning of *jianai* (兼爱). Mozi started with the learning of Confucianism but later abandoned it, finding its ritual rites too trivial, complex and costly. Therefore, he established Mohism, advocating *jianai* (兼爱) as the very core of his thought, economy of expenditure and exalting the worthy being its two main pillars. Besides, his thinking includes reverence for the sky, the sprits, uniformity, on the one hand, and anti-fatalism, anti-music, simplicity in funerals, on the other. *jianai* (兼爱) is thus better translated as inclusive love or impartial love to avoid Christian connotation.

There are three basic arguments in support of the principle of *jianai* (兼爱). First, *jianai* (兼爱) brings social order. According to Mozi, the cause of social disorder is the lack of mutual love (*xiangai* 相爱):

Feudal lords each love their own state but do not love other states. Therefore, they attack other states in order to benefit their own state. Disorder in the world is entirely this and nothing else. If we examine this, from what source does it arise? In all cases it is due to lack of mutual love.[19]

Mozi thus encouraged the love of others. If people could learn to love others as they love themselves, they would mutually benefit. In his words, if there is inclusively mutual love in the world, then there is order, whereas, if there is exchange of mutual hatred, then there is disorder. This applies at all levels of society, in the family, in the community and between states. In this sense, *jianai* (兼爱) is equal treatment of each other without distinction.

Second, *jianai* (兼爱) benefits the world. For a man of *ren* (仁), his way to conduct affairs is to promote what benefits the world and eliminate what harms it. What harms the world? Mozi wrote:

---

[18] Ibid., p. 176.

[19] [澳]伊恩・约翰斯顿:《墨子全译，香港:香港中文大学出版社，2010年，第133页[Ian Johnston, trans. and annotated (2010), *The Mozi: A Complete Translation*, Hong Kong: Chinese University Press, p. 133].

'...if states attack each other, if houses usurp each other, if people harm each other, if there is not kindness and loyalty between rulers and ministers, if there is not love and filiality between fathers and sons, if there is not concord and harmony between older and younger brothers, then this is harmful to the world.'[20]

Lack of mutual love, or loving oneself to the exclusion of others, is at the root of all these problems. That everyone must love others is the only solution. In Mozi's words: 'It can be changed by the methods of inclusively mutual love and exchange of mutual benefit.'[21]

Third, jian (兼), meaning inclusive, is a way to Mozi. That draws our attention to the comparison of 'inclusive' and 'discriminating' or 'partial'. In his own words: 'Inclusiveness is the means of changing discrimination.'[22] If people are 'inclusive' rather than 'discriminating', then they will regard others as they do themselves. So, if 'inclusiveness' is established, there is great benefit to the world; conversely, if 'discrimination' is established, there is great harm to the world. So we must certainly distinguish and name those in the world who love people and benefit people because it is their inclusive love that gives rise to the world's great benefits.

How can *jianai* (兼爱) be put into practice? From what the sages in the ancient times wrote on bamboo and silk, what they carved in metal and stone, what they engraved on [ceremonial] plates and bowls to hand down to their descendants of later generations, Mozi came to know that the first four sage kings personally practised it. He cited the story of King Wen of the Zhou dynasty in the Great Oath (Tai Shi), saying: 'King Wen was like the sun and the moon, creating light and bringing its brightness to the four regions and to the western lands.'[23] To Mozi's interpretation, this speaks of the wide extent and greatness of King Wen's inclusive love of the world being like the sun and moon, which illuminate all parts of the world without discrimination. This was King Wen's 'inclusiveness' and is what Mozi means when he speaks of 'inclusive', taking King Wen as his model.

It is worth noting that Mozi saw *jianai* (兼爱) as *ren* (仁), but there is a nuance between the two. The former emphasizes the practice of love without distinctions while the latter stresses hierarchical order, with the practice of love towards oneself and then extending beyond the self-world. The concept of *jianai* (兼爱) is undifferentiated love.

6.1.4 The cooperative spirit in China's English media in combatting COVID-19 crisis: an overview

This paper selects five major English media outlets in China as the object of study. They are China Daily, Global Times, CGTN, Xinhuanet.com/English

[20] Ibid., p. 137.
[21] Ibid, p. 139. Here benefit is for all.
[22] Ibid, p. 147.
[23] Ibid, p. 157.

and China.org.cn/English, official media outlets at the national level, all devoted to building connections between China and the rest of the world. The emergence of these English media outlets is a significant sign of China's opening-up policy since the early 1980s and of China embracing the world in the hope of promoting global communication and cooperation worldwide.

China Daily was established in 1981 with the support of The Age, an Australian daily newspaper published in Melbourne, Australia. Originally it was aimed at foreigners in China, such as businesspeople, students, tourists and diplomats. Now, as the biggest national English-language newspaper, China Daily has developed into a multimedia platform including newspapers, websites and apps with a strong presence on Facebook, Twitter, SinaWeibo and WeChat, serving more than 200 million readers all over the world. It takes 'Connecting China Connecting the World' as its mission.

Global Times was founded in 2009 with the main purpose of helping the outside world understand China's rapid changes. It is best known for its innovation, tackling issues once thought sensitive and tough, such as child AIDS victims, urban renewal, forced demolition, the fight against corruption, China's use of the death penalty, the challenges of forming a new international order and the nation's growing wealth gap. The paper has often been seen overseas as nationalistic for providing insightful reports on important international issues from Chinese perspectives.

CGTN, China Global Television Network, was launched in 2016. It is the international division of CCTV, which – along with CNR, China National Radio and CRI, China Radio International – is now collectively known as the China Media Group. CGTN seeks to report the news both in China and around the world from a global perspective. It aims to provide more balanced reporting, with a focus on nations, regions and stories that are often underreported by other international media. Its slogan is 'See the Difference'.

Xinhuanet, established in 1997 by Xinhua News Agency, is a comprehensive service-oriented news information portal, the most influential online medium in China and the Chinese-language website of world influence. Xinhuanet has 31 local channels and releases global news and information 24 hours a day in English, French, Spanish, Russian, Arabic, Japanese, Korean, German, Tibetan, Uyghur and Mongolian. It leads by far other domestic online media organizations in originality and re-posting rates concerning major news events. It speaks for China and of China, with the modest hope to become a news website that is thinking globally and acting locally.

China.org.cn, published in 2000 under the auspices of the State Council Information Office and the China International Publishing Group (CIPG) in Beijing, is the authorized government portal site to China. It offers broad access to up-to-date news about China, with searchable texts of government position papers and a wealth of basic information about Chinese history, politics, economics and culture in English, French, Spanish, German, Japanese, Russian, Arabic, Korean and Esperanto.

This paper has collected a total of 65,600 news items relating to the COVID-19 pandemic in these English media outlets during a six-month period from January to June 2020, entering the key words of COVID-19, coronavirus and Xinfadi, the market in Beijing where new COVID-19 cases were found in June. By further entering the key word 'cooperation', 7,525 news items are obtained, accounting for 11.5% of the total number of pieces.

Media	*China Daily*	*Global Times*	CGTN	Xinhuanet.com/English	China.org.cn/Engish	Total
Number of news relating to COVID-19	8530	8130	6490	30150	12300	65600
Number of news relating to co-operation	1657	1249	699	2618	1302	7525

Table 1: The number of news items related to COVID-19 and the number of news items related to cooperation in each media platform. Source: *China Daily*'s New Media Lab

In an interview with Dr. Zhou Shuchun, publisher and editor-in-chief of *China Daily*, he explained why cooperation is an important message to get across to the global audience. First, cooperation has been the basic principle of China's diplomacy and international strategy. Second, to emphasize cooperation is to take the moral high ground in the interest of China and that of the world as a whole. Third, cooperation is the manifestation of traditional Chinese cultural thoughts.

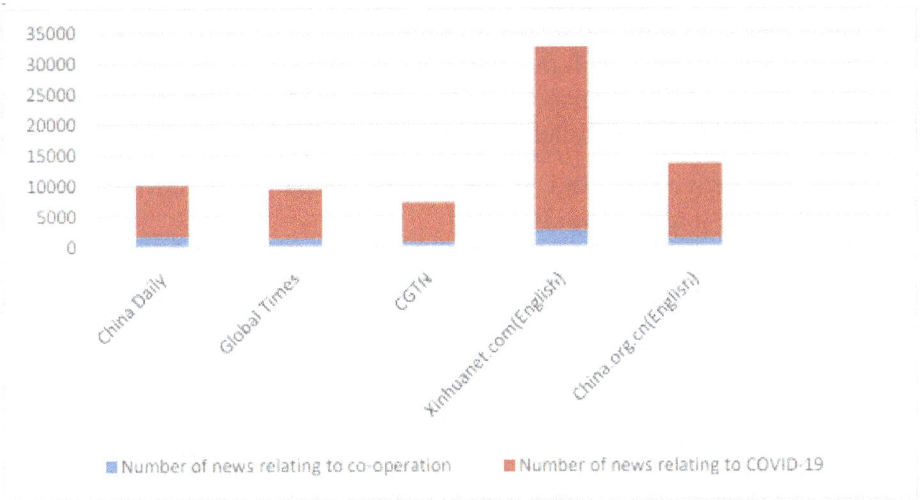

Chart 1: The number of news items related to COVID-19 and the number of news items related to cooperation in each media platform. Source: *China Daily*'s New Media Lab

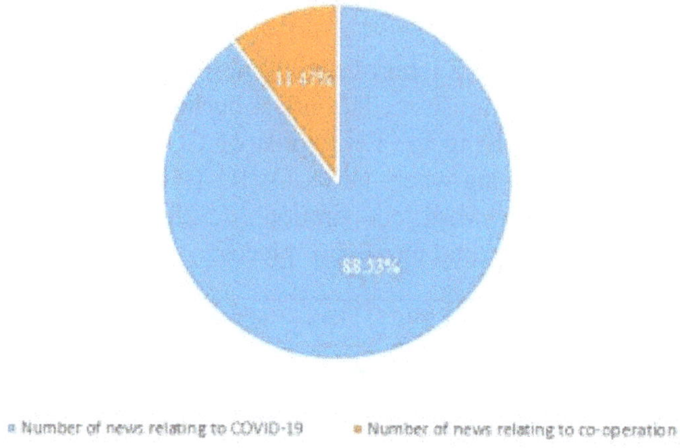

Chart 2: The ratio between news relating to cooperation and news relating to COVID-19

In an interview with Mr. Liu Jiawen, vice president of Xinhuanet.com, he also emphasized the influence of traditional Chinese philosophical thoughts on media and journalistic practice in China. In his eyes, cooperation means two or more countries taking concerted actions to solve an existing problem or reach a common goal. With regard to the COVID-19 crisis, he deems it necessary for all countries to cooperate, for it is not possible for a single country to deal with it successfully. Mr. Liu pointed out that traditional Chinese culture features collective interests before individual interests, stressing not only the principle of not imposing on others what you yourself do not desire, but also kindness, inclusiveness and compassion, etc. Most journalistic practitioners, especially those involved in global journalism, have high moral standards, prioritizing collective interests, being conscious of others' perspectives, having a kind and friendly nature and exhibiting the ability for self-reflection and introspection.

6.1.5 The cooperative spirit in China's English media in combatting the COVID-19 crisis: a textual analysis

The cooperative theme is a frequent occurrence in the reports on the COVID-19 crisis by the selected five media. They have expressed the idea and wish for cooperation with all parts of the world.

CGTN was calling for global cooperation in the manufacture of ventilators. Zhu Min, former deputy managing director of the International Monetary Fund (IMF), was quoted as saying that China has embraced initiatives that call for global cooperation. He said, 'During the pandemic outbreak, ventilators became a rare product everywhere. Many countries started to buy them from China, yet the whole manufacture of ventilators probably requires work from 140 companies at the cost of 50,000 RMB (7,070 USD) each. Thus we need companies from China, South Korea, the United States, Switzerland and many others to work together.'[24]

[24] Experts endorse multilateral cooperation in post-COVID-19 era. CGTN, 24/06/2020. See: https://

China Daily quoted Gao Fu, director of the Chinese Center for Disease Control and Prevention, who expressed his fond wish for cooperation with the international community. He told media that he has been in touch with arriving WHO experts on epidemic response measures, as he coordinates research efforts in Hubei province and oversees developments in vaccines and drugs. Gao said China has always upheld transparent, open and responsible principles when handling such situations and is actively seeking and expanding cooperation with the international community.[25]

China Daily reported on the strong traditional ties between China and ASEAN members. Although the COVID-19 outbreak will affect China–ASEAN cooperation in different fields in the short term, Sino–ASEAN cooperation may not suffer in the long run, since China's strict measures to contain the outbreak are producing results and an increasing number of industries in Chinese provinces and cities are resuming production. *China Daily* further explained that, thanks to their long-established friendship, some ASEAN member states have vowed to jointly fight the epidemic with China despite being affected by the novel coronavirus outbreak. And although the World Health Organization has declared the coronavirus outbreak a public health emergency of international concern, ASEAN members have expressed confidence in and support for China's measures to contain the epidemic.[26]

CGTN also reported on China's ties with other Asian countries. Chinese State Councillor and Foreign Minister Wang Yi was quoted as saying in a phone call with Rasit Meredow, deputy chairman of the Cabinet of Ministers and minister of Foreign Affairs of Turkmenistan, that 'unity and cooperation are the best weapons to overcome the pandemic'. Wang Yi said that 'China is willing to strengthen communication and cooperation in international affairs with Turkmenistan, firmly support each other and safeguard the common interests of both sides.'[27]

Sino–European cooperation is also a frequently occurring theme. For example, CGTN pointed out that 'maintaining frank and honest exchanges and keeping open-minded as to divergences' set out the prerequisite for meaningful cooperation between China and Europe.[28] However, CGTN stressed harmony between differences, saying that 'focusing on cooperation by no means suggests that both sides should or would neglect the disagreements'.[29]

news.cgtn.com/news/2020-06-24/World-experts-endorse-multilateral-cooperation-in-post-COVID-19-era-RAml5Ir2vK/index.html.

[25] ZHANG Zhihao, China, WHO collaborating to conquer disease, *China Daily*, 17/02/2020. See: http://www.chinadaily.com.cn/a/202002/17/WS5e49d110a310128217277e7f.html.

[26] WANG Kan, China–ASEAN won't be affected in the long run, *China Daily*, 27/02/2020. See: http://www.chinadaily.com.cn/a/202002/27/WS5e56ff16a31012821727a9a4.html.

[27] Ibid.

[28] HU Hong, Cooperation remains the theme for Sino–European relations, CGTN, 24-Jun-2020. See: https://news.cgtn.com/news/2020-06-24/Cooperation-remains-the-theme-for-Sino-European-relations-RzMpQa2dqM/index.html.

[29] Ibid.

Another example is *China Daily's* report on President Xi Jinping's telephone conversations with French President Emmanuel Macron and German Chancellor Angela Merkel ahead of the Lunar New Year. Xi expressed the hope that 'China stands ready to work with the international community to effectively curb the spread of the pneumonia cases caused by a new strain of coronavirus to uphold global health security, and China and Germany could become partners who depend on each other despite their ideological differences.'[30] China.org.cn/English quoted the Chinese ambassador to the UK, Liu Xiaoming, as saying that 'When Brexit is done and COVID-19 is over, China and the UK will continue deepening cooperation in areas such as financial services, trade and investment.'[31]

There are also reports calling for cooperation with Africa. Xinhuanet.com/English quoted the white paper 'Fighting COVID-19: China in Action' released by China's State Council Information Office, saying that China has so far sent medical supplies to over 50 African countries and the African Union, dispatched medical experts to the continent, and held several video conferences to share its anti-epidemic experience. China will offer more assistance to African countries in the fight against COVID-19 and continue to do all in its power to offer support.[32] *Global Times* interviewed the Chinese Ambassador to Sudan, Ma Xinmin, who told the reporters that 'China and Sudan are close friends and strategic partners, who over the years have supported and helped each other. And we once again stand shoulder to shoulder in the fight against the COVID-19 pandemic.'[33]

The wish for cooperation with Latin America is clearly expressed. *Global Times* reported on Chinese communities in Brazil. According to the report, in spite of COVID-19 infections, the Brazilian government insisted on keeping its economy going instead of preventing the virus's spread. This approach triggered social concerns, especially among Chinese living in Brazil who are aware of the dangers of the disease. Despite their anxiety, Chinese communities in Brazil have been participating in virus mitigation and have great expectations for China–Brazil cooperation in vaccine development. Cheng Pu, chairman of the Brazil–China Cultural Communication Association, told *Global Times* that Chinese members of the association have donated a million masks and other protective products to local governments, medical institutions and police and sent 8,000 basic food baskets to Brazilians living in poverty.[34]

---

[30] CAO Desheng, Global ties vital to fight coronavirus. *China Daily*, 23/01/2020. See: https://www.chinadaily.com.cn/a/202001/23/WS5e28a12ea310128217272db4_3.html.

[31] China, UK to deepen cooperation in financial services, trade, investment after Brexit: ambassador, Xinhuam 21/06/2020. See: http://www.china.org.cn/world/2020-06/21/content_76186377.htm.

[32] Expert hails China-Africa partnership to combat COVID-19, *Xinhua*, 19/06/2020. See: http://www.xinhuanet.com/english/2020-06/19/c_139152031.htm.

[33] China provides new medical supplies to Sudan to bolster anti-coronavirus fight, Xinhua, 10/06/2020. See: http://www.news.cn/english/africa/2020-06/19/c_139149833.htm.

[34] Brazil-based Chinese merchants assist locals despite own epidemic loss, 2020/6/19. See: https://www.globaltimes.cn/content/1192139.shtml.

With regard to the cooperation with the US, *China Daily* first of all emphasized its importance to the world as well as China by saying that 'When America sneezes, the world catches a cold'.[35] The newspaper further said that, 'while it is hugely important that the Chinese economy is restarting and contributing to global supply chains, it is equally important the American economy remains robust. The US administration must follow the lessons from China and other Asian countries now and significantly increase virus protection and detection, or the world economy will get sick. Political issues need to be put aside and maximum cooperation must be the mantra.'[36]

Only a few examples of the co-operative spirit as represented in China's English media are illustrated here. Cooperation has been the prevalent idea throughout the reports of the five media. The notion of cooperation is not just a media discourse, but rather a true and natural expression of thoughts and feelings of the Chinese nation and its people who have been steeped in Chinese philosophical traditions such as *ren* (仁), water-like virtue (上善若水) and *jianan* (兼爱).

6.1.6 Conclusion

Confucianism, Daoism and Mohism are considered the spiritual homeland for Chinese people, especially the intelligentsia. As a central element of cultural and civic life in Chinese history, the ideas of these major philosophical schools have shaped the soul and character of the Chinese nation and are deeply rooted in the hearts of the Chinese people. As Cheng Yuzhen, professor of Chinese language and literature at Beijing Foreign Studies University, commented, 'We cannot steer away from the trajectory of thinking of influential ancient Chinese philosophers, for their thinking has become the intrinsic spirit of our nation.'[37] Confucius said, 'Is ren (仁) far away from us? You only have to want it and it will come.'[38]

6.2 Has COVID-19 brought globalization to an end?[39]

COVID-19 is a human tragedy. There is no denying that. The latest figures for deaths worldwide from the virus at the time of writing (18/05/20) are 312,646 out of the total of recorded infections of 4,673,809. The repercussions for every sector of life are proving profound. Indeed, some commentators have announced that this is the end of globalization. Well, for a start, I would say that underesti-

[35] Colin Speakman, US needs to step up COVID-19 response, *China Daily,* 0503/2020. See: http://www.chinadaily.com.cn/a/202003/05/WS5e60a01ea31012821727c9bb.html.

[36] Ibid.

[37] 程裕祯：《中国文化要略》（第4版），北京：外语教学与研究出版社，2018年，第90页 [CHENG Yuzheng (2018), *Introduction of Chinese Culture*, Fourth edition, Beijing: Foreign Language Teaching and Research Press, p. 90].

[38] 程昌明注:《论语》，北京：远方出版社，2017年，第12页[CHENG Changming, annotated (2007), *The Analects of Confucius*, Beijing: Yuanfang Press, p. 70.

[39] Martin Albrow, Has COVID-19 brought globalization to an end? In Werner Gephart (ed.), *In the Realm of Corona Normativities*, Frankfurt am Main: Vittorio Klosterman, 2020, pp. 497–502.

mates the impact of COVID-19. It is more than the end of something, it is a beginning, the beginning of a totalization, of which more later. The virus is even more total than global. After all, the global has long been synonymous with the future of human beings on this earth. But the virus looms over the very existence of the human species and all its imaginings of personal life, of empires and existence beyond the planet. The virus penetrates the recesses of individual reality and at the same time shakes the great powers of the world to their foundations. The child is not exempt. 'I want to go out to play with my friends' is a complaint repeated in every household, with no exceptions for class or culture. National leaders nervously check the figures of infections in their land and worry about their standing with their own citizens. China and the USA monitor ever more closely the resulting minutest shifts in their uneasy balance of power.

This is really total, when we learn that Chinese eating habits have to change and no longer will all be served from the same pot. The triple kiss on the Dutch cheeks, the Maori nose rubbing, even the cold handshake of the English, all physical contact greetings are forbidden under the 'social distancing' rules. Actually, 'social distancing' is an inappropriate name for keeping physical space between people. What a government is limiting when it prohibits close personal contact should rightly be called 'physical distancing'. It is demanding increasing space between human bodies. What might more properly be called 'social distancing' are those acts that sustain social relations over ever longer distances, currently conquering physical space as never before.

Ever-increasing varieties of voice and video conversation and conferencing allow us to contact others over any distance. They are now familiar substitutes for presence in the office or even attendance at family events like weddings. These relations at a distance are, however, still social, indeed come much closer to the true sense of the social. The social nature of human beings, celebrated over two millennia ago in Greece by Aristotle and in China by Confucius, now has achieved global recognition for being unlimited by presence or absence. This is true even as the virus emphasizes that also in our natures we are all made of the same physical stuff. The body is rooted to the spot, the social can roam free from such restrictions. We are reaching out to other human beings who could be anywhere in the world in the vivid and renewed recognition that we all belong to a single vulnerable biological species that ultimately has only science between itself and extinction.

This is the world society of the human species as it never has been before. It extends worldwide not simply through the overlapping linkages of neighbouring communities, which has always been a fact of life, but because each one of us has a real or potential link with someone else, no matter how far we are apart. The virus means we sustain our relations with our family and friends even as it forces us to keep our distance from them. By emphasizing absence, it is a paradox that the virus illuminates with still greater clarity the nature of human society. Physical contact or proximity is not of its essence, even if it provides the necessary condition for human reproduction (at least up until *in vitro* fertilization!).

Europeans in particular, with their past experience of incessant movement of people, have long recognized that social relations are not tied to time and place. They have a special history of restlessness, a desire to leave the familiar behind that has been a regular feature of their expansionism and empire building. This is what Michel de Montaigne, French originator of what has come to be known as the essay, observed over 400 years ago: 'I know that the arms of friendship are long enough to reach from one end of the world to the other, and especially this where there is a continual communication of offices.' And he goes on further to describe what is summed up in the old English saying 'Absence makes the heart grow fonder.'

Then it appears at first glance more than a little strange that many commentators have remarked that COVID-19 means the end of globalization. What actually they mainly have in mind is an idea of globalization that restricts it largely to the economic sphere, and in particular to free trade between nations. Ever since its foundation in 1843, *The Economist* has championed free trade between nations and has seen globalization in that light since the term became prominent in the 1980s.

Hence its cover title for May 2020, 'Goodbye globalisation: The dangerous lure of self-sufficiency'. But trade between countries is not everything in the world's economy. When the OECD published a special report on globalization in 1993, it emphasized transnational firms, jumping over tariff boundaries. People migrate to find jobs. They take their tastes with them. Culture and communication are even more global than trade.

'Self-sufficiency' in fact reinforces globalization. What it means is that a product made elsewhere should be made at home. That secures the spread of the product and methods of production. Montaigne pointed that out too when he said the Chinese had printing and artillery a thousand years before his time, so why the great fuss being made then about having them in Europe? Perhaps we should be talking about the globalization of confusion. *The Financial Times* only two months ago featured an article by Robert Armstrong, 'Coronavirus is not a crisis of globalisation'. The *FT* and *The Economist* are two of the most influential publications in the world for business news. When they advance diametrically opposed judgments on the fallout from the virus and its consequences for globalization, we can only conclude something is happening that is spooking global opinion leaders.

Staying cool, consider what could be more globalized than the daily figures of the worldwide spread of the virus that Johns Hopkins University publishes and that I have used at the start of this piece. What of the worldwide interest in what happens in a city in the middle of China? Wuhan is now a familiar place worldwide, when previously outside China most people would have been hard pressed to say which country it was in. That of course depends on global communication, as does the general knowledge that the Tokyo Olympics have had to be postponed for a year. The Olympics of course are a prime example of the long roots of globalization, an idea with antecedents in Ancient Greece, celebrated in Athens for the first time in the modern era in 1896 and now a movement that brings sports of all kinds together in one amazing festival every four years. The global becomes local in the Games itself but is already localized worldwide as they focus the efforts of aspiring athletes, players and participants all over the world for years ahead of them.

The currents that carry globalization forward are fundamentally cultural, the spread of ideas and knowledge in particular, especially in and through science and technology. National boundaries can do little to prevent the spread of knowledge and indeed today the quest for a vaccine for the virus is a shared effort across the globe, where the claims to ownership are insignificant compared with the vast fund of shared knowledge that is at the disposal of all medical scientists from every nation.

So what price these announcements of the end of globalization? What their authors have in mind primarily are the interruptions in supply chains as countries are forced to erect barriers to travel and the movement of goods during the COVID-19 crisis. They also are thinking of the accentuation of geopolitical tensions as national leaderships come under more pressure from the impact of the virus on their citizens. Strengthening national borders, checking the flows of capital, goods and people certainly impedes the growth of international trade and the movement of people in search of work. Many have equated the rise of a single global market with globalization. Certainly there was a period when the drive towards worldwide freedom of trade, dubbed 'neo-liberalism' by its opponents, was regarded as the core of globalization with its corresponding limitation on national governments' options to shape their own economic policies.

But that was a notion of globalization promoted by the interests that benefited most from it, above all by the most powerful nation–state. Complete free trade between countries may result in an overall increase in benefits, but they are distributed unevenly and it is the biggest national economy that gains the most. In the nineteenth century it was the British who championed free trade; in the twentieth the United States used to beat the drum for that kind of globalization; now it is more often China. In point of fact, economic globalization should not be equated with tariff-free trade. When a country imposes duties on imports, it may also encourage foreign companies to locate production of those goods in it, thus creating new centres of local employment. What has been globalized is the product, something Coca-Cola understood early in the story of its worldwide expansion. That kind of corporate globalization has in turn prompted another complaint, that tastes are everywhere becoming standardized, or, in the words of one critic, that the world has become 'flat'. But corporate global strategy may adopt a different approach from Coca-Cola. If you go to a McDonald's in Budapest you can buy goulash or in Beijing Sichuan double chicken burger. Certainly the World Trade Organization-managed reduction of tariffs between countries has helped the growth of supply chains that extend across the world. In the case of sophisticated manufactured products, the components themselves for the assembled item, for instance a motor vehicle, may come from any number of countries. The measures countries take to lessen the impact of COVID-19 may cause interruptions in those chains, but Toyotas will continue to be sold in the United States and Mercedes in China.

Globalization goes on all the time. What doesn't happen is a reduction in the diversity of life and differences between cultures. What doesn't happen is a march to the same destination. There is no single outcome, but there is the continuing experience of multiple cultures in the same place. Technologies of communication have brought the possibility of knowing what is happening to one's closest and dearest even when they are in another continent. They allow us to talk of events in far-off places. One vivid example I used in my *The Global Age* in 1996 was of the 'milk drinking' Ganesh, the Indian god, that was seen in Delhi one day, and sightings were reported worldwide the next. *The Guardian* newspaper at the time called it the first example of global religious fervour propagated by mass telecommunications. The virus emphasizes the nature of social relationships as nothing before has done, even as it highlights the dangers of physical contact with relatives, friends and colleagues working in close proximity. The result has been worldwide transformation of the workplace, in factories, offices, shops, restaurants. In many cases, these places of employment have been closed down altogether. Venues for sport and entertainment, stadiums and theatres have become echo chambers rather than echoing to applause. The underlying principles of many institutions have been brought into question. Justice and the law are not exempt.

The principle of trial by jury has for centuries occupied a central place in the English idea of the administration of justice. The standard way this has been put into practice in a criminal case is in a single court room, where a judge presides, faced by the accused person in the dock and lawyers for the prosecution and defence. A jury of 12 persons, chosen randomly from the general population, also sit together facing the accused. Normally members of the public will be admitted to a gallery above the court proceedings. The way the case proceeds in open court has of course made it a favourite dramatic setting for plays and films, though at times the court empties for the parties to consult one another. The culmination of the trial, beloved by the dramatist, celebrated in the classic film *Twelve Angry Men* starring Henry Fonda, is when the jury withdraws to a separate room in complete privacy to consider its collective verdict, often a protracted discussion that can take hours or even days. COVID-19 has caused the suspension of the whole process.

Only now, eight weeks after the lockdown in the UK, are tentative attempts being made to conduct trials that observe 'social distancing'. Jury members have to sit two metres apart. Lawyers and officials argue about how they can be seated when the court room has not been designed for that kind of spacing. The jury room is now too small. Another court room has to be taken over for the jury's private consultations. The old saying 'Justice delayed is justice denied' is taking on a new virus-related meaning. It spans the world even as it penetrates the intimate spaces of personal life. It is total in its pervasiveness and extent, beyond anything the prophets of globalization could have imagined. This is something other than globalization, distinct in its origin and in its penetration, for each individual. Sometimes a person is affected directly, in their body. They die from catching the virus. You can't die from catching globalization. At other times they have to stay one or two metres away from other people. This is not globalization either, though it is the advice of the World Health Organization or their government.

This is pandemic. In its incidence it is helped by globalization in the sense of the ease with which people can travel these days and therefore multiply their contacts. But it also is quite different in its comprehensive impact. It penetrates every aspect of personal and institutional life. If one wants a term that suggests a process, as globalization does, then totalization would have to be more appropriate. What we experience now is the totalizing moment in human history. The past use of 'total' in writing about social and political affairs has of course been most prominent in the idea of totalitarianism. This cuts across regular thinking about types of government, because it has no direct relation to democracy. We can have open or total types of democracy in the sense that both depend on the will of the people, but in the total case, at its extreme, every institution and all aspects of personal life are subject to inspection and regulation.

The virus has brought the total moment to global society. To understand this we really have to be clear in our minds what the difference is between global and total. 'Global', since its rise in general use ever since the Second World War, refers to the shared fate of our species on this earth. 'Total' means that every aspect of individual and collective life comes under scrutiny and control. You count, inspect and gather all the individual items together to get the total sum. You provide a cover that can accommodate everything when you go global. The total penetrates whatever there is, the global expands to ensure nothing is left out.

COVID-19 has brought the first *total-global* moment, unprecedented in human experience, so far as we know from recorded history. World wars have been approximations to it, but even they have not had the comprehensive impact that the virus is having on daily life everywhere on earth. It is common to say that nothing will ever be the same again. In this time of shock that may seem obvious. But world wars lasted very much longer than the virus has spread up to now and the world did recover enough to triple its population, double-edged of course.

Many of the changes will come from the added impetus to the advance of communication technology precisely because it operates to intensify both the total and the global. Rivalry between states, competition between corporations, individual aspirations for contact and knowledge all add up to a comprehensive digitalization of life. Whether this relentless advance of technology will actually assist or imperil the future of humankind on this earth is a question that remains to be answered after the virus crisis has passed. Our best hope is that we learn lessons from the experience that can be put to good use in averting the worst consequences of climate change. The total may yet help the global.

6.3 The imperative need and necessity to build a community of shared future for mankind are demonstrated by the novel coronavirus[40]

China's President Xi Jinping emphasized that the COVID-19 outbreak is a fresh reminder that mankind rises and falls together when he talked with UN Secretary General Antonio Guterres on the phone on the evening of 12 March. I have a high opinion of this view. It is imperative for all in the world to recognize that mankind has a shared destiny and future and must therefore look out for each other and marshal a collective response to global challenges. At the present time, China offers the world qualities that can mobilize other countries to meet global threats. We must make the planet – our only home – a better place for all. In the same evening, French President Macron said in a speech on television that 'the epidemic, which affects all continents and strikes all European countries, is the most serious health crisis to hit France in a century'. The outbreak of the novel coronavirus disease has vividly and tragically demonstrated what President Xi described as the major change never seen in a century, in which our only choice is to build a community of shared future for mankind.

The coronavirus pandemic has shown to perfection that it is imperative for human beings to work together to meet global challenges and build a community of shared future for mankind. I said, in my interview with CGTN on 6 March, that the Chinese government has done its very best to ensure that they have informed the rest of the world, and also has taken the measures that set an example for everyone. Because the Chinese government depends on the people. And one of the most remarkable things, I think, for the outside world, is how it shows that the Chinese people themselves cooperate, work hard, exercise extraordinary self-discipline and maintain their good spirit throughout the crisis. When it comes to a virus, boundaries don't matter, races don't matter and we are all in a human family. And there is a great example now: even the one family needs leadership, China has given leadership here, and I'm sure will continue to do so.

The crisis is a very big challenge and it does remind us that we are one people in one world with the shared human future. When it comes to a big crisis, we must work together. Cooperation is the fundamental principle on which we can create the global society. We all belong to national societies but we are all equally global citizens too. We all belong together and crises like this just demonstrate that.

---

[40] 马丁·阿尔布劳：序言，《时代之问，中国之答：构建人类命运共同体》，王义桅著，长沙：湖南人民出版社，2021年版 [English translation: Martin Albrow, Foreword of *Questions of the Times, China's Answers: Building a Community with a Shared Future for Mankind*, by WANG Yiwei, Changsha: Hunan People's Publishing House, 2021].

The future of human society depends on cooperation in tackling global issues that threaten its very existence. It is true that the history of human civilization is a history of combatting diseases and no virus has ever beaten us. The challenges will finally be overcome and a better world will be created as long as countries increasingly accept the concept of building a community with shared future for mankind, cooperate closely and act with decisiveness to face the challenges together.

The following lessons can be learnt from the pandemic:

1) Human beings live in a community with a shared future (global civil society or human family);
2) We need leadership (whether from the US or China or any other country or agency: what matters is the issues, not ethnicity or ideology);
3) The Chinese government has shown global leadership when it depends on its people to combat the coronavirus;
4) We need to cooperate on the significant issues concerning human future and safeguard our world together, which means global governance should be managed by all;
5) The way we cooperate is crucial.

Leadership for a common human future requires theory that is free from national prejudices and outdated ideologies and can deliver solutions to problems that confront us all. A truly global perspective actively looks to shape globalization for human purposes and focuses on global issues that threaten the human future. It is neither for nor against globalization, simply wants to make it work for the public good both for countries but also for the world as a whole.

I'm delighted to see that these ideas are elaborated in Professor Wang Yiwei's latest book, *Understanding a Community of Shared Future for Mankind*. I met Professor Wang because of the Belt and Road Initiative and we have become good friends through studying a community of shared future for mankind. When his first English book was released at the London Book Fair on 12 April 2016, I was the commentator. Also, the article, 'Ten Questions on Belt and Road Initiative: Dialogue with the British sociologist Martin Albrow', published in Dialogues on China, the book marking the 70th anniversary of the People's Republic of China, linked our names again.

In the China Media Centre 2019 Spring Seminar in Westminster University, he delivered a speech themed on 'Three dimensions to understand a community of shared future for mankind' and again I was the commentator. I was impressed by his opinion that the concept of a community of shared future for mankind is the joint fruit of the Chinese traditional culture (common destiny of Taoism, mutualism of Confucianism and shared karma of Buddhism) and that of other nations. He believed that the concept means that China's 'peace and harmony' (*he-he*) culture is adapting Marxism to conditions in China and the current world. In fact, my latest book, *China's Role in a Shared Human Future: Towards Theory for Global Leadership*, shares the same inspiration as his book.

I was really touched that he has summarized this book and translated it into English for my review. He argues that the concept of a community of shared future for mankind upgrades the spirit of globalization, replacing the win–lose zero sum game, even the win–win game, with the 'all win or all lose' model. Take the coronavirus pandemic for instance: a country can only be safe and free from fear after all countries are safe and free from fear. It follows that I am delighted to be invited to write a foreword for this book and can recommend its enthusiastic welcome by the whole international community.

6.4 Witnessing China combatting COVID-19: my story in China[41]

When the COVID-19 virus was recognized in Wuhan in January 2020, reactions, not just in the city but in wider China and in the rest of the world, were instantaneous, panic-stricken, courageous, fatalistic, far-sighted, in short a confusion of contradictory responses to a threat carrying life-changing potential for all human beings.

For 30 years previously, the eyes of the world had been on globalization and increasingly had come to see it as double-edged, dividing as much as uniting people within and between countries. President Xi Jinping's shared future for mankind was a call to escape those kinds of deadlocks of the recent past. But no one foresaw that it would be COVID-19 that brought that shared future into the present day in their own time.

Eye-witness accounts are always invaluable sources for understanding the impact of great events. Hence the initiative of President Liu Li and colleagues in the Beijing Language and Culture University deserves our praise for collecting a set of fresh and immediate responses to the virus within little more than a month of its emergence.

The 11 accounts in this book very explicitly bring the shared future into sharp focus for their messages across boundaries, foreigners in China writing home, from Wuhan to the Congo and to Nepal, from Beijing to Sudan and Iran, from Moscow to China. Above all, they address significant others, family and friends, telling them to stay strong, even as their loved one stays to resist the virus.

Typical of these vivid and moving accounts of the experience of living in COVID-19 times is one by the Cambodian student of cyberspace security, Wu Baoquiang. His very direct personal testimony of being quarantined in isolation

---

[41] Editor's note: This is a book review of the English edition of *Battling the Virus: Witnessing China Combatting COVID-19* (2020), LIU Li (Ed,), Nanchang: Jiangxi Education Publishing House; London: Global Century Press [Chinese edition and overseas Chinese editions: 刘利：主编，《战'疫'：我在中国》，南昌：江西教育出版社；同名海外中文版，伦敦：环球世纪出版社，2020年。The review will be published in the *Journal of China in Global and Comparative Perspectives*, Vol. 7, 2021.

in his dormitory in Wuhan includes a period of being very ill with a fever which turned out not to be COVID.

Here he is, writing home as early as 25 February: 'Mummy, I know you want me to get back home. I am the only child in the family. You are afraid I might encounter any danger but I can tell you for sure that your son is safe now.' He goes on to tell how the Cambodian authorities have been in constant contact and guaranteed living expenses for their students in China.

Through all these difficulties, Wu finished writing his graduation thesis and had a message that is replicated in different words by so many of the contributors to the volume: 'When all the people and countries around the world unite together, they can even overcome the greatest difficulties.'

Even as the message goes out that all should cooperate for the benefit of all, along with it often comes admiration for the example that China gives to others through its own efforts. Already within the month, the Congolese Patric Sadi pointed to the sight of the Huoshenshan hospital being built within ten days and long lines of trucks bringing 'charity supplies' from Pujiang County in Sichuan to Wuhan. Romanian Felicia Nina Gherman wrote excitedly to her parents that Beijing municipal government would convert a factory to making 250,000 masks in a day.

The sense of shock comes through as well as intensity of communication. Wang Xiao, Egyptian doctoral student at BLCU, tells how the Spring Festival holidays had to be abruptly cancelled. Then her father, who had always called her once a week from Egypt, eventually began calling her several times a day as he watched often groundless news stories from China. She decided then to post a Facebook message on 31 January to reassure foreigners. That in turn was picked up as a 'hot post' by the Al Jazeera news channel and she became 'the woman of the hour' for the Arabic media. She felt her telling people of her direct experience was a necessary counter to so much fake news that surrounded COVID-19.

Muhammed Hassan from Khartoum in Sudan was also concerned by the rumours that distorted the true situation in China. This too was the topic that the highly experienced CCTV Tunisian journalist Ennis chose to emphasize in her contribution that opens these personal memoirs. For her, COVID-19 provokes reconnections between people. Her message begins: 'A brand new China is around the corner, where high technology, distance learning and telecommuting will become ubiquitous.' The foreign media consistently ignore the 'selfless and fearless dedication of the Chinese people'.

The world's reaction to China's battle with COVID-19 was as mixed as these personal accounts suggest, but there was also admiration and support from other countries. The editors of the volume have chosen to emphasize this by including 16 messages, ('blessings', they are called) from ambassadors of countries with very different political systems and cultures, including, for example, Russia, Germany, Cuba and Armenia. The message of the highest-level UN official in Beijing may serve to cover them all: 'the international community is behind China. Zhongguo jiayou! (Stay strong, China!).'

At the time of writing now, 18 months later, we have ample evidence that China's efforts to contain the virus, not only in Wuhan and Hubei province but also in smaller outbreaks elsewhere, have succeeded through exemplary personal self-discipline, outstanding administrative competence and inspiring leadership. In comparison with the rest of the world, where many countries have experienced precipitous declines in GDP, in 2020 China was the only major economy to maintain positive growth.

The stories in this volume connect us with what it was like to experience a once-in-a-lifetime global event as it was unfolding. In some sense I too was there. If I may end this review on a personal note: my own interest was intense following my visit in November 2019 to Wuhan University for a conference at the School of Marxism and to give a university lecture in November 2019. My host there, and co-author, Professor Jin Wei, recognized at an early stage the global impact of COVID-19. She expressed that at a personal level by sending to me in London a package of face masks – from a friend in China to a friend of China.

This is the COVID message, people are together, even when they must be apart, that this book conveys in each and every contribution. China offers both an example and practical help to the rest of the world. In addition, in the community of a shared future for mankind it also provides a guiding vision.

6.5 UN Chinese Language Day and sinology and the Chinese language during the epidemic[42]

Nihao! Mr President Liu Li, scholars of Beijing Language and Culture University. You have bestowed on me a great honour by inviting me to speak at your launch of the international Cangjie plan. It's a particular honour because saying 'Nihao' almost exhausts my language capacity in Mandarin, and I regret that greatly, but it has not actually impeded my cooperation and friendly exchanges with Chinese citizens and scholars over many, many years. So it is a particular pleasure to be speaking to you from London when you are in Beijing.

Of course, that distance between us is overcome by the simultaneous possibility of communication over the internet. The problem with that is, of course, that you simultaneously get information as well as instantaneous communication as there are many things that are happening at the same time in the world, and we can't all be present at all of them. So, I'm sorry I can't be present even for the video conferencing today but I hope this message will come through to you.

[42] Editor's note: This is a speech delivered at the virtual conference to mark the 11th UN Chinese Language Day, the 2020 International Humanities Forum 'Promoting Sinology and the Chinese Language during the Epidemic' and Ceremony to Launch the International Cangjie Plan, April 19, 2020, organized by Beijing Language and Culture University.

The common threat that brings us together is, of course, the events surrounding COVID-19. That too is a lesson for all of us. A lesson we all have to share in the future, and that future is not necessary a binary one.

It can be a threat. A common threat can bring people together, but there is no guarantee that this will happen. A common goal can bring things together, but not even that guarantees understanding between peoples, because we may go about it in separate ways, competing and contending with one another in striving for that common goal.

Every country in the world wants to defeats the coronavirus but my impression, certainly in my own country, is of the enormous attention being paid to respective different countries in achieving some reductions in the numbers of infections and the reduction in the rates of deaths that can be an attributed to the virus. And sometimes I think, when I see lists of countries, with their relative rates, it's more like looking at some kind of report on the Premier Football League, with China and the United States at the top, vying for the top place, like Liverpool and Manchester United. That is not the way to achieve a common goal that is in all our interests. It's not a way to achieve that win–win situation that we all wish to have.

Now I'm sure in your educational programmes you are stressing the need to understand other cultures, to discover their languages, to learn their languages. At the same time, of course, we can only know a few languages. I'm very limited in my own proficiency. I only have one other language in which I can speak competently and write adequately, and that's the German language. However, it is surprising how just the ability to speak a second language can bring you closer in the world. Because of that second language you may also meet people who also have a second language.

It has been my great pleasure, for instance, to cooperate with a colleague from one of your rival universities I mentioned, the Beijing Foreign Studies University, Professor Zhang Xiaoying. And with her, I have been able to work on research into a German intellectual, one of the great social scientists of the 20th century, because he wrote on China. He died a hundred years ago, and this year is the centenary of his death. He tried to understand China and what it was in their culture and in their development that was different from those of the West.

Professor Zhang and I have gone back to Max Weber and we have looked at the sources he used, translations from Chinese. But because she had Mandarin and I had German and we both had English, our cooperation overcame the difficulties that he certainly had at the time. What this exhibits is the possibility of networking. We can network across the world with overlapping language competences. And through those networks we can achieve multiple goals which satisfy us. And in that network we can carry forward the understanding between peoples that we all wish for.

As I say, the common threat of COVID, the common goal of world supremacy. Neither of those things will guarantee that actually will reach that win–win situation. We have to think in other terms. We have to think in terms of networks, of cross-country ties, of mutual understanding across boundaries, where we can share a goal that does not create rivalry between us. I'm sure your Cangjie programme, your international Cangjie programme, your plan, is going to be a major contribution to that goal, and I wish it every success.

Thank you for inviting me and let me now say it in another phrase that reaches close to the limit of my Chinese language capacity: xiexie, thank you. Goodbye.

6.6 Will the epidemic block the pace of globalization?[43]

LONDON, March 22, 2020 (Xinhua) – China, led by the Communist Party of China (CPC), is marching toward completely building a moderately prosperous society in all respects this year, which is a great accomplishment, said renowned British sociologist Martin Albrow in a recent interview with Xinhua.

Albrow, currently a fellow of the Academy of Social Sciences in Britain, has visited China many times since 1987. 'The success of the party is really taking China forward, rejuvenating China,' he said, adding that the achievement of CPC is a great transformation of the mood of the country. 'We have to look at CPC in relation to the previous hundred years. There were years of, as you say, a century of humiliation. So it's a transformation of the mood of the country. It has created optimism and unity, and those are great achievements in the mood of the country,' the scholar said.

According to Albrow, there are three major reasons for the CPC's success in transforming China.

First, he is impressed that the CPC has been firmly sticking to the path of socialism with Chinese characteristics, which is an 'overriding objective'. 'The CPC has maintained this drive to unify Chinese society, and it continues with that,' Albrow said. The other key, Albrow said, is that the CPC has been pushing forward implementing the reform and opening-up policy over the past more than 40 years, and adopted a very subtle and pragmatic approach to world relations.

'In particular, they have embraced globalization. They've adopted open policy towards the rest of the world, and the reform policy, which allows foreign companies to invest in China and encourages trade with China, but at the same time protects Chinese property rights and ability to control its own affairs. So it's not unqualified globalization,' said Albrow, who is one of the first globalization theorists. He especially mentioned that being enormously cooperative with other nations and international organizations, like the United Nations and the World Trade Organization, is also a very important part of China's success.

---

[43] 张代蕾:"英国知名社会学家：中共改变整个民族精神面貌"，《参考消息》，2021年2月18日，见：http://www.cankaoxiaoxi.com/china/20210218/2435005.shtml [The well-known British sociologist: the CCP changes the spiritual outlook of the entire nation. Interviewed by Zhang Dailei, *Reference News*. 18/02/2021].

The third reason for the CPC's success lies in its capability, said Albrow, who believes China's fight against the COVID-19 pandemic is a fine demonstration of the quality of CPC governance.

'It shows the Communist Party of China is able to mobilize the country as a whole around single goals,' Albrow said.

As far as globalization is concerned, China also gives a good example to the rest of the world, Albrow added. 'I'm thinking of the Belt and Road particularly. This is goal-directed development, not development in accord with some kind of ideological fantasy, not about taking forms of government anyway. I think it is very appropriate for the current situation,' the expert explained. He said, 'Belt and Road provides the world with two important examples of how to build a community of shared future. Firstly, it shows that technologies cross boundaries. They are the products of human ingenuity and efforts that can benefit all who care to make use of them. [Second,] 'it is the exact opposite to isolation. China and the other nations joining in the Belt and Road agreements are using their sovereign rights and power to work towards goals that all can share and help to meet global challenges that face us all.'

He told Xinhua that the world is facing a 'very unsettled environment' for a number of reasons, one of them being the coronavirus pandemic, which 'ought to create global unity because it affects everybody, but in fact it has actually created a lot of tensions.' However, he believes China is able to respond to the global situations wisely, as the CPC and Chinese people are 'very well equipped because they're very pragmatic and very wise.'

6.7 The epidemic highlights the importance of building a community with a shared future for mankind[44]

In a recent interview with Xinhua News Agency, academician of the British Academy of Social Sciences and well-known sociologist Martin Albrow said that responding to major public health events such as COVID-19 requires the collective wisdom and collaboration of all mankind, highlighting the importance of building a community of shared future for mankind.

In a recent interview with Xinhua News Agency, academician of the British Academy of Social Sciences and well-known sociologist Martin Albrow said that responding to major public health events such as COVID-19 requires the collective wisdom and collaboration of all mankind, highlighting the importance of building a community of shared future for mankind.

[44] 张代蕾、桂涛：专访：疫情凸显构建人类命运共同体重要性——访英国知名社会学家阿尔布劳，《新华网》，2020年2月18日，杨晓强 译，见：http://www.xinhuanet.com/world/2020-02/18/c_1125590775.htm [English translation: ZHANG Dailei, GUI Tao, interview with Martin Albrow, a well-known British sociologist: The epidemic highlights the importance of building a community with a shared future for mankind, *Xinhua Net*, 18/02/2020. Translated by YANG Xiaoqiang].

Albrow was one of the first scholars to put forward the concept of 'globalization'. At the age of 82, he has devoted himself to studying China's governance system in recent years and has authored the book *China's Role in a Shared Human Future: Towards Theory for Global Leadership*.

He said that global crises such as infectious disease epidemics and climate change have shown mankind the degree of interdependence and close contact with one another, making people aware of the necessity of cooperation and sharing and building a community of shared future for mankind. He supported China's efforts in responding to COVID-19 and praised the information exchange and sharing between China and international institutions such as the World Health Organization. He said that the Chinese government's powerful measures to prevent and control the spread of COVID-19 impressed him, and the rapid construction of two hospitals was also a miracle. He paid tribute to the medical staff fighting on the front line of the epidemic. 'Chinese medical staff work day and night, regardless of danger, even at the cost of their lives,' he said. 'They have provided tremendous support for dealing with this crisis. I believe the whole world will see and recognize the Chinese people's efforts.'

Albrow said that, in the face of COVID-19, all countries in the world need to work together to effectively curb the spread of the disease and finally develop a vaccine to completely defeat it. 'In a sense, this will be a beneficial impact of the epidemic and help build a community of shared future for mankind.' He believes that the key to building such a community of shared future lies in global cooperation and achieving common goals through common projects, which is more important than establishing multinational institutions. He believes that China is capable of taking a leading role in these cooperative projects.

Responsible editor: CHENG Lan

6.8 China's fight against the epidemic is a global model, using its own actions to interpret the importance of building a community with a shared future for mankind[45]

International Online report (reporter Liang Tao): Martin Albrow, a renowned sociologist of the British Academy of Social Sciences, said China has made great efforts to cope with COVID-19, serving as a model for the world. With its own actions, China has interpreted the importance and major role of building a community with a shared future for mankind.

Professor Martin Albrow told reporters in an interview that China has set a good example for the global fight against the epidemic, and that the excellent qual-

[45] 梁弢，英国社会学家表示 中国抗击疫情堪称全球典范 用自身行动诠释构建人类命运共同体重要性，《国际在线》，2020年3月8日，李可亦 译，见：http://cn.chinadaily.com.cn/a/202003/08/WS5e646256a3107bb6b57a5162.html [English translation: LIANG Tao, British sociologist said that China's fight against the epidemic is a global model, using its own actions to interpret the importance of building a community with a shared future for mankind, *China Radio International Online*, 08/03/2020. Translated by LI Keyi].

ity of the Chinese people has once again impressed the world. Albrow said, 'The Chinese government has done everything to the best of its capacity to respond to the epidemic. They inform the world of the epidemic in time, and the measures they have taken have set a good example for the world. The Chinese government relies on the whole population. In my opinion, China's deepest impression from its fight against the epidemic is how the Chinese people unite, work together, are highly self-disciplined and have always maintained a positive and optimistic spirit in the face of the crisis. Therefore, I think the efforts of the Chinese people and the Chinese government in fighting the epidemic are a global model.'

Professor Albrow pointed out that the COVID-19 outbreak currently occurs in many countries around the world. Although all countries adopt different response strategies and measures because of different administrative systems, China's experience provides a lesson for all countries.

Professor Albrow, 82, was one of the first scholars to propose the idea of 'globalization'. He has spent many years studying China's national governance system and is the author of *China's Role in a Shared Human Future: Towards Theory for Global Leadership*. Professor Albrow believes that in the face of COVID-19, China has explained with its own actions the importance of building a community with a shared future for mankind. Albrow said, 'The virus is mysterious and terrible, can devour lives; this is a huge misfortune. But it also reminds us that we live in a world and in the same community with a shared future for mankind. Indeed, the virus has no borders and takes no account of race. But we are a big family of humans, and I think that's a good example. In such a big family, leadership needs to stand up, and China is playing such a leadership role, and I believe China will continue to do so.'

Professor Albrow believes that the fight will provide solid impetus for cooperation to tackle global crises such as climate change. Albrow said, 'I think in some ways, this 'battle' against the novel coronavirus will unite the world. As I stress, the practical action of cooperation will bring about more examples of cooperation. I am very sure that this global crisis will lead us to focus on other global crises. I am therefore very sure that global climate change will also really gain momentum from this fight against the novel coronavirus. My overall feeling is that the outcome of the fight against the epidemic will be conducive to promoting global cooperation in the future response to the crisis.'

PART III

Globalization of Chinese Social Sciences

DOI https://doi.org/10.24103/GCSS6.en.2021.7

Chapter 7
Academic and social missions in China[1]

This chapter starts with a description of the author's interests in China and engagements with Chinese sociological circles from the 1960s to the early 1990s, covering both his academic and his social missions. In the past two or more decades, the author has been interested most in nurturing relations with students and colleagues in China and exchanging views and information on the developing interaction between China and the rest of the world. They can be viewed from his writing and activities in China and the UK on China related work and matters. It shows the author's intellectual appetite for carrying on both academic and social missions throughout his academic career. This section is followed by two sections on Engagements with Chinese through foreign studies circles (7.2) and Engagements with Chinese mainstream academia (7.3), both of which are aimed at encouraging Chinese scholars to carry out their academic mission. The last section is Engagement with Chinese media (7.4), which supports our social mission to promote understanding between China and the world.

7.1 A Chinese episode in the globalization of sociology[2]

A volume celebrating Fei Xiaotong's immense achievements may well emphasize his understanding of China, but, in the framework of a global sociology, that is bound to lead towards an understanding of a wider and a better world. It has indeed already done so. Writing a short book introducing sociology to a general public, I cited Fei as the sociologist whose work has produced the greatest effect on the greatest number of people anywhere.[3]

My reasoning was based on the cumulative influence that his research had exercised over the years on the introduction of the responsibility system in Chinese agriculture. He was a creative co-author at the outset of the long story of the massive release of personal and collective energies which continues to be told in China today, and which is now spreading its influence worldwide. 'For China today, for the world tomorrow': that has to be the direction of those energies in

---

[1] Editor's note: All the descriptions for the connections between each section have been inserted in this chapter.

[2] Editor's note: This invited paper was included in *Fei Xiaotong Studies* (2016), Vol. 2. Eds. Feuchtwang, Chang and Zhou, London: Global Century Press and Beijing: New World Press, pp.79–90. It has also appeared in the *Journal of China in Global and Comparative Perspectives* (2016), Vol. 2, 2016, pp. 78–89, and as a Postscript in *China's Role in a Shared Human Future: Towards Theory for Global Leadership* (2018), by Martin Albrow, London: Global Century Press, pp.166–175.

[3] Albrow (1999a), *Sociology; The Basics,* p. 64.

the social sciences too. The brief memoir that follows will relate an early episode in such a story as it happened in sociology from the standpoint of a participant.

As a graduate student at the London School of Economics working on Max Weber, I was familiar with his seminal study of the religion of China.[4] But my first acquaintance with contemporary Chinese scholarship and with Fei's work was inspired in 1960 by that fine anthropologist Maurice Freedman. Because, as a rather green student in his graduate seminar, I rashly admitted a schoolboy enthusiasm for Arthur Waley's translations of Chinese poetry, he asked me to prepare a paper on Chinese social institutions. He thus led me into the mysteries (for a Westerner) of *li* via his student Sybille van der Sprenkel's thesis on Chinese law.[5]

It was a big ask of someone whose first degree was in Western history, and an entry in my diary for January 20, 1960 reads, 'Desperation over this paper on China – contemplate giving up – why must every little setback appear a cosmic issue?' But a day later Maurice changed it all. The diary continues, 'Paper delivered – generous praise, excessive pleasure.' His kind treatment of the resulting paper was an important ingredient in my later confident belief that sociology could build a firm bridge across the West–East cultural divides – and, yes, the youthful diary writer was right, bridging those divides will determine the human future and, in that anthropocentric sense, is 'cosmic'.[6]

A fuller test of that confidence came in the 1980s after I was asked to become the founding editor of a new journal for the International Sociological Association (ISA), *International Sociology*. This was part of a renewed drive by the ISA to strengthen bridges between the 'three worlds', capitalist, socialist and developing. It reflected, and took advantage of, the lowering of international barriers at that time to the free exchange of information and ideas. Liberalization of communist regimes was being promoted in the Soviet Union by President Mikhail Gorbachev through perestroika.

In China, reform was being led by senior leader Deng Xiaoping, Chairman and General Secretary Hu Yaobang and Premier Zhao Ziyang through the responsibility system in agriculture. This was the geopolitical and cultural climate in which the Executive Committee of the ISA, first under its president, Fernando Cardoso, subsequently President of Brazil, and then under his successor, Margaret Archer of the University of Warwick, determined to realize sociology's potential as a universalizing agency for creating one world.

The journal aimed, in Cardoso's words, 'to offer the reader a more global and comprehensive view of contemporary sociology' but to do that 'by showing

4 Weber (1951), *The Religion of China* [Chinese edition: (德)韦伯：《中国宗教》中译本《儒教与道教》，王容芬译，北京：商务印书馆，1999年版].

5 van der Sprenkel (1963), A Sociological Analysis of Chinese Legal Institutions.', *American Journal of Sociology*, Volume 68, Number 5.

6 An extended autobiographical account of the atmosphere of the LSE at that time and the stages of a journey through global sociology back to it again in the Global Governance Centre can be found in Mathieu Deflem's volume *Sociologists in a Global Age* (2007).

pluralistic paths of concern in sociology rooted in different historical and cultural traditions'.[7] It was therefore my privilege as its editor to follow the discipline wherever in the world it led. One direction was China, partly because of the happy accident that I was already working in partnership with a significant player in China's drive to modernize, the State Family Planning Commission.

In 1979, the Chinese Government and the United Nations Fund for Population Activities had signed a Memorandum of Understanding that led to in-country assistance for family planning programmes and cooperation with multilateral agencies including the International Planned Parenthood Federation and with training centres overseas.[8] Within that framework, the Population Centre of University College Cardiff provided courses for mid-career officials in the population programmes of developing countries and the State Family Planning Commission of China was one of the agencies that each year sent us two or three of their staff for a Diploma or Master's Degree in Population Policies. Such was the strategic significance of their work for the direction of China's population policies that we were honoured by the visit to Cardiff of the minister in charge of the Commission, Wang Wei, in February 1987.[9]

In November 1987, accompanied by our former student, friend and translator, Li Yong, my wife, Sue Owen, who lectured at the Centre on the economics of ageing, and I, as Director of the Centre, had the privilege of being conducted on visits to offices and sites of the Commission's work in Beijing, Nanjing and Hangzhou and neighbouring villages. We lectured in Nanjing College for Family Planning Administrators on 'The Education of Population Programme Professionals: The Cardiff Philosophy' (Albrow) and on 'Fertility Decline and Female Labour Force participation in the West' (Owen). In Hangzhou University we gave a joint lecture on 'The Old and the Young: the Contemporary Western Crisis'.[10]

At the same time, my visit to China provided a wonderful opportunity to renew an invitation to Chinese sociologists to join in the ISA's efforts to internationalize the discipline. I was deputed by Margaret Archer to represent the Association on my visit and met with Ding Weizhi, Deputy Secretary of the Chinese Academy of Social Sciences, and Professor Lu Xueyi, Deputy Director of the Academy's Institute of Sociology, to discuss Chinese membership of the Association.

---

[7] Fernando H. Cardoso (1986), Foreword, *International Sociology*, 1(1).

[8] Government of China (1987). Leaflet: 'Family Planning Program in China 1987'.

[9] In the newspaper *Western Mail* (February 26, 1987), Charles Hymas, under the headline 'Experts of birth control on visit', wrote, 'A Chinese leader with the toughest family planning job in the world got the chance of some on-the-spot population analysis on a visit to South Wales yesterday.' Wang Wei was pictured viewing computer population projections and the story told how 16 officials from the State Family Planning Commission had studied at the Cardiff Population Centre over the previous five years.

[10] An unpublished account of the tour was circulated as 'Report of an Observational Tour of the Family Planning Programme of the People's Republic of China' by Martin Albrow and Susan Owen, 25/11/87.

There was a history to these talks. The ISA had for some time been seeking to bring the Chinese Sociological Research Society, of which Professor Fei Xiaotong was president, into full membership, and therefore to represent sociology for the People's Republic of China. A formal invitation was sent in August 1985 and repeated in February 1986 and Fei came to the World Congress in Delhi that year and discussed the matter with the ISA's president, Fernando Cardoso.

The talks came to nothing because of the sensitive issue of concurrent membership of the Chinese Sociological Association of Taiwan. That was still the situation in November 1987 and, in explaining it, Professor Margaret Archer, the new President of the ISA, wished me well in my discussions with the Chinese sociologists, writing, 'If you could somehow find your way through this wood, you will have accomplished a major geopolitical miracle in sociological terms'.[11]

It was clear to me that such a miracle was beyond my powers, but equally my experience of working relations with Chinese officials in the population field showed there was always the possibility of finding ways of cooperating across political boundaries if we tried to find areas of common interest and values.

Sociology had been suspended in 1952, politically prohibited in 1959 and re-established in China in 1979 when Deng declared that 'we neglected the study of political science, law, sociology and international politics, and it is now essential for us to catch up' (Dai, 1993a: 92).

The Chinese Sociological Association was founded in 1979 and there was a growing enthusiasm for the subject in official circles and rapid expansion in its provision in the 1980s. The State Education Commission commissioned a report in 1986 on the future demand for sociologists from the Departments of Sociology of Nankai University and of the Shanghai College of Liberal Arts. It was published in the new journal *Shehuixue Yanjiu* (*Sociological Studies*) in July 1987, concluding that 798 postgraduates and 1,423 first-degree holders were urgently needed across government, the Party, in journalism and publishing, in large enterprises and in education.[12] The climate was therefore favourable to an approach in 1987 that invited collaborative work rather than the formal institutional agreements that the ISA had previously been seeking.

The fortunate basis for that collaboration was the new journal I edited and, with the enthusiastic support of Lu Xueyi, who visited us in Cardiff with his colleague Dai Kejing,[13] we were able to establish a productive publication

[11] Private communication from Margaret Archer, 13 October 1987.

[12] Nankai University Investigation Group, 1989.

[13] Editor's note: In 1988, when the author was President of the British Sociological Association (BSA), he invited Professor LU Xueyi and his colleague Ms DAI Kejing to visit the UK for a month. According to Deborah Cole, they visited the Welsh Folk Museum and expressed their particular interest in rural development and family life. Lu suggested that China should have such a folk life museum that could show people what life used to be and how it has developed and improved. See 'Chinese scholars praised our village folk museum', News of Wales, *Western Mail*, October 27, 1988.

arrangement which included Dai becoming an Associate Editor for *International Sociology*. She and I, with the generous agreement of its editor, Wang Yuming, worked together to publish five papers in English from *Shehuixue Yanjiu* in 1989 and 1990, including the report on the demand for sociology graduates. *Shehuixue Yanjiu* started publication in January 1986, appeared every two months and usually included about 20 articles in each issue, so choosing just five to appear in *International Sociology* was an invidious task. What we tried to do was to find a balance between papers reporting research on Chinese society, such as market towns[14] and social security,[15] and ones that reflected on China's place in the contemporary world, social modernization[16] and the dual structure of Chinese society.[17]

A further three papers by Dai on rural women,[18] LI Lulu, Yang Xiao and WANG Fengyu on stratification,[19] and LU Jianjua (1991) on workers' expectations of management,[20] appeared in the last issue of *International Sociology* that I edited. These gave me particular pleasure because the latter two papers had been selected by a Chinese jury for the ISA's Competition for Young Sociologists and Lu's was one of the five eventual winners from the worldwide field of 335 entries.[21]

Under Dai's careful editorial scrutiny, the journal was able over the years to publish a series of academic papers from Chinese sociologists working in China. I stress 'Chinese working in China' because the philosophy underlying the journal was that there should be no political, cultural or linguistic barriers to publication. This may well appear to be the policy for so many Western so-called 'international' academic journals, but in practice those barriers exist, especially the linguistic one that requires authors to write in perfect English.

Our policy was that no paper would be rejected on language grounds, which meant that we had to assess papers in the language of their origin first.[22] Dai's bilingualism was invaluable for the journal, as it was when she translated Fei's LSE

---

[14] YE Kelin, ZOU Nongjian, YE Nanke (1989), The Establishment of Market Town Sociology with Chinese Characteristics, *International Sociology*, 4(4).

[15] CHEN Liangjin (1990), Social Developmental Mechanisms and Social Security Functions.' *International Sociology*, 5(1).

[16] LI Lulu (1989), Theoretical Theses on 'Social Modernization', *International Sociology*, 4(4).

[17] PAN Jianxiong (1990), The Dual Structure of Chinese Culture and Its Influence on Modern Chinese Society, *International Sociology*, 5(1).

[18] DAI Kejing (1991), The Life Experience and Status of Chinese Rural Women from Observation of Three Age Groups, *International Sociology*, 6(1).

[19] LI Lulu, YANG Xiao and WANG Fengyu (1991), The Structure of Social Stratification and the Modernization Process in Contemporary China, *International Sociology*, 6(1).

[20] LU Jianhua (1991), Chinese Workers' High Expectations of Enterprise Managers, *International Sociology*, 6(1).

[21] Daniel Bertaux (1990), Designing the Worldwide Competition, *International Sociology*, 5(4).

[22] Martin Albrow (1991), Internationalism as a Publication Project: Experience in Editing an International Sociological Journal, *Current Sociology*, 39(1).

doctorate into Chinese in 1986, a volume which had previously been regarded as 'criminal evidence' of 'a widespread pernicious influence' in the Cultural Revolution when he was detained in the 'cowshed' or sent for 'retraining' in the 'cadre school'.[23]

But bridging the language barrier was only one aspect of the way we conceived of the sociological mission at the time. A culminating moment came in 1990 with the World Congress of Sociology in Bielefeld, advertised with the theme 'Sociology for One World: Unity and Diversity'. Archer used that title for her presidential address,[24] in which she argued for the universality of human reason, rejecting both a false unitary perspective on the world, whether as modernization or postmodernism, and also a relativism which postulated unbridgeable gulfs between cultures. Sociology, she argued, showed how global mechanisms combined with regional circumstances to create a diversity of novel configurations. Globalization was then not the effect of a new world on the old but part of the interaction of new and old to create a different world.

'Sociology for One World' had been the title of an editorial article I wrote earlier for the second volume of *International Sociology*, in which I argued that the drive for indigenous sociologies was not a retreat from the programme of a universal science.[25] I also touched on the practical consequences of such a vision for selecting papers for the journal. One of the more contentious conclusions I drew in effect was that intellectual excellence alone was not the sole criterion for publication. Stated so baldly, this caused considerable debate. My position was, and remains, that the universalizing mission of sociology requires knowledge to be grown from multiple viewpoints. 'The corpus of sociological knowledge is enriched by contributions from representatives of groups with distinctive social experience'[26]

Let me illustrate the implications of this policy in practical terms, with a necessarily invented example. Let us suppose there are 20 papers, all rated good, competing for space in one issue of a journal that can publish only ten. The 'best' 15 papers are by Western men and women on features of industrialized societies: there are three by women on women's issues in the West and two by non-Westerners, one by a man, one by a woman, in each case on issues from their own cultures. What do I choose for publication? On the basis of my principle of representing diversity, I choose six of the 15, two of the three on women's issues, and both the non-Western papers. Nine of the best papers will have to go elsewhere. Now, of course, you can query the premise of this example as follows: Why would the best papers all be by Westerners? To which my reply is that this simply represents the

[23] DAI Kejing (1993b), Portrait: Fei Xiaotong 1910 –, *International Sociology*, 8(2).

[24] Margaret Archer (1991), Presidential Address: Sociology for one world: unity and diversity, *International Sociology*, 6(2).

[25] Martin Albrow (1987b), Sociology for One World, *International Sociology*, 2(1).

[26] Ibid., p. 7.

subterranean, often subliminal processes and judgments made on language, networks, reputations and orthodox paradigms of research, which time and again will bias the judgment of what is 'best' and will lead to the exclusion of whole areas that sociology needs to take into account.

Diversity as a policy promotes the intellectual comprehensiveness and innovative excellence of the discipline as a whole, as opposed to what happens when we work as if seeking the winners of a competition between individuals. Of course when, as happened with Lu Jianjua, a non-Westerner wins a competition dominated by Westerners, there is double reason for rejoicing.[27] Even there, however, note well that we published papers explicitly to represent the younger generation of sociologists. There were older people who did not make the age limit of under 35, and were correspondingly excluded, who otherwise would have appeared in print. No apologies!

I won't carry this abstract argument further into ever deeper territory in this short memoir. Suffice it to say that it can be pursued up to, and including, ultimate assumptions about how knowledge is gained, what it is for and, indeed, what it is. And the course of that argument would take us into and beyond ideological issues about competition and collective wisdom. For these reasons, debates about editorial decisions on the content of a journal are never purely 'academic'.

Elsewhere, commenting on the editorial policy of *International Sociology*, I expressed this view provocatively and concretely: 'There is, therefore, something which the young female Indian sociologist working in her own city can give to sociology which is beyond the capacity of the senior male American sociologist working in the same place.'[28]

And further, for an illustration of the consequences of that policy for Chinese sociology we can refer to the statistics of papers received and accepted by the journal in its first four years, as reported in volume 39 of *Current Sociology*.[29] From the United States, 55 papers were received and 18 accepted, from the USSR, six and one respectively, and from China, six received, six accepted.

Enough said. I want rather to dwell on the relatively limited topic (though still enormous in its own right) of the contribution that the Chinese collaboration made to the globalization of sociology at that time and how we can construe it now. It was only then that the discipline was beginning to reflect on the consequences of globalization for itself. The term 'globalization' was already being domesticated in the language of sociology in papers from 1985 onwards by Roland Robertson.[30] He was emphasizing consciousness of the globe as an element in the creation of global society, a product of his own dual interest in the sociology of religion and in international relations.

---

[27] LU Jianjua (1991), Ibid.

[28] Albrow (1991), 'Internationalism as a Publication Project,' Ibid. p. 111.

[29] Ibid., pp 116–118.

[30] Robertson (1992), *Globalization: Social Theory and Global Culture*, London: SAGE Publications.

In the pages of *International Sociology,* Piotr Sztompka was another pointing to the globalization of society as involving the internationalization of sociology and a revision of older ideas of comparative method.[31] Zsuzsa Hegedus pointed to the new planetary orientation of 1980s movements, 'conflictualizing' global issues and effectively 'globalizing' individuals, something she referred to as empowerment and globalization.[32]

It was papers such as these that prompted me to recommend to the ISA that the volume to be presented to the delegates at the Madrid World Congress should be drawn from papers published in the journal and bear the title *Globalization, Knowledge and Society*.[33] I believe this was the first time that 'globalization' figured in an English book title. The volume could not have been compiled without the work of Elizabeth King, who had given editorial support from the early planning of the journal and continued through to her tragically early death.[34] In a way, her own biography, spanning Germany, Switzerland, the UK and Greece, epitomized the way I conceptualized the globalization of sociology in the Introduction to the volume: 'It results from the freedom individual sociologists have to work with other individuals anywhere on the globe and to appreciate the worldwide processes within which and on which they work.'[35]

That rather general-sounding formulation actually was intended to represent a concrete stage beyond two others in the development of sociology, which, in succession, were the 'internationalism' and 'indigenization' of the discipline. The former was a post-Second World War phenomenon associated with modernization in both American and socialist thought, and the latter primarily an assertion of autonomy and the values of traditional culture in Third World societies. The volume reflected both of those orientations but pointed also to an emergent one of a globalized sociology, where there is a diversity of sociological dialects and special visions within a worldwide shared discourse.

While not explicit at that point, my reflections drew on understandings that fitted with and were enhanced by what I was learning about Chinese sociology. LI Lulu emphasized that the combination of a huge population, an ancient culture and socialism meant China was bound to develop a distinctive kind of modernization, but he and colleagues in a later paper argued that the old hierarchical culture still inhibited the creativity required for a successful non-Western modernization.[36] In Pan Jianxiong's account of the dual structure of ancient Chinese culture, its com-

---

[31] Piotr Sztompka (1988), Conceptual Frameworks in Comparative Inquiry: Divergent or Convergent, *International Sociology*, 3(3).

[32] Zsuzsa Hegedus (1989), Social Movements and Social Change in Self-Creative Society, *International Sociology*, 4(1).

[33] Martin Albrow and Elizabeth King (1990), *Globalization, Knowledge and Society: Readings from International Sociology*, London: Sage.

[34] Martin Albrow (1998), Obituary: Elizabeth King, 1949-98, *International Sociology*, 13(4).

[35] Albrow and King (1990), op. cit., p.7.

[36] Li (1989); Li, Yang and Wang (1991), Ibid..

bination of autocracy and a secular humanism meant that a conformity in ethics and mutual goodwill provided stability but also a barrier to Western modernization.[37] These accounts captured cultural specifics but did not yet address the way they could frame the development of sociology.

A later round-table discussion led by Dai directly addressed the conceptual problems of a Chinese sociology under globalized conditions.[38] Dai wrote of a 'bumper harvest' for sociology in the previous decade, recording 15 universities where there was a department of sociology and 31 specialized research institutes. That compares with the Nankai report of 1987, which detailed only five university departments and three research institutes. She reported on the third meeting of the Board of Directors of the Chinese Sociological Association in August 1990, which emphasized the need to integrate theory and practice with the goal of creating a Chinese sociology, and where Fei stressed an overwhelming need for further development.

In the other papers of that symposium we find a discussion of the Sinification and globalization of sociology that could almost be taken as a textbook case of the issues involved in indigenization. Bettina Gransow surveyed the different tendencies in intensive debates among Chinese sociologists in Taiwan, Hong Kong, the United States and the People's Republic. She concluded that 'the endeavour towards the sinicization of sociology led to a learning process about sociology's cultural and civilizational ties, a learning process which sharpened the senses for the relative limits set within the context of cultural semantic patterns, even if a universal approach was taken.'[39]

For Chan Hoiman,[40] commenting on Gransow, this debate about globalization and Sinification reflected a wider anxiety about the universalistic credentials of sociology, ones which we saw that Archer was concerned to reassert, and which for Chan would be advanced through a reflexive sociology, one that continually reflected on its foundations under the pressure of indigenizing and globalizing forces. Such a sociology, as advocated by Alvin Gouldner and Pierre Bourdieu, would be one of perpetual self-rejuvenation.

And that is an appropriate point to end this short account of an episode in the globalization of sociology, because the reflexivity of a discipline is fundamental to the advance of knowledge and it continues apace. But the case of this particular encounter between China and a globalizing sociology reveals something about both sociology and reflexivity.

There is a big difference between the reflexivity that arises out of self-examination and the reflectiveness induced through partnership in conversation where

[37] Pan (1990), Ibid..

[38] DAI Kejing (1993a), The Vicissitudes of Sociology in China, *International Sociology,* 8(1).

[39] Bettina Gransow (1993), Chinese Sociology: Globalization and Sinicization, *International Sociology,* 8(1).

[40] Chan Hoiman (1993), Some Metasociological Notes on the Sinicization of Sociology, *International Sociology,* 8(1).

each party reflects on itself and on the other. What I think we managed by introducing Chinese sociology into *International Sociology* was to bring the in-culture self-examination into an arena of multiple exchanges. It highlights cultural differences while simultaneously enhancing mutual understanding.

What does this say about universality, the quality regarded as fundamental to true knowledge? Within sociology, we may employ mathematical and statistical methods that are acknowledged to have universal validity, but we fail to find the invariant relations that characterize the natural sciences. A goal of shared understandings between all human beings is not achieved by means of a science akin to that of the natural world but only through multiple encounters that are bound always to cross cultural and linguistic barriers.

The shared understandings we arrive at often arise from the recognition of a particular patterning of underlying elements that one culture selects out as strategic, the separate components of which, however, can be identified in any culture. When we recognize such a pattern in another culture, because those individual components are familiar to us in our own, we also see its potential for us in our own culture and often seek to replicate it. We discover possibilities for ourselves through understanding others. The history of East–West relations is therefore one of experimenting with each other's ways of life.

It is in this light that I see in sociology the distinction in early German theory between *Gemeinschaft* and *Gesellschaft*, which has generated a wealth of finer distinctions in English. While the original opposition remains embedded in German thought and experience and has no exact equivalent in English, which is why we retain the German terms in English-language publications, it represents a configuration of thought and feeling that may be identifiable in English-speaking cultures but never precisely replicable, and for those who speak both languages it is obvious there can be no exact equivalent.[41]

We can expect many more such examples the more the discipline recognizes indigenous roots to social thought. Recently, Xiangqun Chang's account of the prevalence and durability of *Li shang wanglai* in a Chinese village has provided a fine example of identifying the irreducible distinctiveness of culturally transmitted patterns of social relations.[42] And yet we can still see that this is one possible pattern of social relations, culturally defined in China, but not without approximations elsewhere.

The understanding we achieve of *Li shang wanglai* and its place in Chinese society through Chang's work illuminates cognate patterns, resemblances and differences, in other cultures. This is what is conveyed through her development of it

[41] Editor's note: The author's reflections could be ended here without reading Chang's book, which was published in 2010. Although there is a gap in the author's interests and engagement in China from 1996 to 2010, this chapter presents relevant writings chronologically.

[42] Xiangqun Chang (2010), *Guanxi or Li shang wanglai? : Reciprocity, Social Support Networks, Social Creativity in a Chinese Village,* Taipei: Airiti Press.

as an analytical concept in conjunction with ideas of reciprocity and networks. In comparative work, it therefore operates for us in Weberian terms as an ideal type. Underlying this intelligibility are generic ideas of individual people, acting in social relations with each other. These are translatable into any language, belonging to a universal sociological thesaurus that conveys an unconfined diversity in the concrete manifestations of those relations in social life.

The most elementary features of the human condition are recognizable across cultures, are pre-linguistic and are shared with other species – birth, bonding, nurture, reproduction, health, death among others – and these enable us to cross cultures in our understanding. We replicate the universal features of our species as much, or even more, as we meet foreigners than we do in engaging with our own countrymen, when we are confined by the oddities of our own culture. Chinese and Westerners are of one humankind and we can rejoice in finding difference and similarity in each other.

But there is another moment in the globalization of sociology, and indeed of globalization in general, namely, that whatever differences there are between our cultures, there are supervening issues that affect the human future on this earth. Both climate change and nuclear security are challenges that require cooperation across all boundaries.

Whatever the unity sociology has found *in and through* diversity, it now has to find unity *beyond* diversity in facing the global challenges. This is what animated my concern 'to respect all peoples as potential sources of wisdom for our own time. Already the global age is the first period in human history when both sexes and all peoples have gone a considerable way towards asserting their equal right to make their contribution to the common stock of human knowledge.'[43]

In the 1980s, the problem of how we understand each other was uppermost in our drive to globalize sociology. Since then, the need to cooperate to solve global challenges has become a more urgent priority. We cannot dwell forever on the problems of understanding each other before we work together in a common cause. In that sense, achieving an understanding adequate for the challenges facing humankind collectively is a proper ambition for sociology in our times. That has to be the main thrust of a globalized sociology today, and I am as confident of Chinese sociologists as of any national body of sociologists that they will be major contributors to that joint endeavour.

7.2 Engagements with Chinese through foreign studies circles

7.2.1 Beijing Foreign Studies University (BFSU)

Like American anthropologist Marshall Sahlins (1930–2021), Honorary Doctorate at the London School of Economics and Political Science (LSE), and sociologist Craig Calhoun, former LSE Director, who visited Beijing Foreign

[43] Albrow (1996), p. 6.

Studies University (BFSU) in the 1970s and 1980s, respectively, the author too, in his re-engagement with China, lectured at BFSU from 2009 to 2013 and beyond.

On one occasion, the author was invited to be a co-supervisor of a PhD candidate, ZHANG Xiaoying, from BFSU. She helped arrange the lecture featured in 7.2.1.1. After she obtained her PhD and published her thesis, *The Economist's Construction of Globalization (1985–2010): A Narrative Analysis with a Chinese Perspective* (2012), her work relationship with the author continued. The author was invited as Visiting Professor at BFSU and gave two lecture series (see 7.2.1.2 and 7.2.1.3).

They are not only co-authors of academic articles (see 2018, Chapters 12 and 13, and 2.1, or 7.2.1.4), but also the author contributed the journal article 'Bridging the divides – China's role in a fragmenting world' for the newly founded journal *Global Communication*, which Zhang edits (2018, Chapter 4, or 7.2.1.4). This book includes their joint article 'The moral foundation of the cooperative spirit in China's English media in combatting the COVID-19 crisis' (see 6.1).

7.2.1.1 The first lecture on globalization to senior-year Chinese students via BFSU staff[44]

In his first lecture to senior-year Chinese students, the author explained the important changes that are taking place in the world today from the perspective of globalization. He said that 'globalization' means the integration of people from all over the world into one society, the global society. In this society, people use the potential of technology to narrow the distance between them, the world can interact and communicate and has undergone real changes because of this. These changes are mainly manifested in changes in transport and tourism; in telecommunications; in the integration of production and consumption on a global scale; in the establishment of a global financial system; in the development of global governance, and in the strengthening of international dependence, which must be resolved through joint cooperation. Problems encountered are human identification with environmental, food and energy issues; the reconstruction of communities; and the emergence of a global society. It is in these changes that the relationship between countries has become closer, which also shows that when globality replaces modernity, the country, government, economy, culture and community are no longer the centre, and each country must cooperate with all the others, seeking common development. The speed of globalization is unprecedented.[45]

---

[44] Editor's note: This lecture was arranged and interpreted by ZHANG Xiaying at BFSU. She still co-authors some articles with the author, e.g. 'The Moral Foundation of the Co-operative Spirit in China's English Media in Combatting the COVID-19 Crisis' (6.2 in this book).

[45] 陈海霞：英国著名学者马丁·阿尔布劳教授来我院讲学，北京新圆明职业学院 (现北京艺术传媒职业学院) 网站，30/11/2009，见：http://www.ymyu.com/show.php?id=8027 [English translation: CHEN Haixia, Professor Martin Albrow, a famous British scholar, came to our school to give a lecture, Beijing Xinyuanming Vocational College News (now Beijing Art and Media Vocational College), 30/11/2009].

7.2.1.2 Lecture series one: current issues of globalization at BFSU[46]

Lecture 1: The shock of the globe

1) The idea of the world has a long history in Western thought: it is not the earth but the sum of our experience. Sometimes our world is our home, our country, sometimes all countries and times. But to make sense of that world we tell stories and globalization has been the story of our time for the last 20 years, for the Western world trying to make sense of its past and find a direction to the future, a master or grand narrative (Lyotard). As story, globalization has narrators, actors, settings, plot, events, themes. It is a story people enact in their lives, so also a drama. But equally it seeks to be history, a story of real events and processes. Let us call the first 'discursive reality', the second 'material reality', recognizing the two are interwoven.
2) A master narrative, but also new, so what did it replace? Taking the West as the main subject, there is a previous account, namely the story of the modern, of progress and increasing control of the world around us, beginning roughly five hundred years ago with the idea that science gave us truth about the world and could also be applied to make a better world (Francis Bacon). The Enlightenment that followed was accompanied by imperial expansion, the consolidation of the state system (1648 Peace of Westphalia), the secularization of power, emphasis on human rights and subsequently capitalism and democratization – all seen as aspects of modernity.
3) Is globalization just the latest stage in this narrative of progress? Or a new story? I say it is a new story, but to explain this we need to look at features of the old one. The linkage between science and the story was so strong that there was a general belief that the story itself reflected underlying scientific laws (Comte, Marx, Darwinism). Progress was inevitable on this account. Something had to happen to shake that belief.
4) A series of shocks in the twentieth century undermined the belief in progress, among them the economic crash of 1929, two world wars, the Holocaust, dropping atomic bombs on Hiroshima and Nagasaki (Arnold Toynbee) and the oil price shock of the 70s (Niall Ferguson) These shocks were very material, but directly affected the discursive reality, the old story of modern progress in two main ways. The first was to enforce the recognition that nothing in history is inevitable (Karl Popper). There is always the unexpected. The second was that modernity itself was double-sided, with a negative, destructive, even demonic aspect (Zygmunt Bauman).
5) There are several responses to this. One is to argue the West is in decline, civilization as we know it is breaking up, there is no overarching narrative and

[46] Editor's note: From 2012 the author was invited as Visiting Professor at BFSU. These lectures were delivered in April 2012.

what we have is postmodernity. Another is to try to retain the thrust of a progressive modernization but to recast it in global terms, hence globalization. A third is to say we have entered a new age with its own defining characteristics, a global age.

Lecture 2: Globally speaking

1) Let me turn to what I called 'discursive reality', the story of our time which becomes a fact in our lives, but which we can both deny or reshape in our telling of it. It is like language, existing through a collective use, but always individually shaped. Changes in language tell us much about changes in our world and make up much of what the eighteenth century called 'the spirit of the age'. The globe has come to be one of the most important images and a source of linguistic invention.
2) By public discourse, we mean the language and communication of public life, which sets the terms in which we discuss the main features of our society, its values, distribution of power, wealth and the collective good. Any change in public discourse signifies material changes in those areas and a redirection of human attention and effort. So, the modern age was ushered in by the debate between 'ancients' and 'moderns'. 'Bureaucracy' was a new word in the eighteenth century. A significant shift in the nineteenth century was reflected in the invention of the word 'international'.
3) Prior to the invention of 'globalization', the globe had an important place in the Western world view. The ancient Greeks realized the earth was round and measured its circumference, and the image of the globe was used to represent both heaven and earth. The ambition of the early modern seafarers to circumnavigate the globe was both economic and a quest for knowledge of ultimate boundaries. The globe then symbolized completeness, 'all human life is there', as in Shakespeare's theatre, or in Walt Whitman's 'globe of globes', the aspiration of a 'United States' to which all peoples migrated.
4) In the post-1945 period, 'global' came to be used as opposed to 'world', 'universal' or 'international' because it signified unity in diversity better than earlier concepts and because the globe itself and human life on it appeared to be threatened by human activities. In the 1960s, advances in communication prompted the coining of the term 'global village' and the image of the earth seen from space reinforced global imagery. The globe, peace and green movements became intertwined, a cultural shift.
5) Capitalism responded to and used that cultural shift to promote global brands, to expand markets overseas. Coca-Cola was a main brand leader in that respect. Corporations developed global strategies both for distribution and production overseas and globalization was the term promoted by the Harvard Business School to denote the general movement of capitalistic interests beyond national boundaries.

6) Globalization was originally used in political science circles to denote the coming together of a single world political system, and when it involved active policy it was called 'globalism'. Sociologists used it to refer to the shift to a global society and emergence of global culture, writing of globality to refer to the global condition, rather than the implicit process involve in globalization. But the meaning of globalization as the ongoing creation of a single global market came to be dominant in the 1990s, and a major feature of the political discourse of the time, as the leading economic powers sought to extend the scope and penetration of capitalist interests across boundaries. American and British politicians adopted globalization as a political programme and the economic theory behind it came to be known as the Washington consensus, or neo-liberalism. In that context, it became the key concept in a global public discourse.

Lecture 3: How does globalization affect wealth and inequality?

1) We have seen how the discursive reality came to shape the material world. The global involved a redirection of general human interests but its language then was appropriated by powerful national and class interests, so that globalization became part of Western ideology. But those interests create material effects, and there is worldwide attention devoted to estimating and evaluating those effects. The interests behind globalization as the creation of global free markets claim that the effects are beneficial when we take the population of the world as a whole into account.
2) Marx long ago predicted that capitalism required the continual expansion of markets to cover the globe. He saw as a necessary accompaniment the creation of an international working men's movement. But nation–states have worked to forestall that through a combination of domestic welfare programmes and protecting corporate interests, reinforcing it across boundaries through bodies like the World Trade Organization. In parallel with economic globalization, we have seen the rise of global regulation.
3) Globalization has early on been seen in a contradictory relation with the state, first in breaching state boundaries and requiring great cooperation, even loss of sovereignty, on the other hand in requiring the extension of state regulation and competition between states. Competition between states is often expressed in terms of GDP and standard of living.
4) In terms of GDP, the wealth of the world has increased, but inequality between countries has increased too. Inequality within countries has increased still faster, even if their average wealth has increased. The overall verdict is that globalization increases wealth and even brings people out of poverty but also increases inequality within and between countries.

5) However, GDP is only a monetary measure and takes no account of changes in lifestyle and quality of life. Personal happiness and the good society are not even mainly dependent on money and wealth, even though they may help. Just as historically capitalism gave rise to opposition, so too globalization, seen as the furtherance of capitalism, has been heavily criticized.

Lecture 4: Can globalization be controlled?

1) From the outset, globalization is seen as a process with material outcomes but also as policy, a chosen direction. It was true of corporations, then of countries. As material outcome it could be seen as threat, as Clinton originally did with Japan, but then he turned it to advantage by treating it as a policy enhancing American power, corporate interests and financial capital, but also American culture spreading across the world. Globalization was equated with Americanization and that was the same as Westernization.
2) Opposition to globalization from the beginning included traditional anti-capitalist voices, labour unions, socialist parties and also from countries most exposed to the United States. Canada, France and Latin America were home to particularly strong protests and it was no coincidence that the biggest anti-globalization protest was in Seattle in 1999, causing the suspension of the World Trade Organization meeting. This led to the formation of protest networks and gatherings known as World Social Forums, set up to rival and counter the world economic forums in Davos. We see then the beginning of a global politics based in a rudimentary class division.
3) Anti-capitalist and anti-globalization movements in fact were continuing in a long-established process of transnational networking, which had promoted campaigns on human rights, safeguarding the environment and world peace since the 1960s. 'Think globally, act locally' was a popular slogan. In the 1990s, this was conceptualized as global civil society, the sphere of activity outside government control and not governed by business interests. Civil society is a concept with a long tradition in the West. It has been extended to cover non-governmental organizations as well as to citizen initiatives, and has even extended into the United Nations with observer status for civil society organizations.
4) What is obvious from the worldwide debate about globalization and its impact is that the rhetoric has largely been dominated by capitalist interests and the idea of society as a foundation for human welfare, and socialism as the creed which safeguards the overall interests of society and treats wealth creation as only one sector among many. The problem for socialism is that it has been closely associated with national governments. When globalization is viewed as a transnational force for economic benefit, the social factors have no corresponding counterweight, except 'global civil society', which has no common guiding philosophy. Indeed, what governments provide increasingly

is security and often repression rather than welfare to balance the disruptive effects of globalization on social order.

Lecture 5: Is everything in the world becoming the same?

1) Neo-liberal globalization has raised the spectre of American domination, but has balanced that with an account of the benefits of free trade. But along with the idea of Westernization has come the image of consumerism, mass market and standardization of taste, summed up in the idea of McDonaldization.
2) Americanization was preceded by Westernization in the early twentieth century, as in Turkey and Japan, and here it was an attempt both to import Western technology, but also Western ideas. Is this homogenization?
3) Americanization has been associated particularly with consumerism, Coca-Cola, McDonald's and Hollywood. In each of these, it is important to see how they adapt to local tastes and also seek to internationalize their management. In the case of Hollywood, it has been accused of being anti-American, the movie American Beauty being presented as a case, and is best seen as global culture. This is epigenesis.
4) Global Culture is underpinned by global communication. Here the spread of science and technology proceeds relentlessly and it was this that the OECD originally saw as globalization, before the emphasis on free markets. We do see standardization in major products like airplanes, container ships and communication needs shared standards. Hence international standards organization have been founded.
5) But ability to travel, to come together across boundaries, creates social networks of vast scope. Time–space compression makes it possible for everyone to be in the one place at any one time. The internet is a common resource, worldwide. Does this create homogeneity?

Lecture 6: What is new and different?

1) New communications make it possible to sustain relationships at a distance as never before and facilitate the preservation of identities in far off places. Diaspora means ethnic identity especially preserved at geographical distance, Jews, Poles, Chinese, favoured by adherence to traditional identity conferring culture, religion or language.
2) Widespread immigration puts pressure on states to produce multicultural policies, the extreme case being the United States, generating a secular constitution, emphasis on individual rights, stress on national tradition. The rise of the modern state connected with the invention of tradition.
3) At the same time as multiculturalism, one has hyphenated identities and hybridization and fusion to create something new. This is seen in fusion foods, fashions, music, art and architecture. This again is something that has been happening for centuries – e.g. Vermeer's hat.

4) Under pressure of fashion, consumerism, choices, individualism is enhanced. In purely sociological terms (Simmel), the multiplicity of groups to which people can affiliate, increases the possibility of each person having a unique social profile. Individualism is therefore a function of plural identities.
5) For some this is all the chaos of postmodernism, with no clear standards of taste or propriety. For others the quest for unity, purpose and meaning in life becomes ever more pressing.

Lecture 7: Is a conflict of civilizations inevitable?

1) Problem of order always appears relevant in the face of a chaos. The classic Western statement is Thomas Hobbes, who, faced with religious conflict, stressed consensus around a single authority with sole control of violence, a view backed by Max Weber.
2) There has always been an alternative vision, a society based on agreement and tolerance of difference. After the Second World War, this vision has been entrenched in the United Nations: states hold means of violence, their cooperation leads to international order.
3) The issue of what holds a state together does not go away, however, and the West has emphasized core values, axial values which underpin the rest, which nonetheless are at bottom irrational. But the threat of war between states has always been there, especially if emphasis is placed on core differences. The idea of civilization explains how states can cohere across boundaries but at the same time differ on basic values.
4) The idea of civilization was stressed by Toynbee in a survey of world history, where he says the West is in decline, under challenge from the rest. Huntington too suggested that conflict between civilizations is inevitable.
5) But the United Nations idea, and the fact that core human values are universal, like health and education, has led to the development of global governance, and with the pressure of global issues there has been increasing accord between states. Which will win? Conflict or collaboration?

Lecture 8: Cooperation, invisible hand and Chinese harmony

1) The West developed another view on what holds society together apart from coercion and agreement. Response to the heavy hand of state in economic affairs was the idea of the 'invisible hand'. If all pursued their own interest, made what they were best at doing and exchanged the fruits of their labours in a free market, then it would be to the benefit of all. The wealth of nations would increase, Adam Smith's notion, the ideology of the West, represented in the pages of *The Economist*, later absorbed into globalization.
2) The problems in this idea long ago were pointed out by Marx who saw how industrialization led to the concentration of wealth in a few hands. Markets

led to the polarization of classes, the social problem which the West responded to with the welfare state. He, however, also observed that the division of labour and the development of factory organization depended on cooperation, something more basic than even exchange.

3) We therefore confront basic building blocks of any society and sets of social relations of whatever nature: cooperation, conflict, tolerance, exchange and consensus. The balance between these varies from society to society.
4) In the West, cooperation has led to collaboration, organization around goals, looking to the future. In this respect, China has emphasized more allowing for good outcomes to arise from harmonious relations, and concentrating less on goals.
5) The challenges to the globe suggest an alternative that combines both Western and Chinese models, namely harmonious relations between collaborators in meeting global challenges such as climate change, security, poverty and depletion of natural resources.

7.2.1.3 Lecture series two: Beyond the global crisis at BFSU[47]

Lecture 1. The End of the West

Introduction

It is my privilege to be able to talk about the present:

- as an academic,
- or public intellectual,
- or as a Westerner in China.

The series is called 'Beyond the global crisis' – the worst economic crisis since the 1930s. It is called 'global': is this just the West's term for its own decline?

Decline of the West

- This is an old theme going as far back as the work of Oswald Spengler
- Loss of faith in progress, as described in the work of Weber
- The disaster of two world wars and nuclear bombs
- Toynbee resumed the theme

Parochial nation–states ruin each other by war and statecraft of Italian city state efficiency [note communitarian like nature of Toynbee's social entities]. He said that in 1929 it was already possible to see world unification. Western society is not 'history'. But by 1929 only Western society was in its growth stage (technology was essential to the West), but by 1952 he adds the Islamic world. He sees individual liberty as the core of Western post-Christian liberalism. By 1961, he

[47] Editor's note: These lectures were delivered in April 2013. The late Professor ZHENG Hangsheng (1936–2014), former Vice-President of Renmin University of China and former President of Chinese Sociological Association (CSA), invited the author to give lectures at Renmin University. However, this request was unfulfilled owing to Professor Zheng's sudden death.

sees no possibility of a unifying military world power. 'I see no pattern to which all civilizations conform, unlike Spengler (1969: 519). The West has unified the world technologically (ibid.: 528). The West has its demonic side. The Russians and Chinese borrowed communism from the West. The Atomic Age calls for a rise in standards of behaviour (ibid.: 535). Greater social justice is being achieved (ibid.: 591).

Capitalism and socialism

During the Cold War 1945–1989, the West set itself against state socialist countries. But socialism is a Western thing. Then came the triumph of capitalism and the 'West' began to exclude Europe: the split between the United States and the UK on one hand and Germany/France on the other was deep.

Was South America Western? Are the BRICS Western? Capitalism has no home.

The global market and culture are not Western

The USA, having gone global, has lost leadership, helping to create a global culture. 'Think globally, act locally' is an invitation to go beyond territorial definitions. The globe became a reference point for global challenges. We learned that we must collaborate with the appropriate holders of power (Gideon Rachman: 'The West has lost in Afghanistan', *Financial Times*, March 27, 2012).

Global leadership

Anglo-Americans obsessed with leadership. In nineteenth century they were with heroes, in the twentieth with charismatics. Then role models. There are other possibilities: believers, followers, colleagues or comrades? What applies to individuals applies to countries and cultures. Each culture can make a distinctive contribution to solving global problems.

Lecture 2: Responsibility for the crisis

Attributable causes for the crisis – greed, criminality, misunderstanding, lack of regulation – all point to human faults, but others point to systemic features over which no one has control, namely that expectations can be dashed by events.

There are at least four great ways of avoiding responsibility:

1) Distortion of karma
2) The Chinese sense of Tao, going with the flow, as in the Laozi, perverted by the legalists to justify the ruler just being there (Jullien, 2004: 99)
3) The Western market philosophy, the hidden hand
4) The West shifting blame between collective and individual – the blame game

It is a myth that pre-modern countries had no sense of responsibility. Evans Pritchard studied the Azande of Sudan and found every unfortunate happening was explained in terms of the mix of human and natural events; no one can claim a witch made someone commit adultery. It is the particularity of misfortune that attracts witchcraft speculation. Corporate and personal responsibility were also common in pre-modern societies (Moore, 1972). In traditional India, karma is actually an ethic of responsibility – attributing consequences to actions. In the contemporary world, it is the blame game.

Among Western leaders, Barack Obama, in accepting the Democratic nomination for President, declared 'individual and mutual responsibility – that's the essence of America's promise'[48] and in his inauguration as President spoke of an 'era of responsibility'.[49] Angela Merkel has said that the question facing Germany was how it wanted to live responsibly in a global world.[50] Nicolas Sarkozy has asserted a European interest in arguments on responsibility for the damage to the environment.[51] In the United Kingdom, as a general election comes closer, Prime Minister Brown and Opposition leader David Cameron compete in making responsibility central to their messages. Gordon Brown claimed to have saved the West. The Icelanders are charging their ex-prime minister.

In the West, issue surfaces in organizations. There is a collective purpose, hence no one person is responsible. There is responsibility but it is diffused. Individuals are cogs in the machine, as with the concentration camps and the Milgram experiments.

A sense of responsibility attaches to the global and local. But to whom are we accountable in the global sphere? Is it an excuse not to be accountable, but to whom should we answer? The Civil Service in the UK has been drawn into this now. The traditional doctrine of ministerial responsibility is breaking down; see the Hodge: O'Donnell dispute.

We need to locate responsibility in people, both as individuals and as they share in collective responsibility. The nation–state cannot assume exclusive control on responsibility. And if we are responsible to the nation–state, then also we have rights from it and it continues over generations. Hence the benefits of membership of the nation must also oblige one to accept blame. Britain is to blame for the national humiliation of China in the nineteenth century: I apologise.

But then to what do I belong, and how do I negotiate conflicting demands? This will be the theme of my next lecture, the search for integrity.

References

Jullien, Francois (2004), *A Treatise on Efficacy: Between Western and Chinese Thinking*. Honolulu: University of Hawaii Press.

[48] Acceptance speech at Democratic Convention, 28/08/008, see: http://www.barackobama.com/2008/08/28/remarks_of_senator_barack_obam_108.php.

[49] Obama's inaugural speech, 20 January 2009. CNN, See: http://www.cnn.com/2009/POLITICS/01/20/obama.politics/index.html.

[50] Speech in Königswinter on the occasion of the 60th anniversary of the *Rheinische Merkur* 13/06/06.

[51] 'Le Principe de responsabilité, enjeu européen selon Sarkozy. *Le Monde* 27/10/07.

Moore, Sally (1972), 'Legal liability and evolutionary interpretation: some aspects of strict liability, self-help and collective responsibility'. In: Max Gluckman (ed.) *The Allocation of Responsibility*, Manchester: Manchester University Press, pp. 51–108.

Wadley, Susan S. and Bruce W. Derr (1989), 'Eating Sins in Karimpur', *Contributions to Indian Sociology* (N.S.) 23(1): 131–148.

Lecture 3: Searching for integrity

If responsibility is a current watchword, so is integrity.

Examples

An alternative might be to make a brazen claim to it, as seems to be the case with Joe the Plumber. When a local Ohio man Samuel Joseph Wurzelbacher became an overnight celebrity in October 2008 by challenging presidential candidate Obama on his campaign tour, he probably did not know what he was letting himself in for. He objected to Obama's tax plans for small businesses on the grounds that he was a hardworking plumber looking to buy a business with a turnover of over a quarter of a million dollars.

Obama entered into a conversation with him on camera, beginning a rather laboured explanation of his tax policies. Wurzelbacher stood his ground. He became 'Joe the Plumber' and three days later was cited 21 times by the other candidate, John McCain, in the third Presidential Debate as an example of the harm his opponent's tax plans would wreak on America.

The problem was that Joe the Plumber was not all he claimed and seemed to be. Instant fame brought rapid retribution. The news channel CNN anchor presenter confronted Joe two weeks later with not being a licensed plumber at all, with owing taxes and having nowhere near the resources that would enable him to buy a business with that kind of turnover. 'Why do you vet me out, and not Obama?' Wurzelbacher complained, to which the response was, 'You are no longer Joe, a private person, you have endorsed a candidate.'

The suspension of privacy follows on from stepping onto the public political stage. Celebrities are not allowed, it appears, to have a private life, and indeed that has been the cornerstone for any defence the press makes for intrusion into personal lives as the current furore in Britain around phone hacking by News International makes clear.

Perhaps that episode decided Joe that, since his private life was now public anyway, if he couldn't beat them he would join them. Almost to the day, three years after his initial fame, he announced on October 25, 2011 that he would stand as a candidate for the House of Representatives seat for his local area. His press release stated, 'I want to prove that regular people can run, win and keep their integrity intact' (*The Guardian*, 26/10/2011, p. 21).

There is a double paradox here. One is obvious. Why would anyone draw attention to integrity when he has shown himself to be most vulnerable on that issue? To which the answer might be that, if the divide between the public and private is eliminated, then the contradictions between the two disappear. The integrity of the politician is affirmed exactly by appearing full frontal, warts and all, before the public. An example of this tactic is provided by Newt Gingrich, notorious for mistakes in relations with women, who acknowledges his faults and resumes his run for the Republican presidential candidacy in 2011.

But, if that sort of full disclosure is required for public integrity, the second paradox is that Wurzelbacher implicitly wants to prove that 'regular' guys like him are not going to be like the imposters who usually strut the political stage. Thereby he re-establishes a divide, but this time in a different place, locating integrity not in the private sphere but in the masses as opposed to an elite. In this way, he taps the deep disaffection with the political class that pervades American public opinion today.

At the time of writing, we have to wait to see what happens with Joe, whether his political prospects have been damaged or not by the early challenge to his new reputation. They may or may not be, because no one has shown any connection between political success and integrity.

'Internet threat to jury integrity', headline in an MSN web newscast (9/12/11)

'Michel Platini said he had "no doubts whatsoever about the integrity of the match"' *The Guardian* (9/12/11)

'Having two identities for yourself is an example of lack of integrity', Mark Zuckerberg, *Financial Times* (22/11/11)

'The shapers of the American mortgage finance system hoped to achieve the security of government ownership, the integrity of local banking and the ingenuity of Wall Street. Instead they got the ingenuity of government, the security of local banking and the integrity of Wall Street, David Frum, former White house speechwriter cited in *The Economist* (15/10/11)

'Leading with Integrity: Engaging Hearts as well as Minds', title of 'Tomorrow's Value Lecture' given by Joe Garner, Deputy CEO, HSBC Bank PLC, 19/10/11.

'If only these qualities could be matched by an understanding of journalistic integrity', Sir Harold Evans, former editor of the Sunday Times on Rupert Murdoch in *The Guardian* (19/9/11).

- How much are we entitled to know about someone else?
- Are there limits to what we should disclose about ourselves and others?
- Can we assume as many identities as we like?
- How far are we responsible for what others do in our name?

Lecture 4. The possibility of global justice

Justice is a primordial value, deeply rooted in the human psyche, relevant from family to playground, to law and order, to global justice.

In the West, there is a deep split between justice as represented in law and justice as fair distribution in society. Thomas Hobbes (Leviathan, 1651) saw justice as established only by and through law. But a longer tradition held that justice was established by God or nature, the order of things. The former develops in the direction of legal codes of rights and responsibilities and ways of resolving disputes and breaking of codes. The latter in the direction of action to change the relations enshrined in law.

In the Middle Ages, these were combined as in Aquinas' 'law is the rational ordering of things that concern the common good'. A split in modernity was characterized as the conflict between substantive and formal rationality (Max Weber). Equality before the law cannot guarantee common good. It may enshrine gross disparities of wealth. 'There is no law unless it be just': Aquinas quotes St. Augustine, adding (129) 'so the validity of a law depends on its justice'. And Aquinas makes it clear that the validity of a law depends on its contribution to general welfare; he allows for change and implicitly for campaigns to change the law.

Aquinas again: 'The scope of justice is to regulate men in their relations with others' (165).

Justice not confined to the nation–state in a globalizing world. Justice is never full and complete, and it is demanded when it is defective or absent. It is the sense of injustice that leads to demands for justice.

Example: Women and laws (Aisha Shaheed) (GCS, pp. 96–97)

There must also be the possibility of redress, restitution and forgiveness at the collective level

Example: Australian treatment of Aborigines.

Anti-slavery movement

But justice extends beyond grievance and encompasses the good society.

7.2.1.4 Contributing to a journal article

On behalf of a newly founded Chinese journal *Global Communication,* ZHANG Xiaoying invited the author to contribute an article, 'Bridging the divides – China's role in a fragmenting world.'[52]

7.2.1.5 Two joint journal articles

The author and ZHANG Xiaoying delivered a paper jointly at the international conference 'Max Weber and China: Culture, Law and Capitalism', at the School of Oriental and African Studies, University of London, 5–6 September 2013. They published a paper, 'Weber, China and the world: in search of transcultural communication' in the *Journal of China in Global and Comparative Perspectives*, Volume 2, 2016, pp.32-53. They also published a paper, 'Weber and the concept of adaptation: the case of Confucian ethics' in *Max Weber Studies*, 2014(2), pp. 199–226. Both articles have been included as Chapters 12 and 13 in

[52] Editor's note: It was published as Chapter 4 of *China's Role in a Shared Common Future: Towards Theory of Global Leadership*, London: Global Century Press, 2018, pp. 36–48 [Chinese version: 马丁・阿尔布劳：弥合分歧——中国在分化的世界中的角色，译者王晓健，校对宋毅，《国际传播》，2016年第一期，第21-31页 (Martin Albrow (2016), Bridging the divides – China's role in a fragmenting world, *Global Communication*, Vol. 1: (1):21-31)].

China's Role in a Shared Common Future: Towards Theory of Global Leadership, London: Global Century Press, 2018, pp. 36–48.

7.2.1.6 The moral foundation of the cooperative spirit in China's English media in combatting the COVID-19 crisis (see 6.1)

7.2.2 Beijing Language and Cultural Studies (BLCU)

While participating in the 6th Global China Dialogue in 2019, Professor XU Baofeng of Beijing Language and Culture University (BLCU), invited the author to be a Visiting Distinguished Professor at BLCU. Although to date COVID-19 has stopped this from happening, the author worked with the BLCU in a number of ways.

7.2.2.1 China's contribution to the future of governance (see 3.1)

7.2.2.2 The prospects of the Belt and Road Initiative in the post-pandemic era: a dialogue in the Guangming International Forum (see 4.2)

7.2.2.3 Witnessing China combatting COVID-19: my story in China (see 6.4)

7.2.2.4 UN Chinese Language Day and sinology and the Chinese language during the epidemic (see 6.5)

7.2.2.5 Funding for publications on China (9.6)

BLCU offered the author the post of Visiting Distinguished Professor from 2020 to 2022. The programme included translation of the author's English-language book into Chinese and writing about China based on the author's field trips in China. Global Century Press received funding BLCU for the translation and for publishing the overseas Chinese edition of *China's Role in a Shared Human Future*.

However, as a result of the COVID-19 pandemic, the offer of Professorship was cancelled and the funding terminated.

7.3. Engagement with Chinese mainstream academia

After nearly two decades absent from Chinese mainstream academia, the author has re-engaged with Chinese sociological circles since 2013. This started with three seminars at the Chinese Academy of Social Sciences (CASS), Peking University and Tsinghua University, then Jilin University, Wuhan University; a proposed lecture tour of nationwide universities was interrupted by COVID-19.

7.3.1 Abstracts of three seminars at CASS, Peking University and Tsinghua University

7.3.1.1 Inequality in the global age – Institute of Sociology, Chinese Academy of Social Sciences[53]

[53] Editor's note: On April 3, 2013, a seminar was held at the Institute of Sociology, Chinese Academy of Social Science (CASS), Beijing, China. Based on the author's understanding of the

Classical sociological work focused on specific forms of social structural inequality, such as class or status or the distribution of wealth and goods. Equality was manifested in informal state relations with citizens. This reflected a stage in state–capital relations. Now international rank ordering is a major interest, and within- and between-country inequalities are both in focus while inequalities between people in a global frame have no state-secured equivalent to citizenship. And global capital is increasing in-country inequality. Sociological understanding of the direction of these developments must focus on equality/inequality as a universally applied indicator in all life sectors and recognize competing demands for inequality as much as equality. It is unlikely that the coming period will show the kind of congruence between life sectors, demands for equality and state interests that gave rise to the Western welfare state. States will need to respond to demands to rectify injustice rather than seek to engineer equality.

7.3.1.2 Theoretical Approaches to the Concept of Global Society – Peking University[54]

According to Albrow, widespread recognition that human society is no longer simply a collection of nation–states clearly poses problems for sociology, given that its research agenda has been dictated by national needs. Simple projection of ideas of national social structure to a global level will not work. Formal

nature of the institution, he presented a seminar entitled 'Global Discourse and Public Policy'. Abstract: The Western reception of the language of the globe in academic and public life (global, globalism, globality, globalization) marks an underlying long-term cultural shift quite as important as the historic onset of modernity and justifies recognition of a global age. It has meant a re-orientation of public policy in which economic interests in globalization have been confused with global public policy goals. Each country experiences this confusion differently but the future of the human species depends on the achievement of clarity on specific national responsibilities towards global welfare. For this to happen, global discourse itself requires critical examination in relation to any country's statement of public policy goals. This seminar was chaired by the then Director of the Institute of Sociology, Professor LI Peijin. Former Director and long-standing President. Professor LU Xueyi (1933–2013) participated in the seminar. Sadly, one month later Professor Lu suddenly passed away. The tribute from the British Sociological Association (BSA) said: 'The British Sociological Association has learned with great sadness of the unexpected death of Professor Lu Xueyi, Honorary President of the Chinese Sociological Association. We wish to convey our deep condolences to his family and to the Chinese Sociological Association on the loss of such a distinguished scholar and great servant of sociology. May his work continue to inspire the next generation of sociologists.' The author, Honorary Vice-President of BSA, also sent his condolences: 'In memory of Professor Lu Xueyi. My dear friend's death fills me with deep sadness, coming so soon after our reunion in Beijing. I shall always remember our conversations with the greatest of pleasure and extend my heartfelt sympathies to all his family and friends who share in both happy memories and grief for a great man.' See Tribute to Professor LU Xueyi, Contributors, Appendix C, in Xiangqun Chang (Ed.) (2014), *Society Building: A China model of social development*, London: Global Century Press, p. 156.

[54] Editor's note: On March 27, 2013, Professor Martin Albrow gave a lecture to the Department of Sociology, Peking University, Beijing, China. Professor XIE Lizhong, the then head of the department, chaired the seminar.

approaches to social relations and networks fit with the Weberian method, but the close relation between his concepts of legitimacy and the state are difficult to reconcile with a world without a central government. Durkheimian approaches can grasp public opinion and mobilization of collective entities but appear tied to national or sub-national entities. We will not get an adequate sociological theory of global society until we have rehabilitated collective action in our thinking and established the linkages between civil society actors, global movements and organized social entities up to and including global society as a whole.

7.3.1.3 The Challenge of Transculturality for the USA and China – Tsinghua University[55]

The USA and China have worldviews that extend far beyond their relations with each other. The USA has often regarded globalization as a simple extension of its own experience. Worldviews in general are ethnocentric. *Tianxia* is also based in Chinese experience, a world of harmony contrasting with American tension between individual and community. Transculturality involves not just exchange between cultures but the creation of new culture beyond them. The worldviews of the USA and China were each developed originally in a transcultural experience. When the USA and China reach out to the rest of the world, they are creating a new transcultural space where global governance can grow. Americans have a problem with the idea of global governance that depends on equality between nation–states; the Chinese have a problem because it lacks a central authority. Projects may serve global governance more effectively than preconceived ideas. A pragmatic universalism may replace the universals of national worldviews.

7.3.2 Jilin University

After the 2nd Global China Dialogue in 2015, Professor BING Zheng, the then Vice-President of Jilin University, engaged the author in a number of ways.

7.3.2.1 Pragmatic universalism and the quest for global governance

Jilin University organized the international conference 'Globalization: Social Change and Cultural Construction' at Jilin University on August 12/13, 2016. The author was invited to give a speech entitled 'Pragmatic universalism and the quest for global governance' (2018, Chapter 8).[56]

7.3.2.2 A panel discussion on 'Globalization and China's contribution'[57]

[55] Editor's note: This was an invited lecture which was delivered on the October 25, 2016. The full paper has been published as Chapter 7, *China's Role in a Shared Human Future: Towards Theory for Global Leadership* (2018), by Martin Albrow. London: Global Century Press, pp. 58–66.

[56] See Martin Albrow (2018), *China's Role in a Shared Human Future: Towards Theory for Global Leadership* (2018), by Martin Albrow, London: Global Century Press, pp. 67–76.

[57] Editor's note: 1) A panel discussion was held during this conference among Martin Albrow, Seung Kuk Kim, BING Zheng and Yanjie Bian. The Chinese version is published with the title 'Globalization and China's Contribution' as an introduction (pp. 4–5), under which there are four

Different understandings of the meaning of globalization

As we all know, there are different understandings of the words globalization and global age, which usually cause much debate. So the dialogue began from this basic problem.

Professor Martin Albrow talked about it first. He is one of three scholars who introduced the concept of globalization and he visited China in order in part to build relationships with the Chinese academy in 1987.

Obviously this is just one globalized individual's of view that contrasts the individual as a singular person with the global world as a whole. So I think it is probably very immodest to do this but it is socially necessary because the problem that we have in the world is that even the individual now is capable of disrupting the whole world. The relationship of individuals to the totality of the earth and human species is much more sensitive than it has ever been. Individuals now are capable of creating the most enormous destruction that overhangs all of us and which has led to the development of the discourse of the global. That was what originally focused my thinking on what people were saying, on the utterances of people, politicians and the influential leaders' opinion. They were using the word 'global'.

The 1980s were important to me personally because I was asked then to become the first editor of the journal *International Sociology*, which reflected the diversity of world sociology and allowed more points of view to be presented. When the World Congress of Sociology took place in 1990 in Madrid, we decided we needed a conference volume that every delegate to the congress would get. It should be collections of papers from the journal from those four years, so it would familiarize delegates with the journal and we needed an overall theme and agreed the title *Globalization, Knowledge and Society*. That was the first book ever published with globalization in its title. That was the conference volume for the 1990's world congress. Now, the importance of it was that every delegate had

---

separate titles authored by each panellist. The first one is 'Pragmatic Universalism and the Challenges of the Global Age', by Martin Albrow (pp. 5–8). The abstract of this group of papers and short bios of the panellists in English can be seen on pp. 125 126, *Chinese Social Science Evaluation*, 2017 (01) (《中国社会科学评价》2017年第1期，作者：马丁·阿尔布劳、金成国、邴正、边燕杰；翻译：李文珍、褚国飞、王建峰). The English version is the original panel discussion reflecting the impromptu nature of the debate, the text of which has been copyedited for publication here. 2) According to the editors of the journal, the 'International Conference with the theme "Globalization: Social Change and Cultural Construction" was held on August 13, 2016 at Jilin University. At the conference, the editorial office of the Chinese Social Science Review organized a dialogue on the sociological implications of globalization and invited as speakers Martin Albrow, Emeritus Professor of the University of Wales, Fellow of British Academy of Social Sciences and former President of the British Sociological Association; Seung Kuk Kim, Professor at Pusan National University, president of the Korea Institute of Marine Research; Yanjie Bian, Professor at the University of Minnesota and dean of the School of Humanities at Xi'an Jiaotong University; and BING Zheng, Professor at the Sociology Department at Jilin University and deputy President of Jilin University. The dialogue was moderated by Professor Yanjie Bian.'

it, 4,000 sociologists from all over the world got a book entitled *Globalization, Knowledge and Society*, and publishers would give their right arm for a publishing opportunity like that, and it meant that the notion of globalization was spread worldwide.

There was also Anthony Giddens. Anthony Giddens visited California for a year as a visiting professor, and there he gave a very famous course of lectures, very important and influential, called 'The Consequences of Modernity', with globalization as a main theme. The book of that name came out in 1992, though the lectures stemmed from the 1980s. So here we are, we have three interventions in the discourse of globalization from sociologists simultaneously, effectively as Robert Merton wrote about in respect of simultaneous scientific inventions. We were working independently, although I can tell you of a strange coincidence. The three of us were all graduate students at the London School of Economics, at exactly the same time, in October 1959, and we would sit together discussing around a table in the graduate student common room. That was a complete coincidence, because I assure you the three of us came to work on globalization three decades later completely independently, and with completely different perspectives.

We were working on different ideas in any case. Already at that time in the early 1990s there were different ideas about globalization. I was talking about sociology as an example of globalization under global political conditions, unity and diversity. I was talking really about the narrative of the global in the world as a whole and asking why we are talking about globalization. Because when you considered what people were saying about globalization, they were saying many of the things we had talked about for very long time. It was the word 'globalization' that was the innovation, not the event.

That set me thinking, because in my heart I am still a historian. That was my BA degree. I then asked myself what was the event that prompted people to talk in different way. And I went back to Arnold Toynbee, and for him the great event was the dropping of the bombs on Hiroshima and Nagasaki. It was the end of modernity, the end of the modern age for him, because the modern age was built on the idea of progress, advancement. And now we realized that we could destroy the world. And for him, this was the beginning of what he called the post-modern. He invented the word, the post-modern. But the time I was thinking about was 1990 and for me the post-modern was already past. In this sense, you have the moderns and post-moderns fighting each other. But I said no. We don't live in post-modernity. We live in a new age. What is the new age to be called? It is the global age.

Robertson, Giddens and I have very different views of globalization. Giddens's view of globalization is the extension of modernity, it is the tie-up between technology and new communications, and it is the world becoming one place through interconnection. All this is true; all this is happening. Robertson, as I have already explained, had the idea of the long historical development of a single global society. My concept of globalization can take us in many, many different directions, because it doesn't produce a single society and it produces multiple diversities. You can globalize markets and you can globalize regulation, you can globalize nationalism, you can globalize religion and you can globalize Buddhism. Globalization takes us in no particular direction. But what we do have is a global age, where you have the development of a global society, a global culture and a global social structure. You have in a fact a global society that exists apart from and over and above national societies.

Professor Seung Kuk KIM gave other opinions:

My view of globalization may represent the ordinary, commonsense understanding available in the academic world. First, I would like to start with history. Globalization started from the beginning of human civilization. As you know, in the beginning our life was nomadic, from one area to another area. If we see such a kind of moment in group, we call it a kind of population movement, population shifting from one area to another area. Then, once an agrarian society took the place of hunting, a lot of unpredictable conflicts and wars took place. War was a kind of impetus for globalization. So, it is built into a kind of empire, based on military conquest. This is, I think, the first stage of globalization in our history, together with some forms of overseas trade by businessmen. Then we may turn our attention to religious missionary actors, from Western Christian countries to the Islamic world. This is a kind of religious globalization. Wishing for an absolute eternity, they are destined to spread such a belief all over the world.

And the second stage may be characterized by a political militarism together with economic impetus. The formation of the world capitalist system was already described by Wallerstein. From the 16th century, the capitalism that was built in Western Europe, in cooperation with some convenient river routes and some cheap resources in eastern Europe, tried to go beyond Europe to Africa. The world capitalist system came into being. In another perspective, we call it an extensional world capitalism system and imperialism or colonialism. I think it was in the 19th century or the 20th century that what I call political–military globalization arose, together with economic globalization, social globalization and religious globalization.

In the later 20th century or 21st century, we may identify the energy of the masses and the understanding of IT, internet technology, which made globalization much easier. So, in this sense, I would like to define the core meaning of globalization in the present time as a kind of networking by information technology or global networking. Networking facilitates our interactions throughout the world and the flow of all kinds of human products, such as knowledge, religions, even viruses, diseases and crimes. All are easily globalized with the use of networking technologies. So I would like to identify three dimensions: networking, increased interaction and consequences.

Within the process of globalization, it is therefore just a coming together with globalization. In this sense, it is a consequence, but, in the other sense, it is part of globalization.

Professor Bing Zheng portrayed an image of globalization in China and the thoughts and opinions of Chinese scholars.

Karl Marx said in the *Communist Manifesto* that capitalism emerges really across the boundaries of nations, cultures and so forth because commodities and services grow constantly. That was Karl Marx's perspective on globalization, which has been influential on Chinese sociology; 150 years ago, Marx had predicted that capitalism was going to develop around the world, although he didn't use the word 'globalization'. Entering the global age and living in globalization, as a sociologist in China, I would like to say that we really admire Karl Marx for his judgment and his vision of the future and capitalism.

From foreign sociological perspectives, we understand that the whole world has two kinds of attitudes towards globalization, for and against. Interestingly, that is represented in China as well: for and against globalization.

The main school of thought in China is for globalization, because the majority of Chinese scholars, politicians and economists actually believe that the Chinese economy will go on expanding and that globalization will be good for China. From 1978 to 2013, Chinese GDP grew at an annual rate of 9.8 percent, and the volume of production multiplied several times, according to Bing Zheng, from 400 billion￥ to 10,000 billion￥.

But some are worried that globalization will generate negative consequences for China. Sociologists tend to be influenced by two theories, one being the dependency theory and other the world system theory put forward by Immanuel Wallerstein. Some Chinese scholars believe that globalization is led by American capitalists and therefore automatically globalization is going to have certain bad consequences for China and for late-developing countries.

The major concern is that capital access is going to be accumulated, which will benefit countries such as the USA, with the result that China will be damaged by a rapid increase of inequality in income and wealth, which of course affects everyone. This is the first negative consequence.

The second negative consequence for China is official corruption as a by-product of inequality. This has already been very much visible in China, and Chinese government registration has made it very hard to correct that.

Two concerns are the economy and culture. Globalization should be defined as cultural change, which could be adversely impacted by what may be called modern culture. China is still under the influence of traditional culture, which, one way or another, is going to be affected negatively.

As Professor Martin said in his presentation, in his books, 'culture globalizes without national boundaries', so the values and the norms cut across the boundaries and diffuse around the world. The pattern of that diffusion is that, wherever you have high information technology, you learn certain things from other countries, which occupies the major social space.

One piece of evidence to demonstrate the imbalance is in the diffusion of cultural exchange. The stronger culture influences the weaker culture. For example, a lot of English words and phrases such as WTO, NBA, MBA or laser have become part of daily Chinese, whereas Chinese words tend to have little impact on Western culture, such as *gongfu* and *guanxi*, or Mao Zedong's phrases about educating kids: 'study hard, make progress every day', which in Chinglish becomes 'good good study, day day up' in a word-for-word translation. Thus, the Chinese language's impact on English is much smaller than English phrases' influence on Chinese.

In terms of values, there are two schools of thought emerging in China. One is universalism, that is, whatever values become universal in the Western world should become universal in China. The other is cultural conservatism, or radical nationalism, which promotes the defence of the traditional culture. Both are strong in China now.

Diversity *vs* Integrity, Locality *vs* Globalization

Professor Kim discussed the topic as below.

There are three consequences of the globalization. The first is regionalization. Here I would like to define in narrow terms regionalization as making regional blocs, such as EU, ASEAN or APEC. Since the world is globalized and changing, each individual country should find something to mobilize energy and to belong to a global category. So they choose it as you mentioned as global strategy. They naturally try to form a regional bloc. This is the one consequence. Another consequence, mostly in cultural terms, is glocalization. Maybe we see glocalization as a kind of way or trend from outside, but we have our own values and traditions in everything. So here all interaction called glocalization occurs. But I would like to define the most important character of globalization in cultural terms as hybridization. Globalization can go in any way, in all directions. It means everything, diplomacy, and unexpected things, desirable and undesirable things, made together and coexisting indefinitely. That situation is what I like to call hybridization. But Bing Zheng called it cultural pluralism. They are very similar. Here I try to tell you some historical character of globalization, the three core meanings of globalization and consequences of globalization.

Professor Kim introduced East Asian individualism:

I would like to make three points to make my idea properly understood. First, now it is time for us to discard or go beyond the binary assumption that the West is individualistic while the East is collectivistic. Here, Parsons seems to be misleading us when he talked about the pattern variables. He said the collectivistic

Orient is traditional, and individual orientation is modern. He seems to mean that individualism is better than collectivism. That is misleading. Sometimes it is right, but sometimes it is not.

The second point is: I do not want to deny or totally criticize contributions or merits of Western individualism. It is very useful to emphasize a point of sobriety in an individual, or an individual's potential or an individual's this or that. That is the merit or contribution of Western individualism.

The third, in this sense I would like to try to justify or glorify Eastern individualism. Eastern individualism has some other dimensions and possibilities to make our society better. So in a final sense, we may need a kind of creative intuition or hybridization between Western individualism and Eastern individualism. But at the present, we do not know much about trends and possibilities of eastern Asian individualism. Those are my three points.

What are the contrasting points to Western individualism? Here I would like also to specify three. First, eastern Asian individualism has no master like God in heaven or Jesus Christ as the son of God. But I would like to be speaking of Jesus Christ as the son of a human. So I am not an anti-Christ. I label him as the son of a human. So there is no master. That is eastern Asian individualism.

Second, as a consequence, there is no original sin. According to Christianity, we are all human beings, predestined or condemned. So in this sense, in Western individualism, the Westerners are thinking of immortality as a kind of material human being. So the individual person is God means the whole person is in heaven, or in the alternative of the other world.

But eastern Asian individualism doesn't assume such a kind of outward departure, there is just the here and now. There is no heaven after death in the future.

So these three points constitute the three merits or characteristics of eastern Asian individualism. First is the ontological dimension. Since eastern Asian individualism has no master, we are individual self-masters. It means we are also the indispensable part of our life. We have no master to rely on or to depend on. Second, in the social dimension, we are not an isolated person in the world. The eastern Asian concept of an individual is not an isolated individual but a linked or networked individual. Although he is unique, he is destined to be networked with others. Finally, behaviourally, individualism is supposed to follow the doctrines suggested by the Holy Bible. But in eastern Asian individualism, he should develop himself or idealize himself by his own self-maintenance, which in Confucianism is *xiushen* (修身). I think these are the three merits of eastern Asian individualism.

Professor Martin Albrow introduced pragmatic universalism, which is another kind of answer for the conflict between globalization and locality:

Pragmatic universalism was a concept which I first used in my book *The Global Age*. Thank you for the opportunity to expand on it in a more prominent way than I have done in the past, because I find it particularly appropriate to raise it in the Chinese context.

The American philosophy of pragmatism really has had a strong influence on Europeans, Nevertheless, I think it has particular affinities with various kinds of Chinese thinking. Because pragmatism is a philosophy which says the words we use and the principles we express only capture reality in a tentative, inexact way. We can never grasp reality wholly with words. And to understand each other, we can't rely on words, we have to do other things. This is why practice comes first.

The great German writer Goethe wrote a very famous play called *Faust* where we find Faust himself musing and speculating around what idea is the most fundamental. You know in the Christian Bible it says, 'In the beginning was the word'. Goethe had Faust say, 'In the beginning was the word?' Maybe not. 'In the beginning was the deed.' Doing things comes before language. The underlying spirit of pragmatism is that what we do matters. That's easily compatible with the tradition of Chinese philosophy, of course, the way you live your life. Confucianism is about the way of living. Western pragmatism has been joined, in my experience, with science and technology. Nonetheless, it comes to the same in essence. It is about doing things first.

It is no accident that the philosopher John Dewey, the great founder of pragmatism, came to China, Of course. For two years he taught here in Beijing (1920–1921). Professor SUN Youzhong at Beijing Foreign Studies University went to the United States to write in his doctorate on the relation of Dewey's thinking to China. The point about pragmatism is that it means that any statements of principles are compossible. They are subject to correction in practice and in deed.

That's one element of pragmatic universalism. The other element I probably take from Emile Durkheim. In his lectures on education he was concerned to promote the coherent nation–state, to encourage patriotism. From 1900 to 1919, Europeans agreed to be patriots (that's why they made war on each other!). Nationalism was very strong then. Durkheim argued that every national system of education must promote national values, but it had to find in them what was universal, as true for now and all time. So a national education had to promote universal values.

Every nation is different. So if every nation promotes universal values and yet they are different, how do we compromise between them? This is where pragmatism comes in. You have to come to a compromise. You have to work with each other. One of the great things in the world at the moment is that in working together, we have generated new concepts, new understandings. I think one of the most important is the idea of sustainability which is shared across nations, shared by governments, by activists, by global society. Sustainability, that comes out of the dialogue of nations. The United Nations made dialogue one of the core notions in the 1980s and1990s. We all talk about dialogue now. In dialogue, you come to understandings, but more importantly in deeds you actually show how you can work together. If you can work together, it doesn't matter if you speak different languages. A lecture I gave in the United States on Durkheim's pragmatic universalism was published a couple years ago in my book *Global Age Essays on Social and Cultural Change.* Chinese thinking, Western sociology, American philosophy, put them together, for me the result is pragmatic universalism.

I don't advance something to change the world. I think that's the way the world is working now. I promoted the idea of the global age not because I invented the term 'global age', but because this was the way the world was working. I may add a further point to that, the things that concern me here suggest maybe we are moving from the global age to the digital age. Just as Professor Kim has mentioned, communication, networking, and whatever these may represent.

I used to do many Google searches on globalization and global age. It's a very simple thing to do. Done at different points of time, you could see the global age displacing the nuclear age or the atomic age. Now the digital age has actually, based on Google searches, displaced the global age. Now what does that mean?

Here, I draw on a concept Daniel Bell made famous, 'axial values'. He argued that every national culture, every society, has core principles, central values that is equal to axial values. Also the word axial has been used by historians, when they talked of the few hundred years when Confucius lived, when Aristotle was writing, the great philosophers who lived before the Christian era. But at the same time, the axial values of the global age arose out of the severe threat to the human species as a whole, with the totality of our existence. This is why I preferred the globality concept to that of globalization. The globality of the human species under threat marks our time that is called the global age.

What is the core of the digital age? It's best technology, it means getting to know somebody or other possibly the other side of the world. We chat using Facebook or whatever, we focus down on social human relationships and technology. Is there anything else to the digital age? A possibility is the idea you can actually change human nature. You might actually create new kinds of human beings through the use of technology. That's a long, long way from the concerns of the global age. And the way the global age faces the digital age is as important a conflict as that between modernity and postmodernity.

Professor BING Zheng used the concept of the cultural pluralism to express the relationship of the diversity and integrity:

The Chinese response to the meaning of globalization can be furthered in the second question, That's my own concept of cultural pluralism, I mean plural cultural hybrid. Common nations have plural cultures.

I believe that scholars or people today have wrong assumptions that each culture emerges as very pure, one culture, uniform culture, that's wrong because you really study the emergence of world cultures. You will find each one of those cultures is the cooperation of a lot of different things.

For example, people regularly assume that Western culture or Western civilization comes from just one origin. That is wrong. If you really study Western civilization or Western culture, you will know it not only originates from ancient Egyptian culture and the great Roman culture but also includes Babylon, Arabian and some other cultures.

For China, the same assumption was held by people wrongly as well, for example; a lot of people assume that Chinese culture emerged in the relatively isolated place of China and East Asia, without influence from other cultures. That is wrong.

Although Chinese culture did not interact with the Western culture and Middle Eastern culture, indeed it had a strong interaction with ploughing culture and the nomadic culture from Mongolia.

Under the surface of the core values of the Chinese culture, it appears to be really rooted in agricultural production. Yet when you really study more deeply, you will find a lot of core values of Chinese culture actually one way or another were influenced by the hunting society. And from assimilation they learn a lot and really adjusted how they reckoned things. Today the core traditional value of Chinese culture would one way or another reflect the influence of cooperation between hunting culture and agricultural culture.

For example, I have studied Chinese culture for many years, and my thinking is that three fundamental elements are components of Chinese culture. The first is centralization of political power. The second is a concentrated huge military reserve so that they can mobilize to launch a war or against the invasion from other cultures. The third is a so-called uniform system of hierarchy of the whole nation. All of the three actually formed not just because of agricultural production but because of the interaction with Mongolia and other societies that the nation will have to build that way; otherwise, it is going to collapse.

If you study the histories all around the world, you will find that a lot of countries went through the second period with agriculture that is really the basis of the economy, but none of those cultures really became like China, a huge empire, China became the empire because of the interaction with Mongolians.

A particular reason historically is at the Western and northern sides of China, there are numerous hunting societies or tribal societies, who each are totally military and can mobilize very quickly to attack China. The Chinese of course couldn't be unified otherwise without hierarchy and a single nation would collapse, because in ancient times Mongolia developed tribal society with the skill that out of one million people, more than half are military. And they really had a strong military.

Professor Martin Albrow believed that this is a quite important and different view from that of Karl August Wittfogel, which is dominant in the Western world.

Professor BING Zheng said that he agreed with a British scholar Toynbee. Toynbee said that civilization responds to the environment, and the Chinese environment is Mongolia, the hunting societies, so China would have to be big enough to respond to the possible military invasions, and that really occurred.

For more than two thousand years, China really was in that environment. The hunting society could invade China and in time they needed to invade and of course as they had a military close to one million, therefore China needed at least a one million military reserve in order to defend themselves. For that one million military reserve, they needed several times the agricultural population to support that, and from the Qin dynasty to the Ming dynasty, on average China had a 50 million population and that size could support more than one million military, which is exactly why he understood China was a big empire for a long time. So cultural ideology of course supported the unification and one hierarchy against cultural pluralism. Any separation would be bad for Chinese civilization. Therefore, Chinese culture is a perfect example of the way culture forms in response to the interaction between one culture and another. Chinese culture is not really pure.

Suggestion for Chinese probable contribution to the globalization

Professor Martin Albrow expressed his beliefs:

'For me, what does globalization mean for China? It means that China is inevitably part of this globalizing world, inevitably part of the global society, and it can exercise influence on the direction of that global society from its own special historical experience. That historical experience is more powerful today than the experience of any other country and I am not excluding the USA because it goes back thousands of years. It has adopted a Western ideology of Marxism, and it brings the two together in very dialectical and creative way. Now that has to be and can be put to good use for the world as a whole, because the Chinese country, state and people are the single largest coherent agency in the world today, and the most successful agency in the world. That needs to be put to the use of the global society.

I'm delighted that the Chinese seems to have adopted the notion of governance. And it seems the term doesn't come from the government. Because this is not government. Governance comes from the people and the sense of order underpins the government. The problem means that we live in a complicated world. It's not the order within villages. It is governance of multiple villages we are concerned with. You have to work hard to get these people together to create something.

Governance of the global as a whole has many layers. In Chinese civilization's history we are used to talking of many layers from the family to emperor, or through the village, the town and province. It's many layered, but it also includes multiple differences, accommodating different ethnicities. Of course, Professor Fei was very concerned with minorities in China and wrote about them. The experience of order then is one which is intrinsically hierarchical.

But it does require an understanding of hierarchy by those in different positions of the hierarchy, too. It has to understand that the people who operate at the level of the global governance doing institutional turns for 192 nations are doing quite different jobs from those people who are working driving a taxi in Beijing.

They have to have some kind of mutual understanding and respect. This is why good national leaders very frequently say 'I was talking to this person I met in the store the other day', and 'I was talking with him about the price of the milk'. But when a British leader was asked by an interviewer whether he knew the price of the milk today, he didn't know. That was a measure of the distance between the top and the bottom, which contributed to the British Brexit.

So good governance should practise the fundamental pragmatic universalism in the fact itself, not just in principle. Pragmatic universalism means practice, it's what you do when you meet people with other principles. So I don't think the Chinese will make the American mistake of imposing monetarist policies on other countries but will make the effort to work with all of the people. And that is a very fine example for the rest of the world. China, I trust, will work with and practical pragmatic universalism.

There are risks in lack of self-confidence. The Chinese have lived through dramatic events, experienced many things especially since 1908, and maybe there is a little bit of lack of confidence, but that will change. But I am very hopeful. The best hope for new global prospects comes from China. It is not bound by the institutions of the international monetary order and One Belt One Road is really about working together in common projects for the coming age, which is the wonderful thing to promote nationally.

China can make a unique contribution to the world and to global sociology, precisely because it is new for the rest of the world and different, but it has its own well-established sense of itself. The world has not experienced the same strength of Chinese culture since the 18th century. In the 18th century the Western world was full of Chinese products, Chinese silk, Chinese furniture, Chinese thinking. Chinese thinkers in the 18th century had quite a strong influence on Western economic thought. The more research is done, the more you realize the influence that China in the 18th century had. The time comes again for China to have the same influence. Reflections on the nature of society, all theories and related problems come from the world as a whole, because the problems confront the world as a whole. There are no problems just for Chinese, just for East Asians or Americans.

If we don't have Chinese thinking about global problems, the world will suffer. The world needs Chinese thinking on global problems. Professor LI Peilin talked about global inequality, this is a fundamental contribution, a contribution from a perspective that is both global and Chinese. The concept *guanxi* is generalized as the notion in terms of the relationship between people who create a little network solidarity, and the world will need the concept from China to understand themselves. Similarly, Americans obviously can contribute concepts from American experience.

So the concept derives from your own country and you need to promote it in the rest of the world. *Guanxi* is a very obvious one, but the other concepts associated with Chinese Confucian thought contribute to soft power and the rest of the world does learn from that, as well as from the thinking of ancient Chinese military strategist Sun Zi, from which many people are learning in the West. What you are doing today is important for the rest of the world. I and my colleague Professor Xiangqun Chang try to do this to help promote Chinese sociology in the West.

Professor BING Zheng also mentioned confidence:

The lesson we learn from the review of Chinese history and world history is that every culture is really the mixing of the media culture elements. Therefore, entering the global age living today, I am really against anything that is called cultural conservatism or radical nationalism; none of that would work in the face of the global age. So that is why I raised the concept of a cultural pluralism hybrid. Chinese culture should not build the walls to defend itself, but it should make open interaction and therefore absorb whatever good advantages from other cultures to rebuild the fencing of its own culture. This culture is not the Chinese–Chinese culture; it is the mixing of Chinese and non-Chinese.

In the way of culture exchange in diffusion there is always possibility that your own culture is assimilated into another culture and your culture is gone, so you have to have cultural confidence, you must raise national confidence in your own culture because otherwise your culture one way or another would be merged into some other cultures.

Culture scholars or socialists should really do one thing, that is to guide own people to the train of culture exchange, that is the job to do.

So culture confidence is guided by a third one, integrity.

Finally, coexistence. To explain coexistence, we can use the four phrases that Professor Fei Xiaotong said: 'value what you value, value others' value and value what we commonly value and therefore the society will be harmonized'.

7.3.3 Wuhan University

During the period when she was Visiting Professor at Kings College London, JIN Wei conducted an interview of the author (see 7.3.3.1).

After returning to Wuhan University, Jinwei invited the author to be a keynote speaker at the 4th International Conference on 'Marxism and Socialism in the 21st Century', November 15/17, 2019 at Wuhan University. On the same trip, the author gave a lecture 'What the world can gain from China's global leadership' (see 3.9). Both his speech 'Spirit in Chinese culture and Western culture today' (see 9.3) and a joint article 'Spirit (精神 *jingshen*) as a key contemporary Chinese concept (see 9.2)' were published in the *Journal of China in Global and Comparative Perspectives*, Vol. 7, 2021.

7.3.3.1 Globalization and China's development path: an interview with Professor Martin Albrow, Fellow of the Academy of Social Sciences[58]

[58] 金伟：全球化与中国的发展道路——访英国社会科学院院士马丁·阿尔布劳教授，《马克思主义理论学科研究》，2019年，第5期 [English translation: JIN Wei, Interview of Martin

The latest evolution of globalization and its impact on us

Jin: Professor Martin Albrow, thank you for agreeing to this interview with me. What interests me first of all is that as a leading expert on globalization, you have suggested that one can now think of human society having entered a fourth stage of globalization. What is the difference between this and the previous stages of globalization? What are the characteristics of the present?

Albrow: Well, that's a very interesting question, because it raises two issues, and nearly all discussion of globalization raises these two issues. They are: 'When did we start to use the word globalization?' And 'When can we think about globalization in those terms?' Or, put another way: 'When did globalization begin in the sense of the word as we use it now? And what changed in the world so that we began to use the word?

What happened in history and how do we talk about history? Those two things move independently of each other, you see. There's one sense in which globalization existed long before the word was invented, and the word only became current in the 1970s. So globalization in the sense it was used in 1970 meant simply that the world is becoming one place: everything is becoming more and more connected to each other. Now that sense of the world becoming more and more connected to each other was identified a long time before the word. The most famous example I suppose is the work of Karl Marx and Friedrich Engels, when they talked about the growth of the world's market: how capital expanded to cover the whole world. They regarded the expansion of capital as inherent to capitalism as such. Well, that's not different from what was later called globalization.

Now, why did globalization get called globalization in 1970s? Well, I think it has a lot to do with the prevalence of the word 'global.' People talked a lot about global after the end of the Second World War and one of the very main reasons, of course, was the fact of the dropping of the atomic bombs: the sense of a threat to the earth; that threat was a global threat; it was a threat to the globe. So the word global became very popular and it wasn't long before global generated globalization, just like the word modern generates modernization.

Now you then have to see how globalization develops. Along with the development of the concept in the 1980s, globalization was largely appropriated by the business world when they talked about the globalization of markets. And so in the 1980s globalization was almost identified with what Marx was talking about, expansion of the global economy.

In the 1990s, however, globalization was taken up by the politicians, particularly in the United States, Britain and Europe. Those people were President Bill Clinton and Prime Minister Tony Blair; they made globalization a kind of transformation of the modern: it was the next stage of modernization; it was closely linked with technologies of communication. Then if you like, it's the third stage

Albrow. *Marxist Theoretical Research*, 2019(5)].

of globalization; and then of course when we come into the 21st century, their optimism which belongs to Clinton and Blair received a very nasty blow with the destruction of the Twin Towers in 2002 and "9/11" as it was called. and with that, globalization in a sense became a battleground, a battleground between civilizations; and in some senses the coming together of the world as one place has been associated with conflict ever since. You might say the fourth stage of globalization can be called 'the conflicts of globalization' because they seem to follow one after the other.

I think as far as the globe is concerned, certainly the development of the digital and digitalization has obviously resulted in the increasing intensity of ties between people and corporations across the globe. So we have had an intensification of connectivity. However, it also is connected to the decline in the sense of the global, if by the global; one means a focus on the globe as a whole, because the digital is a matter of the keyboard, the keyboard and not the globe. So to some extent the digital is taking our attention away from globalization, even as it brings people closer together. Here you might say the difference between the processes, the real processes in the world, and the language of the globe—that difference is getting bigger and bigger again.

Jin: With Brexit and Trump Presidency, What do you think of the current wave of anti-globalization? Some would say there will be a 'slowbalization' in the coming decades, what do you think? What role should China play in the latest globalization?

Albrow: Well, you see in the 1990s we had a global anti-globalization and it was very much directed against the growth of global capitalism. I remember very well: December 1999 and the meeting of the World Trade Organization in Seattle, which had to be called off because of the protesters arriving from all over North America and from even wider areas. Protesters actually prevented the meeting from taking place. President Clinton was prevented from attending and said afterwards, 'Well, I think maybe the protesters have a point.' And this was the beginning really of a recognition on the part of all those who were promoting globalization as the new world of a global economy run by Western international institutions. This brought them up with a start and they recognized this isn't all going in one direction; there is a strong anti-globalization movement. And it was a movement, which in the terms of the sociologist Geoffrey Pleyers became an 'alter global' movement.

An alter-global movement is not anti-globalization. What it's saying is we need globalization to be of a different kind altogether now. Later in the first decade of the 21st century that altered globalization, which was led by largely young middle class people, gradually moved into a more general opposition to globalization from people who were not having any advantages from globalization. So whereas anti-globalization has begun as an intellectual movement, later in the first decade of the 21st century, it starts to become a popular movement called populism. Populism basically is an appeal to people who feel they've been left behind. Indeed, these people feel they've been left out even by the previous anti-globalization people because they were intellectuals. And it became very much a divide between the intellectual professional moneyed classes of society against the rest. And an underlying reason of course is that while globalization has brought huge increases in wealth worldwide; within individual countries it's increased inequality and that increase of inequality within the country puts a great deal of strain on the political systems. Now some people have called it 'slowbalization'. Yes, that's right. But in a way what they're concentrating on is simply the reaction of national governments to these populist demands; therefore governments are trying to restrict free trade, putting tariffs on and so on.

Now China's got a special place in all this because, of course, you could argue the one country which is being in the lead and has benefited most from globalization has been China. China is the country which has grown most; China is the country where the middle class has expanded in a vast way and China has contributed to world trade like no other country has done. Now the problem is for China that the reactions against globalization in the rest of the world mean that China has to redirect its attention. Up to now it has been using globalization to its own advantage. From now on it's got to redirect itself and to some extent to use globalization in a different way. Of course, that different way—the One Belt and One Road is not globalization. It's something a bit different.

Jin: What do you think of Brexit? What do you think of the British future?

Albrow: Well, I think Britain is the country where the inner conflicts that arise out of globalization have some of the most intense effects. You see, Britain since Tony Blair and indeed even since the Prime Minister Margaret Thatcher has claimed to be and aims to be a global country. Well, no, Britain is a small country. And for Britain to be global and to open itself up to the global economy is quite a dangerous thing. And one of the things which of course has put greater strain on Britain is that this has proved successful in economic terms, but in part because of the huge amount of immigration from elsewhere: people coming from other countries who are wanting to contribute to and benefit from an economic growth in Britain, that has put pressure on traditional communities and, if you like, simply old-fashioned conservative people, older people who don't like to see so many immigrants. It's very straightforward in that respect.

So Britain, I think, is, if you like, in the eye of the storm of globalization, it's the country which has experienced the most intensive effects and its political system is not very well designed to cope with this, because arguably the system best adapted to cope with this might be one where you had a very strong leader and a very unified political class. But all that has happened in Britain is that it has diffused the political class; it has fractured, fragmented in all kinds of different directions.

The successful way of the reform and opening-up policy in China

Jin: I know you have deep and sincere feelings for China, you first went to China in 1987, after this you have been to China more than 10 times. Could you talk about your intuitive feelings about China's development and change? What do you think of China's achievements, and what are the main reasons for such achievements?

Albrow: Well, my experience of China has given me great reason for being astonished. The developments of your country in those 32 years since 1987 have been quite astonishing; lots of them come to me as visual images. You know, when you visit a country, it's the visual images which remain with you. And my images of my first visits were, well, no cars or very, very few cars; there was one ring road in Beijing; everyone was on bicycles; everyone was in Chairman Mao suits, and then as I was the guest of the State Family Planning Commission, in the countryside what was so impressive was the hard work of the people; their dedication to the task in hand. And I observed how very dutifully they fulfilled the requirements of the one child policy. It was very moving in its way, this commitment to a national task. And the people I met were convinced that they were contributing to the rebirth of China. So that sense of going forward was there already. Of course the reason was that Secretary Deng Xiaoping had already opened up in 1978, so it was already in full swing.

I think what one sees is the continuation of what I first experienced in 1987: a growth of conviction that China is being rejuvenated and will have its proper place in the world, which is to be really at least one of the two leading powers in the world. I think clearly the Communist Party has given a direction and an ideological coherence to people's behaviour, which is missing of course in Western countries. So there is a single-mindedness in the country. But I think there's something else which underlies this, which is the unity of Chinese culture around its discourse, its way of speaking and writing. Its way of speaking and writing is unique in the world: the combination of the Chinese characters with all kinds of different dialects of course. But that gives a kind of profound unity. And I think that underlies the coherence of the society and culture, and that is a requirement for the party. So, at a trivial level, you see this represented in the street signs, the slogans in the street signs, where you see single characters there. Now, in the West you can't represent political ideas in that way, in that visual way that you can in China. So I think that that's a very superficial level, but it's something which reveals a profound underlying unity in Chinese culture, which the Communist Party has developed for the purposes of national rejuvenation.

Jin: What do you think of China's reform and opening-up under socialism with Chinese characteristics?

Albrow: Well, the first thing one has to say is that you had the benefit of the wisdom and the experience of a remarkable political leader, which was Deng Xiaoping. I think we all have to ask what would have happened if Deng Xiaoping hadn't resolved that China should take a new direction, by opening itself up to the world? Could any other leader have done what he did? I don't know. He enjoyed an enormous amount of influence and prestige among the people around him. And he was really what in the West the social scientist Max Weber called a charismatic figure. And he of course got the support and help of large numbers of comrades, sociologists for instance. We sociologists are particularly proud of the fact that one of the people he listened to was the Chinese anthropologist and sociologist Fei Xiaotong and it was Fei who advocated the responsibility system in agriculture and that was one of the pioneering things which led to the acceptance that private property in China was not a bad thing. You needed private property to motivate people so that they could contribute to the common good; you needed a balance of the private and the public, and Deng Xiaoping understood that and he understood that the way in which you would therefore increase China's wealth would be by allowing people to benefit from their own work and then to be able to contribute to the national effort by the export of the things they made that other people and the rest of the world would want.

So, linking China with the rest of the world was closely connected with the hard work of the individual member of the community, with the peasant: the peasants' work and opening up were connected to each other, and then of course the factories have developed and all the movement into the towns. Now the opening up has continued since 1987 without a significant break, and of course initially led to enormous growth rates of 10 percent and more per annum in the gross national product of China. It's now declined to 6 percent, but that compared with the West is still enormous.

Now, a lot of Western critics of course have said 'Well, of course, this means that China does not have any true communism or socialism, that it is a form of state capitalism.' And the answer to that comes from Chinese theoreticians who find their ideas expressed in the phrase 'socialism with Chinese characteristics'. That is actually a very profound saying because what that recognizes is that socialism is not an abstract set of idea; socialism is something developed in practice and therefore in practice it happens within cultures. Every country will have its own characteristics, whether it's a socialist country or a capitalist country: this is the importance of national culture.

So, China takes very seriously its own distinctive culture and, as I was saying, in response to your earlier question: China's culture has got a very, very special characteristic, in the way it's built up on a language which has its characters. Now, those characters have got enormous history behind them and fundamental ideas are launched in those characters. So, when we talked about "*li*" (礼): it is very difficult to translate into English because it covers everything from rules and rituals and virtue and the proper way of doing things. It can be translated in so many different ways, but those different senses all form great unity and they go back deep into China's past. The West can't have anything equivalent to that.

The theoretical contribution of Xi's *The Governance of China* to the development of China's road and global governance

Jin: You mentioned we should examine Xi's The Governance of China as a serious theoretical contribution to global governance. Why would you say that? What do you think is the major contribution of Xi's philosophy to governance?

Albrow: The first things that struck me when I first saw the English translation of President Xi's speeches – the title of the book made my heart leap because he was using in the translation the old European word 'governance': it's a word in French and in English. And governance is a term that goes back several hundred years and it's not quite the same as government, because governance is the creation of order in a society. And the creation of order in a society is not simply a matter of governments. I think this is the important lesson that we should draw from President Xi's speeches, which is that he's looking at the problems of social order, the maintenance of social order, the direction in which society should go, the bringing together of people's motivation into a national purpose. All those things he's bringing together under the heading of governance, that I think in a way develops an idea of governance for use for any country really; takes it out of a Western context and makes it even a universal notion.

And to do that, I think, Xi shows through his speeches that you must operate with ideas of quite high complexity and even abstractness as well. So, some of the ideas which he promotes repeatedly, a very high level in ideas indeed, the concept of values, for instance, which of course are fixed in contemporary thought in the 12 socialist values. The concept of values he talks about so frequently is a very high-level concept. He does the same thing with concepts like responsibility, with rule and with the people, for instance. And those notions are not just, shall we say, 'rhetorical empty phrases'. They are profoundly related to each other. So you relate the Party to the people, to power, to rule, to values and so on. And all the time through his speeches you see the way he's trying to integrate theoretical ideas with the practice of people's everyday lives. This is the remarkable nature of those speeches and I believe there is no political leader in the West who has that same grasp of the relationship between ideas which are the subject of very focused academic thought and the kinds of things people talk about in their everyday lives. He does that. Of course, some of it is his own, very special talent in this area. He is what in the West we used to call in the 18th century a 'Philosopher King'; that was in the period when your kings used to approach a thinker like Voltaire or Thomas Hobbes and say 'Tell us the big ideas and we will try to learn from them.'

Well, of course, Xi takes ideas from all of those around him. He's got a profound sense of the intellectual drive that's necessary to lead a great society in the contemporary world. So this is the significance for the governance of China of those speeches. It is the unification of theoretical ideas with the everyday practices of getting things done. Yes, right the way down to, you know, invoking the spirit of the ordinary citizen to get on with their work. Yes.

Jin: We know you are studying the Chinese spirit. How do you interpret the concept? How do Westerners use the idea of spirit? What can the West learn from the Chinese spirit?

Albrow: I think I probably noticed this for the first time—it hit me, as it were, when I was looking at an official document which was published as the appendix to a book written about One Belt and One Road by the eminent Chinese diplomat and professor, Professor Wang Yiwei. At the end of his book he outlined the vision and proposed actions on jointly building the Silk Road economic belt and the 21st-century maritime Silk Road. And this was an official document that was published by the Ministry Foreign Affairs and Ministry of Commerce. In the very first two paragraphs of this, it speaks about the 'Silk Road spirit'. It speaks of thousands of years of the Silk Road spirit and then invokes peace and cooperation, openness and inclusiveness, mutual learning and mutual benefit. All of this was passed from generation to generation. And it goes on to say that the Silk Road spirit symbolizes communication and cooperation between the East and the West. And then the official document says 'it is all the more important for us today in our new era to carry on the Silk Road spirit'.

No, you wouldn't ever get an official document in the West that started off talking about spirit in this way. So then I looked at the speeches that President Xi gave in The Governance of China and there he's talking about the spirit of China and also about the spirit of the Long March, for instance. Then I realized spirit was everywhere and I realized I needed to have more expert advice on this. So I turned to my colleague, Professor JIN Wei, from Wuhan University. And she very kindly started to research the use of spirit in contemporary public discourse in China. What is clear is the huge scope of references to spirit: it might be the spirit of the Long March or it might be the spirit of Shanghai; it could be the spirit of some famous comrade. Then it's intended to bring about enthusiasm and commitment and energy in the people who commit themselves to that spirit; it's an example to them, to behave in that way; it's a communication to them of something that was important in the past which took people forward to achieve new things. So this reference to the spirit is something that's pervasive in Chinese life and it contrasts enormously of course with the West. With the Chinese spirit, you can have the spirit for China as a whole, one of renewal, renovation and committing energy to the national good, the life of the whole community, taking it forward, realizing the Chinese dream.

Now, in the West we don't talk of spirit in this way, at least not in politics, not in political discourse; you don't get politicians saying. 'We must harness the spirit of Waterloo or the spirit of the Second World War.' It doesn't happen. Indeed if they were to do that, I think people would say, 'Oh, they're trying to deceive us. They're trying to bring us to think in terms which are no longer relevant.' And I suppose the deep reason in the West is because spirit was associated with religion, specifically with organised religions. It was attacked, of course, in the

18th and 19th centuries by the growing secularism, opposition to the churches and by growing materialism, even though it wasn't the materialism of Karl Marx, for instance. Karl Marx recognized the spiritual side of human life. What was against the old sense of the spirit was, of course, people lost faith in the old religions. And when they threw the old religions away, they threw the spirits as well. So the West has in its secularization lost a lot of its moral integration, it's lost a lot of its sense of a mission in life. The West has been de-spiritualized and spiritualization has been taken out of the West.

By comparison, China is a spiritual place and that gives it energy. Well, when I say this I can say this to a Chinese audience and they will understand. I don't think people in the West understand this at all. They think of China as materialist because it's ruled by a Communist Party: and the Communist Party is Marxist; and Marxism is materialist, then obviously the Chinese don't have any spirit. In fact the exact opposite is the case.

Jin: What do you think of Xi's formula for global governance, a community of common destiny? How do we discover common values?

Albrow: Yes, it's extremely interesting how President Xi develops the idea of a community of common destiny, common destiny for humankind, for the human species. That notion arises out of, I think, a sense that the peoples of the world with all their different cultures, nonetheless, have common challenges; and those challenges mean that people have to work together. The community of common destiny is one where the peoples of the world cooperate with each other. Now, one of the things that interests me greatly is the fact that when we consider these 12 socialist values, cooperation is not one of those values. Cooperation is actually outside the set of socialist values for China. And I think there is a good reason for that, because the cooperation which is necessary between peoples is not actually produced by common values. It's produced by challenges, by the sense that we're all under threat; and in responding to that threat we have to work with each other to increase our strength and power. So the community of common destiny is not actually the result of common values, it's the result of cooperating to meet global challenges. I think this is very clear in reading The Governance of China, because it operates on common values, whereas the governance of the globe operates on the basis of responding to global challenges: a very subtle important difference which is never explicitly stated in the way I've stated it. But I think it is implicit in the account that Xi gives. China, on the other hand, has common values and those common values have been produced out of working together and the sense of belonging to each other.

Jin: Yes. What do you think is the challenge for One Belt and One Road? How should China deal with these challenges?

Albrow: Well, of course, it's very presumptuous for a foreigner to try to tell Chinese people what Belt and Road is. I'm sure they know much better than I do. But fundamentally, as I understand it, the Belt and Road Initiative arises out of speeches that President Xi gave originally, I think, as long ago as 2013. And they were put together with a number of initiatives, which are to improve communications between China and neighbouring countries, and those would be road communications and maritime communications, communications in the air. The idea with Belt and Road is that, with good communications, you'll increase trade between people, make trade possible. And as a result of trade exchange of goods, people will get to know each other and it will generate a many ideas of common purpose; and it will generate lots of well-being and wealth and value in the countries concerned. So Belt and Road is there to increase, first of all, the economic well-being of the countries along the road.

Secondly, a further reason is it will increase communication across and between different cultures. Now you may ask 'Well, how will that work in practice?', because communications across cultures is the big challenge or was the big challenge. I mean if you think back in the West, you may have had very good communications between, say, France and Germany, railroads crossing the boundary and so on, yet they still went to war with each other. So the big challenge is to ensure that the relationship between the countries which are linked by Belt and Road is also a peaceful, a cooperative relationship, one which understands mere economic exchange does not in itself produce harmony between nations; all it does is to ensure that what is good in one country is transferred to another and vice versa. Each country sees it is in its own interests to enter into economic exchange, but that doesn't mean they necessarily value the contact with that country or agree with the people in those countries. That is the big challenge for Belt and Road, not the building of the airport and the roads and the ships, because countries are very easily able to agree on them. People know how to make ships, and it's a knowledge which is spread around the world. So that's no problem. It's building on that to produce peace between nations, that's where the big challenge will be.

Jin: So how should China deal with this challenge?

Albrow: Well, this is the big question. I think one of the things that China can do is to spread knowledge of China, of course, to welcome those people who come to China for trade and offer them the cultural experiences. Secondly, to encourage Chinese people who go to these countries along the Belt and Road to interact with people in those countries, to set up schools for instance, to encourage the learning of Chinese. And also of course, importantly, recently President Xi has encouraged this: also for Chinese people just to learn the languages of the countries that they go to and to increase the learning of foreign languages in China, because up to the recent times, every Chinese child has been learning English. But now I believe it should be possible to learn not only another language, but in some cases to say 'I don't want to learn more English. I want in fact to learn more Russian or Hindi or an African language.'

Jin: I think after I came here I found some Western media disparaged China, when President Xi Jinping talked about the Chinese story and the good Chinese voice. What do you think is the problem with China's external communication, and what good advice do you have?

Albrow: Well, I think the first thing to recognize that there's no point in denying this, that in the West there is a great deal of misunderstanding and suspicion of China, and the origins of this go back of course to the original founding of the Chinese People's Republic. They go back to periods even before that, back even to the 19th century when China was under imperial rule and the Ching dynasty. So the roots of the suspicions of China are very deep, although, and I should stress this, it is not inevitable. If one goes back further in Chinese history to the 18th century, Europe was full of people who admired China enormously. It was a period when a European philosopher like Voltaire was saying China has got the wisdom of the East; they can teach us so much. In the West now the change that took place in the 19th century, I'm very sad to say, was in very large part produced by imperialism and especially by British imperialism. And I always as a British citizen apologize, on behalf of my citizens, fellow citizens, for the damage which was done to China in the 19th century.

I think you rightly talk about it as your century of humiliation and I'm terribly ashamed of the fact that it was British actions, above all, which produce that sense of humiliation. I'm glad to say that my reception always in China is very gracious and kind and it seems you have a huge capacity for forgiveness. But that capacity for forgiveness is not matched in the West. The West is still of the view that China is ruled by an authoritarian regime, because it is ruled by a Communist Party now. It's important for Chinese people to recognize that for the West the prime experience of communism was in the Cold War with the Soviet Union; and there is no doubt in the minds of the West that the Soviet Union was a totalitarian dictatorship, and that it had to be conquered and eliminated. The unfortunate thing is that the Soviet experience in Russia was the dominant impression that people have of communism in the West. Now for the Chinese to overcome those impressions, well certainly, they have to stress all kinds of things which will resonate with the West; and I think they have to be quite bold now. So I say this, the Chinese people should not be shy about talking about the Party. They should go abroad and they should tell the world what the Party does in China and for China. And at one and the same time, they have to take on board, and I think there are signs that China is doing this, they have to take on board a discussion about the nature of democracy, because I think for the first time, for, let's say, a hundred years or more, the West is now very uncertain about the way its own democracies work; and that they are possibly beginning to be prepared to hear what Chinese thinkers say about democracy, because there's no reason at all why the representative democracies of the West should be allowed to take the concept of democracy and call it their own.

The idea of democracy is worldwide. Every culture in the world has got access to the idea of democracy, whether it's China or India, Polynesia or Africa. The idea of democracy after all is only people in a community arriving at a collective will, that's all it is. And it has existed worldwide. That notion is something which in China is of course associated particularly with the Party and the relationship of the Party to the people. And that relationship has to be expressed in terms of democracy.

So I would be arrogant to give advice, but my suggestion to the Chinese leadership is to be proud of your own democracy, and to promote its discussion worldwide. And I think that will do more than anything else to get the rest of the world accustomed to the fact the China is a community with a people which is committed to its own culture, and that it organizes itself on principles which are as profound and as well grounded as any that exist in the rest of the world. Now engaging in that way is I think the best possible way for China to make its voice heard. I mean, it's doing lots of good things at the moment, the Confucius Institutes of course, excellent thing, I benefited myself from the Confucius Institute in London. But I would suggest what needs to go further than that is not a question of saying 'We want to impose Chinese values on the rest of the world', not at all. It's a question of engaging with ideas of democracy which come from all quarters, all parts of the world, and making sure that China's voice is heard among them.

Jin: Could you give us an introduction to the new book you are writing? What is the main content of it? When will it probably be published?

Albrow: Well, of course, you're asking for a lot here because if I told you everything that was in the book, then I wouldn't need to write it because other people would start to write it. So all I can tell you is it focuses on a question and that is: 'Has the global age come to an end?', and it looks at all the contemporary problems of populism, of globalization, of digitalization and conflicts between civilizations; so it treats all of those things. But I hope it offers a different angle from other people. After all, it's written in terms of an age that is already a bit different. When you write about an age, you write about the spirit of an age as well, just as in the 18th century Voltaire wrote about the spirit of an age. Now one of the things you have to point to, I'm afraid, is conflicts: there are conflicts within the spirit of the time and a lot of that has to be drawn out of everyday action and everyday conflicts. And also one has to do this in a way which is as objective as possible. Now, to be objective in the contemporary world, to my mind, is not to try to be, shall we say, scientifically universal, because when it comes to looking at cultures, objectivity is very different.

But what one can try to do is to look from the outside in. how it does look from the outside in? With contemporary cultures, where is that outside? What in previous times would be called the Archimedean point: the Archimedes said, you know, if you wanted to move the earth, you would have to get a point so far away that to lever it would be beyond the earth. The Archimedean point: at the point where you could shift things of huge weight.

Well, the Archimedean point I suggest in looking at contemporary cultures, yes, it's the globe. If you take a position where you say the interests of the globe mean the challenges to human beings everywhere, the challenges of climate change in particular, the challenge of the nuclear security, the challenge that the internet presents to everyone, those challenges are global and not national. Though every country has to deal with them, but if you look at them as global challenges, then you look at the different solutions that different countries have and the ways they can cooperate with each other in order to solve them.

So what I try to promote is the idea that in the social sciences today when one's looking at the condition of the world as a whole, we shouldn't be attempting to work on so-called 'universal' principles. We should take the challenges to the globe and see what solutions we can find to those challenges. And in the course of that we may find principles which are relatively universal. Sometimes I've called them simply transcultural, because they cover every country. And the prime example that I use for a universal solution that every culture seems to have drawn out of the global challenge is the concept and value of sustainability. I don't think there's anyone, any culture in the world which doesn't have access to that notion. It's still controversial, but nonetheless has just become universal. So here the global approach has produced something, which is universal, which every country can approach, and no country can say 'This is ours. This is ours and doesn't belong to someone else.' You know, so this is my methodology. If you like the method, the methodology of working on global challenges, developing global governance, understanding between cultures, all those things I believe can fall into place as a result. So that underpins the book that I'm writing at the moment. And you asked when it might come out. Well, it comes out when I finish it.

7.3.3.2 What the world can gain from China's global leadership (see 3.9)

7.3.3.3 Spirit (精神 *jingshen*) as a key contemporary Chinese concept (see 9.2)

7.3.3.4 Spirit in Chinese culture and Western culture today (see 9.3)

7.3.4 Renmin University

Since the launch of *The Belt and Road Initiative: What Will China Offer the World in its Rise?* by WANG Yiwei in 2016, the author and Professor WANG Yiwei of Renmin University undertook some joint publications. In 2018, Wang posed 10 questions to the author on the Belt and Road Initiative. The dialogue has been included in *Dialogue on China,* published by Renmin University of China, 2019, pp. 75–102, and in this book (see 4.1). Two years later, Wang posed 10 questions to the author on Xi Jinping's community of shared future for mankind. They reflected the author's slightly different thinking. For his answers, see 1.2. Wang's answers are too long to be translated into English and included in this book. The author also wrote a Foreword for Wang's book (see 6.3).

7.3.4.1 Dialogue on BRI with WANG Yiwei (see 4.1)

7.3.4.2 Ten questions on Xi Jinping's community of shared future for mankind (see 1.2)

7.3.4.3 The imperative need to build a community of shared future for mankind is demonstrated by the novel coronavirus (see 6.3)

7.3.4.4 Participating in editorial work for the author's two books

Wang is a co-editor of the overseas Chinese edition of *China's Role in a Shared Common Future*, published by Global Century Press, London, 2021. His student LIU Xuejun helped with the editorial work of the above book by making detailed comparative notes between the overseas Chinese edition and the mainland Chinese edition, published by Commercial Press, Beijing, 2020. She also collected a large amount of material for the creation of this book.

7.3.5 Yunan Minzu University

The author presented letters of appointment to Centre Directors of the Global China Academy at the 5th Global China Dialogue in 2018. The Himalayan Civilization Comparative Studies Centre (HCCSC) was one of the Centres. In past years, Professor SHEN Haimei, Director of Nepal Research Centre at Yunnan Minzu University (UMU) has been involved in our work.

7.3.5.1 Translation of Chinese media interviews of the author into English

With help from SHEN Haimei a GCA-UMU volunteer team was formed by some of her PhD and Masters students in 2021. They did Chinese-English translations of all journalists' interviews of the author (5.5, 6.7, 6.8, 7.4.2.2, 7.4.2.3, 7.4.2.5) for this book.

7.3.5.2 Co-editor of Global China Dialogue Proceedings, Vol. 7

The volunteer team also translated most of the speakers' abstracts, short biographies and speech notes from English to Chinese for the production of the 7th Global China Dialogue (GCD VII) dual language programmes. After the GCD VII they transcribed English texts from most of the video records and translated them into Chinese for editing the GCD VII proceedings in both English and Chinese. SHEN Haimei became a co-editor for the GCD VII proceedings together with the author and the editor of the book (8.3.1.3).

7.3.6 Tongji University – The globalization era and China: Concepts, Contexts, Problems and Orientations: an interview with the British sociologist Martin Albrow / WANG Xin[59]

[59] Editor's note: This interview was conducted in 2018 when Professor WANG Xin was a Visiting Fellow in the UK. Between February and May 2021, the interviewer followed up some questions via email. This English version will be published in the *Journal of China in Global and Comparative Perspectives*, vol. 8, 2022 [Chinese version: 王鑫: "全球化时代与中国：概念、语境、问题与面向——英国社会学家马丁·阿尔布劳教授访谈",《国外社会科学》, 2021年第6期, 第54-60页 (*Social Sciences Abroad*, No. 6, 2021, pp. 54-60)].

Abstract: As one of the initiators of the concept of 'globalization', Professor Martin Albrow, a British sociologist, further clarified, in an interview, the connotations, framework and future development of globalization, to provide a more accurate and refined concept for international communication and other studies. Professor Albrow corrected some misunderstandings of the concepts of globalization and anti-globalization in a diachronic and synchronic context, and on the premise of the theory on how to create a positive national image in international communication and how to spread the national image from both theoretical and practical perspectives.

Keywords: globalization, anti-globalization, international communication, national image, post-epidemic era

Interviewer: Tenured professor Wang Xin, School of Arts and Media, Tongji University, PRC

Wang: Hello, Professor Albrow, thank you very much for granting me this interview. The world is undergoing tremendous changes every day. As a big developing country, China, in the context of globalization, plays an important role both in the economic field and in the political structure. China is also eager to prove itself to the world, so it pays special attention to its national image. That is why I wanted to have an interview with you. On the one hand, I want to know more about your thinking about globalization, and, on the other hand, how does China act in the global context? Because my main research is the construction of China's international image from a global perspective and how China tells the world about itself, I will also ask questions on this aspect.

Albrow: That's fine with me.

Theory and Reality: Concept, Connotation and Context of Globalization

Wang: As we know, you are the initiator of the concept of globalization. Globalization has become one of the powerful concepts to explain various experiences and problems in today's world. As a sociologist, what prompts you to focus on and think about globalization? How do you think of the context of globalization today and the commonalities and differences when you put forward this concept?

Albrow: Well, Professor Wang, thank you for asking me to answer your questions, which sound very interesting. Now, to your first question, let me just correct a little bit what you say: I didn't invent the concept of globalization and it's very difficult to know who used the word 'globalization' first. It was probably somewhere in the late 1960s, and then in 1972 an American political scientist, Georg Modelsk, used the word 'globalization' to refer to basically the world becoming one place, so it was used in a very general sense, basically for the world having increasing unity about it, and for some time is that was how it was used in academic life. There was a professor in America, Roland Robertson who had written academic papers about globalization, but I was the first person to put the word 'globalization' in the title of a book called Globalization Knowledge and Society, an edited volume where I brought together papers which had been written by sociologists from all over the world. They were put together in this one volume and it was given to all the delegates to the World Congress of Sociology in 1990 in Madrid, so 4,000 delegates got a copy of this book. They came from all over the world, so you could say this was the launch of globalization as a concept. To that extent, I can say I had a big part in promoting the concept for the first time, but I didn't invent the word. Now, in the 1990s, the concept of globalization came to be used very much by American public speakers talking about the unification of the world's financial institutions and the worldwide extension of the free market economy. So, that was how globalization was presented to the world largely by Americans in the 1990s. To a lesser extent, it was tied up with the ideas of international communication. The world was becoming a smaller place with the growth of the internet, which had been invented by the late 1990s, and also of course satellite communication. All those things enhanced the development of society, so people were talking about globalization as an interconnected world. In addition, I would prefer to keep economic globalization distinct from other forms of globalization. I know President Xi always talks about economic globalization and not just globalization simply, which is very good, because the simple sense of globalization is much more connected with what Chinese would prefer to call connectivity, the world becoming one place again, so in this sense we are coming back to the original meaning of globalization from the 1970s, the world becoming one place.

Wang: Thank you for letting me know the history of the concept of globalization. In 2001, your book *The Global Age* was published in China, which had a lot of influence. More than ten years have passed. If you reflect on your understanding of globalization at the time, do you think there is a correction, or a more in-depth thinking? If you define the concept of 'globalization' again now, how would you define it?

Albrow: Well, I think if I talk about globalization now, it's the meaning that I wrote in the book *The Global Age* that was published in English first in 1996, but what I said in that book was that there were several meanings attached to globalization and those meanings were shifting. We just talked about one globalization, in the sense of increased connectivity of the world, and everybody communicating with everybody else. And then of course economic globalization, which is the development of economic relationships and the free market and so on.

With those different meanings I also tried to suggest that the notion of the global should be distinguished from globalization as such. In fact, what I argue in my book *The Global Age* is that a sense of the globe came before the idea of globalization, and that sense of the globe became very, very prominent after the

Second World War. As a result of it, the world was under threat and it was not just under threat politically, it was under threat actually, in particular from nuclear warfare. When I was young, I saw the pictures of the atomic bombs dropped on Hiroshima and Nagasaki Japan in 1945. I was eight years old, and I can remember seeing the great mushroom cloud. People talked about the globe as something under threat. Now, the words 'global issues' became very prominent, in particular in the work of a Canadian, Marshall McLuhan, who invented that phrase which everyone knows – 'the global village'.

Wang: If from a diachronic perspective, in the process of globalization, is the change in the world pattern consistent with your theoretical presupposition? What do you think your interpretation framework is about how to build a better global society?

Albrow: The global village concept came before globalization, so when we think about the globe, it is not the same as globalization. It is the same as human beings belonging to one family, and that family is under threat sometimes from its own members but also from things outside. One is the nuclear problem, which you might say is related to quarrels between countries. The other thing was increasingly becoming recognized from the 1970s – the fact that human beings could destroy the planet on which they live. So global issues are quite different from globalization. For me, the global age is defined by the sense of the globe under threat and the fact that human beings have to work together to solve global problems. The work that I do is primarily about how can the world come together to solve global problems, and globalization as such is sometimes part of the answer, sometimes part of the problem, but it is not the answer. What I've just answered follows nicely on the last one, because globalization as such doesn't take us anywhere in particular, especially if you think of globalization as connectivity. Suppose I say the world becomes more and more connected, what sort of world is that? We don't know, we don't know whether that means we live a better life or a worse life. Do we quarrel with each other more or less? Do we eat more or less? Do we drop more bombs or fewer bombs? None of those questions is answered by saying the world has increasing connectivity. What we have to say is: how are we going to use these kinds of activities? What's the purpose of it and what is the crucial factor? For me, the only good purpose is to solve this huge problem of the world being under threat from climate change and secondly nuclear threat. My answer to that is this is not solved by globalization, it's solved by the great powers of the world coming together and agreeing with each other on how to solve it.

Globalization, anti-globalization and post-COVID-19 era: Social changes and commonality in the age of globalization

Wang: Globalization has a long historical process. Different countries play different roles in different stages of globalization. They have different standpoints and attitudes towards globalization. How do you treat these differences?

Albrow: The differences are seen in terms of the interests of the countries concerned. Understandably, countries which think they stand to gain from globalization will promote it. So, in the 1990s, the Americans felt we are the winners with globalization because we will open the world to our goods and our capital. They advanced globalization as the solution to global issues but secretly they thought it's to our advantage. So, the way countries respond to globalization will be dictated by whether they feel it's in their interests.

China has always been very clever with globalization, when judging whether it is to her advantage or not. When it is, they're saying economic globalization is a good thing. The Chinese definitely have gained a great deal from it in recent years, but I would say, as I wrote in a piece for *China Daily*, globalization is not necessarily in the interests of a country. For instance, globalization can produce huge differences in wealth. Now, that's happening in Britain. We can say that globalization is quite responsible for the divisions in Britain today. On one side is the increase of huge wealth and on the other are those being left behind. Overall, globalization may have been to the disadvantage of the United Kingdom.

Wang: Just like the Industrial Revolution, Britain was also one of the biggest beneficiaries, Globalization will also bring opportunities to some countries, but also make some countries lose opportunities. 'Anti-globalization' is another trend. In the process of 'globalization' in the depth of development, do you think that 'anti-globalization' is the most significant impact on what aspects of globalization, and what is the most vulnerable place of the globalization concept? What do you think is the logical basis of 'anti-globalization'? Under the changing global order, does it constitute a powerful 'reaction' to 'globalization'?

Albrow: Well, anti-globalization began in the 1990s and it was against the American free trade policy and to some degree against the expansion of American culture generally, so it was a reaction against the United States. It particularly became very strong in France initially, but very quickly it merged with what you could call the Western anti-capitalist movement. So an anti-globalization movement exploded in Seattle in 1999, where the WTO meeting was halted by anti-globalization protests against the free trade ideology, that is, the neo-liberal ideology of the United States and the feeling that free trade was damaging the interests of traditional industry and agriculture in other countries. In France, there was a feeling that globalization was an attack on French culture and French agriculture, and French activists even attacked McDonald's restaurants. So the anti-globalization movement grew in the way that it merged with a general sense of anti-capitalism in the West and with the sense of nationalism. Both anti-capitalism and nationalism were the two sides of the anti-globalization movement. Now, when countries put up tariffs against free trade they think it's in their own interests. To some extent, what they're doing is in line with what anti-globalization activists want. So you can think of the anti-globalization movement as an anti-free trade movement. However, after a while, even the anti-globalization people realised that they were in a sense promoting globalization because they were organising all over the world. So they were a worldwide movement, which is a global movement. They were saying we can't just be against globalization, we must change globalization, making it valuable for countries instead of attacking them. So that's what's changed in anti-globalization.

In fact, that is a little point I would like to share. For many of the Chinese commentators on the West, they may think the West is a unity. In fact, the West is not a unity, and it never has been. It's always been full of diversity and conflicts. The United States was founded by people who left Europe, because they were in conflict with the regimes in Europe. It was founded by people who were opposed to Europe. So when you think of the West, think of internal conflict in the West. All the time, the West doesn't speak with one voice, it has many voices. There are many voices in the West on globalization and anti-globalization. For China, it is very important to realize that. I think clever people in China do understand, sometimes you have to work with some people in the West, sometimes cooperating with others in the West who are moving towards change.

Wang: As a result of the COVID-19 epidemic, the world is in lockdown. Globalization has undergone a major change, which may change the world pattern of nearly 40 years. Do you think in the post-epidemic era, globalization will return to the previous form? What if there is a post-globalization era? What do you think will be the characteristics of this era?

Albrow: Of course the impact of COVID-19 has been dramatic and worldwide. As far as economic globalization is concerned, there is clearly a disruption both of trade in goods and travel between countries. But I doubt very much that it will halt the movement of capital between countries, and indeed may even increase it as countries aim to be more self-sufficient and investors react to the disruption of supply chains. Technology transfer will continue and cyber technologies will advance worldwide. Indeed, what the pandemic has done is give a shock to old established working practices worldwide. We are seeing an extraordinary expansion of out of office work, city centres are being transformed and COVID-19 has massively accelerated all changes that are carried by the internet and new information technology. Paradoxically, the nation–state will become even more active in seeking to control these changes for the advantage of its own citizens, while at the same time being impelled by public opinion to join with other states and agencies to address global issues.

Wang: You have a book on *Global Age Essays on Social and Cultural Change*, which deals with the cultural issues of the era of the globalization. What do you think is the basis for effective communication among people from different countries, regions and cultures in the age of globalization? You highly praise Mr Fei Xiaotong's statement that 'every form of beauty has its uniqueness; precious is to appreciate other forms of beauty with openness; if beauty represents itself with diversity and integrity, the world will be blessed with harmony and unity.' In fact, the premise of 'world harmony' is to be able to achieve 'precious is to appreciate other forms of beauty with openness and if beauty represents itself with diversity and integrity'. In fact, it means respecting differences and respecting the diverse composition of the world. But in fact, whether American culture prevails globally or the world is culturally Eurocentric, it makes the idea of 'beauty and communication' almost a utopia. What is your understanding?

Albrow: Coming to your question of harmony, certainly I do think the Chinese concept of harmony is the concept the world needs today, especially Europe and United States, because what harmony does is to arrange for the reconciliation of different viewpoints and different values. The West is often talking about values, and China talks about values all the time. But, most importantly, values themselves can conflict with each other. Therefore, they need to have a higher value that will reconcile them together. That's the value of harmony, which can bring different values together. As one of the things I said recently in an interview, I think that is very striking if you look at the 12 socialist values in China, 24 characters, 12 values. The word 'cooperation' is not there and the reason is that 'cooperation' itself is not so much value as a strategy. You are forced to cooperate if you want the world to continue properly. It's not really a value in its own right. Harmony is the value which brings cooperation together. So I think the Chinese are working towards finding a way for the different peoples and different cultures to live together to respect differences and not to have a single world culture. The only thing I would say is that, as the world works together, we will find out that new values are generated relating neither just to harmony nor just to diversity. For instance, a value which the whole world will agree on is sustainability – the sustainability of the planet. The whole world can and will agree on the preservation of the planet and this is a reason for communication between cultures. So, however different their cultural backgrounds may be in their communication with each other, they will create new values and that's the most important thing

The Era of Globalization and China: National role and national image

Wang: In the report about you in the Chinese media, it was mentioned that you said it was a bit of a pity that you 'didn't learn Chinese earlier'. Why do you have such feelings? Does this mean that you re-examine the particularity of China in the era of globalization? What kind of role do you think China has played in the era of globalization?

Albrow: Well, I think it's very simple. I certainly regret that I never learned Chinese until recent years, when I have learned a bit. But if I had learned it when I first became interested in China, that would have been wonderful. I can't deny that China brings different ways of thinking. It's very related to its language and towards the way it writes and thinks. Chinese people think differently and the concepts that you have do not match one-for-one with Western concepts. They are different. If you take the concept *li*, which is translated just as 'law', it extends far further than law. It's not just law in Western senses, it's also about the right kind of behaviour, doing things to fit the situation, finding the right way for doing things. But in English it gets translated as law. Chinese concepts don't match Western concepts, which is one of the most important contributions you can make to the world, because you can recognize there are different ways of appreciating the world, and if you can bridge and understand them, you can get a world where we can work on things together. Well, what is China's role particularly in the area of globalization? I think it is to bring people together around the notion of harmony, and in the end, I hope, to bring, in particular, America into an agreement on how to manage global governance.

Wang: I noticed that you came to China for the first time in 1987. This is 30 years ago. Your most recent monograph, *China's Role in a Shared Human Future: Towards Theory for Global Leadership* is still about China. Your concern for China is due to China's role in the process of 'globalization', or is there any other opportunity? In your opinion, what has changed in the course of globalization in the past 30 years?

Albrow: Well, you know, I came to China in 1987, because I had been teaching Chinese students. Some of them were actually mid-career officials from the State Family Planning Commission. I came to China to look at the family planning programme and the One-Child policy. I had another tour in 1988 as well, being taken around Chinese villages and talking with Chinese officials. Obviously, I was able to observe a lot about China. One of the things that impressed me most was the sense of common purpose, since everybody worked together to the same end, because that was 10 years after Deng Xiao Ping came up with the opening-up policy. China had already looked to the outside world and so I was very impressed with how well I was treated and how welcome I was, so my later contact with China was always based on this assumption that Chinese people are very welcoming and always pleased to see me, which was lovely and still is. I have just come from Beijing from the Second Belt and Road International Forum, and that was a wonderful event; I received quite a lot of publicity there. Well, what has changed is obviously the confidence Chinese people have towards the rest of the world. The Chinese reform and opening up gave people more opportunities to go out and Chinese people now increasingly come into the rest of the world and of course they are taking back as well to their own country. So they welcome advances in technology and they develop them. I was amazed when I was in China three or four year ago by the use of contactless card to pay for things. It was more advanced in China than in Britain. So, what impresses you obviously if you go to China regularly, as I've done for many years, is the rate of change. And the major task for China to manage that change is to keep society on a level basis, not to allow things to get out of control, because following technology can also be very dangerous, because technology can destroy values as much as it can take them forwards. I think the Chinese leadership is very aware of the fact that it's got to make sure that technology fits with Chinese values and with the development of China where society comes first, the technology comes after.

Wang: The 'globalization' you mentioned includes five dimensions: the global environmental consequences caused by all human activities; the loss of security caused by weapons of global destruction; the globality of communication systems; the emergence of global economic phenomena and the reflectiveness of globalism, where people and groups have been globally identified as themselves. How do you think China has adapted well in the five areas you mentioned, and then how do you come to the conclusion of 'moving towards global leadership'?

Albrow: This was very interesting, because I don't remember where I wrote about the five dimensions of globalization. But anyway, it's fair count, I think, of different dimensions of globalization. Overall, I think China is aware of them and reacts in each of these areas. I think the whole point is that China does look at them as a whole, and it does consider global issues and various aspects of globalization together, which is the first requirement of moving towards global leadership. You have to recognize the globe and its constitution as a whole. You have to have a sense of global society, a sense of where your country is in that global society, and then you have to have a sense of what global society needs. All those things are true of China and more so than any other big country. I mean, smaller countries may have that sense, but then they can't do so much. For instance, if you take a small country like Lithuania, there are only three million people there. But they are aware of these issues in the same way that China is? What can three million people do compared with 1.4 billion? So, it's the power China has to meet these challenges and also the basis for China to play its global leading role. Population is not sufficient; then it has to have a strategy for global leadership and that's what I like to think I might help. I hope my writing will be in that direction to making suggestions about global leadership.

Wang: I hope your new monograph will be finished and published soon. In fact, there are still major differences in the evaluation of China's 'Belt and Road' between the countries of the world, and there are also some negative voices. China attaches great importance to the image of being a responsible country in the process of globalization. What do you think about these issues?

Albrow: For instance, I just completed writing, with Professor WANG Yiwei, a piece about the challenges of Belt and Road. It is a dialogue between us and to be published soon. There, I've answered questions like: Is Belt and Road simply a geopolitical strategy for increasing power? Does Belt and Road create a debt trap for nations? Is Belt and Road environmentally destructive? and so on. There are answers to all of these. For instance, the debt trap issues, there's no more reason why China is creating a debt trap for countries which negotiate agreements on

Belt and Road. I don't see any evidence for China creating conditions in which people talk of a debt trap. Now, sometimes, people, for reasons out of their own control, are unable to pay back what they owe. That happens. Now China would have to recognize that, when you lend money to people, it's always a risk that they can't pay it back. I trust if that were to happen in the case of Belt and Road, China would treat those cases with considerable respect, generosity and good sense in dealing with a country which had fallen behind in its payments. I don't see any reason to think that the Chinese programme of investing in the infrastructure of the country is creating a debt trap. Now, on the geopolitical strategy, obviously, Belt and Road increases Chinese power. I don't think it increases Chinese power in a negative way. I don't think it's a question of what is called zero sum game. China put it as win–win strategy, both sides win. And I don't even see it's to the disadvantage of United State if China stabilizes the world around, if it makes it stronger and at the same time makes the whole of Southeast Asia stronger and more stable. That's a good thing, so I think for all the complaints about Belt and Road, there are answers in my points. China's record in global governance is extremely good. I see no reason to think that Belt and Road is not going to contribute to world peace and I am confident that it is a real experiment, if you like, in using globalization, for the interest of the world as a whole.

Wang: In the era of globalization, China can't do without the world and the world can't do without China. Could you please talk about how China should shape its image as a big country in the uncertain world and which aspects deserve special attention?

Albrow: Well, there are two sides, the one is clearly that China has an immensely good record on delivering projects. China has shown to the world that it is such big country that it can do so much more for the world, the power and effectiveness of China as a single global player. That's important. The other side is that China is different from all the other players, because it has a unique culture and a unique frame of moral political values which is different from the rest of the world, and it can show the rest of the world you don't have to be the same, you can approach the solution to global problems from your own cultural standpoint. The great thing about China is that it is so different from the West. Even though it adopts Western technologies, it develops technologies that belong to the world. Nonetheless, the values associated with those are still Chinese values. That's the great example to the world that, even if we go ahead in the same direction on technology, we can still retain our own values and contribute to the world. That's the great benefit China can give to the world.

Wang: What kind of China do you think the world needs in the post-pandemic era? In fact, China's success in fighting the pandemic has not helped China to build a better international image. There are still many unrealistic comments about China. What do you think about this issue?

Albrow: China's success in fighting the pandemic has paradoxically drawn more attention to its own system of governance and in a way drawn attention away from the value of its engagement with the rest of the world. China's success arises from its distinctive mix of modern theory and ancient culture, socialism with Chinese characteristics, and neither side of this equation receives extensive understanding in the rest of the world, and the West's response is still burdened with old Cold War attitudes. The world has arrived at a particularly volatile moment, and much depends on the wisdom of the current leadership of the great powers, China included. We have to hope that they see more to gain from cooperation than they do from conflict.

Wang: Thank you for agreeing to this interview. Your clarification of globalization, your interpretation of globalization and anti-globalization issues in the context of history and our times, and your answers and suggestions on how China can play its own role in globalization, build its own image, and solve its own and the world's problems have given me a lot of inspiration for thinking.

Albrow: It has been an enjoyable communication for me and I hope this can help you as well.

7.4 Promoting understanding of China in the world

In recent years, some Chinese scholars have regarded some of the author's publications as 'public intellectual' work, because they did not see much of his scholarly work. In fact, the author performed a public intellectual role for promoting understanding of China in the world, thereby fulfilling an intellectual's social mission. The author was introduced to overseas Chinese readers through an interview in 2012. After the 2nd Global China Dialogue in 2015, the author was introduced to Chinese mainstream society by an interview with a journalist at Xianhua News Agency in 2017. Afterwards he was invited by Chinese media, think tanks and government officials to make speeches at China-related conferences, to conduct interviews and to write book reviews. This session consists of two parts: writing about China and global governance, by the author (Chapter 5), and interviews by media in both Chinese and English.

7.4.1 Writings about China and global governance[60]

- 5.1 China's contribution to the future of governance
- 5.2 Diversity and cooperation in the shared future
- 5.3 Provincial development, global vision: Xi Jinping in Zhejiang
- 5.4 Help for the world
- 5.5 Reflections for the 70th anniversary of the founding of the People's Republic of China

---

[60] This list of popular writing came from chapter 5 of this book.

5.6 Can the world follow China's democratic path?

5.7 National solidarity under conditions of globalization: the theoretical basis of Xi Jinping's *The Governance of China*

5.8 The significance of China's social governance to the world

5.9 What the world can gain from China's global leadership

5.10 Remarks on the CCP's 100th anniversary celebrations

5.11 Remarks on the PRC's 72nd anniversary celebrations

The above works are the author's observations and reflections on China and global governance. It includes journal articles, newspaper articles, book reviews, conference speeches and remarks made at special events.

7.4.2 Interviews by Chinese media

7.4.2.1 Martin: a cool eye observing the 'global age'[61]

In the global era, people are mainly acting as world citizens. The vitality and diversity of the global era depend on the care of its citizens.

Martin Albrow, a renowned British sociologist and professor of social science research at Roehampton University, London, has been to China five times. He served as the chief researcher of China in Comparative Perspective Network at the London School of Economics and has conducted in-depth research on China. He is extremely encouraged by China's development in recent years.

The Sun City of China, where tradition and fashion coexist

When Martin first came to China in 1987, what impressed him most was the endless flow of bicycles on the streets of Beijing. In recent years, every trip Martin has made to China has given him a different impression. In April 2012, Martin and his friends visited Dezhou in Shandong province, known as the 'Sun City of China'. The solar energy industry of Dezhou sprouted in the 1990s. In less than 20 years, the solar energy industry has developed from the original stand-alone production of solar water heaters to the production of solar water heating systems, from the individual use of residential households to the integration of solar energy utilization and construction projects, from solar thermal utilization to solar high-temperature power generation and photovoltaic power generation.

In 2010, Texas successfully hosted the 4th World Solar City Conference, where government representatives, experts and scholars from all over the world gathered to provide advice and suggestions on promoting new energy development and global sustainable development. With strong support from the government, Dezhou is creating a 'green city' model for renewable energy in the world. 'Dezhou has formed a unique urban landscape as China's Sun City, providing a

[61] 高晶，马丁：冷眼观察"全球时代"，《国际人才交流》，2012年第8期。徐海燕译 [English translation: GAO Jing, Martin: A cool eye observing the 'global age'. *International Talent Exchange*. No. 8, 2012. Translated by XU Haiyan].

good platform for increasingly frequent exchanges between countries and closer international cooperation in the global era,' Martin said.

In addition, Martin went to a farmer's home in Dezhou to experience the life of a Chinese farmer. Here, Martin experienced the simplicity and hospitality of local farmers. 'I made dumplings with everyone and it was a very pleasant experience, but I still felt the unequal status of women in the family. When I sat down to eat with the man host, the hostess was still busy in the kitchen.' The visit coincided with the annual Pear Garden Festival, where the whole village, young and old, saw foreigners for the first time. Everyone was pleasantly surprised and slightly curious, and Martin became the focus of the whole village. 'I visited the magnificent and modernized Solar Valley, then drove to a farmer's home not far away, and experienced the traditional way of life in rural China. This is a very typical epitome of China's rapid economic development – the era when tradition and modernity coexist.'

The concepts of traditional Chinese culture are worth learning from

Martin has a deep love for traditional Chinese culture, which has researched in depth. Martin repeatedly mentions the concept of harmony, which is wholly consistent with China's position on globalization. 'China has a long history and has always been advocating Confucian culture, proposing the concept of harmony and stressing harmony in diversity. These are very good ideas and should be better understood and accepted around the world,' Martin said. 'I have always thought that Confucius Institutes have done a very good job of promoting themselves around the world. Through Confucius Institutes, the Western countries gradually have a clearer and deeper understanding about China, which is very helpful for better communication between China and the world.'

Since the world's first Confucius Institute was established in South Korea in November 2004, more than 100 Confucius Institutes have been established in more than 40 countries around the world, becoming a global brand and platform to spread Chinese culture and promote Chinese language teaching. Adhering to the Confucian concepts of 'harmony is precious' and 'harmony in diversity', Confucian Institutes promote the exchange and integration of Chinese and foreign cultures and aim to build a harmonious world with lasting peace and common prosperity.

'Unlike many Western countries, China's special national condition encourages the Communist Party of China to take greater responsibility. The government of CPC is similar to the architecture of a large multinational company, and the functional agencies under the leadership of the government are equivalent to various departments within the company, through the establishment of a perfect mechanism for communication and coordination, whereby the government reaches the ultimate goal of public service. For example, the successful hosting of the 2008 Summer Olympics in Beijing and the rescue work in the earthquake of Yushu, Sichuan Province, fully demonstrate the unmatched advantage of the

Chinese government to "mobilize the strength of the whole country to accomplish major tasks",' Martin added. 'The traditional Chinese cultural concepts such as "harmony between man and nature", "unremitting self-improvement" and "virtue and benevolence are cherished" are all worthy of learning and a reference for other countries.'

The global age and the world citizen

In his book *The Global Age: States and Society beyond Modernity*, Professor Martin Albrow describes the important changes taking place in the world today from the perspective of globalization. He states that 'globalization' is the integration of people from all over the world into one society, the global community. In this society, people have taken advantage of the potential of technology to bring one another closer, to interact and communicate, and the world has actually changed. These changes are mainly manifested in changes in the means of transport, tourism and telecommunications; the convergence of production and consumption on a global scale; the establishment of a global financial system; the development of global governance and the strengthening of international dependence requiring joint efforts to solve problems; human recognition of issues such as environment, food and energy; community refactoring; and the emergence of a global society. It is in these changes that relations between countries have become closer. The changes also demonstrate that, when modernity is replaced by globalization, the state, government, economy, culture and community are no longer central, and countries must seek common development through cooperation.

Globalization is not the popularization of Western countries but the equal exchange between countries. As a result, the pace of globalization is unprecedented. Despite some anti-globalization voices, history is progressing and the process is irreversible.

In Martin's view, the impact of globalization on the contradictions inherent in modernity has actually liberated society, and in the global era it will become increasingly difficult to determine individual identity by ethnicity, gender, age and so on. People are mainly behaving as world citizens, and the vitality and diversity of the global era depend on their care.

Martin thinks, looking to the future, even in the era of globalization, talent cultivation in the countries around the world is inseparable from international cooperation; various forms of youth exchanges and cooperation, such as volunteer projects, can provide the future elites with a broader platform for understanding the world and enhancing the friendship between teenagers of different countries. The UK is one of the most mature countries in the world for volunteer service. In recent years, more and more Chinese students have joined these international volunteer projects to help other people in need, which is very good news.

Martin spoke positively of Chinese students studying in the UK. 'On the whole, Chinese students are studious, working very hard, but most of the time they stay in relatively closed circles and don't like to interact with other students.

In the UK, schools are taking active steps to help them meet more friends, such as arranging Chinese students and foreign students to live in the same dormitory and holding lively parties, etc.'

7.4.2.2 Why I started to learn Chinese when I was 79 years old: an interview with Martin Albrow, one of the first advocates of globalization[62]

Martin Albrow is not like an eighty-year-old at all, because he is healthy, full of energy and has a bright, sharp intellect. He didn't feel tired, even though our conversation lasted two and a half hours. He can quickly and accurately, from memory alone, find the book, photo or material he wants in his three 'book walls'.

Albrow, a member of the British Academy of Social Sciences, is internationally renowned for his initiatives and research on the theory of globalization. Today, there is always a copy of the English edition of Xi Jinping's *The Governance of China* on his desk. He is preparing an article for the book to be published when he goes to a conference in Germany next month. Once a week, he also takes the light rail to the Confucius Institute in downtown London for a Chinese language class.

Albrow loves Chinese ancient poetry and he has visited China many times to learn about China's national conditions. In particular, he believes that, for the West, 'Chinese socialism' is a key to knowing and understanding Chinese policy.

Learning Chinese from the age of 79

Albrow is very famous in international academic circles, and he is often equated with the concept of 'globalization'. He is one of the first three scholars to propose 'globalization', and he established himself as a pioneer in the field of globalization studies in the 1990s with his book *The Global Age: State and Society beyond Modernity*.

He is a former president of the British Sociological Association and the founder and former editor-in-chief of the leading sociological journal *International Sociology*. After his retirement, Albrow has never stopped his academic research and continues to write and work on a voluntary basis for the Global China Academy, an affiliate of the British Academy of Social Sciences. In July this year, he went to China to attend an international academic conference. Next month, he will travel to Germany for another conference.

'Keep learning, in order to keep people active in their thinking' is an idea he stressed to the reporter several times during the interview. Last year, at the age of 79, he started to learn Chinese, and has been attending Chinese classes once a

---

[62] 张代蕾："全球化"概念首倡者阿尔布劳：我为什么从７９岁开始学中文，《新华网》，2017年10月13日。贺佳乐　译，见：http://www.xinhuanet.com/world/2017-10/13/c_1121799017.htm [English translation: ZHANG Dailei, Why I started to learn Chinese when I was 79 years old: An interview with Martin Albrow, one of the first advocates of globalization. *Xinhua Net*, 13.10.2017. Translated by HE Jiale, 13/10/2017].

week for a year. He keeps a thick stack of Chinese tutorials in his study. Turning one over at random, there are his notes on listening to the lessons recorded in pencil.

Albrow says he had an 'unexplainable interest in China' since he was a child. At the age of 18, as a high school student, he wrote a dozen-page essay after school titled 'History of China'. But interest was interest; he didn't ever think to learn Chinese until later.

'There are too few lessons, once a week now. I still only use Chinese to say, "My name is Martin, I'm a professor",' he exclaimed. 'I wasn't able to learn Chinese earlier; it's a great regret in my life.'

In Albrow's opinion, Chinese is a completely different language, representing another way of thinking and worldview. 'If I had started learning it at the age of 18, it would have been a great asset in my life.'

Come to China to understand Chinese characteristics

Before receiving his PhD in sociology from Cambridge University, Albrow took up posts at the University of Reading and Cardiff University. While working at the Centre for Population Studies at Cardiff University, he was invited by the Chinese to visit China for the first time in 1987. The purpose of his visit was to conduct a sociological investigation into the family planning policies that were being implemented in China at the time.

During his first trip to China, Albrow visited Beijing, Nanjing, Hangzhou and several villages in Jiangsu and Zhejiang. At that time, some experiences with 'Chinese characteristics' made him realize the great difference between Eastern and Western cultures, but this did not prevent him from observing and understanding China in an unbiased and objective way.

After this fieldwork, Albrow realized that some people in the West at that time had an unfair view of China's family planning policy. In the report on his visit to China submitted to Cardiff University, he wrote: 'China's fertility policy stems from its unique national conditions, which is the basis for understanding this policy ... [which] can't be evaluated in isolation from its Chinese characteristics ... "Socialism with Chinese characteristics" is the most useful key to understanding this policy.'

Albrow's understanding and friendly attitude towards China also reflects the 'pragmatic universalism' that he advocates in his academic research. He believes that, in the era of globalization, it is not enough for subjects of different cultures to understand one another by language alone. Subjects with different value systems should learn to seek common ground while reserving differences, and respect and cooperate with one another.

Albrow believes that this guideline is very much in line with the concept advocated by the famous Chinese sociologist Fei Xiaotong: 'Appreciate the values of others as you value your own, and the world will become a harmonious whole.'

Since 1987, Albrow has visited China nearly 10 times, and since 2012, he has been giving annual lectures on globalization at Beijing Foreign Studies University as a visiting professor. Each time he returns to the UK from China, he brings back a few souvenirs. In his home, there are Qing dynasty ceramic pots, flower and bird ink paintings, etc., and several stacks of Chinese books on his shelves, including *Cai Gen Tan* (a collection of aphoristic essays on life from the Ming dynasty), *Moment in Peking* and *China Urbanization*.

Albrow said to the reporter, 'I am not an expert in the study of China, I am just a good friend of China.'

A book that inspires new research

Since 2015, Albrow has added a bright 'Chinese colour' to his academic career – becoming a British expert who has studied Xi Jinping's *The Governance of China*.

When the English version of the book was published in UK, Albrow, as an expert of the Global China Academy, attended the press briefing and gave a speech. Since then, he has been invited to give several lectures on the book, and he himself has become increasingly interested in it.

'I like this book not only because it is about China, and not only because it contains huge amounts of information for Western readers, but also, for a sociologist like me, its content stimulates thought. The depth of thought in this book is unmatched by books written by leaders from the West.'

Now, Albrow has a new research project: a comparative research project on China and the West based on *The Governance of China*. 'I believe it will be a very meaningful and rewarding study.'

On Albrow's desk, the thick book is filled with colourful sticky notes marking what he is reading and studying. He turns to one of the pages and points to the English word for 'community of destiny' and asks the reporter to write it down in Hanyu Pinyin.

'*Ming – Yun – Gong – Tong – Ti*.' He took the book and read it in Pinyin. 'It's wonderful!' he said happily.

Editor: YANG Ting

7.4.2.3 Enhance mutual understanding with common targets: an interview with Martin Albrow, Fellow of the Academy of Social Sciences in the UK[63]

He has white hair and a reddish face, quick thinking and a strong spirit. Professor Martin Albrow, an 80-year-old Fellow of the British Academy of Social Sciences and Honorary Vice-President of the British Sociological Association,

[63] 强薇：用共同的目标增进理解——访英国社会科学院院士马丁·阿尔布劳，《人民日报》2018年04月23日03版。赵凯 译 [English translation: QIANG Wei, Enhance mutual understanding with common targets: Interview with Martin Albrow, Fellow of the Academy of Social Sciences in the UK. *China Daily*, 23/04/2018. Translated by ZHAO Kai, see: http://world.people.com.cn/n1/2018/0423/c1002-29942051.html].

speaks endlessly about China. Professor Albrow is one of the first advocates of the concept of 'globalization' and one of the most authoritative experts in the study of globalization theory in the world.

As early as the 1990s, he discussed in depth the role of globalization in modern society in his *The Global Age: State and Society beyond Modernity*.

In recent years, he has been observing China's social development and its role on the international stage, and the results of his research are contained in his book *China's Role in a Shared Human Future*. On the occasion of the release of this book, our reporter conducted an exclusive interview with him.

'Chairman Xi Jinping's initiative to build a community with a shared future for mankind gave me the idea of writing such a book to discuss China's future development,' Albrow said. 'Chairman Xi's speech always combines theory, history and reality. I am very impressed by such a leader who draws nourishment from the nation's excellent traditions, grasps the connotation of the Chinese nation's spirit as a whole and provides new solutions for global governance.' The concept of building a community with a shared future for mankind allowed Professor Albrow to understand the new connotations and extension of globalization. 'The scope of a community with a shared human future is undoubtedly greater than globalization, and globalization will continue to advance.'

Regarding the doubts about globalization in some countries and anti-globalization stances such as trade protectionism, Albrow said: 'Globalization will bring some negative effects, but China has always remained calm and actively seeks solutions to help globalization promote economic growth in all countries.'

The Belt and Road Initiative is an interpretation of globalization from a Chinese perspective, and infrastructure construction is a key driving force for global economic development. 'Now, whether globalization can continue to deepen, and whether countries with very different historical and cultural backgrounds can eliminate differences and increase understanding are closely related questions.'

'I heard this sentence decades ago: "Half of the people in the world don't know how the other half live." This sentence motivates me to work hard to eliminate this barrier that divides the world into two.' Albrow said that his life's work is to allow different cultures to communicate across barriers.

'Every country has its own characteristics. In my opinion, China has set an example for other countries, that is, to maintain cooperation and seek common development with countries around the world on the basis of studying its own national conditions and finding a path that suits its own development.' Albrow also emphasized in his book that the Belt and Road Initiative proposed by China in recent years shows how China has become an emerging power in the world and how to fundamentally help the world to bridge differences. This initiative will become a way to promote global peace and cooperation. 'Different countries can share the same goal, which is more conducive to cooperation,' Albrow said.

7.4.2.4 China's contribution to globalization is of strategic significance[64]

China has offered key components of a global strategy for tackling global challenges as the world enters a new era of so-called 'globalization 4.0,' said a leading British expert.

'The new stage is a transformation of the world. It is a clash between an older global age and a coming, already come, digital age," said Martin Albrow, a renowned sociologist and a pioneer of the theory of globalization.

'That's the real transformation which is going on at the moment, and which the world has not yet been able to manage because it can't see it clearly enough,' Albrow told Xinhua ahead of an annual gathering of world leaders and business elites in the Swiss resort of Davos.

'One "tremendously important contribution" by China in dealing with global challenges is the very pragmatic Chinese approach, in line with the famous Chinese saying "take truth from facts",' said Albrow.

'It stresses that you have to deal with the problems as they arise at the moment. And you do this in a non-ideological manner, you do it pragmatically, you do it as the facts dictate,' he said.

'The second [contribution] is the stress in China's outlook on the world on cooperation, that we won't be able to handle global issues unless we cooperate,' said Albrow.

'Globalization itself is not something that any one person has invented or designed. It is the aggregate effect of human actions and policies,' he said. 'The effect is so big that you have to have collective leadership and the people working as a whole.'

Finally, China is leading the world in stressing that every country, regardless of its size, contributes differently and can make a contribution toward this collective effort, said the British expert.

The World Economic Forum, which is scheduled to start on Tuesday in Davos, is themed 'Globalization 4.0: Shaping a Global Architecture in the Age of the Fourth Industrial Revolution'.

About 3,000 leaders from all parts of society are expected to discuss how to build more inclusive societies and better protect vulnerable communities as globalization undergoes such major transformations amid reshifts of global power and the rapid development of new technologies.

One major solution offered by China to help tackle global challenges and build an open and more inclusive economy is the Belt and Road Initiative, said Albrow.

---

[64] Jin Jing and ZHANG Dailei. Interview: China offers key strategy for tackling challenges in new globalization, *Xinhua Net*, 21/1/2019. See: http://www.xinhuanet.com/english/2019-01/21/c_137762187.htm.

Proposed by China in 2013, the initiative is aimed at building a trade and infrastructure network connecting Asia with Europe and Africa along and beyond the ancient trade routes of the Silk Road.

Albrow recalled that Chinese President Xi Jinping had said in a speech two years ago at the Davos economic forum that the global economy is 'the big ocean that you cannot escape from' and any attempt to retreat back to isolation runs counter to the historical trend.

'The Chinese leadership generally has a very clear-sighted idea of globalization which the world can benefit from,' said Albrow.

'The image of an ocean is a very apt image,' said Albrow, noting that one can either sail on an ocean or try to retreat for fear of tides.

'We have to first of all understand our own position. Then we have to decide what are the best uses we can make of it ... This [the Belt and Road Initiative] is not dictated by economic globalization,' he added.

Author of the book *China's Role in a Shared Human Future*, Albrow said the proposal by the Chinese president to build a community with shared future for mankind is deeply rooted in Chinese culture and dates back centuries.

'That is a crucial contribution that Chinese thought can make towards an improvement of the world situation, not just globalization, but across the board,' he said.

Meanwhile, the sociologist called on the international community to strengthen the rules-based world order which he said is 'fundamental' for cooperation to tackle challenges.

There is a huge responsibility on world leaders to address global problems together, such as the rising threat of protectionism and climate change, he said.

'The rules-based multilateral world order is fundamental for ensuring that we all speak from the same page, we have basic understandings of how we work together,' he said.

(Xinhua reporter Larry Neild also contributed to the story.)

7.4.2.5 Will globalization be stopped?[65]

In a coffee shop, I met Martin Albrow, an 82-year-old Englishman. He is a well-known sociologist and the one of the first three scholars to promote the idea of 'globalization'. He is internationally renowned for advocating and studying globalization theories. British academic circles call Albrow the initiator of the concept of the 'global era', and he has established a pioneering position in the field of globalization research.

The theme of this interview, which took place at Crystal Palace in south-east London, is 'the future of globalization'.

[65] 桂涛：全球化会停止吗？《经济参考报》，2019年3月19日。吴佩桦 译，见：http://www.jjckb.cn/2019-03/19/c_137905864.htm [English translate: GUI Tao, Will globalisation to be stopped? *Economic Information Daily*, 19/03/2019. Translated by WU Peihua].

Crystal Palace was once an icon of the flourishing British Empire. In the mid-nineteenth century, Britain built this palace, with steel as the skeleton and glass as the main construction material, for the Great Exhibition of the Works of Industry of All Nations. The building was called Crystal Palace because it was transparent, bright and spacious. It was the vital symbol of the Industrial Revolution and the worldwide hegemony of Britain. Crystal Palace no longer exists, having burnt down in 1936. Today, Britain is also much occupied with 'Brexit', its departure from the European Union, which is universally interpreted by the media as a severe blow to European regional integration. 'Brexit' and the 'withdrawal' of America from the world stage are considered as the dilemma of globalization after decades of mushrooming growth.

'Will globalization to be stopped?' I threw this question at Albrow, who has been studying globalization for most of his life.

'If you think that globalization is a purely economic event, then it can be said that globalization does have factors that slow it down,' he answered, 'but the driving force behind world integration is not only the exchange of goods and production; actually, it is also the exchange of knowledge, especially the category of knowledge that can calculate with artificial intelligence on the internet. And the amazing speed of the development of communication technology. To a certain extent, globalization is becoming faster and faster.'

We talked about the concept of 'slow globalization' recently put forward by the British *The Economist* magazine. Some economists agree that if the period of 1990 to 2010 could be called the golden age of globalization, globalization's development is gradually slowing. The main factors involved include, for example, the fact that transport costs are no longer declining, multinationals are being challenged by local firms, and it is difficult to sell services across borders. Albrow thinks that new technology enables people around the world to talk to one other and create things together, leading to a fresh global technology. Therefore, globalization is not a narrow economic issue but means total communication among human beings.

'Is it fair to say that, even if there is a slowing of global economic integration, it will not hinder the tendency of globalization to move on. Yes, even the trade war or "Brexit" can't stop globalization,' he said. 'In fact, I do not think that any institution of human making could slow globalization's development.'

Albrow's optimism about the course of globalization is derived from his grasp of human activity as a veteran sociologist. While some argue that globalization has made our world more single and homogeneous, Albrow argues that globalization has brought human society more diversity by giving people more choices in migration and lifestyle.

He mentioned a movie called American Beauty, which is about neighbourhood relationships and life in a small town in America. It is considered a typical American movie, containing solely American images and starring only American actors. 'But in fact, the film director is a Briton from Portugal, and the production team comes from all over the world. It's not a product of American culture, but a critique and attack on American culture,' Albrow said. He believes that, although it is in the United States, Hollywood is a global phenomenon and an outcome of globalization. Americans do not really realize that globalization is also potentially destructive to the United States.

7.4.2.6 No-deal Brexit a big problem for UK and Europe[66]

LONDON, March 13 (Xinhua) – After British Prime Minister Theresa May's Brexit deal was rejected by lawmakers on Tuesday night, a no-deal Brexit will be put to the vote on Wednesday.

However, a leading academic said a no-deal Brexit could be a big problem for Britain and the European Union (EU).

'I think a no-deal Brexit is a pretty big problem for the UK but not for the world,' Professor Martin Albrow told Xinhua in an exclusive interview.

Albrow is a figure of authority within the academic community. He was among the first sociology academics in British universities, and his studies of German sociologist Max Weber and of globalization are highly regarded.

A no-deal Brexit could still be an occurrence on March 29, when the formal Brexit process of Article 50 expires.

In addition to a negotiated deal, an extension of Article 50 and even a second referendum are still possibilities.

'It will be damaging to the European economy. I've seen analyses which suggest there will be a definite measurable decline in European productivity,' said Albrow.

'Britain is about the second largest economy within Europe and so if it removes itself and tariffs go up and so on, that would be damaging.'

In 1996 Albrow published his book *The Global Age: State and Society beyond Modernity*, which examined the challenges facing the modern world as it stood on the edge of a new era that challenged the concept of nation states and the role of modernity.

Twenty years later and Albrow's work seems to have been an early account of the tensions of globalism and the challenges of the 21st century.

Brexit reveals crisis threatening British social cohesion

'The people who will suffer most, clearly, are the British,' Albrow said. 'They will suffer because Brexit will represent a failure to recognize the realities of the world we live in – and if you fail to recognize realities you're very confused.'

Albrow forecast a time of 'great confusion' in British politics and daily life: 'People will not have any clear idea of where Britain is in the world.'

---

[66] GUI Tao, Peter Barker, ZHANG Dailei, Interview, *Xinhua Net*, 13/03/2019. See: http://www.xinhuanet.com/english/2019-03-13/c_137892328.htm.

Confusion would be built on a foundation of differing groups in society with very different views of what direction the future should take.

'The people who want Brexit are a coalition of completely different opposite viewers. One side of the Brexiters are saying, yes, let's get out of the European Union and then we will go everywhere, we will trade everywhere, we will be free at last,' Albrow said.

These supporters of trade and free markets and global opportunities had backed Brexit alongside another group of people who were opposed to foreigners in general.

'There are people who voted for Brexit saying there are too many foreigners here, we don't want all this immigration, look what they're doing to this country. I can't walk through the streets in my town and see a white person.'

Albrow said these people and the people who want a global market are at the opposite ends of the political spectrum. 'There will be huge confusion after Brexit because you will have left, right, little Englanders, globalizers all facing each other without any clear direction for the country at all. So, all I can say is after a no-deal Brexit, there will be utter confusion. The only thing, I think, which can solve the present situation realistically is probably to resume the deal negotiated with the European Union. But the trouble is the deal suits no one.'

Stronger union is needed

The exit of one of the EU's largest economies and one of its most significant political and diplomatic nations may not be a weakening of the EU but an opportunity for it.

Albrow said: 'It could encourage the EU to become stronger, more integrated, and recognize that it does have weaknesses and that it needs to coordinate itself better. I think it's fair to say that the British government wants the European Union to be strong. It's in no one's interest for the Union to be weak. So if all sides agree that it is a win–win situation, if Britain and the EU can agree, the EU will be stronger. That's one possibility.'

On the other hand, he added, there is the possibility – and everyone must be afraid of this – that the same forces which led Britain to leave will encourage others in the EU to leave. And there are several countries where there are anti-EU, anti-globalization, anti-establishment movements.

7.4.2.7 Global crisis highlights importance of building community with a shared future for mankind[67]

LONDON, Feb. 18 (Xinhua). It is in times of global crisis, like the current outbreak of the novel coronavirus disease (COVID-19), that human beings can best realize their common humanity and shared common interests, said world-renowned sociologist Martin Albrow.

[67] ZHANG Dailei, GUI Tao and Larry Neil. Interview. Xinhua Net. 18/2/2020. See: http://www.xinhuanet.com/english/2020-02/18/c_138796189.htm.

In a recent interview with Xinhua, the 82-year-old British academic said disasters show how dependent we are on each other 'in a worldwide sense' and thus demonstrate the need to build a community with shared future for mankind, a concept that was forged and developed by China.

He commended China for its responses and efforts to global challenges such as the outbreak of the virus, saying there is no way the rest of the world can ignore COVID-19.

'Something like coronavirus, or in a previous time, SARS, for instance, requires a global response because the virus doesn't respect national boundaries,' he told Xinhua, adding that he does not share the view that China has been slow in responding to the COVID-19.

'I think the Chinese response has been entirely appropriate,' he said. 'Chinese health workers are working overtime and at great cost to themselves. Many health workers are putting themselves in danger when they are actually treating people who are suffering from the virus.'

'I'm quite sure that in China today there is huge support for the workers who are handling this terrible crisis. And I believe the rest of the world too will be looking to China and recognizing what enormous efforts the Chinese people are making for each other,' said Albrow, also Fellow of the Academy of Social Sciences.

Albrow, who is renowned for his works on globalization and civil society, said he hopes the COVID-19 outbreak can help bring the world together in the fight against the virus, producing a vaccine and eventually overcoming it.

'That, in a sense, will contribute to the shared future for mankind,' he noted.

Speaking of building a community with shared future, Albrow said people-to-people communication is fundamental in a world society where people are increasingly interdependent, with connectivity increasing all the time.

'We should do everything to facilitate communication between people across borders, to create a much better general understanding of different cultures, different customs and so on. This can't be done through governments building walls between countries,' he said.

7.4.2.8 The approaches of China and the United States to globalization are different[68]

'During the bottom-up process of the globalization of China, the main drivers are those projects aimed at improving the living situations of people, so as to achieve conditions similar to those of moderately developed countries. It is totally different from that of the US, especially Wall Street, which benefits its shareholders and the rich,' said Martin Albrow, when he was interviewed by this newspaper.

---

[68] 桂涛、杨婉晨：中国的全球化过程是提高百姓生活，与美国为富人牟利完全不同，《参考消息》，2019年4月24日。杨博、韩志豪　译，见：http://www.globalview.cn/html/global/info_31282.html [GUI Tao, YANG Wanchen, The approaches of China and the United States to globalization are different, *Reference News*, 24/04/2019. Translated by YANG Bo, Ivan Hon].

Martin Albrow FAcSS has an international reputation because of his advocacy and study of theories of globalization. The concept of 'globalization' was first used in the title of a book, *Globalization, Knowledge and Society*, which he edited. As one of the earliest three scholars that pursued concepts of 'globalization', he also initiated the concept of the 'global age', which further consolidated his leading position in this research field. Martin Albrow was the President of the British Sociological Association and the founding and former editor-in-chief of *International Sociology*. Since his retirement, he has held positions of visiting professor or senior researcher in numerous countries. Our reporter interviewed Albrow yesterday.

Reference News: Is the world undergoing unprecedented profound and complex changes?

Albrow: Global changes have happened faster than ever before. Nowadays, China and the US are two most important powers, and the destiny of the world is really dependent on the degrees of coordination achieved by the two countries. In addition, the world is also in the process of globalization. Its consequences have significantly determined those traditional connections, communities and associations. Therefore, globalization is actually very destructive, or extremely destructive for specific countries. Aiming to protect countries themselves, governments have to carefully recognize the advantages and disadvantages of globalization. A few years ago, I published a paper, whose content was roughly that 'globalization does not always benefit the development of countries, except for effective governance by national governments'. I believe this is what China is doing now, ensuring that globalization will not disturb the stable development of domestic society.

Reference News: Is the effective self-governance of China in the face of globalization a part of global change?

Albrow: As we all know, there are important trade negotiations between China and the US, and their success or failure means a lot for the global future. Because it is not just about trading, but also their understanding about shared interests. If they could not reach an agreement about trading issues, they will also not do so for other issues. In other words, if you cannot agree that the other has attained the things you also want, probably you will not agree any actions of the other. Trading is the basis of global construction, so the China–US trading negotiation is really important.

Let us go back to views of Adam Smith and earlier classical economists: wealth will grow when each part could contribute their best advantages to others during trading. Chinese products are cheap and good quality, and American people have strong demand for these products, so China could make substantial amounts of dollars from such trade while at the same time raising demand further. How will China use such money? One of methods is to invest in the Belt and Road Initiative. This understanding makes sense only if we acknowledge that the world is one. To take an example, this is like a whole family living in a house: we could get together and discuss ways to deal with domestic problems, so these are global issues. But at the same time, frictions inevitably happen because of living together, and these can be dangerous.

Reference News: From a historical perspective, how many major changes have taken place in the past few centuries?

Albrow: From the 18th century to the mid-19th century, the Industrial Revolution created a new class system and structure, what we call the working class, or the proletariat, as Marx called it. The information industrial revolution has brought a transformation of production and communication. The technologies of telegraph, phone, radio and television have actually generated a kind of new public thought; it is the second great revolution. Today, we are in the third one.

Reference News: What should China do during such global change?

Albrow: First, China has to realize that it cannot manage globalization at the moment, nor can it split itself off from globalization, as China is one country of the world. If you are managing globalization, it means you are opening to the world. Of course, China's change is based on the understanding that China has to be open, so you know what an important point it was when Deng Xiaoping put forward the reform and opening up in 1978. Therefore, communication with other countries is the basis of managing globalization.

Otherwise, managing Chinese interests around the world can also help other countries adapt to globalization. This means that China will participate in all international institutions, while simultaneously defending its own boundaries – not only the physical borders but also those in China's daily life. Some countries have more difficulty than others; for example, China possesses a critical asset, the Chinese language, to protect its autonomy and cultural distinction.

Reference News: As you said, styles of globalization of China and the US are different.

Albrow: I think that during the bottom-up process of globalization in China, the main drivers are those projects aimed at improving the living situations of people, so as to achieve the conditions of moderately developed countries. It is totally different with the US, especially Wall Street, which benefits its shareholders and the rich. Plainly speaking, American globalization is transmitting American ideas of how the world should be operating: they perceive globalization as the way to derive benefits for themselves. America misunderstands the nature of globalization.

Reference News: In the process of globalization, how has the United States performed?

Albrow: The United States has always believed that globalization is beneficial to the extension of the US market logic. The extension of this logic and the expansion of the international market will surely give advantages to the US. Since Americans own the most wealth in the world, they are the centre of global decision-making, they occupy the dominant position in the International Monetary Fund, they are the main donor country of the World Bank, and so on. Since the 1980s, Americans have always believed that globalization is their way of shaping the world.

What they still do not understand is that other aspects of globalization, especially the globalized culture and market, are not actually controlled by any one country. They are not even controlled by the United States. Americans sometimes also feel that they have been betrayed by globalization.

Hollywood is a global phenomenon because they make films for the largest world market. So, they do not only consider the US market, what they consider is the global market. People who work there come from all over the world. Americans have not truly realized that globalization is also potentially destructive to the United States, unless they can handle it properly.

Reference News: But the United States has also begun to realize this problem and has begun to take action.

Albrow: They may have already changed. In fact, Donald Trump understood that globalization means the unemployment of American steel workers. The question is how he would deal with this problem. He wanted to deal with it through a trade war; at least, that is what he said. But now, I think, even he has recently begun to understand that trade wars cannot solve the problems of globalization, while other measures must be taken, for example, providing employment opportunities for redundant steel workers. However, this is not the traditional American way. They do not have a so-called 'welfare society'.

Reference News: How does Europe respond to the changes brought by globalization?

Albrow: Europe has encountered great difficulties in handling this matter. The current 'yellow vest' movement of France is a typical example, and it is also the continuation of France's hostility to globalization in the 1990s. In that era, the French were also full of hostility towards the arrival of McDonald's. French farm owner José Bové launched a populist movement against globalization around himself. Therefore, since globalization became a reality, the French have been working hard to manage globalization. They have not found a suitable solution, but in fact the economic condition of France is not bad.

On the other hand, the establishment of the European Union is also an important result of globalization. The European Union is a European common market, and a sufficiently large trading entity. It is very important to world trade and it can set conditions for world trade. Therefore, it is a group of free trade protectionism. To a certain extent, it reflects the socialist values of Europe, and so Europe has more socialism.

Therefore, Europe as a whole has managed globalization quite effectively, even though there are differences among different countries, while there are also many problems. The immigration problem is also an important result of globalization. The current immigration problem largely stems from the war in the Middle East. Now you can even connect the war in the Middle East with globalization, but I think it is more the clash of civilizations and their past tense relations.

No country can stop globalization.

Reference News: What is the current general trend of globalization? Is it stagnating, or is it starting to become 'slow globalization', as *The Economist* said?

Albrow: It depends on how broad a concept of globalization you adopt. If you think that globalization is a purely economic matter, then you can say that factors have emerged in globalization that make it slow down.

However, the driving force of world integration is not only the exchange of goods and production; it is actually also the exchange of knowledge, especially the kind of knowledge that is calculated through artificial intelligence on the internet. On this measure, globalization is becoming faster and faster, because these technologies allow people from all over the world to talk with each other, create things together, as well as create a kind of new global technology for humanity. Therefore, it is no longer an economic problem in the narrow sense. It is more comprehensive exchanges between humans.

Reference News: Can it be said that, even if global economic integration slows down, it will not hinder the forward development of globalization trend?

Albrow: That is correct. Trade war or 'Brexit' cannot stop globalization. In fact, I do not think any human institution can slow down the development of globalization. Even if Americans say today that they will no longer use the internet and computers, this will not affect globalization.

What should we do if countries set up trade barriers between each other? Companies will move to other countries to invest and produce in those countries. This is what the Coca-Cola Company did at the beginning of China's opening to the outside world. Coca-Cola Company did not export Coca-Cola to China, and they opened a bottling plant there. There are numerous ways in which capital itself can overcome trade barriers. Of course, countries can also try to control capital. However, in addition to stopping the flow of capital, they must also stop the flow of people, and then stop the flow of ideas. I think there is no way to stop globalization.

Reference News: What is the driving force behind globalization?

Albrow: It is the sum of human activities. I think people have not yet understood this point. Globalization will not take us to any particular place. It sees the sum of human activities as an open future and an open past. What I want to emphasize is, globalization seems to produce a unified homogeneous world in a certain way, but the reality is not that. On the contrary, globalization will produce diversity. Market globalization is actually just the exponential increase of each person's choices. In the context of globalization, there are more and more choices open to individuals. Only if you want, you can leave the place you are in and go to another place.

'One Belt One Road' creates the Chinese brand.

Reference News: What do you think of China's 'One Belt One Road' initiative?

Albrow: The 'One Belt, One Road' is a very viable project, which aims to increase the possibility of connecting China and its neighbouring countries through various means, such as railways, air flights, oceans and means in a broader sense. Therefore, it is a set of practical systems for establishing relations between China and other countries.

The Belt and Road Initiative is obviously closely related to global economic integration. Its main purpose is to tighten ties with other countries through increasing the common interests with neighbouring countries.

I think the Belt and Road is a very good way of marketing. It is also a good way of creating the brand of China's activities and China's contribution to the world economy.

7.4.2.9 CPC's success in transforming China great accomplishment[69]

LONDON, March 22 (Xinhua). China, led by the Communist Party of China (CPC), is marching towards completely building a moderately prosperous society in all respects this year, which is a great accomplishment, said renowned British sociologist Martin Albrow in a recent interview with Xinhua.

Albrow, currently a Fellow of the Academy of Social Sciences in Britain, has visited China many times since 1987.

'The success of the party is really taking China forward, rejuvenating China,' he said, adding that the achievement of CPC is a great transformation of the mood of the country.

'We have to look at CPC in relation to the previous hundred years. There were years of, as you say, a century of humiliation. So it's a transformation of the mood of the country. It has created optimism and unity, and those are great achievements in the mood of the country,' the scholar said.

According to Albrow, there are three major reasons for CPC's success in transforming China.

First, he is impressed that the CPC has been firmly sticking to the path of socialism with Chinese characteristics, which is an 'overriding objective'.

'The CPC has maintained this drive to unify Chinese society, and it continues with that,' Albrow said.

---

[69] ZHANG Dailei, Interview: CPC's success in transforming China great accomplishment: British sociologist. *Xinhua Net* 22/03/2021. See: http://www.xinhuanet.com/english/2021-03/22/c_139827392.htm.

The other key is, Albrow said, the CPC has been pushing forward implementing the reform and opening-up policy over the past more than 40 years, and adopted a very subtle and pragmatic approach to world relations.

'In particular, they have embraced globalization. They've adopted open policy towards the rest of the world, and the reform policy, which allows foreign companies to invest in China and encourages trade with China, but at the same time protects Chinese property rights and ability to control its own affairs. So it's not unqualified globalization,' said Albrow, who is one of the first globalization theorists.

He especially mentioned that being enormously cooperative with other nations and international organizations, like the United Nations and the World Trade Organization, is also a very important part of China's success.

The third reason for the CPC's success lies in its capability, said Albrow, who believes China's fighting against the COVID-19 pandemic is a good example to demonstrate the features of CPC governance.

'It shows the Communist Party of China is able to mobilize the country as a whole around single goals,' Albrow said.

As far as globalization is concerned, China also gives a good example to the rest of the world, Albrow added.

'I'm thinking of the Belt and Road particularly. This is goal-directed development, not development in accord with some kind of ideological fantasy, not about in taking forms of government anyway. I think it is very appropriate for the current situation,' the expert explained.

He said, 'Belt and Road provides the world with two important examples of how to build a community of shared future. Firstly, it shows that technologies cross boundaries. They are the products of human ingenuity and efforts that can benefit all who care to make use of them.'

Secondly, 'it is the exact opposite to isolation. China and the other nations joining in the Belt and Road agreements are using their sovereign rights and power to work towards goals that all can share and help to meet global challenges that face us all.'

He told Xinhua that the world is facing a 'very unsettled environment' for a number of reasons, one of them is the coronavirus pandemic, which 'ought to create global unity because it affects everybody, but in fact it has actually created a lot of tensions.'

However, he believes China is able to respond to the global situations wisely, as the CPC and Chinese people are 'very well equipped because they're very pragmatic and very wise.'

7.4.2.10 Intercivilizational dialogue project 'West–East Talk' / Martin Albrow and PENG Dawei[70]

Peng: So let's talk a little bit about the pandemic. I want to know what impact did the COVID-19 pandemic have on the development of globalization? The question is, will we eventually come back to the world we are familiar with before the pandemic?

Albrow: Well, the short answer to that is no. We will not, because we never go back to the world as it was. There are many things that happen in the world which have only indirect relationship to the pandemic. They're not the things which are normally associated with globalization either. So the most important developments in the world concern technology and the extraordinary increase in the pace of technological development.

Now, the pandemic itself throws light on that in the sense that worldwide, we have scientists working on the viruses and developing vaccines, exchanging information. This, if you like, is a global process and illustrates the advance of globalization, at least in the sphere of science, technology and the rest. So the driving force behind what happens in the world today comes not from, shall we say, the attempts to create a global system of government, nor does it result from the sudden impact of COVID. It results from this underlying pressure, towards increased technical control, not just of disease, but also of climate and in advance of weaponry.

Peng: You are probably have the most authority to talk about Max Weber in the whole English-speaking world. Max Weber made a comparison between China's Confucianism religion and the Christian religion in Europe, in the West. And he concluded that that's what contributed to the development of capitalism in the West and the absence of it in China. What's your opinion on Weber's theory in this sense?

Albrow: That's a very complex and interesting question relating very directly to the debates and scholarships surrounding Max Weber's work ever since he wrote. And we've only just passed the centenary of his death. And he was writing about China in the last 10 years of his life. So we're talking about a period from 1910 to 1920, roughly. And in that period of time, he did actually somewhat change his view on China. And what he wrote about China did develop over time. So I think one should distinguish various elements of that.

---

[70] Editor's note: This is a transcript of the online dialogue between the author and Mr Peng Dawei, chief reporter of the German branch of China News Service and deputy director of China News Network Research Institute in November 2021. The edited version will be published as subtitles on the video column of the 'W.E. Talk (West East Talk)' in China News Service http://www.ecns.cn/z/2021-10-20/detail-ihasacat0473694.shtml, but no date is given for publication before this book was completed.

Certainly, his first interest was to compare Confucian ideology with Puritanism. That was his first interest. And in that respect, his argument was, well, Puritanism gave that extra impulse to capitalism in the West. It wasn't so much that Confucianism was an obstacle. It just didn't actually promote capitalism. It was just rather neutral. There were, however, elements in traditional Chinese culture that he pointed to, which he did think were a hindrance to the development of capitalism. And these he broadly summed up under the heading of superstition, that is practices related to festivals, related to family history, related to one's relation to the soil, all those things, which had nothing directly to do with Confucianism. Indeed, you can argue, they went back beyond Confucianism. So there is a difference in Weber's emphasis. Confucianism, I would say, according to my reading, is a neutral factor, *vis-à-vis* capitalism. What was more hostile to the development capitalism was, as I say, traditional practices in daily life which he called superstition.

Now, over time, however, he recognized the impact of industrialism in China itself and recognized that there were Chinese capitalist industrialists. And so in his last set of lectures on economic history he pointed out, just wait until the Chinese businessman get the potential of railways in their heads, and we will see what's going to happen in China. In other words, he didn't see any fundamental obstacle to capitalism in China. And certainly, the influence of China of Confucianism on my reading is for Weber entirely neutral; what is missing is what we had in the West for him, which was this extra motivation provided by the belief that unless you were successful in life, you wouldn't go to heaven.

Now, it is my belief that he was saying something important there. And certainly, the Reformation and its consequences are very important for the development of Western culture.

Peng: So I maybe add one point, there is still an on ongoing debate whether Confucianism is a religion or not. But I would say that whether we are talking about capitalism or Confucianism or Taoism, I think China's ruling party is not denying any factor from elements from the long tradition of this this country.

Which goes to my next question about this very interesting comparison. What do you think of the Western practices in this fight against epidemic? And should the West actually learn something from China, or could it have learned something from China?

Albrow: In a way. I think the answer to that question is related to the answer that I gave to your previous question. Of course, I see the Confucian ethic, certainly, as a very important aspect of China's old cultural tradition; certainly the two are intimately connected. And I also would say that the practices associated with Confucianism, in particular, and emphasis on learning the ancient books, rising in society through education, are still very deep factors in Chinese society. And one of the things I'm going to mention in the speech I'm giving on 10th December is that the West should not forget the fact that the Chinese Communist party builds on traditions in China, which go back thousands of years. And in particular, that tradition of rising in society through knowledge and education. The Communist Party is also an educational movement, and it foregrounds cultural values, ethical factors, ahead of purely, shall we say, economic factors.

And that's crucial, I think, for the West to understand. And it does mean that when you respond to something like the pandemic, you actually appeal to a general sense of consensus around social values. So the Party is drawing on China's tradition. And in that extent, I would agree with Martin Jacques that we should never forget the historic foundation of a Chinese social order.

I would add that what the Communist Party does is, in addition to that, provide a very strong driving force from the centre. So the central control of Chinese society is obviously immensely more effective, particular with modern technologies and so immensely more effective than it ever could have been in imperial times. And that makes a huge difference.

Peng: Recently, two concepts, one is the clash of civilizations, another is the Thucydides trap, are often mentioned these days. So what do you think of these two concepts? And do you think that China can really achieve a peaceful rise without a major war with anyone?

Albrow: The clash of civilizations thesis associated with the American author Samuel Huntington does depend on deep differences between cultures. Now, I don't actually subscribe to that thesis, because I think cultures can coexist, exchange and coexist in relative peace with each other as well. They may conflict. But it's not intrinsic to the notion that cultures are different. You can have cultures that are different, and they coexist. Now, the Thucydides trap, on the other hand, is much more concerned with strategic realities, rather than cultural realities. It is concerned with the fact that if you have two parties striving for dominance in a single world, it's going to be extremely difficult for them, not to come into conflict with each other. And that I think is a much more plausible danger, risk for the world than anything to do with clash of cultures.

Now, are we in danger of reaching the Thucydides trap? We will be if the world coalesces into two single camps. Sometimes it's thought that we had that situation between the West and Soviet Russia. But an actual fact, it wasn't between two camps there and you had, in fact, three worlds. We should recall you had the two rival parties, but then you had a huge part of the world, which was relatively neutral, if you like, between the two. And that, in the end, was one of the reasons that we never fell into the Thucydides trap. With the present world, there is a real risk, because I think that with the political and economic reach of both United States and China there is a danger of the world dividing into two camps. There is no third world out there.

Now, the counterweight to that argument is, if you like, the global integration of the world, in particular, around technologies, and to some extent, consumption patterns, exchange of people and all the rest of it. So I don't think this Thucydides trap is necessarily our future. If we focus our attentions on those things that are common to us, and those things that are common to us include very large elements of, if you like, a global way of life, which transcends all cultures, this brings us together and to some degree, I think, does mitigate against those groups and societies who are continually looking outside and wanting conflict.

Those groups are much more vocal in the West than they are in China for the some of the reasons we've looked at already. China is much more a consensual society. Therefore, hostility towards the West such as it is, will be, if you like, shared, rather than in pockets of people who are calling for war. Obviously, there is a difference between Chinese society and Western societies in terms of the degree of integration. And those differences, coupled with the global similarities, lead me to think we should not be too pessimistic about the Thucydides trap. What I am worried about more is, if you like, conflict arising out of accidents, conflicts arising out of, for instance, the rise of artificial technology and weapons.

The rise of artificial technology and weaponry is immensely dangerous, because we can easily reach the point where they become autonomous. And weapons will bring nations into conflict without them actually wanting it. That is the real risk, which the whole world should be concentrating on. In other words, not strategic issues, but the consequences of new technological risks.

Peng: If I may paraphrase your opinion strongly, it is that we should not maybe always stick to the old-fashioned geopolitical point of view, but we should maybe focus more on AI and other new technologies and trying to govern it as a global community. We try to have dialogue, have communications to manage those newly funded emerging technologies.

Albrow: You've summed it up very well. Thank you.

Peng: Yeah. And my next question is somehow related also to your first book, because it mentioned the role of Belt and Road Initiative, which was initiated by China. But we see nowadays, for example (I'm based in Germany) in German newspapers every day, there's a criticism of Belt and Road, whether China is, for example, taking over Uganda or taking over south-eastern Europe, and so on. What do you think of those criticisms? Why should the outside world not see Belt and Road as a threat?

Albrow: I think that this is a case of a contagion of the transference, of thinking about China, into areas where China is operating very much as other powers operate when they have money to invest. The Belt and Road programme is a massive investment programme. It's an investment based upon the credit which China has in the world's markets. From that point of view, I don't see it as any different from, let's say, the development programmes the West operated in the 1970s, 1980s and 1990s. Those too were subject to criticism because any kind of economic development will be judged according to the benefits which result for the country where the development takes place and the benefits which result for the people who invest. China will expect to get benefits from Belt and Road. It wouldn't do it otherwise. But then it also has to persuade, and does persuade, the countries which get the investment in the airports and the ports and the railways that these are also important for the development of their country.

So I don't think the criticisms of Belt and Road are really, in principle, any different from the criticisms which are always directed at foreign investment in any country. That's my view.

Peng: Okay, thanks. And the next question also looks like a follow-up question, but in your book, China's Role in a Shared Human Future: Towards Theory for Global Leadership, you discuss how China will reshape the future of globalization. And I think many business leaders also believe that the 21st century will be a so-called Asian century. Actually, yesterday I talked with Mr Stephen Perry, the president of the 48 Group, who also told me that he strongly believed that Asia will be the centre of the world. It will no longer be Europe or America, but Asia.

But the real question is that, actually, the big idea in the title of your book is that it's about global leadership, because leadership translated into Chinese is '*Ling Dao Li*', which means the power to lead, which sounds a little bit like Joseph Nye or Donald Trump. Because when Donald Trump talks about leadership, he basically means that, in this room, I am the boss. You all have to listen to me. That's what American leadership is really about. But I understand that you were writing about a different type of leadership. The real question is, if there will be an Asian century, is the West ready for such a century or is the West happy about that?

Albrow: I think if there is an Asian century, I would suspect that it would be rather short-lived. The West as such is unlikely to exist in the way it does now. The West is entirely fragmented and there are many forces at work there. I think, for instance, if we are looking 20, 30 years ahead, then we might well be talking of an African century as much as an Asian century. The paths of development in the world are such that if you are looking for those parts of the world where there are resources, where there are people and where all the energy is, then I would have thought 20 or 30 years from now it's more likely to be in Africa than anywhere else.

But the West itself, insofar as we speak of the West at the moment, seems to cover most of the world. It will absolutely fragment. It won't be regarded as an entity in the way that the Americans would like it to be. Indeed, the current efforts of the American president Biden to create some kind of league of democracies already verges on the laughable in the sense that basically he seems to want anyone to join it who happens not to like China. It doesn't seem to matter what kind of politics they have, doesn't matter what kind of regime. I think the idea of an integrated West really is out of date. And from that point of view, Chinese leadership now, I think, is best applied in the global institutions, getting them to focus on global goals, getting them to look at practical projects and setting an example to the world, for instance, in handling global warming and developing solar power and so on.

China has got the resources and the political system which enables it to make big decisions and come to those decisions rapidly and put them into effect. That is the comparative advantage that China has *vis-à-vis* the rest of the world.

Peng: My question is: Why is it so important for the world to never close the door on exchange in the intellectual sense?

Albrow: Exchange, intellectually, is the basis for the advance of understanding each other, but also for the development of science and knowledge generally. So we can only work and develop collectively if we understand each other.

Now, one of the very big problems in the West is fragmentation, which historically I take back a very long way, but certainly crucially into the 15th, 16th centuries. It replicates itself time and time again. So when you look at a country like the United States, it is immensely varied internally. There will be groups of people there who are immensely hostile to Asian people, immensely hostile to Black people, immensely hostile to Spanish people and so on. And unfortunately, there is an element in it, if you like, of human beings' hostility towards the stranger, and that hostility can become focused in smaller groups.

Well, the United States was built on small groups who immigrated and, therefore, suspicion towards the outsider has been a factor within American society. What the United States does as a collective is attempt to create a wider community which will incorporate these groups competing with each other. It's an immensely difficult job. And again, I think looking at that from China, I think you need to understand that deep hostility to the stranger which is built into the United States.

But at the same time, there have been immense efforts to create institutional structures, which will actually contain it. The United States alternates between periods where sometimes it contains it, sometimes it doesn't. At the moment, I think it's in a very dangerous period. And I don't think the world at large realizes just how close the United States came with the end of the Trump presidency, how close it came to what could have been a civil war. Very, very close.

Indeed, that wouldn't have been the result of the majority opinion. It would have been the result of the driving force of minorities who have created within themselves immense hostility towards the rest of the world and towards their neighbours. So it's those structural factors in Western countries, but in particular in the United States, which call for a great deal of understanding on the part of Chinese people.

Peng: I would like to know what your take is on common prosperity.

Albrow: Creating common prosperity is something where governments have a very important part, because if we rely simply on the energies and the skills of the population, unfortunately, everything that we understand from economic science would suggest that you will get the development of monopolies.

You'll get the development of very powerful people who will start to control others, in spite of everybody working very hard. Chinese people, I think, do have hard work built into that culture. They are very hardworking people. Max Weber pointed that out. And this was one of the reasons Max Weber thought that China could eventually become a big economic power.

You see, unless you do have policies to redress the imbalances that result from unrestrained pursuit of profit, unless you have policies which will redistribute in one way or another, unless your policies will create a public area, then, of course, a common prosperity will not result.

China is a very interesting case in the last 50 or so years, because, 50 years ago, there was very little of the kind that you could call a welfare state. From very little indeed, over the last 50 years, the amount of public support for education and health has increased all the time. That is an important factor in the creation of a common prosperity. So, you've got the ingredients in China for a highly prosperous nation. You've got a hardworking population and at the same time you've got, I think, an administration which understands the need every so often to redress the balance of the rich and powerful in favour of those who have been less successful in economic competition. Because we have to understand that hard work alone does not create wealth. It's also competition. And I think, again, Chinese administration has shown a great deal of wisdom in the way it's managed competition for the benefits of the population as a whole.

Peng: Since 2012, socialism with Chinese characteristics has entered a new era. And could you please tell us your thinking on the past 10 years of China's development? What's the most important development in China?

Albrow: I think one of the important features of the last 10 years has been, if you like, raising the profile of the Party to represent values of a broadly moral, social and ethical kind, and therefore using the Party very much as the social conscience of the nation as a whole. The more the Party itself can accept that role and at the same time be accepted in general, as, if you like, the conscience – and that, to my mind, is what has been happening in the last 10 years – then the future looks very good.

DOI https://doi.org/10.24103/GCSS6.en.2021.8

Chapter 8
Academic and social missions for Chinese scholars in the UK[1]

The author was Honorary Senior Fellow at the Centre for Global Governance (CGG) at the London School of Economics and Political Science (LSE). However, the CGG was closed after the LSE–Gaddafi affair in 2011, after which the author worked, in an honorary capacity, for the China in Comparative Perspective Network (CCPN) at the LSE. As a social theorist, he provided theoretical guidance from a global perspective, in addition to China in a comparative perspective. The changing of names from CCPN Global to Global China Academy (GCA) and from *JCCP* (*Journal of China in Comparative Perspective*) to *JCGCP* (*Journal of China in Global and Comparative Perspectives*) reflects the author's strong influence over the past decade.

This chapter consists of three sections. 8.1 summarizes the author's contributions to GCA on three occasions with his three mini speeches on December 10, 2021 at the British Academy. 8.2 demonstrates the author's contributions to GCP's publications from journal articles, dialogues with or interviews by scholars and media, book reviews, prefaces for books, book series proposals, book editing, and the sole-author's books themselves. These contributions have greatly helped GCA to fulfil its academic mission.

With regards to its social mission, 8.3 demonstrates the author's contributions in the seven forums of the Global China Dialogue (GCD) series from 2014 to 2021. More broadly, the author advanced the idea of 'China for global', which has been a guideline for the GCA to participate in building a global society and participating in global governance with Chinese knowledge resources (2018, Chapters 1, 2, 3, 5, 9).

8.1 Global China Academy

Three mini speeches have been included in this section. They were made by the author at the 7th Global China Dialogue (GCD VII) and associated events on December 10, 2021, at the British Academy. They are: an announcement of the launch of the Global China Academy (GCA) at the Opening session, the launch of his book *China and the Shared Human Future*, by Martin Albrow, published by Global Century Press (GCP) at the Closing session, and a further event to launch the GCA at the dinner. Altogether they well summarize the author's views on and contributions to Global China Academy, including its Global Century Press and Global China Dialogue series.

---

[1] Editor's note: All the descriptions in this chapter have been inserted by the Editor of the book.

8.1.1 Speech notes on receiving a Certificate of Appreciation at the announcement of the launch of GCA

At the end of the Opening session of the GCD VII, Professor Tony McEnery FAcSS and FRSA, Council Member, Academy of Social Sciences, Distinguished Professor of English Language and Linguistics at Lancaster University, Chair of Global China Academy Council and Founding Fellow, announced the launch of the Global China Academy (GCA). He also presented a Certificate of Appreciation to Emeritus Professor Martin Albrow FAcSS. He read, 'Upon your retirement as Honorary President of the Global China Academy, for your academic guidance in fostering and nurturing the Academy and the Global Century Press, and for your intellectual input and activities in supporting and participating in the first seven Global China Dialogue forums. Your dedicated efforts and service are greatly appreciated.'

The author expressed his thanks as follows: 'I am very surprised. It couldn't have been done without the cooperation of so many people. Above all, the founder of the Global China Dialogue, the Academy and all the rest, Professor Xiangqun Chang. It's really she who should be getting this certificate, but I am glad to be associated with this particular certificate. Thank you very much, Xiangqun, and thank you all for supporting these dialogues. It's been many years. Now and it's come to the seventh. We've been planning for 10 years and I thought it would be a very good thing for the next ten years to be able to hand the reins to Professor McEnery here. I'm truly grateful to you. Thank you very much.'

8.1.2 Speech at the launch of the *China and the Shared Human Future* at the GCD VII

The *China and the Shared Human Future* book launch was held at the end of the Closing session of the GCD VII. Speakers included the author, the editor and a reviewer of this book. The reviewer was Professor Robin Cohen, Senior Research Fellow at Kellogg College, Emeritus Professor of Global and Development Studies; Former Director of the International Migration Institute, University of Oxford; Life Fellow of Global China Academy.

The author started with the following remarks: 'Well, I think it's an extraordinary privilege to be able to promote my book at the end of this conference. I won't say any more about it at all. I just want to thank the Global China Academy for allowing me to end my career on a high note.

I began it 60 years ago in October 1961: that was my first professional appointment. I travelled down to Leicester with a friend from the LSE. He was called Tony (Anthony) Giddens, and the two of us together started our careers then. Mine has had a different trajectory. In 1987, the institution I worked for went bankrupt, and ever since I have moved from place to place and I think since then I have worked in 14 institutions. And the Global China Academy is the summit of my achievement.

I'm announcing today my retirement. I'm retiring from professional life but I'm going to continue writing the things I want to write about, not for academics or the academic world, but, I hope, for the general readership. Thank you all very much indeed for giving me this wonderful occasion, especially Xiangqun, thank you all very much.'

8.1.3 Recorded message as Honorary Founding President for the GCA founding event

The launch of GCA event was held at the dinner. It was chaired by Professor LI Wei FAE FBA FAcSS FRSA, Director and Dean of Institute of Education, University College London; Non-executive Chair of Global China Academy Council and Founding Fellow. Together with some absent Founding Fellows and Life Fellows including the Honorary Founding President of GCA in the session of video presentations, the author's pre-recorded video speech was played.

'This is a very good moment when we are enjoying the 7th Global China Dialogue. When we're looking at the reform of global governance, to think of the Global China Academy as the creation of Professor Xiangqun Chang and many others who have helped over the last 10 years or so to build something which will contribute in a lasting way to understanding between China and the rest of the world. The basic philosophy behind it is that we understand each other better if we do things together. The creation of the Global China Academy and the Global Century Press are, I think, practical things which can contribute to this greater understanding.

It's been a huge pleasure for me over recent years to be able to help in this project. I do wish it every success in the coming decade and hopefully even longer than that. So it's with great pleasure that I say that. I welcome and hope for the increasing success of the Global China Academy over the coming years. Good luck to you all. And thank you very much for the chance that I've had to help towards it. Thank you, goodbye.'

8.2 Global Century Press

8.2.1 Contributing to the *Journal of China in Global and Comparative perspectives* (JCGCP)

8.2.1.1 A Chinese episode in the globalization of sociology (see 7.1)

8.2.1.2 Max Weber, China and the World: in search of transcultural communication (with ZHANG Xiaoying, see Book 1, Chapter 12)

8.2.1.3 Spirit (精神 *jingshen*) as a key contemporary Chinese concept (with JIN Wei, see 9.2)

8.2.1.4 Dialogue on BRI with WANG Yiwei on the BRI (see 4.1)

8.2.1.5 The prospects of the BRI in the post-pandemic era: a dialogue with XU Baofeng in the Guangming International Forum (see 4.2)

8.2.1.6 'West-East talk': Intercivilizational dialogue with PENG Dawei (see 7.4.2.10)

8.2.1.7 The globalization era and China: concepts, contexts, problems and orientations: an interview by WANG Xin (see 7.3.5)

8.2.1.8 Review article: Chinese social theory in global social science Knowledge Flows and Chinese Social Theory (see 9.1)

8.2.1.9 Book review: Witnessing China combatting COVID-19: my story in China (see 6.4)

8.2.1.10 Book review: *After the Event*[2]

After the Event: The Transmission of Grievous Loss in Germany, China and Taiwan. By Stephan Feuchtwang. New York and Oxford: Berghahn Books, 2011. (Hbk) 240pp. £55.

This is a complex book, to be read in different ways for varied purposes. Above all it is the creation of a memory about memory, and is very personal as a result. It contains three separate studies in one book, and it might be best initially to treat each separately.

The first is a study of the Great Leap Forward famine in China, 1958–61, drawing on the author's own fieldwork as an anthropologist and sinologist, working with Professor WANG Mingming of Peking University in the Quanzhou area of southern Fujian province. The core data came from 34 interviews with village people in 2004. But the written account draws on information from the author's long engagement with China, from co-workers and correspondents over the years from 2002 onwards, from written records and historical and literary treatments of the period of the famine, and extending back and forth into the history of Communist China and earlier.

These diverse materials are held together in much the same way as memory works, through highlighting signal events, holding a recurrent theme, finding a motif and creating a narrative with an underlying explanation for the way things turned out the way they did. A theme that holds the story together is that Party cadres remember differently; for them it is an issue of responsibility, whom to blame, but their past 'aggravated indifference' to the hardship of the people extends into disdain for them in the present. For the others, the Great Leap Forward merges into a general recollection of past hardship survived, a mixture of pride and shame for what they have gone through. The younger generation prefers to bury the failure of enforced collectivization under a return to interpersonal loyalties, revival of ritual and a determined enjoyment of prosperity that conceals an underlying insecurity. The famine is buried but not dead.

---

[2] This book review was published in the *Journal of China in Global and Comparative Perspectives*, Vol.2 2016, pp. 123–125.

The second account is of events much smaller in scale and less well known to the rest of the world. Beginning on December 29, 1952, secret police and the army of the ruling Chinese Nationalist Party swooped on the village of Luku in the Shiding area of Taiwan on the grounds that it was a hotbed of communism, detaining most of the men and some women, and executing many. It was the main incident in a 40-year period of martial law that began in 1947, since named the

'White Terror'. Only after 1987 was it possible to refer to the Luku incident, as detailed elsewhere by a co-researcher of Professor Feuchtwang, Shih Fang-long, as the 'The White Terror Incidents in Taiwan' in Albrow and Secklingen (2011).

The poignancy of the subsequent public disclosure for Feuchtwang was that he had been conducting his first anthropological fieldwork in Shiding in 1968, and not a hint of the Luku incident had come to his attention at the time, even though he had been there for 17 months and his respondents must have been fully aware of it. In the late 1980s, a period of gradual recognition of the wrongs suffered during the White Terror began. History books were revised, books of interviews with Luku survivors were published and in 2000 a monument to the victims was erected. Parallel to this official history, families distance themselves from it while seeking to restore their own continuity with the past through new burials or re-claiming their old land. Yet Feuchtwang as the visitor and researcher found the past was turning into a museum for the locals that had little to do with the reality of the Luku incident, which is still shrouded in the complexities of Taiwanese politics – even the name Luku is disappearing from the maps.

The third story is the Third Reich. This, of course, is on a different scale altogether, in terms of both the available historical record and the national and international processing of truth, guilt, shame and reconciliation. The author's personal involvement extends from his family's flight from Germany when he was two years old to the present day. He retells the diverse acknowledgments of the past in West and East Germany, by non-Jews and Jews, interviewing and asking himself questions, and then turning to what it is to come from a mixed Jewish family living in Germany and being brought up in England. Here his interviews become conversations, in which his respondents question him. He admits to being plagued by 'a sense of obligation to my Jewish heritage' (183). He finds that family stories are told with reference to public events. Of course, at issue must be whether they get them right: the Nazis did not 'win power electorally' (35) – their best result in the last free elections in March 1932 before Hitler came to power was 33% of the votes; a misprint (161) dates the Balfour Declaration as 1948 and not 1917. The reflections that introduce and conclude these three studies explore the theme of the interweaving of personal and public narrative, and the whole book is a valuable contribution to understanding how collective and individual fates are registered in a single story even when it is hardly possible for any organized collectivity to enforce the kinds of claims on individuals that Hitler, Mao or Stalin could make.

But it is difficult to hold it all together and one wonders whether Feuchtwang's materials might not have been better absorbed into autobiography.

That could be a great book, illustrating to a coming generation how a scholarly career is never as important as the struggle for one's own identity, both in it and outside.

References

Albrow, M. and H. Seckinelgin (Eds) (2011). *Global Civil Society 2011: Globality and the Absence of Justice*. Houndmills: Palgrave Macmillan.

8.2.1.11 Book review: *What has been lost in Contemporary China*?[3]

What Has Been Lost in Contemporary China? Lixing Chen. Translated by Enxi Chang. London: Global Century Press, 2018. 140pp.

There has to be a warm welcome for the first book in a series that will explore the emerging new cultures of our time. These arise out of the multiple exchanges between cultures, but are owned by none of them. For this series, China will be an essential part of the mix.

The editors, Professors Lixing Chen and Xiangqun Chang. have chosen the Chinese metaphor of 'Three Eyes' as the series title to emphasize its commitment to viewing cultures from the inside, but also from a standpoint outside them, yet that still is cultural.

The Three Eyes are not seeking the kind of objectivity that Western culture has tried to claim for itself over the centuries. They acknowledge only the advantage of seeing things from several sides at once. The editors are both born Chinese, but based for many years overseas, Chen in Japan, Chang in the United Kingdom, and their aim is to bring Chinese thought into the transcultural conversation.

Transculturality as a concept may only have been coined by a Cuban anthropologist in the 1950s, Fernando Ortiz, but the processes it refers to are as old as culture itself. Instead of focusing attention on the unique and distinctive features that separate one culture from another, it emphasizes the other equally important property of culture, its continual potential for generating novelty in the processes of human communication.

In recent times, the internet has become almost the paradigm case of transculturality, a medium potentially accessible to all, belonging to none. But it is only the latest technical extension over unlimited space of the human ability to communicate through signs and symbols. The current feverish debates about its control are a vivid illustration that boundaries between cultures are themselves cultural products, readily erected, just as easily crossed or dismantled.

At a time when China is in the forefront of attempts to regulate internet access, it is particularly appropriate that this series will put China under the gaze

[3] This book review was published in the *Journal of China in Global and Comparative Perspectives*, Vol. 6, 2020 [Chinese version: 马丁·阿尔布劳：书评，《当代中国失去为什么？》（英文版），陈立行 著，常恩悉 译,《全球中国比较研究》, 2019年，第二期)].

of the three eyes, finding in its past and present experience of the wider world a contribution to a general understanding of the direction of our time.

Lixing Chen's book is a wonderful testimony to the personal experience of transculturality and the relentless pace and turmoil associated with it in her lifetime. Intellectuals in the past, like Voltaire or Hegel, sought to grasp their time with terms like 'spirit of the age'. We do the same with 'culture', covering the activities of countless millions, but in the end these abstractions can only gain their validity by relating to individual lives.

Chen is a sociologist. She has lived and researched in China, the United States and Japan for long periods, as well as for shorter times in many countries. As a former President of the Japan–China Sociological Society, she has profound understanding of what divides people as well as what brings them together.

The author of *What Has Been Lost in Contemporary China?* combines mature reflections on the meaning of many years of direct experience of different cultures with the accumulated wisdom of a career working with ideas. The result and purpose of this book is to provide a text both accessible and attractive to the general reader as well as challenging and provocative for scholars. It demonstrates the importance of senior scholars having the courage to offer insight into their personal lives as well as their knowledge to a wider public.

For the search for meaning in life is shared by everyone. The accumulation of experience can lead to wisdom, the value of which has been long recognized in Chinese culture. Sharing the personal journey makes it accessible to all. Notable examples that come to mind of those in the West who have shared that experience include Max Weber and John Kenneth Galbraith. Chen can be proud to follow in such footsteps.

There are poignant personal stories here. She and her daughter of 11 years old went shopping in Nanjing one day and passed a disabled beggar in the street. The little girl asked if she could give him 5 yuan. Her mother hurried her along, only to find that the child no longer wanted to buy anything for herself, and, on returning home, her great-grandmother even suggested the beggar might have intentionally crippled himself. The child's anger and distraught response to this suggestion led Chen to relent and take her back to the beggar to give him the 5 yuan (p. 68).

This personal incident leads Chen to reflect on the shared universal value underlying Confucian 'compassion', Western 'philanthropism' and Buddhist 'benevolence' and to find in the child the basics of 'what makes someone human'. Theory is embedded here, not as a sequence of arid propositions, but as a narrative thread that links human beings to their place in the world. So, what has been lost in China today? The question mark is very important here. For the answer is complex, indeed perhaps at the end the answer is open.

Chen laments the ubiquitous rent-seeking that she associates with public ownership. At the same time, she finds the market economy gratifying decadent tastes in Japan, England and the US as well as in China (p. 85). It seems that both socialism and markets feed the same vices. Perhaps it is modernity as such that deserves the blame, and, as the author points out, 'modernization is a double-edged sword' (p. 93).

China has achieved Zhou Enlai's Four Modernizations, in industry, agriculture, technology and defence, but, Chen argues, has yet to find the institutionalized public space on which integrity in Western societies depends. Was that ever there in China? Chen's account gives us plenty to chew over: during the period of the Republic, one aged informant tells her, people were polite and honest (p. 71); now bribes ease the way to becoming a student union official (p.78); 'family-first' has always been the centre of Chinese people's lives; now it militates against the formation of a public space (p. 88).

This is vivid, trenchant cultural criticism, from a comparative standpoint, seeking values that stand the test of time for any society. In a revealing 'Afterword', the author tells us the theme of what China has lost has preoccupied her ever since 2008 when she penned a newspaper article 'The Olympics don't just belong to China'(see Appendix 1).

But, in effect, she has arrived at a rather more nuanced view after working in Japan since she has come to recognize so much of Japanese qualities derive from the same sources as traditional Chinese culture – harmony, mutual trust and self-discipline.

This indeed fits more with the general tenor of her argument, since, although twice she speaks of the abolition of the lineage system (pp. 55, 90), this might apply to the extraordinary rapid collectivization of land tenure of 1955–57, but it does not reflect the emphatic endorsement of duties within the family in the Marriage Law of 1950 that was re-enacted in 1981.

The clan spirit persists in the sense of family obligation between the generations. This China has not lost. Even private property has regained a place in Chinese culture. Effectively, then, and on the evidence of her book, Chen has reached the point where she may be ready to offer reasons to expect a better future.

We can then hope she will rephrase her question for her next book. Perhaps the title will be *How Can Chinese Characteristics Humanize Modernity*? Since she is prepared to share so much of herself and opens her scholarship to a wider public, it ought to be just as readable and challenging as this book is. We can be encouraged in this hope by her willingness to co-edit a series that looks to the creativity of transculturality and makes China the central case study. The several volumes that she and Xiangqun Chang inform us are already planned give every reason for optimism.

This volume promises much for the general attractiveness of the Three Eyes series. Its accessibility for the general reader benefits too from the easy, colloquial English that the translator, Enxi Chang, contributes. She has the direct, contemporary style of the younger generation that fits very well with the purposes of the series.

8.2.2 Contributing to book series

Currently, GCP publishes six book series that encourage the study of China in global and comparative perspectives. The author made contributions to four of them. They are 'Chinese Concepts' (see 8.2.2.1, 8.2.2.2), 'Globalization of Chinese Social Sciences' (see 8.2.2.3, 8.2.4.1, 8.2.4.2), 'Understanding China and the World' (8.2.3, 8.2.5), 'Transcultural experiences with "three eyes"' (8.2.1.9, 8.2.1.11).

8.2.2.1 Proposing a book series for Chinese thought /concepts[4]

Although Chinese economic development has attracted world attention and the diverse nature of both China and the Chinese has been universally acknowledged, China's achievement in the social sciences occupies an insignificant position in the human knowledge system. Over the past century, Chinese scholars have made extraordinary efforts in introducing the theories and methods of Western sociology into the study of Chinese society. In the last 30 years, Chinese social scientists, in their studies of Chinese society, have managed to either extract concepts from Chinese cultural resources such as '*bao*' (reciprocation), '*mianzi*' (face) and '*guanxi*' (deferential relationship) or replenish the existing concepts with Chinese elements such as reciprocity or social exchange.

Just as the Chinese economy has developed from merely manufacturing to a mix of solid production and R & D development, social study in China should also shift its focus from the mere import of Western thoughts to the export and contribution to the world of some of the Chinese achievements in social studies. Our proposal is to edit a series entitled 'Social Science Keywords' from a Chinese perspective. It will cover a wide range of topics including sociology, anthropology, politics, law, economics, economic history, management, social policies, international relations and gender studies. The purpose of the series is to rewrite keywords of social science disciplines in order to renew outdated concepts in relevant textbooks in the West. By offering a uniquely Chinese perspective on the study of social sciences, the editors hope that their work can stimulate genuine global dialogue between cultures and thus add value to the world knowledge system.

Each volume would consist of three key concepts and each concept should be from 25,000 to 30,000 words. Based on their understanding of social sciences key concepts in the West, the writers, Chinese scholars inside or outside China, would draw on their own cultural resources for theories and concepts that address problems of worldwide concern. Using empirical research methods, they would integrate Chinese concepts into Western social science studies and thus present an alternative to the solely Western frame of thought. This series should be scholarly but also strive for maximum readability and usability. The series should have

[4] Editor's note: Based on this proposal the editor and the author developed a book series 'Chinese Concepts'. The first volume of this book series was for promoting a Chinese concept of 'society building'.

both Chinese and English versions, targeting a wide range of audiences such as Chinese, overseas Chinese and all those who are interested in China and Chinese culture and society. It also can serve as ideal supplementary materials for foreigners who study Chinese.

The editors of the series are Martin Albrow, Xiangqun Chang and ZHANG Xiaoying. We will invite specialists worldwide to form the editorial board. On the one hand, they will be asked to make comments or review the books; on the other hand, it is hoped the book series will be included in their reading lists for teaching and research. We would edit the series jointly, Chang being responsible for identifying Chinese authors in the social sciences based on her long experience of comparative studies between China and the West, and Zhang for organizing the translation and editing of the books into English based on her expertise. Albrow will be responsible for assessing the viability and quality of the English translation. We will invite specialists worldwide to form the editorial board. The complete works, with the approval of the four editors, will then be recommended to the editorial board and submitted to the publisher for proofreading.

The series can start from September 2013 and is scheduled to be completed in the next five years. To guarantee the quality of the book, every book will go through the three-step procedure of the publishing house. The book is allowed to be published only when it meets the requirements. Appendix 2 includes some of the disciplines and relevant key concepts for your reference. Those who are interested in submitting their own books should kindly submit their CV (200 words), abstract and key words (1,000 words) before December 2012.

Albrow also wrote a book review for *What Has Been Lost in Contemporary China* (8.1.2.6). It is Volume 1 of the Transculturality with 'Three Eyes book series (General Preface of the series introducing the reasons for producing this series), edited jointly by Lixing Chen, Professor of Sociology, Kwansei Gakuin University, and former President of Japan–China Sociological Society, Japan, and Xiangqun Chang, President of Global China Academy and Honorary Professor of University College London, UK. It is published by Global Century Press from 2017.

8.2.2.2 Foreword 1 for *Society Building: A China Model of Social Development*[5]

This book is not just about building society or society building, it is a contribution to it. Indeed, the main contribution social sciences make to society is to bring to it the consciousness of self that enables self-direction. But which self, which society, do we, social scientists, help to build? If it is China we observe, are

[5] Martin Albrow, Foreword 1, in Xiangqun Chang (Ed) (2015), *Society Building: A China Model of Social Development*, Chinese Concepts Book Series, Vol.1. London: Global Century Press and Beijing: New World Press, pp.XXIII–XXV [Chinese edition: (英)常向群 主编：《社会建设——中国社会发展的一种模式》，徐海燕等译，伦敦：环球世纪出版社；北京：新世界出版社，2015年].

there not many societies, many selves? – ethnicities, provinces, cities, churches, families, businesses, the Party and parties, inside the territory of the People's Republic and outside, Hong Kong and Taiwan, Malaysia and Singapore, London and New York?

It was ever so, not a matter of the territorial boundaries, or even of what a nation–state government controls. Wise public policy finds what is creative and productive in society and registers and secures the aspirations of the people while ensuring collective security in the international arena. A society that governments serve builds itself in its own way and there is no universal model. Shigeto Sonoda in this volume illustrates effectively the diversity of attachment that populations have towards the regimes of so-called Confucian societies of the Far East.

States supply the frame for very different kinds of society. The constitutional differences between states are minor compared with the profound differences that underpin daily life in, say, the United States, India, China, Brazil and Iran. These are differences within differences, where the country/city divide takes on a quite different value in each country, where class and ethnic affiliation crosscut occupation and religion differently in each, and all have their characteristic way of handling established and outsiders.

The reader will find in these pages ample recognition of the diversity and complexity of Chinese society in central/local relations, country and city, market and guanxi, characteristic diversity, different from diversities elsewhere in the world, as for instance in the hukou registration system, and now overlaid by forces of globalization with differential impacts arising precisely out of these differences.

The reader will find in these pages ample recognition of the diversity and complexity of Chinese society in central/local relations, country and city, market and guanxi, characteristic diversity, different from diversities elsewhere in the world, as for instance in the hukou registration system, and now overlaid by forces of globalization with differential impacts arising precisely out of these differences.

The same production technology will destroy a traditional household structure in one part of the world and create a new one elsewhere. The new communications technology can lay waste the shopping streets of Western countries and create businesses in Indian villages. Xiangqun Chang's study of a Chinese migrant community in London shows how it can change from being marginal or central to its own self and to the outside under constantly changing social and environmental conditions. In theoretical terms, this is what Laurence Roulleau-Berger calls here the 'recodification of grammars of recognition'.

The many different kinds of globalization, economic, scientific, technological, informational and recreational, have challenged national governments to rethink what is inside and outside their own societies and to redefine the points at which intervention can be effective. In the 1990s, when globalization was equated by both Wall Street and its opponents with neo-liberal economic policies, it was fashionable to foresee the end of the nation–state. But it has since become clear, and in this respect China has led the way, that an openness to new products and outlooks in society even as they register and react to the way the wider world is changing. They have to be clearer about their own role. They have to become smarter and more strategic, to match the increasing empowerment of their own people. They will digest outside opinion but this may mean precisely not accepting some universal prescription from outside experts, be it IMF or any others.

The strategic state, as the description implies, is engaged in finding guiding ideas and, in reflecting on globalization, is bound to examine its own identity in a global society. The very openness of national societies and the interrelations of their own people with others worldwide compel the recognition of a transnational reality to society which goes far beyond old modern conceptions of international relations. I think this is what Flemming Christiansen expresses when he examines how 'China is equipped to create growth within a non-imperialist and ecologically cost-neutral scenario'.

National governments are local in a global society, but with an autonomous capacity beyond what they allow their own local governments. Globalization may force changes in that respect too but, more importantly, at the level of global society, the imperative for a government is to express a collective identity in a meaningful way that can persuade its own people that it has a contribution to make, and in turn they have one too, to the global community of which they are all a part. Were it not for the past history of the term, we might call this national ideology, which is neither the expression of a class interest nor an imperialist nationalism.

I think this is implicit in much of what the Chinese government has been seeking to do over recent years and which the scholarly analyses in this book reflect. Parama Sinha Palit's account of the concerted effort to make China both a global education hub and to provide opportunities for education abroad is consistent with ideas of 'soft power' but also meets the aspirations of its own families that look beyond national borders. Bettina Gransow proposes that China's infrastructure projects at home and abroad have to meet not just development goals but also need to validate normative ideas of good governance and a harmonious world.

This book, then, is a snapshot of Chinese steps along a way that national societies everywhere have to tread and which has no inherent endpoint. The society building that is happening is the establishment of China in a developing global society which has already moved beyond old questions of who rules the world or which is the best economic system to ones of how national societies can address global issues that transcend boundaries and on which it is in their common interest to cooperate. If states can find their own way of contributing to these ends, if their peoples are persuaded that there is a commitment by their states to the future welfare of humankind, we may soon recognize building global society as the next stage in China's development.

8.2.2.3 Preface to *A Record of Launching Martin Albrow's Book China's Role in a Shared Human Future*

This book is published entirely thanks to Professor Xiangqun Chang's initiative, with the able assistance of Costanza Pernigotti. I stress this aspect of its origin in order to reduce my own embarrassment. There always has to be a touch of arrogance that brings a writer to offer up a book to the public. But to write a preface to a book that focuses on the launch of his own book! That requires whatever reserves of humility I may have left, as well as special justification.

The launch process is a practical example of what the globalization of Chinese social sciences involves. It is not simply the outcome of intensive discussion between Global Century Press, New World Press and the Commercial Press in China.

As the following pages illustrate, it has involved a great variety of exchanges between scholars, public officials, journalists, photographers, editors, reviewers and businesspeople. They have all been engaged in the globalization process and I believe this book provides a valuable documentation of their contribution to it.

It is their work that is represented in the following pages and I have here the opportunity to express my deep gratitude for all that they have done to make the publication of *China's Role in a Shared Human Future: Towards Theory for Global Leadership* a success.

They have all been working towards a 'shared human future'. This is the point about the globalization of Chinese social sciences. It is to contribute to a common global goal, sharing scholarly and scientific achievements with the rest of the world.

Striving for global goals requires us to be ready to take account of the approach of any other culture. I consider myself a sociologist who is proud to be called a friend of China. But any fruit of my work arises out of dialogue with Chinese social scientists about the future of global society and not from my limited knowledge of China.

The 'shared human future' will arise from transcultural dialogue and cooperation, rather than from any attempt to fix a universal set of principles. This applies in science as much as in practical affairs.

I am glad that we emphasized this point at the very outset of sociological concern for globalization in the pioneering set of papers by international sociologists that I edited with Elizabeth King for the Madrid World Congress of Sociology in 1990 (*Globalization, Knowledge and Society*, London: Sage, pp. 8–10).

From this point of view, I am happy to offer a new contribution to this volume, namely a paper prepared for a succeeding World Congress of Sociology, 28 years later, this time in Toronto.

It adds to an argument for Xi Jinping's *Governance of China* that will be found in my speeches in this volume, namely that the Chinese leadership is demonstrating a social scientific sophistication that enables it to have a clearer vision of what makes a 'shared human future' possible.

8.2.2.4 Book reviews for 'Transcultural experiences with "three eyes"' book series

The author wrote two book reviews for the 'Transcultural experiences with "three eyes"' book series. They are:

What Has Been Lost in Contemporary China, Volume 1 (see 8.2.1.11).

Battling the Virus: Witnessing China Combating COVID-19, Volume 5 (see 6.4).

This book series is edited jointly by Lixing Chen, Professor of Sociology, Kwansei Gakuin University, and former President of Japan–China Sociological Society, Japan, and Xiangqun Chang, President of Global China Academy and Honorary Professor of University College London, UK. It is published by Global Century Press from 2017.

8.2.3 Contributing to edit the book of *Max Weber and China: Culture, Law and Capitalism*

8.2.3.1 Preface: The Continuing Relevance of Max Weber[6]

When the editors of this volume were planning the conference on Max Weber and China in 2013, we had in mind the 150th anniversary of his birth. Now, as we come to publish a selection of the papers from the event held at the School of Oriental and African Studies in London, UK, we are commemorating the centenary of his death. But celebrating Weber's life and career is not the main reason for this book.

The events of the intervening period have impressed on us the need to make the fruits of contemporary Weber scholarship on China available to a wider readership, especially in China where his intellectual contribution as a theoretician is increasingly recognized as complementary to that of Marx and socialist political economy.

It is not just a matter of the poetic parallels between the last five years and the period leading up to Weber's death. He died in the aftermath of the Spanish flu. We are surviving and quaking at the impact of the coronavirus, even as we cling anxiously to our academic calling in politically unstable times. By heroic contrast, he took an early and eager part in the catastrophic World War of 1914–18, but, even in its worst times, continued with his study of China, pursuing an ever-expanding agenda for his social and political theory.

No other social scientist since Weber has sustained an intellectual programme as wide-ranging, comprehensive and productive as he did in his short career, covering the role of the public intellectual, the meta-theoretical foundations of social science, the historical origins and development of capitalist society, the compar-

[6] This is a draft Preface for the book of the conference *Max Weber and China: Culture, Law and Capitalism*. It will be co-edited by the by Martin Albrow, Ernest Caldwell, Xiangqun Chang, Athena Leoussi and Sam Whimster, to be published by Global Century Press in 2023.

ative study of civilizations and the analytical elements for any science of society – all this accompanied by vigorous interventions in political debates. Ironically, not long before his death, he was concerned to give career advice to students, typically both encouraging and admonitory, in his most famous two lectures on science and politics as professions.

Faced with such an output, scholars repeatedly and rightly enter into detailed engagement with issues that concerned him at particular points of time. It is still worthwhile to examine his account of the social conditions of workers in the eastern German territory in the late 19th century and the political consequences he drew from it. But he moved on from there.

Endlessly and rightly, we reconsider his arguments in his study of the Protestant ethic and spirit of capitalism, but he continually revised his position, as he did also in the work he felt impelled to undertake as a result, namely protracted enquiries into the society, economy and culture of non-Western civilizations, and in particular of China.

But the development of his thought was not only driven by intellectual logic and scientific enquiry. The impact of changes in the world in his own time and his recognition of the continuing transformation of human society came to pervade even his most rarefied analytical work. He felt compelled to sustain an equal interest in universal concepts of rationality even as he advanced an overarching account of historical development as the cumulative systematization of human endeavours, and which, in line with the new-fangled scientific management of his time, he called the process of rationalization.

The ever-changing nature of the world around him increasingly became a driving force in his own enquiries. It also came to influence his own outlook on life. The young expert on the political economy of Wilhelmine Germany may easily be assigned to what today we may call neo-liberal nationalism, but, while he never changed his view that revolutions only brought disaster, he often expressed sympathy with socialist aspirations.

When it came to China, he adopted early in his studies the view of the eminent sinologist J. J. M. de Groot that magic was a core element of Chinese culture and that this was an insuperable impediment to the growth of anything like capitalism. In contrast, near the end of his life, as a footnote to his lectures on economic history, he observed that the economic interests of the mandarin class led them to set in motion the development of railways in China, and this was sufficient to overcome any traditional cultural obstacles as in Confucianism.

While Weber never conducted a distinct study of its modern development, his whole work after 1911 was peppered with references to China and there seems little doubt that political upheavals there were food for his accounts of bureaucracy, legitimation and charisma as well as of religion. For instance, one incidental reference to the significance of reading and writing for the traditional Chinese official having a decisive influence on the whole development of culture was an insight into conditions that apply equally today in indicating the continuity of the Communist regime with its ancient past.

China study accompanied movements in his conceptual framework too. In earlier work, he had emphasized in sub-Darwinian fashion the adaptation of behaviour and beliefs to circumstances. In the course of his study of China, he came to raise values to a major causal factor and stressed both the way they could shape circumstances and the perpetual and increasing tension between distinct value spheres in the course of their development. These tensions he also detected in and experienced in his personal life, and generalized to be a general feature of the world of his time.

Analytically, the shift in his outlook was most notable in the introduction of the category of value rationality as one of his four types of action. His earlier thinking had allowed only for ends/means or technical rationality, emotional and traditional action. It was a conceptual innovation that accompanied an elaboration of the idea of rationalization as a historical process encompassing and driving the development of the modern world. Advancing technologies, intensifying value conflict: what more succinct account of history up to our own time could there be?

Rationality was detected as the core feature of bureaucracy from a very early point in his work, as was evident for him in what he recognized as the ideal type case in his native Germany. But it was a view reinforced by the application of scientific methods in the Taylor system of industrial management, and Weber's ever-ready observation for cross-sector affinities saw it too in the development of music and, of course, in financial accounting.

In that spirit of finding fundamental historical forces, there surely can be little doubt that for Weber, in our own time, the most fateful technical developments will have been the computer, the internet and artificial intelligence, and he would have examined their ramifying relations with global capital as the driving force in changes in our social and cultural conditions.

These are genuinely the continuation of the processes he described as rationalization, but what they leave open is the balance between factors that Weber saw as perennially in play at any stage of development, and in particular between a stable political system based on the legitimacy of the rulers and the emergence of a charismatic figure calling for change or revolution.

Analytically, the shift in his outlook was most notable in the introduction of the category of value rationality as one of his four types of action. His earlier thinking had allowed only for ends/means or technical rationality, emotional and traditional action. It was a conceptual innovation that accompanied an elaboration of the idea of rationalization as a historical process encompassing and driving the development of the modern world. Advancing technologies, intensifying value conflict: what more succinct account of history up to our own time could there be?

Rationality was detected as the core feature of bureaucracy from a very early point in his work, as was evident for him in what he recognized as the ideal type case in his native Germany. But it was a view reinforced by the application of scientific methods in the Taylor system of industrial management, and Weber's ever-ready observation for cross-sector affinities saw it too in the development of music and, of course, in financial accounting.

In that spirit of finding fundamental historical forces, there surely can be little doubt that for Weber, in our own time, the most fateful technical developments will have been the computer, the internet and artificial intelligence, and he would have examined their ramifying relations with global capital as the driving force in changes in our social and cultural conditions.

These are genuinely the continuation of the processes he described as rationalization, but what they leave open is the balance between factors that Weber saw as perennially in play at any stage of development, and in particular between a stable political system based on the legitimacy of the rulers and the emergence of a charismatic figure calling for change or revolution.

But this is a relatively minor issue for a Weberian frame of reference. He points to profound, historically based cultural differences between the West and China as the determinants of the directions that each will take in response to capitalism and technological advances. He could not foresee either economic globalization or the Chinese Communist Party, but in each case his method would have highlighted deep historically rooted cultural contrasts, such as between competitive aspiration for success on the one hand and consensual respect for authority on the other.

We are convinced that it is the contrasts between the cultures of China and the West, as they face common global threats to human existence and pursue distinctive paths in responding to advancing technologies, that make the comparative historical investigation and conceptual analysis that Weber conducted part of a common human heritage from which we can all benefit.

The papers in this volume bear testimony to the fruitfulness of following Weberian lines of enquiry into China's past for understanding its present, and at the same time provide fine examples of scholarship in pursuit of truth. We commend them to our readers, as citizens of their own country and equally citizens of the same world.

8.2.3.2 Report on the conference 'Max Weber and China', 2014

The author proposed an international conference entitled 'Max Weber and China: Culture, Law and Capitalism'. In his proposal, he wrote, 'Max Weber is not only celebrated as a founder of modern social science but also for his view that modern capitalism was the achievement of a uniquely Western rationalism. His celebrated study of China argued that its legal institutions and ethical and religious culture had prevented a similar development there. But he also drew on his knowledge of China in developing his ideas of bureaucracy, authority and legitimacy.'

'The economic success of China over the last 30 years represents for some the biggest challenge yet to Weber's account of its culture, to his theory of capitalism and to the methods he employed in arriving at his account. But it also brings into question the self-image of the West and the idea of modernity. The conference we are announcing will bring scholars from the social sciences and humanities together in a West/East dialogue central both to mutual understanding between China and the West and to an exploration of the possible varieties of capitalism.' Based on CCPN Global, he engaged with the Weber Studies Group of the British Sociological Association (BSA), the journal of *Max Weber Studies* and the Centre for Chinese Studies of SOAS, University of London where the successful conference was held.

China, the West and the Future of Global Capitalism – or Not?[7]

'The future of the global economic system depends on the West's relations with China.'[8] On 5–6 September, the conference entitled 'Max Weber and China: Culture, Law and Capitalism', was successfully held at SOAS, University of London. Nearly a hundred social scientists from China and around the world re-examined Weber's thesis and asked how far his pioneering social scientific methods can illuminate the very different conditions of economic growth today. After the conference, we received praise from some conference participants: 'A great triumph!' 'A significant conference!' 'A fantastic conference!' 'An intellectually productive conference!'

Dr Hong Bo, Reader in the Financial Economics Department of Financial & Management Studies at SOAS, University of London, chaired the Opening session; Professor Paul Webley, SOAS Director, made welcoming remarks and introduced SOAS as the world's leading institution for the study of Asia, Africa and the Middle East; Professor Martin Albrow, Fellow of Käte Hamburger Centre for Advanced Study, University of Bonn, Germany and Honorary Vice-President, British Sociological Association (BSA), pointed out that we have joined together out of shared scholarly interest in the conference theme, not as part of a programme mandated by big associations or institutions, and expressed his gratitude to SOAS, to some Conference Programme Committee members and to everyone participating who played key roles in hosting and organizing this conference.

Keynote speeches

There were four keynote speeches in this conference, arranged in the morning and afternoon on 5 and 6 September. Wolfgang Schluchter, Professor Emeritus of Sociology and Director of the Marsilius-Kolleg, University of Heidelberg, Germany, made a keynote speech entitled 'How ideas become effective in history:

[7] The idea of the conference was initiated by the author at CCPN Global. The author engaged with the Weber Study Group, the British Sociological Association (BSA), the journal Max Weber Studies, whereas the editor engaged with SOAS, where the event was held. This report was summarized by the editor and posted on the CCPN Global website.

[8] SOAS news, China, the west and the future of global capitalism. See: https://www.soas.ac.uk/news/newsitem86398.html.

Max Weber on Confucianism and beyond'. He made an important clarification of Weber's usage of Confucianism, 'the most pronounced counter- example to ascetic Protestantism, seemingly similar from the outside, but totally different from the inside'. So, Confucianism is included in his attempt to provide a sociology and typology of religious rationalism. Confucianism is also used as a backdrop to understand the singularity of Western development. This speech also served as the first Max Weber Studies Annual Lecture. It was chaired by its Editor Sam Whimster, Professor of Sociology and Global Policy Institute, London, UK

Although Professor Su Guoxun was absent from the conference for health reasons, his speech was delivered at the conference by Dr Xiaoying Zhang (Beijing Foreign Studies University, China). Su, the foremost Chinese expert on Weber from the Chinese Academy of Social Sciences and Harbin Engineering University, pointed out some of the misconceptions that led Weber to misinterpret certain elements of Chinese culture and sought to develop more refined methods of intercivilizational analysis. The audience raised many critical and interested questions. Professor Xiangqun Chang (CCPN Global and SOAS), chair of the session, offered to convey all the criticisms, comments, questions and feedback to Professor Su and seek his responses and, it is hoped, to publish an 'absent dialogue' between a Chinese scholar and the Western Weberians in the conference special issue of the Journal of China in Comparative Perspective in 2014.

Professor Martin Albrow, held up a new edition of the *Max Weber: The Protestant Ethic and the Spirit of Capitalism*, translated and introduced by Stephen Kalberg, when introducing Professor Kalberg as Keynote speaker from Boston University, USA. Kalberg argued for the continued relevance of Weber's systemic approach to the comparative analysis of civilizations. He made a critical reappraisal of Weberian theory and its contemporary relevance, which can be seen from his book *Max Weber's Comparative–Historical Sociology* (2012). Many interesting questions were raised by the audience.

The last Keynote speaker was Professor Gary Hamilton, University of Washington, USA. Professor Wolfgang Schluchter chaired this session. He acknowledged two things that he learned from Hamilton on studies of Weber. One is that Hamilton's work on family-based capitalism in Asia reveals to him that Weber's insistence that capitalism requires a separation between firms and families was not accurate for Asia. Another is that he agreed that Weber made a mistake equating patria potestas and *xiao* (孝) in his comparison of traditional Chinese and Roman societies. When Schluchter mentioned this, he showed the newly published From the Soil: *The Foundation of Chinese Society* (*Xiangtu Zhongguo*) in Chinese and English. The editor of the Chinese–English edition of From the Soil is the same person who organized a dialogue between Gary Hamilton and Xiangqun Chang on Fei's contributions to world anthropology and global sociology for commemorating the centenary of Professor Fei Xiaotong's birth in 2010. The abridged version is published in Anthropology Today, No. 6, 2011. The completed version is available in print in *Journal of China in Global and Comparative Perspectives* (JCGCP), Vol. 2, 2016.

In his presentation, Hamilton showed pictures of a single and multiple ripplesin a pond to demonstrate *chaxugeju* as 'the differential mode of association' and 'everyone is the centre of their own circle of relationships'. In his earlier paper he put his corrections on Weber's view between xiao and patria potestas by using Fei Xiaotong's concepts *chaxugeju* (差序格局) and *tuantugeju* (团体格局) into a larger framework (published in the first ever issue of *JCGCP*, Vol. 1, 2015).

All the major articles in this issue of *JCGCP* are related to Fei's From the Soil. It was published in Chinese in 1947 and the English version became available in 1992, but it is still relevant today because many important later generations of Chinese scholars' work has been built on it. Even Hamilton, translator of the book, had overlooked and did not fully appreciate some major points made by Fei Xiaotong in this book (Chang, Vol. 2, 2016, *JCGCP*). A more substantial work on *chaxugeju* by Stephan Feuchtwang is entitled 'Social egoism and individualism: Surprises and questions from a Western anthropologist of China – Reading Professor Fei Xiaotong's contrast between China and the West'. It was written 15 years after the English version *From the Soil* was published in *JCGCP*.

After the conference, Hamilton said that 'the conference made me aware about how much remains to be done to build a framework for the comparative study of China'.

Plenary sessions

There were three joint plenary sessions. Dr Athena Leoussi, Co-Director of European Studies, University of Reading, UK, chaired the first joint plenary session. Athar Hussain, Professor and Director of the Asia Research Centre at the London School of Economics and Political Science (LSE), UK, showed how examination selection in Chinese schools favoured the well-established who could afford to give their children extra coaching for a marking scheme that ranked students; this worked against the children of the poor and the internal migrant. Professor Sam Whimster, Editor of *Max Weber Studies*, gave a presentation on Weberian social economics, arguing that Weber's typology had to be unpacked and applied to case studies. Weber did this for Russia in 1906; we have to do this for China today. He suggested that Weber's key concepts, such as economic power, the legal power of disposition, appropriation, the forms of the division of labour, the forms of organization, the nation and its state and societalization, can be used to analyse Chinese economic development over the last decades in its own terms, and not judged against a normative model of what proper capitalism should be.

The second joint plenary session was chaired by Dr Peter Flügel, Reader in the Study of Religions at the Department of the Study of Religions, SOAS, UK. Bryna Goodman, Professor of History and Director of Asian Studies, University of Oregon, USA, gave a talk entitled 'Not a Club for Ethical Culture': Politics,

Law and Capitalism in Early Chinese Stock Exchanges Selection'. Using the 1921 Shanghai Stock Exchange bubble as a case study, she 'examine[d] a public controversy over these issues in the form of a public debate between individual businessmen and the Shanghai Chamber of Commerce over issues of economic development, freedom, and national sovereignty'. This mirrored the issues raised by Weber's own defence of the stock exchanges in the Kaiserreich in the 1890s. Afterwards, Karen Turner, Professor of History and Research Scholar, College of the Holy Cross at the Harvard Law School, EALS, USA, talked about 'Religion in the service of the state: A reassessment of Weber's view of the Chinese tradition'. She 'analyzed how excavated texts and revisionist views of transmitted texts reveal that a high level of formal rationality shaped the Chinese bureaucracy in the formative era of the imperial state', and demonstrated that the Chinese, much earlier than the West, developed an efficient blueprint, sanctioned by sacred texts, for managing the economy to serve the state'. In her remarks she observed that Confucian officials were mostly self-serving and not prepared to make sacrifices for fundamental change.

The third joint plenary session was chaired by Dr Carlos Frade, Senior Lecturer in Sociology, University of Salford and Chair of the Weber Studies Group, British Sociological Association (BSA), UK. This session combined two co-presenters. Judith Farquhar, Max Palevsky Professor of Anthropology, Department of Anthropology, University of Chicago, USA, presented a joint paper with Dr Lili Lai, Senior Lecturer, Medical Humanities Institute, Health Sciences Centre, Peking University, China, entitled 'National Medicines in China: Institutional Rationality and Healing Charisma'. From their empirical studies they found that 'being social, no regime can ever be purely 'rational'' because 'rational systems of medical information cannot, in the end, be external to medical art or 'healing charisma''. They sought to show that the rational and the non-rational have a co-constitutive relationship, not just in theory, but in historical practice in China'. This paper prompted many questions. Wolfgang Schluchter suggested that 'charisma' was a political concept that presupposed a personal relationship of leader and follower. Against this, the speakers referred to the magical- charismatic practices as described by Stephan Feuchtwang and WANG Mingming (*Grassroots Charisma: Four Local Leaders in China*, 2001). Both cases are examples of how Weber's 'Charisma' can be used as either a real term or in an 'imaginative way' by empirical studies in China. It seems there are two views on charisma. This illustrated a tendency in the conference for papers that sought a strict application to the Chinese context, and those that favoured a more imaginative use of Weberian concepts when faced with that same context?

The last joint plenary session was presented jointly by Professor Martin Albrow and Dr Xiaoying Zhang, Associate Professor and Head of Journalism Department, Vice Dean of School of English and International Studies, Beijing Foreign Studies University, China. The title is 'World beyond worlds: Max Weber,

China and the 'impartial spectator". This presentation was a kind of dialogue: Albrow explained how the ideas of 'world' have a central place in Max Weber's comparative studies of religion. Zhang introduced the Chinese view of the world (*shijie* 世界 and *tianxia* 天下). Other thinkers like John Dewey and Bertrand Russell, who had both lived and taught in China, thus also appreciated a different world from the West. They provided 'a shared account of a different world as a better alternative to discarding the idea of the world altogether'. As the author of *The Global Age*, Albrow turned his attention to 'world' as can be seen from the book series 'Chinese Thoughts for a New World Order -- A Series of Works in English by Chinese Scholars in Humanities and Social Sciences in Comparative Perspective' that he proposed. One of the books that was mentioned by Zhang in her talk is Global System by ZHAO Tingyang, which provides a Chinese perspective on the world-system.

Streams

The conference received nearly 50 paper submissions, including from joint authors. Apart from the plenary speeches and absent presenters of papers, the rest of the 30 papers were divided into 10 streams. They are: Re-reading Weber, On Rationalization in Weber, Confucianism and the Work Ethic, Law in China, Chinese Law in Comparative Perspective, Modernity and the Rise of China, Revisiting Weber on the Modern Chinese Economy, The Chinese State and Market Socialism, Chinese Enterprise, and Chinese Investment.

One interesting presentation was given by Professor Hong Qian, Director of the Institution for Global Symbiosis, China, entitled 'Weber's Capitalist Spirit and the Symbiosis Values'. Qian made a comparison between Karl Marx and Max Weber and believes the former used 'the critical weapon' and 'weapons of criticism' to examine capitalism; whereas the latter, Weber, discussed the internal relationship between the Protestant ethic and the spirit of capitalism. He then made a simple comparison between capitalist and socialist societies. He pointed out that 'capitalism encountered the limits of its self-development, antagonism and being treated negatively. As a result, when dealing with the relations between human beings and nature, humans and humans, and humans and themselves, the Protestant ethic and Weber's capitalism spirit encountered a great predicament,' whereas socialism in China appeared as 'state capitalism'.

He concluded that 'either socializing capitalism or capitalizing socialism' won't work. Based on his research and experience, the integration of ancient Oriental wisdom and contemporary biological symbiogenesis findings, Qian proposed a Chinese philosophical idea of 'symbiotic values' in the context of global ecology. It can be simply expressed as 'live and let live'. This idea has been acknowledged by the new generation of leaders in China. He suggested that it can be used as a principle to deal with the three major relationships in the world: man and nature, man and man, man and himself. In order to implement the 'symbiotic values' Qian proposed 'A decalogue by symbiosis' with 333 Chinese characters.

Q & A sessions

After each speech or presentation at either plenary or stream there are always Q & A sessions. They are equally important. It was the engagement of enthusiastic participants and the contributions of the speakers that made the conference so intellectually stimulating.

Closing session

The closing session started with a plenary panel entitled 'The Future of Capitalism'. It was organized and chaired by Professor Sam Whimster from the Global Policy Institute. Scott Lash, Professor of Sociology and Director of Centre for Cultural Studies at Goldsmiths, London, presented arguments from his new book *China Constructing Capitalism: Economic Life and Urban Change*, of which he is co-author. China is either regarded as falling short of Western business standards, e.g. property and contract law, or as hell-bent on its own version of neo-liberalism. Instead, Lash argued that, while neo-liberal economic life is individualized and disembedded, the China model is relational and situated. Also, its vast urban change has to be seen as a new form of 'local state capitalism'. Weber's instrumental rationality has to be reconceptualized as a new type of substantive rationality, an argument extending to ethics. The question to the panel then became whether China represents a divergent model of capitalism. Stephen Chan OBE, Professor of International Relations at SOAS and editor of *The Morality of China in Africa: The Middle Kingdom and the Dark Continent*, said that China placed great store in essential features of the global order: the Westphalian notion of the sovereignty of the state and its membership of the WTO. On matters of trade with Africa, Chinese officials applied an extremely hard-headed cost-benefit analysis of their objectives. Ann Lee, adjunct professor of economics and finance at NYU and author of *What the US Can Learn from China*, took a more convergent view, noting that China in its vigorous new initiatives did not suffer from the dysfunctionality of the current US. Martin Jacques, author of the controversial bestseller *When China Rules the World: The End of the Western World and the Birth of a New Global Order*, argued that on present trends China will soon become the dominant global power; for example, just how long do we expect the international ascendancy of the US dollar to last? It then becomes fanciful to suppose that China will abide by a model and rules established in the West. The recent financial crisis, still unresolved, shows both the weakness of the West and the need for new departures, and indeed, as Martin Albrow noted, are we not entering a universalized information age? The extensive and lively Q&A session recalled Max Weber's own stipulations on the rationality structures required for a successful modernity and that the dynamic of capitalism is marked by inherent tensions and dangers.

Finally, there was a small session for Closing Remarks. It was chaired by Mr Ernest Caldwell, Lecturer in Chinese Law, SOAS. Professor Stephen Chan, representing SOAS, thanked everybody whose participation in different ways made a great success of the conference. It reminded him of the first time when he read Max Weber in 1973, how much more understanding he gained and how helpful it had been with his research over the past four decades. Professor Xiangqun Chang, Director of CCPN Global and Research Associate of Centre for Chinese Studies, SOAS, University of London, UK, offered a long list of thanks to all the people who helped the conference directly, indirectly, physically, spiritually, intellectually, financially and so on. Xiangqun quoted a Chinese saying 'When we drink water from the well, we shall never forget the person who digs the well' (吃水不忘挖井人). Thanks went to: Professor Stephan Feuchtwang, founding Director of the China in Comparative Perspective Network (CCPN) and Editor-in-chief of the *Journal of China in Comparative Perspective* (*JCCP*) when they were both at LSE. Both CCPN Global's and JCCP's involvement in the Weber and China conference had benefited greatly from Stephan's input; Professor Elisabeth Croll, for arranging for Xiangqun Chang to be a Research Associate at SOAS's Centre of Chinese Studies in 2006, without which link we would not have been able to hold the conference at SOAS; Professor Martin Albrow, for proposing to co-host the Weber and China conference when he acted as the Principal Research Associate of CCPN at LSE (2011–13) and led the conference's Programme Committee which organized the conference successfully; SOAS's colleagues: Dr Tian Yuan Tan, the current Director of the Centre for Chinese Studies, Professor Michel Hockx, the Founding Director of the new SOAS China Institute, Professor Julia Strauss, Dr Hong Bo, Mr Ernest Caldwell, Professor Paul Webley, Professor Stephen Chan, Dr Andrea Janku, Dr Peter Flügel, Dr Carol Tan and Ms Jane Savory, the Manager of SOAS's Centres and Programme Office, for their support in different ways throughout the conference; other Conference Programme Committee members (apart from the above mentioned): Professor John Breuilly and Dr Kent Deng of LSE, who were a part of the inception of the conference, Professor Sam Whimster, Editor of *Max Weber Studies*, Dr Carlos Frade, Chair of the Weber Study Group, BSA, Dr Athena Leoussi, Co-director of the European Studies Programme of the University of Reading, for their intellectual input and emotional support; other organizers and sponsors: Professor Letian Zhang, of Fudan University, the Co-director of CCPN Global, Professor Daming Zhou of Sun Yat-sen University and the Guest Editor of JCGCP, and Mr Michael Sheringham, who runs the Arthur Probsthain Bookshop, for their organization and sponsorship of the conference, for their organizational and financial support; and all the volunteers: Mimi Ajibade, Anlan Chen, Wewei Chen, Mieke Houvenaghel, Farwa Sial, Ghayda Nawres from SOAS, and Xiaojing Sun from CCPN Global and Bristol University, for all their help during the conference. Xiangqun then expressed her gratitude with the Chinese phrase that 'When everybody adds fuel, the flames rise high' (众人拾柴火焰高) to all the conference participants including keynote speakers, panellists of the closing session, plenary speakers, all the panel speakers and participants for their enthusiasm and energy to make this conference so intellectually productive.

As a Chinese saying puts it, there is no feast under heaven (*tianxia*) that can last forever (天下没有不散的筵席), which means, of course, that all good things must come to an end. Conferences are indeed intellectual feasts. We hope, after you return home, the visible or invisible images, imaginative thinking or memories of the Weber and China conference and its spirit will stay with you…

* * *

Articles generated from the conference had been published in two academic journals: *Max Weber Studies* (Vol. 14, Nos. 1 and 2) and *JCGCP* (Vols. 3 and 4), as well as other journals.

The author and co-author contributed an article to each journal. They are 'Max Weber, China and the world: in search of transcultural communication' (*Journal of China in Global and Comparative Perspectives*, Vol. 2, 2016, pp. 32–53), and 'Weber and the concept of adaptation: the case of Confucian ethics (*Max Weber Studies* 14.2, 199–226.)'. Both articles have been included in *China's Role in a Shared Human Future: Towards Theory for Global Leadership*, Globalization of Chinese Social Sciences book series No. 4, London: Global Century Press.

The selected papers will be edited by the conference organizers jointly and published in English and Chinese in 2023 (see 8.2.3).

8.2.4 Contributing two books

8.2.4.1 *China's Role in a Shared Human Future: Towards Theory for Global Leadership*

One of the unique features of Global Century Press is its book series. Having proposed the book series 'Chinese Thoughts' or 'Chinese Concepts', the author also helped in the development of the 'Globalization of Chinese Social Sciences' book series. His book *China's Role in a Shared Human Future: Towards Theory for Global Leadership* is Vol. 4 of this series. This book series is edited by Xiangqun Chang (2018, Appendix for General Preface of the series), and published by Global Century Press from 2016.

8.2.4.2 *China and the Shared Human Future: Exploring Common Values and Goals*

The current book, *China and the Shared Human Future: Exploring Common Values and Goals* is Vol. 6 of the 'Globalization of Chinese Social Sciences', edited by Xiangqun Chang, published by Global Century Press from 2016.

8.2.5 Promoting a Chinese book on rural education to the world

8.2.5.1 Donating royalties to fund its English translation and published in overseas Chinese and English editions

The author donated his advance royalties of £7,500 for the publication of two books in English and Chinese editions in mainland China, as well his fees for writing a preface for a book (3.2), to fund the publication of the English edition *Levelling the Mountain-high Gap: Lessons from China's Leading Rural Educators*. It was edited by Visionary Education at the China Association for NGO Cooperation (CANGO) and published by China Economic Publishing House, 2020.

This will be the first NGO book from China to go abroad. Since its launch in 2008, Visionary Education has been efficiently run by volunteers. Visionary Education includes two flagship sections, 'Global Leadership Fellowship for Headmasters in Mountain Regions in China' and 'I SEE Initiative'. The former has attracted the participation of nearly 200 headmasters from all over China, and the latter has benefited tens of thousands of students. In 2020, China triumphed in its fight against poverty, and the relative poverty problem that had plagued the Chinese people for thousands of years has been historically brought to an end. At this key historical point, Visionary Education invited more than 50 outstanding headmasters from mountainous areas to share their experiences of school governance, management strategies, innovative practices, forward-looking thinking, educational challenges and corresponding countermeasures. It is expected to help more rural educators in China and provide a paradigm and reference for educational poverty alleviation in impoverished societies worldwide.

This book has been translated into English by DU Yichao. It has been included in Volume 4 of the 'Understanding China and the World Series', published by Global Century Press as Overseas Chinese and English editions in 2022.

8.2.5.2 Writing a preface for *Levelling the Mountain-high Gap: Lessons from China's Leading Rural Educators* (see 3.3)

8.3 Global China Dialogue series

CCPN Global, the predecessor of Global China Academy (GCA), held the 1st Global China Dialogue (GCD) in 2014, with the theme 'The experience of China's modernization from a comparative perspective' in London. The author not only added a global perspective to the dialogue and provided an introduction with six themes to form a series of annual forums but also contributed to all the GCDs as an organizer and speaker. He regards the GCDs as a platform to enable GCA to participate in global governance, thereby fulfilling our social mission.

8.3.1 Contributing to developing Global China Dialogue series

8.3.1.1 Introduction and themes of Global China Dialogue series

Martin Albrow and Xiangqun Chang

World in Turmoil

The road to peace and development is strewn with numerous risks and challenges. The international system and order are in constant flux, and there are profound shifts in the balance of power. All countries, whether developing or developed, are having to adapt to this ever-shifting international and social environment, while the process of modernization in some countries has been interrupted or has spilled out to create global turmoil as a result of the conflicts and contradictions brought about by cultural, religious and social transformation. At the same time, rapid developments in technology and society have had a profound impact on patterns of thinking, behaviour and interaction and on the moral principles of different countries and groups. They have also constantly challenged established ideas of good governance, including the functions of government in the globalization era and the pros and cons of the participation of non-government organizations. The changes and challenges are myriad: digital technology, mobile communications and the popularization of the internet, the coexistence of cultural homogenization and diversity, ethnic and religious conflicts, the collision between giant multinational corporations and national sovereignty, changes in social norms as a result of scientific innovations, the decisive influence of regional economies on national economic development, the constraints of climate change and the discovery and adoption of new energy source. Cultural diversity and transculturalism have become part of people's daily life.

Confronted with such challenges, national leaders devise development strategies that reflect both the status quo and their long-term goals. Business leaders and entrepreneurs also invest substantial resources in studying the impact of the changing international economy and financial order on the development of enterprises. Experts and scholars focus on the efficiency of global governance and cultural factors that have quietly exerted great influence, and explore how culture and ideology enhance global and social governance.

Such efforts and initiatives are moves in the same direction: towards reaching an in-depth understanding of the knowledge systems of the human community and the development of a 'global cultural sphere' beyond any single culture, state or nationality, under the condition of global governance. Thus, the theme of the development and governance of China, Europe and the world has gradually become one of the key research interests of scholars worldwide.

China in a Changing World

China and the Chinese people are making an important contribution to the world order and shaping a global society. What are the important global issues that concern China? What are the Chinese ways of thinking and doing things with respect to global issues? We wish to engage Western audiences in dialogues on topics that arise from these questions, including development, education, economics, migration, the family, the environment, public health, human security and global governance. For nearly three decades, China has been implementing a 'going out'(走出去) policy to encourage its enterprises to invest overseas. The policy embraces not only the economy but also finance, language, culture, sciences, technology, social sciences, publishing and the media, and under its provisions an international investment bank (亚投行) has been established. Through his visits to 55 countries, President Xi Jinping himself has promoted the Belt and Road (B&R 一带一路) regional development strategy and China's governance model (治国 理政). In his recent visit to the UK, he said, 'As our capabilities grow, we shall shoulder more responsibilities to the best of our ability and contribute China's wisdom and strength to the world's economic growth and global governance.' In his keynote speech at the United Nations Office in Geneva in January 2017, Xi Jinping clarified the basic principles of China's participation in global governance. They are: to stay committed to building a world of lasting peace through dialogue and consultation, build a world of common security and common prosperity through win–win cooperation, create an open and inclusive world through exchanges and mutual learning, and make our world clean and beautiful by pursuing green and low-carbon development.

The Global China Dialogue Series (GCDs)

In order to jointly achieve these goals and tackle the problems we all face, dialogue between China and the world is essential. The Global China Dialogue series (GCDs) focuses on these issues, aiming to enhance public understanding of current global affairs and common interests through public dialogue and discussion between Chinese and non-Chinese academics, experts, professionals and practitioners and interested laypeople, from interdisciplinary and comparative perspectives.

In addition to universities, research institutions and professional think tanks, the GCDs also work closely with Chinese and other governments, international organizations, media and publishing units to track global hot topics over the long term. It provides a high-end platform for the global public interests of China and Chinese participation in building a global society and a comprehensive governance of such a society.

The GCDs are an ongoing creative social activity, bringing Chinese and Western scholars and opinion leaders together to explore transculturality and cultural generativity, contributing to the development of a 'global cultural sphere' beyond any single culture, state or nationality.

The GCDs also develop the rules of 'civilized dialogue', encouraging both sides to listen to the other, understand cultural differences, respect local customs, accept different perspectives and acknowledge the common destiny of humanity. In particular, it explores new global governance, encompassing national governments, international organizations, multinational companies, NGOs and citizens, with a mission to build a harmonious, symbiosis-based human destiny community.

The past and future programmes of the series have been developed working within the framework of the UN's Sustainable Development Goals (SDGs), which accord with UNESCO's mission of defending peace and the conditions for building sustainable development world through creative intelligence, as follows:

2014 GCD I: The Experience of China's Modernization from a Comparative Perspective

2015 GCD II: Transculturality and New Global Governance
2016 GCD III: Sustainability and Global Governance for Climate Change
2017 GCD IV: The Belt and Road (B&R) – Transcultural Cooperation for Shared Goals
2018 GCD V: Governance for Global Justice
2019 GCD VI: Governance for World Peace
2020 GCD VII: Reforming Global Governance

8.3.1.2 General Preface to the Global China Dialogue Proceedings[9]

In this time of turmoil, when the world political order is so fragmented and the fate of our species is in question as never before, dialogue may seem a less than practical way to find solutions to global issues.

In fact, dialogue is the absolutely essential precondition for the cooperation that alone can produce the changes the world requires. No country on its own, however powerful, is up to the task and only the power that collective action generates can be adequate.

But even the most powerful actors have to be persuaded that there is a common task in which all must play their part. The rise of China means there is a new candidate for a global leadership role. For that reason, the rest of the world needs to appreciate what China can contribute, and China owes it to the world to explain how it will make a difference. That can only be done through dialogue.

The Global China Dialogues invite Chinese scholars, scientists, entrepreneurs and public figures to share their insights on global issues with their counterparts in other countries and to debate with them how best to go forward in partnership.

They will converge on problems of climate change, migration, poverty, inequality, justice, rights, trafficking, corruption and the whole range of issues that good governance of the globe must cover, and they will do so from multiple perspectives.

The participants in these dialogues will not come exclusively from one discipline, profession or sector. They will not be required to represent an official viewpoint of any kind, though they will be free to do so. What they will share is a commitment to working with colleagues from other cultures and the conviction that cultural divides can be bridged in a common cause.

Professor Xiangqun Chang shares that conviction and has demonstrated her commitment to the cause by initiating the Global China Dialogues and bringing together the voices of the contributors in this volume of proceedings. Her innovative energy and their fresh and uninhibited engagement combine to demonstrate to the world the rich potential of Chinese perspectives on global issues juxtaposed with those of their international counterparts.

---

[9] Editor's note: This General Preface was invited for the *Global China Dialogue Proceeding* series in 2015.

8.3.1.3 Co-editor of *Global China Dialogue Proceedings*, Vol. 7. It will be co-edited with Xiangqun Chang and SHEN Haimei[10]

8.3.2 Participating in the Global China Dialogue series

8.3.2.1 The Experience of China's Modernization from a Comparative Perspective – The 1st GCD I (Global China Dialogue I), 2014

The author began his dialogue with a global perspective. He said: 'I won't start with a global perspective; I'll start with a European one. Let's go back to the origin to the idea of the "modern", because that idea has undergone many changes in the course of the history of Europe, and it really takes off at a very crucial time in East–West relations, round about 1700, when there were these very enlightened Jesuit priests going to China and taking Western science there and bringing Chinese ethics back. And the great Western philosopher (thought of by Bertrand Russell as the greatest European philosopher) Gottfried Leibniz said; "We may be superior at this point in terms of science, but China is superior in terms of ethics." Now, what did "modern" mean for him and other people at that time? It meant rational, not given over to religious dogma, indeed, opposed to religious dogma and especially the application of science, the development of science and indeed, what Leibniz hoped for was, by examining the origins of the Chinese script he would find something which cohered with and was compatible with the new Binary Arithmetic which he'd developed. Leibniz not only invented the Calculus, which some of you know, he also invented Binary Arithmetic, which is the basis of modern computing; there's a genius for you, and he was hoping for China and Europe to find that common core of understanding for the world.

Now, I would suggest in there we have a lesson for today and the future of modernity, let's forget the bit that comes in between, all this stuff about capitalism – it wasn't about capitalism at all, the idea of the "modern" was the rational, the reasonable and human beings all finding their common humanity; now, that's the basis we need for global governance, the sense that every nation, every civilization can contribute, and of course, the contribution of China in the future is going to be, I would say, the most fundamental because in a sense, it is the newest when we're thinking about global governance, that is, it is the newest contributor because it is the only civilization which, for a very long time, was in the shadow of the West – no longer, no longer. So what we look forward to, and I'm sure this Forum looks forward to, is that joining together of civilizations in creating a general global humanity.'

---

[10] Editor's note: Although the author was not Chair of the Organising Committee, he was involved in heavily in organising the 7th Global China Dialogue. Afterwards he offered to be a co-editor of the *GCD Proceedings*, Vol. 7. Professor SHEN Haimei of Yunnan Minzu University offered encouragement and with her volunteer team not only translated all the speech notes before the GCD VII, but also transcribed and translated all the video records afterwards. It will be published in 2022.

At the end the author said: 'I just wanted to come back to the question of understanding other cultures and understanding other people. I think the outcome of all the academic research there's ever been suggests that we can never understand another person or another culture completely. The other remains mysterious, and the search for that can become self-defeating and frustrating, and that extends even into the area of learning from each other. The best things that we can learn from each other are when we do things together, and I think the prospects for global governance are best if we think in terms of projects for the future, reforming what we've got, creating better things and collaborating with each other in those things, and not to assume that collaboration with each other means we understand each other perfectly, because that's not the case, you can collaborate very effectively with other people even when you don't understand them and I think that is a very crucial thing to recall. Remember, the scenes of the greatest World Wars have been hitherto between people who understood each other extremely well! The interaction between Germany and Britain before 1914 was intense, huge cultural exchanges going on. That didn't prevent war. So collaboration and cooperation is something different, from trying to understand the other completely, and I think that's something in my own personal experience and my academic work, I've come to that conclusion, I work in a field which is called interpretative sociology, the sociology of understanding, and this has been a great project within the academic study of sociology. I think the main thing you learn from that is that you don't ever understand completely, just as you never understand another language completely and you don't even understand your own language completely, so don't let's go down the road of thinking there is that perfect understanding, let's just work together instead.'

8.3.2.2 Transculturality and New Global Governance – The GCD II, 2015

At the opening session the author made the following remarks:

'It's a great pleasure. Many thanks to Counsellor Xiang Xiaowei and to the rest of the panel. It's a very happy circumstance for me because on this panel I represent the British Sociological Association, which is one of the hosts for this meeting, one of the honorary hosts. We in the Association would like to congratulate Professor Xiangqun Chang for organizing this conference, and for making it a part of the Anglo–Chinese Year of Culture, which has been a very active ongoing series of events. Even today, a very high-level Chinese delegation is meeting with our minister, competing obviously with this event, but there are so many things going on simultaneously. Let me say just a little bit, though, about sociology, in this context, because one of the things sociology tries to do is to bring people together. Believe it or not, sociology is about the social, and one of the great pleasures of my career has been regular contact with Chinese colleagues since the 1980s.

That's why it's a particular pleasure also to welcome Professor Bing Zheng here, who is Vice-President of the Chinese Sociological Association, so welcome from our side, and I can say also that I knew your previous President of the Chinese Sociological Association rather well, because I was his host back in the 1980s, when he came to Britain and he was on a fact-finding tour. He was a specialist in rural sociology, and he is an example of possible cross-cultural misunderstanding. Transculturality deals with misunderstanding and understanding. When he came, he said he wanted to meet "Welsh peasants", and those who know British history will know that the term "peasant" went out of British discourse around the 16th or 17th century. We didn't have peasants after that. He wanted to meet a Welsh peasant. Well, the nearest I could get to that was to take him to a farm in mid-Wales, to a sheep farmer who on his own looked after about 200 sheep, but my guest, Professor Lu, was mystified with the fact that the sheep farmer had a big barn, and in the big barn he had a collection of old Alfa Romeo cars. This sheep farmer collected cars.

Now, you can get the same misunderstanding in reverse. Later in the 1980s, I was a guest of the state family planning commission of China, because at the time I was director of a population centre, and your country used to send us Chinese officials to have training, a Master's programme in population policies. This was back in the 1980s; these exchanges had been going on for a long time and I had the privilege of being taken to a Chinese village in order to observe family planning as it was on the ground, and I was taken, with my interpreter, who had been my student in Cardiff, where I was teaching at the time, into the house of a large family. I wanted to conduct an interview and there were eight or nine people to interview; I thought, I want to interview the most senior woman in the family. I wanted to interview her on my own, I said. Discussion. Talking to each other. The translator turning to me and saying, "Is that really what you want?" And he turned back to them and he told them, and they all started to roar with laughter. I don't know what his interpretation was, but anyway, I said, "Why are they all laughing?", and he said, "They are all laughing at Western individualism." [laughter] I wanted to interview somebody on my own, and why should I want to do that? – because the opinion in the household would be the same; it wouldn't matter whom I had an interview with. That was the thing. So the misunderstandings go both ways. This conference is about trying to bridge those understandings, and, with the development of new concepts of transculturality, we owe so much to Professor Yu Shuo, who is here and I am sure we should have an extremely instructive programme. So let me repeat: welcome everybody, and I trust we should have a very, very vigorous discussion, not just here but also during coffee and lunch. Thank you very much."

Speech at Panel I Introducing 'transculturality' and new global governance[11]

'Following the horror of the terrorist attacks in Paris, the unanimous resolution 2249 of the United Nations Security Council on 19 November 2015, call-

[11] This speech is included as Chapter 9 with the title 'Can there be a public philosophy for global governance' in *China's Role in a Shared Human Future*, by Martin Albrow, London: Global Century Press, 2018, pp, 77–80 [Chinese edition: (英)马丁・阿尔布劳：《中国在人类命运共同体中的角色——走向全球领导力理论》，北京：商务印书馆，2020年；同名海外中文版，伦敦：环球世纪出版社，2021年].

ing upon member states "to redouble and coordinate their efforts to prevent and suppress terrorist acts committed by ISIL in the world", reminds us what global governance is really about. It concerns the creation of unity and order among the diversity of nations.

Governance and diversity are intimately connected. The earliest constitutional treatise in the English language was written in the 15th century by the king's Chief Justice, Sir John Fortescue. Under the title it acquired a little later, The Governance of England, on its very first page it cites St Thomas Aquinas and his account of diversity, using that very word, and it sounds historical and contemporary, from lands as different as Scotland, Flanders and, strikingly to us, Egypt and even Libya.

That diversity was the source for a stock of ideas about good governance applied in Fortescue's own country. We at this conference are concerned with the way that governance ideas hold all countries together. Just add the word "global".

Following the great American writer Walter Lippmann, I am going to call those ideas "public philosophy". What he wrote in 1954 is as relevant today as it was then. In the face of what he quotes as "a plurality of incompatible faiths", he lays claim to "a body of positive principles and precepts which a good citizen cannot deny or ignore". For us, just insert "global" before "citizen".

What Professor Yu has invited us to do is to review these ideas through the lens of culture or, more specifically, transculturality. I think this is a particularly good way of bringing into the open the difficulties of finding principles bridging incompatible fates, especially as the focus on culture confronts us with a particular modern antithesis of culture versus principle. For we are accustomed to associate culture with difference, imagination, innovation indeed with the ever potent source of diversity.

So when this conference links culture and governance, we may feel acute discomfort Samuel Huntington's *The Clash of Civilizations* prompted us to regard culture as the challenge to any kind of ordering of the globe. Social critics have taught us to regard another kind of clash between generations as "counterculture", social deviance as subculture and postmodernism as the cultural subversion of any established culture. Now, as we move to "trans"-culture, we can sense all the ambiguity and confusion contained in that prefix "trans-", now central to the new discourse of fluid gender and sexuality.

It was not always so. In the mid-19th century, the British civil servant Matthew Arnold wrote a celebrated attack on the progressive ideas of his time. He called it *Culture and Anarchy*. Culture for him meant the realization of the highest values and these were to be located in the citizen's aspiration to the order which would realize these, namely the state, "the organ of our collective best self". Arnold claimed not to have a philosophy but in basing order in the citizen's culture he was grounding ideas in the people's conscience.

I make no apologies for bringing old and even ancient texts to bear on global governance, for they illustrate an essential point for me, namely that governance is an abiding, never-ending issue for human civilization. It is best considered as the active production of the kind of order in society that allows people to live secure, fulfilling and creative lives, a cultural life. It has historically been created in many societies, in different periods with very distinct cultures. It is fundamentally a kind of decentred order in much the same way as a natural language is ordered and has rules, but arises out of conversations between innumerable multiple partners. Any central control that is exercised is very much after the event.

If only for the reason that it contributes indirectly or directly to this theme, we should welcome the fact that President Xi Jinping's speeches have been assembled under the title *The Governance of China* (2016). In citing the West's ancient texts, I'm only imitating him. Xi quotes the ancient Chinese classics thus:

"The people are the foundation of the state"; "Everyone is responsible for his country's rise and fall"; "Govern the country with virtue and educate the people with culture". These are, he writes, "the core socialist values" and, I quote him again, "they carry forward the fine traditional Chinese culture, draw on the best of world civilization and reflect the spirit of the times."

Dr Xi – in this context let us give him his correct academic title – Dr Xi is advancing his own sophisticated sociological understanding and effectively carrying forward the significant contribution to steering Chinese society and economy that the doyen of Chinese sociology, Fei Xiaotong, pioneered in the Chinese Academy of Social Sciences under Deng Xiaoping.

Xi's example has particular relevance to transculturality and new global governance. He is not simply offering an alternative governance model. But in the spirit of his book we can draw on "the best of world civilizations and reflect the spirit of the times". We can address the potential claim of values, responsibility, principles, rights, etc., to universality, but acknowledge their very interpretation in different countries.

Ideas which occupy a strategic organizing position within the total vocabulary of public order in a society the sociologist Daniel Bell's called "axial principles". "Harmony" has long been central to Chinese reflection on human relations with each other and with nature. The American dream of aspiration and self-improvement contributed to the rise of the United States and its 20th-century domination of the global economy. Xi both borrows and adapts that when he promotes a distinct Chinese dream.

Could any one national axial principle serve in that position for global society? My own gut feeling is that it's unlikely. The Chinese emphasis on harmony arose in the context of a rural society, where the well-being of the population was intimately connected with the intelligent adaptation of and to the natural world. The American emphasis on individual aspiration to rise in and contribute to society was the product of a history of migrants finding a new world and creating a new society. When these two cultures encounter each other, misunderstanding as much as understanding arises when the emphasis is placed on distinctive historical experience.

At the beginning of the 18th century, Leibniz, the great German philosopher, sought to solve this dilemma by seeking a universal language, finding affinities between the Yijing and the binary arithmetic he invented. His astonishing perception is, to this day, I believe, better appreciated in China than in the West. Since then, however, both East and West are coming together in a more sensitive appreciation of the limits of cross-cultural understanding.

Professor Yu's concept of transcultural generativity captures the multiple possible outcomes of encounters between cultures, multiculturalism, adaptation and hybridity, to name a few current fashionable terms. What she advances is, as I understand it, the possibility of a broader cultural sphere that transcends all the others, and one image they each share.

I suggest that this sphere arises out of cultural encounters engaged in common tasks, practical issues that call for cooperation, as in Resolution 2249; as in the agreement on the Millennium Development Goals and the coming Sustainable Development Agenda; as in, we hope, the coming agreement in Paris on combating the effects of climate change.

It is these very practical issues in relations between cultures that inspired the American philosophical tradition of pragmatism which its most celebrated representative, John Dewey, detected in the 1920s in Chinese Daoist thought. The processes involved in cultural encounters are resolved in practice, not in theory, yet out of those practices arise new insights. This is transcultural generativity. It is a process I have called pragmatic universalism, not the universal acceptance of an idea, but the universality of the belief that others seek universality. We are all looking for it together. It's the basis of tolerance, dialogue, of communicative rationality, in Jürgen Habermas's terms.

When we recognize that global governance is the ordering of global society, then we need to understand that it is conducted through the continual reappraisal of the concepts that inform that order. The global dialogue is one where public philosophy is embedded, where the ideas of justice, harmony, diversity, rights and respect regulate cooperation for sustainability, well-being, truth and reconciliation.

These are only a small sift from a harvest of concepts that fill the discourse of leaders in all walks of life. Obama, Xi, Putin, Merkel, Cameron, Hollande all gather at leaders' meetings, as Colin Bradford has observed so closely, to speak a language that their officials develop as a continuous narrative between nations. But it is informed by concepts that are shared now throughout global civil society, from the community leader to the cyber activist. This is the public philosophy of our time, belonging to all, commanded by none. Thank you very much.'

8.3.2.3 Sustainability and Global Governance for Climate Change – The GCD III, 2016

At the GCD III the author organized the panel IV Delivering the UN's Sustainable Development Goals and acted as chair and discussant of the panel. He began, 'It's a huge pleasure for me to be able to chair this panel, called Delivering the UN's Sustainable Development Goals. It's a particular pleasure because I know all the panellists, in fact, they are all friends of mine. I think you'll allow me [to] say a little something about each one of them, which is not actually in the programme. You didn't know I was going to say any of these things, did you? Geoffrey, for instance, believe it or not, for his ground-breaking book published in 2013, *Alter-Globalization: Becoming Actors in the Global Age* (Polity, 2010), interviewed between five and six hundred young activists. He tells me he attended no fewer than 10 World Social Forums. Those of you who know World Social Forums will realize what an achievement that was. He spent much of his time in Mexico; although, of course, his first language is French, he speaks English and Spanish. Now and again, he lives very close to the Dutch border in Belgium, I think now and again he speaks a little bit of Walloon, and also German. This is Geoffrey, who published his book in 2013.

Then, after we shall have Joy Zhang, I have known Joy not quite so long as Geoffrey, who I think introduced me to her. She's a lecturer at the University of Kent, but what she's so modest about, doesn't tell you at all, and I will reveal now, [is that] she's a qualified medical doctor from the University of Peking. It's very good to have a doctor in the house, you'll all agree. She also published a very fine book in 2013, called *Green Politics in China: Environmental Governance and State-Society Relations*.

And finally, in this all-star cast, we have Olaf Corry. Olaf is both Danish and British and has published fundamental work on global governance, in particular his notion of governance objects He is establishing a conceptual framework that is distinct from governance studies, and it's called *Constructing a Global Polity: Theory, Discourse and Governance*, also published in 2013. So, each of them published a great book in the year 2013. The final, private thing about him that I am going to reveal, and he doesn't know I am going to reveal, is that he was the chief speech writer for the Danish opposition leader, I think in 2009, and so successful was he that she became the prime minister after he finished his job of writing her speeches. So, this is our panel. Geoffrey will begin with his talk "New Meanings of Global. How Environmental Movements and Challenges Have Shaped the 'Global' in the Early 21st Century".'

The speakers and their presentations were:

- The new meaning of the global. how environmental movements and challenges have shapes the 'global' in the early 21st century, Professor Geoffrey Pleyers, FNRS-University of Louvain, Director of Global College, University of Louvain, Belgium
- Social uptake on the notion of sustainability in China, Dr Joy Zhang, Senior Lecturer in Sociology, School of Social Policy, Sociology and Social Research, University of Kent, UK
- Societal multiplicity in the global polity: conditions for achieving Sustainable Development Goals, Professor Olaf Corry, Department of Political Science, University of Copenhagen, Denmark

8.3.2.4 The Belt and Road (B&R) – Transcultural Cooperation for Shared Goals – The GCD IV, 2017

Harmonizing Goals and Values: The challenge for the Belt and Road[12]

'As one of the organizing committee of this, the 4th Global China Dialogue, may I extend the warmest welcome to our distinguished visitors from the rest of the world and, in particular, from the People's Republic of China.

You have joined us at the midpoint of our series of seven Dialogues. Some of you have already taken part in our debates and demonstrated that your country is a key contributor to the developing awareness of the need for a new global order.

You will notice from our programme that the Dialogues began with China considered in a comparative perspective. They will conclude in three years' time with the reform of global governance.

These are the departure and destination points in our journey over seven years and I would argue that, so far, we have kept pace, if somewhat breathlessly, with the hectic rate of changes in the world around us. We hope we make our own small contribution to ensuring that those changes can be positive.

In 2014 we were reflecting the Western recognition that China's opening-up policy signalled a distinctive and innovative approach to development. Last year we focused on one of the major demands for cooperation across boundaries, namely combating climate change. This year we generalize our concerns to all goals.

We engage in our dialogue at a time when there is a reassertion of nation-state sovereignty within the global order. Some detect in that a dismantling of the multilateral systems that have been built so laboriously over the decades since 1945. It is irresponsible to dismiss those fears as groundless.

Yet, by contrast, this very event here in London is built on something other than national sovereignty. We share a belief in the constructive potential of dialogue, we are concerned to contribute to a global order that extends to all humankind. We recognize dangers that confront us all.

These common understandings exist, even though we may be citizens of countries with leaders who proclaim their own country comes first. What we enjoy here, therefore, is what we have emphasized in our previous dialogues, and will do so again in this one, a transcultural experience. With our feet on our countries' earth we lift our eyes to a heaven we all hope to share.

We are then halfway on a journey that takes us towards a reshaped global order, with a developing understanding that sovereign countries will each be able to make their distinctive contribution to it. In the case of China it has become such a powerful agency it can exercise a decisive influence on the emerging shape of that order.

Belt and Road, announced by President Xi Jinping only four years ago, is already a unique contribution, referencing in its name the historic ties between

[12] The speeches here are included in Chapter 3 in *China's Role in a Shared Human Future*, by Martin Albrow, London: Global Century Press, 2018, pp. 32–36.

China, East and West, avoiding in that way the summary, soulless anagrams that dominate the language of global governance.

This is not to say China is not also an experienced participant user of the multilateral governance alphabet, in APEC, ASEAN, BRICS, G20, IAEA, IMF, UN and UNESCO and so on. But none of these can offer the poetic resonance and cross-cultural backstory of Belt and Road. This evokes a family history, the family of nations. Of course China also takes initiatives that extend the multilateral model, for instance by founding the Asian Infrastructure Investment Bank. The financial backing of the AIIB provides a vital function for Belt and Road projects.

But those projects are much more than the financial guarantees that support them. They have an engagement in the culture of the partner countries that no amount of financial leveraging can match.

When China agrees with Kazakhstan to begin the Bright Road Initiative, or with Vietnam on the One Economic Circle, or with the UK to support the Northern Powerhouse, technology and infrastructure are core components. But in each case the demand for these initiatives arises also out of the felt needs of the people in their local environments with their distinct cultural heritages.

Sea trade between France and China began in 1698 with the sailing of the ship Amphitrite from La Rochelle to Canton. This September, the Committee for Sailing in La Rochelle joined with the International Yacht Club in Dalian to establish there a French-style school of sailing. Connections made through trade and the opportunities for contact it brings link similar lifestyles from cultures far distant from one another in a mutual understanding of what they each value.

President Xi opened the Belt and Road Forum for International Cooperation in Beijing on 14 May with a keynote speech that included five principles that should steer the Belt and Road Initiative to greater success. They asked for cooperation along five roads: to peace; to prosperity; to opening up; of innovation; connecting different civilizations.

He elaborated the fifth of these, connecting different civilizations, in the following way: 'exchange will replace estrangement, mutual learning will replace clashes, and coexistence will replace a sense of superiority. This will boost mutual understanding, mutual respect and trust among different countries.'

Let us consider the very basic grounding of these connections. In the beginning there is a shared project to build a road, or a railway, or a port. There is clear goal with a specific understood benefit. Our understanding of why others build roads is as intuitive and immediate as our understanding of why birds build nests. Infrastructure is only the forbidding term we use for something as basic as providing the conditions for safeguarding the long-term necessities of social life.

Thus, it is not just for economic reasons that the response of all major economies in recent years since the financial crisis of 2008 has been to invest in infrastructure. Within a country it is possible to achieve political consensus around the renewal of basic requirements for transport and travel. It is a public good delivering benefits to all social classes, even if under capitalism they are distributed as profit for some and wages for others.

But the President of the People's Republic of China is challenging us to see Belt and Road not just as a sharing of technologies for common goals but as a journey towards greater understanding between cultures. Infrastructure across boundaries, crossing seas, linking far distant lands has the potential to create that wider sense of community of a shared future that he has often held up to us as the direction in which we must all travel.

I have little doubt that it is by taking steps along this road that people can begin to tackle the problems that are genuinely global in their reach. The experience of shared technology for common goals is a good preparation for cooperating in sustainable development. We can hope too that it may aid in the spread of nuclear technologies for peaceful use.

This is what President Xi calls "policy connectivity". We can add that it is genuinely public policy for the global age quite distinct from what is so often regarded as its hallmark, namely globalization.

For me it is quite significant that he confines the use of that term to 'economic globalization', by which we can refer to all those processes that create a single market and promote the worldwide spread of production methods and consumption of goods.

Belt and Road is something else. It is the extension of connectivity that encourages the local culture to find its common features with others and to contribute its distinctive qualities to shaping common ventures. This is what he calls "people-to-people connectivity".

Of course, the advocacy of Belt and Road is also the outstanding example of China "going global". Moreover the scope and ambition of the ideas that underpin it make it the most comprehensive initiative for shaping the future global order since the international agreement on the Sustainable Development Goals.

What distinguishes Belt and Road from the SDGs is that it emphasizes processes rather than targets, learning rather than repetition, and innovation rather than standardization. Every country can contribute its own way of going global once it opens up as China has done. The SDGs are still an essential feature of the multilateral system, but Belt and Road is their counterpart contribution to the global order of the family of nations.

This is why I am not as dispirited as so many are by the current worldwide

"my country first" movement. It can also lead to more intensive engagement with global issues, even, at its most paradoxical, to competitive striving to contribute most to their solution. It does not deny cooperation (the "art of the deal"!) or friendship with other countries.

But the most powerful feature of Belt and Road compared with current contributions to shaping the world order is its consistent determination to bring relevant theoretical ideas into close alignment with the practical problems facing humankind.

It pins the abstract vocabulary of culture, exchange, cooperation, connectivity, coexistence and interdependence to the map of our world today or, as Xi describes it, "in this increasingly multipolar, economically globalized, digitized and culturally diversified world".

I can think of no better way to describe the current state of the world with no more than seven descriptors! (Perhaps that could spark a competition for this Dialogue: "Find seven words to describe our human condition at this time.")

At the same time let us not underestimate the challenge that Belt and Road is taking up. Even as it applauds cultural diversity and aims to find common cause in joint projects, it is facing values that many see as imperilled and announce they will defend "to the death".

One only has to think of one of the most contested areas in development policies, population planning. India and China have long looked over one another's shoulders at their respective efforts. China's one-child family policy began in 1979 and was largely effective until it was recently replaced with a two-child policy.

By contrast, India has struggled since the 1950s with a variety of policies in different states, with very different reactions, even trying compulsory sterilization in the mid-1970s, contributing to a national emergency and the attempted assassination of Sanjay Gandhi, the Prime Minister's son who was held largely responsible for the population policies of the time.

These are not insurmountable problems. I recall touring Bangladesh's population programme in the 1980s and finding close cooperation between religious Imams, the state and women's cooperatives. I cherish still my photograph of a Centre for Conjugal Beatitude where family planning knowledge was available to local men and women.

Values are rooted in the historic experience of peoples, shape their identity, daily lives and plans. They differ from the mundane, short-lived practicality of goals. Even when there are common values between nations they can be divisive. Sovereignty is the most obvious example.

For these reasons, in the coming Global Dialogues we will be addressing the issues that arise when shared values result in conflict, how we can transcend competing ideas of justice, overcome the inequalities that endanger peace and reform the current system of global governance.

With these objectives in mind, I believe that One Belt One Road is showing the world a pre-eminently practical way forward with the greatest chance of significant progress in achieving them at the present time. Let us therefore enjoy this day as one where we share in its hopeful endeavour.'

8.3.2.5 Governance for Global Justice – The GCD V, 2018

Closing Remarks

'We have enjoyed today an amazing coverage of the issues involved in viewing justice globally! What extraordinary stimulus there has been for reflection and creativity over the coming year, for us all, looking forward to GCD VI.

Next year we will develop many of the insights we have gleaned from today's discussions. That is entirely natural and to be expected, since justice is a foundation for the governance of peace, the theme of GCD VI. That Dialogue in turn will prepare for the culmination of this whole series of dialogues, the reform of global governance. This indeed has been our purpose from the very beginning of the Dialogues, five years ago.

Justice is at the heart of human society, of its survival and sustainability. It is on an equal level with cooperation, our Dialogue theme last year, as a societal universal, foundational for social relationships.

That was apparent in so many of the contributions presented today and in the discussions that have followed. At the same time we have never been able to avoid the recurring issue that the universality of justice, its presence in every society is accompanied by an equally diverse view of what it is.

That has not prevented us from engaging in fruitful debate. We allow for each other's interpretations in a spirit of respect and tolerance, without necessarily accepting their arguments, and certainly without believing they can be applied to our own societies.

The way China interprets *yi* depends on Chinese history, culture and contemporary issues. Similarly the West's idea of justice has special features, and those in turn are developed differently between traditions of Anglo-Saxon common law and the Roman law based traditions of continental Europe. They also all echo the ancient Greek image of the goddess of justice, Dike, bearing the balance or scales, which find the true weight to give to competing claims. That idea of balance is also familiar in Chinese culture.

Yi and justice, justice, *Gerechtigkeit* share a sense of finding the balance between people in a way that conforms to basic values. Underlying these differences in emphasis there is a basic thrust towards finding what is right and what can overcome conflicts between peoples.

There is one big difference however that should be uppermost in all considerations of global governance, namely the emphasis in modern Western history on law, as a system of rules enforced by authority. Very often they are equated. The history of this is long and complex.

A crucial moment came at the beginning of the modern nation–state system when Thomas Hobbes, after allowing for natural justice predating any national laws, went on to say that no law coming from a sovereign power could be unjust. The death sentence on natural justice was then later declared by Jeremy Bentham when he called natural law nonsense on stilts.

But when we come to big issues of justice that concern us all today, unwillingness to atone for past crimes against humanity, the unfair exploitation of natural resources, the way the very rich escape national taxation, the inhuman treatment of refugees, these are not addressed by regular legal systems. And if law is to tackle them it has to be established on the basis of a prior, sometimes unacknowledged, agreement on justice.

In Confucian thinking *yi* and *li* are intertwined and, operating together, their equivalent in the West is much more the processes associated with peace and reconciliation or with arbitration than with law courts and litigation, which in Chinese are best rendered by *fa*.

Whether we begin with *fa*, *li*, and *yi* or law, equity and justice, we are dealing with the constructs that civilizations develop to meet universal features of the human condition. Different civilizations never fully reconcile their differences, and there are good reasons for this that cannot detain us here, but in a spirit of recognizing them, with respect and tolerance, we approach an outlook of pragmatic universalism that can inspire the reform of global governance.

In that spirit, and in all the optimism we can gather, let us look forward to GCD VI.

Finally that "spirit" and "optimism": they alone are not enough. Also indispensable are the extraordinary reserves of knowledge, energy, care and attention to detail that Professor Xiangqun Chang has devoted to making the Global China Dialogues a reality every year. A formal thanks is not enough, so let us conclude by showing our appreciation in a resounding way.'

8.3.2.6 Governance for World Peace – The GCD VI, 2019

The author acted as chair of the Organizing Committee and adviser to the GCD VI. The theme of the Dialogue was Governance for World Peace. It highlighted crucial settings for the international cooperation that is required for reform to take place, based on the resolution of long-standing conflicts.

Keeping to the format of previous GCDs, GCD VI had four panel sessions in one day, allowing short presentations and ample time for Q & A. Each session had a balanced panel of one or two Chinese and two or three participants from the rest of the world. We also planned two pre-Dialogue and two post-Dialogue symposiums, all on the same theme of 'Globalization of Chinese social sciences.'

There were four themes or panels. They are:

- Mediation and peace-making in civil conflicts
- Belt and Road and tension reduction between countries and cultures
- China's role in multilateral peacekeeping
- Civilizational values and the promotion of peace

Each presentation or discussion clearly involved a very different scenario, and each conformed to the Chinese 'red line': no interference in the internal affairs of another country. However, any reform of global governance inevitably calls for understanding of the internal affairs of other countries. This conundrum was at the heart of the debates in the GCDs.

The theme of the seventh GCD (GCD VII) was Reforming Global Governance. It would be co-organized with the Institute of Global Common Development, Tsinghua University, and would take place in Beijing in October 2020.[13]

The author also acted as chair at both the Opening and Closing sessions.

[13] Due to COVID-19 the GCD VII had been postponed to 2021 and held in London (see 8.3.2.7).

8.3.2.7 Reforming Global Governance – The GCD VII, 2021

China's Place in Tomorrow's World[14]

'Reforming global governance is our theme today. But you will notice from the programme of this 7th Global China Dialogue that reforming institutions is only one quarter of our concern. This is because we consider governance to be more than institutions. It is the creation and maintenance of the kind of order in society that allows people to shape their own lives and realize their dreams.

The United Nations institutions, then, and all the international and multilateral agreements that span the globe, are not the only source of global governance. It rests, as does the order of any society, on the shared beliefs and practices of its people, in this case the peoples of the world, taken in their entirety. For this reason the example of China's governance becomes ever more important.

The contribution that China will make to the world of tomorrow arises from its own unique form of governance with roots in millennia of history. Looking at China, wondering at its rise in the last 50 years, the West speculates endlessly on the causes of this success.

Could it be that it has stolen Western ideas? Or, more positively, could the residues of age-old philosophies supply the secret ingredient? Could it even be that Chinese calligraphy, far from being an antique hangover, actually empowers national culture?

Yet, few in the West, apart from committed Marxists, will suggest that Chinese success may also have something to do with the Party, the Communist Party of the People's Republic of China. After all, how can that be compatible with the long history? Often there is some kind of tacit agreement not to mention the Party. As if it would go away if we ignore it for long enough!

Occasionally a reckless voice is heard, such as Trump's Mike Pompeo, declaring the Party to be the most dangerous entity in the world today. Otherwise it is thought of as a recent anomaly, detached from China's past, and, as such, sure to pass away soon. Nothing could be further from the reality.

Let us dispose first of the idea that it is a novel quirk of the present day. The Party has celebrated its centenary this year. It predates the United Nations, saw the rise and fall of the Soviet Union, observed the end of the British Empire, and witnessed the passing of the American century.

But the Communist Party of China is not just old, relative to much of the rest of the world. I am going to argue it has developed through building on the inherent features of a unique civilization, long predating what we call the West.

China has always been different. It has a history of predominantly centralized administration over many centuries. It grafted education on to social status.

[14] Keynote speech at the 7th Global China Dialogue, December 10, 2021 at the British Academy. An abridged version entitled 'Nation shows how to put moral principles into action', was published in *China Daily Global* 14/12/2021. See: https://www.chinadaily.com.cn/a/202112/14/WS61b7f814a310cdd39bc7b2af.html.

Its governance system perpetuated the life-long study and practice of traditional culture on the part of its personnel and all who aspired to office.

Although associated with the name of Confucius, that culture is rooted in a moral code governing family life and social relations that has permeated Chinese society since time immemorial. The Director of the Kings College London Lau China Institute, Kerry Brown has written convincingly of how the Party struggles to come to terms with China's past, and how, in those very efforts, it reproduces abiding features of China's social order.

It was President Xi, in his speech of May 31, who gave this order its most recent expression when he said the thoughts and spirit behind the China story convey a message of home, harmony, health and hope.

Such is the special emphasis in Chinese culture on the embodiment of rules in relationships, the fusion of moral principles with social interaction, that our very own Global China Academy President, Xiangqun Chang, has suggested that only a neologism in English, "recipropriety", could begin to convey this unique cultural character of Chinese social relations.

A shared moral code for everyday life, inspiring society's governance at every level, has not prevailed in the West since the Roman Catholic Church supplied it for mediaeval rulers. In China the failed experiment of the republican system a century ago was the only brief interruption in its traditional fusion of morality with governance.

The Party's watchword, "Socialism with Chinese characteristics", is as easily understood in China as a message of continuity as it is misunderstood in the West as a break with the past. With more than 90 million members, the Party features at every level of social organization, from the village or the factory up to the highest levels of government, as the contemporary guardian of Chinese values and moral order.

* * *

China boasts a versatile governance system that responds to the changes of the present. Matching principles with pragmatism, it rivals the fabled frameworks of the West, summed up widely as "liberal" or "representative democracy".

If one mistakenly treats China's present system as a momentary anomaly, then the converse and equivalent mistake is to regard the Western order as the long standing and abiding expression of universal values.

Certainly, the slogan of liberty, equality and fraternity is over 200 years old and has worldwide appeal to this day. But it hardly produces stability. France is now into its 5th Republic. Of course the United States boasts of its Declaration of Independence and its commitment to democracy. But that didn't prevent a savage civil war and a persisting culture of discrimination against the descendants of the revolutionary leaders' slaves.

As for attempts to install Western inspired democratic institutions in other countries, the example of the Weimar Republic in Germany after the First World War, should have been sufficient warning of the hubris lying in wait for victorious powers. Within fifteen years the democratically elected German leader set in train the most murderous regime of modern times.

Populism is a perennial danger in democracies and was one reason why in ancient Greece, often regarded in the West as the fountain-head of democratic ideas, its philosophers distrusted pure democracy. They recognized the ever-present risk democracy posed to any social order that enabled people to live their lives and follow their dreams with a sense of security.

There should be a much more general awareness than there is that the United States was on the brink of a populist coup only a year ago. Probably only the courage of its Vice-President Mike Pence, who defended the rights of Congress and refused to challenge the result of the Presidential election of 2020, prevented a disaster.

Institutional frameworks for governance cannot guarantee there will be no risk of the mass mobilization that populists inspire. Social order can be undermined by a felt loss of security, declining standards of living, and a general sense that established institutions only protect corrupt officials who exploit ordinary people. Contemporary economic and technological transformations only exacerbate that sense of the fragility of social and political order in our time.

Every social and political order depends fundamentally on a widespread belief in its legitimacy if it is to survive, but additionally it must provide the conditions for its citizens to enjoy the material and spiritual wellbeing they seek in their personal lives. In our time the forces of capital and technology constantly transform those conditions.

* * *

The Communist Party of China has assumed the responsibility to supervise and control those forces that in the West spawn the multiple competing and conflicting groups of civil society. In this respect the regime, where the Party has enjoyed the confidence of the Chinese people over the last fifty years, can claim to have been outstandingly successful.

Of course, this is not to say that the Communist Party has not gone through difficult times. It had to fight both foreign invaders and a civil war before the People's Republic could be founded, and the erratic period of the so-called Cultural Revolution showed how a populist message could be self-destructive.

Recognizing that institutions in themselves cannot deliver such results, we ought then to seek alternative reasons for the Chinese achievement. We may find some help to do that by considering a characteristic distinction drawn in the West between the public, business and third sectors, otherwise expressed as state, economy and civil society.

Within the law everything is allowed for civil society, including efforts to change the law. It reflects potentially limitless diversity. Equally it allows for an endless scope for conflict, extending even into the innermost privacy of the family.

My discipline, sociology, has long accepted endemic conflict as inherent in modern society and even viewed it as intrinsic to society's survival. The theory emerging in the early 20th century tells how varied group memberships of individuals create overlapping networks of relationships, a "web of group affiliations", and how institutions develop both to manage the conflicts that arise between them.

Conflict is consequently given a positive gloss in the idea of the institutionalization of conflict. For example, the anglophile sociologist, Ralf Dahrendorf, former EU Commissioner for external affairs and Director of the LSE, (briefly my supervisor in the Germany of 1961) used to applaud the UK for its positive attitude to conflict compared with the aversion to it in his native country.

But this "institutionalization of conflict" can mean equally that conflict is promoted as much as it is managed. It becomes an intrinsic component of the political process of the West, and society is always its hostage. The supreme irony of the theory is that the period in which it originated ended in the bloodbath of the First World War.

To understand China's place in the world today we have to recognize how peculiar the West is. Its celebration of individual freedom is also an exposure of the person to the contradictions of capitalism and the forces of unrestrained technological advance.

The West's democratic institutions, grounded in the unique identity of particular individuals, equally facilitate, manage and, in effect, promote the conflicts that arise within and between competing groups. The CPC by contrast aims to manage China's democratic processes and protect citizens from the free play of the forces of economic and technological advance that in the West are so disruptive.

Those same forces that provoke conflict, populism and threaten democratic institutions are at work in China too. The measures announced earlier this year to restrain the giants of technology and limit excessive accumulations of personal wealth are the most recent evidence of China's unique governance system at work.

It is a system that escapes the conventional categories of Western political thought. "Technocracy" has been one Western term attempting to convey the transformed nature of modern governance. This expresses well the new power of the expert over people's lives, just as 'bureaucracy' was invented in the 18th century as the word for the rising power of the public official. For China my suggestion has been that a new term is needed. "Humanocracy" comes closer to conveying the society-wide pervasive relations between the people and the Party, and the Party's role in guarding social values.

* * *

The sweep of my concerns today has covered contrasts between two types of societal governance systems that distinguish the two great civilizations of the West and China. For the future of both, and for the world as a whole, they have to cooperate.

China already has committed itself fully to the multilateral institutions of the global governance system. Unlike the other superpower, it does not regard them as optional arrangements it can join and leave at will.

But the present global institutions owe more to the model of institution building that characterizes the Western nation state, namely through agencies, representative or otherwise, that manage conflicts between rival parties. They are also vulnerable to institutional capture by an official class of functionaries owing allegiance only to those institutions and their own careers. Cooperation between China and the West has other, quite different possibilities.

The world needs the virtues of China's own governance system to be applied to global governance. In the West there are many groups outside the multilateral institutions who are vocal in their demands for solutions to global problems.

My modest suggestion is that China should extend its reach to the civil society groups of the West who have self-declared global missions, whether on climate change, protection of animal species, the rights of refugees, open source publishing or a host of other issues.

This will not in itself represent a change of direction for China's own non-governmental organizations. They have been bonded into a wide-ranging official administrative framework since the founding of the China Association for NGO Cooperation (CANGO) in 1992. It has continued to help them to develop closer relations with their counterparts throughout the world.

In this context we have a paradox in that the fragmented governance systems of Western countries can have also have positive outcomes. The diversity of their civil societies has allowed the emergence of a multiplicity of associations of self-described global citizens dedicated to issues of peace, sustainability, climate change and to our continued existence on this planet. It was their concerns that Mary Kaldor's and David Held's late-lamented LSE Global Governance Centre and its annual publication *Global Civil Society* addressed in the first decade of this millennium.

China has proven through its attainment of national goals, notably this year in the Party's First Centenary Goal of achieving moderate prosperity for all, how its governance delivers results. Its Belt and Road Initiative is extending this capacity to mobilize people for collective goals far beyond its borders. If China now invites global civil society to join with it in transnational partnerships to meet the global challenges of our time we will soon see the development of an alternative kind of global governance.

This reform would make a credible advance towards the achievement of the goals on which our survival on this planet depends. It is in goal orientation rather than institution building that China demonstrates the distinctive cultural capacity of its governance. Its own system, people, party and the state, continues to prove how an alternative to Western models of representative government can prosper.'

DOI https://doi.org/10.24103/GCSS6.en.2021.9

Chapter 9
Towards social theory with Chinese characteristics

While globalization has given enormous impetus to theoretical work on contemporary social, political and economic change, it is also the case that exploring the nature of human society, detecting the elements and processes underlying people's activities in common, has always driven the sociologist's quest for knowledge. 'Integrity' and 'spirit' are offered here as two possible additions to the list of sociological universals. That the quest never ends may be illustrated by the author's career-long, never-to-be-concluded engagement with Max Weber's ideas.

9.1 Chinese social theory in global social science[1]

In a globalizing world, the aim of social science has to be the increase of mutual understanding between peoples and cultures that are thrown together, whether they want it or not, to overcome conflict and to enhance the possibilities of cooperative responses to the global challenges that confront them all. It is the urgency of the need to cooperate under current conditions that makes intensive examination of the impediments to it so important. Ethnocentrism, the inability to view another culture except through the lens of one's own, is the major impediment that comparative studies seek to remove. A particular aim is to correct the widely acknowledged limitations of dominant social science concepts embedded in the historical experience of the West. Xiaoying Qi provides us with an exemplary study of the way the wealth of Chinese intellectual traditions can be brought into critical engagement with Western paradigms to develop common conceptual resources that will be to the benefit of all peoples.

A great virtue of this book lies in demonstrating the worth of a multiplicity of methods for disentangling the transcultural potential of concepts from their cultural roots. The author brings an impressively equipped toolbox to her chosen task, to show how 'Western or metropolitan social theory might be reconstituted through the incorporation of particular relevant Chinese concepts' (7). The first half of the book is devoted to exploring and documenting transcultural flows. In the first chapter, we read an account of the institutional and linguistic hegemony of Western theories and concepts; the second is a case study of the treatment of *guanxi* in 214 Western management journal articles. There follows an account of the reception and use of Western concepts by Chinese intellectual entrepreneurs

[1] Editor's note: This piece is a review of *Chinese Social Theory in Global Social Science: Knowledge Flows and Chinese Social Theory*, by Xiaoying Qi (2014), New York and Abingdon: Routledge (hardback), 260 pp. £85. It was published in the *Journal of China in Global and Comparative Perspectives*, Vol .1, 2015, pp. 143–146.

between 1842 and 1949 and then the fourth chapter depicts the historical interplay of continuity and transformation, from the reception of Buddhism onwards, that makes up the intellectual heritage that is called Chinese today.

The second half of the book offers three examples for the incorporation of Chinese concepts into mainstream social theory. The first is one that has already been received in the West extensively, namely 'face' (*lian* and *mianzi*). The second explains how *xin* (heart/mind) transcends the Western dichotomy of reason and emotion. The third develops a concept of 'paradoxical integration' (*xiangfan xianghe* or *xiangfan yiti*) derived from the classic Daoist text *Daodejing*. The very different ways in which each of these concepts resonates with cognate ideas in Western thought stand out in Dr Qi's account and it is one of its great merits that she does not attempt to suggest that there is any simple rule of thumb by which Chinese ideas can be assimilated in the West. Each case involves a unique cultural encounter.

But there are lessons to be drawn for the general tasks of comparative social science in this study of the actual and possible contributions of Chinese concepts to a universally accessible and applicable repertoire. We can identify elementary analytical components for any cultural frame of thought: them and us, living and dead, connected and disconnected, cause and effect, the same and different, new and old and so on, the human commonalities so emphatically stressed by Lévi-Strauss (1966) in declaring that the savage mind works by the same logic as ours today.

Yet there are endless variations in the configuration of such basic elements of culture and this is true for social relations too. The result is different prominence being accorded to a particular configuration of elements according to the culture in which it is situated. The vendetta in southern Italian culture as an organising principle of clan relations has near equivalents in other societies, although it may not have acquired in them the recognition as a distinct phenomenon that is accorded a name. Similarly, *guanxi*, when defined (that is dissected into elements) by Qi, as 'carefully constructed and maintained relations between persons that carry mutual obligations and benefits', may render very effectively relations in Western societies that are only alluded to in terms of 'influence', 'patronage', 'old-boy network' or corruption. None of these terms is adequate to describe, for instance, what the British magazine *Private Eye* specializes in revealing, favours given and returned that are outside any formal relations. *Guanxi* is closer to the target of its satire than any other single concept and discloses the ambiguities in public morality lying below the surface of British culture.

The example of 'face', popularized in his account of 'Chinese characteristics' by the American missionary Arthur H. Smith (1894), illustrates a quite different kind of cross-cultural flow. His book went through 15 editions and was an important source for Max Weber's (1951) study of Chinese religion. It led to the *Oxford English Dictionary* including 'to lose face' in its Supplement with the note '[tr. Chinese *diulien*]'. Yet, while Smith saw it as the key to Chinese character, Qi shows that it was he who first attracted the attention of Chinese scholars to it and there is now an extensive social scientific discussion of face in Chinese. Qi points Chinese social theory in global social science here to the intellectual entrepreneurship required to effect this kind of exchange of concepts between cultures and rightly assigns her own work to it.

In the chapter on reason and emotion, Qi bravely tackles a strategic distinction in Western thought and makes the case for their effective integration in the Chinese concept of *xin*, documenting its shared recognition in the long series of major thinkers from Guanzi (683–642 BCE) through Laozi, Confucius and Mencius up to Dai Zhen (1723–1777). Serving for the Western comparison, Max Weber is singled out as a prime representative of the view that emotions are irrational.

The contrast between West and East is strongly drawn and richly informative on *xin*. There are, however, two qualifications that should be entered. While the author is explicit about the pitfalls of postulating an undifferentiated West or East, in this chapter there is a marked asymmetry between the treatment of them, one that is not infrequent in West/East comparisons, namely classic Chinese thought is contrasted with modern Western, whereas the rich diversity of classic and European thought up to the eighteenth century is neglected. The legacy of Aristotle extends beyond logic into ethics and his concepts of virtue and the mean combine reason and emotion, just as does the Christian idea of the soul. Here it would help if Qi made more extensive use of Alasdair MacIntyre's (e.g. 1967: 64) work than she does.

The other qualification relates to the treatment of Max Weber as a proxy for Western thought as a whole. It is true that he opposes rational action to emotion, but this is an analytical distinction within an account that is concerned to identify the features of Western modernity. The main focus of his work is the explanation of formal institutionalized rationalities in the state, economy, science and religion, and to account for the revolutionary impact of modern capitalism. He is above all the theorist of modernity, and for him the traditional societies of West and East equally displayed their own kinds of rationalism. Once modern capitalism had gained its momentum in the West, he had no doubt that the East would be able to adopt its main features – as indeed it has. If we are going to assimilate the Eastern classics to enrich a shared world culture, we need to draw on pre-modern Western ideas also and in this respect set limits on modernity, both before and after the dominance it achieved in the nineteenth and early twentieth centuries, a viewpoint I advance with the concept of the global age (Albrow, 2014).

This is a position that requires the advance of new concepts for a new age and, under conditions of globalization, despite the hegemony in science of the English language, it is certain that insights based on the vast intellectual heritage of China and its unique historical development will increasingly enrich a store of concepts belonging to the world community of social scientists. It is a process that will include the revision of old concepts as well as the invention of new ones. Qi's last chapter illustrates this very effectively. It advances the idea of paradoxical integration (*xiangfan xianghe* and *xiangfan yiti*), drawing on the Daoist tradition, 'the non-contradictory or non-destructive correspondence of opposites in a single thing or event at a given moment of time' (210). She suggests that it is particularly helpful methodologically for identifying some of the paradoxes of globalization, as with Roland Robertson's (1992) 'glocalization' and Bryan Turner's 'enclave society' (2007). A similar critical approach to older concepts has allowed Xiangqun Chang (2010) to advance the concept of *lishang-wanglai* for a more precise analytical approach to reciprocal social relationships in *guanxi*. The overriding point is that Chinese social theory will not stay in the past but change with the changing times. This indeed is the conclusion Qi reaches: 'transformations in Chinese culture paradoxically draw upon enduring properties of a Chinese intellectual heritage that provides the means through which such change is achieved' (227).

In a short review one can only begin to suggest the depth of scholarship and richness of argument and insight that this book contains. It not only provides an extensive exploration of sources for Chinese social theory but also exemplifies the way in which a truly global social science can continue to develop through comparative studies of concept formation. There is more than ample proof here that the author will be in the forefront of those who take this programme forward. This book should be on the reading lists for all courses in comparative sociology or anthropology and is essential for courses in social theory or philosophy of social science where there is a main concern (as there should be!) to combat Western ethnocentrism. To this end, I would urge the publishers, if they have not already done so, to prepare for paperback publication at a price students can afford.

References

Albrow, Martin (2014), *Global Age Essays on Social and Cultural Change*. Frankfurt am Main: Vittorio Klostermann.

Chang, Xiangqun (2010), *Guanxi or li shang wanglai?: Reciprocity, Social Support Networks, & Social Creativity in a Chinese Village*. Taipei: Airiti Press.

Lévi-Strauss, Claude (1966), *The Savage Mind*. London: Weidenfeld and Nicolson.

MacIntyre, Alasdair (1967), *A Short History of Ethics*. London: Routledge & Kegan Paul.

Robertson, Roland (1992), *Globalization. Social Theory and Global Culture*. London: Sage.

Smith, Arthur H. (1894), *Chinese Characteristics*. New York: Fleming H. Revell.

Turner, Bryan. S. (2007), 'The enclave society: towards a sociology of immobility', *European Journal of Social Theory* 10(2): 287–303.

Weber, Max (1951), *The Religion of China: Confucianism and Taoism*. Translated and edited by H. H. Gerth. Glencoe, IL: Free Press.

9.2 Spirit (精神 *jingshen*) as a key contemporary Chinese concept[2]

Martin Albrow and JIN Wei

Abstract: The ancient concept of spirit 精神 (*jingshen*) occupies a pivotal place within contemporary Chinese political discourse for which there is no equivalent in the West. Older Christian and subsequent Enlightenment usage of spirit, culminating in Hegel's thought, was displaced by crude materialism, utilitarianism and scientific positivism. The Chinese spirit today is based in the thought of Mao, Deng and Xi, inspires patriotism and combines the socialist core values, path, power and discourse. All kinds of human action exhibit spirit. It is manifested in the Party, in the Long March, by Comrade Jiao Yulu, by Shanghai city, by space exploration. In public discourse, three main types may be distinguished, the exemplary individual, the paradigmatic deed and the collective inspiration. Spirit in China provides the connectedness of community and common purpose that the West struggles to rediscover. In responding to global challenges together, China and the West may share a spirit that transcends their differences.

Keywords: spirit (精神, *jīng shén*, *jingshen*), China, the West, materialism, socialism, values, party, discourse, connectedness

9.2.1 Introduction

For Western readers, the frequent reference to 'spirit' in Chinese public discourse may resemble an incidental rhetorical flourish. It is much more than that. For instance, the Preface of the original action plan for the Belt and Road Initiative cited 'the Silk Road spirit' twice in its very first paragraph.[3]

That spirit was defined as 'peace and cooperation, openness and inclusiveness, mutual learning and mutual benefit'. All contributed to the advance of human civilization, the prosperity of the countries along the Road and cooperation between East and West.

'Spirit', *jing sheng*, 精神, is deeply embedded in Chinese language and world view, intimately related to other pivotal concepts like *dao lu*, the path, and *hua yu,* language.

By contrast, 'spirit' in the West has had a much more contested history. Often tied to religious dogma, it has been central to a binary world view: the spiritual versus the material. It has variously been the focus of a philosophy of history and the target of historical materialism.

In this paper, we will first briefly illustrate the varying and contradictory places that spirit has occupied in Western thought. We will then examine the histo-

[2] This paper is published in the *Journal of China in Global and Comparative Perspectives*, Vol. 7, 2021.

[3] Wang Yiwei (2016), *The Belt and Road Initiative: What China will offer the world in its rise.* Beijing: New World Press, p. 189.

ry and general concept of *jingshen*, the specific Chinese spirit, the party spirit, and review examples of spirits as portrayed in Chinese leaders' speeches, and organize them under three main categories.

This examination of its current Chinese use reveals the multiple contexts where it directs the readers' or listeners' attention to an exemplary reality that should shape their future conduct. We shall argue that 'spirit' in Chinese thought is an integrating concept, combining the passion of individuals, the dynamic of events and the collective will of social entities.

Each of these manifestations of spirit may be invoked to energize human activity, link it with powerful antecedents and provide for direction into the future. We will then make a general comment about their function in Chinese socialism today, and conclude with a brief comparison with Western political discourse and the difficulties it faces through the lack of an equivalent concept.

9.2.2 The Western binary divide of spirit and matter

The Latin *spiritus* (*esprit* in French, *Geist* in German, spirit in English) in the Western mediaeval Christian world view was opposed to the material world, both as realized in the individual soul and in being recognized as the property of God. In the doctrine of the Trinity, the Holy Spirit was integral to the nature of God, both as creator of the world and as brought to earth in the person of Christ.

The result was that communal activity beyond the Church had no independent spiritual existence. The nearest the early Christian spirit came to a collective presence was in the role the apostles of Christ assumed, filling the void between individual and God. It was a role subsequently claimed by the Catholic Church, but it was not unchallenged.

Indeed a millennium after the birth of Christ, for nearly five hundred years, there was a movement known as the Free Spirit or Spiritual Liberty moving territorially through northern Europe, adopting no settled doctrine but drawing upon marginal and disaffected individuals to join in the spiritual experience of small groups. The Church which denounced them as heretics was to be replaced 'by their own community, seen as the vessel of the Holy Spirit'.[4] As such they have been described as the remote forerunners of the bohemian intelligentsia of modern times following Bakunin and Nietzsche.[5]

The translation of the Bible into the vernacular at the beginning of the modern period was an important factor in the challenge to the Church of the Protestant Reformation of the 16th century. In this case the reliance on the printed text provided greater focus of attention than the ecstasy of the Free Spirit. It served to invoke the spiritual power of the congregation as a collective sharing in the Holy Spirit but was also opposed to the spiritual authority of the priesthood.

---

4 Norman Cohn (1970), *The Pursuit of Millennium*, London: Paladin, p. 150.

5 Ibid., p. 148.

The vernacular connotations of the various translations of '*spiritus*' as 'spirit', '*esprit*' and '*Geist*' could only help to encourage speculation about the nature of spirit. It developed into a critical debate that inaugurated what was often called the age of reason, or the Enlightenment, when spirit was detached from religious doctrine.[6]

For the 18th-century philosophers, the Enlightenment spirit was no longer the preserve of religion. But it would be a mistake, frequently made, to assume that they denied its place in religious motivation or indeed the importance of spirit more generally in human affairs. The target of their critical rationalism was religious dogma and intolerance as promoted by the Church of their day.

The consequence was to release spirit from institutional religion and to allow it a presence not just in people but in the environments and circumstances of their lives. There could be an '*esprit du temps*' ('spirit of the age'), as in Voltaire's account of the Age of Louis XIV.[7] This was a notion that was bound up with the growing sense of the novelty of their time and the special nature of their history that was gripping European intellectuals.[8]

Going beyond both dogma and religious boundaries was also tied up with the West's encounter with other cultures. This culminated in the mid-eighteenth century in the defining work of that period, written by the French aristocrat, Charles-Louis Montesquieu (1689–1755), *De l'Esprit des Lois* (On the Spirit of the Laws), 1748. Without denying a pure and universal realm of spirit beyond human reach, he argued from the vast diversity of laws in different cultures that the different material conditions under which human beings live meant their spirit took on equally varied forms.

Spirit, then, in general, beyond religion, became a prime talking point. Writing in 1754, the German commentator on the French ideas of the time, Baron Grimm, wrote that everything seemed to have a spirit: 'the fine arts, Montaigne, Fontenelle, the day, not to mention the spirit of the laws'.[9]

In this intellectual climate, a young radical was inspired to challenge assumptions behind the chatter and to write of spirit in general. Claude-Adrien Helvétius, (1715–1771) wrote *De L'Esprit* (1758), arguing that spirit derived from

[6] The differences between everyday equivalents of 'spiritus' give rise to variations in its interpretation in the different languages. Goethe was reported as saying 'The French *esprit* is close to what we Germans call *Witz* (wit). Our *Geist* is perhaps what the French would express with *esprit* and âme (soul)'. He went on to suggest that a notion of 'productivity' was contained in the German *Geist*, and to express this the French had to introduce the word *génie* (genius) as a supplement to '*esprit*' (*Goethe im Gespräch*, ed. E. Grumach (1960), Frankfurt and Hamburg: Fischer, p. 122)..

[7] Friedrich Meinecke's account of the rise of historical thinking in Europe says of Voltaire that he wanted to summarize the unique features of a time, a people or a structure with a general name and that was 'esprit' (1959, *Die Entstehung des Historismus*, Munich: Oldenbourg, p. 101).

[8] It gained lasting currency beyond France. The English essayist William Hazlitt's book *The Spirit of the Age, or Contemporary Portraits* (1824) was a set of appreciations of major literary figures of his time.

[9] Baron Friedrich Melchior Grimm (1754), *Correspondance littéraire, philosophique et critique*, Vol 2.

a combination of physical sensation and memory and then drawing the conclusion that only education could reconcile individual interests to the general welfare of society.

In effect, Helvétius deconstructed spirit and redirected the arguments around it to support the expansion of public education and minimize the evils of poverty and inequality. The radical nature of his book led both to its public burning and corresponding fame. Its immediate effect was to contribute to the ferment of ideas that led up to the French Revolution. It won him the longer-term reputation of being one of the originators of modern materialism.

In reaction to that radicalism and the political upheavals that followed, spirit was taken in a diametrically opposite direction in the philosophy of G. W. F. Hegel (1770–1831). It became, in the guise of human reason, the driving force of history, culminating in the Western civilization and Prussian state of his time.

Considered thus, as the decisive factor in the advance of human civilization, spirit had reached the supreme intellectual height of Western public discourse. It is difficult today to appreciate the influence that Hegel's idea had at the beginning of the nineteenth century, but the extent of its dominance can be seen in an equivalent rejection that exercises its influence in the West to this day.

Spirit, in its treatment by Hegel's followers, became the property of the philosopher, the intellectual opposed to the mass of ordinary people. In his early writing, Karl Marx rejected the philosophical views of the young Hegelians. In *The Holy Family* (1845), he summed up his rejection of Hegel's conception of history: 'The history of mankind becomes the history of the Abstract Spirit of mankind, hence a spirit far removed from the real man.' [10]

In the second decade of the twenty-first century, we can still recognize that divide in the populist revolt against the established order of rationalized society. Marx's and Engels's historical materialism rejected the binary opposition of the spiritual and material, by emphasizing the struggle of human beings to bring the material conditions of their lives under control. Spirit, then, was not the exclusive domain of a group of privileged intellectuals.

We should stress that this was not the crude materialism of Helvétius. Marx had read and cited him, but he never reduced spirit to physical factors. He had no difficulty in accepting that there was a spiritual side to class struggle. For example, in a newspaper article of June 5, 1857, he commented on the 'different spirit among the Chinese now to what they showed in the war of 1840 to '42'.[11]

It was not the historical materialism of Marx and Engels that deprived spirit of its place in Western public discourse. It was the advance of crude utilitarianism and scientific positivism that combined to push spirit back into the confines of

[10] Karl Marx and Friedrich Engels (1975), *Collected Works*, Vol. 4. London: Lawrence and Wishart. p. 85.

[11] *Marx on China: Articles for the New York Daily Tribune*, 1968. London: Lawrence and Wishart, p. 48.

churches and cults. In the social sciences, spirit was in practice deconstructed in the vocabulary of ideas, ideology, culture and ethos. Hegel's *Geist* was translated as 'mind' and soon was assimilated into the study of consciousness and the brain.

In Germany, *Geist* survived for longer, as in the *Geisteswissenschaften* (sciences of the spirit, hardly translatable into English, and best rendered as the 'humanities') with a vigorous debate about their nature before the First World War. But the adoption of *Volksgeist* (spirit of the people) for the nationalism of the early twentieth century deprived it of any wider application beyond the German cultural territory.[12]

9.2.3 The Chinese definition of spirit (精神 *jingshen*)

The contrast between the West's binary approach to spirit with the place of spirit in Chinese civilization is profound and goes to the heart of the difficulties Western people have in understanding China up to the present day.

9.2.3.1 A classical definition

Spirit refers to the spirit of human beings relative to the human body.

> 《吕氏春秋·尽数》：'圣人察阴阳之宜，辨万物之利，以便生，故精神安乎形，而年寿得长焉。'[13]

This sentence is quoted from 'Lü's Commentaries of History' which was compiled by Lü Buwei who was the Prime Minister of Qin country in the late Warring States period around 239BC. Its meaning is 'Saints can observe the good of *yin* and *yang,* to distinguish the good of all things, in order to live, so the spirit can match the shape, and they have a long life.'

9.2.3.2 The Chinese spirit today (中国精神 *zhongguo jingshen*)

The Chinese spirit is the spirit of unity and solidarity, peace-loving, industrious and courageous, unremitting self-improvement and innovation with reform as the core of patriotism.[14]

'Chinese spirit' is guided by Marxism, Mao Zedong Thought, Deng Xiaoping theory, the important thought of 'Three represents', the Scientific View of Development and Xi's Thought on Socialism with Chinese Characteristics for a New Era. These are the essence of the socialist core value system, taking the socialist core values as the core connotation, and embodying the socialist concepts of honour and disgrace.[15]

---

[12] *Zeitgeist*, however, has lasted longer and even survives in English text where an author wants to convey the meaning without using the inadmissible 'spirit of the age'.

[13] 吕不韦著，陈奇猷校释:《吕氏春秋新校释》，上海古籍出版社2002年版，第138页[Lü Buwei (2002), *Lü's Commentaries of History*, Shanghai: Shanghai Ancient Books Publishing House, p. 138].

[14] 吴潜涛:《中国精神教育读本》，北京：人民出版社, 2014年，第6页 [Wu Qiantao, (2014), *Chinese Spiritual Education Reading Book*, Beijing: People's Publishing House, p. 6].

[15] Ibid., p. 5.

The Chinese spirit then combines core features of human thought and action to provide a direction into the future and an inspiration for all who follow its path.[16] These core features include:

Chinese values 中国价值 (*zhongguo jiazhi*) refers to socialist core values.

Chinese path 中国道路 (*zhongguo daolu*) refers to the road of socialism with Chinese characteristics.

Chinese power (or strength) 中国力量 (*zhongguo liliang*). Xi Jinping has repeatedly pointed out that Chinese power is developed in the unity and struggle of all Chinese people under the correct leadership of the Communist Party of China.

Chinese discourse 中国话语 (*zhongguo huayu*). China needs its own discourse to make itself understood around the world. To build the system of Chinese discourse, China must decide such basic questions as: 'who is talking?', 'how to talk?', 'what should be said?' and 'why is one speaking?'. In building Chinese discourse the ideal state is the self-building and appearance of the discourse about China. It is important to reveal the characteristics of China and get rid of the demonization of China by the West.

9.2.3.2 Party spirit

Party spirit is synonymous with party character 党性 (*dangxing*), the inherent nature and characteristic of political parties. It is the highest and most concentrated manifestation of the nature of class through concrete practice in the long-term political struggle. It is also contained in the programmes and policies of political parties and demonstrated in their political activities. Political parties demand of their party members that they continue to strengthen the party spirit so that their political objectives can be successfully realized. Political parties in terms of their performance and requirements of party spirit vary in their different situations and national conditions.

While bourgeois political parties may deny they have a special party spirit and boast of being non-party or supra-party, in fact, their real spirit and main performance are to maintain capitalist private ownership and bourgeois rule as the supreme interests and the highest goal of the parties, unscrupulous activities to carry out everything they wish for, for the party to seize the leadership of the country.

The proletariat openly affirms its party spirit, which is the class nature, the basic idea of Marxism on the party spirit. In the *Communist Manifesto*, Marx pointed out that the different characteristics of the Communist Party and other proletarian political parties are as follows: 'On the one hand, in the struggle of the proletarians of all countries, the Communists emphasize and adhere to the common interests of the entire proletariat, regardless of the nation; on the other hand, at all stages of development experienced by the struggle of the proletariat, the communists always represent the interests of the whole movement.'[17]

---

[16] Xi Jinping (2014), *The Governance of China*. Beijing: Foreign Languages Press, p. 47.

[17] 《马克思恩格斯文集》，北京： 人民出版社，1995年第315页 [Marx and Engels (1995),

The CPC has always attached importance to party spirit. In January 1941, the CPC Central Committee put forward the issue of strengthening party education and party spirit.[18]

> In the new period of socialist construction, the party has carried out a more in-depth exploration, summed up in the following points: adhering to the socialist road, adhering to the dictatorship of the proletariat, adhering to the leadership of the Communist Party, adhering to Marxist–Leninist Mao Zedong Thought, insisting on reform and opening up, striving for the construction of a socialist modern power; combining theory with practice, everything starts from reality and is seeking truth from facts; all for the benefit of the people of all ethnic groups in China, to serve them wholeheartedly, to work closely with the masses, to resolutely eliminate corruption, to oppose often, not to harm the interests of the State and the people for the benefit of personal interests and small groups; we should resist and overcome the decadent ideas of capitalism, the remnants of feudalism and other non-proletarian ideas, conscientiously criticize and self-criticize, adhere to the party's democratic centralism and strengthen organizational discipline, and constantly improve the party's leadership over State power and the whole socialist cause.

Party spirit is, in a broad sense, the inherent nature of political parties. In a narrow sense, it refers to the specific characteristics of the party as realized by individual party members, that is, in their political personality. The Party Constitution provides the standard and yardstick for party members and cadres to strengthen their achievements, and cadres should have a high degree of respect for and abide by the Constitution. Xi Jinping said:

> Adhere to the spirit of the Communists to pursue Party spirit, [which] is the cornerstone of the CPC members of *lisheng* (立身), *liye* (立业), *liyan* (立言) and *lide* (立德), firm ideals and beliefs, adhere to the spiritual pursuit of the Communists, [which] has always been the foundation of the Communists to settle down.[19]

9.2.3.4 Types of spirit

In contemporary China, spirit is frequently invoked in the speeches of political leaders and in widely circulated slogans. They may point to the example provided by outstanding people, to particular deeds that should provide standards for action and to events that have demonstrated the power of the spirit. Very broadly,

---

Marx and Engels Anthology, Beijing: People's Publishing House, p. 315].

[18] 中共中央文献研究室，中央档案馆编，《建党以来重要文献选编(1921-1949)》，第18卷，北京：中央文献出版社，2011年第70页 [CPC Central Literature Research Office and Central Archives (Eds.) (2011), Selected important documents since the founding of the Party (1921–1949), Vol. 18, Beijing: Central Literature Press, p. 70.

[19] 习近平：在河北省委常委班子专题民主生活会上讲话，《新华网》，2013年9月25日，见: http://www.xinhuanet.com/politics/xxjxs/2020-01/10/c_1125447211.htm [Xi Jinping spoke on the special democratic Life of the Standing Committee of the Hebei Provincial Committee, *Xinhua Net*, 25/09/2013].

then, we can identify three types of Chinese spirit in the discourse of today, the exemplary individual, the paradigmatic deed and the collective inspiration.

1. T*he Exemplary Individual*

    a) *Lei Feng spirit*

    Lei Feng was born in December 1940 and was a Soldier of the Chinese People's Liberation Army. In August 1962, Lei Feng died in the line of duty. In his speech commemorating the 30th anniversary of Comrade Lei Feng's inscription, Comrade Hu Jintao proposed the 'Lei Feng spirit', meaning dedication to hard work, positive progress, self-improvement, with […] dedication to national and collective interests everywhere, mutual respect, a good social attitude of helping one another, being honest and trustworthy and being harmonious.[20]

    b) *Jiao Yulu comrade spirit*

    Xi Jinping's speech on April 1, 2009 during a conversation with cadres and masses during the investigation of Lankao County, Henan Province, put forward the Jiao Yulu spirit as 'serv[ic]e to the people, hard work, scientific truth-seeking, selfless dedication', the heart of all the people, but not his own, The spirit of public servants, investigation and research adhere to all from the actual truth-seeking spirit, to meet the difficulties: not afraid of hardship, not afraid of risk,[21] revolutionaries with selfless dedication, integrity, diligence for the people, for the Party and the People's cause.

2. *The Paradigmatic Deed*

    a) *The 'Red Boat spirit'*

    At the beginning of August 1921, the First National Congress of the Communist Party of China concluded successfully on a cruise ship in Nanhu lake, Jiaxing, Zhejiang Province, with the solemn proclamation of the birth of the Communist Party of China. The cruise ship thus won the name of a permanent Chinese revolutionary – Red Boat.

    Xi Jinping put forward in the *Guangming Daily* on June 21, 2005 the specific content of the 'Red Ship Spirit', saying it was groundbreaking, daring to be the first, had pioneering spirit, firm ideals, an indomitable spirit of struggle, work for the public, loyalty and dedication to the people.[22]

---

20 《人民日报》社论：发扬光大雷锋精神，2003年3月5日，见：https://www.bcu.edu.cn/xyzt/info/1025/1144.htm [*People's Daily* editorial: Carry forward the spirit of Lei Feng, 05/03/2003].

21 习近平：结合新的实际 大力弘扬焦裕禄精神，《河南日报》，2009年05月14日，见：http://www.ce.cn/xwzx/gnsz/szyw/200905/14/t20090514_19076080.shtml [Xi Jinping's speech during a discussion with cadres and masses during the investigation of Lankao County, Henan Province, *Henan Daily,* 14/05/2009].

22 习近平：弘扬'红船精神'走在时代前列，《光明日报》，2005年6月21日 [Xi Jinping: Carry forward the 'Red Boat spirit' to walk at the forefront of the times, *Guangming Daily*, 21/6/2005].

b) *The spirit of the Long March*

From October 1934 to October 1936, the first, second, fourth and 25th armies of the Red Army carried out a Long March. During the journey, the Red Army soldiers and the enemy engaged in more than 600 battles, across nearly hundreds of rivers, climbing more than 40 dangerous and snow-covered mountains, of which several were more than 4,000 metres above sea level, through the vast grassland known as the 'Death Trap', with tenacious will to extend the limits of human survival. The Red Army generals staged a magnificent war drama in world military history, and created a human miracle. In his speech on October 21, 2016 commemorating the 80th anniversary of the Red Army's Long March, Xi Jinping expressed the connotation of the Long March spirit: to take the fundamental interests of the people of the whole country and the Chinese nation above all, to strengthen the ideals and beliefs of the revolution, to firmly believe that the cause of justice is bound to prevail, to save the people from salvation, not to be afraid of any difficulties and obstacles, to honour the spirit of sacrifice, to insist on independence, seeking truth from facts, the spirit of close unity, relying closely on the people, with the people, suffering and striving, the spirit of hard work.[23]

c) *Jinggangshan spirit*

The Jinggangshan spirit was born in the Jinggangshan area. After the Great Revolution failed, Comrade Mao Zedong and Zhu De, as well as the leaders of the party and the Red Army, led by example, urging Jinggangshan civil and military personnel to overcome all kinds of difficulties and hardships, breaking the siege and blockade. At this critical moment in history, CPC adhered to seeking truth from facts and research, combined the basic principles of Marxism with the concrete practice of the Chinese revolution, and, with its fearless revolutionary courage, has created a unique path of Chinese revolution that surrounds the city with the countryside and seized power, always believing in and relying on the people, caring for and helping the people, with the broad masses of the people maintaining flesh-and-blood ties, only to win the support of the people, so that the Jinggangshan revolutionary area has been consolidated and expanded.

Xi Jinping put forward the specific contents of Jinggangshan in his speech during investigation and research in Jiangxi in 2016: firmly persistent pursuit of ideals, seeking truth from facts, hard struggle to overcome difficulties, relying on the people to seek victory.[24]

---

23 习近平：《在纪念红军长征胜利80周年大会上的讲话》，北京：人民出版社，2016年第9页 [Xi Jinping. Speech at the 80th anniversary conference in commemoration of the Red Army's Long March, Beijing: People's Publishing House, 2016, p. 9].

24 《人民日报》记者：习近平春节前夕赴江西看望慰问广大干部群众，祝全国各族人民健康快乐吉祥祝改革发展人民生活蒸蒸日上，《人民日报》，2016年02月04日，见： http://

3. *The Collective inspiration*

a) *The spirit of 'atomic and hydrogen bombs and man-made satellites'*

October 16, 1964: China's first atomic bomb explosion was successful. October 27, 1966: China's first ground-to-ground missile with a nuclear warhead was successful. June 17, 1967: China's first hydrogen bomb air explosion test was successful. April 24, 1970: China's first manmade satellite launch was successful. This is an extraordinary human miracle created by the Chinese people in their journey to climb the peak of modern science and technology.

Comrade Jiang Zemin presented the meaning of the 'atomic and hydrogen bombs and manmade satellites' spirit in his speech on September 18, 1999 in recognition of the scientific and technological experts who made outstanding contributions to the development of such bombs and satellites, which is to love the motherland, selfless dedication, self-reliance, hard work, vigorous coordination and the courage to climb.[25]

b) *The Daquing spirit*

Comrade Jiang Zemin's speech at the inspection of Daqing oilfield on February 25–27, 1990 put forward the 'daqing spirit', which is patriotic, entrepreneurial, truth-seeking, dedicated and patriotic; bearing in mind the patriotic spirit of winning glory for the country and vying for the nation; entrepreneurship; independent, self-reliant spirit of hard work; truth-seeking; emphasis on science; the overall spirit of the mind, dedicated to the country.[26]

c) *The spirit of space*

In his speech celebrating the success of the sixth manned space flight conference on November 26, 2005, Hu Jintao stated that the spirit of space is particularly capable of suffering, especially able to fight, especially able to tackle, especially dedicated.

'Especially able to endure hardship' is a true portrayal of the hard work of Chinese spaceflight people.

---

politics.people.com.cn/n1/2016/0204/c1024-28109316.html [*People's Daily* Reporter (2016,), Xi Jinping went to Jiangxi on the Spring Festival's Eve to visit the cadres and the masses. He wishes the people of all ethnic groups in the country health, happiness and good luck, and the further reform and development of a prosperous life. *People's Daily*, 4/2/2016].

25 江泽民：在表彰为研制'两弹一星'作出突出贡献的科技专家大会上的讲话，《新华网》, 2014年09月28日，见：http://news.12371.cn/2014/09/28/ARTI1411888182032814.shtml [Jiang Zemin: The speech at the Conference of scientific and technological experts who made outstanding contributions to the development of 'atomic and hydrogen bombs and manmade satellites', *Xinhua Net*, 28/09/2014].

26 朱舒坤：大庆精神的由来与发展，《人民政协报》, 2016年12月29日 [Zhu Shukun (2016), The origin and development of the Daqing spirit, *People's Political Consultative Conference Newspaper*, 29/12/2016].

'Especially able to fight' is a true portrayal of Chinese spacefaring, all-conquering man.

'Special ability to tackle problems' is a true portrayal of Chinese spaceflight people exploring innovation.

'Special dedication' is a true portrayal of the selfless sacrifice of Chinese spaceflight people.[27]

d) *The spirit of flood fighting*

The spirit of flood fighting or 'flood resistance' is the lofty spirit formed by the unprecedented cohesion of the national civil and military in their the victory over the 1998 floods in the Yangtze River, Nenjiang, Songhua River and other areas. On September 29, 1998, Jiang Zemin summed up the spirit of flood fighting in his speech at the National Summary and Commendation Conference on Flood and Rescue, namely united, not afraid of difficulties, tenacious struggle, perseverance, winning victory.[28] The essence of the spirit of flood fighting is to take the communist spirit of unselfish and unmatched as the soul, to take the overall consciousness of the people's interests, national interests and overall interests first as the core, and to unite and work together – 'one side is difficult, eight sides support' – all linked in the socialist big collaboration spirit; to be unafraid of difficulties, undaunted.

e) *Shanghai spirit 上海精神 (Shanghai jingshen)*

The Shanghai Cooperation Organization, referred to as the SCO, is a permanent intergovernmental international organization proclaimed by the People's Republic of China, the Republic of Kazakhstan, the Kyrgyz Republic, the Russian Federation, the Republic of Tajikistan and the Republic of Uzbekistan in Shanghai, China, on June 15, 2001. When the SCO was formally established, the Heads of State of the Member States clearly stated in the 'founding declaration' of the 'Shanghai Five' process, the formation of the 'Shanghai spirit' of 'mutual trust, mutual benefit, equality, consultation, respect for diverse civilizations and seeking common development' as its basic content, which became the norm of mutual relations among SCO member States in the new century. It is not only the foundation of the 'Shanghai Five-nation Mechanism', but also the soul of the Shanghai Cooperation Organization. Just 20 words contain rich comprehensive and profound connotations, forming

---

[27] 胡锦涛：在庆祝神七载人航天飞行成功大会上的讲话，共产党员网，2008年11月7日，见: https://news.12371.cn/2014/09/28/ARTI1411888326205833.shtml [Hu Jintao: Speech at the conference to celebrate the success of the Shenzhou seventh manned space flight, *CPC Members Net*, 7/11/2008].

[28] 江泽民：《江泽民文选》第一卷，北京：人民出版社，2006年第230页 [Jiang Zeming (2006), Selected Works of Jiang Zemin, Vol. II, Beijing: People's Publishing House, p. 230].

a complete organic whole, reflecting the new national security and development concept of each member State, and representing the correct direction of development in international relations. The Shanghai spirit is included in the 2018 annual international politics category of ten most popular languages.[29]

f) *Shanghai City spirit* 上海城市精神 *(Shanghai chengshi jingshen)*
This is different from the Shanghai spirit. The Shanghai City spirit refers to the spirit of Shanghai city, openness (海纳百川 *haina baichuan*), the pursuit of excellence (追求卓越 *zhuiqiu zhuoyue*), enlightened wisdom (开明睿智 *kaiming ruizhi*), modesty and gentleness (大气谦和 *daqi qianhe*).
The spirit of Shanghai city was first officially determined on the basis of a great discussion of the city's 2003 years of developing spiritual civilization, for 'openness' and 'the pursuit of excellence' – eight words.
At the Ninth Party Congress in Shanghai in May 2007, Xi Jinping, then secretary of the Shanghai Municipal Committee, proposed 'cultivating the spirit of the city with the Times' in his report on behalf of the eighth Shanghai Municipal Committee of the CPC, adding the expressions of 'enlightened wisdom' and 'modesty and gentleness'.
In November 2011, 16 plenary meetings of the CPC Shanghai Municipal Committee proposed the value orientation of justice (公正 *gongzheng*), tolerance (包容 *baorong*), responsibility (责任 *zeren*) and integrity (诚信 *chengxing*).[30]

9.2.4 What the West can learn from the Chinese spirit

It is too simple to say that 'spirit' lost its hold on Western thought with secularization. As we have seen, spirit pervaded Western discourse into the nineteenth century and it was only the combined assaults of positivism and bourgeois materialism that loosened its grip on the imagination. But it was the combination of the growth of the social sciences with the rejection and suppression of non-Christian belief systems that excluded spirit from serious intellectual consideration in the West.

'Myth' is a sceptical near equivalent. 'Culture' serves to bundle up many of the aspects of spirit that can be separated from human agency, like symbols, language and knowledge. But what is it that gives life to language? Perhaps Western

29 习近平：上合组织新型国际关系的典范，共产党员网，2018年06月06日，见：https://news.12371.cn/2018/06/06/ARTI1528265207829989.shtml [Xi Jinping: A model of the SCO's new type of international relations, *CPC Members Net,* 06/66/2018].

30 习近平：在上海市第九次党代会上的报告，上海市人民政府网，2007年05月24日，见：http://www.gov.cn/gzdt/2007-05/24/content_624657.htm [Xi Jinping's report at the Ninth Party Conference in Shanghai, Shanghai Municipal People's Government website, 24/05/2007].

organizations come nearest to appealing to spirit with their mission statements, but this is to provide competitive advantage rather than to evoke wider human sympathies.

Perhaps the most famous use of 'spirit' in Western social science was Max Weber's account in his book *The Protestant Ethic and the Spirit of Capitalism* (2011 [1904/5]).[31] There he treated the reader to an extended illustration of what that spirit meant by citing a lengthy passage from the 'Advice to a Young Tradesman' (1748) by the celebrated American writer and diplomat, Benjamin Franklin. He followed it by developing his distinctive 'ideal type' methodology to distinguish separate components of that 'spirit', the word enclosed in quotation marks to indicate it belonged to everyday non-scientific language. When he wanted to refer to the components of spirit he employed terms like 'ethos' or 'ethic'. And that remained his preferred usage throughout his work.

This was the beginning of Weber's protracted concern to develop precise social science concepts for the analysis of such complex cultural and historical entities that might be referred to as spirit. But this inclination to treat 'spirit' as an everyday, non-technical term has reinforced the trend to regard it more as a convenient general label rather than an entity with any historical force.

Books with titles like *The Spirit of America*[32] or *The Spirit Level*[33] leave the idea of spirit unanalysed. A notable exception is Stephen Kalberg's *Searching for the Spirit of American Democracy*[34] , which adopts ideal type methodology to point to a historically rooted set of values and beliefs that together make up a unique spirit of democracy in the United States.

The prevalence and prominence of spirit in Chinese usage today should encourage the West to take a close interest, if not for spiritual reasons, at least for self-interest, since, in our view, it is a vital and unrecognized factor in the Chinese rejuvenation.

Spirit provides the mobilization of resources and engagement with the world that means that the human species becomes an agent in evolution. It coordinates the factors of motivation, energy, knowledge and morality that provide the power and direction of human agency, individual and collective.

All these elements are alluded to, as we have seen, in the core features of the Chinese spirit (*Zhongguo jingshen*) to which successive Chinese leaders, Mao, Deng and Xi, have contributed their ideas. We have detailed a few of the numerous instances where the Chinese spirit has been represented in a very specific, often dramatic way, and have suggested a preliminary classification into three types, namely the spirits of the exemplary individual, of the paradigmatic deed and of the collective inspiration.

---

[31] Max Weber (1904/5; 2011), trans. Stephen Kalberg, New York: Oxford University Press.

[32] William J. Bennett (1997), New York: Touchstone Books.

[33] Richard Wilkinson and Kate Pickett (2009), London: Penguin Books.

[34] Stephen Kalberg (2014), Boulder, CO: Paradigm Publishers. I am grateful to Kalberg for well-taken comments on an earlier draft of this section.

These types never exist in isolation from one another, for they all bear the imprint of the Chinese spirit and each feeds into the other. For instance, Comrade Jiao Yulu's example of hard work and service to the people replicated elements of the paradigmatic experience of the Long March. In turn, its spirit of sacrifice and seeking truth from facts was what Comrade Jiang Zemin highlighted in his inspection of the Daqing oilfield over fifty years. The Chinese spirit exists then in an ever-expanding web of events and experiences that feed on one another and amplify the bonds of collective identity.

Reference to spirit draws attention to connectedness and the ongoing process of making connections. Those connections are not just with and between people. They are created and perpetuated with and through environments, both natural and cultural.

Even the hydrogen bomb then realizes a human dream and is an aspect of the wider human spirit that finds a home in the Chinese spirit too. Spirit does not then deny the potential that human beings have for misusing their creativity and will always struggle against its denial. But without spirit we cannot recognize and reject its negation.

There are two lessons for the West that we would draw when we compare the Western experience of spirit with the Chinese. The first is that the early separation of the spirit in the West between God on the one hand and the individual on the other minimized the collective and inherently connecting element in human life that spirit confers on community and common purpose and that is so evident in the Chinese case. As a result, community is continually being lost and rediscovered and lost again in the Western experience.

The second lesson is one that both West and China can work on together and indeed engage in shared learning, for connectedness in the contemporary global society faced with the challenges to existence on this earth requires cooperation and a sense of a shared fate as never before.

Far-sighted thinkers who bridge some of the artificial distinctions between scientific disciplines and bridge the gap between them and our collective sense of the shared future recognize the essential affinity between connectedness and spiritual experience.

One example is provided by Rupert Sheldrake, who, in many books and recently in *Science and Spiritual Practices*, concludes that the experiences that were once associated with organized religion are now part of a rediscovery of the importance of the spiritual in everyday life.[35] Our connectedness with plants and natural life in general, musical performances, travel and ritual, giving and receiving gratitude, meditation are all part of a wider retrieval of spirit.

China has a long-term advantage in appreciating the importance of spirit. Today in an ever-changing world, facing unprecedented challenges, that advantage

[35] Rupert Sheldrake (2017), *Science and Spiritual Practices: Reconnecting through Direct Experience*. London: Coronet Books.

can only be put to appropriate use by connecting with the West and developing a new, shared spiritual experience of the common human destiny.

9.3 Spirit in Chinese culture and Western culture today[36]

Martin Albrow and JIN Wei

Our paper begins with what for the West is a paradox. Chinese leaders frequently refer to the spirit of something when they want to encourage the people to greater efforts.

Westerners find this difficult, because for them spirit has long had religious overtones and they know China is a secular state and Marxism rejects organized religion. So, where does this Chinese spirit come from?, they will ask.

Chinese people may equally ask how it is that in the West, where spirit has long been associated with religion and where religious freedom is regarded as a human right, political leaders rarely call upon spirit to motivate their followers.

This paper aims to provide an initial examination of this contrast between the West and China. It concludes by arguing that, in Marx's rejection of the spiritual/material dichotomy, we find a theoretical solution that supports the long-established place of spirit in Chinese discourse.

In the early years of this century when President Xi Jinping was a senior official in Zhejiang Province, he emphasized spirit in many of the articles he wrote for the *Zhejiang Daily*. Newly translated for the benefit of Western readers, those articles are collected under the title *Zhejiang, China: A New Vision for Development*.

Martin Albrow's speech at its launch in Frankfurt last month declared it was a statement of the 'governing philosophy of the Scientific Outlook on Development'. Spirit belongs to that philosophy. Xi refers to it in this volume no fewer than 69 times, sometimes as a quality of human effort, as in 'a realistic and pragmatic spirit', sometimes to emphasize a collective response, as in 'the spirit of typhoon relief', or as the property of a collective entity, as in 'the Party spirit.'

In our wider account of spirit in Chinese culture, we have made a similar threefold distinction between the spirit of exemplary individuals, such as comrade Lei Feng, the spirit of paradigmatic deeds, as with the 'Red Boat spirit', or the Long March, and the collective inspiration, as with the spirit of flood fighting or the Shanghai spirit.

But perhaps the most emphatic evidence of the significance of spirit in Chinese public discourse is that a Provincial Committee of the CPC in Zhejiang regarded it as so important that it provided a definition of its province's spirit in a plenary session in July 2000. It ran as follows: 'the pursuit of self-improvement, perseverance, innovation and pragmatism'. Xi repeated those very words in an

---

[36] The English paper is published in the *Journal of China in Global and Comparative Perspectives*, vol. 7, 2021 [Chinese version: 马丁·阿尔布劳、金伟，万蕊嘉 译，中西方文化中的'精神'，《文化软实力研究》，2019，4(6): 5-7].

article on February 5, 2006, entitled 'The Zhejiang Spirit that Keeps Abreast of the Times' and then elaborated on it to include qualities of honesty and harmoniousness, open-mindedness and strength.

It was the Zhejiang spirit that he argued was summoned up in the response to typhoons in September 2005. The spirit of typhoon relief enriched the Zhejiang spirit. It added, among other things, a consciousness of unity as well as a belief in one's own responsibility, bringing a fighting spirit as well as strict discipline (op. cit., p. 263).

In the terms of narrative analysis, spirit then is a trope, an often-repeated allusion to an image that illuminates connections between different experiences or events. But a turn to narrative analysis can divert attention away from the importance of spirit within social scientific work. It is a real factor in social life.

Karl Marx resolutely followed the path of science from his earliest encounters with the young Hegelian movement. In *The German Ideology*, he contrasted the materialist conception of history with the idealist that turned it into the progressive coming to consciousness of spirit. As is well known, he rejected emphatically the way the young Hegelians, following their master, turned history into a story of the 'abstract spirit of mankind'.

That statement has been often been misunderstood. The key word is 'abstract'. It is abstraction that removes spirit from the real man. But spirit is a quality of the real man. The spiritual and the material are brought together in the practical energies of human beings.

Marx's method meant he could refer without any awkwardness to spirit in historical contexts. In *The German Ideology*, Marx and Engels wrote of the way all classes in eighteenth-century France had been captured by the commercial spirit (MECW 5: 411). Marx wrote an article for the *New York Daily Tribune* for March 7–8, 1853, where he commented on British politics and an unreformed Parliament in terms that could almost apply today. He wrote that a speech by the Lord Chancellor Cranworth combined both the 'true spirit of Whiggery' and the 'true spirit of Aristocracy' (MECW 11: 517). Engels wrote in the *New York Daily Tribune* of the spirit of the Chinese people in 1857 compared with what they had shown in 1842 (*Marx on China: Articles for the New York Daily Tribune*, Lawrence and Wishart, London, p. 48).

These easy ways in which Marx was able to allude to spirit arose out of his early Paris manuscripts and his intensive engagement with the ideas of both idealists and early materialists. Then he emphasized the artificial nature of their opposition and pointed to its resolution in the practical activities of human beings. Philosophy created an antithesis that could not be solved theoretically but only in real life: 'Spirituality and materiality – their antithetical character' (MECW 3: 302).

Let us summarize. The spiritual and the material are two sides of real things, things which may exist in nature, in human affairs or in technology. In this respect, a forest, a community or a satellite all are real and have both material and spiritual sides. When we consider the human community, we observe relations between people, both the purposes and values they attach to it and the practical ways they produce its goods and collective facilities.

What has happened to spirit in the West? Now we are going to generalize in a way that one can do in a conference that allows ideas to be advanced, criticized, refined or rejected, as the case may be. We have not done the exhaustive research on *jing sheng* or on spirit in the West. But we can advance some hypotheses.

The first is that Marx and Engels did largely succeed in demolishing the Hegelian edifice, and the idea of spirit as the driving force of human history lost credibility.

The second is that the Christian religion managed to retain a hold on spirit as its special property to the exclusion of non-believers.

The third is that the advance of industry and the triumph of technological civilization gave a prestige to experimental science that relies on a mechanistic and atomistic positivism.

These are big claims in a short speech and, rather than attempting to elaborate them, we will simply refer to what has been called the most important social scientific text of the twentieth century, Max Weber's *Protestant Ethic and the Spirit of Capitalism.* There we find spirit headlined. But examine how he treats it. Rather than attempting to summarize the main features of capitalism, he illustrates what he calls an ideal type by referring to the writing of a prominent eighteenth-century American personality, Benjamin Franklin. He selects a number of passages he regards as most expressive of the capitalist spirit and these together serve as his ideal type, to be used subsequently in his comparative studies of the ethics of world religions.

But the way he uses it in those studies is to disaggregate the components and point to them singly in other contexts. So he finds no sense of salvation in Confucianism, no limits on greed in general in Asian religion (the Chinese mandarins were notably avaricious), no inner-worldly asceticism that characterized Protestantism.

When, a few years later, he revised his original account to be published in book form, he defined the spirit of capitalism as a 'norm-bounded lifestyle dressed up as an 'ethic''. Ethic is in quotation marks; so also is spirit. Indeed with those quotation marks he discloses his discomfort for using a term that escaped scientific usage. He did the same elsewhere when he wrote of bureaucratic spirit or of the Prussian spirit.

We will suggest here that Weber's approach is symptomatic of a Western ambivalence towards referencing spirit precisely because it has been separated from real human practices. In this respect too, it is noteworthy that he adopted the widely circulated Western view at the time that Chinese religion was a realm of magic and spirit worship.

One authority on whom Weber drew at one point declared that the Chinese never knew logical contradictories, they couldn't perceive that two forms of belief are mutually exclusive (A. H. Smith, *Chinese Characteristics*, p. 295). It is that unity of opposites that Marx was declaring necessary to overcome the division between the spiritual and the material.

When the Chinese government today declares that the Silk Road spirit has for thousands of years from generation to generation linked civilizations, it is referencing a human product, a combination of human activities that persist in their interconnectedness. It is not a set of ideas detached from human practices.

In calling on the spirit of the Long March or the spirit of typhoon relief, the Chinese leadership is not simply adopting Marx's rejection of spiritual/material dichotomy, but is expressing a world view with origins deep in Chinese history and culture. This world we inhabit is a spiritual world.

9.4 Book review: *Principles and Laws in World Politics*

Principles and Laws in World Politics: Classical Chinese Perspectives on Global Conflict, by Walter Lee, World Scientific Publishing, Singapore. 2022. Pp. xxv + 495.

This is an extraordinarily opportune time to publish a book that brings China and the rest of the world together in one intellectual framework for world peace. It is not only the right time, it is even more the right book, since it delivers much more than the title promises. Walter Lee is Assistant Professor in the School of Arts and Social Sciences at the Hong Kong Metropolitan University. He was an intern in the United Nations, and a visiting scholar at the Chinese Academy of Social Sciences. He is to be congratulated for his courage in using this experience, both to illuminate scholarly traditions of thinking on international relations, and to demand imaginative innovation that can match the seriousness of the current global crisis.

Many authors have in recent years sought to draw on the centuries of Chinese wisdom to inform and enlighten those Western outlooks that are blind to their own limitations. François Jullien's explorations in his *A Treatise on Efficacy* (2004 [1996]) and *In Praise of Blandness* (2008 {1991]) spring to mind as outstanding examples of this genre. He writes as an independent philosopher, working within and amplifying the scope of traditional Chinese schools of thought for our common world today.

Xiaoying Qi's *Knowledge Flows and Chinese Social Theory* (2014, reviewed by this author for the *Journal of China in Global and Comparative Perspectives*, vol.1, 2015), showed successfully how ancient and enduring Chinese concepts such as xin could bridge the binary conflicts in Western thought between reason and emotion. Drawing on a wealth of scholarly sources, she then demonstrated how a new concept of 'paradoxical integration' (*xiangfan xianghe* or *xiangfan yiti*).

The editor of this book, Xiangqun Chang, conducted intensive field work in the same village that the doyen of Chinese social science, Fei Xiaotong made famous, yielding an original concept that expands the conceptual scope both of Western discussions of reciprocity and understanding of Chinese social relations in her *Guanxi or Li shang wanglai* (2010). Her examination of the way Chinese social support networks, underpinned as they are by a distinct catechism of principles that can be applied to every situation, introduces a new range of issues for Western thinking on social ethics.

It is an indication of how broad the stream is that carries these studies forward that they are wholly independent of each other in terms of their own academic support networks. This point may help us to appreciate how it is that Walter Lee can write a book that neither comments on, nor even refers to any of these different, and yet outstanding contributions to Western understanding of China, and still he contrives to produce a brilliant assessment of what is needed today for a new approach to world peace that can accommodate vastly different world views.

How has Lee achieved this? In spite of the title of his book, suggesting a prime concern for past thought, in fact the spur to his endeavours is the contemporary world situation and the need to go beyond simplistic attempts to reconcile the USA and China. He cites the readiness of political elites in the West to ditch their own high flown principles and undermine institutions like the International Criminal Court when it suits them.

At the same time he is inspired by a human quality, prized in China, also appreciated to a lesser extent in the West, namely the need to respond to circumstances, to be inventive, creative and explore novelty that meets the exigencies of the moment. Roughly covered by the term pragmatism, this goes beyond any set of principles, indeed it requires principles always to be reviewed in the light of experience. It is no accident that the celebrated exponent of that new-fangled philosophy, pragmatism, in the United States, John Dewey, was also feted in China where he lived and taught for two years from 1919-21.

Lee has a vision, the imagination for a 'post-liberal emancipated Leviathan'. His definition of this counter-factual necessity for any future settled world order needs to be quoted in full. It is 'an almighty political authority which exercises awe and force to restore and maintain order, as well as enshrines globally negotiated values of common conscience and reinvented cosmopolitanism' (p. 13). It is certainly an all-embracing vision, of both doctrine and forces, and it is projected over an indefinite future, looking forward to a world that is not just encompassed by and divided up into the community of nation states, but one where other types of authority might develop. For the moment, however, we have to work with the system of sovereign states.

Lee has every sympathy with demands for dialogue between the nations, but he is also emphatic that dialogue is not enough. His 'emancipated Leviathan' has to guarantee that parties to conflict look inward to find common moral principles. He cites Tsinghua University Professor Yan Xuetong's advocacy of 'moral realism' or the 'kingly way' (yangdo) as an authority for his own advocacy of an international order that covers the whole world, and not just US/China relations.

It reminds us of the reaction to the Thomas Hobbes original Leviathan that in the succeeding century resulted in the popular notion of the 'philosopher king'.

These are the motivating ideas that take Walter Lee through the huge literature on the tradition of Chinese Confucian-Legalism. He shows how it has underpinned ruling elite ideologies in imperial China (as jingxue), in Mao's time, and potentially today in 'socialism with Chinese characteristics. It leaves him pessimistic about its possibility as a basis for reconciling West and East, for allowing shared humanitarian interventions, or for winning China friends in the international community. He calls for reinterpretations of classical Chinese canons and a renewal of the creative spirit of Chinese civilization. He applauds as an example none other than the Nordic Network on Chinese Thought, evidence enough that China is penetrating the minds of distant other cultures. The Nordic Network has produced a 'Lapland Manifesto of Confucianism' (Kallio, Lodén, Torbjörn & Nojonen (accessible at https://www.ulapland.fi/loader.aspx?id=2a63c6e8-fab3-467c-a5b0-a49e5222b6ee). Its authors applaud a 3,000 year Confucian tradition as relevant for the human predicament today as it has always been.

This is an entry point into the globality of our time, the vulnerability of our species to its own inventiveness and the renewed risk of mutual self-destruction that was ushered in by the Hiroshima and Nagasaki bombs. Our present crisis in March 2022, accelerated beyond anything even that Lee imagined in writing this book, certainly requires all of the soft-power construction, 'global, cross-civilizational, and cross-disciplinary effort' he calls for. It appeals too to the wisdom of the 'emancipated Leviathan'.

Wisdom involves responding to the demands of the day with the accumulated experience of the past, and reacting appropriately to the unique circumstances of the particular moment. From this point of view today it is the relation of friendship between two great powers where the maximum leverage is possible for producing a solution to the crisis in Crimea. This is not a West/East relationship issue. It arises out of the past thousands of years of Asian history.

Sufficient said, to indicate the scope of Walter Lee's own imagination and the contribution he makes in this book to take the debate about the future world order to a new level. The title is justified by the entirely appropriate place the book can gain in the booklists for conventional IR courses. Its content blows those conventions apart.

9.5 Some thoughts on integrity

A vivid example of present-day emphasis on integrity has been provided in the numerous references to it during the 2020 US Presidential election. It reminds the author that he was writing a book on integrity when we first met 11 years ago. He has been engaging since then with Chinese scholars trying to add understandings from a Chinese perspective. He used 'integrity' seven times, mainly referring to honesty (诚信 *chengxi*), one of China's 12 core socialist values, in his previous book, *China's Role in a Shared Human Future* (2018). In the present book, 'integrity' has been used no fewe than 62 times. Sections 7.1.1 to 7.1.4 consist of related attempts in this book to preserve the relative integrity of its exploration with Chinese and non-Chinese perspectives. It is hoped that this unfinished work will pique interest in the study of integrity.[37]

9.5.1 Integrity in cultural perspective[38]

Just to remind ourselves, the word 'integrity' originates from the Latin adjective *integer*, meaning whole or complete. In this light, integrity can be seen as the sense of wholeness deriving from consistency of character based on values, beliefs and principles people claim to hold. A person of integrity is thus one who acts according to a personal value system, a set of values and standards that people can observe as consistent with expectations.

In that sense, integrity may have varying connotations in different contexts, as the core group of values may differ from culture to culture. In a culture of individualism such as exists in the West, the core principles that make up the wholeness may be independence, initiative and self-responsibility, qualities required for the pursuit of one's own happiness but that also contribute to being seen as a unique individual.

By contrast, in a culture which sees the group, be it the nation, community or state, as more important than the individual and requires personal sacrifice for the common good, the basic quality of wholeness may be self-sacrifice, the subordination of one's interests to those of others. This is seen to be a code of custom, morality and laws, which social members observe in their life in common.

Taking for example a culture that has profoundly different roots from those in West, namely China, the translation of the word 'integrity' in the above sense presents quite a challenge. While the dominant translation of the word is '完整' (wholeness), it is sometimes translated into '正直' (uprightness) and '诚实' (honesty), and at other times translated into '诚信' (good faith) or '操守' (moral principle).

This set of Chinese equivalents are closely related, and it is worth considering a prime example of a combination of qualities that has the completeness that matches the Western idea of high integrity. Traditionally in Chinese culture, there has been very high esteem accorded to someone who is known as a *junzi* (完人), usually translated as 'consummate man'.

A little knowledge of Confucius' teaching may help here. When his student Zilu asked him what a consummate man was, he said: 'He is witty like Zang Wuzhong (politician), unselfish like Men Gongchuo (high-ranking official), courageous like Bian Zuangzi (soldier), versatile like Ran Qiu (Confucius' student). In

[37] Editor's note: This introductory paragraph was written by the Editor.

[38] Editor's note: Some Chinese input in this piece came from ZHANG Xiaoying at Beijing Foreign Studies University, when she was Visiting Fellow at the University of Cambridge in 2011.

addition, he emphasizes rites and music.' Then he added: 'Can a consummate man today adhere to such high standards? If he is not in the hunt for ill-gotten gains, willing to sacrifice his own life in times of calamity and keeps his promise even in perpetually difficult situations, he can be called a consummate person.'

The contemporary Chinese philosopher Feng Youlan goes further to explain what a consummate man means. A man of integrity lives in the *tian* (the sky) and *di* (the earth) realm. He consciously regards himself not only a member of his society, but also a member of the *yuzhou* (cosmos). Besides the duties of a citizen or a social member, he must also be a consummate person, who knows clearly about *Dao*, denoting *Tong* (getting through without obstruction). He does not care about transient worldly success or failure. He overcame the feeling of selfishness and understood the limits of worldly affairs, so that his virtue realizes the goal of melting in and combining with the virtue of nature.

That combination of 'virtue with nature' points to the other aspect of the wholeness of traditional Chinese culture. Life was to be led in harmony with nature and in that context *zhongguo* meant the central kingdom, administered by a sovereign power, and the Emperor whose task it was to safeguard that harmony. Civil strife and natural disasters, floods or famine would be sufficient cause for him to lose the mandate from Heaven.

Both at the level of the person and the civilization, traditional China had ideas that expressed both completeness and values, and therefore in a Western understanding there was a sense of integrity, without its ever being brought into focus as a general concept. When we compare the historical experience of China with the West, we can understand why. Completeness and values in the West were constantly lost and renewed, derived from one social entity and reconstituted in another.

This contrast is not so much a matter of West and East but one of traditional cultures versus the modern, or possibly even of Rome versus the rest. For instance, if we consider a culture relatively free from Latinization, that of Wales, we find in its language no single term for integrity. *Gonestrwydd* (honesty, truthfulness), *cywirdeb* (rightness, correctness) and *uniondeb* (straightness, directness) are all listed by the Welsh Academy English–Welsh Dictionary as possible translations of 'integrity', but asking a Welsh speaker to translate them into English is unlikely to get 'integrity' as the answer.[39]

The general concept of integrity in the languages derived from Latin, where it signifies a completeness of any entity and in the human case explicitly refers to values, thus has a history that is tied up with the development of the West. We can infer further that the frequency of its use in contemporary life and its controversial character are intimately connected with the growing flux of social entities and the fraught nature of personal identity in current conditions.

[39] I am indebted to the late Reverend Dr. Hugh Matthews of Cardiff for his explanation of the Welsh usage.

9.5.2 Other attempts

Searching for Integrity is the third lecture in the lecture series titled Beyond the global crisis. Other titles of lectures are The end of the West, Responsibility for the crisis, and The possibility of global justice. They were delivered in April 2013 at the Beijing Foreign Studies University (BFSU). See 8.2.2 in this book.

Diversity vs. integrity, locality vs. globalization (see 8.3.2.2) is a panel discussion in Globalization and China's Contribution (8.3.2).

Integrity. This is one of the 10 themes that the author developed under 6.2 Goals, Values and Endemic Conflicts in the New Global Culture in this book. They are The autonomy of culture, Cultural differentiation, Transculturality, Pragmatic universalism, Negotiated identities, Integrity, Global culture, Globalism versus populism, Agency and responsibility, and Global citizenship. This paper was originally published as a chapter in *Challenges of Globalization and Prospects for an Inter-civilizational World Order*, ed. Ino Rossi, Switzerland: Springer Nature Switzerland, 2020. pp. 143–156.

9.6 Respect for the 'harmony but difference' between people is essential[40]

1) *Could you please tell me the difference between the two concepts of 'globalization' and 'the unity of the world'?*

'Unity of the world' is a state of affairs or condition that refers to the harmony and coexistence of people on this earth. 'Globalization' is a process whereby something expands or travels from its original location across the globe. It has no necessary relation to the unity of the world, and can even work against it.

2) *The article points out that the relationship between philosophical social science and national construction is very close. What do you think is the main reason for the lack of idea system structure in the Western world?*

There are many, complex reasons so to pick out the main one is difficult, but I suppose one has to highlight the system of representative democracy that puts ideas that appeal to the average member of the public at the centre of political leaders' concerns.

3) *Why can the the Belt and Road Initiative transcend the limitations of the formation of an ethnocentric worldview? How can China avoid being seen as a replica of American-style globalization?*

BRI is a project-based collection of agreements with other nations that focus on shared interests in building infrastructure. As such, it does not have a world view that belongs to any one country, only one that can be shared by any country in the world.

---

[40] Editor's note: This interview with the author was conducted by a journalist at the *Xinhua Daily*. The English text is provided by the author. The Chinese translation was published in *Xinhua Daily*, 30 May 2020, see http://xh.xhby.net/mp3/pc/c/202006/12/c787499.html].

4) *Hollywood culture has gradually become an indispensable part of global culture in the process of globalization. Will this damage the traditional culture of all countries?*

No, because Hollywood is transcultural, that is, it exists in a sphere that is not part of any culture. It has long transcended the United States, and belonging to global culture does not threaten national cultures. Think how national cultures can co-exist with local cultures.

5) *'Transcultural' runs through the book. What do you think is the biggest difference between it and 'cross cultural'?*

Cross-cultural is used ambiguously, sometimes meaning 'transcultural' in the sense I have used it above, but more often referring to relations between two or more cultures, sometimes to their points of fusion or hybridity. The lack of precision is why I generally avoid its use.

6) *What lessons can China learn from British exit from the European Union on the road of building a community with a shared future for humanity?*

I'm not sure any country can look to Britain for lessons these days, except, and this I suppose is the reason for your question, a lesson of what not to do. That lesson is for any country, not just China, and China does not need it because it exemplifies what Brexit denied, namely, the importance of maintaining multilateral relations, building alliances and working towards common goals.

7) *In your article, you pointed out eight qualities, namely 'execution, efficiency, reasonableness, respect, reciprocity, respect, transcendence, innovation'. Why do you particularly emphasize respect, reciprocity and innovation?*

These are values that the present-day world emphasizes because they most fit its contemporary condition, threatened by global challenges that affect us all. So, innovation is in huge demand to find the technologies to combat climate change, but also to handle the deep social tensions produced by unthinking pursuit of economic globalization. Reciprocity is necessary to stimulate and intensify the cooperation needed to meet those challenges. Respect is vital to allow the differences between people that can generate alternative solutions to those challenges.

8) *You have helped a great deal of Chinese sociologists publish papers in international journals, which is very important and effective for 'Chinese social science' to go global. What was your original intention?*

My intention was just that, for Chinese social science to go global. That meant taking its place among all national sociologies as an equal partner but able also to contribute its own distinctive perspective. Unity in diversity was the watchword.

9) *Why do you think it is the best time for China, the 'Middle Kingdom', to appear on the global centre stage?*

China has now achieved parity or at least second place to the United States on all kinds of economic measures. Beyond that, it now represents the most coherent, single-minded nation–state, with an ability to achieve its targets that is unparalleled in the contemporary world. As such, it is the Middle Kingdom of the new global order and the rest of the world is in urgent need for it to assume leadership and set an example on a whole range of issues, health, clean energy, social security, transport and digital security, to name just a few.

10) *Specific cultural contacts have brought about various new problems. How can social order solve the problem of cultural changes?*

We come back to respect and reciprocity. Cultures must always be alert to power difference between them and acknowledge rights on both sides.

11) *In your opinion, the reference to 'the Chinese Dream' emulates the American Dream from a certain angle. Does it fully address issues such as rights, social conflicts, class divisions and market failures?*

If the implication of your question is that the American Dream addresses them, then that must certainly be denied. The issues you mention are all ones that the American Dream provokes, precisely because its emphasis on individual success above all results in the marginalization of all who are not 'successful' in the terms of the Dream, namely have not become prosperous. The Chinese Dream emphasizes prosperity but it is a shared and relative prosperity, one that does not depend on pushing others back. It does indeed attempt to address precisely the issues on which the American Dream fails – but of course it has a lot of work to do still.

12) *In a time when we have multi-culture, since common values cannot guarantee mutual understanding and harmonious coexistence, does a public philosophy of global governance exist? Will such a philosophical system also have exclusiveness?*

The present public philosophy, such as it is, inhabits mainly the multilateral institutions, above all the United Nations agencies. It rightly emphasizes the shared goals of nations in the SDGs and the principles of the UN Charter. But a lot of work has to be done to co-opt the support of civil society and non-state cultures and to deal with every increasing corporate power and inequality. The need is to develop well-understood ways of shaping a global order that is more than just an association of nation–states. But it will also be one where debate and criticism are integral aspects of its capacity to cope with change.

13) *'Community of shared future' is rooted in Chinese culture, which is quite different from the core value system of the United States. How can we achieve shared development and enjoy benefits together, rather than cultural mutual understanding?*

Well, of course, my paradoxical answer is that we should downplay perfect mutual understanding, something that can never achieved, and emphasize joint projects where there is mutual advantage that each side can understand. People with different values can well cooperate for shared goals, like building railways or even developing shared internet platforms! We have to hope they see their own interests are served by joint projects.

Thank you for your questions!

9.7 *The Global* Tianxia (GTX)[41]

Author's preface

In an earlier book, *China's Role in a Shared Human Future*, I aimed to provide directions towards a theory for global leadership. The need for global leadership increases daily. The world requires clear-sighted focus on the issues that endanger our life on this earth and at the same time the resources and the capabilities to deliver solutions. I proposed that China alone was in a position to assume that global leadership. This is a big challenge to the West and in particular to the United States, which has always assumed it had the vision and provided the direction, resources and capabilities to lead the world. My aim is to examine why this is no longer the case, how the West has lost its way, become fragmented and disillusioned while ignoring the global challenges. Instead it should look to China.

China, since the founding of the People's Republic, has been striving to recover the position in the world that is appropriate for its size, population and historic culture. It has chosen its own unique path of development, even as the rest of the world around it has changed, and in that journey it has adapted many of the achievements of the West for its own benefit while rejecting its conceptions of liberal democracy. The reaction in the West has been a mixture of disbelief, suspicion and outright hostility combined with both admiration and apprehension. In particular, it cannot see how it is possible for a country to succeed when it rejects the West's cherished beliefs, its conviction that it follows both universal values and economic truths.

This book aims to cut through the West's bewilderment. It points to factors outside the usual ones that are regarded as necessary for economic success and social stability. It recognizes the fundamental contribution made to China's rise by the Communist Party and it points to the crucial significance that theoretical thinking has had for China's achievements. In this respect, the recognition of Xi Jinping thought as the third pillar for China's ideology along with the thought of Mao Zedong and Deng Xiaoping entrenches theory as a key element in its future direction. This recognition of the functions of theory for defining a vision for the future and the exercise of leadership in its pursuit underpins the main purpose of this book. I believe only decisive leadership, coupled with the capacity to deliver on clearly conceived goals, can deliver the policies and measures the world needs to combat global warming and the other global issues that endanger our existence

41 Editor's note: This was a book proposal invited by Commercial Press in 2020. It was suggested that the book be backed up with field visits in China. Owing to the COVID-19 pandemic, the project was abandoned.

on this earth. President Xi has already declared China's commitment to the world community of a shared future. Taking this forward needs a theory for global governance that equates to his own theory for China.

In a book written in the 1990s, *The Global Age*, I argued the time was defined above all by global issues like climate change rather than by the globalization that the West was trumpeting abroad, and I put a big emphasis on a worldwide change of outlook among citizens challenging their governments to come up with solutions to climate change. Now that very global age is diminished in the face of digital developments that seem to deflect attention from the existential issues. If the global age is to endure, then it needs the most powerful single agency in the world to commit itself to the task. This is my standpoint, a global point of view, beyond any particular country, East or West, but asking China to come to the rescue of all on the planet.

Introduction

Global issues, above all climate change, confront the world as a whole and for the first time the human species must act as one. But we have to use our intelligence. Civilization has developed through discovery and solving problems. The classic account of Arnold Toynbee told how civilizations fell when they failed to respond to an existential challenge. Now it is human civilization as a whole that meets such a challenge.

This book has three parts. It first describes the nature of the challenge and the condition of a world in no fit shape to meet it. Second, it brings together the concepts, perspectives and theories that can guide a new global leadership. Third, it shows how they inform the necessary response to overcome that challenge – and points to China as the agency best qualified to ensure the effectiveness of that response.

Part 1 The global challenge

1) The climate change crisis
2) Global issues – social, economic and environmental
3) Globalization in the dock
4.) The rise of populism
5) The fragmentation of the West
6) Clashing civilizations
7) Digital escapism
8) Chaotic connectivity
9) Multipolar confusion
10) World in denial

Part 2 Theory for practice

11) Renovating theory
12) Democracy versus capitalism
13) Conflict, law and institutions
14) The Chinese spirit
15) West/East views and the globe
16) Pragmatic universalism
17) Collective agency
18) Power, projects and leadership
19) Principles for new global governance
20) Shaping global society

Part 3 Rising to the challenge: China's role

21) Mao, Deng and Xi: theoretical leadership
22) Socialism with Chinese characteristics
23) Setting the example: energy policy
24) Belt and Road
25) Multilateralism
26) Leveraging cultural diversity
27) Exporting Chinese culture
28) Cooperation for global goals
29) Global governance reformed
30) The global *tianxia*

Appendix
Basic information about
China's Role in a Shared Human Future: Towards Theory for Global Leadership

1. Foreword by Anthony Giddens

Professor Martin Albrow is one of the foremost sociologists in the English-speaking world and one of the greatest experts on globalization, perhaps the most significant driving force of our times. In his pioneering work *The Global Age* (1996), written when the term 'globalization' itself was quite new, he set out the main dimensions of the profound changes that had begun to transform world society. In its most fundamental meaning, 'globalization' refers to the intensifying interdependence of individuals, institutions and states across the globe.

One dimension is economic – the spread of a world marketplace, a massively complex division of labour between and within companies and their workforces, coupled with financial institutions of global scope. However, globalization is also political and cultural. Increasing globalization confers many benefits, at the same time as it opens up new stresses and strains. Think, for example, of the case of China itself which, when the country opened itself out to the wider world some three decades ago, travelled all the way from mass starvation to a level of prosperity that once would have seemed inconceivable. There are still many who live close to the breadline. Yet in China's prospering cities today one of the main health issues is the very opposite: rising levels of obesity, a condition not of scarcity but of abundance.

Many in current times speak of globalization going into reverse. The reverberations of the global economic crisis are still being felt, especially in Western countries. Whole segments of those countries have not shared in the rising levels of abundance experienced by the majority. There are significant cultural divisions too. Cosmopolitan values – a welcoming of cultural diversity, equality between the sexes and a comfort with geographical mobility – have flowered in many larger cities. In other regions, especially those that have not shared in rising prosperity, there has been a marked reaction against these values. Resentment against immigration, hostile or racist attitudes towards 'foreigners', and towards ethnic or cultural minorities, has again become commonplace. These are the attitudes that have helped fuel the rise of populist parties in the West, parties which explicitly set themselves against globalization and wish to return to the more traditional nation-state. The most significant consequence in global terms is the ascent of Donald Trump to power in the United States, a leader who wants to reverse what he sees as America's declining power and who blames globalization for the US's problems rather than seeing it as the source of its relative prosperity.

Make no mistake, however: globalization has not gone into reverse and short of calamity there is no chance of its doing so. Whatever its stresses and strains, the world is more and more interdependent every day. One of the prime reasons is the rise of the digital revolution, which has moved globalization – i.e. interdependence – to a wholly different level. The celebrated Canadian thinker Marshall McLuhan, writing many years ago at the outset of the digital revolution, coined the term 'global village' to describe the trajectory of world society. How right he was, but even he could never have guessed how far that process would develop. Consider on the level of everyday life. Someone takes a plane to London. That trip takes only some ten hours or so, an everyday miracle which depends upon global satellite systems circling high above the earth. On arrival she calls her parents on her smartphone. It is another everyday miracle. She can see them and vice versa; and they can talk almost as if they were in the same room. Moreover, they can do so almost for nothing. And of course political leaders and billions of other ordinary people can do the same thing.

The global village is what I call a 'high opportunity, high risk' world, where we do not know in advance how that balance of opportunity and risk will play out. The opportunities are everywhere, China's rise to world influence, and probably world leadership, being among them. They are of a scale that human beings have not experienced before, as witnessed in myriad scientific and technological advances, moving faster than ever before precisely because of globalization. To take just one example, this could be an era of massive innovation in medicine, because of the capacity of scientists to collaborate across the world and be in instantaneous communication with one another. Yet the risks are also without precedent in previous periods of history, in some large part because they too are globalized – we just do not know at this point whether as a species we can deal with the combined threats of climate change, a world population approaching ten billion, the proliferation of nuclear weapons, mass migration and the potential for global pandemics.

In this book Albrow does a remarkable job of shedding light on these extraordinary changes and on the pivotal role that China is likely to have in shaping their further evolution. As the United States pulls back from its former global role, China not only can, but must, assume a pivotal position in shaping world society for the better. The progress of the Belt and Road Initiative will be only one element in determining whether China's new world role will help heal divisions and promote peaceful global cooperation. That initiative has to demonstrate that it is a vehicle for free cooperation, not an imposition of sectional power.

Albrow fruitfully deploys the thinking of Xi Jinping in showing how all this might be achieved, but links that thinking in an impressive way with Western traditions, old and new. Max Weber, who a century ago sought to pinpoint the cultural origins of Western capitalism, at the same time was fascinated with Eastern religion and culture. His writings, the author shows, still provide core ideas for a rethinking of global cooperation today. We should reject the idea that our hypermodern world can be stabilized and pacified only by hypermodern concepts and technologies. Almost the contrary is the case. In rediscovering the deep roots of shared civilizational values, we can shape a global ethics that can be the foundation of a resurgence of global cooperation.

2. Contents

3. Other info

Product details

Language: English and Chinese
Publisher: London: Global Century Press (2018)
ISBN 978-1-910334-34-8 (paperback, English)
DOI https://doi.org/10.24103/GCSS.en.pb.2018
ISBN 978-1-910334-35-5 (hardback, English)
DOI https://doi.org/10.24103/GCSS.en.hb.2018
ISBN 978-1-910334-36-2 (paperback, Chinese)
DOI https://doi.org/10.24103/GCSS.ch.pb.2018
ISBN 978-1-910334-37-9 (hardback, Chinese)
DOI https://doi.org/10.24103/GCSS.ch.hb.2018
The Mainland China English edition is published by the New World Press 2019
The Mainland China Chinese edition is published by the Commercial Press 2020
The Hong Kong English and Chinese editions are published by the Hong Kong Commercial Press 2022

Abstract

This book is about China's role in the world to come and includes the author's recent explorations of China's readiness to assume a global leadership role. The book effectively links the study of Max Weber, an important Western theorist during the global transformation of the nineteenth to twentieth centuries, with the study of Xi Jinping's thinking during the global transformation from the twentieth to the twenty-first century. According to the author, on the one hand, Western classical theory can still provide the core ideas for rethinking today's global cooperation. On the other hand, Xi Jinping's 'The Belt and Road' initiative, though only a very recent attempt to show how China as a new player in the world can help to heal its divisions, has as its foundation Xi's thinking on the governance of China, which has demonstrated that the initiative will serve as a means to promote global peace and cooperation rather than strengthen great power rivalries. The author believes that we can shape global ethics in the process of rediscovering the deep roots of common civilized values that will underpin the global cooperative recovery. This book will be translated and available in Chinese. It is expected it will help a wider readership from China and other countries and regions to understand China and how it can contribute to the shared human future.

Reviews

> What is the process of incorporation of Chinese ideas and thinking into a transcultural public social science? Is the Belt and Road project the successor to Western economic globalization? Is Asia going to be the continent that works through the dilemmas of sustainable modernity? Martin Albrow is one of the very few social scientists who has the authority, experience and ambition to give us the answers, in this rich collection of essays.
>
> —Professor Sam Whimster, Editor, Max Weber Studies

> Professor Albrow's book provides a fascinating counterpoint to Western-centric notions of China as a 'rising power'. It is unique in providing a globalist view of how China understands its new role and how its leadership is already fundamentally reshaping the architecture of the world in the 21st century. China is becoming a global nation and this book explains how. In the process, sinology and global governance scholarship just got more properly global.
>
> —Associate Professor Olaf Corry, PhD, University of Copenhagen

A group of book reviews were published in the *Journal of China in Global and Comparative Perspectives (JCGCP)*, vol. 6, 2020.

Index

Numbers

A

B

C

D

E

F

N

O

P

Q

R

S

T

U

V

W

X

Y

Z

Dual language information from Global Century Press

About the book

1 Abstract and about the author

About the book

China and the Shared Human Future: *Exploring Common Values and Goals* serves as a companion to Martin Albrow's previous book *China's Role in the Shared Common Future: Towards Theory for Global Leadership* (2018). It consists of essential selections of work on the theory and practice of globalization (Chapter 2) by the author, the British social theorist and pioneer of global studies, based on his 60-year academic career, which lays a solid theoretical foundation for this book. In the past 10 years, the author has paid much attention to the issue of global governance and China. The editor collected almost all the author's complete works in Chapters 3–6 including, academic papers and writings, newspaper articles, lectures, speech notes in academic and public conferences, academic and media dialogues or interviews and remarks for China's special occasions during this period. Together, they showcase the author's bidirectional engagements with Chinese academia, politics, publishers and media on practical themes such as fighting COVID-19, the BRI and lifting the Chinese out of poverty. They offer an insight into how China participates in the shaping of a global society, enabling readers to grasp the author's thoughts and opinions in the context of China in a global setting.

Based on the creative idea of the 'globalization of Chinese social sciences', the editor has brought together a large number of examples of the help given by the author over the past 40 years to Chinese scholars and professionals to fulfil their academic and social missions in China and the UK (Chapters 7–8). The last chapter exemplifies how to develop social theory with Chinese characteristics. In all, the book aims to encourage the globalization of Chinese social sciences and their incorporation into the sum of human knowledge.

About the author

Martin Albrow FAcSS is founding and past Honorary President of the Global China Academy (2012-2021), UK; non-resident Senior Fellow at the Käte Hamburger Center for Advanced Studies 'Law as Culture', Bonn University, Germany. He became Emeritus Professor at the University of Wales in 1989 and has held senior visiting positions at various institutions across the world. He is a former President of the British Sociological Association. He was editor of the journal Sociology and founding editor of International Sociology. His *The Global Age: State and*

Society beyond Modernity (1996) won the European Amalfi Prize in 1997. Other books include *Bureaucracy* (1970), *Max Weber's Construction of Social Theory* (1990), *Globalization, Knowledge and Society* (1990, ed. with E. King), the first book with the keyword 'globalization' in the title (book reviewed by Roland Robertson, *Contemporary Sociology*, Vol. 21, No. 1, Jan. 1992), *Do Organizations Have Feelings?* (1997), *Sociology: The Basics* (1999), *Global Civil Society* (co-editor) in 2006/7, 2007/8 and 2011, *Global Age Essays on Social and Cultural Change* (2014) and *China's Role in a Shared Human Future: Towards Theory for Global Leadership* (2018).

About the editor

Xiangqun Chang FRSA is Founding Fellow and President of Global China Academy, Editor-in-Chief of Global Century Press, Honorary Professor of University College London (2015–20), UK; Distinguished Professor of Nankai University, China. Her publications amount to three million words, including *Guanxi or Li shang wanglai? Reciprocity, Social Support Networks and Social Creativity in a Chinese Village* in English (2010) and Chinese (2009). She is Editor of the *Journal China in Global and Comparative Perspectives* (English and Chinese Editions), and Editor or Co-Editor of six series of books (in English and Chinese): 'Chinese Concepts', 'Globalization of Chinese Social Sciences', 'Understanding China and the World', 'China and Chinese in Comparative Perspectives', 'Cutting Edge and Frontiers', 'Transcultural Experiences with "Three Eyes"' and 'Global Chinese Dialogue Proceedings'.

2 Table of contents (see page v)

3 About the book series

The phrase 'globalization of Chinese social sciences' came out of a discussion, with Professor Stephan Feuchtwang at the London School of Economics in 2010, about the title of a book commemorating the 100th anniversary of Professor Fei Xiaotong's (Fei Hsiao-tung) birth. The first volume (in both English and Chinese) was published in 2014 by Global China Press alone and, in 2015, jointly with New World Press. The dissemination of 'Chinese social sciences' covers a very wide range, in which the promotion of Fei Xiaotong's work is only the first step. We therefore decided to use 'Globalization of Chinese Social Sciences' as the name of a book series to promote representative Chinese social scientific works and nearly a century of efforts made by social scientists both inside and outside China. See more details from the General Preface by the Editor of the book series. This is the sixth book in the *Globalization of Chines Social Sciences* book series, edited by Professor Xiangqun Chang, Honorary Professor of University College London (2015-20); President of Global China Academy, UK.

Other books in the *Globalization of Chinese Social Sciences* series

Series Editor: Xiangqun Chang

Title: *Fei Xiaotong Studies*
Editors: S. Feuchtwang, X. Chang and D. Zhou
Series No.: Vol. 1
Language: English; Chinese
London: Global Century Press (2016)
ISBN 978-1-910334-05-8 (English hardback)
ISBN 978-1-910334-06-5 (English paperback)
ISBN 978-1-910334-07-2 (Chinese hardback)
ISBN 978-1-910334-04-1 (Chinese paperback)
DOI https://doi.org/10.24103/GCSS1.en.2015
DOI https://doi.org/10.24103/GCSS1.cn.2015

Title: *Fei Xiaotong Studies*
Editors: S. Feuchtwang, X. Chang and D. Zhou
Series No.: Vol. 2
Language: English; Chinese
London: Global Century Press (2016)
ISBN 978-1-910334-11-9 (English hardback)
ISBN 978-1-910334-10-2 (English paperback)
ISBN 978-1-910334-09-6 (Chinese hardback)
ISBN 978-1-910334-08-9 (Chinese paperback)
DOI https://doi.org/10.24103/GCSS2.en.2016
DOI https://doi.org/10.24103/GCSS2.cn.2016

Title: *Fei Xiaotong Studies*
Editors: S. Feuchtwang, X. Chang and D. Zhou
Series No.: Vol. 3
Language: English; Chinese
London: Global Century Press (2015)
ISBN 978-1-910334-15-7 (English hardback)
ISBN 978-1-910334-14-0 (English paperback)
ISBN 978-1-910334-13-3 (Chinese hardback)
ISBN 978-1-910334-12-6 (Chinese paperback)
DOI https://doi.org/10.24103/GCSS3.en.2017
DOI https://doi.org/10.24103/GCSS3.en.2017

Title: *China's Role in a Shared Human Future: Towards Theory for Global Leadership*
Author: Martin Albrow
Series No.: Vol. 4
Language: English; Chinese
London: Global Century Press (2018)
ISBN 978-1-910334-35-5 (English hardback)
ISBN 978-1-910334-34-8 (English paperback)
ISBN 978-1-910334-37-9 (Chinese hardback)
ISBN 978-1-910334-36-2 (Chinese paperback)
DOI https://doi.org/10.24103/GCSS4.en.2018
DOI https://doi.org/10.24103/GCSS4.cn.2018

Title: *A Record of Launching Martin Albrow's Book: China's Role in a Shared Human Future*
Editors: Xiangqun Chang and Costanza Pernigotti
Series No.: Vol. 5
Language: English; Chinese
London: Global Century Press (2019)
ISBN 978-1-910334-62-1 (English paperback)
ISBN 978-1-910334-63-8 (Chinese paperback)
DOI https://doi.org/10.24103/GCSS5.en.2019
DOI https://doi.org/10.24103/GCSS5.cn.2019

环球世纪出版社双语信息

关于本书

1 提要和作者

本书提要

本书是《中国在人类命运共同体中的角色：走向全球领导力理论》（2018，马丁·阿尔布劳著）一书的姊妹篇。英国社会理论家、全球研究首创者之一马丁·阿尔布劳在其60年的学术生涯之际、精选的其全球化理论与实践的重要著作，为本书奠定了坚实的理论基础（第二章）。近10年来，作者重点关注了全球治理与中国的重大议题。本书编者结集的这一时期作者发表的几乎全部的学术论文、书籍章节、报刊文章、教学、参加国内外学术等会议的讲稿、与学者和媒体的对话及访谈，及与中国相关的特殊议题的发言（第3–6章）。展示了作者在"一带一路"倡议、中国脱贫和抗击新冠病毒肺炎等实践主题等方面与中国学术界、政界、出版界和媒体界双向交流的成果。为读者提供了客观地把握作者在全球与中国语境下的学术思想和观点，以及对中国如何参与形塑全球社会及其治理的深刻洞见。过去的40年来，作者对国内外中国学者给予了各种各样的帮助。基于"中国社会科学全球化"的创意，本书编者整理了作者分别在中国和英国帮助中国学者及专业人士履行学术与社会使命的大量实例（第7–8章）。最后一章展示如何发展具有中国特色的社会理论，旨在鼓励在构建人类知识大厦中推动中国社会科学全球化的进程。

作者简介

马丁·阿尔布劳，英国社会科学院院士（FAcSS），全球中国学术院荣誉创始及前荣誉院长（2012–2021)；德国波恩大学卡特汉堡"法律文化"高研院非驻院高级研究员。1989年成为威尔士大学（卡迪夫）荣休教授前为该校社会理论系讲座教授。此后，他在许多机构任访问教授，其中包括慕尼黑的埃里克·沃格林讲席教授、伦敦政治经济学院、纽约州立大学石溪分校，华盛顿特区的伍德罗威尔逊国际学者中心，以及北京外国语大学客座教授。曾任英国社会学学会会长，主编《社会学》期刊，创刊并主编《国际社会学》期刊。其《全球化时代：国家与超越现代性的社会》（1996年）获得欧洲阿马尔菲奖。其他著作包括《科层制》（1970年）《马克斯·韦伯的社会理论建构》（1990年）《全球化、知识与社会》（1990年，与E.金合编）《组织是否有感情？》（1997年）《社会学基础》（1999年）《全球公民社会》（合作主编，2006年7月，2007年8月和2011年）《论全球时代的社会和文化变迁》（2014年）《中国在人类命运共同体中的角色——走向全球领导力理论》（2018）。

编者简介

常向群教授，英国皇家艺术院院士（FRSA），全球中国学术院创院院士和院长，伦敦大学学院荣誉教授（2015–20）；中国南开大学特聘教授。她发表的中英文著述约300余万字，其代表作为《马克思主义社会学论稿》(2018/1992)，《关系抑或礼尚往来：江村的互惠社会支持网和社会创造的研究》(2009和2010英汉两个版本)。该书研发了一个有中国特色的互惠、互动、社会关系和社会网络的模型，借用并改造中国古典的和民间常用的"礼尚往来"用法，锤炼出的一个基于"礼仪资本"的具有普适价值的分析概念："互适"(recipropriety)，被国际社会学协会（ISA）学术委员会选为全球的影响"应对动荡的二十一世纪的社会学"的15位社会学家之一。她还是环球世纪出版社总编，主编《全球中国比较研究》（英汉两个版本）等学术期刊及多套系列丛书，如"中国社会科学全球化""中华概念""读懂中国与世界"，合作主编"中国与中华比较视野""新锐与前沿""'三只眼'转文化丛书""全球中国对话文集"等。

2 目录

3 本系列丛书及其它书籍

本系列丛书简介

"中国社会科学的全球化"一词源于2010年与伦敦经济学院王斯福(Stephan Feuchtwang) 教授关于纪念费孝通教授诞辰100周年的书名的讨论。其第一卷（英文和中文版）于2014年由环球世纪出版社独立出版，并于2015年与新世界出版社联合出版。“中国社会科学”的内容范围非常广，推介费孝通先生的研究只是第一步。因此，我们决定以“中国社会科学的全球化”为丛书名称，以推介具有代表性的关于中国社会科学著作。近一个世纪以来，国内外社会科学工作者在不同程度上推动中国社会科学走出去或曰中国社会科学全球化做了很多努力。更多详情见丛书主编的总序。本书是“中国社会科学全球化”丛书的第六本。该丛书由英国伦敦大学学院荣誉教授（2015–20）、全球中国学术院院长常向群教授主编，由环球世纪出版社于2015年开始出版。

《中国社会科学全球化》丛书的其他书籍

系列主编：[英]常向群

书名：《费孝通研究》
编者：[英] 王斯福（S. Feuchtwang）[英]常向群 周大鸣
系列编号：第1卷
语言：英文；中文
伦敦：环球世纪出版社（2015年）

ISBN 978-1-910334-05-8（英文版 精装）
ISBN 978-1-910334-06-5（英文版 平装）
ISBN 978-1-910334-07-2（中文版 精装）
ISBN 978-1-910334-04-1（中文版 平装）
DOI https://doi.org/10.24103/GCSS1.en.2015
DOI https://doi.org/10.24103/GCSS1.cn.2015

书名：《费孝通研究》
编者：[英] 王斯福（S. Feuchtwang）[英]常向群 周大鸣
系列编号：第2卷
语言：英文；中文
伦敦：环球世纪出版社（2016年）

ISBN 978-1-910334-11-9（英文版 精装）
ISBN 978-1-910334-10-2（英文版 平装）
ISBN 978-1-910334-09-6（中文版 精装）
ISBN 978-1-910334-08-9（中文版 平装）
DOI https://doi.org/10.24103/GCSS2.en.2016
DOI https://doi.org/10.24103/GCSS2.cn.2016

书名：《费孝通研究》
编者：[英] 王斯福（S. Feuchtwang）[英]常向群　周大鸣
系列编号：第3卷
语言：英文；中文
伦敦：环球世纪出版社（2018年）
ISBN 978-1-910334-15-7（英文版 精装）
ISBN 978-1-910334-14-0（英文版 平装）
ISBN 978-1-910334-13-3（中文版 精装）
ISBN 978-1-910334-12-6（中文版 平装）
DOI https://doi.org/10.24103/GCSS3.en.2017
DOI https://doi.org/10.24103/GCSS3.cn.2017

书名：《中国在人类命运共同体中的角色：
走向全球领导力理论》
作者：马丁·阿尔布劳
编者：常向群
系列编号：第4卷
语言：英文；中文
伦敦：环球世纪出版社（2018年）
ISBN 978-1-910334-35-5（英文版 精装）
ISBN 978-1-910334-34-8（英文版 平装）
ISBN 978-1-910334-37-9（中文版 精装）
ISBN 978-1-910334-36-2（中文版 平装）
DOI https://doi.org/10.24103/GCSS4.en.2018
DOI https://doi.org/10.24103/GCSS4.cn.2018

书名：《马丁·阿尔布劳<中国在人类命运共同体中的角色>新书发布纪实》
编者：[英] 常向群 [意] 裴可诗（Costanza Pernigotti）
系列编号：第5卷
语言：英文；中文
伦敦：环球世纪出版社（2019年）
ISBN 978-1-910334-62-1（英文版 平装）
ISBN 978-1-910334-63-8（中文版 平装）
DOI https://doi.org/10.24103/GCSS5.en.2019
DOI https://doi.org/10.24103/GCSS5.cn.2019

Milton Keynes UK
Ingram Content Group UK Ltd.
UKHW050140130124
435947UK00005B/31